ECONOMIC ISSUES
FOR CONSUMERS

Fourth Edition

ECONOMIC ISSUES
FOR CONSUMERS

Fourth Edition

ROGER LEROY MILLER
University of Miami

WEST PUBLISHING COMPANY
St. Paul New York Los Angeles San Francisco

Copy Editing: Susan Jones
Art: Brenda Booth
Cover Photograph: D. J. Farr
Composition: Parkwood Composition Services

50 West Kellogg Boulevard
P.O. Box 43526
St. Paul, Minnesota 55164

Printed in the United States of America

Library of Congress Cataloging in Publication Data
Miller, Roger LeRoy.
Economic issues for consumers.
Includes bibliographies and indexes.
1. Finance, Personal. 2. Consumer education.
I. Title.
HG179.M48 1984 332.024 83-21793
ISBN 0-314-77928-0

CREDITS

xxxii, 1 Frank Siteman, EKM-Nepenthe; 4 Jeffrey Grosscup; 10, 11 Paul Sequeira, Photo Researchers; 18 Fujhira, Monkmeyer Press; 23, 24 Hazel Hankin, Stock, Boston; 34, 35 Carol Bernson; 42, 43 Hugh Rogers, Monkmeyer Press; 47 Freda Leinwand, Monkmeyer Press; 61 Tom Barnett; 69 Jeffrey Grosscup; 74, 75 David Bellak, Jeroboam; 77 Tom Barnett; 83 George E. Jones III, Photo Researchers; 92, 93 Steve Malone, Jeroboam; 98 Hella Hammid, Photo Researchers; 101 David R. Frazier, Photo Researchers; 105, 107 Jean-Claude LeJeune; 110, 111 (c) bildagentur alphapress, Jeroboam; 116 EKM-Nepenthe; 118 Jeffrey Grosscup; 124, 125 Frank Siteman, EKM-Nepenthe; 130, 131 Tom Ballard, EKM-Nepenthe; 133 Tom Ballard, EKM-Nepenthe; 140 Jeffrey Grosscup; 143, 144 Frank Siteman, Jeroboam; 148, 149 Brenda Booth; 160 Budd Gray, Jeroboam; 167, 169 Kent Reno, Jeroboam; 172, 173 (c) bildagentur alphapress, Jeroboam; 178, 183 Robert V. Eckert, Jr., EKM-Nepenthe; 186, 187 Tom Ballard, EKM-Nepenthe; 192, 193 Brenda Booth; 197 Tom Ballard, EKM-Nepenthe; 203 (c) Bruce Kliewe, Jeroboam; 206, 207 Jeffrey Grosscup; 212, 213 Michael Hayman, Photo Researchers; 218 Tom Ballard, EKM-Nepenthe; 225 Ray Solomon, Monkmeyer Press; 231, 232 EKM-Nepenthe; 244, 245 John Stewart, Mead Paper; 250 Robert Eckert, EKM-Nepenthe; 254 Tom Ballard, EKM-Nepenthe; 266, 268 (c) Bruce Kliewe, Jeroboam; 274, 275 Robert Eckert, EKM-Nepenthe; 280 Carolyn A. McKeone, Freelance Photographers Guild; 288, 289 Tom Ballard, EKM-Nepenthe; 294, 295 James J. Mejuto, Freelance Photographers Guild; 302 Robert V. Eckert, Jr., EKM-Nepenthe; 316, 318 Mimi Forsyth, Monkmeyer Press; 331, 334 Dick Powers, Freelance Photographers Guild; 338, 339 Litton Microwave

(Credits continued on p. 566)

CONTENTS
in Brief

CONTENTS

Chapter 4

Chapter 5

Consumer Issue D
HOW TO CHOOSE AND START A CAREER 124

Chapter 8
YOU HAVE TO LIVE WITH WHAT YOU HAVE 131

Consumer Issue E
HOW TO BUDGET YOUR LIMITED INCOME 143

Chapter 9
THE HIGH COST OF LIVING 149

Consumer Issue L
BUYING, SELLING, AND INSURING A PLACE TO LIVE 316

Consumer Issue M
RENTING A PLACE TO LIVE 331

PREFACE

The mid-1980s are already upon us. The economic and political landscape is constantly changing so that what was critical a few years ago may not be critical today. That is exactly how many consumers felt in the first few years of 1980, when they considered the phenomenon of inflation. During the first few years of this decade, the rate of inflation dropped dramatically from what it had been over the previous ten years. Some consumers and politicians started believing that inflation had gone away. But then, by 1984, many prices started to rise again. Consider another serious problem of the 1970s—the energy crisis. Indeed, for a time, it was considered to be the most pressing problem facing the American consumer. It is still a problem today, of course. Prices at the gas pump are high—of that there can be no question. But, when corrected for inflation, gas prices are not as high as they were a decade ago. Other prices, though, are continuing to skyrocket. This is particularly true of medical care expenses. All of the above demonstrate that consumer economics remains a complex subject. Discovering the best way to earn and to spend one's money will remain a stumbling block for the majority of Americans. The quest to become a rational consumer must continue into the mid- and late 1980s.

THE FORMAT OF THE BOOK—CHAPTERS AND ISSUES

You will notice a somewhat unusual format throughout the following pages. I have attempted to present the major areas of consumer economics in chapter form. At the end of many of these chapters, a Consumer Issue has been presented. For example, after an explanation of what inflation is and how it affects the consumer, an Issue outlines how the individual can best protect himself or herself against the ravages of inflation. As another example, after the chapter on food, a Consumer Issue outlines the steps that the individual can take to become a better foodshopper. To a large extent, the consumer issues offer more practical advice than do the chapters.

PEDAGOGICAL AIDS

Students will find a number of pedagogical aids in both the chapters and the consumer issues. Each chapter begins with a Chapter Preview that indicates to the reader what will be covered. Then, to "ease the blow" of the new terminology, a Glossary of Terms that might not be known to the reader is presented before the actual text begins. At the end of each chapter, there is a point-by-point Summary that can be used for review. Then, the Questions for Thought and Discussion that follow the Summary may be used as the basis for class discussion, or as the basis for individual thought or even group discussions without the aid of an instructor. Things to Do lists some projects that a class can do as a group, or that individuals can do at the request of the professor or on their own. Finally, Selected Readings presents some alternative sources of reading for those students who wish further explanations of certain sections of the chapter.

The consumer issues have basically the same pedagogical devices, except that there is no Preview and the Issue Summary gives more practical hints on certain consumer decision-making problems.

ILLUSTRATIVE MATERIALS

You will notice a wide use of illustrative materials—photographs, charts, and cartoons. In my experience, visualization of certain ideas not only aids the student in understanding the material but also makes the task of reading the text more enjoyable.

KEY CHANGES IN THE FOURTH EDITION

So much has happened since the publication of the third edition that a large number of changes were necessary to keep this text the most up-to-date on the market today and to make it the most usable book possible for rational consumers.

A New Chapter and a New Issue

Our complex society is getting even more complex. The ability of the consumer to protect him- or herself has taken on new dimensions and has become more difficult. Because of this, I felt it necessary to add a separate chapter on consumer fraud. Chapter 4 is entitled *The Many Faces of Fraud*. It includes the following:

- **False and deceptive advertising.**
- **Interstate land sales regulation.**
- **Health care and therapeutic devices, as well as weight-reduction programs.**
- **Mail-order problems.**
- **Pyramid schemes.**

The chapter ends with a checklist on how to avoid consumer frauds.

A NEW ISSUE We are indeed in the age of the computer. The computer will become as commonplace as the TV during most of our lifetimes. Currently 200,000 personal computers are being sold per month. It seems appropriate that Issue O, *Buying a Personal Home Computer,* be added. In this Issue, you will learn about the different parts of the personal computer system, how to buy a computer, where to look for it, and what to have put in the written sales contract. *Economic Issues for Consumers* has entered the computer age.

Other Changes

The following chapters and issues had significant changes made:

Chapter 3 The Information Glut: Has an expanded discussion of brand-name loyalty and how it connects with market power. The new view at the Federal Trade Commission subsequent to the Reagan administration's change in policies towards the consumer is also presented.

Chapter 5 Making Up Your Mind: Significant additional discussion on value clarification and the difference between values and value judgments. Industrial-age versus post-industrial-age consumer values are discussed.

Chapter 7 The Consumer As Wage Earner: Where the jobs will and will not be in the future through 1990.

Issue E How to Budget Your Limited Income: Greatly simplified with budgeting forms that are easier for students to use.

Chapter 9 The High Cost of Living: New theories on the causes of inflation, as well as discussions of the problems and the accuracy of various price indices. A section on calculating your own price index.

Chapter 11 Banks and the Banking System: A completely reworked and updated view of the banking system including NOW accounts, Super-NOW accounts, money market deposit accounts (MMDA's), and debit cards.

Issue H Coping with Banks and Their Services: How to settle a complaint with a bank. Rules for dealing with electronic banking.

Chapter 12 The Overextended American: Update on the sources of credit and important changes in the Truth-in-Lending Act.

Chapter 15 Putting a Roof over Your Head: How to calculate whether to buy or to rent. Shared appreciation and other creative financing schemes.

Chapter 17 Getting There by Car is Half the Worry: The cost savings of used versus new cars. Automobile financial responsibility, and a table of the compulsory insurance liability limits in each state.

Chapter 20 Saving: A new discussion of available saving instruments, including floating-rate deposit accounts and money market deposit accounts.

Issue T How to Be a Rational Investor: Now includes full cash management, reading quotations on the New York Stock Exchange, over-the-counter market and the bond markets.

Of course, all tables, charts and graphs have been thoroughly updated. All references have been updated, rechecked, and edited wherever necessary.

SUPPLEMENTARY MATERIALS

A practical and easy to understand *Student Workbook* has again been provided by Dr. Phillis Basile. Students using it will find the text material more interesting and better presented. The Workbook will also allow students to apply the principles of rational decision making to practical problems.

The *Instructor's Manual* has been expanded and improved by Professor Judy Farris. She has added and changed test items where necessary. The tests have answers included.

ACKNOWLEDGMENTS

Major reviewers who offered detailed criticism for the first, second, and third editions were as follows:

Professor Howard Alsey
Department of Home Economics
Arkansas State University

Professor Joseph E. Barr
Department of Economics—Chairman
Farmingham State College
Massachusetts

Professor Phillis B. Basile
Orange Coast College
California

Professor Harold R. Boadway
Department of Economics
Moraine Valley Community College
Illinois

Professor Jean S. Bowers
Department of Home Economics
Ohio State University

Professor Margaret Jane Brennan
College of Home Economics
Western Michigan University

Professor Kay P. Edwards
Brigham Young University

Professor Judy Farris
College of Home Economics
South Dakota State University

Professor Barbara Follosco
Department of Home Economics
Los Angeles Valley College

Professor David G. Garraty
Thomas Nelson Community College
Virginia

Professor Linda Graham
Department of Economics
Wichita State University
Kansas

Professor Ron Hartje
School of Business
SOUK Valley College

Professor Ann R. Hiatt
University of North Carolina
at Greensboro

Professor James O. Hill
Department of Economics
Vincennes University

Professor Hilda Jo Jennings
Department of Home Economics—Chairman
Northern Arizona University

Professor William L. Johnston
Oklahoma State University

Professor Ann Lawson
Department of Marketing/Economics
Thomas Nelson Community College
Virginia

Professor Geraldine Olson
Department of Home Economics
Oregon State University

Professor James Poley
Department of Business
City College of San Francisco
California

Professor Rose Reha
Department of Business Education

St. Cloud State University
Minnesota

Professor Shirley Schecter
Department of Home Economics
Queens College
New York

Professor Jolene Scriven
Department of Business Education
Northern Illinois University

Professor Eugene Silberberg
Department of Economics
University of Washington

Professor Nancy Z. Spillman
Department of Economics
Los Angeles Trade-Technical College

Professor Faye Taylor
Department of Home Economics
University of Utah

Professor Margil Vanderhoff
Department of Home Economics
Indiana University

Professor Frank A. Viggiano, Jr.
Department of Economics
Indiana University of Pennsylvania

Professor Joseph Wurmli
School of Business
Hillsborough Community College
Florida

Professor Prudence Zalewski
California State Polytechnic University
San Luis Obispo

Fourth edition reviewers were:

Judy L. Allen
Southwest Texas State University

Esther McCabe
The University of Connecticut

Claudia J. Peck
Oklahoma State University

Reuben E. Slesinger
University of Pittsburgh

Merle E. Taylor
Santa Barbara City College
California

Mary Ann Van Slyke
North Central Technical Institute
Wisconsin

It goes without saying that I am extremely appreciative of the tremendous help that the above reviewers provided to me. Without them, I believe that this Fourth Edition would not be as complete and accurate as I believe it now is.

I have found through the years that the best way I can improve on what I write is by soliciting the comments of those who use my texts. I therefore stand ready to answer any and all comments, criticisms, or questions relating to what follows in this book. It is with the help of those who want the best for their students that I can find out what is best for the ultimate reader of *Economic Issues for Consumers*.

RLM
Coral Gables, 1984

CHAPTER
THE AGE OF THE CONSUMER

You consume; I consume; we all consume—in one way or another. As consumers, we number at least 230 million in the United States alone. The dollar value of what we consume is staggering. In 1984, the estimate is $2.2 trillion. That comes to over $25,000 for every household in the U. S.

CHAPTER PREVIEW

- What are some of the characteristics of our consumer-oriented society?
- What is scarcity, and why does it necessitate choices?
- What rights and responsibilities do consumers have today?
- Is there a need for consumer education?

CONSUMERS
Individuals who purchase (or are given), use, maintain, and dispose of products and services in their final form in an attempt to achieve the highest level of satisfaction possible with their income limitation.

You consume; I consume; we all consume—in one way or another. As **consumers**, we number at least 230 million in the United States alone. The dollar value of what we consume is staggering. In 1984, the estimate is $2.2 trillion. That comes to over $25,000 for every household in the United States.

What do we buy as consumers? In a word, everything. Our purchases include goods as varied as eighteen-karat gold wristwatches, toothpicks, racehorses, four-bedroom houses, televisions, hamburgers, filet mignon, and goldfish bowls. Exhibit 1-1 lists some of the broad categories of goods and services for which we spend our money each year.

SCARCITY AND THE CONSUMER

SCARCITY
A term used to indicate that no society has enough resources to satisfy everyone's wants and desires at a zero price for those resources.

Even though we spend those billions year in and year out, that in no way means we have unlimited resources. Our nation and, indeed, the world, are faced with **scarcity**: No society has enough resources to satisfy everyone's wants and desires at a zero price for those resources. Even if you were the person on earth, you would face scarcity; that is, you would not have an unlimited amount of time to enjoy your wealth and would have to choose among many ways to spend your time.

Scarcity forces us as consumers to make *choices* all the time. We must choose how we spend our time, how we spend our labor power (that is, what kind of job we do), and how we spend our income (our purchasing power). Life would be simple without scarcity, and you and I would not have to bother about consumer economics. In a world without scarcity, choices would not have to be made. But we haven't reached nirvana yet, and that is why a knowledge of consumer economics is essential for maximizing the satisfaction we can derive from being consumers.

A MORE COMPLEX LIFE

Certainly, today's consumer products and, therefore, today's living experiences seem incredibly more complex than those of our ancestors. When the United States was young, life was indeed hard, but it certainly did not appear to be as complicated as it does today. For almost everyone, it was either do or die—eke out a bare existence tilling the ground or starve to death. At that time, over 90 percent of the population was engaged in agriculture. One of the most complicated aspects of life then was coping with the extremes of weather. Of course, all the day-to-day problems involved in human relationships existed then as they do now and as they will in the future. But, as both consumers and producers, Americans had fewer choices to make and, as a result, faced less complicated decision making. Times have changed. Today, less than 5 percent of the population is engaged in agricultural production, and we are richer than we were when this country was founded. The number and variety of products available to us seem to approach infinity, and the number of different types of economic pursuits we can engage in seems overwhelming.

EXHIBIT 1–1

Personal Consumption Expenditures by Major Type, 1983

This table shows an actual tabulation of the billions of dollars that are spent by American consumers on various categories of goods and services. (The last category, "All others," includes everything that was not listed specifically.) You can check the latest issue of the *Survey of Current Business* to find out how much personal consumption expenditures have grown since 1983.

TOTAL SUBCATEGORIES: (in billions)	$2,151.3	PERCENTAGE OF TOTAL 100.0
Automobiles and parts	134.5	6.25
Furniture and household equipment	100.5	4.67
Food and beverages	420.1	19.53
Clothing and shoes	126.3	5.87
Gasoline and oil	90.9	4.22
Housing services	321.4	14.94
Household operation services	134.6	6.26
Transportation	76.7	3.56
All others	746.3	34.70

SOURCE: *Survey of Current Business*, October 1983.

OUR COMPLEX SOCIETY

Technology changes every day and, according to some, at such a rapid pace that it has made day-to-day living more difficult. If you do not know from one minute to the next what technological advance is going to alter your optimal choices as a consumer, then you obviously need guidance. Some observers believe that increased technology, leading to an increased number of product choices, creates decision overload. Remember, though, that, in the United States, technology responds not to the absolute dictates of some higher power but, rather, to the profit incentives that rest on the desires of consumers taken as a whole. Technology will develop products for consumers to buy; but if no consumer wants to buy them, there is no profit in continuing production (unless the government decides to subsidize such production).

If you were only able to choose products out of either a 1908 Sears, Roebuck catalog or a current one, most of you probably would pick a current catalog because the number of choices would be so much greater and the items available so much closer to your tastes and preferences. Today you cannot buy many of the things listed in the 1908 catalog—buggies, horseshoes, tapeworm remedies, and so on. There are, however, even more things that you can buy today that you could not buy in 1908. Technology is obviously both a curse and a blessing.

It is not, however, an uncontrolled monster. As a matter of fact, technology has sometimes simplified rather than complicated our lives. For example, the newest jet airplanes are enormously sophisticated compared to airplanes of, say, twenty years ago. But in spite of this complexity of contemporary aircraft, today's pilots do little more than make certain that the computer that runs the

plane is working right. The machinery the pilots are operating is extremely complex and, of course, their responsibility for lives and expensive machinery is great, but pilots' tasks are not too complicated once they have mastered them. In other words, technology can provide us with very complex and sophisticated products that are not difficult to use. Is our life more complicated or less complicated because we have these products? Only you can ultimately decide.

Consumers also face a host of modern problems. Most of us live in polluted environments in urban areas where we suffer more respiratory diseases than we used to and where crime rates are escalating. We also have trouble getting to and from our places of work because of horrendous traffic jams. Being a consumer is clearly not just going to the marketplace to buy an item, taking it home, and using it. Being a consumer involves seeking a higher **quality of life.**

QUALITY OF LIFE
All the attributes of life that citizens subjectively determine to be beneficial, including, but not limited to, air quality, amount of noise, natural vegetation, surrounding cleanliness, range of cultural activities, and so on.

WHERE THE CONSUMER FITS INTO THE ECONOMY

Our complex economy consists of many sectors. One can place the consumer in the grander scheme of things by looking at the circular flow of income and product illustrated in Exhibit 1–2. Here we show the circular flow of income from businesses to households via the market for productive services. These productive services include those obtainable from labor, land, and capital.

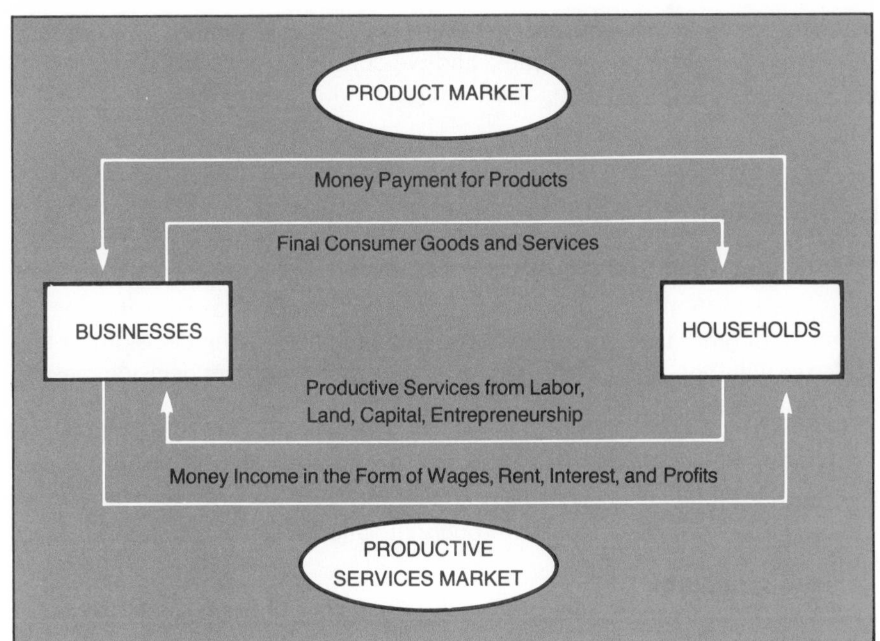

EXHIBIT 1–2
The Circular Flow of Income and Product

The consumer fits into the circular flow of income and product by providing productive services to businesses and by purchasing businesses' final goods and services. In this diagram, productive services derived from labor, land, capital, and entrepreneurship flow from households to businesses, which in turn pay for those services in the form of wages, rent, interest, and profits. Businesses provide final consumer goods and services, and households provide money payment for those products in the product market.

Households are paid by businesses in the form of wages, rents, and interest. Entrepreneurs—those who take risks in setting up new businesses—receive profits. In the upper part of the circular-flow diagram, businesses provide households with consumer goods and services. When households pay for those consumer goods and services in the product market, businesses receive income.

WE ARE NOT JUST CONSUMERS

Because we usually do not get something for nothing, most of us, at one time or another, have to work. That is, we have to act as employees, or producers. In fact, there are about 115 million of us in the measured labor force who earn incomes as professors, flight attendants, truck drivers, typists, engineers, artists, construction workers, businesspersons, fashion consultants, or as any of a great number of other types of workers. Additionally, many, such as homemakers, work to provide services for family members but are not given monetary payments. Those of us who are paid to work for a living receive wages, or salaries, that account for about 75 percent of all the income generated in any one year in the American economy. The other 25 percent of that income goes to those of us who own things such as land, stocks, bonds, oil wells, and apartment buildings.

Most of us are, therefore, consumers, employees, and/or **capitalists.** We consume in order to survive and be happy; we work in order to receive the income necessary to buy what we want; and we often obtain income from our savings, whether in the form of shares of stocks or houses. In fact, more than 40 million Americans have directly purchased shares in American corporations; another 85 million indirectly own shares through their pension plans.

CAPITALIST
An individual who owns all or part of an income-producing asset.

Consumers recently have obtained rights they never before enjoyed.

In addition to being consumers, employees, and/or capitalists, we are also citizens. We vote on public issues, and we consume goods and services that are provided by federal, state, and local governments.

THE PROBLEMS FACING TODAY'S CONSUMER

Consumers constantly face problems that they must solve in some way. It is not enough to think in terms of getting the best goods with your income. A multitude of other factors enter into every buying and saving decision. In this book, we will look at a wide variety of areas where consumer decision making is critical. These include purchases of major items such as food, clothing, housing and equipment, transportation, and medical care. We will look at insurance, saving, and investing, as well as at retirement and the leisure society. The responsibilities of the business community and the government to you, the consumer, will be stressed throughout, and we also will look at your responsibilities as a consumer.

Consumer Rights

As we will see in the following chapter, consumers recently have obtained rights they never before enjoyed. In our complex, consumer-oriented society, we have witnessed a consumerist movement that has involved governments at all levels and received the attention and support of recent presidents. In 1962, John F. Kennedy sent the first consumer protection and interest program to Congress. In that message, he stated four consumer rights:

1. **The right to safety**—a protection against goods that are dangerous to life or health.
2. **The right to be informed**—not only to discover fraud but also to make rational choices.
3. **The right to choose**—a restatement of the need for many firms in a competitive market and for protection by government where such competition no longer exists.
4. **The right to be heard**—the right of consumers to have their interests heard when governmental policy decisions are being made.

To these four rights, subsequent presidents have added others. For example, Lyndon Baines Johnson added:

5. **The right to a decent environment.**

President Gerald Ford added:

6. **The right to consumer education.**

Finally, to the preceding rights most consumer representatives would add one more:

7. **The right to reasonable redress for physical damages suffered when using a product.**

CONSUMER RESPONSIBILITIES

It would be unfair merely to list a set of consumer rights without also indicating that consumers have responsibilities, too. No president has yet produced a list of them, and probably no two consumer organizations would agree on the same set of responsibilities. Nonetheless, there are some obvious areas of responsibility about which most of us would agree.

1. A responsibility to be honest.
2. A responsibility to give correct information when, for example, the consumer is filling out an application for a loan or is trading in a used car. More bluntly, consumers shouldn't lie, since they do not believe salespeople should.
3. A responsibility to report defective goods both to the seller and the manufacturer. Consumers thus can inform manufacturers of problems the latter may not have known about and also allow manufacturers to inform other consumers who might be using defective and dangerous products. This is a particularly important responsibility with respect to automobiles and electrical equipment.
4. A responsibility to report wrongs incurred in consumer dealings. These should be reported to appropriate government agencies and to private organizations responsible for monitoring various aspects of the marketplace.

In the real world of today, consumers must obtain information in order to make rational choices.

RATIONAL CONSUMER DECISION MAKING

Rational consumer decision making, or the decision making of households, occurs in both the product market (households as demanders of goods and services) and in the productive resources market (households as suppliers of labor, land, capital, and entrepreneurial ability). In both markets, rational consumer decision making involves at least six steps:

1. Defining the need to make a decision.
2. Searching for the alternatives.
3. Obtaining information about the alternatives.
4. Weighing the alternatives.
5. Making a choice.
6. Reviewing the choice and evaluating its success.

Essentially, then, decision making involves planning, reading, comparing, and choosing alternatives.

Every consumer who goes through this process always should keep the following three important principles in mind.

1. Because your time is scarce and valuable, consider it a resource that must be used wisely.
2. Information about products and services is valuable and important, but costly to obtain. You have to use your time and sometimes a portion of your income to obtain information about alternatives, so there is an *optimum* amount of information to obtain (as opposed to an *infinite* amount). That is to say, the optimum amount of information is not too much and not too little, just the ideal amount. You will find out how to determine this amount later in the text.

3. Every choice you make necessarily means that you give up something, whether it be the use of your time or the use of your income. Remember, we live in a world of scarcity. That means that you will constantly face trade-offs—giving up one thing to have another.

THE LACK OF PERFECT COMPETITION AND THE NEED FOR CONSUMER EDUCATION

In a world of perfect competition in both the productive resource market and the product market, consumers, in their roles as providers of productive resources and as consumers of products, don't have much to worry about—because in a world of perfect competition, information is perfect, and all products of strictly equal quality are sold at the same price. But a world of perfect competition does not exist. It is simply a model that economists have found useful for making certain predictions in certain markets.

In the real world of today, consumers must obtain information in order to make rational choices. Moreover, the lack of perfect competition creates a need for market intervention by governmental authorities. (That doesn't mean that all government intervention is beneficial to consumers, though.)

Most of the topics that follow concentrate on household decision making. These involve, for example, budgeting one's limited income, consuming energy, obtaining efficient banking services, deciding on the use of credit, and purchasing food, housing, clothing, transportation, and insurance. To some extent, the larger issues that affect the economy as a whole are also examined. These include the consumer movement, inflation, saving, and government spending and taxing.

Clearly, the age of the consumer is upon us. We hope that the age of the informed consumer is not too far away.

SUMMARY

1. We are all consumers who purchase a variety of goods and services.
2. We live in a world of scarcity, which requires us to make choices about the use of our limited resources: time and income.
3. We are not just consumers; we are also employees, producers, capitalists, and citizens who vote and enjoy publicly offered goods and services.
4. Today, consumers have rights relating to safety, information, choice, the ability to be heard by policymakers, a decent environment, and reasonable redress for consequential physical damages from using a product.
5. Consumers have a responsibility not to steal or lie, to report defective products to sellers and manufacturers, and to report wrongs incurred in consumer dealings to appropriate government agencies and private monitoring organizations.
6. Consumers fit into the circular flow of income and product as members of households that provide productive resources to firms and, in turn, as individuals who are paid money income by firms. Consumers in households also purchase the output of businesses and make money payments to businesses for those purchases.
7. Rational consumer decision making involves deciding that a need exists, searching for alternatives, obtaining information about those alternatives, weighing them, making a choice, and reviewing the choice and evaluating its success.

8. All choices involve costs in time or effort or income or a combination of those three.

QUESTIONS FOR THOUGHT AND DISCUSSION

1. Can you think of any individuals in our society who are not consumers?
2. Does a consumer's decision about what productive services to offer in the resource market influence how that consumer acts in the product market?
3. Is there a limit to how complex consumer products can become?
4. Can you think of any choices that you make as a consumer that do not involve trade-offs?

THINGS TO DO

1. See if you can add to the list of consumer rights given in this chapter.
2. Keep a running tabulation on general consumer principles that will be presented throughout this book.

SELECTED READINGS

Clark, Lincoln H., ed. *Consumer Behavior—The Dynamics of Consumer Reactions.* New York: New York University Press, 1958.

Markin, R. J., Jr. *Consumer Behavior: A Cognitive Orientation.* New York: Macmillan Publishing Co., 1974.

Miller, Roger Leroy and Pulsinelli, Robert. *Understanding Economics.* St. Paul: West Publishing Company, 1983.

Raymond, Charles K. "The Economists' Mythical Consumer." In *Consumer Behavior and Behavioral Sciences,* edited by S. H. Britt. New York: John Wiley & Sons, 1966.

Wilcox, Suzanne D. *The Educated Consumer: An Analysis of Curriculum Needs in Consumer Education.* Washington, D.C.: U.S. Office of Education, No. 30, October 1979.

CHAPTER
THE CONSUMER GETS A VOICE*

*I am deeply indebted to Professor Phillis Basile for her help on this chapter and the following Issue. She is responsible for much of what follows.

Like the police officer who tries to break up a family fight . . . the concept of consumer protection is constantly in the middle of an argument between those who believe in competition in the marketplace and those who believe in consumer activism.

CHAPTER PREVIEW

- Is the consumer movement a new one?
- What are antitrust policies all about, and how do they affect the consumer?
- How do state and local consumer-protection agencies compare with federal ones?
- Can the private sector do anything to protect the consumer?
- What is the essence of consumer-activist groups?
- What are the innovations in providing legal assistance to consumers?

Like the police officer who tries to break up a family fight and suddenly finds himself the target of both the husband and the wife, the concept of consumer protection is constantly in the middle of an argument. On one side are those who believe that the only needed consumer protection arises out of competition in the marketplace and that consumer protection insults consumers by implying that they are helpless. On the other side are those who believe that consumerism, or consumer activism, is needed to counteract the lack of competition in the marketplace. Although most people have become aware of consumer protection only in recent years, it has a long history.

A HISTORY OF CONSUMER PROTECTION

The earliest forms of consumer protection were really attempts to make market protection effective. Because there are many buyers and sellers in a competitive market, no one buyer or seller can individually influence the price of a particular good. We assume that buyers and sellers know what they are doing and are familiar with the product for which they are bargaining. But even if they know what they are bargaining for, it may be difficult to determine exactly how much they are bargaining for and how much they are getting. And so, from earliest recorded times, we have found ourselves involved in the setting of standards of weights and measures.

Policing Standards

Once standards of weights and measures were established, the next problem was enforcement. The second development in consumer protection, then, was policing these standards. Once fraud in the marketplace had been made illegal, the market had to be policed and the police work evaluated. Thus, the courts and administrative bodies came into the consumer-protection system. The principle supported here is competition. If enough consumers have enough information, they can protect themselves in the marketplace.

Business Wanted Them, Too

But even this system was not purely a consumer-protection system because consumers were not particularly influential in monitoring the standards of weights and measures, the policing system, and the courts. Rather, producers found themselves engaged in competition they deemed detrimental to their own interests. Remember, everyone is a consumer. We tend to think of consumers in supermarkets, department stores, car showrooms, and so on; that is, we think of the consumer role only at the retail level. But businesses are also consumers when they buy goods and services to use in further production. Businesses, then, have two reasons for being interested in the enforcement of standards:

1. To protect themselves when they go into the market to buy, and
2. To protect themselves against fraudulent competitors who may be more successful in selling to the individual consumer than the traditional business.

ANTIMONOPOLY POLICIES

At the same time that standards were being set and enforced, another concept was emerging: antimonopoly, or **antitrust, policies** established by the government. The rights of buyers and other competitors had long been protected in **common law** because the courts refused to enforce monopolistic contracts. But before the Sherman Antitrust Act was passed in 1890, there had been no stated public policy (in the form of **statute law**) that **monopoly** and price fixing were unacceptable in the American economy. Although this legislation was designed to protect the interests of all competing producers in the market, it had consumer implications as well: In order for competition to exist, the market must have many buyers and sellers so that no one alone can influence price.

At the turn of the century, consumer protection as it is understood today did not exist. Rules to provide protection for the seller as a competitor in the marketplace had only an incidental effect on consumers because the information and antimonopoly requirements might make it easier for consumers to operate in the market. In the years between 1900 and World War I, however, a distinct change occurred, not only in the consumer area but throughout the society and economy of the period. This was the period of the "muckrakers", the period of the first wage-and-hour laws, the period of the first women's and minors' protective legislation, and the period in which the first federal law designed specifically to protect consumers was passed. The latter was the Food and Drug Act of 1906, which dealt with the production, transportation, and sale of foods, drugs, and medicines.

ANTITRUST POLICIES
Government policies designed to prevent business monopolies. Antitrust policies are aimed at establishing and maintaining competition in business to assure the consumer fair prices and goods of adequate quality.

COMMON LAW
The unwritten system of law governing people's rights and duties, based on custom and fixed principles of justice. Common law is the foundation of both the English and U.S. legal systems (excluding Louisiana, where law is based on the Napoleonic Code).

STATUTE LAW
Law created by lawmakers, such as members of Congress or members of state legislative bodies.

MONOPOLY
A form of market structure in which one firm dominates the total sales of a good or service.

Food and Drug Act

Although thirty years earlier Congress had made fraud through the mails illegal, the emphasis remained on the transaction at the retail level of the marketplace. Upton Sinclair's book, *The Jungle,* awoke the general public to the fact that consumer protection meant more than information at the point of sale. In that book, Sinclair graphically described to the buying public the squalor that existed in the meat-packing business. Groups began seeking some form of "consumer protection" in products that were processed prior to arrival at the marketplace. Eventually, Congress reacted by passing the Food and Drug Act of 1906, as well as the Meat Inspection Act of that same year.

But the Food and Drug Act of 1906 was not the beginning of a strong, continuous surge in consumer interest or in consumer protection. Not until 1914 was the Federal Trade Commission Act passed to provide administrative machinery to enforce antitrust laws and to spell out unfair methods of competition, including deceptive advertising. And it was thirty-two years later that the 1938 Food, Drug and Cosmetic Act was passed to strengthen the protective features of the 1906 legislation.

The passage of the 1938 legislation was the last significant federal activity on the consumer-protection issue until 1958. In the following years, a flood of legislative activity occurred at federal, state, and local levels. Between 1965 and 1975, more than twice as many laws were passed in the consumer areas than had been passed in the previous ninety years.

Why the Renewed Interest in the Consumer?

What happened to rekindle the interest in consumer protection? Some people attribute the renewed interest to Ralph Nader, whose 1965 book *Unsafe at Any Speed* brought to public attention the issue of automobile safety. Yet Upton Sinclair's *The Jungle,* which preceded the passage of the Food and Drug Act of 1906, and Stewart Chase's *Your Money's Worth,* which preceded the sporadic consumerist activity in the 1930s, had not led to continuing consumer protection activity. Something else was operating in the system, and that something else, according to some, was the complexity of modern economic life. By the early 1960s, the American public had felt the impact of the technology explosion as it affected production, transportation, and information systems. The developments in plastics, frozen foods, and dried foods had made preprocessing and prepackaging an everyday fact of American life. The American automobile had become a complex, accessory-loaded machine that the buyer could no longer easily understand. Consumers found themselves at the center of an increasing mass of information. Accompanying this expansion was the depersonalization of the modern American marketplace.

In making buying decisions, consumers spend much time seeking and evaluating information. In a relatively simple system, consumers may know enough about the products they are buying and enough about the sellers of those products to feel comfortable about making a good decision. But with today's complex technology, seeking information may be a time-consuming job. To know enough to make completely satisfactory consumer decisions in every field takes a lifetime.

This, by the way, is not a new thought. Wesley Mitchell, a prominent economist of the turn of the century, pointed out in a 1912 article, "The Backward Art of Spending Money," the difference between a business firm, which hires experts to carry out its many functions, and the family unit, which makes the same and even more complex decisions through a single buyer or two. Mitchell concluded that if the family had developed as well as the production unit, by now we would have homemakers who specialize in each of the different aspects of family buying.

In effect, consumers in the 1960s began to ask the government to perform some of these functions by establishing standards of packaging and disclosure that would enable them readily to compare claims from many sellers. There was also a strong movement to provide government standards of safety so that consumers could eliminate such concerns from their information-gathering tasks.

PROTECTION AFTER THE FACT

The legal system that had developed over the years was not geared to handle the problems of millions of individuals with small sums of money at stake, each sum important to the individual but no one amount large enough to pay for the costs of litigation. A mounting sense of helpless frustration led consumers to look for a new form of consumer protection: protection *after* the fact. The new emphasis in consumer protection became *consumer redress:* the right of every consumer legitimately to air grievances and to seek satisfaction for damages incurred through a system that would not penalize the consumer because the individual sum involved was small. This was not the same as the earlier consumer protection against fraud. We consumers now asked for redress, not because we had been deliberately defrauded but because the complexity of the marketplace had made it impossible, in our eyes, for us to protect ourselves adequately before the fact of purchase.

The new emphasis in consumer protection became *consumer redress:* the right of every consumer legitimately to air grievances and to seek satisfaction for damages

THE PRESIDENTS SPEAK UP

Chapter 1 mentioned that President John F. Kennedy sent a consumer protection program to Congress in 1962. Presidents Lyndon Johnson and Richard Nixon reaffirmed these consumer rights, and the strong tide of consumer legislation at the federal level continued. In 1977, President Jimmy Carter asked for more legislation.

To some extent, the election of Ronald Reagan to the presidency heralded a change in the executive attitude toward the consumer movement. Reagan and his advisers had announced well before the election that the business world was overregulated. According to the school of economic thought guiding the Reagan administration, the consumer can take care of him- or herself better than government can. Also, according to this school of thought, competition in the marketplace would eventually eliminate most market imperfections. Hence, during the early 1980s, the federal government reduced its role in protecting the consumer.

Legislation, of course, is not the end of the story. Legislation must be administered, and the administration must be efficient if the concept of consumer protection is to be effective. In 1964, President Lyndon Johnson made a gesture in this direction when he appointed the first special presidential assistant for consumer affairs. Although this person, a member of the staff of the Office of the President, had no direct authority, the fact that such a position existed made certain that consumer interests would have some representation at the federal policy level. The office was continued by President Nixon in 1973, when it was transferred to the Department of Health, Education, and Welfare, now the Department of Health and Human Services.

Consumer Affairs Council and Coordination of Consumer Programs

The Consumer Affairs Council is composed of representatives of the twelve cabinet-level departments and is chaired by the president's special assistant for consumer affairs. The Consumer Affairs Council was established by an executive order signed by President Carter on September 26, 1979. That order established a comprehensive federal policy to guide agencies in responding to consumer issues. It was also meant to stimulate the growth of a more effective group of federal employees by giving them additional tools with which to serve consumers. In addition to establishing the Consumer Affairs Council, the executive order required that, by June 9, 1980, each agency must have a consumer program designed to satisfy the needs and interests of consumers. The order also required that each agency have a consumer staff and educate its staff in the principles underlying the executive order. Not every agency was made subject to the executive order; for example, independent agencies were exempt.

STATE AND LOCAL GOVERNMENTS AND PRIVATE CONSUMER PROTECTION

We have spent considerable time detailing the history and developments in federal consumer protection in the United States. And while federal action clearly illustrates the national importance of an issue, the adoption of a federal policy is often the result of prolonged activity at the state and local government levels or in the private sector of the economy. This has been especially true of consumer-protection policy. In fact, some states, localities, and private groups have gone far beyond the limits now set by federal policy.

State and local governments have always been involved in setting standards of weights and measures and marketing standards, as well as standards that define the term *fraud*. Even today, enforcement of consumer-fraud statutes is left largely to state and local governments. Many areas of fraud are commonly dealt with under state and local criminal-fraud statutes arising out of the criminal-fraud case decisions of earlier years. Furthermore, in the areas of credit, insurance, health and sanitation, and all issues concerning contract rights, mainly state governments have enacted legislation dealing with consumer problems. In fact, state response has sometimes come much earlier than federal response. For example, as early as 1959, both New York and California had legislation on the books to protect the rights of consumers in credit transactions. And not until Massachusetts passed the first truth-in-lending law was federal action on this important issue likely to succeed. When the federal Consumer Credit Protection Act (truth-in-lending) was passed in 1968, Massachusetts became, in effect, a pilot case for the national legislation.

Sources of Private-Sector Consumer Information

How does the private sector of the economy fit in with the public activities for consumer protection? As you might expect, activity in the private sector has been varied and, in many cases, short-lived and uncertain in its effect. But in some specific areas, private activities have been critical. The first of these is product testing. Although the federal government has only very recently begun to test products and to reveal test results in a form that aids consumers in their purchasing decisions, private product-testing groups have been active for a long time. Consumers Union and Consumers' Research, Inc., exist primarily to provide consumers with information on products they may buy.[1]

Other product-testing groups exist not solely to assist consumers, but their activities do produce information that consumers can use. The American Standards Association, for example, is a private agency that was organized in 1918 to develop standards and testing methods to be used by manufacturers. By

1. See Chapter 3 for further information on these organizations.

setting a uniform level of performance, these standards and testing methods can protect manufacturers against unfair competition. But they also provide protection to the consumers who buy products, the safety of which may be important. Using the standards developed by the ASA, other private laboratories or testing groups certify the efficiency and/or safety of such items as electrical and gas appliances, textiles, and many other products. In addition to product testing at the manufacturing level there is a wide range of product testing by retailers who are eager to perform a consumer service and to provide themselves with a competitive advantage.

We mustn't place too much stock, however, in the "seals of approval" that appear on numerous products. Two of the most well-known are the Underwriter's Laboratory, or UL, label and the Good Housekeeping "seal of approval."

UNDERWRITER'S LABORATORY. Most household appliances display the UL label, and many manufacturers emphasize its presence in their advertising. The UL label, however, only certifies that the products or appliances do not have the potential of causing fire, electric shock, or accident. Underwriter's Laboratory does not evaluate the actual quality of the appliances you are purchasing. Nor does the UL label mean that the product has been compared to its competitors and proved better. Moreover, the only way the UL label can be obtained is for the manufacturer either to submit the product and pay a fee or agree to a specified control procedure. In order to keep the UL label, the manufacturer must pay a yearly fee. Some companies decide not to pay that fee but still produce perfectly sound products.

Recently, the Underwriter's Laboratory has begun to test marine equipment (for example, life preservers), medical equipment (for example, adjustable hospital beds), and other items. UL also now tests products to determine if they present general safety hazards; for example, it might test a particular electric coffee pot to see if the lid falls off when it is tipped, although this has nothing to do with the product's electrical performance. Recently, UL has required manufacturers to include safety tips in the use and care manuals for products it approves.

GOOD HOUSEKEEPING SEAL. More than thirty-five years ago, the Federal Trade Commission required Good Housekeeping to eliminate the term "seal of approval." Nonetheless, for many consumers, the seal continues to convey approval. Good Housekeeping does not test the full quality of a product; presumably, it only determines whether the product or service submitted by a manufacturer for advertisement in *Good Housekeeping* magazine will live up to the claims made in the advertisement.

In principle, if the Good Housekeeping seal is on a product, you can receive a refund or replacement if that product proves defective. But no product is tested by the Good Housekeeping Institute Laboratories in New York City unless the product is to be advertised in the magazine. Before a manufacturer can use the Good Housekeeping seal, it must guarantee to the magazine that the volume of advertising placed in *Good Housekeeping* is equivalent to its ad volume in other media (or at least two columns a year).

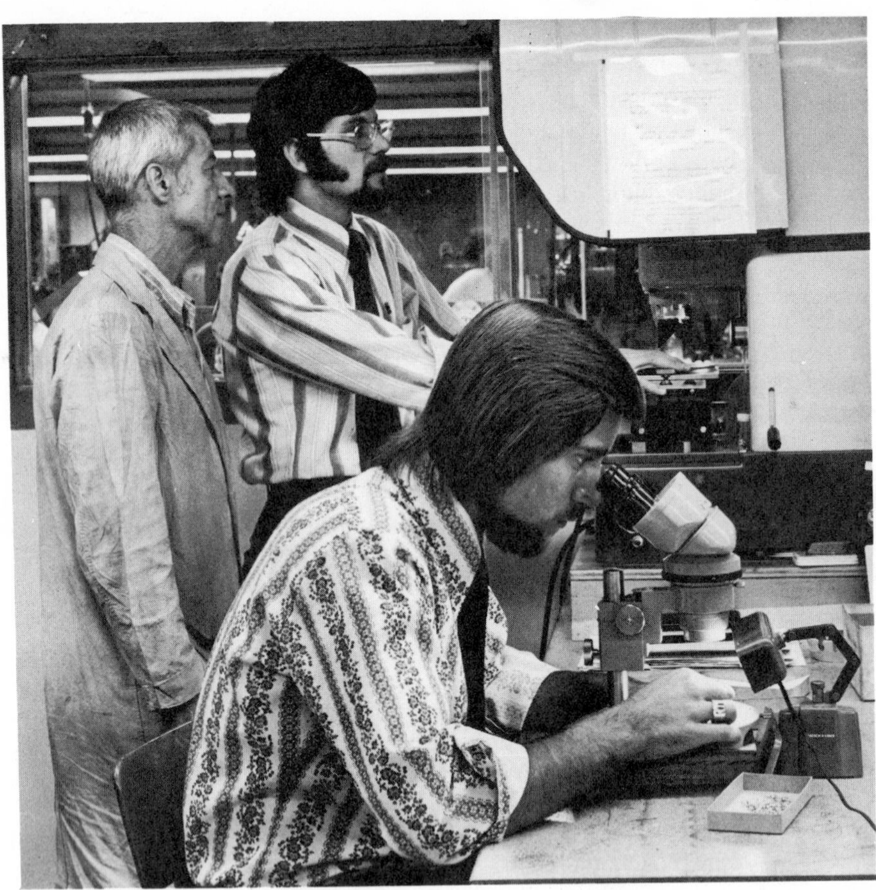

Private Industry Self-Regulation

We are observing an increase in the willingness of industry to regulate itself. Self-regulation involves the creation of a set of standards for an industry's products or services, publication of those standards, and their subsequent enforcement. For example, fabric and furniture manufacturers have set up their own flammability standards. It appears that private industry often would rather regulate itself than submit to government regulation.

RECOVERY OF DAMAGES

Recovery of damages for the individual consumer is a major issue in the consumer-protection movement today. States have generally provided this kind of service only in areas that have presented special problems. For example, California has provided for registration, for disclosure standards, and for administrative procedures on consumer grievances about service and repair for radios and TVs, automobiles, and major appliances. In cities and counties all over the country, concern about consumer damages has been expressed more broadly, as local government agencies mediate disputes between consumers and sellers.

The makeup and the authority of these local agencies vary dramatically. In some areas, authority is lodged in an "old line" agency, such as the Bureau of Weights and Measures, which already has operations in the consumer field. In other cases, the agency is attached to a social services department. But in its most effective form, the local consumer agency is independent and owes responsibility to no one but consumers and the public at large.

In its most effective form, the local consumer agency is independent and owes responsibility to no one but consumers and the public at large.

PRIVATE AGENCIES

Local private agencies are new participants in the public area of consumer protection. Probably the best known of such private agencies is the Better Business Bureau, which is business supported. The National Better Business Bureau has been in existence since 1916 and has local affiliates in all major cities and counties. Its purposes are:

1. To provide information on products and selling practices to consumers,
2. To provide businesspeople with a source of localized standards for acceptable business practices, and
3. To provide a technique for mediating grievances between consumers and sellers.

Because the Better Business Bureau has no enforcement powers, all actions must be voluntary. And because the Better Business Bureau is dependent on the business community for its membership, it cannot afford to antagonize that community. The weaknesses in the voluntary system were felt most strongly when the consumer movement began to press for protection, not only against the fly-by-night, illegal, fraudulent firm but against marketing practices that were generally accepted by the business community. Once consumers began to seek redress for damages suffered from exaggerated advertising, ineffective warranties and guarantees, safety hazards, and poor consumer choices due to market structure, the private business organization was unable to police its members effectively. But the Better Business Bureau continues to survive and to thrive as it seeks to improve communication with the consumer. For example, the Better Business Bureau's arbitration program has been expanding[2] in an attempt to deal more formally with the issue of consumer redress for grievances against sellers and producers of goods and services.

Don't get the impression, though, that the Better Business Bureau in your community is a truly effective consumer agency. In many communities, the BBB simply keeps files on businesses regarding consumer complaints.

Although the Better Business Bureau is the oldest of the private agencies that seek to mediate grievances, it is by no means the only one. As consumerism has grown, the media have been both criticized for their performance and mobilized for consumer protection. The media have been criticized for the type of advertising they have carried and for their lack of interest in providing time for countercommercials or public-service information. But newspapers, radio stations, and TV stations have all been in the forefront of the movement to help consumers who have legitimate complaints by providing column space or air time for consumer action, and they have been highly successful in

2. See Consumer Issue A for more details.

obtaining results for consumers able to make use of them. Affiliates of both the ABC and NBC networks have run regular consumer reports and consumer-action series, as have many independent television stations. These programs typically use publicity as a powerful weapon to resolve the consumer's grievance.

Looking back, we can see that the concept of consumer protection started as a set of standards to protect both buyers and sellers in a fair exchange. Next, standards were set for health and safety, primarily to protect consumers. Later, both consumers and businesses were protected against fraud. And, finally, the emphasis fell on the techniques of marketing and the problems of consumers in finding their way through the maze of technological detail in a highly industrialized society. No longer are consumers to be protected only up to the point of purchase; protection past the point of purchase is now a goal. This new area of consumer protection involves groups that seek, both publicly and privately, to provide mechanisms for settling consumer grievances without litigation.

ACTIVE CONSUMER GROUPS

We noted at the beginning of the chapter that many people find the term "consumer protection" insufficient, if not insulting; instead, they seek consumer-policy participation. While Ralph Nader, both through his own activities and those of organizations he has inspired, has become the symbol of consumer activism in the 1960s and 1970s, consumer organization at the state and local levels actually began long before Nader appeared on the scene. And although the consumer cooperative movement has never successfully defeated the corporation as a business form, it has succeeded in helping a few consumers solve some of their problems.

During the 1930s, consumer groups sprang up all over the country as many people found it necessary to stretch a precious few dollars to cover basic living needs. The big burst of consumerism, of course, occurred in the 1960s, and, by the early 1970s, organizations existed at state and local levels throughout the country. In 1967, the Consumer Federation of America was formed to coordinate the efforts of such groups at the national level. Local consumer-activist groups have aggressively pressed for legislation on credit, packaging, no-fault insurance, and adequate labeling of food and drugs. They have been active as well in seeking protection of consumers in such fields of major abuse as automobile and appliance repair services.

While acting at their own levels to seek redress for consumers who feel they have been damaged in private transactions, the state and local groups also have worked to provide education and representation to consumers in hearings before government legislative and administrative bodies. The ultimate goal of these groups is consumer participation in government policy decisions. In addition, they seek for consumers the strength to participate indirectly in the policy decisions of business firms by using their power in the marketplace and by acting as a single group. Thus, at least some consumers seek to participate in the functioning of the marketplace in the same way that large corporations and major trade unions do.

The development of this kind of consumer activism is significant because it illustrates that consumers also can have points of view. In any public policy issue, there may be a business interest, a labor interest, and a consumer interest. The price of food, for example, is a major issue that has involved all these interests in recent years. The question is: What is the public interest? From this point of view, where is consumer protection heading? What issues must be resolved as we expand, or try to expand, the concept of consumer protection?

There are many ways to obtain satisfaction when you, the consumer, feel you have been wronged in the marketplace. In Consumer Issue A, we outline the steps you should take and the agencies you can contact for help.

SUMMARY

1. One of the first consumer-protection activities was the formation of standards of weights and measures, which then had to be monitored and enforced.
2. Businesses were interested in enforcing such standards to protect themselves when buying materials or products and also to protect themselves against fraudulent competitors.
3. Among the first purely consumer-oriented activities were antitrust or antimonopoly policies aimed at preventing or breaking up existing monopolies that fixed prices at higher than competitive levels to the detriment of the consumer.
4. Although the first Food and Drug Act was passed in 1906, not until the 1938 Food, Drug and Cosmetic Act did consumer protection receive active federal government support. The most recent development in the consumer movement is consumer redress after a wrong has been committed.
5. In the 1960s and 1970s, starting during the administration of President Kennedy and extending through that of President Carter, the rights of consumers and the need for increased consumer protection have been popular topics for our chief executives. The election of Ronald Reagan changed the emphasis in favor of less government regulation of business.
6. The best-known private agencies are Consumers Union and Consumers' Research, Inc., both established chiefly to provide information to consumers. In addition, branches of the Better Business Bureau attempt to help consumers as well as business people, but they are not effective consumer-protection agencies. There are also private testing agencies, such as the American Standards Association and Underwriter's Laboratory.
7. State and local agencies have recently introduced means to help consumers recover damages for fraudulent business activities. At the very minimum, local government mediators act in disputes between consumers and sellers and often refer both parties to an appropriate agency if specific laws have, in fact, been violated.
8. Recently, consumer-activist groups have engaged in consumer advocacy at all levels of government. Their ultimate goal—consumer participation in the policy decisions of business firms—may be realized when certain segments of the marketplace can unite to become a single advocacy group.

QUESTIONS FOR THOUGHT AND DISCUSSION

1. Why is the consumer movement thought to be relatively new, even though it started many years ago?
2. Exactly what are antimonopoly policies? Why do monopolies hurt the consumer? (Hint: Look up the Sherman Act.)
3. What is the difference between consumer protection before the fact and consumer protection after the fact?

4. If you had to set up a model consumer-protection act, what would you include in it?
5. What do you think the current administration's stand on consumer protection is?
6. Do you think the consumer movement is still as strong as it was a few years ago?
7. Should the government engage in product testing and present the results of those tests to consumers?
8. What private sources of consumer information do you use in making your decisions about what to buy?

THINGS TO DO

1. Research and outline the history of consumer activism back to its origins in England. What groups have been around longest? What principles of consumerism have endured?
2. If you know a lawyer, talk to him or her about recent developments in laws affecting the consumer and the "sanctity" of contracts entered into by both consumer and seller.
3. Call your local Better Business Bureau and ask for its booklet describing the bureau and all the areas in which it is active. If there is no Better Business Bureau in your area, contact the local chamber of commerce.
4. Obtain a list of the books produced by Ralph Nader and his associates. Read one or two of them and then read Upton Sinclair's *The Jungle*. Do you see any similarities? Have manufacturing practices improved or worsened in the United States?

SELECTED READINGS

Aaker, David A. and Day, George S. *Consumerism: Search for the Consumer Interest*. New York: The Free Press, 1974.

Best, Arthur. *When Consumers Complain*. New York: Columbia University Press, 1981.

"Consumer Information; Federal Agencies and Information Centers." *Consumer Reports,* December 1979, pp. 355–59.

Faber, Doris. *Enough! The Revolt of the American Consumer*. New York: Farrar, Strauss & Giroux, 1972.

Fornell, Claes. "Increasing the Organizational Influence of Corporate Consumer Affairs Departments." *Journal of Consumer Affairs,* Winter 1981.

Magnuson, Warren. *The Dark Side of the Marketplace,* 2d ed. Englewood Cliffs, N.J.: Prentice-Hall, 1972.

Nader, Ralph, ed. *The Consumer and Corporate Accountability*. New York: Harcourt Brace Jovanovich, 1973.

Consumer ISSUE  

HOW TO GET HELP FOR CONSUMER PROBLEMS

GLOSSARY

INJUNCTION—A legal order requiring that an activity be stopped.

Knowing what kinds of services are available is the first step toward taking advantage of consumer-service agencies. Generally, government agencies and private voluntary and business groups provide the following four consumer services.

1. Information to consumers before a purchase is made. This service includes standard setting, inspection, investigation of marketing techniques, product testing, labeling and other disclosure legislation, publication of results, and formal teaching.

2. Aid to consumers after purchase is made, generally through the enforcement of public policy to prevent repeated unsatisfactory or fraudulent practices. This service includes accepting complaints, investigating the complaints, possibly instituting legal proceedings followed by a judgment, and imposing either an **injunction** against the action or a penalty for breaking the law. This kind of action does not help individual consumers make up their own losses.

3. Redress to individual consumers for their individual losses as a result of purchases. This involves a complaint, an investigation, possibly publicity or mediation, sometimes settlement, or legal action followed by a judgment and enforcement of it.

4. Representation of consumers in issues with a consumer interest before a legislative body, government administrative agencies, and private business leadership. Here again, this generally concerns the complaint, investigation and research regarding the complaint and the problem it reflects, and the subsequent development and publication of plans for its remedy. Often this results in changes in legislation.

WHERE TO GO

There are at least thirty-seven federal agencies involved in consumer issues and even more state, local, and private agencies with which you might have to deal. We will be primarily concerned with the problems you face when something goes wrong, rather than with gathering information before you buy a product. But even this limitation does not significantly reduce the number of agencies or organizations with which you will have to contend, for many of the agencies that provide information before you buy are the same ones that provide protection after you buy. And, of course, when you are concerned with complaints about products, you will most likely deal with a business firm, of which there are some 12 million in the United States.

A STRATEGY

First, you should always try to figure out a strategy for settling your grievances without going to an outside party. After all, it takes additional time and effort to get a third party involved in your disputes with a seller. Thus, whenever you buy anything, *keep a receipt* if you are worried that there may be problems later. But even before you make the purchase, be certain to *have everything put*

in writing about any take-back provisions, warranties, or guarantees.

Exhibit A-1 shows the chain of complaint. Imagine, for example, that you buy something, and it falls apart a week later. A friendly, polite cali to the store and a talk with the salesperson will tell you immediately whether you will have problems. Many times, reputable stores will either give you an identical article that is in good working condition, repair the one you have, or refund your money. If the salesperson does not agree, then seek out the manager or the owner. If you still do not get satisfaction and if you are dealing with a nationally advertised product or with a large chain store, you may want to write the president or the chairperson of the board directly to complain.[1]

1. In your local library, you can consult *The Consumer's Register of American Business* and *The Directory of Foreign Manufacturers in the United States.*

If you have a complaint about your car, your bank account, airline service, your insurance, a hospital bill, or almost anything else, you'd do well to obtain a free copy of *Consumer's Resource Handbook* from the Consumer Information Center, Department 579L, Pueblo, Colorado 81009. This booklet lists addresses, phone numbers, and individuals at hundreds of companies, federal and state organizations, and Better Business Bureaus whom you can contact to obtain remedial action for your consumer problems. Exhibit A-2 shows a sample copy of an appropriate letter of complaint. Personal letters to the presidents of large companies get quick responses surprisingly often. But sometimes they do not. If your letter-writing effort fails, what is your next recourse?

To answer this question, you may also have to decide how much of your time and other resources you want to expend. Do you just want your money back, or do you

1. Purchase a product and save the sales receipt. Write down the salesperson's name.
2. The product proves to be defective.
3. Visit or call the store and talk to the salesperson.
4. If unsuccessful in dealing with the salesperson to obtain a refund, repair, or new article, find out the manager's name and either call or visit him or her.
5. If unsuccessful with the manager, do the following three things simultaneously:
   a. When dealing with a nationally advertised product or a large retail chain, obtain from your local library the name and address of the president or chairperson of the board and write to him or her directly, enclosing a copy of the letter shown in Exhibit A-2. Make sure that you indicate that you have written to local and state consumer groups.
   b. Write to local and state consumer groups about your problem, enclosing a copy of the letter you sent to the president or chairperson of the board.
   c. Contact national consumer-help agencies and consumer-action panels. For example, there is a Major Appliance Consumer Action Panel (MACAP) discussed in Issue N and an Automobile Consumer Action Panel (AUTOCAP) discussed in Issue P.
6. If still you receive no satisfaction, lodge your complaint with the state attorney general's office.

EXHIBIT A–1
The Chain of Complaint

want to ensure that this never happens again? Some states have special catalogs that tell you how to handle your complaint. For example, the *Complete California Consumer Catalog* is available for $2.50 from the California State Government Publications Section, P.O. Box 20191, Sacramento, California 95820.

GETTING YOUR MONEY BACK

If getting your money back or solving your own problem is your primary goal, then it is probably best to work at the local level. First, you should determine if there is a consumer-affairs agency or a consumer-affairs office in your local government. The telephone book is probably your nearest source of this information; in most major cities today, there is a Yellow Pages listing under "Consumers" of the major public agencies that provide consumer services. A call to the administrative officer of your county or city should also provide information on the availability of public consumer services.

If you find no local consumer agency, look under the state listings; if no listing there looks promising, call the state attorney general's office. That office works closely with consumer agencies because much of the consumer fraud uncovered by consumer agencies is prosecuted through the attorney general's office. Exhibit A–3 lists the addresses of state consumer-protection agencies.

Private Organizations

While your state and your community may have no public consumer-affairs agency or office, there may be a private organization (a consumer organization, a local newspaper, or a radio or television station) that provides a consumer service. You probably will have read or heard about any successful private organization, and you will find it listed in the telephone book. But if you have difficulty locating it, it probably is not yet an effective group, in which case it may not be able to help you resolve your problem. Nonetheless, you might consider joining it to prevent a recurrence of your problem.

Finally, getting your money back may depend on private legal action. If you have to go beyond the small claims court, which we discuss later, to a higher court, you must be prepared to pay legal fees. But even if you can't pay them, don't give up; in many cities, the traditional legal-aid society has been augmented by special legal services for low-income families, and these services often place strong emphasis on consumer problems. In some states, too,

EXHIBIT A–2
How to Lodge a Complaint

Your address
Date

Addressee
Company Name
Street Address
City, State Zip Code

Dear Sir or Madam,

I am writing this letter to inform you of my dissatisfaction with [name of product with serial number or the service performed] which I purchased [the date and location of purchase].

My complaint concerns [the reason(s) for your complaint]. I believe that in all fairness you should [the specific action you desire for satisfaction] in order to resolve this problem.

I sincerely look forward to your reply and a speedy resolution to my complaint. I will allow two weeks before referring this complaint to the appropriate consumer agency.

Yours truly,

Your Name

Enclosures (include copies, not originals, of all related records)
cc: State Attorney General
Better Business Bureau

group legal practices have been approved, and you might obtain help through your union or some other organization that has contracted with such a service. Some college governments have made available to students legal services that permit students to pursue solutions to their consumer problems.

EXHIBIT A–3
State Consumer Protection Agencies

Alabama. Governor's Office of Consumer Protection, 138 Adams Avenue, Montgomery 36130

Alaska. Office of the Attorney General, 420 L Street, Suite 100, Anchorage 99501

Arizona. Economic Protection Division, Department of Law, 200 State Capitol Building, Phoenix 85007

Arkansas. Consumer Protection Division, Justice Building, Little Rock 72201

California. Department of Consumer Affairs, 1020 N Street, Sacramento 95814

Colorado. Assistant Attorney General, 1525 Sherman Street, 3rd Floor, Denver 80203

Connecticut. Department of Consumer Protection, State Office Building, Hartford 06115

Delaware. Consumer Affairs Division, 820 N. French Street, 4th Floor, Wilmington 19801

Florida. Division of Consumer Services, 110 Mayo Bldg., Tallahassee 32304

Georgia. Governor's Office of Consumer Affairs, 225 Peachtree Street, N.E., Suite 400, Atlanta 30303

Hawaii. Consumer Protection, 250 S. King Street, P.O. Box 3767, Honolulu 96811

Idaho. Consumer Protection Division, State Capitol, Boise 83720

Illinois. Consumer Advocate Office, 160 N. Lasalle Street, Room 2010, Chicago 60601

Indiana. Consumer Protection Division, 215 State House, Indianapolis 46204

Iowa. Consumer Protection Division, 1209 E. Court, Des Moines 50319

Kansas. Consumer Protection Division, Kansas Judicial Center, 310 W. 10th, 2nd Floor, Topeka 66612

Kentucky. Consumer Protection Division, Frankfort 40601

Louisiana. Governor's Office of Consumer Protection, P.O. Box 44091, Suite 1218, Capitol Station, Baton Rouge 70804

Maine. Consumer and Antitrust Division, State Office Building, Room 505, Augusta 04333

Maryland. Consumer Protection Division, 131 E. Redwood Street, Baltimore 21202

Massachusetts. Executive Office of Consumer Affairs, John W. McCormack Building, One Ashburton Pl., Boston 02108

Michigan. Consumer Protection Division, 670 Law Building, Lansing 48913

Minnesota. Consumer Protection Division, 102 State Capitol, St. Paul 55155

Mississippi. Consumer Protection Division, Justice Building, P.O. Box 220, Jackson 39205

Missouri. Consumer Protection Division, Supreme Court Building, P.O. Box 899, Jefferson City 65102

Montana. Consumer Affairs Division, 805 N. Main Street, St. Helena 59601

Nebraska. Consumer Protection Division, State House, Lincoln 68509

Nevada. Consumer Affairs Division, 2501 E. Sahara Avenue, 3rd Floor, Las Vegas 89158

New Hampshire. Consumer Protection Division, Statehouse Annex, Concord 00301

New Jersey. Division of Consumer Affairs, 1100 Raymond Blvd., Room 504, Newark 07102

New Mexico. Consumer and Economic Crime Division, P.O. Box 1508, Santa Fe 87501

New York. Consumer Protection Board, 99 Washington Avenue, Albany 12210

North Carolina. Consumer Protection Division, Justice Building, P.O. Box 629, Raleigh 27602

North Dakota. Consumer Fraud Division, State Capitol, 1102 S. Washington, Bismarck 58501

Ohio. Consumer Frauds and Crimes Section, 30 E. Broad Street, Columbus 43215

Oklahoma. Department of Consumer Affairs, Jim Thorpe Building, Room 460, Oklahoma City 73105

Oregon. Consumer Protection Division, 520 S.W. Yamhill Street, Portland 97204

Pennsylvania. Bureau of Consumer Protection, 301 Market Street, 9th Floor, Harrisburg 17101

Rhode Island. Rhode Island Consumers Council, 365 Broadway, Providence 02909

South Carolina. Office of Citizens Service, State House, P.O. Box 11450, Columbia 29211

South Dakota. Department of Commerce and Consumer Affairs, State Capitol, Pierre 57501

Tennessee. Division of Consumer Affairs, Ellington Agriculture Center, P.O. Box 40627, Melrose Station, Nashville 37204

Texas. Consumer Protection Division, P.O. Box 12538, Capitol Station, Austin 78711

Utah. Division of Consumer Affairs, Department of Business Regulation, 330 E. Fourth South, Salt Lake City 84111

Vermont. Consumer Protection Division, 109 State Street, Montpelier 05602

Virginia. Division of Consumer Counsel, 11 S. 12th Street, Suite 308, Richmond 23219

Washington. Consumer Protection and Antitrust Division, 1366 Dexter Horton Building, Seattle 98104

West Virginia. Consumer Protection Division, 3412 Staunton Avenue, S.E., Charleston 25305

Wisconsin. Office of Consumer Protection, State Capitol, Madison 53702

Wyoming. Assistant Attorney General, 123 Capitol Building, Cheyenne 82002.

District of Columbia. Department of Economic Development, Consumer Retail Credit Division, Room 306, 614 "H" Street, N.W., Washington, D.C. 20001

Commonwealth of Puerto Rico. Director of the Consumer Services Administration, P.O. Box 13934, Santurce 00908

Virgin Islands. Consumer Services Administration, P.O. Box 831, Charlotte Amalie, St. Thomas 00801, or Vitraco Mall, Christiansted, St. Croix 008820

SPECIFIC INDUSTRY AGENCIES: THIRD-PARTY INTERVENTION

An increasingly popular way to resolve consumer problems is to allow third parties to settle a dispute between you and the seller of a product or service. Local agencies, trade associations, and individual companies are setting up mediation procedures, most of which are free to consumers. There are basically three types of third-party interveners:

1. **A conciliator,** who simply brings together the parties in a dispute to get them to resolve their differences;
2. **A mediator,** who is in a stronger position and can make nonbinding recommendations and proposals;
3. **An arbitrator,** who makes a decision that can be binding on some or all of the parties. A binding decision can be enforced in a court of law.

Obviously, from the consumer's point of view, the best of all possible worlds is a mediation process that is binding on the business but not on the consumer. This may sound unrealistic, but the arbitration procedures of Ford Motor Company's Consumer Appeals Board and the Homeowners Warranty Corporation (HOW), which provides guarantees on new home construction, operate that way; we will discuss HOW further in Issue L.

Where to Go

Where you go depends on the kind of problem you have. If it is a dispute between you and a local company, going to a local agency makes sense. Ninety-four local Better Business Bureaus across the country provide arbitration. Your county Office of Consumer Affairs will also be able to help. If it is a dispute between you and a manufacturer of a product, then you should find out if there is an arbitration panel for that industry. The names and addresses of such services are given in the chapters on transportation, appliances, and housing. There are arbitration panels for new automobiles, automobile repair services, furniture, new home construction, and major appliances.

CONSUMER HOTLINES

For a specific complaint, you may wish to call the consumer hotline that deals with firms engaged in a particular industry. The following is a list of hotline numbers for many of the industries about which you may raise a consumer issue.

1. **Advertising:** Director, Bureau of Consumer Protection, Federal Trade Commission (202) 523-3727
2. **Air safety:** Community and Consumer Liaison Division, Federal Aviation Administration (202) 426-1960.
3. **Appliances:** Major Appliance Consumer Action Panel (312) 984-5858
4. **Auto problems:** Ford (313) 337-6950; Chrysler (313) 956-5970; American Motors (313) 493-2344
5. **Auto safety:** National Highway Traffic Safety Administration (800) 424-9393
6. **Bus travel:** Consumer Affairs Office, Interstate Commerce Commission (800) 424-9312
7. **Business:** Office of the Ombudsman, Department of Commerce (202) 377-5001
8. **Credit:** Bureau of Consumer Protection, Division of Credit Practice (202) 724-1181 (For bank credit problems, call Housing and Credit Section, Justice Department (202) 724-7396.)
9. **Fraud:** Federal Trade Commission (202) 523-3598
10. **Furniture:** Furniture Industry Consumer Advisory Panel (919) 885-5065
11. **Mail fraud:** Chief Postal Inspector (202) 245-5445
12. **Mail-order problems:** Direct Mail: Marketing Association (212) 687-4977
13. **Movers:** Interstate Commerce Commission (800) 424-9312
14. **Safety at work:** Occupational Safety and Health Administration (202) 523-6091
15. **Stocks and bonds:** Consumer Liaison Office, Securities and Exchange Commission (202) 523-5516
16. **Surgery:** Department of Health and Human Services (800) 331-1000; in Missouri (800) 342-6600; in Oklahoma, call collect (918) 664-8300
17. **Travel:** American Society of Travel Agents (212) 486-0700
18. **Unwanted mail:** Consumer Service Department, Direct Mail Marketing Association (212) 689-4977
19. **Warranties:** Public Reference Branch, Federal Trade Commission (202) 523-3598

THE FEDERAL GOVERNMENT

If your problem concerns a product sold nationally or if it affects a large number of people nationwide, you should appeal to a federal agency.

Office of Consumer Affairs

The Office of Consumer Affairs once advised the president directly but is now part of the Department of

Health and Human Services. For a while, it coordinated all federal activities on behalf of consumers. Although it is still involved in a consumer-education program, many consumer specialists believe that this office has little power today. In any event, if you have complaints about products or services, you can write directly to the Federal Complaint Coordination Center in the Office of Consumer Affairs, 621 Reporters Building, Washington, D.C. 20201; telephone (202) 755-8875.

The Food and Drug Administration (500 Fishers Lane, Rockville, Maryland 20857)

The Food and Drug Administration has regional offices in many cities, and on each office staff is a person specifically charged with consumer services. Many of the FDA's 5,000 employees are technical experts working in specific fields under FDA jurisdiction. Any complaint about a food, drug, or cosmetic that you purchase should be made either to your regional office or directly to Washington, D.C. The agency will ask you for complete information, and its staff is particularly interested in examining the container or the food or drug about which you are complaining. If they believe your complaint is justified, a member of the staff will visit the firm in question to observe its production and packaging procedures. If you do not have the product, you still may complain. The FDA is always interested in receiving consumer reports, even though the complaints may have no legal consequence. Through such reports, the FDA often discovers new problems or new incidences of old problems. In those areas in which the FDA sets and/or enforces standards, consumers can play a very important role. But unless the agency hears from consumers, it may be making avoidable mistakes.

Federal Trade Commission (Washington, D.C. 20580)

The FDA largely enforces standards of product and performance, but the Federal Trade Commission's standards are essentially those of practice—competition in the marketplace; false, misleading, and deceptive advertising by sellers to buyers; and packaging and labeling practices of firms engaged in nonfood sales. In addition, the FDA handles complaints that are subject to federal credit and federal warranty legislation.

The FTC has regional offices and consumer-service representatives in major U.S. cities. It has established a special office to serve consumers, and it provides a wide range of informative pamphlets for them. If you have a complaint for the FTC, you may address it to a regional office or to the Washington, D.C., headquarters. If it believes you have a valid complaint, the FTC will send an investigator out to check with both you and the firm. Typically, the FTC works in two ways. First, it investigates whether or not a particular seller or advertiser has violated a particular law that the agency enforces; if its findings are positive, it takes action to stop the practice by the single firm. Second, the agency looks for new patterns of practice that may mislead consumers; if it finds such patterns, the FTC may attempt to act against an entire industry, rather than a single firm, to stop the practice altogether.

U.S. Department of Agriculture (Washington, D.C. 20250)

Although the U.S. Department of Agriculture primarily provides services to farmers, it also protects consumers in very important ways, notably by inspecting and grading meat, poultry, and fish. In recent years, the agency has also become a primary source of information for consumers on the best ways to spend their food dollars. The USDA does this through its Cooperative Extension Service, operated in conjunction with land-grant universities throughout the United States. Any complaint you have about the grades of meat you buy or the quality of the poultry that is shipped interstate should be reported to your local health department or your local department of agriculture.

The Department of Agriculture provides other services, including the Agricultural Research Service, the Animal and Plant Health Inspection Service, the Economic Research Service, the Food and Nutrition Service, the Forest Service, and the Rural Development Service. If you are interested in any of these services, you can get the appropriate telephone numbers and addresses from the Office of Information, USDA, Washington, D.C. 20250; phone (202) 447-6311.

U.S. Postal Service (Washington, D.C. 20260)

This agency is responsible for investigating mail fraud, unordered merchandise, obscenity in the mails, and other mail-related problems.

Department of Housing and Urban Development (Washington, D.C. 20410)

This agency is responsible for numerous federally subsidized housing programs. You can contact its consumer-affairs coordinator if you have a relevant problem.

Interstate Commerce Commission (Washington, D.C. 20523)

Any complaints you have regarding moving companies, truck shipments, or railroads can be addressed specifically to this agency.

CONSUMER PROTECTION BY THE CPSC

One of the newest federal agencies designed to protect the consumer is the Consumer Product Safety Commission. It was established in 1972 and given sweeping powers to regulate the production and sale of potentially hazardous consumer products. The agency eventually will have a staff of more than 1,000, making it one of the major federal regulatory agencies for consumer protection.

Creating the Agency

Consumer product-safety legislation began in 1953 with the enactment of the Flammable Fabrics Act, designed to protect consumers from hazards created by the use of certain consumer products. Between 1953 and 1972, Congress enacted legislation regulating specific classes rather than broad categories of consumer products. Finally, as a result of the 1970 recommendations of the National Commission on Product Safety, the Consumer Product Safety Act was passed in 1972, creating the CPSC to regulate all potentially hazardous consumer products.

Purposes of the Act

As stated in the act, the CPSC was created:

1. To protect the public against unreasonable risk of injury associated with consumer products;
2. To assist consumers in evaluating the comparative safety of consumer products;
3. To develop uniform safety standards for consumer products and to minimize conflicting state and local regulations; and
4. To promote research and investigation into causes and prevention of product-related deaths, illnesses, and injuries.

Form and Functions of the CPSC

The commission was set up to conduct research on product safety and to maintain a clearinghouse to "collect, investigate, analyze, and disseminate injury data, and information, relating to the causes and prevention of death, injury, and illness associated with consumer products . . . ." To this end, the CPSC immediately started gathering data on the 200 most hazardous consumer products in the nation. The data have been obtained by requiring hospital emergency wards to indicate the particular cause of any injury, illness, or death related to a consumer product. After the initial CPSC survey, the most hazardous consumer product was found to be the bicycle.

The CPSC hoped that the data obtained and the resulting hazard index for consumer products would move manufacturers to improve voluntarily the most hazardous products and forewarn consumers about such products. Exhibit A–4 gives a list of today's top hazards and the corresponding number of reported accidents.

HOW TO CONTACT THE CPSC

If you think there is an unsafe product on the market, or if you have any questions about product hazards and safety, you may want to get in touch directly with the CPSC. The number, toll-free from anywhere in the United States, is (800) 638-2772. You can also write to the Consumer Product Safety Commission in Washington, D.C. 20207 and explain your concern about a particular product or products.

OBTAINING MORE INFORMATION ON FEDERAL CONSUMER SERVICES

The first thing you can do to obtain more information on the availability of federal consumer services is to send for the *Guide to Federal Consumer Services*, publication number (OS) 76-512.

If you do not know which way to turn, you may wish to write or visit a Federal Information Center, whose staff members can give you information about the vast number of federal agencies and programs. Exhibit A-5 is a list of the Federal Information Centers in thirty-eight cities.

EXHIBIT A–4
Today's Top Hazards

SOURCE	NUMBER OF REPORTED ACCIDENTS
Stairs, steps, ramps, and landings	763,000
Bicycles and bicycle equipment	518,000
Baseball-related equipment and apparel	478,000
Football-related equipment and apparel	470,000
Basketball-related equipment and apparel	434,000
Nails, carpet tacks, screws, and thumbtacks	244,000
Chairs, sofas, and sofa beds	236,000
Skating	225,000
Tables (nonglass)	225,000
Architectural glass doors, windows, and panels	208,000
Beds and bunk beds (including springs and frames)	199,000
Playground equipment, swings, slides, seesaws, monkey bars	165,000
Lumber	151,000
Cutlery and knives	140,000
Glass bottles and jars	140,000
Desks, cabinets, and shelves	126,000
Swimming pools and associated equipment (in-ground only)	126,000
Drinking glasses	111,000
Ladders and stools	99,000
Fences	99,000
Soccer	96,000
Cans and other containers	93,000
Bathtubs and shower structures, nonglass bathtub and shower enclosures (except doors, panels)	83,000
Exterior structures and materials (poles, exterior walls)	78,000
Power homeworkshop saws	76,000
Volleyball	75,000
Footwear, outerwear, and clothing accessories	74,000
Tableware and flatware (not including cutlery)	70,000
Balconies, porches, open sliding doors, and floor coverings	69,000
Lawn mowers	68,000
Tennis, badminton, and squash	67,000
Wrestling-related apparel and equipment	66,000
Chain saws	64,000
Fishing-related apparel and equipment	64,000
Gymnastics-related apparel and equipment	62,000
Guns (all types)	60,000

SOURCE: Consumer Product Safety Commission, 1981.

SPECIAL PROBLEMS WITH MAIL-ORDER SALES

Purchasing items by mail has become an increasingly important type of shopping activity. There are three major reasons why catalog sales have more than quintupled in the last three years.

1. Consumers' time is becoming more valuable as we become a richer nation.
2. As state sales taxes increase, it becomes more advantageous to shop by mail to avoid these taxes; in many cases, an item sent from another state remains untaxed.
3. As the price of gasoline continues to rise, shopping by mail becomes relatively more attractive.

The Federal Trade Commission Rules

The Federal Trade Commission has established the following rules to protect you when you shop by mail.

1. If a catalog or ad indicates that the goods will be sent within a certain period, such as a week, they must be sent within that time. When no date is mentioned, the items must be shipped within thirty days.
2. If the item can't be shipped within the specified time or within thirty days, you must be notified and be given a free means of stating what you want to do about the delay; the supplier must provide a toll-free telephone number or a postage-paid postcard.
3. You can cancel an order or agree to the new shipment date. If you cancel, you must receive your refund within seven business days. If you fail to reply and if the delay will be less than thirty days, the company can assume that you agree to the delay. For any delays over thirty days, your money must be refunded if you have not given your consent to the delay.

The preceding rules do not apply to magazine subscriptions, photofinishing services, plants and seeds, COD orders, and credit orders that aren't charged until the goods are shipped.

Hints to Catalog Shoppers

The following is a list of things you might do if you decide to shop by mail.

1. Keep a record of the company from which you order, by writing its name and address on your check stub.
2. Do not send cash; use only checks, money orders, or credit cards.

EXHIBIT A–5
Federal Information Centers

ARIZONA
Phoenix
(602) 261-3313
Federal Building
230 N. 1st Ave. 85025

CALIFORNIA
Los Angeles
(213) 688-3800
Federal Building
300 N. Los Angeles St. 90012
Sacramento
(916) 449-3344
Federal Building
U.S. Courthouse
650 Capitol Mall 95814
San Diego
(714) 293-6030
202 C St. 92101
San Francisco
(415) 556-6600
Federal Building
U.S. Courthouse
450 Golden Gate Ave. 94102

COLORADO
Denver
(303) 837-3602
Federal Building
U.S. Courthouse
1961 Stout St. 80202

DISTRICT OF COLUMBIA
Washington
(202) 755-8660
7th & D Sts. S.W. 20407

FLORIDA
Miami
(305) 350-4155
Federal Building
51 S.W. 1st Ave. 33130
St. Petersburg
(813) 893-3495
William C. Cramer
Federal Building
144 1st Ave. S. 33701

GEORGIA
Atlanta
(404) 526-6891
Federal Building
275 Peachtree St. N.E. 30303

HAWAII
Honolulu
(808) 546-8620
U.S. Post Office
Courthouse & Customhouse
335 Merchant St. 96813

ILLINOIS
Chicago
(312) 353-4242
Everett McKinley
Dirksen Building
219 S. Dearborn St. 60604

INDIANA
Indianapolis
(317) 269-7373
Federal Building
575 N. Pennsylvania St. 46204

KENTUCKY
Louisville
(502) 582-6261
Federal Building
600 Federal Place 40202

LOUISIANA
New Orleans
(504) 589-6696
Federal Building
701 Loyola Ave. 70113

MARYLAND
Baltimore
(301) 962-4980
Federal Building
31 Hopkins Plaza 21201

MASSACHUSETTS
Boston
(617) 223-7121
John F. Kennedy
Federal Building
Government Center 02203

MICHIGAN
Detroit
(313) 226-7016
Federal Building
U.S. Courthouse
231 W. Lafayette St. 48226

MINNESOTA
Minneapolis
(612) 725-2073
Federal Building
U.S. Courthouse
110 S. 4th St. 55401

MISSOURI
Kansas City
(816) 374-2466
Federal Building
601 E. 12th St. 64106
St. Louis
(314) 425-4106
Federal Building
1520 Market St. 63103

NEBRASKA
Omaha
(402) 221-3353
Federal Building
U.S. Post Office & Courthouse
215 N. 17th St. 68102

NEW JERSEY
Newark
(201) 645-3600
Federal Building
970 Broad St. 07102

NEW MEXICO
Albuquerque
(505) 766-3091
Federal Building
U.S. Courthouse
500 Gold Ave., S.W. 87101

NEW YORK
Buffalo
(716) 842-5770
Federal Building
111 W. Huron St. 14202
New York
(212) 264-4464
Federal Office Building
U.S. Customs Court
26 Federal Plaza 10007

OHIO
Cincinnati
(513) 684-2801
Federal Building
550 Main St. 45202
Cleveland
(216) 522-4040
Federal Building
1240 E. 9th St. 44199

OKLAHOMA
Oklahoma City
(405) 231-4868
U.S. Post Office Building
201 N.W. 3rd St. 73102
Tulsa
(918) 584-4193
U.S. Post Office Building
201 N.W. 3rd St.
Oklahoma City 73102

OREGON
Portland
(503) 221-2222
1220 S.W. 3rd Ave. 97204

PENNSYLVANIA
Philadelphia
(215) 597-7042
Federal Building
600 Arch St. 19106
Pittsburgh
(412) 644-3456
Federal Building
1000 Liberty Ave. 15222

TENNESSEE
Memphis
(901) 534-3285
Clifford Davis Federal Building
167 N. Main St. 38103

TEXAS
Fort Worth
(817) 334-3624
Fritz Garland Lanham
Federal Building
819 Taylor St. 76102
Houston
(713) 226-5711
Federal Building
U.S. Courthouse
515 Rusk Ave. 77002

UTAH
Salt Lake City
(801) 524-5353
Federal Building
U.S. Post Office & Courthouse
125 S. State St. 84138

WASHINGTON
Seattle
(206) 442-0570
Federal Building
915 2nd Ave. 98174

If none of the above-mentioned centers is nearby, you may call one of the following local numbers and ask to be connected by a toll-free tie line to a Federal Information Center.

ALABAMA
Birmingham 322-8591
Mobile 438-1421

EXHIBIT A–5 (Continued)
Federal Information Centers

ARIZONA
Tucson 622-1511

ARKANSAS
Little Rock 378-6177

CALIFORNIA
San Jose 275-7422

COLORADO
Colorado Springs 471-9491
Pueblo 544-9523

CONNECTICUT
Hartford 527-2617
New Haven 624-4720

FLORIDA
Fort Lauderdale 522-8531
Jacksonville 354-4756
Tampa 229-7911
West Palm Beach 833-7566

IOWA
Des Moines 282-9091

KANSAS
Topeka 232-7229
Wichita 263-6931

MISSOURI
St. Joseph 233-8206

NEW JERSEY
Trenton 396-4400

NEW MEXICO
Santa Fe 983-7743

NEW YORK
Albany 463-4421
Rochester 546-5075
Syracuse 476-8545

NORTH CAROLINA
Charlotte 376-3600

OHIO
Akron 375-5475
Columbus 221-1014
Dayton 223-7377
Toledo 244-8625

OKLAHOMA
Tulsa 548-4193

PENNSYLVANIA
Scranton 346-7081

RHODE ISLAND
Providence 331-5565

TENNESSEE
Chattanooga 265-8231

TEXAS
Austin 472-5494
Dallas 749-2131
San Antonio

UTAH
Ogden 399-1347

WASHINGTON
Tacoma 383-5230

WISCONSIN
Milwaukee 271-2273

3. Keep a copy of the catalog pictures of the items you selected.
4. Mark on your calendar the date you mailed the order and the date you expect it to arrive.
5. Print your full name and address on the order form.
6. Send your order in immediately (or telephone it in if there is a toll-free number). Catalog companies are often out of stock soon after an item is advertised.
7. Whenever you suspect fraud, contact your nearest postal inspectors.

SUMMARY

1. When you have purchased a faulty product or have been given inadequate services for money spent, you should follow a strategy for redress of your grievance. Even before you purchase any good or service, make sure that all guarantees, warranties, and take-back provisions are in writing. If you are dissatisfied after making a purchase, speak with the person who sold the goods or service to you; if you do not obtain satisfaction there, speak with the store manager or owner; if you're still unsatisfied and if your purchase was a nationally advertised product or was from a large chain store, contact the company president or chairperson of the board. When you cannot obtain satisfaction directly from the company, you may wish to seek out a local consumer-affairs agency or the office of consumer affairs affiliated with your local or state government. In the Yellow Pages, look under "Consumer" to find out if there is such an agency or office in your area, or call the state attorney general's office for information on the appropriate agency in your local or state government.
2. Private organizations may help you, but these are difficult to find in certain areas. A call to your local college or university might work; ask to speak with someone in the department of home economics or the school of business. Also, many campuses have consumer-resource centers.
3. Certain professional organizations and industries have consumer-oriented agencies—for example, the American Medical Association, the American Dental Association, the American Bar Association, the Association of Home Appliance Manufacturers, the Gas Appliance Manufacturers Association, and the National Retail Merchants Association. By contacting one of these associations directly, you may be able to obtain redress for a particular grievance.
4. Each state has the following departments that you can contact directly for help in specific areas: agriculture, public health, occupational licensing, and the attorney general's office. In addition, your local district attorney's office may be helpful in cases of fraud or deceptive advertising.
5. The federal government may be able to assist you or refer you to the appropriate agency at the state or local level. You may wish to contact one of the following: the Office of Consumer Affairs in the Department of Health and Human Services, the Federal Trade Commission, the Food and Drug Administration, the U.S. Department of

Agriculture, the Consumer Product Safety Commission, the Federal Communications Commission, the U.S. Postal Service, the Department of Housing and Urban Development, or the Interstate Commerce Commission.

QUESTIONS FOR THOUGHT AND DISCUSSION

1. Who do you think benefits most from consumer protection agencies?
2. Should there be an agency to inform low-income consumers that other agencies exist to help them?
3. If you were head of the Consumer Product Safety Commission, how would you determine which products should be banned from the market?
4. When do you decide it is time to seek help for a consumer grievance?
5. How do you decide when to seek protection against fraudulent activity on the part of businesses?
6. What is the difference between consumerism and consumer advocacy?

THINGS TO DO

1. Draw up a list of consumer affairs agencies in your area. First look in the Yellow Pages under "Consumer" to see what is listed there. Then contact the district attorney's office. Next contact the state attorney general.
2. Write to various industry organizations, such as the National Retail Merchant's Association. Find out what kind of grievance procedure each has for consumers who feel they have been wronged.

SELECTED READINGS

Consumer Union. *Consumer Reports Annual Buying Guide.* Published annually in December.

Consumer's Resource Handbook. Available free from Consumer Information Center, Department 579L, Pueblo, Colorado 81009.

George, Richard. *The New Consumer Survival Kit.* Boston: Little, Brown & Co., 1978.

Horowitz, David. *Fight Back and Don't Get Ripped Off.* New York: Harper and Row, 1959.

"Mail Fraud Laws." Publication No. P1–10. Available free from post offices or from Consumer Information Center. Pueblo, Colorado 81009.

Newman, Stephen and Kramer, Nancy. *Getting What You Deserve.* Garden City, N.Y.: Doubleday, 1979.

Rosenbloom, Joseph. *Consumer Complaint Guide.* New York: Macmillan Co., 1979.

Rosenbloom, Joseph. *Consumer Protection Guide.* New York: Macmillan Co., 1978.

Rowse, Arthur E. and the staff of Consumer News, Inc. *Help: The Indispensable Almanac of Consumer Information.* New York: Everest House, published annually.

"Shopping by Mail? You're Protected." Available free from the Federal Trade Commission, Washington, D.C. 20580.

Wall, Edward C. *Consumer's Index to Product Evaluations and Information Sources.* New York: Pierian Press, published annually.

Consumer ISSUE 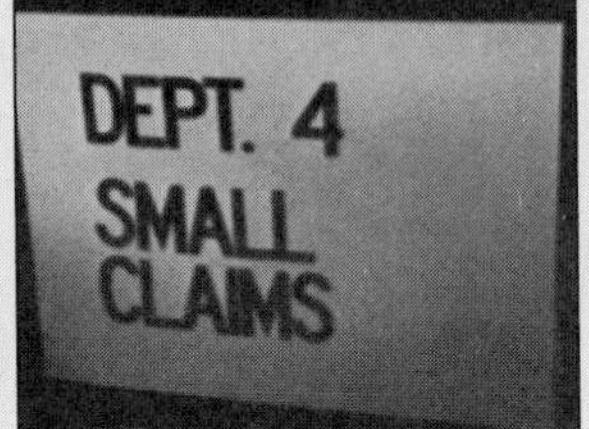 B

HOW TO USE A SMALL CLAIMS COURT

GLOSSARY

LITIGANTS—Those people involved in a lawsuit (called litigation).

PLAINTIFFS—Those who initiate lawsuits.

Did you think that your former landlord cheated you by keeping your security deposit when you moved out? Did a dry cleaner ruin or lose your clothes? Did you make a claim to your insurance company that it refused to pay? Did a company issue you a warranty on one of its products and then charge you for a repair job while the product was still covered?

If you've ever felt helpless in these or similar situations, you needn't have. To right such wrongs, you could have used the small claims court in your area.[1] But because it may take some time, effort, and patience to get on a court calendar, first you should examine some of the possible alternatives, including the use of consumer hot lines available in many states and cities; consumer advocates, who will take up your gripes with the appropriate people and see that the results are publicized; and, in some cities, radio and TV newspersons who narrate complaints over the air. In Consumer Issue A, we discussed other ways you can complain and get redress for your consumer grievances. If you still feel you need judicial help, then you might want to use a small claims court.

1. Called a magistrate's court in some areas and a court not of record in others.

WHY WERE THEY FOUNDED?

In 1913, Roscoe Pound, a noted professor of the Harvard Law School, gave a justification for small claims courts: "It is a *denial of justice* in small causes to drive **litigants** to employ lawyers, and it is a shame to drive them to legal-aid societies to get as charity what the state should give as a right." In most states today, you have the right to use the services of small claims courts to litigate claims of, usually, less than $1000.

BUT YOU HAVE TO WATCH OUT

Complications can arise in small claims court proceedings. In many states, the defendant can automatically and routinely have a case transferred to a regular civil court. In most civil courts, your efforts are useless unless you have an attorney; if a case in which you are plaintiff is transferred to the civil court, you must, therefore, incur the expense of an attorney or drop the suit.

Further, a small claims judgment in your favor does not mean you will get full satisfaction for your loss. The judge may order the defendant to pay you $100 on a $150 claim (which, of course, is still $100 more than you started with). *But no matter what the defendant is ordered to pay you, the small claims court does not act as a collection agency.* Accordingly, you don't always collect when you win. For example, in a 1970 study by Consumers Union, of the sixty-two cases which the consumer plaintiff won, thirteen proved uncollectible. You must realize that a defendant who doesn't show up in court is not likely to

pay. You may be able to obtain a so-called writ of execution from the small claims court if you can show that the defendant is not paying you, but this writ against the defendant's property, bank account, or wages is often ineffective.[2]

Additionally, you must realize that you probably will have to make several trips to the courthouse, and, if the court has no evening session in your area, you may miss time from work. **Plaintiffs**—those bringing the lawsuit—spend between ten and thirty hours on court-related activities, such as filing papers, preparing the case, and so on. Going to court—even small claims court—takes time and energy.

2. Even if a debt is not collectible now, however, it stays on the records. Thus, if the person who lost the judgment in small claims court and who owes you money comes into some assets in the future, you can activate the judgment at that later time.

HOW THESE COURTS WORK

The first thing you do is ask the clerk of the small claims court in your area whether the court can handle your kind of case. For example, some large cities have special courts to handle problems between renters and landlords. While you're at the courthouse, it might prove helpful to sit in on a few cases; that will give you an idea of what to expect when your day in court arrives. Then make sure that the court has jurisdiction over the person or business you wish to sue. Usually the defendant must live, work, or do business in the court's territory. If you're trying to sue an out-of-town firm, you may run into real problems. You probably should go to the state government, usually the secretary of state, to find out where the summons should be sent. Remember that the small claims court does not act as a collection agency; if you're filing suit against a firm that no longer is in business, you'll have a very difficult time collecting.

Make absolutely certain that you have the correct business name and address of the company being sued. Frequently, courts require strict accuracy; if you don't abide by that requirement, the suit is thrown out.

Once you file suit, a summons goes out to the defending party, either by registered mail or in the hands of a sheriff, bailiff, marshal, constable, or sometimes a private citizen. When a company receives the summons, it may decide to resolve the issue out of court; about one-quarter of all cases for which summonses are issued are settled this way. Many times, however, the defendant company may not even show up for the trial, in which case you stand a good chance of winning by default. (But, as we said, no-shows are usually hard to collect from.)

PREPARING FOR TRIAL

How should you prepare for trial? Obviously, if you know a lawyer, seek advice from him or her. In any event, you should have on hand all necessary and pertinent receipts, canceled checks, written estimates, contracts, and any other form of documentary evidence that you can show the judge. Set the entire affair down in chronological order with supporting evidence so you can show the judge

EXHIBIT B–1
Small Claims Courts Characteristics in Selected States

STATE	NAME AND LOCATION OF COURT	MAXIMUM AMOUNT OF SUIT	ARE LAWYERS ORDINARILY ALLOWED?	WHO CAN APPEAL?		WHAT IS THE INITIAL COST TO SUE?
				PLAINTIFF	DEFENDANT	
Alabama	Small Claims Branch of District Court, Birmingham	$5,000	Yes	Yes	Yes	$0–$500, $10.50; $501–$5,000, $25.50
California	Small Claims Branch of Municipal Court, Sacramento	$1,500	No	No	Yes	$5.00+
Colorado	Civil Division of County Court, Denver	$ 500	No	Yes	Yes	$9.00+
Connecticut	Small Claims Branch of Superior Court, Hartford	$ 750	Yes	No	No	$6.00+
Washington, D.C.	Small Claims Branch of Superior Court, Washington, D.C.	$ 750	Yes	Yes	Yes	$3.00
Florida	Civil Division of County Court, Miami	$1,500	Yes	Yes	Yes	$0–99.99, $6.00+ $100–$999, $15.00+ $1,000–$1,500, $20.00+
Georgia	Civil division of County Court, Atlanta	$ 299.99	Yes	Yes	Yes	$0–$99.99, $7.00+; $100–$299.99; $13.00+
Illinois	Small Claims Branch of Municipal Court, Chicago	$1,000	Yes	Yes	Yes	$0–$499.99, $12.00; $500–$1,000, $15.00
Indiana	Small Claims Division of County Court, Indianapolis	$1,500	Yes	Yes	Yes	$20.00
Iowa	Small Claims Division of Associate District Court, Des Moines	$1,000	Yes	Yes	Yes	$9.00+
Kansas	Small Claims Division of Limited Actions County Court, Topeka	$ 500	No	Yes	Yes	$5.00
Kentucky	Small Claims Division of District Court, Louisville	$ 500	Yes	Yes	Yes	$13.58

EXHIBIT B–1 (Continued)

STATE	NAME AND LOCATION OF COURT	MAXIMUM AMOUNT OF SUIT	ARE LAWYERS ORDINARILY ALLOWED?	WHO CAN APPEAL?		WHAT IS THE INITIAL COST TO SUE?
				PLAINTIFF	DEFENDANT	
Louisiana	Small Claims Division of First City Court, New Orleans	$ 300	No	No	Yes	$15.00+
Maine	Small Claims Division of District Court, Augusta	$ 800	Yes	Yes	Yes	$5.10
Maryland	Small Claims Division of District Court, Baltimore	$ 500	Yes	Yes	Yes	$5.00+
Massachusetts	Small Claims Division of Municipal Court, Boston	$ 750	Yes	No	Yes	$4.40
Michigan	Small Claims Division of District Court, Lansing	$ 600	No	No	No	$14.00
Minnesota	Small Claims Division of Municipal Court, St. Paul	$1,000	Yes	Yes	Yes	$3.00
Mississippi	Justice Court, Jackson	$ 500	Yes	Yes	Yes	$25.00+
Missouri	Small Claims Division of Associate Circuit Court, St. Louis	$ 500	Yes	Yes	Yes	$0–99.99, $7.20; $100–$500, $12.20
New Jersey	Small Claims Division of District Court, Trenton	$ 500	Yes	Yes	Yes	$2.70+
New York	Small Claims Division of Civil Court, New York City	$1,000	Yes	Yes	Yes	$3.40
North Carolina	Small Claims Division of District Court, Raleigh	$ 800	Yes	Yes	Yes	$1–$500, $8.00+ $500–$800, $21.00+
Ohio	Small Claims Division of Municipal Court, Cincinnati	$ 500	Yes	Yes	Yes	$6.00+
Oklahoma	Small Claims Division of	$ 600	Yes	Yes	Yes	$7.00+

EXHIBIT B-1 (Continued)

STATE	NAME AND LOCATION OF COURT	MAXIMUM AMOUNT OF SUIT	ARE LAWYERS ORDINARILY ALLOWED?	WHO CAN APPEAL? PLAINTIFF	DEFENDANT	WHAT IS THE INITIAL COST TO SUE?
	County Court, Oklahoma City					
Oregon	Small Claims Division of District Court, Salem	$ 700	No	No	No	$8.00+
Pennsylvania	Small Claims Division of Municipal Court, Philadelphia	$1,000	Yes	Yes	Yes	$11.00
South Carolina	Summons and Complaint Court, Division of Magistrate Court, Columbia	$1,000	Yes	Yes	Yes	$22.00
Tennessee	Civil Division of County General Sessions Court, Nashville	$5,000	Yes	Yes	Yes	$15.75
Texas	Justice Court, Houston	$ ~~150~~ 1000	Yes	Yes	Yes	$8.00
Virginia	Civil Division of District Court, Richmond	$5,000	Yes	Yes	Yes	$5.50
Washington	Small Claims Division of District Justice Court, Seattle	$ 500	No	No	Yes	$1.00+
Wisconsin	Small Claims Division of County Court, Madison	$1,000	Yes	Yes	Yes	$7.50

exactly what happened. Make sure that your dates are accurate; inaccuracies could prejudice your case against you. Make sure you have a copy of the "demand letter"—similar to the one shown in Exhibit A–2—that you sent to the offending party. This document should be no more than two double-spaced-typewritten pages and should clearly summarize the facts, as well as your demands of the other party. It is important that you be able to hand this letter to the judge on trial day. It will not only present your version of the story but also will demonstrate your reasonable approach to the situation.

If you are disputing something such as a repair job, you may have to get a third party—generally someone in the same trade—to testify as an "expert." It is often difficult to get persons to testify against others in their profession, but they may be willing to give written statements, which sometimes are considered acceptable evidence. If possible, when you are suing over disputed workmanship, bring the physical evidence of your claim into court. If, for example, your neighborhood dry cleaner shrank a wool sweater of yours to a size three, be sure and show it to the judge.

WHAT HAPPENS IN COURT

The judge generally will let you present your case in simple language without the help of a lawyer. In fact, in many states neither the plaintiff nor the defendant may have a lawyer present. You may receive the judge's decision immediately or by notice within a few weeks. In some states, you can appeal the case, but, in many situations, the small claims court plaintiff does not have that right. Remember, whatever action you decide to take after the judgment should be weighed against the costs of that action. Your time is not free, and the worry that may be involved in pursuing a lost case further might detract from the potential reward of eventually winning.

If your opponent tries to settle the case out of court, make sure everything is written down so it can be upheld if the offer is withdrawn. You both should sign anything that is written and file it with the court so that the agreement can, in fact, be enforced by the law. It is best to have your opponent appear with you before the judge to outline the settlement terms. Generally, if you win or if you settle out of court, you should be able to get your opponent to pay for the court costs, which range from zero to $25, depending on the state.

WHERE, WHAT, AND HOW MUCH?

Exhibit B–1 briefly summarizes the characteristics of small claims courts in selected states.

To be a truly rational consumer decision maker, you must weigh the potential benefits of going to court against the potential costs. If the potential gain to you means less than the value you place on saving your time and energies, it may be best to forget the whole thing. On the other hand, if you are convinced that your case is just and that you have indeed been cheated out of a significant sum of money, by all means take advantage of the information presented in this Consumer Issue and start the proceedings.

A SUMMARY OF HOW TO HANDLE YOUR CASE

1. Identify your opponent properly.
2. Send a warning letter.
3. Find the correct court.
4. File a claim.
5. Notify the defendant.
6. Assemble the evidence.
7. Consider settling out of court, if possible.
8. Present your case.
9. Remember that a judgment in your favor does not guarantee payment of the claim.

How to Present Your Case in Court

You don't have to try to act like an experienced lawyer when presenting your case. Simply do the following.

1. Stand up when you make your first statements to the judge.
2. Don't read your statements; rather, present them conversationally.
3. Be brief.
4. Don't interrupt your opponent or any of the witnesses
5. If part of your case is difficult to express in words, bring the necessary physical materials, such as a diagram, a faded rug, a battered bicycle tire, and so on.

QUESTIONS FOR THOUGHT AND DISCUSSION

1. In your opinion, who makes the most use of small claims courts?
2. Why should you decide in some cases not to go to a small claims court?
3. Do you think that small claims courts should take on bigger cases? That is, do you think that the maximum amount of money at issue in a suit should be raised in many states? Why or why not?

THINGS TO DO

1. Find out the current maximum amount of money for which you may enter a suit in the small claims court in your state. Are lawyers allowed in small claims courts in your state today? Can both plaintiff and defendant appeal? What does it now cost to sue?
2. Go to a local small claims court and observe some of the action. Do you think that all the cases should have been brought into court? What would determine whether some of them should not have been brought into court?
3. Talk to a lawyer about the advisability of using the small claims court in your area.

SELECTED READINGS

"Caveat Venditor; Suing in Small Claims Court; Advice of D. Matthews." *Time,* September 10, 1973, p. 70.

Price, Howard, et al. *The California Handbook on Small Claims Courts*. Sacramento: Hawthorne Books, Inc., 1972.

"The Role of the Small Claims Court." *Consumer Reports,* November 1979, pp. 666–70.

Warner, Ralph. *Everybody's Guide to Small Claims Court.* New York: Addison Wesley, 1981.

CHAPTER
THE INFORMATION GLUT

Whether you like it or not, every year you are subjected to about 70 billion dollars' worth of producer-generated information about products and services: We call this advertising. . . . In fact, if you are the average TV viewer, you see about 150,000 ads a year on television.

CHAPTER PREVIEW

- Has there been an advertising explosion?
- Who pays for advertising?
- What are the characteristics of informative, as opposed to competitive, advertising?
- How does the Federal Trade Commission operate?
- How do you go about obtaining privately produced information?

ADVERTISING
Producer-generated information about a product or service.

Whether you like it or not, every year you are subjected to about 70 billion dollars' worth of producer-generated information about products and services: we call this **advertising**. Every time you turn on a commercial television station, you are treated to some sort of ad at least every ten to fifteen minutes. In fact, if you are the average TV viewer, you see about 150,000 ads a year on television. When you turn on a commercial radio station, the melodious sound of advertising strikes your ears at least every five minutes. Every time you open your local newspaper, advertisements cross your field of vision. And if that's not enough, you can purchase more information about every good or service you might want to buy: You can buy books on how to invest money in the stock market; how to buy a house, real estate, a car; how to keep fit and trim; how to avoid being defrauded. You name it, and you can buy or get free some bit of information on it. Information is all around us, bombarding us every second of every waking hour—or so it seems.

Obviously, some of this information is useful, and some of it is not. And, just as obviously, more information might sometimes be useful if we could get it at a "reasonable" cost. Information, however, is a valuable commodity, generally requiring resources to provide and to obtain. As a result, we never have *perfect* information about any of the products we buy because it would be too costly to provide.

There is a tremendous variety of sources of information about goods and services. They include:

1. Personal selling by individuals
2. Packaging, advertising, and broadcast promotions
3. Expert professional organizations
4. General news media
5. Friends, relatives, and acquaintances
6. Government standards (for example, grading of meats and vegetables)
7. Nonprofit rating organizations, such as Consumers Union and Consumers' Research, Inc.
8. Private industry rating and evaluation systems

This chapter will examine many of these sources.

HOW MUCH INFORMATION SHOULD WE ACQUIRE?

What we want is reliable information at the "right" price. In our daily lives, we *acquire information up to the point where the cost of acquiring any more would outweigh the benefits of that additional information.* In other words, we engage in rational decision making, which we have defined and briefly discussed in Chapter 1 and will talk more about in Chapter 5. When we decide to go shopping for goods, we may look at advertisements for only a few supermarkets instead of trying to find out the price of specials at all forty-six stores in the city. Why do we look at only a few? Because we have found that it does not pay to look at any more than those few pieces of information. When we go shopping for a new car, we may go to only a few dealers within the immediate area. Why go to only a few and not all? Because, again, we have found that it does not pay to go to all of them.

Some of us may not do any **comparison shopping** at all. We may not even bother to read advertisements or to seek additional information about the goods and services we wish to purchase. Instead, we may decide to shop at a store where only the most expensive brands are carried. Why? Perhaps we are "status-seeking," or perhaps we consider our time too valuable to spend in comparative shopping, in acquiring additional pieces of information. We may believe that high price means high quality, which is possible but not necessarily true. If we shop this way, we may have determined that it is not worth our while to acquire quantities of information, and we are, therefore, essentially nonshoppers.

COMPARISON SHOPPING
A shopping technique that involves comparing the value of different products, both from the same retailer and from different retailers. Comparison shopping involves spending time to acquire information about different sellers and different products.

Information in the form of advertisements relating to products in our economy has been on the upswing, as shown in Exhibit 3–1, which details the expansion of U.S. advertising in its various forms. A detailed look into advertising will show why it pays sellers to advertise, who pays for it, and the problems of false advertising.

THE ADVERTISING EXPLOSION

There must be a fairly good reason why we are subjected to so much advertising and why it is increasing each year. Let's look at it from the advertiser's point of view. Most businesspeople are in business for one reason and one reason only—to make money. Obviously, they wouldn't advertise if they didn't think that advertising could help increase their profits or, at least help maintain their current sales and level of profits. Thus, we can assume that businesspeople

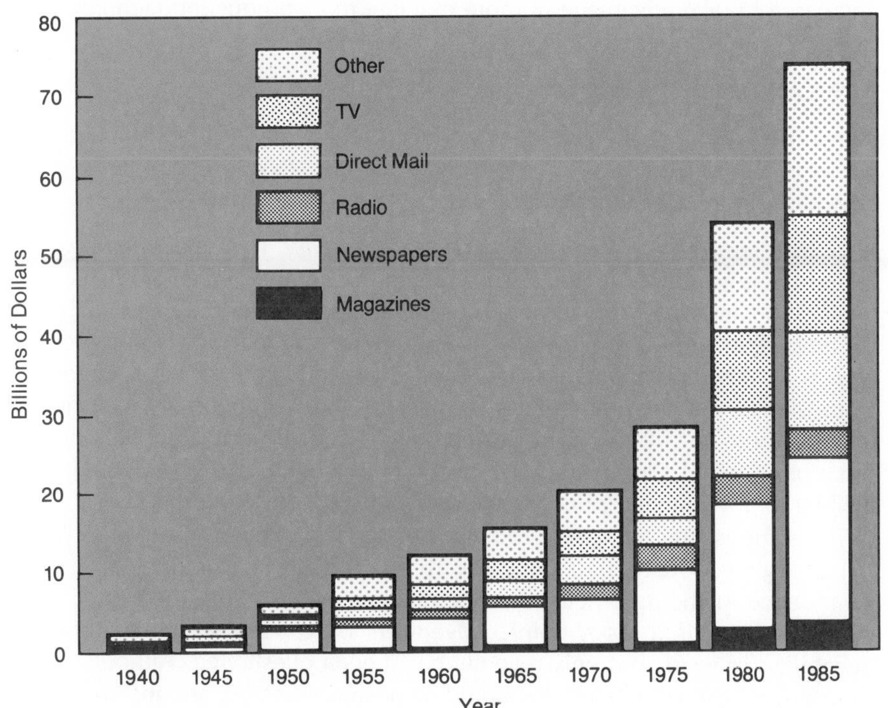

EXHIBIT 3–1
Advertising Expenditures in the United States, 1940–1985.

believe the additional sales they will make through advertising will at least cover the costs of that advertising. So the advertising explosion can be attributed partly to the realization by businesses that increased advertising yields more than enough additional sales to justify the expenditure. Of course, when you look at it this way, you also realize who ultimately pays for advertising.

Who Pays?

Since businesses are out to make money for themselves and are not necessarily altruistic, we can be certain that they are not going to lose money by advertising, at least not intentionally. Only when they make a mistake about the profitability of a particular advertising campaign do they pay for it themselves—by taking a loss on that particular expenditure. In general, however, the cost of advertising is built in to the price of the products we buy. After all, the cost of labor is built in to the price of the products we buy and so are the costs of buildings and machines. There is very little we can do about it, except, of course, to purchase nonadvertised items that are similar in quality to advertised ones and lower in price. And we can do this by shopping at supermarkets that sell nonnational brands of food and other products. But this presents a dilemma: If it is possible to purchase at lower prices nonadvertised products that are identical to advertised products, why do any of us buy nationally advertised brands?

In all fairness, it should be pointed out that the advertising industry claims that the increased sales due to advertising can cause some industries to experience lower per-unit costs. Hence, the consumer benefits when these lower unit costs are passed on. It is claimed that, through advertising, sales can be increased to take advantage of more efficient mass-production techniques.

The Value of Brand Names

Obviously, many of us have decided that well-advertised brand names have value in and of themselves. There are at least three reasons why many of us purchase brand-name products.

1. **Brand names may mean less variance in quality.** If we have learned that brand-name products generally vary less in quality than other products, then the brand name has value for it tells us to anticipate fewer problems. This may be true, for example, with electronic equipment. You may decide to purchase, say, Sony stereo components because you have found out, or have heard from your friends, that the brand name Sony means less likelihood of breakage and repair. Therefore, if you go to a stereo shop and see two amplifiers next to each other, one by an unknown company and the other by Sony, you may be willing to pay a higher price for the nationally advertised brand item.

The same is true for other products and services. People sometimes prefer to pay slightly more for nationally advertised products because they have more confidence in them. Whether or not national brand names and quality are always related is a moot point. Advertisers have been selling brand-name reliability for years, but only recently has it been questioned. Although many consumers have concluded that brand name and reliability are not associated, many others are still willing to pay more for brand-name products.

2. **Brand-name products may offer better warranties.** When something goes wrong with the national-brand product you bought, it may have a superior warranty, and the service you can get for it may be quicker and easier to obtain than service for a nonnational brand. For that reason, you may decide to pay more for the national brand.

3. **National-brand products may be repaired at a larger number of facilities.** It may be more difficult to get nonnational-brand products repaired. This is especially true for automobiles. How many gas stations can help out when a Maserati refuses to start? And even if a mechanic knows how to fix it, how quickly would he or she be able to get the parts?

People sometimes prefer to pay slightly more for nationally advertised products because they have more confidence in them. Whether or not national brand names and quality are always related is a moot point.

Brand-Name Loyalty

The preceding discussion clarifies the reasoning behind brand-name loyalty, which is fostered by national advertising. Brand-name loyalty is rational for some people but not for others. It is up to you to decide whether you wish to pay the higher price for nationally advertised items. Incidentally, many national advertisers produce products (which may be of equal quality) under other names. Comparison shopping may reveal less expensive products made by these national manufacturers with the same features of national-brand items.

The Benefits of Brand Names to the Producer

MARKET POWER
The ability of producers to change price and/or quality without substantially losing sales.

Brand name loyalty is designed specifically to benefit producers. When brand name loyalty occurs on a wide scale, producers gain **market power.** Market power may be defined as the ability of producers to change price and/or quality without substantially losing sales. Every producer has as its goal some degree of market power. In a perfectly competitive environment, no producer has any market power; that is, each producer must take the price of its product as given in the marketplace. In a perfectly competitive world, any producer that raises its prices will lose virtually all sales. But, as pointed out in Chapter 1, for the most part we do not live in a perfectly competitive economy. Rather, producers have various degrees of market power. Brand-name loyalty is just one attempt by those producers to obtain more market power and to make higher profits.

THE UGLY SIDE OF ADVERTISING

There are many critics of advertising because of the abuses that advertisers have heaped upon the American consuming public. The following is a fairly comprehensive list of critics' complaints about advertising.

1. Advertisers play on people's guilt or need for acceptance.
2. Some advertising is abusive and involves the vulgar exploitation of women.
3. A significant amount of advertising is aimed at children who cannot determine its value.
4. Many advertising campaigns use fear to encourage the purchase of the advertised product.
5. Many ads involve the use of questionable testimonials about the product.
6. Finally, many ads are at least somewhat deceptive, such as "going-out-of-business" sales and "freight-damaged" sales.

TYPES OF ADVERTISING

INFORMATIVE ADVERTISING
Advertising that gives useful, factual information about the suitability and quality of a product.

DEFENSIVE (OR COMPETITIVE) ADVERTISING
Advertising that emphasizes brand names and contains little information that is useful for rational consumer decision making. It is used only to allow a producer to maintain a share of the market for that product. An example is cigarette advertising.

Basically, its critics and students place all advertising into two broad catgeories, which sometimes overlap. The first category is **informative advertising,** which presumably is always good; the second is **defensive (competitive) advertising,** which presumably is always bad. (Of course, there is also false, or deceptive, advertising, which we discuss in Chapter 4.)

Informative Advertising

Informative advertising is just what the term says: It simply informs. Consumers see a tremendous amount of informative advertising: supermarkets advertise their prices; stereo shops advertise the brands they sell and their prices; producers advertise new products that were not previously available. In other words, you the consumer are constantly being informed about prices, products, and availability. You can take that information for what it is worth and use it any way you want. You are not asked to believe that a product is better or worse than another one or that a company does a good or a bad job. Rather, you are simply given the relevant information about the key aspects—price and availability—of a good or service.

In the United States, there is a tremendous amount of informative advertising, advertising that even the critics would not suggest we abolish. There are some very unusual products you would never expect to be advertised because the market is so specialized. Did you know, for example, that the producers of multimillion-dollar steam electricity generators send salespeople around to various electric utilities to inform them about the availability and the costs of different types of steam generators? Did you know there are hundreds of specialized trade magazines that treat very narrow fields of interest and that companies in those fields subscribe to them just to find out what is happening and what products are available? There are journals published exclusively for the fields of printing, publishing, electric utilities, leatherworks, paper production, flour milling and so on. In fact, most industries have a trade magazine or two in which very specialized informative ads can be found.

Defensive Advertising

Another kind of advertising is called defensive (competitive) advertising, and, again, it is just what the name implies. Defensive advertising fosters—and is fostered by—brand-name competition. Cigarettes are a good example. Each of the large tobacco companies advertises extensively, but no single company gets an edge on the others through this advertising. If any one company stopped advertising, it would lose sales, but it gains no more by advertising than it would if *no* company advertised at all. This is what defensive advertising is all about.

With any attempt to regulate advertising, we risk eliminating informative advertising. Who, after all, is wise enough to decide what is defensive and what is informative? What is the cutoff point? How could advertising actually be regulated? For example, if you were in charge of deciding the contents of car ads, what would you let manufacturers say? Could they list only obvious characteristics, such as horsepower and tire size? Or would you let a company say that its new model "handled better" because of an improved suspension system? You would have to make countless difficult decisions. The Federal Trade Commission has begun to specify what is and what is not informative advertising, but its rule-making procedures are still being determined.

In recent years, some forms of defensive advertising have come to resemble informative advertising in certain respects—at least if it is done honestly.

Comparative Advertising

Until the last few years, there was very little **comparative advertising**—that is, advertising that actually named competitive brands (not merely Brand X) when comparing them with the advertised brand. For example, Volvo has been compared favorably with other brands of cars, such as Saab and Mercedes.

COMPARATIVE ADVERTISING
Advertising that compares the advertised brand with specific other brands of the same product.

Although many people had thought that such advertising was illegal, it never actually was; but in the past, radio and television stations were either reluctant to broadcast it or refused it altogether. When properly and honestly done, comparative advertising is obviously beneficial to consumers because it saves us the time of doing the comparisons ourselves.

Consumers must be careful, however, because comparative advertising is bound to be selective and show only what the advertiser wants us to know.

Commercial supporters of direct mail contend that it permits more informative advertising because written ads can deal with the subject in more detail than can those that are broadcast for thirty or sixty seconds.

DIRECT-MAIL ADVERTISING

Most of us constantly receive quantities of direct-mail advertising from sellers of goods and services and from fund raisers. A lot of people consider this junk mail, but it is, nevertheless, a big business. Your name is probably on at least 150 lists that are rented or exchanged for other lists. Which list you are on depends on where you live, what type of car you drive, your occupation, what magazines you receive, what charities you contribute to, and so on. Nonprofit organizations, such as educational and public-interest groups, depend upon soliciting via third-class mail to raise 80 percent of their contributions.

Commercial supporters of direct mail contend that it permits more informative advertising because written ads can deal with the subject in more detail than can those that are broadcast for thirty or sixty seconds.

Some companies receive large revenues by renting their direct-mail lists. It is rumored that American Express Company gets over $2 million a year and that *Psychology Today* magazine gets over $1 million a year from their list rentals. Thus, *unless you request otherwise,* whenever you sign up for an American Express card or subscribe to *Psychology Today,* your name is added to a mailing list that subsequently will be rented or exchanged.

Perhaps this is an invasion of privacy, and perhaps you should be given an option to refuse to be thus listed. When you subscribe to something or buy something from an organization that rents lists, it would not be too difficult for that organization to allow you to refuse to have your name rented or exchanged with other firms. *Consumer Reports* told its subscribers in 1976 that they could have their names removed from any list that CR exchanges. American Express, *Ms.* magazine, and Diner's Club also offer this option. If you are truly interested in getting your name removed from direct-mail lists, you can do the following.

1. Write to any organization that uses your name, and ask that it be removed from that list.

2. Complain to the post office about the receipt of mail that you consider pandering. Simply fill out Form 2150; by law, any mailer listed on that form must drop your name from its mailing list.

(Incidentally, there is no universally accepted definition of exactly what "pandering" materials are. The dictionary defines "pander" as providing gratification for others and exploiting their weaknesses. To many, the word also has a sexual connotation. Strictly speaking, mail that panders is not necessarily salacious.)

3. Write to Direct Mail/Marketing Association, Inc., 6 East 43rd Street, New York, New York 10017, and request a Mail Preference Service form. After you have completed and returned it, your name will be removed from lists used by over 400 cooperating mailers who account for 70 percent of direct-mail advertising.

THE FEDERAL TRADE COMMISSION

There are government agencies, both state and federal, that are attempting to control advertising. Since more than half of all advertising is national in its coverage and, therefore, involves interstate commerce, the Federal Trade Commission has control over that advertising. The FTC is organized into two principal operating bureaus: the Bureau of Consumer Protection and the Bureau of Competition. The former has chief responsibility for "monitoring advertising, labeling and deceptive practices, reviewing applications for complaints, draft ing proposed complaints concerning . . . practices and . . . prosecuting cases after the commissioner issues a formal complaint." At each of the FTC's twelve regional offices around the country, a staff of attorneys and specialists in consumer protection is responsible for monitoring advertising and competitive practice over an area of several states. The staff also investigates complaints and suspected violations and tries cases concerning alleged unfair practices in its particular geographical area.

The FTC receives letters or other communications complaining of violations from many sources, including competitors of alleged violators, consumers, consumer organizations, trade associations, better business bureaus, other government organizations, and state and local officials. In addition, the commission staff has an extensive program for monitoring radio and TV commercials, national advertising media, and, through field offices, local advertising media. In the last few years, the FTC has created in major cities consumer-protection coordinating committees that attempt to bring together local, state, and federal consumer-protection officials in a particular geographical area to provide a coordinated, one-stop consumer-complaint service.

Among the many statutes administered by the FTC are several that specifically involve advertising, such as the Wool, Fur, and Textile Fiber Products Labeling Acts of 1939, 1951, and 1958, respectively. In addition, a 1938 amendment to the original FTC Act of 1914 specifically prohibits false advertising of food, drugs, cosmetics, and devices. The lending provisions of the Consumer Credit Protection Act of 1968, administered by the FTC, require full disclosure in advertising that makes claims about credit terms.

CORRECTIVE ADVERTISING

In the 1970s, the FTC strengthened its rulings against what it considers to be false advertising. In a famous case, Profile bread was required to eliminate its advertising claim concerning the weight-reducing qualities of its product. It turned out that the reason Profile bread has fewer calories per slice than other breads is because it is sliced thinner. The FTC required the bakers of Profile bread to spend a specific amount of money to explain, via advertising, that they had indeed presented false information. The manufacturers of Listerine mouthwash and STP motor oil were similarly reprimanded. Listerine had to recant its claims that the product cured sore throats, and STP was required to correct the impression that its motor oil additive could do all the wondrous things, such as greatly extend the life of a car's engine, that the company had claimed.

The FTC also stopped an innovative advertising campaign for Sure deodorant. The ads said, "Put Sure under your left arm and your regular deodorant under your right arm, and we're sure that you'll stay drier with Sure." The majority of Americans are right-handed, and they perspire more under their right arm because they use it more.

The fact is, an impression created by an advertising campaign lasts, no matter what steps are taken to correct it.

Sometimes the FTC's attempt at corrective advertising has surprised the industry in question. For example, the FTC claimed that Wonder bread was wrong in advertising its nutritive value because it implied that Wonder bread is unique. The FTC reasoned that it was not unique because other enriched breads had the same nutritive value. Notice that the FTC did not claim the ads were false or that they misrepresented the product. It simply said that what was claimed was not unique to that product.

Recent studies have raised doubts about the effectiveness of corrective advertising. When corrective advertising has been required, researchers found that such advertising did not change the consumer's view of the product. For example, although Listerine advertised for many years that it helped cure sore throats, a recent survey showed that most consumers of Listerine still believe that it prevents or reduces sore throats due to colds. The fact is, an impression created by an advertising campaign lasts, no matter what steps are taken to correct it.

THE NEW VIEW AT THE FTC

In keeping with Ronald Reagan's free-market philosophy, the natural choice for the head of the FTC in 1980 was a free-market economist, Dr. James Miller. Once Miller became head of the FTC, he installed other advocates of free-market competition as directors of the various departments within the FTC. The result has been a reduction in the amount of FTC regulation of advertising in the United States. For example, Miller and his associates at the FTC have lobbied within Congress to prevent legislation that would have restricted advertising in the funeral business. They also have sabotaged efforts to require used-car dealers to give every prospective purchaser the past repair records of used cars.

The FTC attitude toward regulation in the marketplace in the early 1980s is based on a benefit-cost approach; that is, every potential regulation is examined in light of the benefits that will rebound from it compared to the costs to society. FTC Chairman Miller has even declared that all past regulations should be subjected to a benefit-cost analysis. But problems arise because it is impossible to determine the exact nature and sum of the benefits and of the costs. Calculations depend upon who is counting and what are considered the relevant benefits and costs.

OTHER AGENCIES HELPING YOU OUT

The FTC is not the only agency charged with controlling advertising. There is also the Food and Drug Administration (FDA), the U.S. Postal Service, the Federal Communications Commission (FCC), and the Securities and Exchange Commission (SEC). The basic laws created by these agencies result in some overlapping jurisdiction. Consequently, for example, the FDA and the FTC operate under a voluntary agreement that gives specific areas of authority to each agency and responsibility for policing local advertising problems to state attorneys general's offices.

BUYING PRIVATELY PRODUCED INFORMATION

If you want to buy a product but are not quite sure which brand to purchase, you need not rely solely on manufacturers' advertisements. You can purchase brand-name product information in the form of such publications as *Consumer Reports* and *Consumers' Research Magazine.*

Consumer Reports

Consumer Reports is the publication of Consumers Union, a nonprofit organization chartered in 1936 under the laws of the State of New York. The object of Consumers Union has been to bring more useful information into the seller/buyer relationship so that consumers can buy rationally. The first issue of *Consumer Reports,* in May 1936, went to 3,000 charter subscribers, who were told about the relative costs and nutritional values of breakfast cereals, the fanciful claims made for Alka Seltzer, the hazards of lead toys, and the best buys in women's stockings, toilet soaps, and toothbrushes. Consumers Union's policy has always been to buy goods in the open market and bring them to the lab for objective testing.

Approximately 2½ million subscribers and newsstand buyers now read *Consumer Reports* every month. Consumers Union, which accepts no advertising in its magazine, gives advice on purchasing credit, insurance, and drugs. One major aspect of Consumers Union's testing involves automobiles—which are the best buys, which are safe, which have good brakes, which have safety defects, and so on. Recently, Consumers Union has published articles on such ecological topics as pesticides, phosphates in detergents, and lead in gasolines. It also strongly criticizes government agencies when they act against consumer interests.

If you decide to rely on the recommendations of *Consumer Reports,* you have to realize that it is difficult for their researchers always to present purely objective results. This is not to say that you will get misinformation, but the researchers may sometimes emphasize certain aspects of products that are consistent with their interests and preferences but not with your own. For example, recommendations about cars may give more weight to safety, gas mileage, or comfort than you personally want to give. You may opt for a different car because you prefer styling or low cost as opposed to safety. Even though the occupants of VWs face a higher probability of serious injury in an accident than do occupants of bigger cars, people continue to buy VWs, presumably because they are cheaper. Obviously, you will face this problem of acceptance with any information you obtain, either free or at a price.

In the last analysis, only you can make a decision, and it has to be based in part upon your personal value judgments. If you are not a tireless shopper, you may be content simply to look at *Consumer Reports* for whatever you want to buy, pick either the "best buy" or the top of the line, call your local dealer, and have your selection delivered. You may get some products you dislike but, on average, if your tastes correspond with those of the Consumers Union researchers, you will save considerable time and probably will avoid basically defective products.

Consumers' Research Magazine

Consumers' Research, Inc., founded in 1929, publishes a monthly *Consumers' Research Magazine*, with a readership of several hundred thousand. It contains product ratings, ratings of motion pictures and phonograph records, and short editorials. Like *Consumer Reports*, no advertising income is permitted. The product-testing policy of Consumers' Research often involves borrowing test samples of large, expensive items from manufacturers who sign affidavits that the goods are typical and were selected at random. Some of the goods—for example, typewriters—are rented for testing. Consumers' Research often restricts its tests to brands or goods that are nationally distributed, while Consumers Union sometimes tests brands that are distributed in various high-density localities. It is Consumers' Research policy to service their national and international audience rather than give any special attention to products or brands sold in specific geographical areas. Further, *Consumers' Research Magazine* does not give brand names as "best buys" as does *Consumer Reports*. Both publications pride themselves on stressing safety and efficiency in products, and both have found potentially unsafe products long before any government agency has done so.

Buying Guides

Consumer Reports publishes an annual *Buying Guide* in December; the *Consumers' Research* annual guide appears in October. Both contain a wealth of information on such things as food and nutrition, energy-saving ideas, and the like. Unfortunately, they both suffer from a problem that is impossible to avoid

in a dynamic economy: Certain models that are listed may no longer be available by the time you decide to make a purchase.

At any one time, you can choose from at least a half-dozen other buying guides, such as the *Consumers' Handbook,* edited by Paul Fargas; *Better Times,* edited by Francis Cerra; and the Department of Agriculture's *Shoppers' Guide.* All are uneven in coverage, and none can be recommended unreservedly.

Other Information Sources

There is an increasingly large number of privately produced information sources in addition to those just described. For example, *Money,* a monthly magazine published by Time-Life, is aimed at families of middle income and above. *Money* emphasizes financial management—stocks, bonds, retirement, real-estate investments, and commodities. And it often provides valuable information about making better consumer choices, such as articles about deceptive selling practices, better nutrition for your family, and so on.

Changing Times, the monthly magazine published by the Kiplinger Service for Families, is another source of consumer guidance. Any given issue may provide information on weight-reduction gimmicks, advice about buying insurance, new tax rulings that might affect you, tips on how to get interest on your checking account, and warnings against long-term car loans.

Most major newspapers carry a column by Sylvia Porter or other consumer-information specialist, and specialized regional consumer-information sources are available in different parts of the country.

Better Homes and Gardens, Good Housekeeping, Sunset, Family Circle, and *Woman's Day,* as well as less traditional magazines (*Mother Earth,* for example), give helpful consumer information on such things as money-saving meals, furniture maintenance, and do-it-yourself projects.

SUMMARY

1. Comparative shopping involves acquiring information about alternative sources for a particular product. Because acquiring that information requires using your time and perhaps other resources, such as gas for your automobile, there is a limit to how much comparative shopping you will want to do.
2. Expenditures for advertising in the United States were an estimated $70 billion in 1983.
3. Ultimately, the consumer pays for advertising in the form of a higher-priced product.
4. Individuals often associate brand names with (a) less variance in quality, (b) better warranties, and (c) a larger number of repair facilities.
5. The Federal Trade Commission is empowered to monitor advertising and deceptive practices of businesses. If you think you have been the victim of deceptive advertising, you might want to contact the local bureau of the FTC. The field office can be located by consulting the telephone directory of the closest big city in your state.
6. You can obtain privately produced information about products and services by subscribing to *Consumer Reports, Consumers' Research Magazine, Money, Changing Times, Better Homes and Gardens, Good Housekeeping,* or *Sunset.*

QUESTIONS FOR THOUGHT AND DISCUSSION

1. Do you think that all corrective advertising is necessary?
2. Can advertisers regulate themselves?
3. Do you think there is an end in sight to the advertising explosion?
4. Why do consumers still prefer brand names?
5. Can you distinguish between informative and defensive advertising?
6. Why are there more privately produced sources of information, such as magazines of the *Consumer Reports* type, on the market today than there were, say, fifty years ago?

THINGS TO DO

1. Examine some marketing journals, such as the *Journal of Marketing* and the *Journal of Advertising Research*. What do the authors who write for those magazines believe is necessary for successful advertising?
2. List the products that you buy mainly because of their brand names. Which of those products could you buy at a lower price by switching to a nonbrand name? Why have you chosen a brand name for so long?
3. From the point of view of the consumer, does the corrective advertising you see on television give you information that will change your buying behavior with respect to the product in question?
4. Compare the various informative consumer magazines, such as *Consumer Reports* and *Consumers' Research Magazine, Money,* and *Changing Times*. If you had a limited amount of time, which one or ones would you read most often? Why?

SELECTED READINGS

Advertising Age (various issues).

Allen, Frederick Louis. *Only Yesterday*. New York: Harper & Row, 1931.

Buxton, Edward. *Promise Them Anything*. New York: Stein & Day, 1972.

Consumer Reports (various issues, "The Docket" section).

"How Advertising Affects Price and Quality." *Consumers' Research Magazine,* April 1981.

Levitt, Theodore. "The Morality (?) of Advertising." *Harvard Business Review,* July/August 1970.

Packard, Vance. *The Hidden Persuaders*. New York: David McKay Co., 1957.

"Should an Ad Identify Brand X?" *Business World,* September 24, 1979, p. 156.

Ward, Scott. *Effects of Television Advertising on Children and Adolescents*. Cambridge, Mass.: Marketing Science Institute, July 1971.

Weiss, Ann. *The School on Madison Avenue*. New York: E. P. Dutton, 1980.

CHAPTER
THE MANY FACES OF FRAUD

Fly to Florida FREE Just for Touring Retirement Haven

Don't miss this opportunity to increase your income by thousands of dollars a year!

Guaranteed to Prevent Baldness

Prime Land For Sale!

You CAN Own Your Own Lake Home! Vacation at beautiful Windy Hills FREE

Lose Weight Instantly With Pounds-Away! Not a drug, not a gimmick, this miraculous treatment

Miracle Drug Proven Cure

Lake Lots At Only $100 Per Acre!

FREE WITH PURCHASE

for considering our special offer . . .

Increase your upper body strength in just 10 days with Muscle Bound

In the legal sense, fraud occurs when an individual *knowingly* misrepresents an important fact or fails to tell the consumer about an important fact. The ultimate result of this misrepresentation is that the consumer is somehow cheated.

CHAPTER PREVIEW

- What are some forms of false advertising?
- What, according to the FTC is the most common fraudulent practice by sellers of products?
- How should you deal with door-to-door salespersons?
- What is a cooling-off period?
- How can you avoid deceptive practices of sellers?

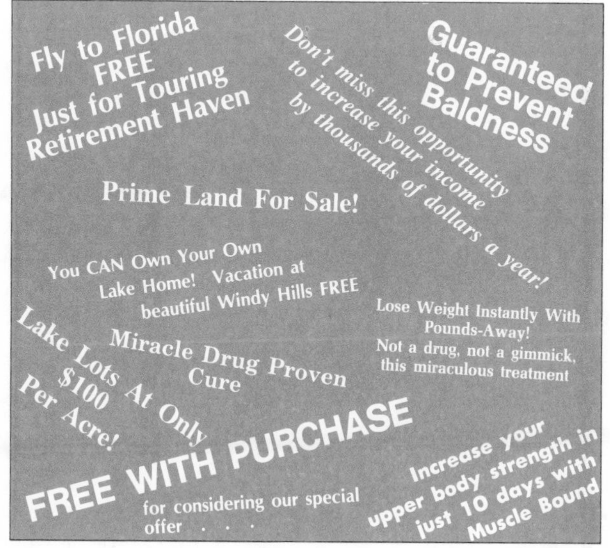

FRAUD
Legally defined as making a false statement of a past or existing fact with knowledge of its falsity, or with reckless indifference as to its truth, with the intent to cause someone to rely upon such a statement.

The formal legal definition of **fraud** is:

> Any misrepresentation either by misstatement or omission knowingly made with the intention of defrauding another, and on which a reasonable person would and does rely to his or her detriment.

Quite a mouthful, isn't it? The essence of this legal definition, however, is quite simple: In the legal sense, fraud occurs when an individual *knowingly* misrepresents an important fact or fails to tell the consumer about an important fact. The ultimate result of this misrepresentation is that the consumer is somehow cheated. In our judicial system, then, fraud is limited to deliberate deceit. In other words, if you believe that you have been defrauded by a seller, for example, you must prove in court that the seller actually had the intent to deceive you. Such proof is often difficult to obtain. Consequently, the best protection against fraud, in the more general sense of the term, is to be aware of the numerous fraudulent schemes that sellers in the marketplace have devised to deceive you.

To be sure, not all observers of the American economic scene believe that much fraud exists. Indeed, most businesspersons, when queried, contend that fraud, if and when it exists, must be short-lived. According to these observers, businesses rely on repeat customers (continuous dealing) to stay in business. Therefore, so the reasoning goes, any businessperson who consistently attempts to use fraudulent means to make higher profits will not have repeat customers. That businessperson will eventually lose money. While this line of reasoning is basically sound, it ignores the fact that, in our complex, multidimensional economy, information is not always reliable. Furthermore, the population being serviced is huge, and this increases the possibility of sellers using unscrupulous selling techniques on many different people throughout the country. This is particularly true in the sale of products through the mails.

In the remainder of this chapter, we will discuss some of the more important fraudulent or semifraudulent schemes. Only by understanding these schemes can you guard yourself against falling victim to them.

FALSE, OR DECEPTIVE, ADVERTISING

Everyone agrees that false advertising is not in the public interest, particularly if it can be stopped without spending too many resources. An example of one of the many types of false advertising should give you an idea of what you have to watch out for.

Bait and Switch: The Case of a Washing Machine

Let's assume that you read in the newspaper that Joe's Appliance Store is having a tremendous sale on the most modern washing machine available. The advertised price is only $199.95. As soon as you walk into the store, a friendly salesperson named Mr. Jones greets you. You are holding the ad, and you ask to see the washing machine it describes. Immediately, Mr. Jones takes you to the washing machine—which is in miserable condition. It is antiquated and covered with a layer of dust. Mr. Jones starts to tell you that you certainly don't

EXHIBIT 4–1
Bait and Switch

want *this* washing machine because it's obviously inferior. He quickly takes you on a tour of the store, showing you several other washing machines, which are in pristine condition compared to the one on sale. Mr. Jones also informs you that the advertised machine is out of stock. You are finally convinced to buy one that you "really need," with five speeds, four water levels, and sixteen settings. Its cost, by the way, is $420.

You have just become the victim of a **bait-and-switch** ploy by the appliance store. The bait was an unrealistically low-priced washing machine. The switch was to a much higher-priced, superior-quality machine. The key to avoid being tricked by this scheme is learning how to recognize the pattern of a bait-and-switch scheme and to walk out when you think you're being duped. No one forces you to take the bait and then accept the switch.

The Federal Trade Commission puts bait and switch at the top of the list of common fraudulent practices or deceptions. Other deceptions include the following.

BAIT AND SWITCH
A selling technique that involves advertising a product at a very attractive price; then informing the consumer, once he or she is in the door, that the advertised product either is not available, is of poor quality, or is not what the consumer "really wants"; and, finally, promoting a more expensive item.

1. **Contest winner.** You are told you have won a contest that you didn't enter, but it turns out you must buy something in order to receive your prize.
2. **Free goods.** You presumably will get something free if you buy something else, but you may be paying a higher price for that "something else" than you would have otherwise.
3. **Merchandise substitution.** In place of what you thought you were buying, the seller substitutes an item of a different variety, make, model, or quality.

Again, there are ways to avoid deceptive practices by sellers or, at least, to reduce their probability. One way is to establish yourself as a steady customer of reputable sellers in your area. Even if such sellers are tempted to cheat you, they will be reluctant to do so because they rely heavily on your repeat purchases for their business.

DOOR-TO-DOOR SALESPERSONS

There are probably more fraudulent practices used in door-to-door sales than in any other type of product selling. The dubious sales pitches used by many salespersons of encyclopedias, vacuum cleaners, land, and even Bibles range from quoting phony list prices of competitive products in order to make their own prices seem reasonable to getting people to sign questionnaires that really are installment credit contracts. So notorious are these techniques that it is not necessary here to go into detail about how door-to-door salespersons ply their trade. The best way to ensure that you never are cheated by door-to-door peddlers is to refuse to deal with them. If they persist, you can always call the police.

This is a good time for you to practice assertiveness. People who are assertive do not often fall prey to bait-and-switch techniques or the high-pressure pitches of door-to-door salespersons. Being assertive, however, does not require that you be rude or obnoxious. Salespersons are human too, so remember your manners, as well as your rights.

Sometimes, of course, door-to-door salespersons may provide you with a product or service that is both useful and a bargain. In fact, certain products are sold only door-to-door and cannot be obtained elsewhere—for example, special types of household cleaning aids and certain cosmetics and toiletries, such as Avon products. If you happen to like these special products, you have no choice but to purchase them from a door-to-door salesperson. In these cases, you obviously are not dealing with someone trying to sign you to a thirty-six-month installment contract on a set of fifty-eight books at a total price of $650. Rather, a smaller amount of money is involved, and you run less risk of losing it. In any event, some door-to-door sales companies, such as Avon and Fuller Brush, have been in business for many years and have established reputations for reliability; the consumer runs no more risk with them than with any other company.

Cooling-Off Periods

Several states now have a "cooling-off" law that must be applied to many, if not all, installment contracts. For example, Ohio has a three-business-day cooling-off period. Say a door-to-door salesperson gets you to sign a contract to purchase a set of encyclopedias and pay for it over thirty-six months; during the following three-day period, you can renege on that contract. Essentially, you are given three days in which to reconsider the commitment, and also to acquire information about alternative means of purchasing the product for which you contracted.

The Federal Trade Commission adopted this cooling-off provision in 1973. It makes it a violation for door-to-door sellers to fail to give consumers three business days to cancel any sale. This rule also applies to the previously mentioned state statutes, so consumers are given the most favorable benefits of the FTC rule and their own state statute. Additionally, the FTC rule requires that the notification be given in Spanish if the oral negotiation was in that language. Exhibit 4–2 is a typical Notice of Cancellation that should be available from any door-to-door salesperson.

There are probably more fraudulent practices used in door-to-door sales than in any other type of product selling.

INTERSTATE LAND SALES

Most of us would like to own a "piece of the country." Some people dream about having a second home. Others consider land one of the best investments available. Unfortunately, prospective real-estate investors have, at one time or another, fallen victim to land scams.

EXHIBIT 4–2
Typical Notice of Cancellation for Door-to-Door Solicitation Sales

(enter date of transaction)

____
(date)

You may cancel this transaction, without any penalty or obligation, within 3 business days from the above date.

If you cancel, any property traded in, any payments made by you under the contract or sale, and any negotiable instrument executed by you will be returned within 10 business days following receipt by the seller of your cancellation notice, and any security interest arising out of the transaction will be cancelled.

If you cancel, you must make available to the seller at your residence, in substantially as good condition as when received, any goods delivered to you under this contract or sale; or you may, if you wish, comply with the instructions of the seller regarding the return shipment of the goods at the seller's expense and risk.

If you do make the goods available to the seller and the seller does not pick them up within 40 days of the date of your notice of cancellation, you may retain or dispose of the goods without any further obligation. If you fail to make the goods available to the seller, or if you agree to return the goods to the seller and fail to do so, then you remain liable for performance of all obligations under the contract.

To cancel this transaction, mail or deliver a signed and dated copy of this cancellation notice or any other written notice, or send a telegram to

____
(name of seller)

at ________________ not later than midnight of ________________
(address of seller's place of business) (date)

I hereby cancel this transaction.

________________ ________________
(date) (buyer's signature)

Land scams used to be fairly easy to execute. A canny buyer would purchase, say, 10,000 acres of low-valued land in the middle of nowhere. The land might be partially under water, as in the Florida Everglades, or in a totally arid region of Arizona or New Mexico. The owner might develop a small section of the 10,000 acres and take photographs to show how beautiful it is. Those publicity pictures would form the basis of an advertising campaign that would probably run nationwide. The development would have an alluring name, such as The Hills of Monte Cristo, or Terra Bella Villages, and the land would be sold at five, ten, or even a hundred times its actual cost. All sales would be transacted over the phone and through the mails. Only when the unsuspecting buyer actually visited the location or attempted to resell the land would he or she discover the fraud.

In 1968, Congress passed the Interstate Land Sales Act, which went into effect in 1969. This act requires anyone engaged in selling or leasing land interstate to register the offering with the Department of Housing and Urban Development (HUD). Unfortunately for consumers, that law was revised in 1979. Today, only a limited amount of information on interstate land sales must be made available to HUD. A large number of land swindles still occur, evidence that the amended law isn't very effective.

The obvious way to prevent land swindles is to investigate before you invest. A good rule of thumb is: Never purchase land sight unseen. If you are nonetheless interested in property being sold by a land development company, obtain the property report from HUD. Remember, though, that HUD does not pass judgment on the true value of the offering.

SELLING HEALTH-CARE MIRACLES

Health may be the primary concern for most Americans, at least at some point in their lives. It is not surprising, then, that Americans fall victim to literally tens of thousands of schemes related to health care each year. Consider a few of them.

Health, Natural, and Organic Foods

Many people are concerned about the chemical nature of their diets and will go to great lengths to obtain particular foods—sometimes even growing their own without the use of chemical fertilizers and pesticides. Most of us are aware that so-called health, natural, and organic foods are more expensive than their counterparts in regular supermarkets. Anything grown "organically" seems to cost more. And anything in a distinctive "health-food" package seems a bit more expensive, too. No wonder sales in the so-called health-food industry are now close to $4 billion a year.

It's up to you to decide whether you want to pay the extra price for a product that may not be worth it. You should, however, be aware of the possibility of being defrauded in your health-food purchases. To increase your awareness of the differences among health, natural, and organic foods, we offer the following broad, although widely accepted, definitions.

1. **Health foods** may include vegetarian and dietetic foods and other products not necessarily free of chemical additives.

2. **Natural foods** do not contain artificial ingredients, preservatives, or emulsifiers.
3. **Organic foods** are grown without the use of chemically formulated fertilizers or pesticides.

The problem with these definitions is that the terms are not defined by law. How do we really know what is natural and healthy? Is it true that organic fertilizers produce more nutritious fruits and vegetables? The Federal Trade Commission attempted to ban the use of such words as *organic, natural,* and *health foods* because of their vagueness and the possibility of deceiving consumers. At the hearing for this regulation, a former nutritionist for the USDA testified that the terms were meaningless. Ruth Leverton stated that foods grown with organic fertilizers are not superior to foods grown with commercial fertilizers. After all, she pointed out, pesticide residues are present in almost all foods, and no food is completely free of them. The proposed ruling was never approved, but the FTC is attempting to formulate new regulations that won't be overruled by representatives of the health-food industry. Until these rules are made public and enforced, anybody can use the terms *health, natural,* and *organic* for anything sold.

There also is a question about the effectiveness of these foods. Most people in medical science believe that you can't expect health miracles just by eating so-called natural foods and taking large quantities of vitamins. In fact, taking too many vitamins—especially vitamins A and D—can be harmful. Most doctors now believe that if you eat a well-balanced diet, you are likely to get all the vitamins you need to stay healthy. Supplements are generally superfluous, but if they make you feel better psychologically, you may still wish to take them.

> **T**he obvious way to prevent land swindles is to investigate before you invest.

The Sale of Therapeutic Devices

Sears, Roebuck catalogs from the early 1900s contain ads for numerous therapeutic devices, such as magnetic copper belts, guaranteed to cure aching backs, rheumatism, arthritis, and the like. You might expect today's sophisticated American consumers to realize that current therapeutic devices are about as effective as those sold in the early 1900s—that is to say, not effective at all. Nonetheless, some sellers of these products do a thriving business. This area of consumer fraud is so obvious that little more need be said about it. Simply ignore any claims that a particular device can cure a host of diseases and general maladies.

Weight Reduction

Millions of dollars are spent each year on miracle weight-reduction pills. But unless those pills actually contain appetite-reducing drugs, which can be sold only by prescription, they are useless. Overweight people seem to have eternal optimism, however, because they continue to buy such pills. Those same people fall victim to unscrupulous physicians and related practitioners (osteopaths, chiropractors, and the like) who claim to have miracle weight-reducing cures. These cranks recommend special diets, and, lo and behold, their naive patients do lose weight immediately. But the trick to these special diets is that they call for a radical reduction in liquid consumption during the first few

Unless a person has a true physiological imbalance, overweight can only be "cured" by burning more calories per day than are consumed per day.

days; when an individual's normal liquid intake is reduced abruptly, that person can lose up to five pounds of water in a few days. Of course, as soon as the normal intake of liquids resumes, the individual's weight increases.

Unless a person has a true physiological imbalance, overweight can only be "cured" by burning more calories per day than are consumed per day. To lose one pound of weight, a body must burn 3,500 calories in excess of those consumed. Until men and women are constructed differently, that simple fact is the true key to weight reduction.

THE HIGH PRICE OF BEAUTY

All people want to look attractive. Consequently, Americans are willing to spend hundreds of millions of dollars a year on cosmetic products, many of which do little, if anything, to enhance physical attractiveness. The more repulsive forms of "beautifiers" are those cosmetic creams containing horse blood serum, shark oil, goat enzymes, chick embryo extracts, and the like. Whenever you see an ad for such products—usually in sensational tabloid-type magazines and newspapers—beware.

Perhaps the most ridiculous of all beauty aids are those that guarantee a reduction in hair loss. So far, there is not one single piece of evidence that any product is effective against baldness. Nonetheless, it is estimated that over $22 million a year are spent on such products. Men and women have only a few choices to alter baldness—wear a toupee or have a hair transplant or a hair-weaving implant.

FOOD STORE FRAUDS

Probably the majority of food stores are managed by honest individuals, but because some are not, you should be aware of the unsavory practices sometimes employed to rob you of the value of your food-buying dollar. The following methods of tampering with the actual weights of foods are not as uncommon as they should be.

1. Adding water to the cereals used in making processed meats, thereby adding the weight of the water (As a result, you pay meat prices for water.)
2. Soaking turkeys, oysters, chickens, and hams in water or juice overnight, thus adding several ounces to their weight
3. Placing rolled-up chicken-neck skins in the breast cavities of the birds (You pay chicken prices for neck skins.)
4. Boring holes in counterpoised weights, reducing them by anywhere from 10 to 20 percent
5. Hooking lead sinkers to the underside of the weighing pan
6. Attaching one or more one-ounce magnets under the scale pan

There are probably numerous other ways you can be short-weighted. It is up to you to figure out if this trick is being played on you. If you think it is happening consistently, you can either shop at a different store or report the dishonest operator to the proper agency, such as the weights and measures inspector in your area.

The easiest way to check the accuracy of all weighed food purchases is to use a reliable household scale. If you find that items have been short-weighted, return them to the store manager. This way, the manager is given a chance to correct an honest error, if it is one. In addition, he or she receives a warning signal that you are a smart shopper who cannot be easily cheated.

If you decide to call your local weights and measures inspector, you can find the appropriate number in your telephone directory Yellow Pages. Be sure that you've saved your purchase so it can be used as evidence. After your accusation has been confirmed by an inspector's purchase in the same store, the offending merchant will be warned or even prosecuted, if he or she is a repeat violator.

AUTOMOBILE SALES

Some automobile sales personnel have dubious reputations, which may or may not be justified. Nonetheless, it pays to be aware of three common techniques used to sell cars—and to extract more money from the gullible consumer.

1. **High-balling.** The salesperson offers you an unreasonably high trade-in value on your car, far more than competitive dealers are willing to pay. The wily salesperson hopes the unwary consumer will think he or she is getting a bargain, but actually the additional price the consumer receives for the trade-in will be included elsewhere in the price of the new car. To avoid being high-balled, assume that you can only get the wholesale or "blue book" value of your car as a trade-in, even if it is in good condition.
2. **Low-balling.** Over the phone, you are told that a particular car can be sold to you at a very low price; that is, you are given a low-ball estimate. When you come to the dealer's showroom, the salesperson tells you that he made a mistake and that the car actually will cost you a few hundred dollars more. Or the salesperson will "pack" the transaction by adding on a number of unreasonable extra charges to make up the difference so that he or she obtains the normal profit on the sale.
3. **Bushing.** Here the salesperson adds on unordered accessories. When you go to pick up your car, you find that it is costing you more than you bargained for because of these accessories, which the salesperson simply claims he or she thought you wanted.

How to Avoid Questionable Auto Sales Practices

Once you reach an agreement with the salesperson, make sure that the exact car and optional equipment that you've selected are listed plainly on the order. Make sure, too, that the order is countersigned by someone in authority, such as the sales manager of the dealership. At a minimum, the following four items should be listed on the order.

1. There will be no increase in price; the price shown at the bottom of the order is the total price to be paid on delivery.
2. There will be no reappraisal of your trade-in.
3. There will be no substitutions of nonfactory equipment for anything that you order on the car.
4. The car will be delivered within a reasonably specific time period.

Finally, don't fall for the "switch" that a salesperson might try to pull. For example, a few days after you place your order, a salesperson might call and

Everybody wants to make a quick buck. If that weren't true, a host of investment frauds would never be able to exist.

tell you that the factory has a backlog of orders and that it will take longer than anticipated to get your car. The salesperson then might say that the identical car has been located at another wholesale source—but with a few unordered options and for about $500 more.

AUTO REPAIR PROBLEMS

Some unscrupulous mechanics try to gyp customers whose cars need repair. One trick is to replace ball joints in the front suspension. An unscrupulous mechanic may put your car on a hoist, turn the wheels to the side, and wiggle them to make it appear that the ball joint is about to jump from the socket. True, these parts do wear out, but they are fairly sturdy, and some movement is acceptable, anywhere from ⅛ to 3⁄16 of an inch. Before you have the ball joints replaced, get the opinion of another mechanic; you may not need that repair job. The same misleading test can be applied to the idler arm, a short piece of metal in the lower steering mechanism of the car.

Another common ploy is to convince you that you need new piston rings because your car's exhaust is smoking; again, get a second opinion. And, finally, if you keep needing to add automatic transmission fluid, that doesn't necessarily mean you need a new transmission or a complete overhaul. Rather, it may mean that you need a new modulator valve in the transmission, a replacement that costs less than $25.

PROBLEMS WITH TV REPAIRS

Since most consumers know little, if anything, about the inner workings of a television set, repair personnel obviously can—and often do—take advantage of such ignorance. TV repair persons often use the low-ball technique to get their feet in the door. They advertise a relatively low price for a complete TV overhaul and then, once in the customer's house, claim that major repairs are necessary. A good rule of thumb is to avoid patronizing repair shops that advertise ridiculously low prices. A good TV technician earns well over $20 an hour, and you can't expect a decent job at less than that.

Perhaps the best way to avoid TV repair swindles is to purchase a reasonably priced service contract on a new set for a relatively long period of time. Today most TV sets have fewer problems than did earlier models. Your set probably incorporates solid-state technology, so when something goes wrong, only a simple exchange of a circuit board is necessary. Given the relatively low price of modern TV sets, it is often better simply to buy a new one when a major repair is actually needed.

BUYING EDUCATION

We all want to improve our lot in life, or so it seems. That's why a $3½ billion home-study education industry can exist in this country. Most home-study programs are legitimate; they are offered by accredited schools and have realistic requirements. But many others teach very little and promise the impos-

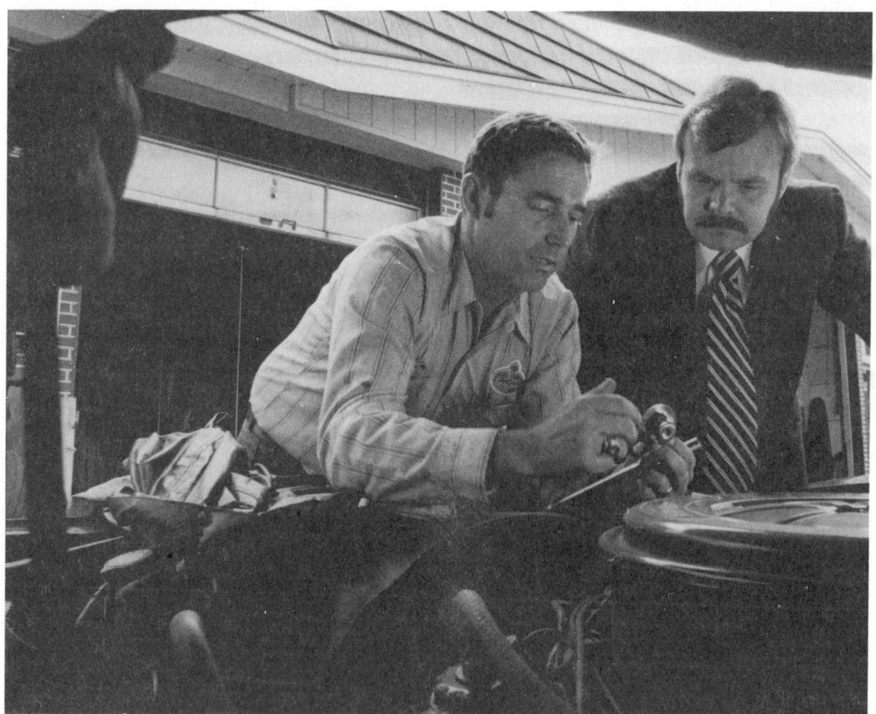

sible. For example, they guarantee that anyone passing their home-study course will obtain a high-paying job in a specific industry. Even though the Federal Trade Commission prohibits false representation of job-placement abilities and the value of the diplomas, problems exist throughout the industry in those areas.

If you are seriously considering investing in a home-study program, investigate those offered by a major college or university in your area. If, on the other hand, you are convinced that a for-profit institution offers a better home-study course, check out exactly what you will be getting for your money. Get names of graduates who have been placed in high-paying jobs after they have completed their studies, and talk to these individuals to find out if the claims of the home-study institution are valid.

PYRAMID SCHEMES

Everybody wants to make a quick buck. If that weren't true, a host of investment frauds would never be able to exist. One investment scam, which seems to come in cycles, rather like locusts, involves the pyramid scheme. If you fall for this one, here's what will happen. You go to a meeting where several people give testimonials about how much money they have made in a particular investment. You, too, are invited to become involved; just ante up an investment fee. Once you pay this fee, you are given a license, or the ability to recruit additional individuals to whom you can sell the right so they can recruit additional individuals. And, of course, they can then sell that right to other

The problem with pyramid schemes is that the only way they will work for you is if you find others willing to buy the licenses for you.

individuals. Hence, the term pyramid. In some cases, the only investment is an investment in the pyramid scheme. In other cases, the pyramid scheme involves the actual sale of a product, such as mink oil, powdered milk, or beauty cream. Your goal is to be at the top of a pyramid with constantly widening base, because you get a cut of everything sold below you on the pyramid.

When a product is actually sold, a pyramid scheme is called multilevel marketing. At the top is the original promoter, who then sells the right, usually at a percentage fee, to a couple of friends, who go out and sell the right to other friends. It all seems to be a very friendly arrangement.

The problem with pyramid schemes is that the only way they will work for you is if you find others willing to buy the licenses for you. Pyramid schemes capitalize on the greater-fool theory: There is always a bigger fool than you out there to help you get richer.

It is true that if you get in at the bottom of a pyramid scheme, you can make lots of money, but the majority of people involved in them don't make much at all. In fact, the average individual who participates in such schemes makes very little, if anything at all.

MAIL-ORDER MADNESS

Direct-mail advertising and so-called space ads placed in magazines and newspapers constitute a significant percentage of all advertising dollars. Also, general mail-order companies head the list in terms of the top ten categories of consumer complaints, as registered by the Council of Better Business Bureaus; Exhibit 4–3 is a list of the ten most common consumer complaints. The inspection service of the U.S. Postal Service estimates that fraudulent mail schemes cost the public close to a billion dollars a year. Here is just a partial list of mail-order scams:

1. Home-improvement fraud
2. Auto-insurance fraud
3. Charity fraud
4. Fake contests
5. Chain-letter schemes
6. Missing-heir schemes

EXHIBIT 4–3
Top Ten Categories of Consumer Complaints

General mail-order companies
Franchised auto dealers
Home-furnishings stores
Magazines ordered by mail
Home-maintenance companies
Independent auto-repair shops
Department stores
Miscellaneous automotive
Television-servicing companies
Insurance companies

SOURCE: Council of Better Business Bureaus, 1981.

Consider one typical mail-order scheme, which involves selling coats of arms. First, you receive from Halbert's, Inc., of Bath, Ohio, a personally addressed letter in which you are offered the "exclusive and particularly beautiful" coat of arms appropriate for families bearing your last name. Should you respond and should Halbert's be unable to find your name in its book of coats of arms, it simply creates a new one, which is no doubt historically invalid. The U.S. Postal Service now requires Halbert's to disclose in its mailings that, when it is unable to locate the historically valid coat of arms, it creates a new one.

Halbert's also is in the business of selling genealogies. For a mere $24.95, you can receive a limited edition of a book that traces the origin and meaning of your last name and gives the facts about others with your last name living in the United States. Your coat of arms is illustrated and interpreted, and you are told how to trace your ancestors. If you decide to pay, you receive a word-processor-generated 100-page booklet filled mainly with general information. Your last name is first mentioned on page 10, there are two paragraphs describing your coat of arms, and there are a number of pages listing people with your last name in various cities in the United States. And that, for almost $25, is all you receive from a mail-order operation the U.S. Postal Service acknowledges is extremely deceptive.

Actually, the majority of items sold through general mail-order companies are useful to the consumer. What you have to watch out for are great deals that you just can't pass up. Anything that seems too good to be true is probably suspect.

WAYS TO AVOID CONSUMER FRAUDS

To avoid falling prey to shady or downright dishonest merchandising and selling practices, you should first be aware of what these more common ploys are. The following guidelines will help you keep your pride and your pocketbook intact.

1. Beware of any free or bargain offers. Remember, there's no such thing as a free lunch.
2. Avoid deals that must be made *immediately*.
3. Be suspicious of any offer that costs "pennies a day" or "less than the price of a daily newspaper". After all, 75 pennies a day is almost $275 a year.
4. Always wait two to three days before signing a contract. Any salesperson who insists that you must sign a contract immediately is someone to avoid.
5. Politely but firmly get rid of fast-talking salespersons who come to your home (announced or unannounced).
6. When a stranger calls or comes to your house claiming to be an inspector, ask for proper identification. When in doubt, insist on calling the appropriate authorities to confirm the inspector's legitimacy. The fact is, virtually no households are visited by legitimate inspectors these days.
7. Avoid bait-and-switch sales practices; don't be traded up.
8. Stay away from anyone who asks you to withdraw cash from your bank account.

SUMMARY

1. Consumer fraud involves the making of a false statement of a past or existing fact with knowledge of its falsity, or with a reckless indifference as to its truth, with the intent to cause someone to rely on such a statement.
2. Proof of fraud by sellers is often difficult to obtain. The best protection against fraud is to be aware of the various fraudulent schemes practiced by sellers in the marketplace.
3. There are many forms of false advertising: bait and switch, dishonest contests, the offer of "free" goods, merchandise substitution, and so on.
4. Bait and switch involves advertising a product at an attractive price; then informing the consumer that the advertised product is either not available, of poor quality, or not what the consumer "really wants"; and, finally, promoting a more expensive item. The Federal Trade Commission puts bait and switch at the top of its list of common fraudulent practices by sellers.

5. Door-to-door salespersons often use questionable selling practices to persuade consumers to buy their products. Such sales often require that the buyer sign an installment contract. The best way to protect yourself from such schemes is never to let a door-to-door salesperson enter your home. It should be noted, however, that there are several reputable firms—for example, Avon and Fuller Brush—that only do business on a door-to-door selling basis.
6. The Federal Trade Commission has adopted a cooling-off provision, which makes it a violation for door-to-door salespersons to fail to give consumers three business days to cancel an installment contract. Many states also have a cooling-off law.
7. Other areas in which fraudulent selling practices have been identified are: interstate land sales; the sales of health-care products, therapeutic devices, weight-reduction items, and beauty products; food retail outlets; automobile sales; auto repair; TV repair; home-study programs; and pyramid schemes.
8. One way to avoid being cheated by food retailers is to measure what you buy with your own scales. Once you find a store that does not cheat you, you can continue to shop there with some assurance of honesty on the part of the retailer. In fact, repeat buying usually will yield high returns because the retailer's income depends largely upon customers who continually come back.
9. General mail-order companies are at the top of the list of consumer complaints about sellers, according to the Council of Better Business Bureaus. The U.S. Postal Service estimates that fraudulent mail schemes cost consumers almost $1 billion annually. Some examples of mail-order schemes are: home-improvement frauds, charity frauds, auto-insurance frauds, phony contests, chain-letter schemes, and missing-heir schemes.

QUESTIONS FOR THOUGHT AND DISCUSSION

1. Do you think that fraud in the marketplace is a major problem? Have you or a member of your family ever been the victim of such a scheme? How did you or they handle the situation?
2. Do you think that businesses can continue to use fraudulent selling techniques indefinitely? Why or why not?
3. Are consumers who shop by mail more likely to be victims of fraudulent selling schemes? Why or why not?

THINGS TO DO

1. When you see what you believe to be a false or misleading ad, write the manufacturer of the advertised product and ask for an explanation. If you are not satisfied with the explanation, ask your local FTC office if the advertising is, in fact, deceptive.
2. Check through several tabloid-type magazines. Make a list of the types of products advertised in these publications. Do many of them carry ads for products that promise amazing improvements in personal appearance, health, and so on? Do you believe any of these products can do what they advertise? Why or why not?

SELECTED READINGS

Carson, Rachel. *The Silent Spring*. New York: Houghton Mifflin, 1962.
Council of Better Business Bureaus Philanthropic Advisory Service, 1150 17th St., N.W., Washington, D.C. 20036 offers a free booklet on major charities.

Feinman, Jeffrey. *The Purple Pages*. New York: Hawthorn Books, 1979.

Handbook of Nonprescription Drugs. Washington, D.C. Published biannually by the American Pharmaceutical Association.

Harris, Marvin. "Why It's Not the Same Old America." *Psychology Today*, 1981. *Help: The Indispensable Almanac of Consumer Information*. New York: Everest House (yearly).

"It's Natural! It's Organic! Or Is It?" *Consumer Reports*, July 1980.

Kallet, Arthur and Schlink, F. J. *100,000,000 Guinea Pigs*. New York: Vanguard Press, 1932.

Lamb, Ruth de Forest. *American Chamber of Horrors*. New York: Farrar & Rinehart, 1936.

Nimmons, D. and Barrett, K. "Don't Be Conned." *Ladies Home Journal*, November 1982, p. 80.

Paulson, Morton C. *The Great Land Hustle*. Chicago: Henry Regnery, 1972.

CHAPTER
MAKING UP YOUR MIND

Even if you were the wealthiest person on earth, you would still have to make decisions. Even if all your material wants could be satisfied at the touch of a button, one valuable resource would still be scarce for you, and that resource is your time.

CHAPTER PREVIEW

- What is involved in rational decision making?
- How do goals affect your consumer choices?
- Why is value clarification important?
- What else determines how you act?
- What determines your buying habits?
- What are some of the aspects of alternative life styles?

Even if you were the wealthiest person on earth, you would still have to make decisions. Even if all your material wants could be satisfied at the touch of a button, one valuable resource would still be scarce for you, and that resource is your time. You have only so much time in a day and so many days in a life. Even in that nirvana of total abundance, you would still be faced with making a choice about the use of your time. You would, therefore, have to learn the art of decision making.

We know that in the real world the art of decision making applies not only to the use of our time but to other resources as well. Intelligent, **rational consumer decision making** thus becomes all the more important. We all face a budget problem, and, since we cannot have everything we want, we must make choices, which we must then act upon in a rational manner. We cannot simply decide to buy a new car. We must also choose what kind of new car to buy—foreign or domestic, small or large, luxury or economy, sedan or station wagon, and so on. We must then decide where to look for the car of our choice and whether to pay cash or buy it on credit. If we use credit, we must decide where to obtain that credit. Decision making is an ongoing process.

RATIONAL CONSUMER DECISION MAKING
Deciding how to buy, where to buy, and what to buy so that the consumer obtains the highest satisfaction from using his or her resources, including both time and money.

EXCHANGE AND RATIONAL DECISION MAKING

All consumer decision making ultimately results in a choice that is accomplished by exchange. When we decide to enter a certain occupation and take a job with a particular firm, we exchange our labor services for that firm's payment of wages. When we decide to buy a TV, we exchange for the set itself the purchasing power implicit in the money paid for it.

In our market economy, there are many ways exchange can be facilitated—by using money instead of trading goods for goods **(barter)**, by the branding of particular products to give certain types of information, by the use of media to transmit product information, and so on. As rational consumers, we try to facilitate our transactions in the marketplace as much as is economically worthwhile. For instance, we may attempt to acquire information that is not provided to us by the seller of the product. Or we may prevail upon private or government agencies to facilitate the exchanges we like to make.

Rational consumer decision making involves understanding both the benefits and the costs of any action. "Cost" is defined here as the **opportunity cost** of doing something. Thus, when you decide to read this book, you are giving up the opportunity of, say, working one more hour at your part-time job. How would you quantify that cost? By seeing what your after-tax earnings would be if you worked one more hour instead of spending one hour reading this book. That would be your opportunity cost. How would you quantify the benefits of reading the book one more hour? Those benefits would be whatever value you placed on the knowledge you receive, the probability of getting a higher grade in your course in consumer economics, and so on. Basically, then, rational consumer decision making means doing a series of **cost/benefit analyses** and choosing those actions that yield the highest net benefits, given your limited time and income. A net benefit is all the benefits of an action totaled together minus all the costs totaled together.

Using cost/benefit analysis to determine your particular most beneficial choices may seem difficult. Whenever your personal values or feelings enter into your

BARTER
The exchange of goods or services without the use of money. If, for example, I give you two pencils for one eraser, you and I have exchanged by way of barter.

OPPORTUNITY COST
The cost of doing something, measured by the most valuable alternative you give up in spending your time and/or money on a particular product or activity. For example, one way to measure the opportunity cost of your reading this book would be to measure the wages you would receive if you were working for pay instead.

COST/BENEFIT ANALYSIS
A way to reach decisions in which all the costs are added up, as well as all the benefits. Using the net benefit approach, if benefits minus costs are greater than zero, then the decision should be positive. Alternatively, if benefits are divided by costs and if the quotient is greater than one, the decision should be positive.

EXHIBIT 5–1
A Typical Decision-Making Process

Should I buy a new car?	What size should I buy?	What body style should I buy?	Automatic or manual transmission?
Yes	Compact	Sports car	Manual

decision making, you will have a difficult time quantifying them. Nonetheless, you are always implicitly making choices on the basis of what is best for you, given the alternatives and the opportunity cost of each alternative.

We can break the decision-making process down into several steps.

1. Define the problem in light of your goals and values.
2. Select and explore possible alternatives; that is, collect information.
3. Evaluate these alternatives in light of the information you have collected.
4. From these alternatives, select the one that seems best to you.
5. Proceed to accept and evaluate your responsibilities after having selected this one alternative.

After you have selected a particular alternative, retain in your memory the results of your decision and draw upon these recollections for future decision-making processes (cost/benefit analyses). For example, suppose that you finally decide to purchase a used, two-door, subcompact car. After several months, you find that you would have been willing to pay a slightly higher price and higher gas and maintenance costs to have a compact car. You should remember this experience and use the information it provides the next time you have to make a cost/benefit analysis of what type of car to buy.

DETERMINING OUR CHOICES: FIRST, A HIERARCHY OF NEEDS

Many factors determine how we make choices in our day-to-day living. One way to approach this determination is to look at a sociopsychological analysis of needs. Sociologist Abraham Maslow did this in his now classic book, *Motivation and Personality*, in which he states that there is an ordering of needs

Using cost/benefit analysis to determine your particular most beneficial choices may seem difficult. Whenever your personal values or feelings enter into your decision making, you will have a difficult time quantifying them.

VALUES
Learned or acquired beliefs that create a strong intellectual and/or emotional response whenever challenged.

VALUE CLARIFICATION
The process by which each individual can determine his or her values.

that represents the priorities established by Western men and women. The following list is comprehensive but not exhaustive, nor is it permanently fixed.

1. **Survival, or physical, needs.** Appetites and physical well-being are primary here. The need for food and drink is basic and must be satisfied, according to Maslow, before attention can be given to other needs.
2. **Safety needs.** Humans require security, dependability, and stability.
3. **Love and a sense of belonging.** At this level, needs begin to be more social and less physiological or body-related. They are also less material and more psychological.
4. **Esteem needs.** Individuals would like to be respected and liked.
5. **Self-actualization.** According to Maslow, self-actualizing individuals experience "peak moments"—moments, and sometimes extended periods, of fulfillment and feelings of oneness with the universe. This need will be fulfilled when all other needs have been met and when the individual feels satisfied with what he or she is doing.

If we accept Maslow's hierarchy of needs and values, then we are able to analyze in our own minds what determines our own choices. Such analysis can lead to better self-awareness, and such improved self-awareness often produces better decisions. Generally, the choices we make depend on the values we hold, the goals we set for ourselves and our family, and the customs of our society.

CLARIFYING OUR VALUES

When you were a child, people probably asked you what you wanted to be in life. You might have said a musician, a mother, a father, an artist, a scientist, a doctor, a lawyer, a flight attendant, a firefighter, or any number of other roles and occupations you might have been aware of at that time. Later on, however, you had to start making some realistic decisions about your future.

For many, this process starts in high school. Should you drop out or stay in? Should you be a vocational-education major or a precollege major? Should you take more or less math? Once you have decided to stay in high school, you face another choice: Should you go on to college after high school or get a job? In either case, you must decide what you really want to do. Once in college, you have to decide on a major. When you graduate (if you do), you must decide where you want to work and how, the amount of free time you want to have, what kinds of risks you want to take, what kinds of people you want to be with, and so on.

Often, however, many of us let ourselves follow what we might call the "path of least resistance." And just as often, in retrospect we decide we have made a mistake. We realize we did not clarify our **values** about life and how to live it. For this reason, career-guidance counselors, psychologists, and sociologists increasingly stress the need for individuals to engage in their own **value clarification.**

Values and Value Judgments

Values can be defined as learned, or acquired, beliefs that create a strong intellectual and/or emotional response whenever challenged. Value clarification, therefore, is the process by which each individual can determine his or her values. We frequently make negative value judgments about other people's behavior. Making value judgments is part of value clarification for each individual, because realizing what one does not like in others indicates what one should like in oneself.

Many of us let ourselves follow what we might call the "path of least resistance." And just as often, in retrospect we decide we have made a mistake.

Industrial Age versus Post-Industrial Age Consumer Values

Dr. Ronald Stampfl has attempted to identify sets of values that were prevalent in the industrial age in the United States, which he defines as the years between 1920 and 1990, compared with those values that consumers will hold after 1990. Here is his list of the different sets of values.[1]

INDUSTRIAL AGE CONSUMER VALUES	POST-INDUSTRIAL AGE CONSUMER VALUES
1. Style and fashion do not relate to function.	1. Functional changes take precedence over style changes.
2. Ownership, particularly of homes and cars, is important.	2. Renting or leasing is just as acceptable as owning.
3. Maximum consumption rates are desirable.	3. Consumption of what is necessary is desirable.
4. Products that can be thrown out are preferred.	4. Recycling is preferred.
5. Social and environmental costs of products are unimportant.	5. Preservation of the environment is important.
6. Economic growth helps everyone and is good.	6. Zero economic growth may be preferable if it creates stability.

According to Stampfl, the difference in value sets will occur because, prior to the 1990s, consumers will have felt that natural resources were all but inexhaustible and that Americans were entitled to an ever-increasing material existence. After 1990, according to Stampfl, persistent pollution problems, energy crises, rising prices, and shortages will cause people to rethink their values.

The years between 1960 and 1990 represent an era of transitional values, when we will gradually move toward post-industrial-age values. In any event, it's easy to see that our values relate to our consumption decisions. As we move toward post-industrial-age values, our decisions about what to buy and in what quantities obviously will change, even if prices and incomes do not. For example, the choice of clothing is influenced by our value system: In the post-industrial-age value system, functional and durable clothing will be preferable to fashionable but less practical clothing.

The Process of Value Clarification

Clarifying our values is an ongoing process. All of us change throughout our lives (or at least we think we do). You're probably not the same person you were five years ago in terms of your values and your view of the world.

1. Ronald W. Stampfl, "Consumer Values in Transition," *Forum*, Spring/Summer 1981.

Sometimes a discussion with your family or friends or even a career-guidance counselor helps clarify the extent of change you have experienced as you mature. When you make decisions, you are weighing values; you are asking yourself, "What is important to me *now*?"

For all of us, the ultimate goal is happiness, which, of course, means different things to different people. How we get there is another matter, but one way to assure that we at least approach our goal is to clarify our values on a regular basis. Change is inevitable, and, as our life situations change, so do our values. Gradual change is generally less painful and less costly than abrupt change. For example, a homemaker of many years who suddenly realizes she can't bear the tedium of keeping house might become so unhappy with her situation that she makes sudden—and disastrous—decisions based upon her newly found values. If, on the other hand, this individual had consistently clarified her values and related them to her actual situation, she could have changed her life style gradually according to those evolving values.

Goals

Goals are linked to our values: A set of values leads to a set of goals. For example, if you place a high value on educational success, your goal may be to graduate from college with honors.

Everybody has goals, whether or not they are well defined. To attain that ultimate and universal goal of happiness, we set numerous subgoals. Yours may be to finish college or to get a good job or to play the guitar well; you may have set goals for your children, if and when you have them; you may have set a goal in your job or your business. These goals will often determine your consumption behavior. If one of your goals is to be relatively well off by the time you are fifty, you may then decide to work hard, spend little, and save a lot. That means you will not be tempted to take long vacations or buy costly housing, at least not in the earlier stages of your career. If, on the other hand, your subgoal is different, you may take those longer vacations, knowing you will pay for them later because your savings will be smaller.

Changing Standards

Changing goals and values can affect our standards as consumers. For example, most of us have changing standards in purchasing items. You may have one standard as an undergraduate student, another standard as a graduate, yet another as a single working person, and, finally, another as a married person.

Individuals change their goals all the time. In fact, experts who specialize in helping people plan for the future often advise clients to set goals for the short run, the intermediate run, and the long run and to revise them often. For example, your short-run goal for the next two months might be to finish a particular project, do well in certain classes, or increase your sales. At the end of the stipulated period, you will be able to see if you attained those goals, and you will make new ones for the next immediate time period. In the intermediate run, your goals may involve improving your tennis game, painting the house, or getting a new car. And then there are the long-run goals—five-year, ten-year, even twenty-year projections into the future. As most people discover, these are often revised according to changes in one's social and professional status.

Goals and planning go hand in hand. Consumer decision making is sometimes based on plans that are themselves based on goals. Planning is sometimes a painful procedure, particularly when a family is involved and numerous diverse interests must be considered. Compromise is always involved in making and following plans. People who tend to "want the stars" invariably have to compromise and face the reality of scarcity.

Consumers who plan in a rational manner may appear to lack spontaneity, and that certainly is one of the costs of planning. But one of the benefits is that goals can often be met—on schedule and to the satisfaction of the planner. If you decide to become a consumer who plans, then you may be able to satisfy many of your desires and needs. But if spontaneity is important in your life, you'll probably chafe at the prospect of laying plans and following them.

Customs

Primitive societies are usually ruled by custom. Even modern societies have customs that determine people's choices. In the United States, custom plays a smaller role in consumer decision making than it does in many other nations. Nonetheless, if you examine your own behavior as a consumer, you may be surprised at the extent to which your decisions depend on established customs. Here are just a few areas of our lives that are dictated more or less by custom:

1. The types and combinations of food we eat
2. The exchange of holiday cards
3. The style of clothes we wear
4. The way we dispose of the dead
5. The types of ceremonies by which we marry

Consider clothes, for example; the two or three nonfunctional buttons on the sleeve of a man's jacket are there simply because of custom. You probably can think of numerous other features of clothing that have no function other than to fit the dictates of custom. Even the fact that men in our society don't wear skirts is dictated by custom; we partly identify sex roles by established dress.

Customs do serve a useful purpose. Without them, we could not predict behavior, and the result would be considerable confusion. By following customs that are in line with our values, we reduce both time and search costs in determining what our behavior should be. Consider the example of Thanksgiving; since custom says that we will have a turkey on Thanksgiving, the decision about what to fix for Thanksgiving dinner has been made for us.

CONSPICUOUS CONSUMPTION

Your consumption patterns also may be determined by your desire to influence others' opinions of you. Many years ago, a famous American economist, Thorstein Veblen, pointed out in his *Theory of the Leisure Class* that many people desire to consume in a conspicuous manner. **Conspicuous consumption,** then, means using the goods and services that we can afford to demonstrate our social worth. The implicit assumption here is that the more we can afford, the worthier we are. Such consumption is based on conformity; the consumer apparently wants to emulate the consumption practices of neighbors and friends.

CONSPICUOUS CONSUMPTION Consumption of goods more for their ability to impress others than for the inherent satisfaction they yield; buying and using consumer goods ostentatiously.

Goals and planning go hand in hand. Consumer decision making is sometimes based on plans that are themselves based on goals.

This type of behavior, also known as "keeping up with the Joneses," is considered undesirable by many because it implies a lack of individuality. Although individuality earns high praise in American society, it tends to be more preached than practiced. The theory of conspicuous consumption fails to explain adequately our consumption activities. People's tastes and values do indeed differ, and today's motivational psychologists no longer credit Veblen's theory with explaining consumption patterns in our economy.

Actually, many families and individuals, especially those with "old money," practice what might be called nonconspicuous consumption. Rather than attempting to flaunt their wealth, they underplay it by purchasing relatively inexpensive cars, clothes, and houses. Some individuals also may display, with pride, their nonconspicuous consumption of such products as faded jeans and well-worn tennis shoes.

BUYING BEHAVIORS

In one respect, there are as many buying behaviors as there are consumers. But for the purpose of analysis and to better understand our own buying behavior, we can categorize them into several broad groups, the three most obvious being impulse buying, habit buying, and planned buying.

Impulse Buying

To buy impulsively is to walk into a store, see something we like, and purchase it without further ado. Merchants exploit impulse buying by displaying whimsical and relatively inexpensive items at the checkout counter. Obviously, impulse buying cannot explain all our buying habits because we have certain needs that must be met if we are to survive, the most obvious being minimum amounts of food and shelter. Thus, we must plan to purchase at least part of what we consume. The rest, however, could conceivably be purchased on the basis of pure spur-of-the-moment impulse. Nonetheless, there is a limit—our income plus our available credit—to impulse buying. Most consumer economists argue against impulse buying because it can undermine a budget and may lead to financial difficulties.

Habit Buying

Many purchases are made as a result of habits acquired through the years. No plans are involved and no impulses either, just the force of habit. A person might stop at a tavern on the way home from work every Friday night. An individual might continue subscribing to, say, a photography magazine even though he or she has long given up the hobby and doesn't even own a camera anymore. Consider, also, that habit buying may be necessary in order to free up time for other buying that requires time and thought. In other words, habit buying isn't necessarily bad (as long as you don't make a habit of it).

Planned Buying

Planned buying, or rational consumer decision making, may lack spontaneity, but it does have the virtue of safety if it is consistent with available resources. Rational consumers generally won't exceed their budgets if they plan to limit their purchases carefully to those items they can afford. But even the best laid plans can go awry. Moreover, some motivational psychologists believe that businesspersons can affect our plans—and certainly our impulsive buying sprees—by means of effective advertising campaigns.

CONSUMER SOVEREIGNTY VERSUS PRODUCER SOVEREIGNTY

Every day in every way, we are bombarded with advertisements as producers attempt to manipulate us into buying their products. How successful are they? Some say very; other say not so much. The saving rate in the United States at least gives some evidence that producers have not made us spend any more now than we did in the past, measured as a percent of our total incomes.

In the ideal world where the consumer is sovereign, we consumers, through our dollars, vote for the products or the services we want most. Those products

In the ideal world where the consumer is sovereign, we consumers, through our dollars, vote for the products or the services we want most.

receiving the most votes yield the highest profits; therefore, they attract the businesspersons' money from other areas in the economy where dollar votes are smaller. In this manner, the profit system directs resources to areas in the economy where they yield the highest value to the population.

Even in this ideal world, however, income may be so unevenly distributed that very few people are commanding large amounts of resources; hence, the dollar voting system does not distribute goods and services the way that society deems best. But, setting aside for the moment the problem of income distribution, the consumer sovereignty issue also rests on an assumption about the economy itself.

That assumption concerns the degree of competitiveness within our economic system. If there is little competition—that is, a great deal of monopoly and severe restrictions on entry into an industry—then a high price will not cause outside resources to flow into that industry. Suppose you produce a medical device that doctors have found very helpful in surgery. If you convince the government to pass a law naming you the only person who can make that medical device, then you have succeeded in restricting entry. Even though you may charge a high price for your device, no one else will be able to take their resources—labor and machines—and compete with you; you have a restricted monopoly. Of course, this is an oversimplified example. But if you believe the United States is composed, more or less, of restricted-entry monopolies, you will have serious doubts about the validity of the consumer sovereignty principle.

Even if all producers want to influence our buying habits, they must somehow collaborate on methods for doing so. Otherwise, competition among them (except in the case of monopolies) will not necessarily lead to any predictable conclusion. Even with sophisticated marketing techniques and heavy doses of advertising, consumers, at least occasionally, have demonstrated their desire to be sovereign. Witness the reluctance of the American woman to accept the midi-skirt, even though the fashion industry pushed them so hard. It has been estimated that nine out of every ten new products fail within one year. This is a staggering figure, considering that thousands of new products are marketed every year in the United States.

Distinguishing between Consumer Choice and Consumer Sovereignty

If the consumer has the freedom to decide what to buy and how to use it, then consumer choice exists. In other words, as long as the consumer is presented with options, he or she has choice. On the other hand, **consumer sovereignty** implies that consumers are the ones who determine those options. A self-sufficient family living in the middle of the wilderness obviously enjoys both choice and sovereignty. It alone decides what to grow, how to make things, and how to divide its time between work and play. It directs the use of available resources and makes choices among what is produced. In our society, the richest one the world has ever seen, there is no question that consumers have choices, literally millions of them. But economists such as John Kenneth Gal-

CONSUMER SOVEREIGNTY
A situation in which consumers ultimately decide which products and styles will survive in the marketplace; that is, producers do not dictate consumer tastes.

braith, as well as more radical Marxists like Paul Baran, believe that consumer sovereignty is essentially dead.[2]

We must also point out that even if consumer choice exists, individuals are forced by law to buy some items. For example, in certain states, it is illegal to drive a car without also purchasing automobile liability insurance. To be sure, individuals in such circumstances could always choose not to drive, but that is really begging the issue. In essence, then, there is a gray area where we are, in effect, forced to purchase certain items. As shown in Exhibit 5–2, consumers actually confront a range of purchasing situations. It is safe to say that we generally are in the middle of that range, somewhere between being forced to purchase and being able to make independent choices.

BUYING AND SEARCHING

Most consumer decision making depends upon information that must be acquired through some searching procedure. The best search procedure is, of course, different for each person, but a general rule for rational consumer decision making can be made: The larger the expected payoff from searching for better information in the marketplace, the greater the cost that should be incurred to acquire the information.

In plain language, that means we probably will spend considerably less time trying to get the best deal on a tube of toothpaste than we will spend trying to get the best deal on a new car. The expected gains from a good deal on toothpaste may be at most a few cents; but on a car the gains may be several hundred dollars. The major difference between rational and so-called irrational buying habits is that the former involves looking at the expected costs and benefits in order to determine the best deal.

Some people, such as doctors, lawyers, and top executives, consider their time so valuable that they seek out very little information. For example, they may purchase many products from an expensive store in their neighborhood. They are willing to pay higher prices because they have found that the store carries relatively higher quality brand names, and they aren't willing to spend additional time searching for alternative sources.

For any one of us, it is not *always* beneficial to spend more time searching for lower price or higher quality in a product. At some point, we have to stop our search. We won't search *every* store in our city for the lowest toothpaste price, even though we know that the next store might offer that lower price. The point at which we stop searching is determined by the information we already have and a comparison of what it will cost to acquire new information against what we expect the benefits to be from that new information.

A study done in Chicago revealed that most people shopping for cars visited only two car dealers. This finding indicates that many consumers realize that searching for the best deal may not mean searching everywhere in a large geographical area. Would you buy a new car from a dealer thirty miles away

2. Paul Baran, "A Marxist View of Consumer Sovereignty," *The Political Economy of Growth.* New York: Monthly Review Press, 1957. For an opposite view, see George Gilder, "Galbraithian Truth and Fallacy," *Forbes,* November 12, 1979, pp. 117–30.

In deciding about your lifestyle, you are forced to make decisions based on incomplete information.

EXHIBIT 5–2
The Range of Consumer Choice and Sovereignty

At one extreme, no one forces us to buy anything; at the other, we are required to purchase an item whether we like it or not. Generally, depending on the situation, we are somewhere in between.

because it costs a hundred dollars less than the same car at a dealership two blocks away? If you have warranty or service problems and must take the car back to the dealer thirty miles away, you will incur time costs, additional gas costs, and probably car rental costs that you would have been spared had you purchased from your local dealer.

Expected potential benefits must be weighed against actual and expected costs. You can become a rational consumer decision maker by remembering, and acting according to, that rule.

YOU ARE IN CONTROL

Remember throughout this discussion that you're the boss: You determine your values and make decisions based on those values. Think about that when you analyze the behavior of others, too. If you consider someone stupid for purchasing a product at a price you deem too high, you may be trying to impose your low time value on that person. Also, you generally impose your values on other people if you consider their purchases to be in poor taste. Their taste is merely a reflection of a value system that is different from yours. Thus, while the preceding tenets of rational consumer decision making are universal, one person's decision making may be rational for that individual but not for someone else. Don't fall into the trap of trying to apply the rules of others to your behavior or your rules to the behavior of others.

FORESIGHT AND HINDSIGHT

In deciding about your lifestyle, you are forced to make decisions based on incomplete information. That is, you can never know how you will feel in the future, what your values will be, or what your job situation will be. Although you lack perfect information, you nonetheless have to make decisions about your future. Years later, you may look back and reflect ruefully on those earlier decisions. Little did you know that you were going to tire quickly of sitting at a desk, or that your business was going to go backrupt, or that you really needed an extra year of bumming around the country before you started to work. Had you known, you probably wouldn't have done things the way you did.

If you regret your decision five years later, remember that hindsight is always more reliable than foresight. Because you can't reverse your past, hindsight is useful only in analyzing your mistakes to help you make better decisions in the future. As trite as it may sound, there's a ring of truth to the saying "Let bygones be bygones." To express this fact about the past, we can use the economists' term **sunk costs:** Sunk costs are gone forever; figuratively, they have sunk to the bottom of the ocean. Stop worrying about them and look to the future. If you can extract some information from mistakes you made in the past, so much the better. But don't chastise yourself for a decision made five years ago if the decision was based on the best information available at the time.

SUNK COSTS
Costs that have been incurred already and that cannot be changed. An example of sunk costs is the initial cost of buying a television set; that cost never changes after purchase, but the cost of running the equipment can change because the longer the set is kept on, the higher the electricity bill will be.

TIME, TIME, TIME

In every possible alternative lifestyle, one element remains constant: the amount of time you have available. The question you must answer is how you want to use that time. A chosen lifestyle may involve being constantly busy, with no time to spend with family or friends and no time for vacations. Successful businesspeople often choose this pace. They use every second of their time to maximize their prestige and income, and they may work so much that they have little time even to spend their growing incomes. Compare these individuals with those who decide to work on a factory assembly line. Their jobs last seven hours a day and may seem boring, but when their shift ends, they can forget their jobs and enjoy their leisure. An assembly-line worker will never have as large an income as a successful executive, but there will be a pay off: the freedom from worry that makes free time truly free.

It is important to look at time as a commodity that you purchase. It is also important to judge the quality of that time. Suppose that you're a busy executive; if you think about your work even when you're at home with your family and friends, that time may have little value to you as leisure. It is not equal to the quality of time you might spend at home on your own interests or those of your friends or family. Once in a while, it's a good idea to evaluate how much time is actually your very own. A change in lifestyles might be in order, one that involves changing firms and limiting your time on the job to thirty-five hours per week instead of the sixty hours per week you spent on your former job.

The same is true for those who decide to devote much of their time to the household. Specialization of tasks may be fine for some but perhaps not for you. Maybe you want to have a part-time job, letting other family members share the household chores with you while you share the responsibility for earning family income. Such possibilities involve a decision about how you, and the others affected, want to use your time. You can wisely make this kind of decision only if you have some general notion about what your values are.

PARKINSON'S LAW

PARKINSON'S LAW
Work will expand to fit the time allowed.

Whatever our values may be and whatever our lifestyle becomes, most of us share a certain psychological trait commonly known as **Parkinson's Law.** Parkinson, a management expert, made an observation that unfortunately seems to have universal validity: *Work expands to fit the time allowed.* If you're aware of Parkinson's Law, you can fight it. If you're not, it may overwhelm you. Say you have allotted yourself four hours to write a report. You had better believe that the report will take you at *least* four hours. However, had you allotted yourself, say, three hours, it would have taken only three hours and probably would not have been any better or worse. In fact, it might have been better because you would have started in earnest immediately instead of twiddling your thumbs, sharpening pencils, and looking at additional reference materials for the first two hours.

Breaking the Law

One way to avoid falling victim to Parkinson's Law is to plan and draw up lists of things to do. The more specialized and specific the lists are, the more efficient people become. For many people, list making is beneficial to accomplishing their goals; as a result, they feel more satisfied with how they spend their lives. Instead of telling yourself that you really ought to read more books, make sure you do it by setting aside some reading time every day. Don't set an unrealistic goal, such as five hours at a sitting, but shoot for something you know you can manage—say, fifteen minutes at a time, four times during the day. You will be surprised at how many books you can read that way. If you really would like to keep up correspondence with old friends, stop putting it off: Set up a specific time and do it.

Another way to make sure you accomplish tasks and use your time efficiently is to reward yourself. A famous writer once did so and increased his output significantly. Because he was an avid smoker and craved nicotine, he decided to reward himself with one cigarette after he finished writing a page. Once his plan was in place, he never missed his deadlines. You may not make the same use of cigarettes, but you might find another appropriate self-reward.

Such a technique can be extended to lifetime planning. You can set goals for each day, each week, each month, each five-year period, and you can keep redefining these goals. Some extremely efficient people always list more goals each day than they know they can achieve. But sometimes they actually accomplish more than they thought they could because their goals provide a strong impetus to complete their tasks.

SUMMARY

1. Because we live in a world of scarcity, we are forced to make choices and, therefore, to involve ourselves in decision making.
2. Rational consumer decision making involves seeking out the most beneficial exchanges. To understand the full opportunity cost of your actions, you must engage in cost/benefit analysis.
3. Decision making involves defining the problem in light of your goals and values, selecting and exploring possible alternatives, evaluating these alternatives, selecting one alternative, and evaluating your responsibilities after selecting this alternative.

4. Your goals, which change from time to time, generally determine the choices you make.

5. Setting goals and laying plans depend upon information acquired during the decision-making process.

6. Some psychologists and sociologists believe we have a hierarchy of needs. For example, Maslow thinks that our needs have the following order of importance: survival, safety, love and a sense of belonging, esteem, and self-actualization.

7. Many of our actions and habits, such as our choice of clothing, are determined by custom.

8. Consumers generally engage in impulse, habit, or planned buying.

9. Information must be acquired before purchases can be made. It is, however, only useful to acquire information up to the point where the expected payoff from searching for more information is not as great as the expected costs of that additional search. The larger the purchase contemplated, the more time you should spend seeking information on the best product and the best financial deal.

10. Hindsight is always twenty/twenty, but what has happened in the past cannot be reversed. It is, however, useful to analyze past decisions and actions to make better decisions in the future.

11. Even if you have decided to accomplish certain goals because they fit in with your values, you may not succeed if you fall prey to Parkinson's Law, which says that work will expand to fit the time allowed. It is your responsibility to manage your personal time most efficiently.

QUESTIONS FOR THOUGHT AND DISCUSSION

1. Can you think of any product, service, or resource that is actually free?

2. Why does scarcity force you to make decisions?

3. How do your goals determine your choices?

4. What are some of the customs of your family or your community that influence your expenditures? How do they differ from the customs of other groups that you have observed?

5. Do you think most people around you engage in some form of conspicuous consumption? Why?

6. Are there any psychological benefits that individuals might obtain from allowing themselves to buy on impulse once in a while?

7. The debate is still raging about whether or not you, the consumer, determine what you buy. Do you feel you have any effect on what producers are willing to produce and offer you for sale?

8. What does the statement that "sunk costs are gone forever" have to do with consumer decision making?

9. Why do you think Parkinson's Law seems so valid?

10. What have been some of the influences helping you to clarify your own values? What are those values? Are they the same as those of your parents, your friends, your neighbors? If they are different, why?

THINGS TO DO

1. Remember a recent consumer decision you made about, say, the purchase of an article of clothing, a book, a record, a TV, a radio, or whatever. Outline the steps you took to reach your final decision. How did you decide what to buy, when to buy it, where to buy, how much to pay, what brand, what

quality, and so on? See if you can draw a chart showing the step-by-step progression of your consumer decision making. In retrospect, was there any point within that process where you should have obtained more information? Why did you fail to obtain more information? After reviewing your decision-making process, do you think it can be improved? How? Do you see a general behavioral pattern that you want to change?

2. Read Vance Packard's *The Hidden Persuaders*. Do you think that book, written a number of years ago, is still valid today? If not, why? Has the world changed so much, or have we become smarter consumers? Has legislation affected anything in advertising that Packard talked about?

3. Write down a set of short-term, intermediate, and long-term goals. Are these the same goals that you had last year, the year before, or the year before that? Do you think you will have the same long-term goals five years from now? If not, why do your goals change? Is there any way you can predict how they will change?

4. List some consumer actions you engage in that are at least partly determined by customs in your family or community.

5. Draw up a list of those things you purchase on impulse and those you plan to purchase very carefully. If the impulse list is long, does that bother you? How could you change your buying behavior? Do you limit impulse buying to low-cost items?

6. Try to determine the way you decide how many places to shop for any particular item. Does your decision depend on the price of the item? Does it depend on your knowledge or lack of knowledge of alternative sources of that item? Is there any way you could make a rule that would tell you when to stop looking for a better deal?

7. List the times when you are most likely to follow the dictates of Parkinson's Law.

8. Recall the last time you went window shopping. What kinds of information did you find (and store in your mind) as a reference point for future decisions? Do you think this is a good way of acquiring information about the goods and services available in your community? Why or why not?

SELECTED READINGS

Arnold, John D. *Make Up Your Mind: The Seven Building Blocks to Better Decisions*. New York: AMACOM, 1978.

Hall, Mary Bowen. *More for Your Money: How to Increase Your Spending Power up to 20% without Increasing Your Income*. New York: Houghton Mifflin, 1981.

Hamilton, David. *The Consumer in Our Economy*. Boston: Houghton Mifflin Co., 1962. See especially Chapters 2 and 3.

Katona, George. *The Powerful Consumer*. New York: McGraw-Hill, 1960.

Maslow, Abraham. *Motivation and Personality*. 2d ed. New York: Harper and Row, 1970.

Morgan, James N. and Duncan, Greg J. *Making Your Choices Count: Economic Principles for Everyday Decisions*. Ann Arbor: University of Michigan Press, 1982.

Packard, Vance. *The Hidden Persuaders*. New York: David McKay Co., 1957.

Packard, Vance. *The Status Seekers*. New York: Pocketbooks, 1959.

Paolucci, Beatrice; Hall, Oliva; and Axinn, Nancy. *Family Decision Making: An Ecosystem Approach*. New York: John Wiley & Sons, 1977.
"Values and Decision Making." *Home Economics Research Abstract,* No. 6 (1968), Washington, D.C.: American Home Economics Association.
Veblen, Thorstein. *The Theory of the Leisure Class*. New York: Macmillan Publishing Co., 1899.

CHAPTER
THE ECONOMICS OF LOVE AND PAIN

It is not surprising that the family occupies a key role in the study of economic and consumption decision making in general. The family, however, is not the sole spending unit in this country, because today there are 14 million one-person households.

CHAPTER PREVIEW

- What is the history of marriage in the Western world?
- What are the economic costs and benefits of marriage and divorce?
- Are women "crypto-servants" in our society?
- What are the economic aspects of women's liberation?

Let's look at the five stages that constitute the life cycle of the average person in American society: (1) the beginning, including all the formative years when you depend mostly on your parents and family members for your well-being; (2) the expanding years, when you start to branch out on your own and are less dependent on your parents; (3) the launching years, when you are settling into your career and starting your own family; (4) middle age, when you reach a peak in your career earnings and when your own children grow up and move away; (5) retirement.

The life cycle starts over again for your offspring when you begin to raise a family. After you have children, raising your family will occupy a large percentage of your time and money for the next twenty years or so. What does this mean? Since a tremendous part of the average person's lifetime is involved in family activities, it is not surprising that the family occupies a key role in the study of economic and consumption decision making in general. The family, however, is not the sole spending unit in this country, because today there are 14 million one-person households. No matter what your present or contemplated living arrangement might be, the principles and rules outlined in this text for your personal economics are going to be valid. Nonetheless, it might be useful to look into the economic aspects of marriage and its counterpart, the dissolution of marriage.

STATE-SANCTIONED LOVING

Marriage is an old institution. In fact, the form it takes in modern Western civilization combines traditions established during the developments of Greek, Roman, Hebrew, and Christian societies. Before the rise of Christianity, the Germanic peoples and the Jews had a type of marriage similar, it seems, to that of the Greeks and Romans. It fitted well into a society composed of kinship groups headed by patriarchal chiefs—fathers with great authority over their grown sons and unmarried daughters and over their sons' families. Every person, male or female, belonged to a clan dominated by a **patriarch.** When a woman married, she was allowed to leave the clan of her birth and enter her husband's clan. Marriage, however, was not a transaction between the two partners involved but between the chiefs of the two clans; the same was true for the dissolution of a marriage. By the time of Jesus, custom and law allowed a marriage to be terminated arbitrarily by the husband but not by the wife.

PATRIARCH
The male head of a family or clan; he assumes an authoritarian role that generally extends not only to his own immediate family but also to the families of his sons.

Some contemporary observers maintain that the institution of marriage was dying out until the 1980s. Divorce statistics indeed indicated a slight downward trend in the percentage of young adults remaining married (but that trend has recently leveled off). In addition, the average age at which people first marry has been increasing throughout the history of the United States. Since marriage remains a viable institution, we will investigate why the marriage contract is such an enduring institution. Perhaps we might better observe that the "traditional" marriage contract is undergoing a transition as it is modified by changing motives and roles.

Estimating Economic Values

It is, of course, easiest for us to look at marriage as an institution in which love plays a primary role. This view reflects our modern culture; in the marriage institutions of past societies, particularly in the East, love had little if anything to do with getting married. But today, at least for most people in this country, love plays a role. In fact, we might consider the major benefit of marriage to be a reduction in the search costs for love and companionship. Once a mate is found and a marriage made, love and companionship (sexual and otherwise) can be obtained with much less effort than must be expended by single individuals in search of the same goals.

Of course, long-term **pair bonds** need not always be legalized by the state in order for people to obtain the benefits of them. Whatever the reason, however, most persons seek legal bonds. Perhaps the state sanctioning of the marriage contract and the difficulty of reneging on that contract give a sense of security to the partners involved. More important, perhaps, are the obvious materialistic reasons for legalizing marriage: to establish clear lines of inheritance of material property and to establish legal responsibility for the care of any children resulting from the marriage (although for this purpose only legally admitted paternity, not marriage, is necessary.)

PAIR BONDS
Generally, male-female relationships in which the two persons involved share in significant mutual activities and life planning.

Marriage: Costs and Benefits

If we are willing to make some fairly general assumptions, we can estimate the economic value of marriage to both men and women. In 1884, long before today's feminist and liberation movements, Friedrich Engels maintained that monogamous marriage as it had developed in the West was little more than a contractual system by which men exploited women.[1] This argument, of course, ignores some of the important features of marriage today. For one thing, the marriage contract is usually voluntary; hence, both parties are presumed to be better off married than unmarried (at least for a while). Marriage also involves **specialization;** members of the family specialize in individual endeavors in order to increase the general welfare of the family unit. Moreover, the homemaker in the family unit, *particularly if he or she does not work for wages or a salary,* receives at least part of the income *not* spent on goods and services that only benefit the money-income-earning family member. In other words, the nonemployed homemaker obtains services from jointly consumed goods, such as houses, cars, and stereo systems, in addition to making his or her own personal consumption expenditures, such as on food and clothing. Of course, he or she does not obtain these goods and services free of charge, because the specialization aspect of the marriage may require that he or she do certain tasks.

SPECIALIZATION
The dividing up of various tasks so that one individual concentrates only on certain tasks while leaving the other individual or individuals time to concentrate on the remaining tasks. Also called the division of labor.

CRYPTO-SERVANTS

The women's liberation movement today is attempting to make known the true costs of marriage to the female partner and, even more, the benefits of marriage to the male. Economist John Kenneth Galbraith believes that considerable social anxiety has arisen from the conversion of women to the role of **crypto-servant** (*crypto* meaning "secret, not seeming"). That is, women are consigned to the function of managing and executing for their families the high level of con-

CRYPTO-SERVANT
John Kenneth Galbraith's name for the woman's role in America. Women are, he says, secret or nonseeming servants—but servants, nevertheless—to the males in our society.

1. Friedrich Engels, *The Origin of the Family, Private Property and the State.* New York: International Publishers, 1942.

sumption the modern economy permits. Galbraith considers this to be a degrading exploitation.

> The conversion of women into a crypto-servant class was an economic accomplishment of the first importance. Menially employed servants were available only to a majority of the preindustrial population; the servant-wife is available, democratically, to almost the entire present male population. Were the workers so employed subject to pecuniary compensation, they would be by far the largest single category in the labor force. The value of the services of housewives has been calculated somewhat impressionistically at roughly one-fourth of total Gross National Product.[2]

Dr. Galbraith has a strong point, but at least some facts contradict the notion that there is an increasing amount of female exploitation within the family unit. For example, from 1950 to 1980 the proportion of married women working or seeking work outside the home rose from 24 to 51 percent. (Of course, this does not mean that women are not exploited outside the family, but we will say more on that later.)

MEASURING THE VALUE OF HOUSEHOLD SERVICES

HOUSEHOLD PRODUCTION All the work, tasks, and organization that go into producing household output, such as feeding the family, clothing the family, providing for shelter, entertainment, and so on.

Both men and women participate in **household production** activities. Traditionally, females have been considered homemakers, but that role is certainly changing. In any event, household work by both men and women represents a significant part of all production in the United States. For example, the dollar value of household work is around 44 percent of gross national product (GNP)—the sum total of all output of final goods and services in the United States per year. Women account for most household work even today, and their value of household work is roughly double their reported money income earnings. The average full-time homemaker contributes approximately $12,500 per year in household services.[3] This estimate was obtained by looking at the market equivalent occupations involved in meal preparation and clean-up, cleaning and gardening, laundry work, home repairs and hobbies, child care and instruction, and shopping. It was estimated, for example, that women spend 33.8 hours per week in household work and that men spend 15.1 hours per week in the same work.

In the United States, the employment status of females influences dramatically the number of weekly hours engaged in household work. When a woman does not work at all, she spends 42.6 hours per week, on average, in household production activities; when she is employed full-time, she spends 20.1 hours per week.

Evidence from other countries, however, contrasts with what happens in the United States. Research shows that when the husband and wife both work, the wife is still saddled with the household activities in France, Poland, and Russia. It was found that the average employed woman spent over two hours a day doing housework, compared to the less than one-half hour a day the man spent doing the cooking, home chores, laundry, and marketing. Employed men and women seem to spend about the same amount of time doing other

2. John Kenneth Galbraith, *Economics and the Public Purpose*. Boston: Houghton-Mifflin, 1973.

3. Peskin, Janice, "Measuring Household Production for the GNP," *Family Economics Review*, No. 3, 1982, pp. 16–25.

household chores, such as gardening, animal care, errands, and shopping. Except for the Soviet Union, employed married women spent more time than men in child care. Since it was presumed that the women worked the same number of hours as the men, it is interesting to note what the women had to give up in order to devote more time to housework and child rearing. They spent less time enjoying the offerings of the mass media, such as radio and television, and also less time participating in study and religion.[4] In other words, they seem to have less choice in the things they do. It will be interesting to see if future similar studies show the same pattern of role-playing rather than role-sharing in the typical household where both parents work. Will the man and woman be true equals?

In the United States, the employment status of females influences dramatically the number of weekly hours engaged in household work.

THE CHANGING ROLE OF WOMEN IN OUR SOCIETY

Women's roles in the United States have changed dramatically over the past fifty years. Not only are there more women working outside the home than there are full-time homemakers, but many women now hold jobs previously held only by men. In particular, married women had a labor force participation rate of only 30.5 percent in 1960, whereas today it is almost 51 percent. The labor force participation rate is obtained by dividing the number of working women, for example, by the number of women sixteen years of age and over. To calculate the labor force participation rate for married women, use as the numerator the number of married women that work and as the denominator the number of married women sixteen years of age and over.

If one compares the situation today with that of fifty years ago, the change is even more striking. Married women's participation in the paid labor force has increased dramatically. Fifty years ago, only one in eight married women was gainfully employed, whereas today more than half of all married women work for pay.

In terms of total dollar earnings, working wives contribute, on average, a little more than 26 percent of total family money income. Those who work full-time twelve months per year, contribute 40 percent or more of family income. Obviously, the economic status of families is enhanced by multiple income earners. Multi-earner families enjoy incomes that are 40 percent or more higher than the incomes of single-earner families. Not surprisingly, multi-earner families have very low incidences of poverty because they are more protected from the risks of unemployment than are single-earner families.

There are, of course, extra expenses in a multi-earner family, but they are more than compensated for by the extra income. One particular "cost" to the two-earner family is the fact that the husband cannot change jobs or be transferred to a different city unless the wife also finds a suitable job in the same location.

VOLUNTARY MARRIAGE DISSOLUTIONS

In some cities in the United States, there are more divorces than marriages on any given day. Look at the vital statistics page in the *Los Angeles Times,* for example. The trend is obvious: Divorces increased, until recently, not only in

4. Alexander Szalai, *The Use of Time.* The Hague: Mouton & Company, 1972, pp. 584–88.

the United States but also in the rest of the world. Exhibit 6–1 shows the per-thousand number of divorces in this country over the past half century.

The dissolution of a marriage is, of course, an economic as well as a non-economic act. Divorce may occur for any number of reasons, some of which may not necessarily correspond with the legal reasons given in court. Couples wishing for more than just a friendship may decide to divorce after they "fall out of love". Or marriages might dissolve because of money problems or the simple incompatibility of two human beings. When children are involved, they, too, feel the effects of the costs and benefits of the decision. Child psychologists have recently discovered that children are often better off living with a single parent than living with both parents in an uncomfortable, disruptive family situation.

The upsurge in divorce may be accounted for by two key changes in American society—one economic, the other social. In the first place, the cost of divorce has declined as legal fees have dropped and the courts have become more lenient about the grounds for divorce. Of course, some states still recognize only such things as provable adultery as grounds for divorce; but others, such as California, Ohio, and Washington, have essentially eliminated the need for seeking any grounds at all when both parties agree to the divorce settlement and when there are no children.

Divorce instruction through the mail is becoming increasingly popular throughout the United States. A number of enterprising companies are even offering do-it-yourself divorce kits. For example, a number of Divorce Yourself franchises have sprung up in New York. The kit they offer costs less than $100 and theoretically saves on lawyers' fees, which, even in an uncontested divorce in a no-fault state, can exceed $500.

The act of divorce has become more acceptable and the treatment of divorcees by friends and colleagues more favorable and, therefore, less costly emotionally. Divorcees may not be treated by all their friends exactly as they were when they were married, but the social stigma once attached to divorce is not nearly as pronounced as it once was.

Another reason for relatively high divorce rates in recent years has often been placed at the feet of the women's liberation movement, an important subject we will discuss later.

MAIL-ORDER DIVORCES

California first allowed no-fault divorce proceedings in 1970; 47 other states now permit no-fault divorce. In 1979, California again led the country by ushering in the era of mail-order divorces. Under the California law, childless couples with limited property who have been married less than two years can divorce by mail and thus avoid court appearances and lawyers' services. Cou-

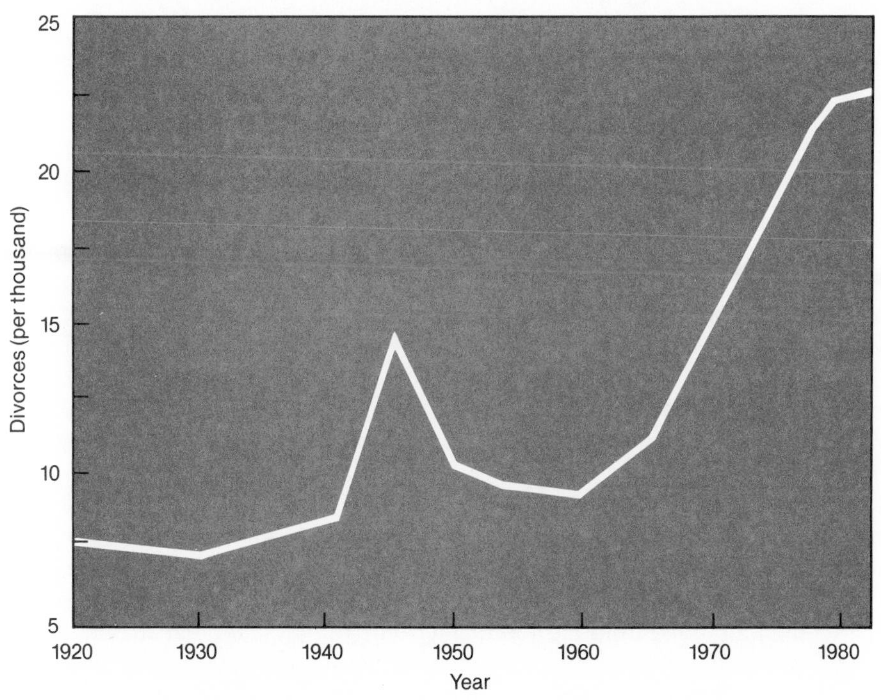

SOURCE: *Current Population Reports, Series P-120*

EXHIBIT 6–1
U.S. Divorces Per 1,000 Females 15 Years or Older

Before World War II, the average was fewer than 9 divorces per 1,000 females. The half decade right after the war saw a rise in divorce rates, which settled down to an average figure of fewer than 10 per 1,000 females from 1950 to about 1963. (Beginning in 1960, figures include Alaska and Hawaii.) Then the rate started rising again, reaching over 15 per 1,000 in the 1970s. (The 1983 figure is an estimate.)

Only 24 percent of ex-husbands continue to pay full alimony and child support after one year.

ples pay a fee of $50 to the state and take responsibility for dividing any jointly owned property. In six months, the divorce is automatically granted by mail. At least fifteen other states are studying the California law and will probably adopt some form of it within the next few years.

THE ECONOMIC COSTS OF DIVORCE

Although the actual costs of getting divorced are decreasing, the procedure still takes a tremendous toll, particularly for women. Only 24 percent of ex-husbands continue to pay full alimony and child support after one year, and divorced women often have a very difficult time attempting to collect from nonpaying ex-spouses. Additionally, there is always the economic cost of adapting to a different life style. Increasingly, divorced women are expected to learn an occupation or start a career in very short order after the divorce. If a woman did not work outside the home during much of her marriage, there may be grave psychological problems when she suddenly is forced to seek paid employment.

NONMARRIAGE AND THE OUTSIDE WORLD

For those women who decide not to marry or who are widowed or divorced, important social and economic pressures await them. Even though the Civil Rights Act of 1964 specifies that it is illegal to discriminate by sex (as well as by race or national origin), not all groups will necessarily be treated equally in the job market or the marketplace in general; nor will they be treated equally by their peers or society in general. Until recently, single women generally had an extremely difficult time obtaining credit—purchasing houses, cars, and so on "on time." In many places, divorced women with children have had, and still have, difficulty renting houses or apartments. Because the single, widowed, or divorced woman has been considered less "stable," entrepreneurs in their role as profit-makers have sought to treat these groups of potential buyers differently from other groups. Prejudice is difficult to eliminate. In the job market, a single woman often faces tremendous barriers, not the least of which are created by the past behavior of single women taken as a whole.

In the past, the life cycle of a woman generally involved getting married and having children, for whom she was expected to care full time. Employers often have been reluctant to hire a young single woman at the same wage rate at which they would hire a man for fear that the woman would eventually quit to get married and raise a family and thus take with her all the specific training the employer had invested in her. This reason for giving less pay to women for equal work is, of course, slowly changing as more and more women continue to work throughout their married and child-rearing years. Many working women are gone from the job market only during late pregnancy and for a few weeks after giving birth; then they reenter the market, leaving the child or children with babysitters or at child-care centers during working hours. Men are also given leave when they experience temporary physical disabilities.

(Recently *both* men and women have been given pregnancy leaves by some employers.)

THE FUTURE OF THE AMERICAN FAMILY

We have seen in this chapter that divorce was increasing until recently. Indeed, marriages end in divorce more often in the United States than anywhere else in the world. Does this mean that the institution of marriage is actually disappearing and, with it, the American family? Some experts believe that this is

indeed the case. They point out that in the past, extended families provided each generation with economic security, emotional nourishment, and social activities. When this nation was founded, Americans made their livings largely from farming, and they often traveled great distances in groups to seek better agricultural conditions. Males traditionally labored in the fields, females in the home. As we became a more industrialized nation, men left the home to work in factories, thus reducing contact with family members. Finally, wives and mothers also began to take jobs outside the home.

MATRIARCHAL FAMILY
A household unit that is headed by a female, as opposed to a patriarchal family headed by a male.

Statistics confirm that even our traditional idea of a nuclear family—consisting of a husband and wife and children—seems to be changing. By 1990, 21 percent of all school-age children will live with one parent. By that same time, 15 percent of all families will be **matriarchal**—that is, headed by a woman—and very likely will be officially classified as poor.

While courts still generally award custody of children to the mother in a divorce action, in recent years there has been a tendency for the father to take custody of one or more of the children. In deciding custody, the court's goal is to do what is best for the child. Thus, the court takes into consideration the child's age, sex, the mental and physical health of all involved parties, and which parent the child indicates he or she would rather live with. Although custody is generally given to only one of the parents, joint custody is becoming more common. In joint custody, both parents are responsible for the child and make decisions together about the child's activities. The child also takes turns living with each of the parents; for example, he or she might reside with the mother for two weeks each month and with the father for the other two weeks. Joint custody can work only if the parents are at least civil to each other. If not, the court will award custody to one of the parents for the welfare of the child.

In spite of the rising divorce rate, interview surveys invariably show that individuals rank "family" near the top in terms of important sources of personal satisfaction.[5] Thus, for those who believe that family life is indeed important, the future may be less grim than recent trends would indicate.

The Family—Another View

If we compare the family structure of American society today with what it actually was and not with what we *think* it was in the past, we get a different picture. A study done by Mary Jo Bane, associate director of the Center for Research on Women at Wellesley College, reveals some interesting findings about the reality of early American family life.

1. The extended family never really existed in the United States on a wide scale. In colonial America, only 6 percent of U.S. households had children, parents, and grandparents. The latest figures in the 1970s show that it's still 6 percent.
2. More families have two parents now (84.3 percent) than in colonial days (70 percent).
3. Divorce may be disrupting families today; death did it in colonial times. As the death rate has dropped, the divorce rate has increased but not at the same rate.

5. See "What Future for the American Family?" *Changing Times,* December 1976, p. 9.

4. Mothers during colonial times, laboring from dawn to dusk doing housework without today's labor-saving machines, apparently did not spend any more time raising their children than working mothers do today.

Professor Bane tells us that yesterday's family was much like today's: "The nuclear family, consisting of parents living with their own children and no other adults, has been the predominant family form in America since the earliest period on which historians have data. . . ." Relationships among relatives appear to have been historically what they are now—that is, "complex patterns of companionship that only occasionally involve sharing bed and board."[6]

SUMMARY

1. In early Eastern and European societies, marriage was a type of economic arrangement negotiated by a family patriarch. In Western society, however, love between the two partners has always been emphasized.
2. Friedrich Engels once said that marriage, as it evolved in the West, was little more than a contractual system whereby men exploited women.
3. Divorce turns out to be relatively costly for many women because only 24 percent of ex-husbands continue to pay full alimony and child support after one year. An additional cost is related to adaptation to a different life style.
4. The economic value of homemakers' services to their families is significant. For example, some economists believe that the typical homemaker's services would cost at least $12,500 a year to replace in the marketplace.
5. Today, women working outside the home contribute 27 percent of all family income.
6. Latest statistics show increasing divorce rates, a larger number of children living with only one parent, and a reduction in the importance of the family. Comparisons of current data, however, with data from colonial times show that the nuclear family is just as strong today as it was then.

QUESTIONS FOR THOUGHT AND DISCUSSION

1. Do you think it is appropriate to study consumer economics within the framework of the family unit? Or would it be better to discuss it for a one-person household?
2. Do you think that the costs outweigh the benefits of marriage? Why or why not?
3. Does specialization necessarily imply that women should do housework and men should work outside the home for money income?
4. Do you think Professor Galbraith's contention that women are crypto-servants in the United States is a valid one? Why or why not?

THINGS TO DO

1. Look at the vital statistics page of your local newspaper to see what the ratio is of marriages to divorces in your community. Go to the library and look at the same page as it appeared in a newspaper of, say, thirty years ago. Has there been any change?
2. Try to figure out how you would measure the implicit—that is, unstated—value of the services of a homemaker. What would you add to the traditional

6. Mary Jo Bane. *Here to Stay: American Families in the Twentieth Century,* New York: Basic Books, 1977.

services, such as housecleaning and preparing meals? Would companionship be included? Would gardening activities? Would your computations change if the person in question enjoyed doing those things?

SELECTED READINGS

Ahern, D. D. and Bliss, Betty. *The Economics of Being a Woman*. New York: McGraw-Hill, 1977.

Bird, Caroline. *The Two-Paycheck Marriage*. New York: Rawson, Wade, 1979.

Briles, Judith. *The Women's Guide to Financial Savvy*. New York: St. Martin's Press, 1981.

Cotton, Dorothy W. *The Case for the Working Mother*. New York: Stein & Day, 1965.

Engels, Friedrich. *The Origins of the Family, Private Property and the State*. New York: International Publishers, 1942.

Galbraith, John Kenneth. *Economics and the Public Purpose*. Boston: Houghton Mifflin, 1973.

Goebel, Karen P. "Time Use and Family Life." *Family Economics Review*, Summer 1981, pp. 20–25.

Robinson, John P. "Household Technology and Household Work." In *Women and Household Labor*, edited by Sarah F. Berk. Beverly Hills, Cal.: Sage Publications, 1980.

Robinson, John P. "Of Time, Dual Careers, and Household Productivity." *Family Economics Review*, No. 3, 1982, pp. 26–30.

Stafford, Frank P. "Women's Use of Time Converging with Men's." *Monthly Labor Review* 103(12), 1980, pp. 57–59.

Strober, Myra H. and Weinberg, Charles B., "Strategies Used by Working and Nonworking Wives to Reduce Time Pressures." *Journal of Consumer Research*, vol. 6, No. 4, 1980, pp. 338–48.

"What You Should Know about Divorce Today." *Consumer Reports*, June 1981, pp. 327–31.

"When Fathers Raise Children Alone." *U.S. News & World Report*, April 12, 1982.

Consumer ISSUE C

MAKING A DECISION ABOUT CHILDREN

GLOSSARY

CONSUMPTION GOOD—A non-income-producing good or service that you use up quickly. A movie, for example, is a consumption good; so are food and similar products.

PRODUCTIVE ASSET—Anything you own that produces income or satisfaction for you. A productive asset might be, for example, a tractor that you use on a farm.

Once a new family unit is formed, its members initially are the husband and wife. The decision of whether to enlarge the family unit must be faced from the very beginning. Long ago, when there was little knowledge about conception and the possibility of its prevention, this decision usually was not even considered; children came when they did, and parents made the best of the situation. Of course, men and women always had the choice of forestalling marriage to a later date, and abstinence has always been, and continues to be, an effective means of preventing conception. Things have changed, though, at least for most people in the United States.

Decisions about when to have children and how many to have can now be considered by both parties in the pair bond. This is a particularly relevant decision to be made in an era when children are not the **productive asset** they used to be. On the farm in the old days, raising children was a means of obtaining needed workers. But today, with less than 5 percent of the population working on farms, children are raised mainly as a **consumption good**—that is, as an investment that will not yield income for the parents later on.

THE COST OF CONSUMING

To figure out rationally the desired family size, a couple might be interested in knowing the expected costs of raising children. Estimates of these costs range from about $85,000 to $200,000 per child. Such costs depend, of course, on the income level of the parents: An upper-class family generally spends more on clothing and education than does a lower-class family. If, however, you expect to be part of a middle-class family and send all your children to college, be prepared to expend the upper-end figure for each child. Many families start providing for a college education as soon as their children are born, by establishing trust funds or investing in insurance programs.

Exhibit C-1 shows estimates of the total cost of raising a child from birth to age eighteen in the north central region of the United States. These costs are further broken down into the average amounts spent for such essentials as food and clothing. In order to obtain a calculation for a college-bound child, add an estimate of the cost of four years at a college or university.

More Costs Involved

None of the cost estimates of raising children takes account of the time cost for the parents. When the responsibility of caring for children prevents the wife or husband from working or from pursuing other interests, a cost is incurred; this is called the opportunity cost of raising children. If the mother or father must give up the opportunity to pursue a career, to get more education, to learn ceramics or photography or whatever, these sacrifices represent a real cost. Boone A. Turchi, a

EXHIBIT C–1
Estimates of the Cost of Raising a Child

The cost of raising urban children: June 1982[1]

REGION AND AGE OF CHILD (YEARS)	TOTAL	FOOD AT HOME[2]	FOOD AWAY FROM HOME	CLOTHING	HOUSING[3]	MEDICAL CARE	EDUCA-TION	TRANSPOR-TATION	ALL OTHER[4]
NORTH CENTRAL:									
Under 1	$ 3,991	$ 545	$ 0	$ 131	$ 1,762	$ 242	$ 0	$ 810	$ 501
1	4,115	669	0	131	1,762	242	0	810	501
2–3	3,832	669	0	212	1,549	242	0	706	454
4–5	4,060	768	129	212	1,549	242	0	706	454
6	4,212	743	129	294	1,469	242	104	706	525
7–9	4,385	916	129	294	1,469	242	104	706	525
10–11	4,559	1,090	129	294	1,469	242	104	706	525
12	4,870	1,115	155	425	1,522	242	104	758	549
13–15	4,994	1,239	155	425	1,522	242	104	758	549
16–17	5,484	1,387	155	588	1,575	242	104	836	597
Total	$81,195	$17,365	$1,962	$5,750	$27,772	$4,356	$1,248	$13,384	$9,358

[1]Annual cost of raising a child from birth to age 18, by age, in a husband-wife family with no more than 5 children, spending at the moderate cost level. For more information on these and additional child cost estimates, see USDA Miscellaneous Publication No. 1411 by Carolyn S. Edwards, "USDA Estimates of the Cost of Raising a Child: A Guide to Their Use and Interpretation." This publication is for sale by the U.S. Government Printing Office, Washington, D.C. 20402.
[2]Includes home-produced food and school lunches.
[3]Includes shelter, fuel, utilities, household operations, furnishings, and equipment.
[4]Includes personal care, recreation, reading, and other miscellaneous expenditures.

SOURCE: *Family Economics Review*, 1982, No. 4.

population specialist at the University of North Carolina, estimated that a woman working in a family with total family earnings of $24,000 a year today will give up approximately $200,000 in terms of the 12,900 salaried hours that she must lose because of her children. However approximate such an estimate is, it does indicate how high the opportunity cost of raising children actually is.

Often left unmentioned in discussions of whether or not to have children are the problems children bring into the family unit. A recent survey by the University of Michigan Institute for Social Research discovered that most women seem to identify the time before the arrival of their first child and after the departure of the last grown child as the happiest times of their marriage. Some sociologists and marriage counselors maintain that childless couples have happier marriages than do parents. At the very least, the married couple probably can expect the birth of the first child to create difficulties in their relationship with one another. In this period, the sexual life of the couple is disrupted. And there is potential for jealousy because much of the time the new mother formerly spent with her partner is now taken up by the child. Not every husband adjusts gracefully to such a change.

It must be anticipated, also, that the arrival of the first child or more children entails considerably more housework. This is particularly true during the first six or so years of each child's life, before the child is able to assume responsibility for his or her own personal care. Couples who are used to immaculate households often have difficulties adjusting to the disorder and even chaos caused by the presence of children, their playmates, and their belongings.

THE COST OF CHILD CARE

In those families where both parents must work, child care is a necessity. Latest figures show that in families with at least one member under six, 2.9 percent of all family spending goes to child care. In single-parent families, however, this figure rises to 7.3 percent, which is certainly not an inconsequential expense. *Finding and Keeping Child Care: A Parent Guide*, the result of a joint project between the Center for Systems and Program Development, Inc., and the Administration for Children, Youth and Families of the Department of Health and Human Services, is available from Day Care Division, Administration for Children, Youth and Families, Department of Health and Human Services, P.O. Box 1182, Washington, D.C. 20013. It is recommended reading for parents seeking child-care guidance.

A SERIOUS DECISION

The decision to become a parent is a momentous one. It means bringing into the world other human beings who must be cared for and loved and for whom the parents will feel a responsibility to raise in a suitable manner. To become parents is to take on the responsibility of fostering a suitable environment for children—that is, of creating an economic, social, and moral foundation for each new member of the family. In the United States, decisions about having children are changing. In 1970, the birth rate was 88 per 1,000 women ages fifteen through forty-four. By 1973, it had dropped to 69 per 1,000 and it was estimated to be about 68 per 1,000 in 1981. A recent survey conducted by the U.S. Department of Commerce indicates that young married women between eighteen and twenty-four plan to have an average of fewer than 2.3 children, compared with the 1965 planned average of 3.1.

FAMILY-PLANNING INFORMATION

A couple seeking family-planning information can look first to their private doctor. If the private doctor is a general practitioner or internist, he or she usually will recommend that the woman see a gynecologist who specializes in these matters. The gynecologist will perform a complete physical examination and will inquire about the woman's medical history in order to suggest the most suitable birth-control technique, such as "the pill," an intrauterine device, a diaphragm, condoms, or some other method. If the couple wants to remain permanently childless, the man can have a vasectomy. Of course, if an unwanted conception occurs, abortion is an alternative; but for many couples, it is an unacceptable one.

Couples unable to afford the services of a private medical practitioner have an alternative in most states. They can go to Planned Parenthood centers where, after the couple attends a class on birth control, volunteer doctors provide them with the contraceptive of their choice at a nominal fee, often no more than the supply cost.

SOCIAL PRESSURES TO BECOME A PARENT

Besides the tax deduction that every child gives to parents, there seems to be a bias in America toward having children. It can be expected that after about two years of marriage, outsiders to the family unit will start to wonder—discreetly, of course—when the children will come. According to Ellen Peck, author of *The Baby Trap,* people exert "ingenious pressures on you to have children. People say you're selfish, that you're missing the greatest things in life or that you're denying your maternal instinct. And the smuggest threat: 'You'll be sorry when you're old.' " Fighting against this bias is a group called the National Organization for Nonparents (NON), which has associated itself with Planned Parenthood and Zero Population Growth (ZPG). Whereas Planned Parenthood

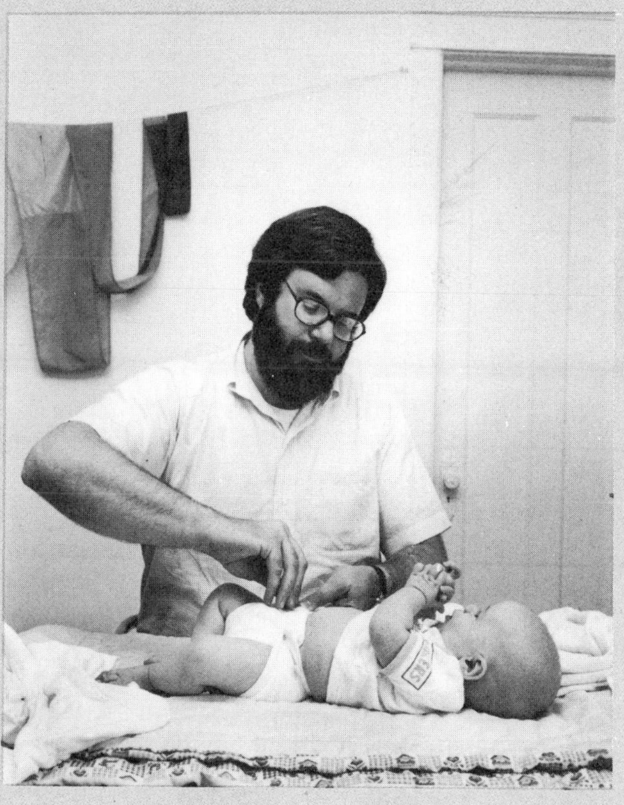

and ZPG recommend that all couples limit themselves to one or two children, NON is asking whether it would not be preferable if some couples had no children at all and others had six or seven. Anthropologist Margaret Mead contended that "childbearing will become a vocation to be pursued by a diminishing group of people who really want to become parents."

Whether NON and Margaret Mead were right remains to be seen, but the pro-child bias in America today is obvious, especially to any married couple who has put off having children for a while or who seeks permanent contraception.

THE JOYS OF PARENTHOOD

When all the cards are counted, however, and even after looking at all the costs just outlined, couples become parents because of the expected joys of raising a child, of watching him or her grow and develop into a young adult. But while it's difficult to put into monetary terms the benefits of having children, the costs remain and must be reckoned with, and the distribution of those costs within the family unit also must be understood. The decision to have children generally works out best when both the man and the woman can agree as to the advisability, the number, and the timing of children. The decision to get married, as well as the decision to have children, must rank highest among the lifetime decisions that most of us face. It is hoped that the information contained in the previous chapter and in this Consumer Issue will help you make the right decision for yourself. (If you are already married and/or have children, these discussions may have given you some retrospective insight into your decisions and their consequences.)

If you decide to become a parent and act upon your decision, then it would be useful for both you and your spouse to take continuing education courses in parenting. Being a parent is a very important job, yet most of us get no training!

SUMMARY

1. Children are no longer the productive asset they used to be when ours was a predominantly agricultural society and children could work on the farm.
2. The costs of raising children include not only all the actual money spent but also the time involved in their upbringing. This time is called the opportunity cost of child raising.
3. The birth rate in the United States has been falling dramatically in the last couple of decades. Its present level will probably give us zero population growth in the not-too-distant future.
4. Family-planning information can be obtained from a general practitioner or internist; specialists, such as gynecologists and obstetricians; and Planned Parenthood centers.

QUESTIONS FOR THOUGHT AND DISCUSSION

1. Currently, families are allowed to deduct $1,000 from income before paying taxes for each dependent child. What do you think would happen to birth rates in the United States if this $1,000 income exemption for dependent children were eliminated?
2. Would it be possible for our society to die out because of an insufficient birth rate?
3. Is there any way you could ever determine whether child-free couples have happier marriages than other couples?
4. When do you think is the best time to have children?
5. Do you think that the social pressures to become a parent are increasing or decreasing?

THINGS TO DO

1. Try to figure out the costs your parents incurred in raising you to age eighteen.
2. Is there any way you could figure out the time cost your parents incurred in your upbringing? If you have children, what are your time costs?
3. Find out the latest U.S. Department of Commerce/Bureau of Census statistics on birth rates. Have our rates actually dropped below those that produce zero population growth? What are the Bureau's projections for the future?

SELECTED READINGS

Barber, Clifton. "Parental Responses to the Empty-Nest Transition." *Journal of Home Economics,* Summer 1981.

Hoover, Mary and Modsen, Charles Jr. *The Responsive Parent: Meeting the Realities of Parenthood Today*. New York: Parents Magazine Press, 1972.

Johnson, Beverly. "Single-Parent Families." *Family Economics Review,* Summer/Fall 1980.

Peck, Ellen. *The Baby Trap*. New York: Bernard Geis Associates, 1971.

CHAPTER
THE CONSUMER AS WAGE EARNER

A basic fact of life is that individuals are generally paid only what they are worth to employers. Education can be viewed, then, as a process of making workers more productive. That's why we can say that, by pursuing your education, you are making an investment in yourself.

CHAPTER PREVIEW

- What does investing in yourself mean?
- What determines how productive you are and, therefore, how much you earn?
- What is the payoff for going to school?
- What are the differences among wages earned in various occupations?

The amount you earn often depends on decisions you have made about education, training, and occupation. To be sure, there are many reasons why different people earn different incomes. Some persons are more clever than others and, as a result, may earn more income than others in a similar position. Some persons have more artistic ability, and this, too, enables them to earn more income than less talented individuals. Some persons prefer riskier jobs at higher rates of pay than others do: If you're willing to work as a welder on top of high-rise buildings, you will certainly make more money than you would as a welder in a ground-floor welding shop. And some people make more money because they inherit a fortune from their families.

But more important, at least for those of you who are now making the investment, is your decision to go to school. That decision will permanently affect the extent of your command over goods and services in your role as a consumer. What exactly does this mean? You may think you've never made an investment in your life, but you'll soon see that you have and, for most of you, not a bad one either.

INVESTING IN YOURSELF

INVESTMENT IN HUMAN CAPITAL
Any activity that makes you more productive. You as an individual can produce just like a machine, which is physical capital. You, on the other hand, are human capital; and when you go to school, you make an investment in yourself because you make yourself better able to perform on the job. You also might become a better decision maker (a more rational consumer) as you gain wider knowledge and more training in evaluating situations and sources of information. Additionally, investment in human capital includes health expenditures.

INCOME
The flow of spendable resources coming into a consumer unit during a given period of time, usually a year.

Few people think it strange or unfair that somebody with a master's degree is paid more than someone with a grade-school diploma. In the first place, the possessor of a master's degree has spent a long time acquiring his or her specialized knowledge; second, the grade-school graduate probably could do little of the work the college graduate does (and, sometimes, vice versa). And a basic fact of life is that individuals are generally paid only what they are worth to employers. Education can be viewed, then, as a process of making workers more productive. That's why we can say that, by pursuing your education, you are making an investment in yourself.

An investment can be defined as giving up something now for something later on. When you make an investment in a business, for example, you take, say, $10,000, put it in the business, and hope to get back more than $10,000 when the business is successful. Going to school, therefore, is a type of investment because you are giving up the opportunity to work during those hours when you are attending school. You hope that the **investment in human capital** (where human capital is simply yourself) will pay off in the future by enabling you to earn a higher **income**. Usually, the longer you go to school, the more new skills you learn. You may become a better thinker; you generally become a more responsible person, at least in working situations. Why, otherwise, would employers pay more for college grads than for high-school grads when they could get the less-educated people to work for them for less money? Education is not all investment, of course. Many students get psychic income—consumption value—out of attending a college or university.

Don't assume, though, that simply going to school will automatically guarantee you a higher income. If you specialize in an activity or a field that no one cares about, the *demand* for your services is going to be minimal. No amount of obscure services you could supply would induce others to hire you at high wages; what ultimately determines the individual's wages or income is the supply and demand for different types of labor.

Wages and Productivity

For any given specialty, the more trained you are, the more productive you will be and, therefore, the higher will be the demand for your services. One way to predict your future income is to analyze how productive you can be in doing something. Employers tend to pay workers their exact worth, no more, no less. (Of course, like any general rule, this one has exceptions.) Thus, anything you can do to make yourself more productive will tend to result in a higher wage rate and higher total lifetime earnings.

Formalized schooling is not the only way to invest in yourself; you can learn on your own by reading and practicing skills, or you can learn on the job. In fact, **on-the-job training** is an excellent way to invest in yourself because it means you increase your productivity. Persons engaged in on-the-job training—for example, as apprentices—are usually paid less during the training and more afterward.

ON-THE-JOB TRAINING
Training that you receive while you are working on a particular job. On-the-job training will increase your productivity and, therefore, your value to your employer.

Ultimately, then, investing in yourself (in your own human capital) requires careful planning. Your investment should increase your productive capacities in areas that the economy demands. If it looks as though computer keypunch operators will be unneeded in the future because of optical-scanning techniques, then you certainly don't want to specialize in computer keypunching. Choosing the right occupation may require that you become informed about future demands for different types of jobs.

THE RATE OF RETURN TO EDUCATION

Although the evidence is overwhelming that an education is valuable, the old saying "Get all the education you can" does not apply equally to everybody. Perennial students, after all, are not big earners. We can offer a general rule, though: Acquire more education as long as the expected benefits at least cover the costs.

Exhibit 7–1 shows the **age/earnings profile** for three levels of degree holders—grade school, high school, and college. Note that the more educated individuals appear higher on the curve. For example, the average high-school graduate at forty years of age may earn 40 percent more than the average grade-school graduate at forty years of age. In dollars and cents, the figures are even more impressive. In Exhibit 7–1, it is obvious that college-degree holders earn more than those with grade-school educations and for a longer period of time.

AGE/EARNINGS PROFILE
The profile of how earnings change with your age. When you're young and just starting out, your earnings are low; as you get older, your earnings increase because you become more productive and work longer hours; finally, your earnings start to decrease.

Often ignored in discussions about college or higher education in general are the noneconomic aspects of the process. Individuals change in some ways when they go to college: Their tastes change, they are exposed to a broader array of possible life styles, and so on. How does one measure the value of these noneconomic goods? It isn't easy. Ultimately, only you, the individual, can measure that for yourself.

The Costs of Education

Of course, our general rule has its limits because it is always more expensive to acquire more education. The main cost of going to college is *not* tuition

EXHIBIT 7–1
Age/Earnings Profile for Selected Degree Holders

SOURCE: U.S. Department of Commerce, Consumer Income Series P-60, No. 74.

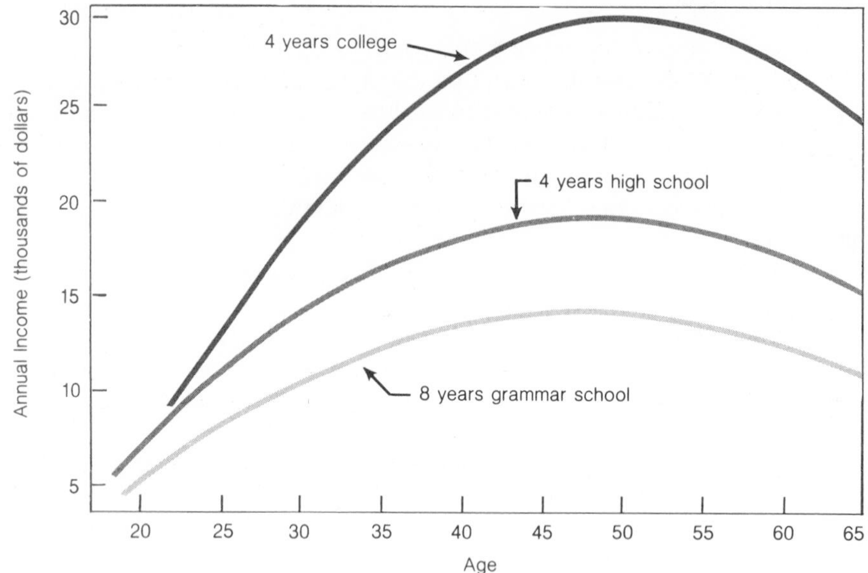

and books. These costs rank second to the cost of foregone income—that is, the *opportunity* cost of not working. In other words, had you decided not to go to college, you could be working full time at some average salary during those four years. But even with the costs of foregone earnings, tuition, and books, the rate of return for investing in education is at least as good as the rate of return for investing in the stock market and certainly higher than putting your savings into a savings and loan association account.[1]

In certain years, of course, some college graduates may have difficulty getting jobs because the erratic movements in business activity alter the demands for different types of college-degree holders. Should this happen to you, it doesn't necessarily mean you specialized in the wrong area during college. Demand fluctuates, and time may prove that you made the right choice after all.

THE CHANGING JOB SCENE

In the 1960s, a college degree could almost guarantee its recipient a managerial job or a professional position. The Bureau of Labor Statistics now predicts that there is a one-in-four chance that students earning college degrees between now and 1985 will wind up in clerical jobs or blue-collar positions, occupations that traditionally have not been filled by college-educated workers. The big change, of course, has been the increase in the *supply* of college-degree holders. In the 1960s, half a million students a year received bachelor's degrees; today, that figure is closer to one million per year.

Although a college degree does not guarantee a good job, the lack of one may bar you from being considered for certain positions. The Bureau of Labor

1. Statistics reflect this is true only for those who were successful at college. See Gary Becker, *Human Capital: A Theoretical and Empirical Analysis, with Special Reference to Education* (New York: Columbia University Press, 1964).

Statistics predicts, for example, that by 1990 over 17 percent of all jobs will be reserved only for college graduates. One big advantage of having a college degree, according to Howard Brown, author of *Investment in Learning,* is that it keeps lifetime options open; it allows for more flexibility in the job market and in response to changing economic conditions. Clearly, a college education enhances your ability to cope with changes in the job market and other economic conditions.

Experts in the field of education now put much more emphasis on the nonmonetary benefits of going to college. There is, of course, no way to put a monetary value on "the educated person" or "the whole person" or on the fact that college introduces you to new people, new ideas, and new ways of thinking. But it does undoubtedly give you intellectual flexibility and fosters self-discovery. College grads do a lot of things differently than do those who have not graduated from college. For example, they read more books, vote more often, participate more in civic organizations, and are more satisfied with their jobs. To end this discussion, here is a purported quote by a professor who taught Harold Macmillan, one of Great Britain's prime ministers: "Except for [those who will become teachers] nothing that you learn in the course of your studies will be of the slightest possible use to you in the afterlife—save only this—that if you work hard and intelligently, you should be able to detect when a man is talking rot, and that, in my view, is the main, if not the sole purpose of education."

In the 1960s, a college degree could almost guarantee its recipient a managerial job or a professional position. Now . . . there is a one-in-four chance that students earning college degrees between now and 1985 will wind up in clerical jobs or blue-collar positions.

THE CHANGING WORLD OF FEMALE ENDEAVORS

Numerous data have been collected to show that women earn less than men. In fact, we often hear that women, on average, earn 60 percent of what men make. Although this figure does not in itself prove that discrimination and sexism operate in the labor market, it does indicate the prospects facing women who work.

The **labor-force participation rate** of females has been rising steadily—from 18.2 percent in 1890 to about 55 percent by 1984; that is, by 1984, 51 percent

LABOR FORCE PARTICIPATION RATE
The percentage of any given group that participates in the labor force. If, for example, 50 million of the 75 million females between the ages of sixteen and sixty-five are working or looking for a job, then the female labor force participation rate would be two-thirds, or 66.67 percent.

EXHIBIT 7–2
Average Lifetime Earnings of Selected Degree Holders

The average lifetime earnings of selected degree holders are given in this table. The difference between eight years of grammar school and four years of college is over $500,000. These figures are averages only and are not corrected for the timing of the income received. (Strictly speaking, these figures should be corrected [discounted] for timing, and all made comparable on a present value basis.)

LEVEL OF EDUCATION	AVERAGE LIFETIME EARNINGS
8 years of grammar school	$1,430,000
4 years of high school	1,627,000
4 years of college	2,062,000

SOURCE: U.S. Department of Commerce.

Numerous data have been collected to show that women earn less than men. In fact, we often hear that women, on average, earn 60 percent of what men make.

of females over the age of sixteen were in the labor force. In light of certain social changes, it's not surprising that this rate has increased for women as a whole. Civil-rights legislation and changing views on the role of women in society have opened to women an increasing number of occupations once restricted to men. There is a growing cadre of women showing up as construction workers, airline pilots, locomotive engineers, police officers, coal miners, and firefighters. For example, in 1974, women numbered only 1,000 of the nation's 200,000 coal miners; today, there are at least 8,000. Ten years ago,

there were no women working as heavy-equipment operators; today, one-half of one percent do that kind of work. In 1982, the number of women corporate officers in the 1,300 largest companies rose to 624, an increase of 34 percent over 1977. Today, almost 8 percent of the nation's working women are managers and administrators. Twelve and one-half percent are professionals.

Lest these numbers give too rosy a picture, note that some statistics show that ten years ago the percentage of women working as managers and administrators was actually slightly higher. Women continue to face sometimes monumental problems in their quest for equality with men in the labor market. To many observers, the status of women in higher positions in the labor force still represents only tokenism.

Sexism has worked two ways, though, and males have been discriminated against in certain occupations. For example, there used to be few, if any, male telephone operators, airline stewards, or high-school home economics teachers. Yet, today, we frequently hear male voices when we call the operator and are served by male stewards on airplanes. But only a few women are in evidence as pilots, air-traffic controllers, and so on. In spite of the complaints that many males have lodged against the women's liberation movement, at least some men have benefitted because the Civil Rights Act of 1964 has eliminated discrimination against males in many occupations.

OCCUPATIONAL WAGE DIFFERENTIALS

At the top of the income ladder shown in Exhibit 7–3 are the so-called professions—medicine, dentistry, and law. Does that necessarily mean you should decide to study medicine, dentistry or law? Obviously not. You could be wasting your time. For example, unless you're able to get into an accredited medical school (and, of course, graduate from it), you cannot legally practice medicine in the United States. The ratio of applicants to acceptances in most medical schools is astounding. Therefore, unless your father is a doctor or you

EXHIBIT 7–3
Median Earnings by Occupation and Sex, 1981

OCCUPATION	MALE	FEMALE
TOTAL	$20,260	$ 7,222
Professional, technical, kindred workers	25,653	12,590
Self-employed	33,738	3,508
Salaried	25,350	12,994
Farmers and farm managers	5,579	1,586
Managers and administrators, exc. farm	25,425	11,867
Self-employed	15,968	4,666
Salaried	26,656	12,789
Clerical and kindred workers	18,938	8,434
Sales workers	22,331	4,069
Craft and kindred workers	20,095	8,641
Service workers	13,990	3,258
Farm laborers and supervisors	8,898	1,465
Laborers, exc. farm	14,449	5,062

SOURCE: U.S. Bureau of the Census, *Current Population Reports*, Series P-60, No. 369.

are an extremely good student in an extremely good school, the odds are against your admission to medical training.

The same is not true of law, however. There are numerous law schools you can attend; you can even learn law at home by mail. Of course, you should not look only at the high salaries in law. To obtain a law degree, you must take three additional years of training after college, and that means three more years of not earning any income. This additional cost means that the rate of return on becoming a lawyer may be no higher than if you chose another career.

Moreover, you may receive a relatively low salary for a number of years before you become a junior partner in a law firm. Even doctors earn relatively low incomes when they start their practices. So, even though the average salary for a particular occupation is very high, don't anticipate that your impressive amount of schooling will make you a nice sum of money right away. To see why this isn't necessarily unfair, we must look at the reasons behind the shape of the typical age/earnings profile, as represented in Exhibit 7–4.

WAGES AND AGES

When you first start a job, you are inexperienced (you might even need on-the-job training), so your employer won't be inclined to pay you as much as he or she would pay a more experienced worker who can be more productive. Gradually, as you become better trained and more productive, and work more hours per week, your wage rate increases (even corrected for inflation). Your employer gets more and more information on your productivity and your reliability from your continuing work record.

Your earnings may peak at age forty-five to fifty-five and then slowly decline until retirement, when you cease work altogether. The age/earnings profile eventually shows a slow downturn because older people generally work fewer hours per week and usually are less productive than middle-aged people.

OCCUPATIONAL CHOICE

Not only are there vast differences among the wages for different occupations, as shown in Exhibit 7–3, there are also vast differences in the qualifications,

EXHIBIT 7–4
Typical Age/Earnings Profile

Within every class of incomes earned, there is usually a typical age/earnings profile. Earnings are lowest when starting out to work at age 18, reach their peak at around 45 to 55, and then taper off until retirement at around 65 when they become zero for most people. The rise in earnings up to age 45 to 55 is usually due to more experience, working longer hours, and better training and schooling (abstracting from general increases in national productivity).

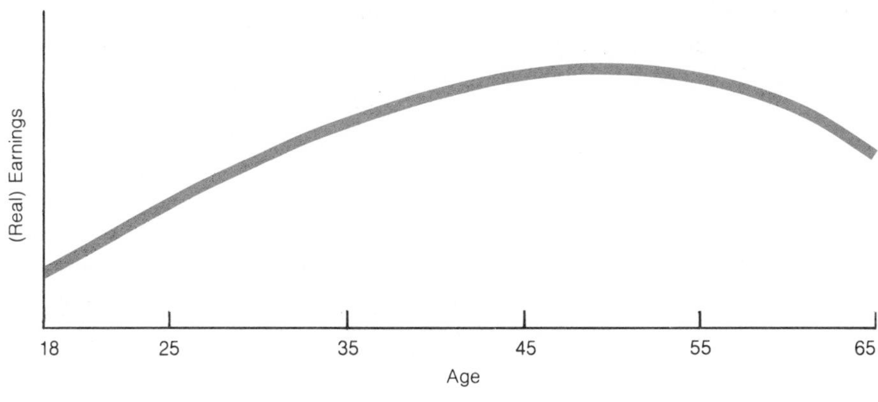

the amount of training, and the type of work required in each occupation. In an occupation with highly variable periods of employment, the average wage rate is relatively higher than in occupations that offer steadier employment; the higher wage rate compensates for the periods of unemployment.

MONEY INCOME
The total amount of actual dollars you receive per week, per month, or per year.

Money income alone is not going to determine whether you make the right career choice. If you have a spirit of independence, you certainly won't be satisfied doing paperwork in a large insurance office, and if you have a spirit of adventure, you'll be restless as a sales clerk. Therefore, you may finally choose an occupation that promises you a lower wage rate than some others but a more acceptable work situation. After all, most of us work the better part of our lives; if we hate our work, we won't be very happy, even if we make quite a bit of income. In other words, the total income you make from an occupation includes more than just money income. It also includes **psychic income**, or the satisfaction derived from your work situation or occupation. Psychic rewards from a job can be more important for some people than monetary payment.

PSYCHIC INCOME
The nonmonetary rewards you receive from doing a particular job; the satisfaction received from using goods and services.

You also have to decide whether or not you want to live in one area for a long period of time. If you become a junior executive in a company that has a history of switching its executives around the country every eighteen months, you'll be very unhappy if you dislike moving. On the other hand, you might be very happy with this transient life style if you want to see the country while you're young.

In some ways, your choice of occupation depends on your values and your desired life style. The occupation you choose may even determine the nature of your consumption—that is, the house you live in or the clothes you wear. It also will determine how much leisure you will have. As you've already seen, very few things come free of charge. If you want a job with more leisure, you generally will have less income to spend than from a job that offers less leisure. If you want a job that is highly stable and risk-free, you will pay for it in the form of a lower income.

REAL INCOME

REAL INCOME
Goods and services that can be purchased with your money income; the purchasing power of your money income.

Your choice of occupation and, in particular, *where* you will work will determine your **real income**—that is, the amount of goods and services you can purchase with your money income. In different cities, you will experience different costs of living, so the same money income will yield a different real income. For example, $1,000 a month generally yields a lower real income in New York City or Honolulu than it does in Peoria or Fresno.

NONMONEY INCOME

In figuring out what your standard of living will be in different types of occupations, you also must look at the nonmoney income that might be available. This refers to goods and services that individuals can obtain without paying money for them. There are several sources of nonmoney income that can make our lives more satisfying and/or comfortable.

1. **Material goods produced at home,** such as those that come from growing our own produce, sewing our own clothes, and cutting firewood from the family lot.
2. **Income from services** in the form of food, clothing, or housing. For example, farm laborers may receive housing accommodations in addition to money income. Ministers are often given food and housing. In fact, the whole category of fringe benefits for wage earners is covered under nonmoney income.
3. **Services provided by family members.** Full-time homemakers provide services to other members of the family for which they do not pay directly. Certain members of the family may do auto repairs, chores around the house, and lawn mowing without pay, thus providing nonmoney income to other family members.
4. **The implicit income or pleasure received from owned items,** such as a house, a car, or furniture. Specifically, if you own a house, you receive considerable pleasure from living in it. You could approximate the value of that pleasure by seeing what it would cost to rent the house.
5. **Barter income.** If you are able to exchange goods for services, goods for goods, or services for goods without resorting to the use of money or the marketplace, this can constitute part of your nonmoney income. Farmers, for example, can grow crops on their land and then trade them with other people for, say, furniture or clothes.
6. **Social income.** Such income is available largely at public expense and includes public-health clinics, libraries, parks, public education, roads, and fire and police protection.

In order to estimate your total income, it would be necessary to add up monetary income, the value of psychic income, and the value of all the nonmoney income you receive.

Just because an occupation will experience the greatest job growth in this decade doesn't necessarily mean you should plan to enter that occupation.

WHERE THE JOBS WILL AND WILL NOT BE THROUGH 1990

Forget for the moment the current economic situation. As of this writing, unemployment is as high as it has been in years. By the time you use this text, though, unemployment may have fallen, and the economic outlook for the nation may appear rosy.The current economic situation, however, is not that important in making your career choice. Rather, you must look to the future to determine where the greatest demand will be for different occupations. The U.S. Department of Labor has devised a way to help you. The results of its study of employment trends through 1990 are presented in Exhibits 7–5 and 7–6. Just because an occupation will experience the greatest job growth in this decade doesn't necessarily mean you should plan to enter that occupation. Rather, your choice of occupation may be influenced if you know where the jobs will be. You still want to maximize your happiness factor in your work, so you should choose an occupation that you think you're going to enjoy.

SUMMARY

1. Many income differences are the result of inherent differences in human beings, but they also are determined by the amount of training and education

EXHIBIT 7–5
Occupations That Will Experience the Greatest Job Growth

	JOB GROWTH, 1980–1990		JOB GROWTH, 1980–1990
Secretaries	700,000	Bookkeepers	157,000
Nurses' aides, orderlies	508,000	Guards, doorkeepers	153,000
Janitors	501,000	Warehouse stock clerks	142,000
Sales clerks	479,000	Computer-systems analysts	139,000
Cashiers	452,000	Store managers	139,000
Nurses	437,000	Physicians	135,000
Truckdrivers	415,000	Utility repairers	134,000
Fast-food restaurant workers	400,000	Computer operators	132,000
General office clerks	377,000	Child-care workers	125,000
Waiters, waitresses	360,000	Welders	123,000
Elementary-school teachers	251,000	Sales-floor stock clerks	120,000
Kitchen helpers	231,000	Electrical engineers	115,000
Accountants, auditors	221,000	Computer programmers	112,000
Building-trades helpers	212,000	Electricians	109,000
Automobile mechanics	206,000	Bank tellers	108,000
Blue-collar supervisors	206,000	Electrical, electronic technicians	107,000
Typists	187,000	Lawyers	107,000
Licensed practical nurses	185,000	Real-estate agents	102,000
Carpenters	173,000		

EXHIBIT 7–6
Occupations That Will Experience the Greatest Job Reductions

	JOB REDUCTIONS, 1980–1990
Farmers	246,000
Farm laborers	235,000
Secondary-school teachers	173,000
College, university teachers	55,000
Maids, servants	29,000
Graduate assistants	24,000
Compositors, typesetters	13,000
Shoemaking-machine operators	11,000
Clergy	9,000
Postal clerks	6,000
Central office repairers	3,000
Ticket agents	2,000
Taxi drivers	2,000

an individual has obtained, the amount of on-the-job training, and the riskiness of the occupation.

2. Going to school is an investment in human capital because it makes you, the human, more productive in the future. Generally, your investment in human capital should pay off in the form of a higher wage later on.

3. You should, however, specialize in an activity that is in demand and for which there is not a surplus of supply. Hence, choosing your occupation requires predicting both the demand and the supply for that particular occupation in the future.

4. Generally, individuals are paid according to their productivity. Therefore, anything that raises an individual's productivity may ultimately lead to a higher income.

5. The rate of return on education is as high as the rate of return on investing in other things. A college-degree holder may make as much as half a million dollars more on average than a person who has graduated from grade school.

6. The greatest cost of going to college is the opportunity cost of not being able to work and to make an income during those years.

7. An individual's wages (corrected for inflation) are usually lowest when the individual first enters the labor force. That's because he or she is least productive then.

8. In determining your standard of living, it is important to include nonmoney income, which includes, but is not limited to, goods produced at home, services produced at home, and social income from government-provided goods and services.

QUESTIONS FOR THOUGHT AND DISCUSSION

1. What are some of the most important factors that contribute to differences in income?
2. Have you ever considered going to school as an investment in your own human capital?
3. Is the act of going to college pure investment or not?
4. Does it seem fair that some students specialize in areas in which they cannot get a job once they get a degree? What would you do about that situation?
5. Why does the government subsidize so much higher education?
6. Do you think college is a good investment?
7. What is the most important cost of going to college?

THINGS TO DO

1. At the career-guidance center of your college or university, look through some books on occupations that you could enter, and make a list of the highest-paid occupations. Then ask someone in the center whether or not you would be eligible for those occupations. Try to determine why you would or would not.
2. Get the latest data from the Department of Commerce on lifetime earnings of various degree holders. Is it still worthwhile for individuals to complete college?
3. Check the latest edition of the *Occupational Outlook Handbook* (issued quarterly by the Bureau of Labor Statistics, U.S. Department of Labor) for a forecast of your chosen career.

SELECTED READINGS

Becker, Gary. *Human Capital: A Theoretical and Empirical Analysis with Special Reference to Education*. New York: Columbia University Press, 1964.

Berg, Ivar E. *Education and Jobs; The Great Training Robbery*. New York: Center for Urban Education, Praeger, 1970.

Bird, Caroline. *The Case Against College*. New York: David McKay, 1975.

Gilder, George. *Wealth and Poverty*. New York: Bantam, 1982.

Iris, B., and Barrett, G. V. "Some Relations between Job and Life Satisfaction and Job Importance." *Journal of Applied Psychology,* August 1972, pp. 301–304.

"Job Prestige: The Duncan Scale." *Psychology Today,* July 1979, p. 34.

"Many Recent Grads Who Got Good Jobs Are Now Losing Them." *The Wall Street Journal,* September 17, 1982, p. 1.

U.S. Bureau of Labor Statistics. *Occupational Outlook Handbook*. Washington, D.C.: U.S. Government Printing Office. Published annually.

Waite, Linda. "U.S. Women at Work." *Population Bulletin,* May 1981.

Consumer ISSUE D

HOW TO CHOOSE AND START A CAREER

GLOSSARY

RESUMÉ—A brief summary of your education, training, and honors that you give to a prospective employer.

HOW TO CHOOSE AND START A CAREER

The choice of a career will determine, to a large extent, your future income, but the choice of a career is not based on money alone.

APTITUDE MAY DETERMINE YOUR CAREER

Many individuals have specific aptitudes and abilities that lend themselves to specific careers; others do not. It would be futile to choose a career as a concert violinist if you had no aptitude for music. Virtually all specialty occupations that might be labeled "glamourous" or "artistic" require special talents. This is also true for professional sports. Many individuals want careers in these areas but cannot and, indeed, should not seek them because they lack the appropriate abilities.

On the other hand, you can, with relatively little risk, try out a few of these areas. In effect, it is possible to test your aptitude when you are young. At this time, you can decide whether you should take the considerable risk of choosing a "glamourous" career.

You can also consider the possibility of choosing such a career without necessarily attempting to be in the spotlight. If you would love to be in the theater but realize during your second year in college that you just don't have any natural acting talent, you can still enter that profession. You might train as a technician, an assistant producer, or a cameraperson.

In such careers as law, medicine, engineering, accounting, and others, aptitude is still crucial. The competition for good jobs (and even entrance to professional schools) is keen. If you are considering these careers, it would be appropriate to take aptitude tests well in advance. Most colleges and universities have services that can, either free or for a small fee, provide you with such tests.

GETTING INFORMATION ABOUT AN OCCUPATION

There are at least four publications you can consult to get information concerning career outlooks.

1. The Encyclopedia of Careers and Vocational Guidance is a two-volume work published by J.G. Ferguson Company of Chicago and distributed by Doubleday & Company. These two volumes contain general information on vocational testing, interviewing, and the like. In addition, there is information on jobs and professions that do not require college training.

2. The Occupational Outlook for College Graduates is a publication of the U.S. Department of Labor. Annually, it surveys the job outlook for college graduates and describes each profession in terms of training required, salaries, working conditions, and the nature of work. This publication may help you avoid choosing a career for which there will be no demand in the future.

3. The Occupational Thesaurus may be obtained from Everett A. Teal, Lehigh University, Bethlehem, Pennsylvania. This two-volume work lists employment areas for which college majors are qualified. There are specific job-skill categories, arranged according to demand, for different industries.

4. The College Placement Annual is published by the College Placement Council, Inc., P.O. Box 2263, Bethlehem, Pennsylvania. It gives job information for college graduates and alphabetically lists all major private employers in the United States, as well as government agencies. A unique employment index lists employers by occupations that are needed in the region the employer serves.

WHERE TO OBTAIN MORE JOB INFORMATION

The following are some places where you can obtain additional job information.

1. College or university placement centers. Virtually every college and university has some type of placement center. For college students, this might be the first place to look for job information. Placement centers have career consultants and vocational guidance counselors, as well as facilities for providing interviews between prospective graduates and recruiters from major firms and government agencies.

2. State employment agencies. All fifty states have state employment offices. There are more than 1,800 employment offices operating in conjunction with the U.S. Employment Service of the Department of Labor. These employment services charge no fee and make placements for all types of jobs; some even provide free career guidance and aptitude tests.

3. Specialized placement services. Employers seeking women to hire and women seeking jobs may consult some of the various special job-matching services, including:

a. Catalyst National Network, 14 E. 60th Street, New York, New York 10022. This organization provides listings and resumés of managerial and professional applicants.

b. Talent Search Skills Bank, Office of Voluntary Programs, Equal Opportunity Commission, 1800 G Street N.W., Washington, D.C. 20506. This office maintains a file on minority female applicants and their skills.

c. National Federation of Business and Professional Women's Clubs, Inc., 2012 Massachusetts Avenue N.W., Washington, D.C. 20036. This organization operates a talent bank to help women find positions in educational institutions, private industry, and government.

4. "Help-wanted" ads in newspapers and professional or trade journals. Virtually every newspaper in the country has ads listing vacancies for various jobs. There are also job vacancies listed in trade and professional journals. Since these usually require that you apply by mail, an impressive resumé is imperative.

5. Private employment agencies. You can register with an agency and wait to be called, or apply directly for a job that is advertised in a periodical. Agencies generally require you to sign a contract that obligates you to pay a fee if the agency places you. Read these contracts carefully; the small print may reveal that you owe the agency the fee even if you're fired after one week. Agency fees may run from 5 to 15 percent of your annual starting salary. In the upper-income job brackets, agency fees can sometimes be as much as 30 percent of your first year's salary. Those agencies that receive their commissions from employers usually are free to applicants.

For guidance on agencies in your chosen field, look at *Employment Directions,* which lists agencies by specialty in forty-nine states and five foreign countries. You can order this from the National Employment Association, 2000 K Street N.W., Washington, D.C. 20006.

PREPARING A WINNING RESUMÉ

For almost all job applications, you must submit a **resumé**. Because personnel officers in corporations must read thousands of them every year, your resumé should create the best possible impression in order to give you a competitive edge over other job seekers. Remember, your resumé is an advertisement for yourself.

Keep It Brief

Since your resumé is, in large part, bait for the interview, it need not be an entire dossier, starting out with letters of commendation from your junior-high-school principal. Nor should it list your every accomplishment, information about your outside interests, or the backgrounds of your parents.

Presentation of Your Resumé

Your resumé should be typed on one or more sheets of high-quality rag bond. A good resumé is usually professionally printed, not photocopied. Remember, the appearance of a resumé is like the appearance you will make for an interview: First impressions count in both cases.

The Format of a Resumé

You needn't write a resumé as if it were an application for college. In other words, don't put the word NAME before your name. The fewer headlines, the better, but you can divide your resumé into sections, such as education, experience, publications, honors and awards pertinent to the work you are applying for, and special interests.

EXPERIENCE. On your resumé, list your job experience, either in reverse chronological order or according to functional headings, such as sales, teaching, or administration.

EDUCATION. In this section, list appropriate institutional degrees and certificates. If you went to college, you need not mention high school unless it was a special kind. If you transferred to three or four different colleges, you need not list all of them, only the one from which you received your degree; doing otherwise might cause a prospective employer to think you were unstable.

The Do's and Don't's of Resumé Preparation

Experts in the field of resumé preparation offer the following guidelines.

1. Make sure you proofread your resumé so that there are no typographical or spelling errors.
2. Make sure that there are no errors in grammar. When in doubt, ask someone who knows.
3. First impressions are important. Therefore, don't use colored or perfumed paper, and don't include a picture of yourself on the front.
4. Describe yourself honestly. Don't exaggerate. If you're young, be candid about your experience—or lack of it.
5. Don't cram your resumé with useless information.
6. Don't have your resumé typeset because that gives the impression that you think you'll be unemployed for a long period.
7. State very succinctly and clearly a job or career objective.

Once your resumé earns you an interview, consider these other pointers that can improve your chances to land the job.

HOW TO BE INTERVIEWED

Remember that the personnel officer for the company interviews many prospective employees. You must somehow convince the interviewer that you are as good as or better than anyone else who is being considered for the job. Basically, your interview should be constructed to convince the prospective employer that you will fulfill his or her needs. In order to do that, you must find out, beforehand, about the company, the job requirements, and, if possible, your interviewer.

Some Pointers on Successful Interviews

Here are some suggestions for a successful interview.

1. Be on time.
2. Come with a list of your qualifications.
3. Always maintain eye contact and listen attentively.
4. Be honest and frank, but don't make derogatory comments about a previous employer.
5. Let your interviewer offer you information on benefits, salary, and agency fees (if any).
6. Find out all you can about your potential employer as well as what that employer will want to know about you.
7. Dress appropriately; first impressions are important.

OBTAINING INFORMATION ABOUT PROSPECTIVE COMPANIES

Prior to the interview, you should find out some facts about the company. This can be done by looking at some of the following sources:

1. *Moody's Manuals*
2. *Fitch Corporation Manuals*
3. *Thomas' Register of American Manufacturers*
4. *MacRae's Blue Book*
5. Company annual reports

SOME FINAL POINTERS ON JOB HUNTING

The key to success in job hunting is motivation. If you are motivated, you will follow many of the suggestions in this section. If you feel that you need some more professional advice, consider seeking the services of a professional resumé writer, generally someone associated with a private employment-counseling firm. If you need help with interviews, practice with a friend or with someone who works in the placement center at your college or university. Without a doubt, job hunting requires a great deal of effort.

SUMMARY

1. Aptitude can determine which career you pursue. It is important to determine early in life whether you have the appropriate aptitude for specialized careers, such as professional sports and the arts.
2. You can obtain information on occupations from *The Encyclopedia of Careers and Vocational Guidance*, *The Occupational Outlook for College Graduates*, *The Occupational Thesaurus*, and *The College Placement Annual*.
3. You can obtain further information on jobs from private employment agencies, state employment agencies, your local college placement centers, and "help-wanted" ads in newspapers and professional journals.
4. A resumé is bait for an interview. It should be a brief outline of your experience and education, not your entire life history.

5. Successful interviewing requires that you follow a few rules. Among the most important are these: Be on time, be honest and frank, and obtain information about the company before the interview.

QUESTIONS FOR THOUGHT AND DISCUSSION

1. Can you think of a way to measure your aptitude for a career you are considering?
2. Who can use the services of a college or university employment office?
3. What individuals should seek the aid of private employment agencies in finding a job?

THINGS TO DO

1. Find out as much information as you can about the occupation you think you want to enter.
2. Make up a sample resumé. What do you think is lacking in it in terms of what will impress a potential employer?

SELECTED READINGS

Angel, Juvenal L. *The Complete Resume Book and Job Getter's Guide.* New York: Pocket Books, Inc., 1982.

Berry, K. D. "Career Can Be Satisfying." *Essence,* August 1979, p. 28.

Bolles, Richard Nelson. *What Color Is Your Parachute?* Berkeley, CA: Ten Speed Press, 1979 (revised edition).

Greiff, Barrie and Munter, Preston. *Trade-offs: Executive, Family, and Organizational Life.* New York: New American Library, 1980.

Haldane, Bernhard. *Career Satisfaction and Success: A Guide to Job Freedom.* New York: American Management Association, 1974.

CHAPTER

YOU HAVE TO LIVE WITH WHAT YOU HAVE

American consumers are rich. . . . We are rich compared with the British consumer, the Indian consumer, the African consumer, or the Venezuelan consumer. The average per capita income in the United States is considerably higher than in most other countries in the world.

CHAPTER PREVIEW

- Why do we budget?
- How can a budget become part of democratic decision making for the family spending unit?
- What do typical family budgets look like?
- How can you fit a budget into a lifetime plan?

American consumers are rich. That is, we are rich compared with the British consumer, the Indian consumer, the African consumer, the Spanish consumer, or the Venezuelan consumer. The average per capita income in the United States is considerably higher than in most other countries in the world.

But per capita income does not tell the story we want to tell. Exhibit 8–1 shows the different percentages of U.S. families that make particular amounts of income, ranging all the way from poverty to extreme opulence. Most of us find ourselves somewhere in the middle range. We're not destitute, because we do have some form of income, but, on the other hand, we're not David Rockefeller or Hugh Hefner either.

All of us, though, whether rich or poor, have something in common: We can't buy everything we'd like to buy. In other words, we all face the universal problem of scarcity. All of us operate within a limited budget. Because everyone faces this universal problem of scarce resources, we can better understand why personal money management is important for all of us, no matter what our income level.

WHY FIGURE OUT A BUDGET OR SPENDING PLAN?

If you find yourself at either end of the income spectrum, you may think it a waste of time to formulate a budget. Of course, if you have no income, a budget won't be of concern to you. And if you have a seemingly unlimited amount of income, you won't have to formulate a budget either. Most of us, however, lie somewhere in between. Because we have limited incomes, every action that involves spending part of that income means sacrificing something else. Economists term this the opportunity cost of spending. For example, if you decide to spend more on entertainment, you will have less left over for all the other things in your budget. In other words, every spending decision involves an opportunity cost: You are giving up the opportunity of spending that income on something else. Why? Simply because you have a limited budget and, as a result, because you face a problem of scarcity. As you read the rest of this chapter, remember that the first objective of budgeting is to encourage *disciplined spending;* the second objective is to reduce the amount of money wasted through needless expenditures.

EXHIBIT 8–1
Money Income of Families by Income Level, 1983

TOTAL MONEY INCOME	NUMBER (THOUSANDS)	PERCENT DISTRIBUTION
Under 5,000	8,770	10.5
5,000–9,999	12,445	14.9
10,000–14,999	12,028	14.4
15,000–19,999	10,274	12.3
20,000–24,999	9,522	11.4
25,000–34,999	14,367	17.2
35,000–49,999	10,107	12.1
50,000 and over	6,014	7.2
TOTAL	83,527	100.0

SOURCE: U.S. Bureau of Census, *Current Population Reports*, Series P-60, No. 105, 1–4.

Planning a budget and attempting to follow it forces the issue of scarcity and opportunity cost out into the open. Budgeting also forces decision making and the establishment of priorities. If you include a trip to Mexico in your budget, you will realize that somewhere along the line another item or items must be cut out. A budget, then, helps you manage your money in a more or less systematic and rational manner. It is also a control mechanism that causes you to be aware of the decisions you are actually making—decisions that are being made even if you don't wish to acknowledge them. Some of you may be able to determine instantaneously the **trade-offs** (opportunity costs) involved every time you make a purchase. But most of us would benefit from a budget. With it, we may be able to hold in check undirected spending activities that can lead to unhappiness and, occasionally, financial disaster.

TRADE-OFFS
The giving up of one thing to have another. In order to get a desired good or service, it is necessary, in a world of scarcity, to trade off some other desired good or service. Every trade-off involves a sacrifice.

With a budget, you can consume according to the values that you clarified when you established your lifetime spending and saving goals.

Setting up financial goals is an important step in budget formulation. Without even considering the possibility of financial disaster, a household will have specific future financial goals. For example, your family may wish to save enough money for a down payment on a bigger house. Budgeting a specified amount to be saved each month will make attainment of this financial goal more likely than will using a haphazard approach.

An understanding of value clarification, which we discussed in Chapter 5, will help you understand the importance of budget formulation. With a budget, you can consume according to the values that you clarified when you established your lifetime spending and saving goals. A budget also reduces dissent in a household where money may be a difficult subject.

DEMOCRATIC DECISION MAKING

If, in your situation, more than one person is affected by how each month's income is spent, then you have to choose how decisions will be made. Will decision making be unilateral or dictatorial? Will decision making be democratic? That is, will everybody involved participate? This problem arises not only in traditional family situations but also in communal and group-living situations. If you decide on a unilateral approach, then those whose lives are affected may, at one time or another, feel cheated, left out, or imposed upon.

It is important to work out money problems within the family unit because many families fight about money. A recent survey by Yankelovich, Skelly, and White found that 54 percent of the families interviewed argued about money, and those that were hard-pressed by financial problems argued about money 65 percent of the time. The study also showed that families who often fought about money were unable to communicate freely and frankly on money matters. All surveys show that money is the first or second most frequent cause of fights among couples. The formulation of a spending plan can increase harmony within any living situation because it forces those involved to consider the desires, needs, preferences, and complaints of others. Each time a major economic decision has to be made, democratic decision making will involve everybody in the process. On the other hand, when only one person makes budget decisions, the situation is akin to tyranny. In most families today, the so-called male breadwinner is no longer automatically allowed all the decision-making powers simply because he brings home the "bread." After all, the homemaker also contributes to the total implicit income of the family—to the tune of at least $12,500 a year in a family of four. If a wife is contributing implicit income, even though it is not in the form of dollars brought home in a paycheck, she, too, will want to help formulate the budget and, therefore, the lifetime goals and plans of the family unit. In some states, such as Washington, the wife has a legal right to share in controlling family finances. That is, either partner is empowered to act independently on behalf of the "community"; this law does not apply in a few specified instances in which the signatures of both spouses are required, such as signing a mortgage when a house is purchased.

The Family Council

Often, in truly democratic households, a family council meets to make the budget. At this time, everybody airs his or her desires, and everyone, including children, faces the problem of scarcity and the trade-offs that have to be made with a fixed income. Everybody must realize at the onset that no one person's every desire will be satisfied. Many decisions are mutually exclusive; if, for example, a new TV is purchased, it may be impossible to buy a new ten-speed bike. If the family unit decides to trade in the old clunker for a brand new sedan, there may be no vacation in the mountains that year. The beauty of the democratic family-council budget-making process is that everybody's cards can be laid on the table—and the biggest card of all, of course, is the fixed amount of income that the family has to spend. As a result, even the parents may have a better sense of the opportunity costs of their actions and the effects of these trade-offs on other members of the family. Moreover, differences in values often surface during family discussions of money management. It is important for all concerned to understand and respect other family members' values.

Viewed in this light, the budget-making process has another, separate goal: Not only can it hold in check undirected spending and prevent financial crises, it also can help solidify family relationships. Lack of money is the basic cause of so many marital squabbles that democratization of the spending process would seem to be a natural desire of all families that wish to have unity, tranquility, and harmony within the household.

A number of marriage counselors have proposed some specific guidelines about how to handle money matters within a family.

1. **Try the democratic decision-making meeting on an informal basis.** If the casual approach doesn't work, hold a formal meeting at a set time and place. Different family members should preside over the meetings. Such meetings are more successful if instituted when the children are young; adolescents may balk at the idea unless they have grown up with this system.
2. **Write it down.** Communication on paper may be easier than verbal communication. If there is a quarrel about family spending priorities, have each family member write down a list of priorities in descending order and then compare them.
3. **Record and then listen to the family money fights on cassettes.** Frequently, those who argue don't really hear themselves.
4. **Negotiate a contract.** The bargain-making process encourages participants to give a little and take a little.

No matter how democratic the process may be, there always will be problems with children, particularly when they enter their teens and want to assert their independence (and with adults, too, who wish to assert *their* independence).

HOW DOES THE TYPICAL HOUSEHOLD ALLOCATE ITS INCOME?

Averages sometimes can be deceiving. But it may be instructive for you to see how typical households in the United States allocate their disposable (after-tax) incomes to the many competing demands. The U.S. Department of Labor, Bureau of Labor Statistics, has for some time obtained survey data on the spending patterns of households of various income levels. Exhibit 8–2, a pie graph, shows how an average American family spends its "take-home" income. A large chunk usually goes for housing services (including utilities and maintenance). Equal to that expenditure, and sometimes even larger, is the chunk

EXHIBIT 8–2
Average American Family Budget (Based on Annual Budgets for a Four-Person Urban Family, Intermediate Level of Living, 1983)

The average American family spends about 30 percent of its after-tax disposable income on housing and almost one-third of its disposable income on food. The rest is divided among transportation, clothing, medical care, personal care, and other expenses.

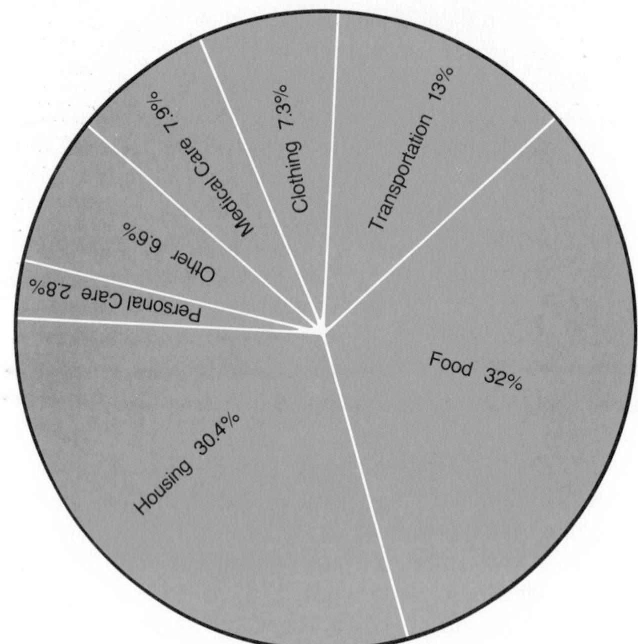

SOURCE: U.S. Department of Labor, Bureau of Labor Statistics.

of income that goes for food. Food and housing often account for over 60 percent of the average American family's nontax expenditures in any one year.

This may seem to be a frightfully large percentage, but it isn't when compared with that of other countries. Exhibit 8–3 shows the percentage of total income spent on just food in different countries of the world. Notice that there seems to be a relationship between the percentage of income spent on food and the level of development of the country. In fact, for a fairly accurate measure of how prosperous a country is, look at what percentage of each family's budget goes for food; with few exceptions, the larger the percentage, the less developed the country.

In Exhibit 8–4, you can see that personal care, clothing, and medical care constitute another large chunk of each family's budget in the United States. Medical care alone represents an increasingly large percentage of total U.S. consumption spending; we will discuss the reasons for this increase and the future of medical-care expenditures in Chapter 18. And, in Chapter 22, we will discuss how taxes, unfortunately for many of us, usurp an ever-increasing amount of our income.

For the average American, an increasingly large fraction of every dollar earned goes to federal, state, and local taxes. Some of those tax monies are returned in the form of **transfer payments**, such as Social Security benefits and unemployment compensation, but the remainder is still a large fraction of total income in the United States.

TRANSFER PAYMENTS
Payments made by the government to individuals for which no current services are rendered. A transfer payment might be a Social Security check or an unemployment check.

Different Budget Levels

The makeup of the various budget categories changes as we go from lower-income to higher-income spenders. Exhibit 8–4 shows the U.S. Department of Labor's latest estimates of what it takes to live on a low-, medium-, or high-income budget for a hypothetical family of four. (Note that these estimates say nothing about what the incomes in the United States actually are.) As income goes up, food spending falls and housing expenditures rise as percentages of total income. That means that, as our incomes increase, we buy proportionally more housing and proportionally less food. Housing, then, is often considered after a certain point to be a **luxury good**, for people buy a disproportionate amount of it as they become wealthier. Food, on the other hand, has the opposite characteristic and is, therefore, considered a necessity.

LUXURY GOOD A good whose purchase increases more than in proportion to increases in income. Jewelry, gourmet foods, and sports cars usually fall into this category.

We have to be careful of such labels as luxury and necessity, however, because they have some subjective connotations. One person's luxury may be another person's necessity, and vice versa. Most of us have a hard time determining our own values and goals, let alone those of other people. But that's exactly what we do when we consider somebody else's spending to be wasted on so-called luxury items or frivolous consumption. After all, since we purchase "satisfaction," and not the items per se, who can judge what another's derived satisfaction is?

EXHIBIT 8–3
Percentage of Total Income Spent on Food in Selected Countries

As much as 60 to 70 percent, or more, of total income is spent on food by some less developed nations, such as Uganda, which spends 79 percent of total income on food.

COUNTRY	PERCENT TOTAL FOOD EXPENDITURES/ TOTAL INCOME
Argentina	40
Brazil	37
Chile	64
France	36
Honduras	41
Hungary	42
Indonesia	60
Japan	27
Kenya	38
Korea	49
Malawi	40
Netherlands	29
Pakistan	51
Philippines	63
Poland	45
Saudi Arabia	74
Somalia	60
Spain	49
Sudan	70
Switzerland	21
Thailand	55
Tunisia	50
Uganda	79
United Kingdom	28
Venezuela	25
Yugoslavia	35

SOURCE: FAO Review of Food Consumption Surveys, 1980.

BUDGET MAKING, GOALS, AND VALUE CLARIFICATION

In Chapter 5, we discussed value clarification—how you decide what your goals are, what your values are, and what they mean with respect to how you should spend your time. Ultimately, this all relates to what kind of life you want to lead. Now you can put this abstract problem into perspective by applying it to an actual dollars-and-cents decision-making process—budget formulation. When you sit down alone or with the other members of your spending unit, you have to consider the values that you place on the various things you want to do with the income available. To be able to clarify your values, you first have to formulate your goals and those of the spending unit as a whole. Then you must set *priorities* among your goals. These priorities will be related to three general types of goals you probably will set for yourself or your household—short-term, intermediate, and long-term.

Consider an example. Your long-term goal is for all members of your family to become as physically fit as possible. This long-term goal may, therefore, dictate short-term and intermediate-term goals. As a short-term goal, you may decide to buy jogging uniforms for wet-weather running for every member of your family within the next month. As an intermediate-term goal, you may decide that, within a year, all members of your family will be in sufficient shape to run a ten-kilometer race.

Consider another possible long-term goal—that of acquiring a genuine appreciation of the arts for yourself and your family. That long-term goal may dictate certain short-term goals, such as going to a museum once a month or purchasing art-appreciation books. An intermediate-term goal might be to save enough money to purchase season tickets for next year's opera.

More basically, you may have the goal of seeing that your family is well nourished and adequately housed or that it has sufficient medical protection or safe, comfortable transportation. Here, however, your goals may involve choices. To have a well-nourished family, you may have to stint on housing; to have medical protection, you may have to stint on transportation needs.

To be able to clarify your values, you first have to formulate your goals and those of the spending unit as a whole.

Essentially, everybody's main goal is to be happy. The problem is clarifying your values enough so that you can establish goals that, taken together, will spell happiness for you and for those around you. When you formulate a budget, you can see exactly what these goals cost. You are forced to rethink and to reformulate your values when you realize that they are either unattainable or extremely costly, in the sense that you must forego other desired or necessary things.

TRADE-OFFS

Many families and other spending units frequently encounter problems when they must make budgetary trade-offs. The key to understanding these problems is the realization that nature is stingy and does not give us everything we want. That is, nature makes things scarce for us, and, ultimately, that scarcity is reflected in the income of the spending unit—an income that is insufficient to satisfy everyone's desires and wants and needs.

For example, assume that you and the other members of the spending unit have decided that physical fitness is an important value you wish to maintain and that your goal for the next several years is good health, stamina, and athletic prowess for all family members. There are many ways you can accomplish this goal. Jogging is probably the cheapest way of building stamina; after the initial outlay for warm, weatherproof suits for the winter and sturdy running shoes, there is nothing else to buy. But not everybody can be satisfied

EXHIBIT 8–4
Summary of Annual Budgets for a Four-Person Family at Three Levels of Living, Urban United States.

	LOW BUDGET	MEDIUM BUDGET	HIGH BUDGET	ITEM AS A PERCENTAGE OF TOTAL BUDGET		
COMPONENT	LOWER	INTERMEDIATE	HIGHER	LOWER	INTERMEDIATE	HIGHER
Total Budget	$15,323	$25,407	$38,060			
Total family consumption	12,069	18,240	25,008			
Food	4,545	5,843	7,366	30%	23%	19%
Housing	2,817	5,546	8,423	18	22	22
Transportation	1,311	2,372	3,075	9	9	8
Clothing	937	1,333	1,947	6	5	5
Personal care	379	508	719	2	2	2
Medical care	1,436	1,443	1,505	9	6	4
Other family consumption[1]	644	1,196	1,972	4	5	5
Other items[2]	621	1,021	1,718	4	4	5
Taxes and deductions	2,632	6,146	11,333	17	24	30
Social Security and disability	1,036	1,703	1,993	7	7	5
Personal income taxes	1,596	4,443	9,340	10	17	25

NOTE: Because of rounding, sums of individual items may not equal totals.

[1]Other family consumption includes average costs for reading, recreation, tobacco products, alcoholic beverages, education, and miscellaneous expenditures.
[2]Other items include allowances for gifts and contributions, life insurance, and occupational expenses.

SOURCE: U.S. Department of Labor, Bureau of Labor Statistics, 1982.

with jogging; or, even if they are, they may want to engage in more competitive sports. While the children may be able to engage in certain sports that make no additional demands on the family's budget, the parents might wish to participate in other sports, such as tennis or golf, for which equipment must be purchased and fees paid for the use of courts or greens.

By making budgeting a family affair, everyone involved knows the exact costs of attaining the goals that resulted from the family's clarification of values. Those members of the spending unit who will feel cheated if the parents decide to play tennis indoors during the winter can express their feelings, and perhaps a compromise can be reached. Individual values may conflict when a budget is formulated this way, and compromises may be necessary. If compromise is accomplished in a democratic way through the formulation of monthly budgets, those in conflict may be willing to yield because they know they will gain in the future.

Goal definition and value clarification are integral parts of budget formulation and may be considered the only ways to design a satisfactory budget that works. Remember, though, a budget should not be considered a straitjacket but, rather, an indication of direction that will change, depending on changes in individual and family situations.

Lifetime planning actually is based on the establishment and subsequent accomplishment of both mundane and lofty goals.

FITTING IT ALL INTO A LIFETIME PLAN

Today there is much talk about early retirement and the decisions that must be made if it is to be a happy period. There is also much talk about how increased leisure time will be spent and the need to purchase more leisure-related products. These matters should be considered as part of a lifetime plan, one that is revised periodically to take account of changing values, income, and consumption situations.

Lifetime planning actually is based on the establishment and subsequent accomplishment of both mundane and lofty goals. As a consumer, you might begin your planning by drawing up monthly and yearly lists of goals, tasks, and ideas. The monthly list, for example, would tell you when to schedule maintenance on your car, when to have services performed on household appliances, what days sales are coming up at various stores, and so on. The yearly list, of course, can do the same thing but probably will be more general and less specific.

Your long-term goals, those you hope to achieve in five, ten, or even fifteen years, will be much broader and will have to be revised to remain realistic. Your five-year goal may be to obtain a bachelor's degree, to learn how to ski or play tennis better, to become fluent in Spanish, or to become an active participant in a minority-affairs program. To attain those goals, you have to lay your yearly, monthly, weekly, and even daily plans with your future firmly in mind. Every once in a while, you have to take stock of your current position and your progress toward the various goals contained in the different plans. You probably will want to include in your evaluation those members of the spending unit who would be most affected by the different plans.

Periodically, you should confer with all members of the family spending unit to determine where each stands and where the family as a whole wants to be a year from now, five years from now, and so on. If a new house with a view of the ocean is what everyone really wants, you might decide to devise a program to attain that goal. That program might require sacrificing many consumption expenditures over the next few years in order to save up the down payment on that house. But if the family is united in its desire to meet that goal, the sacrifices may be made quite willingly.

Long-range planning is quite simple in concept but sometimes difficult to put into operation, mainly because people don't always like to face the reality of what is entailed in attaining certain goals. For example, the only way to consume more goods and services is to make more income, and, in most cases,

the only way you can make more income is to become more productive in your job or to change jobs. That may involve going to night school, taking additional training, or working on weekends. If you're aware of such requirements, then you may be more willing to accept the cost of attaining a particular goal for yourself and/or your family.

SUMMARY

1. Even the richest among us do not have an unlimited budget and must, therefore, make choices.
2. Budgeting, or making a spending plan, forces you to realize that you face the constraint of a limited income and that you must make trade-offs among those things you desire to purchase.
3. Democratic decision making within a spending unit may mean that the entire family helps design the budget.
4. A typical household in the United States spends about 30 percent of its after-tax income on housing and about one-third on food. As a family's income goes up, the percentage spent on food decreases and the percentage spent on housing increases.
5. Goals should be set according to your priorities. Short-term, intermediate, and long-term goals must be realistic, and striving to attain them may involve making trade-offs.

QUESTIONS FOR THOUGHT AND DISCUSSION

1. Do you know anybody who does not face a budget constraint?
2. Do you think citizens of the United States have different problems working within their budget constraints than do citizens of India or Turkey?
3. It is sometimes argued that budget making and time planning reduce spontaneity. Do you agree or disagree? Is there any way the two can be reconciled?
4. Democratic decision making by way of a family council sounds old-fashioned to many individuals. What might be a more modern alternative?
5. How much voice do you think a teenager should have in family budget making?
6. Why do Americans spend more on housing than on food as their incomes increase?
7. Why must trade-offs be made?
8. "If I only had 50 percent more income, I could buy everything I wanted." Evaluate this statement. Have you ever made it? Has it proved to be true?
9. Although very few people do serious lifetime planning, don't most individuals implicitly have a "plan"?

THINGS TO DO

1. With the help of your reference librarian, go back to the earliest publication you can find from the Department of Labor, Bureau of Labor Statistics, and see what the average American family budget looked like then. How has it changed over the years? Are we spending more or less on food? On housing? What about taxes?
2. Make a detailed list of your short-term, intermediate, and long-term goals. How do these goals fit in with your overall values?

SELECTED READINGS

Amling, Frederick and Drems, William G. *The Dow Jones-Irwin Guide to Personal Financial Planning*. New York: Dow Jones-Irwin, 1982.

Dichter, Ernest. *Strategy of Desire*. New York: Doubleday, 1960.

Kilgore, James E. *Dollars and Sense: Making Your Money Work for You and Your Family*. New York: Abingdon Press, 1982.

Kraft, Barbara. *Costs of Living: A Budget Program to Manage Your Money*. New York: A & W Press, 1982.

Margolius, Sidney. *How to Make the Most of Your Money*. New York: Appleton-Century-Crofts, 1969.

Rosefsky, Robert. *Financial Planning for the Young Family*. Chicago: Follett, 1978.

Consumer ISSUE  

HOW TO BUDGET YOUR LIMITED INCOME

GLOSSARY

FIXED EXPENSES—Expenses that occur at specific times and cannot be altered. Once a house is purchased or rented, a house payment is considered a fixed expense; so is a car payment.

FLEXIBLE EXPENSES—Expenses that can be changed in the short run. The amount of money you spend on food can be considered a flexible expense because you can buy higher- or lower-quality food than you now are buying. These are also known as variable expenses.

Once you decide to do some positive money management, you must figure out a budget and try to follow it. Your budget, remember, is a planning tool to help you reduce undirected spending. This Consumer Issue looks at two different types of budgets for two different situations—one for college students and the other for those not in college.

STEPS IN BUDGET MAKING

Very briefly, after you determine your income and goals, you should follow these basic steps to create a spending plan.

1. Analyze past spending by keeping records for a month or two.
2. Determine **fixed expenses**, such as rent and any other contractual payments that must be made, even if they come infrequently (such as insurance and taxes).
3. Determine **flexible expenses**, such as those for food and clothing.
4. Balance your fixed and flexible expenditures with your available income. If a surplus exists, you can apply it toward achieving your goals. If there is a deficit, then you must reexamine your flexible expenditures. You can also reexamine fixed expenses with a view toward reducing them in the future.

Note that so-called fixed expenses are only philosophically fixed in the short run. In the longer run, everything is essentially flexible or variable. You can adjust your fixed expenses by changing your standard of living, if necessary.

THE IMPORTANCE OF KEEPING RECORDS

Budget making, whether you are a college student, a single person living alone, or the head of a family, will be useless if you don't keep records. The only way to make sure that you are carrying out the plans implicit in your budget is to maintain records that show what you actually are spending. The ultimate way to maintain records is to write everything down, but that becomes time-consuming and, therefore, costly. Another way to keep records is to write checks for everything. Records also are important in case of a problem with a faulty product or service or with the Internal Revenue Service.

Which Records to Keep at Home

The following are eleven types of records you should keep at home. Not all these records are directly related to budget making; some should be kept so you can document insurable losses, lost credit cards, and the like.

1. Income. Keep paycheck stubs, records of self-employment income, W-2 Forms (given to you at the end of the year by your employer[s]), and 1099 Forms, which indicate interest, dividends, and so on earned during the year.

2. Most canceled checks. Keep these at least one year; for tax purposes, a minimum of three years is advisable.

3. Insurance policies. Automobile, homeowners, fire, health, life, and other policies should be retained indefinitely.

4. Large purchases. All receipts and canceled checks for autos, furniture, equipment, appliances, stereos, and so on should be kept as long as you own the item.

5. Home improvements. All receipts and canceled checks must be kept until you are no longer a homeowner. You can reduce taxes this way.

6. Investment transactions. A register of all stock transactions and confirmations of purchases and sales sent to you by brokers, as well as any receipts, should be maintained.

7. Tax-deductible items. Canceled checks and receipts for interest, taxes, contributions, business expenses, medical and dental expenses, and drugs should be kept at least three years after the tax-filing deadline for the year in which the expenses occurred.

8. Tax returns. Copies of all returns, worksheets, and schedules should be kept for three years after the tax-filing deadline.

9. Information on valuables. Canceled checks and receipts for art, antiques, and jewelry and appraisals of these items should be kept as long as you own them, plus three years after any sale, for income-tax purposes.

10. Credit cards. All credit-card numbers, company telephone numbers and/or addresses, and/or prepaid envelopes to notify of loss or theft should be retained and updated constantly.

11. Other current documents. Warranties, loan contracts, service contracts, and so on should be retained.

Things to Keep in a Safe Deposit Box

You will want to keep a number of items in a safe deposit box. Although they don't specifically relate to budget making, these items are part of sensible and complete record keeping.

1. Personal documents. Birth certificates, marriage certificate, military records, naturalization papers.

2. Securities and properties. Deeds to a house or other property, car titles, stock certificates, extra copies of insurance policies, bonds.

3. Wills. All current wills. Originals should be kept by those who will carry out the will.

4. Inventory of personal and household items. Make a complete record and update it in case of loss or damage. Take photographs and perhaps make a tape-recorded inventory.

A SIMPLIFIED THREE-TO-FOUR-STEP APPROACH TO BUDGETING

The object of budgeting is to reconcile unlimited wants with limited income. You can take a simple three-step approach to this reconciliation.

1. Keep a record of expenditures for at least one month.
2. Review records to see if spending is consistent with your goals.
3. Reallocate dollars to ensure that you reach your identified goals.

There is also a possible fourth step—to monitor new spending patterns for a while via record keeping to see if you are deviating from new identified goals. The whole concept of reconciling unlimited wants with limited income is to impose self-discipline, which does indeed play a major role in financial management.

WORKING WITH FIXED AND FLEXIBLE EXPENSES—CONSTRUCTING A ONE-MONTH BUDGET WORKSHEET

In order to construct a one-month budget worksheet, you must first determine your available income. If you are receiving spendable income from your parents or relatives or from a scholarship or fellowship, then you know right away what is available to you every month. If you are earning your income, however, you must estimate your gross income and then calculate your net income as is done in Exhibit E–1.

To estimate gross income, simply multiply the number of hours you work times your hourly wage rate times four weeks. To calculate net income, deduct withholding (income taxes) of approximately 15 percent. Social Security contributions will take away another 7 percent (approximately). Now you have total taxes withheld. You must further subtract other deductions, such as medical insurance payments and the like.

Estimating Fixed Expenses

Exhibit E–2 can be used to estimate your fixed expenses.

Estimating Flexible Expenses

Flexible expenses include food, clothing, entertainment, and the like. For most students, food constitutes at least one-third of total expenditures, so you'll have to estimate your total food budget per week. Exhibit E–3 shows an example of a budget worksheet for figuring flexible expenses.

EXHIBIT E–1
Calculating Net Income

To find your net income, simply compute the following:

GROSS INCOME = $ (hours worked × hourly wage × four weeks) − taxes ($) = $ − deductions ($)

FIXED EXPENSES	ESTIMATED AMOUNT FOR SINGLE PERSON	IF LIVING WITH ROOMMATE, DIVIDE BY 2
Rent	$____	$____
Utilities	$____	____
Telephone	____	____
Furnishings	____	____
Car payments	____	____
Insurance	____	____
Car	____	____
Life	____	____
Other	____	____
Savings	____	____
Funds for short-term goal	____	____
Emergency	____	____
TOTAL FIXED EXPENSES FOR ONE MONTH	$____	$____

EXHIBIT E-2
Estimating Fixed Expenses

RECONCILING YOUR MONTHLY NET INCOME WITH YOUR MONTHLY TOTAL EXPENSES

In Exhibit E–4, you can fill in your gross income and then your net income. To find out your total expenses, also fill in your fixed and your flexible expenses.

Whenever the difference between your income and expenses is positive, you are adding to your savings. Whenever the difference is negative, you clearly are reducing your savings.

COMPUTER BUDGETING SERVICES

Certain banks now offer monthly computerized budget accounts for a fee ranging from three to six dollars per month. One such service, called "Money Minder," is offered by the United States National Bank of Oregon (P.O. Box 3460, Portland, Oregon 97208). All computerized systems offer major budget classifications with a specific code number that you mark on each check and deposit slip. For a higher fee, you can choose up to 1,000 individually selected income and expense categories. The monthly report will give you, at a minimum, the following information:

1. Total income and expenses by category
2. Number of items in each category
3. Percentage of total income and expenses by category for month
4. Percentage of total income and expenses by category for that year to the month in question

Some systems even allow you the option of budget comparisions. They will, for example, compare a fixed amount you had budgeted for a particular category with what you actually spent.

Also, after you have used the system for at least thirteen months, you can request a previous-year comparison that permits you to see the change from last year's totals for each classification. Such automated budgeting systems eliminate some of the drudgery often associated with financial planning.

BUDGET REVIEWS

Every successful budget requires a review of what has happened. You must be aware, however, that the money spent during the first several months in a particular category may be a very different amount from the money budgeted. That is to be expected; the budget will become more realistic as the process continues. Every few months,

EXHIBIT E–3
Estimating Flexible Expenses

TOTAL FOOD EXPENSE FOR ONE MONTH (Multiply total cost for one week by 4; if single, divide total cost by 2.)	$________
Eating out	________
Household items (miscellaneous items)	________
Transportation (includes gas, oil, etc.)	________
Clothing	________
Medical care	________
Personal items (soaps, shampoos, etc.)	________
Gifts (birthdays, holidays, etc.)	________
Recreation	________
Miscellaneous (hobbies, etc.)	________
TOTAL FLEXIBLE EXPENSES	________
Add to this amount your total fixed expenses	+ ________
TOTAL EXPENSES	$________

NOTE: Your net income amount and your total expenses must be equal. Reevaluate your budget items until they are.

GROSS INCOME	$ ______	
Minus taxes and deductions	______	
NET INCOME		$ ______
ESTIMATED EXPENSES		
Flexible Expenses		
Food	$ ______	
Eating out	______	
Household	______	
Transportation	______	
Clothing	______	
Medical care	______	
Personal items	______	
Gifts	______	
Recreation	______	
Miscellaneous	______	
Total Flexible Expenses		$ ______
Fixed Expenses:		
Rent	$ ______	
Utilities	______	
Telephone	______	
Furnishings	______	
Car payments	______	
Car insurance	______	
Life insurance	______	
Savings	______	
Funds for short-term goal	______	
Emergency	______	
Total Fixed Expenses		$ ______
TOTAL EXPENSES		$ ______
DIFFERENCE BETWEEN INCOME AND EXPENSES		$ ______

EXHIBIT E–4
Calculating Your Monthly Budget

analyze your budget to see which categories are seriously out of line with reality.

It's also a good idea to rethink the budget process itself every few months. With time, you and/or the spending unit can predict relatively accurately what size each budget category should be. Then the decision makers can determine for each category whether the maximum amount of satisfaction is being obtained from the budgeted income. If it isn't, perhaps one category should be expanded while one or more is contracted. Thus, a budget will be continuously updated to reflect the spending unit's understanding of the level of satisfaction it is receiving from each budget category. Additionally, family changes will cause changes in budget categories. For instance, when children grow up, expenditure patterns change for the family unit, and when a homemaker goes to work, other expenditure patterns change.

SUMMARY

1. Budget making requires keeping records, determining fixed and flexible expenses, balancing fixed plus flexible expenses with available income, and, finally, reorganizing and redetermining priorities if there is a budget surplus or deficit.
2. A cash forecast for each month can be estimated and then compared with what actually happened after the fact. Any difference signals excessive spending and must be made up.
3. Record keeping is essential to effective budgeting. Perhaps the easiest way to keep records is to use a checking account and save the canceled checks.

QUESTIONS FOR THOUGHT AND DISCUSSION

1. Do you feel that a budget is worthwhile for young people? When would it not be worthwhile?
2. Does making a cash forecast seem too time-consuming for you?
3. What individuals would be most likely to benefit from making detailed budgets?
4. Is it possible to live your entire life without worrying about meeting your budget?

THINGS TO DO

1. Write down a goals statement that will tell you where you want to go.
2. Make out an income statement.
3. Make out a budget.

SELECTED READINGS

Burkett, Larry. *The Financial Planning Workbook*. New York: The Moody Press, 1982.
Daly, M. "Family Money Management." See issues of *Better Homes & Gardens.*
"A Guide to Budgeting for the Family." U.S. Department of Agriculture, *Home and Garden Bulletin,* No. 108. Washington, D.C.: U.S. Government Printing Office, 1980.
Priest, Alice. *The Family Budget Book*. Boston: Lorenz Press, 1978.

CHAPTER
THE HIGH COST OF LIVING

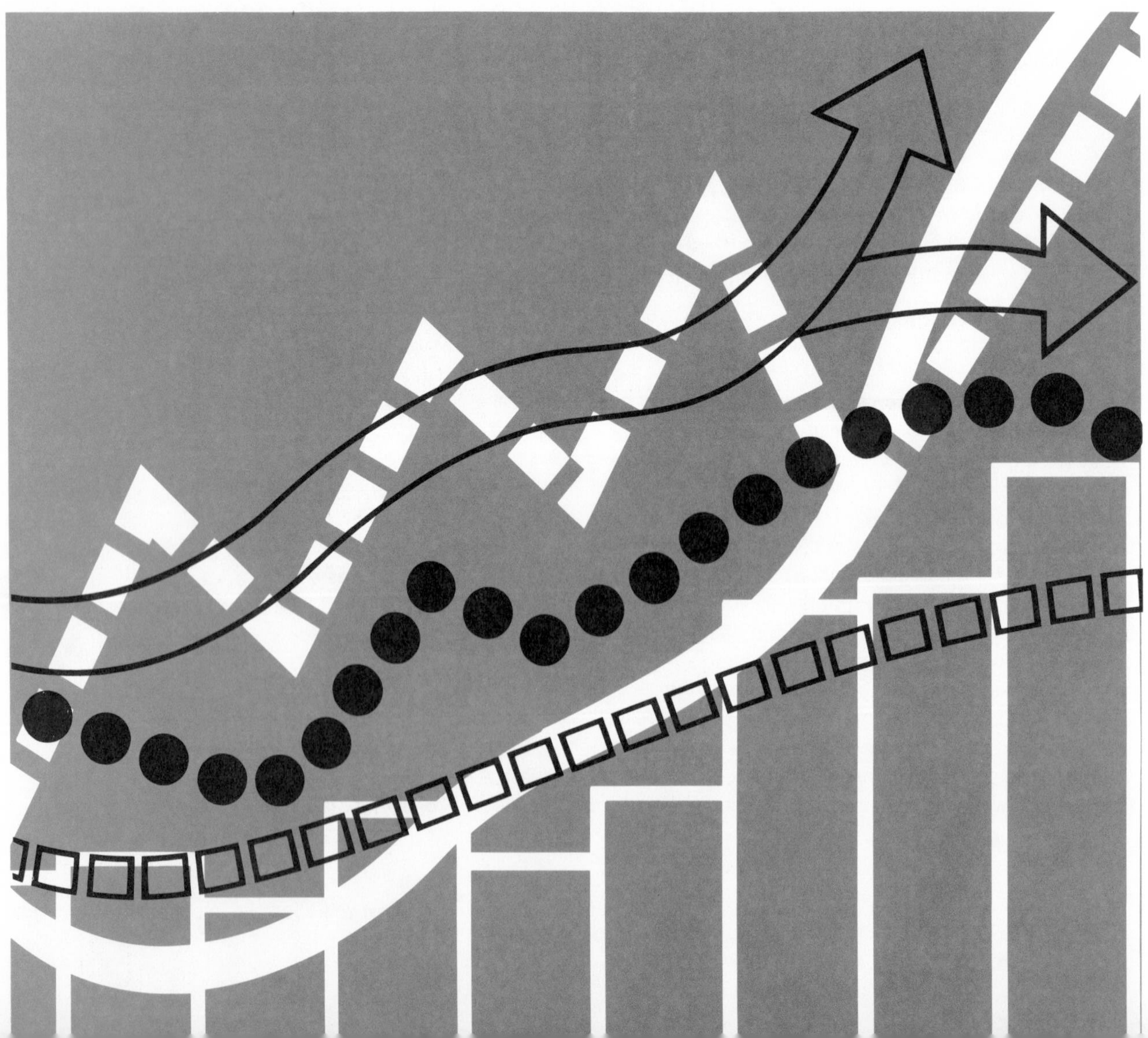

We've all been aware—often painfully so—of the constant increase in the cost of living in the United States. Rising prices now seem as inevitable as death and taxes. We are continually reminded that today's dollar is worth only 18 percent of 1939's dollar.

CHAPTER PREVIEW

- What has been the history of prices in the United States?
- How does inflation in the United States compare to that in the rest of the world?
- Does inflation hurt everybody equally?
- Why is it important to look at *relative* prices?
- What has happened to income as prices have risen?
- What is the effect of inflation on interest rates?
- How does inflation affect your income taxes?

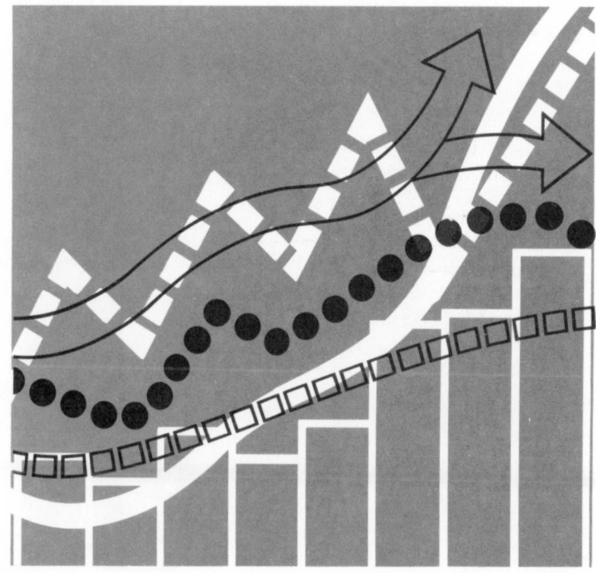

We've all been aware—often painfully so—of the constant increase in the cost of living in the United States. Rising prices now seem as inevitable as death and taxes. We are continually reminded by newspaper and magazine articles that today's dollar is worth only 18 percent of 1939's dollar. Although prices have not always risen at such rapid annual rates, they have been rising at a compounded rate of 1 percent per year from 1867 to the 1980s. The pace of **inflation** (defined as a *sustained* rise in the weighted average of all prices), however, has not been even.

INFLATION
A sustained rise in the weighted average of all prices.

HISTORY OF PRICES

The erratic behavior of prices is shown in Exhibit 9–1. After shooting up at a rate of 25 percent per year during and after the Civil War, the price index *fell* at the rate of 5.4 percent from 1867 to 1879. That is equivalent to a halving of the price level in less than fifteen years. Strangely enough, during those

EXHIBIT 9–1
History of Prices in the United States, 1770–1981

Here we see the wholesale price index for the past two centuries. Prices have not always been rising, even though the experience of the past few years might lead us to that conclusion. Almost every war in our history has been associated with a rise in the wholesale price index. (The figure for 1983 is an estimate.)

SOURCE: U.S. Department of Commerce.

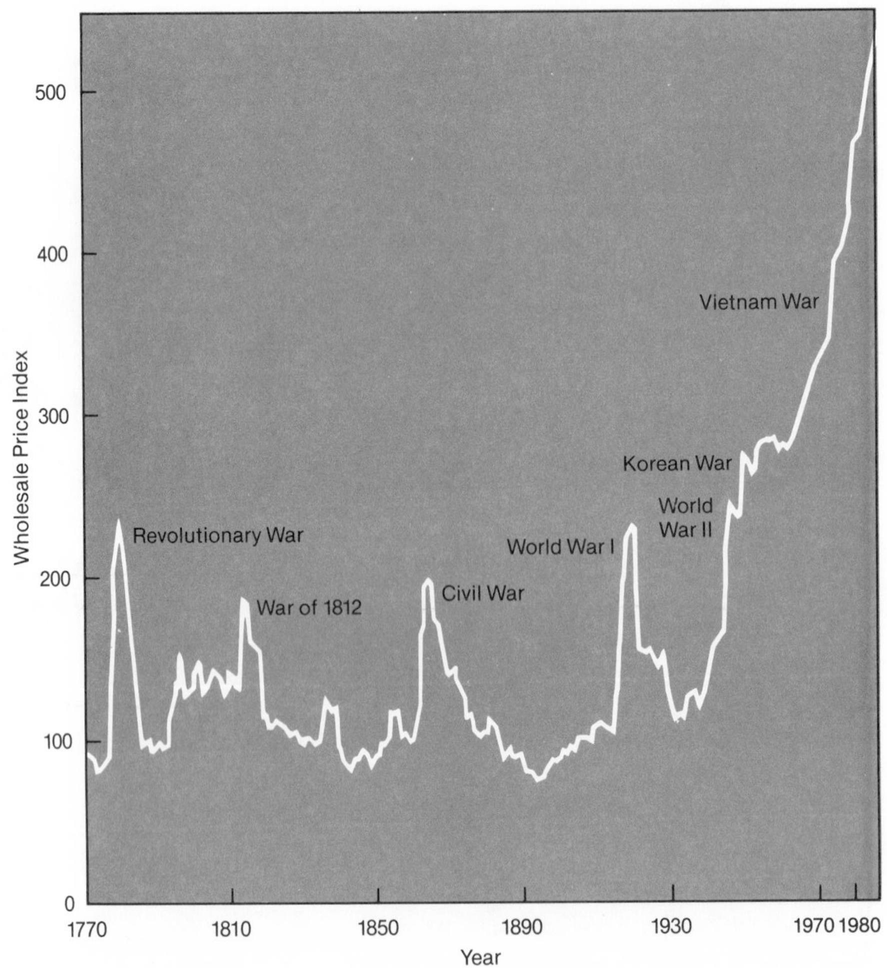

years of falling prices, farmers and businesspersons cried out for higher prices—inflation and "greenbackism," as higher prices were later called. Farmers thought that inflation would cause the prices of their products to rise faster than the prices of the products they bought. Politicians apparently didn't listen very well, however, for prices continued to fall, averaging a decline of 1 percent per year from 1879 to 1897. Prices then rose 6 percent per year until World War I. For several years after the war, prices fell drastically and then remained fairly stable until the Great Depression, which started in 1929. Wholesale prices dropped at an average annual rate of 8 percent from the stock market crash until Roosevelt declared a "banking holiday" in March 1933. Roosevelt's attempts to raise prices were successful, and there was general inflation until 1937. Then prices leveled off until the beginning of World War II.

The rate of price rises during World War II was lower than the rates of price increases during both the Civil War and World War I. The wholesale price index rose 118 percent from August 1939 through August 1948—about 9 percent per year. From 1948 until the mid-1960s, prices remained quite stable except for a jump during the Korean War at the beginning of the 1950s. Since the Vietnam involvement around 1965, inflation has accelerated.

EXHIBIT 9–2
Cost of an Average House If 8 Percent Annual Inflation Continues for Ten Years

YEAR	COST OF HOUSE
1984	$ 78,000
1985	84,240
1986	90,979
1987	98,258
1988	106,118
1989	114,608
1990	123,776
1991	133,678
1992	144,372
1993	155,922
1994	168,396

WHAT INFLATION MEANS TO YOU

Inflation is defined as a rise in the weighted average of all prices year in and year out. It also can be defined as the reduction in the purchasing power of the dollars that you have and earn. To see where inflation will lead prices in the future, look at Exhibit 9–2, which shows what the price of an average house might be in ten years. If it is $78,000 in 1984 and the rate of inflation is 8 percent a year, by 1994 the average American family will have to come up with more than $168,000 for that dwelling.

When comparing salaries in the past with salaries today, it is important to take account of inflation. Exhibit 9–3 shows how inflation erodes a paycheck; if take-home pay in 1950 was $10,000, in 1983 it would have to be $43,518 just to stay even.

INFLATION IN OTHER COUNTRIES

The United States is not alone in its history of rising prices. Inflation seems to be a worldwide problem, as can be seen in Exhibit 9–4. In fact, our rate of inflation is minor compared to rates in many other countries. Some countries have had periods of **hyperinflation** that make our wartime episodes look like ripples in the monetary ocean. In 1939, Hungary's price index was set at 100; by January 1946, it was almost 5,500,000. A half year later, it was 20,000,000,000,000, or 2×10^{13}! This means that a commodity with a 1939 price tag of 100 forints would have cost 5,500,000 forints in January 1946; by August of the same year, it would have cost 20,000,000,000,000 forints. Imagine having to push a wheelbarrow full of money to the store just to buy a loaf of bread.

HYPERINFLATION
An inflation that has gotten out of hand. The United States experienced hyperinflation in the South during the Civil War. Germany experienced hyperinflation after World War I; it took wheelbarrows full of German marks to buy a loaf of bread.

There are as many theories of inflation as there are people who want to express their opinions about the subject.

THEORIES ABOUT THE CAUSES OF INFLATION

Rather than talk about the causes of inflation, we should discuss the *theories* of the causes of inflation. There is no one generally accepted cause of inflation but, rather, only models of how inflation occurs in this economy and elsewhere.

There are as many theories of inflation as there are people who want to express their opinions about the subject. Often we hear that inflation occurs because of rising prices. That is clearly not a theory of inflation but mere tautology or truism. Having defined inflation as a sustained rise in the weighted average of all prices, it is definitely true that we will have rising prices in a time of inflation. The informed consumer won't fall into the trap of accepting a restated definition as an explanation for inflation.

Another attempt to explain inflation focuses on components of the price index that are rising fastest and estimates what the index would be if the items were omitted. As expected, the index rises at a lower rate. Sometimes the lower rate is called the *underlying rate of inflation*. Sometimes the argument focuses on special circumstances that cause some prices to rise at a high rate and on the belief that the measurement of the high-rising prices is defective.

The opposite approach—of removing the least rapidly rising prices from the index is, however—usually ignored. In addition, the special-circumstances argument is not applied to prices that rise slowly; it also ignores the question of what would have happened to other prices if some had not risen as quickly. For example, if food and energy prices had not risen so rapidly, would other prices have risen faster because money would have been spent on those other items instead?

RELATIVE PRICES The price of something relative to the price of other things. For example, if the price of apples increases 50 percent and the price of oranges increases 100 percent, then even though apples may have a higher absolute price, they have a lower relative price with respect to oranges.

The key point is the distinction between absolute and **relative prices.** Inflation is a rise in the weighted average of *all* prices and is not explained by relative price movements. Some prices rise faster than the average and some rise slower than the average, reflecting *relative* price changes. Arguments that focus on a subset of prices—for example, on some rapidly rising prices—do not explain the phenomenon of inflation. In fact, the effect of some rapidly rising prices relative to the average of all prices could be offset by other prices that are falling. On balance, the *relative* price change could leave the average level of all prices unchanged or lower rather than higher.

Here we will explain the three major theories of inflation: (1) demand pulls prices up—*demand-pull inflation;* (2) input costs push up the price of final products—*cost-push inflation;* and (3) too many dollars chase too few goods—a *monetary theory of inflation*.

Demand-Pull Theory of Inflation

When total demand in the economy is rising while the available supply of goods is limited, demand-pull inflation occurs. Goods and services may be in "short" supply, either because the economy is being fully utilized or because the economy cannot grow fast enough to meet the growing economywide demand. As the result of either, the general level of prices rises.

Cost-Push Inflation

The cost-push inflation theory of price increases has gained credence. It attempts to explain why prices rise when the economy is *not* at full employment.

The cost-push inflation theory apparently explains both "creeping" inflation and the inflation that the United States experienced during its 1969–70 and 1973–75 recessions. Three different factors are involved in the cost-push inflation theory: union power, big business monopoly power, and higher raw materials prices.

UNION POWER. Many people feel that unions are responsible for inflation. Their reasoning is as follows. Unions decide to demand a wage hike that is not warranted by increases in their productivity. Because the unions are so powerful, employers must give in to their demands for higher wages. When the employers have to pay these higher wages, their costs are higher. To maintain their usual profit margin, these businesspeople raise their prices. This type of cost-push inflation seemingly can occur even when there is no excess demand for goods and even when the economy is operating below capacity at under-full employment. The union-power argument rests on the unions having monopolistic market power in their labor markets. In other words, it is argued that some unions are so strong that they can impose wage increases on employers even when those wage increases are not consistent with increases in the productivity of their labor.

BIG BUSINESS MONOPOLY POWER. The other variant of the cost-push theory is that inflation occurs when the monopoly power of big business allows them to push up prices. Powerful corporations are alleged to be able to raise their prices whenever they want to increase their profits. Each time these corporations raise prices to increase their profits, the cost of living goes up. Workers demand higher wages to make up for the loss in their standard of living, thereby giving the corporations an excuse to raise prices again, and so goes a vicious cycle of price-wage increases.

RAW-MATERIALS COST-PUSH INFLATION. Since the beginning of increasingly high prices for all forms of energy, a relatively new type of cost-push inflation has

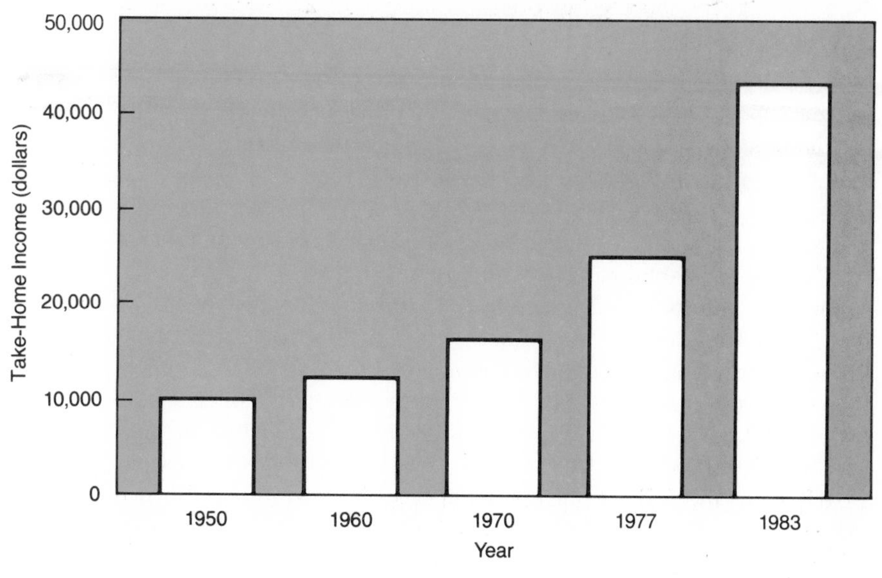

EXHIBIT 9–3
The Erosion by Inflation: What You Need to Stay Even

EXHIBIT 9–4
World Rates of Inflation, 1981 and 1982

COUNTRY	1981	1982
Japan	4.3%	1.8%
Netherlands	7.2%	4.3%
Austria	6.4%	4.7%
West Germany	6.3%	4.6%
Britain	12.0%	5.4%
United States	8.9%	3.9%
Industrial nations	9.3%	6.1%*
Canada	12.1%	9.3%
Belgium	8.2%	8.1%
Sweden	9.2%	9.6%
Denmark	12.2%	9.0%
Spain	14.4%	14.0%
Italy	16.4%	16.4%
France	14.0%	9.7%

*From November to November.

SOURCES: International Monetary Fund, Organization for Economic Cooperation and Development.

been suggested. It is termed raw-materials cost-push inflation because the costs of raw materials seem to keep rising. Coal is more expensive, so is petroleum, so is natural gas, and so are a lot of other inputs into basic production processes.

Whether it be union power, big business monopoly power, or higher raw materials prices, the resultant increased cost of production pushes prices up—hence, the term cost-push inflation. One solution offered as a way to stop, or at least slow down, cost-push inflation is wage and price controls. In analyzing these controls later, we will see that they have not done much to reduce the inflation that plagues the economy.

A Monetary Theory of Inflation

A third theory of inflation is that it is a monetary phenomenon. This theory indicates that the growth of the money supply in circulation exerts a strong influence on total spending in the economy. In simplified form, the monetary theory is this: When individuals, taken together, find that they are holding cash balances—dollars plus any checking-type account balances—that are greater than desired, these individuals, together, will spend the excess cash balances on goods, services, and financial assets, hence bidding up the prices of these items.

According to the monetary view of inflation, the only way for higher prices to persist—a sustained rise in the weighted average of all prices—is for the money supply in circulation to grow faster than the real sector of the economy. Those who hold this view of inflation believe that, in the long run, it is impossible to have inflation if the rate of growth of the money supply is held constant at some rate that is consistent with no inflation.

WHO IS HURT BY INFLATION?

Do we necessarily suffer because of inflation, and, if so, is the suffering "equitably" distributed? Although we have observed that falling prices (deflation) generally bring misery, inflation certainly doesn't always mean prosperity. Even if it did, not everyone would benefit. When prices rise unexpectedly or more than expected, those persons who have given credit to others are repaid in "cheaper" dollars—that is, dollars that cannot buy as much as before. When the price level goes up unexpectedly, any obligation fixed in terms of **nominal dollars** will cause creditors to lose and debtors to gain. The moral, of course, might be to borrow all you can if you expect an inflation that nobody else expects.

NOMINAL DOLLARS
Dollars measured by their face value and not by their purchasing power.

If everyone anticipates rising prices, the cost of borrowing (interest rate) will rise. People who lend money will demand higher interest rates as compensation. They know that if prices rise, the money they are repaid will buy less than when they lent it. If a person lends $12,500 (enough money to buy a Buick Riviera) when prices are rising, by the time that person is repaid $12,500 may only buy a used Malibu. Debtors anticipating this decreased purchasing power will pay the higher interest rate. If you know that prices will rise 8 percent by the end of next year, you won't lend money unless you are compensated for the loss in purchasing power. You will charge 8 percent more than if you had expected no inflation: instead of 3 or 4 percent interest, you will demand 11 or 12 percent.

Pocket Money

All of us, in some sense, are bondholders because we carry cash with us. A dollar bill is basically a noninterest-bearing bond from the government. Its expiration date is infinity, and it pays zero cents a year in interest. Anyone holding cash during an inflation loses part of his or her real (as opposed to nominal) wealth when prices rise. The real value of your cash is what it can be traded for—what it can buy. When the price level goes up, the same amount of cash no longer buys as much. If you kept an average checking account balance (which is considered as cash) of $100 in 1982, its purchasing power would have fallen approximately 5 percent by the end of the year.

Inflation, therefore, causes people to lose purchasing power in proportion to the amount of cash—currency and checking account balances—they generally keep on hand. The only way to avoid this loss of purchasing power is to keep no cash balances. But life without cash can be very inconvenient.

Inflation causes people to lose purchasing power in proportion to the amount of cash—currency and checking account balances—they generally keep on hand.

RISING PRICES AND YOU—CONSTRUCTING A PRICE INDEX

All this information about inflation may be interesting, but, of course, what you want to know is how inflation affects you. You know that prices are rising, for that is the definition of inflation. How much prices are rising is more specifically applicable to decisions you make. In order to find out what is happening to the average of all prices in the United States, you can consult the **Consumer Price Index (CPI)**.

CONSUMER PRICE INDEX (CPI) A price index based on a "fixed representative market basket" of about 400 goods and services purchased by about 80 percent of the population.

The CPI is an index of the prices of a fixed representative market basket of goods and services in eighty-five urban areas. The index represents the prices of everything people buy for day-to-day living—food, clothing, shelter, automobiles, homes, home furnishings, household supplies, medical care, recreational goods, legal services, hair care, rent, repair costs, transportation fares, public utility rates, and so on. All taxes, such as sales, excise, and real estate, that are directly associated with the purchase and ownership of an item are included in the price. Income taxes and other taxes such as Social Security taxes are excluded. Statisticians attempt to keep the quantity and quality of these items unchanged between major revisions of the index so that only price changes are measured.[1] Prices are collected from over 18,000 tenants, 24,000 retail establishments, and 18,000 housing units for property taxes in eighty-five urban areas throughout the country.

For a number of years, the Consumer Price Index was based on a 1960–61 survey of a market basket of goods and services purchased by individuals. More recently, it has reflected spending patterns based on a 1972–73 survey. Changes in individual spending patterns were taken into account in revising the CPI. For example, the revised Consumer Price Index includes an "Index for Urban Wage Earners and Clerical Workers" that represents the items typically purchased and prices typically paid by about 40 percent of the population. The Bureau of Labor Statistics (BLS) also publishes an "Index for All Urban Consumers" that reflects the buying habits of all urban households. It reflects the buying habits of 80 percent of the population, including professional workers, the self-employed, wage earners and clerical workers, the poor, the

1. Although quality changes do occur between major revisions of the index, these changes are difficult to take into account.

unemployed, and retired persons. The Bureau of Labor Statistics began publishing indexes for both population groups in 1978. Before 1978, the Consumer Price Index covered only the spending patterns of urban wage earners and clerical workers.

Annualizing Monthly Data

Every month, the U.S. Department of Labor's Bureau of Labor Statistics releases information on the Consumer Price Index that can be reported in two different ways—on a monthly basis or on an annualized basis. Thus, the Bureau of Labor Statistics may state that prices for the previous month rose 1.1 percent or that prices rose at an *annualized rate* of 13.2 percent (12 × 1.1 percent). Occasionally, the annualized rate is mistakenly reported as the monthly rate, in which case the uninformed consumer might erroneously think that last month's prices rose 13.2 percent. Clearly, they didn't. They rose only 1.1 percent.

THE PRODUCER PRICE INDEXES

The Producer Price Index (formerly the Wholesale Price Index) is similar to the CPI except that it measures changes in the average prices of goods sold in primary markets by producers of commodities in all stages of processing. At present, it includes price quotations for about 2,800 items from producers and manufacturers. No services are included in the Producer Price Index (PPI) market basket.

The Producer Price Indexes are organized into three major categories or sectors: (1) *stage of processing*—products are differentiated by class of buyer and degree of fabrication—that is, finished goods, intermediate (semifinished) goods, and crude goods; (2) *type of commodity*—products are distinguished by similarity of end-use or material composition; and (3) *industry sector*—products are also set apart by producing industry as defined in the Standard Industrial Classification system.[2]

PROBLEMS AND ACCURACY OF VARIOUS PRICE INDEXES

Obviously, no price index, however constructed, can be completely accurate.[3] The consumer should be alert to particular problems that occur with these indexes in order to interpret correctly the government's publication of these data. For example, the BLS constantly must point out that changes in the CPI do not represent changes in maintaining a standard of living. The BLS never

2. U.S. Department of Labor, Bureau of Labor Statistics, *Escalation and Producer Price Indexes: A Guide for Contracting Parties,* Report 570. Washington, D.C.: U.S. Government Printing Office, September 1979.

3. For a general discussion of the effects of inflation on statistics, see also Geoffrey Moore, "Inflation and Statistics," *Contemporary Economic Problems 1980*. Washington, D.C.: American Enterprise Institute, pp. 167–92.

states that the changes in the CPI represent changes in the cost of living. If the CPI is not a gauge of current living costs, what is it? It is simply a measure of the change in prices of a fixed representative market basket of goods and services purchased by a typical urban worker's family in 1972 and 1973.

Consumers, however, do not actually continue to purchase a given set of products in fixed quantities, because prices, tastes, and incomes change over time. Since 1972 and 1973, consumers have reacted to changes in the relative prices of housing, energy, and food by purchasing proportionately smaller amounts of those products. Therefore, too much weight is given to those goods whose prices have risen since the base year relative to other goods. Such a problem exists with all price indexes using base-year quantities. But because the cost to the Department of Labor of constructing a price index every year with current-year quantities purchased would be astronomical, we can't expect the government to revise its Consumer Price Index yearly to reflect the different proportions of goods purchased by the typical urban household. Perhaps some gross changes could be accounted for, however. For example, the CPI assumes that consumers spend the same proportion of their incomes on energy, even though the price rise of energy has substantially altered the consumer's typical expenditure and use patterns since the 1973 survey.

Consumers do not actually continue to purchase a given set of products in fixed quantities, because prices, tastes, and incomes change over time.

Some Problems with the Producer Price Index

The Producer Price Index reflects some double counting. By counting some prices over and over again, it gives them more weight than they deserve. For example, a change in the price of raw cotton will appear first as a crude material, will again be reflected in the price of cloth, and will then be reflected in the price of clothing. This pyramiding overemphasizes crude material price changes and can cause the PPI to behave quite erratically, especially when the prices of basic materials are changing. Thus, the informed consumer will know not to overemphasize abrupt changes in the PPI that are due to relatively modest changes in prices of raw material.

Some prices reported in the PPI reflect list rather than transactions prices. Because list prices do not reflect the actual prices at which exchanges occur, they do not reflect the smoother transition that may occur as prices move from old to new list prices. Instead, the prices shown in the index may be overly slow to show change, and, when they are changed, the change may appear very abrupt.

Biases Imparted to All Indexes

Biases may be imparted to all price indexes because of improper accounting for changes in quality. For example, at the same nominal price a good is actually cheaper if its quality has been improved. Alternatively, at the same nominal price a good is actually more expensive if its quality has fallen. It is difficult for government statisticians to take quality into account.

It is also difficult for government statisticians to take into account the introduction of new products, such as personal home computers, color televisions, and other consumer products that may not have been widely marketed when the original market was surveyed during the base year.

In order to make rational decisions you should know how fast the price of one product has risen relative to the price of another product.

HOW TO INTERPRET THE CONSUMER PRICE INDEX

The current Consumer Price Index has a base year of 1967. That means that, in 1967, the base was 100. If you hear that the Consumer Price Index is, for example, 300, that means that, since 1967, the CPI has increased threefold. The representative market basket of goods in 1967 would cost 300 percent more if the price index today were 300.

Typically, you will hear about changes in the Consumer Price Index. If the index is, say, 300 on December 31 this year and it hits 330 on December 31 of next year, then the CPI has increased 10 percent. That means that the fixed representative market basket of goods will cost the consumer 10 percent more, on average, one year hence.

CALCULATING YOUR OWN CPI

The Consumer Price Index that accurately reflects changes in the costs of things you buy may be different from the one announced in the news every month. There are two reasons why your CPI may differ from the national average.

1. You may live in a city that has experienced a higher or lower price rise than the national average. For example, at the beginning of this decade, the national average increase in the CPI was 14.7 percent for all U.S. cities. If you lived in New York, it was only 11.9 percent, but if you lived in Los Angeles, it was 17.7 percent and in Dallas-Fort Worth, 19.1 percent.
2. The proportion of your budget that goes to the various major categories used in computing the CPI may be different than the fixed representative market basket of goods proportions that the Department of Labor uses.

Relative Prices

The Consumer Price Index tells you what is happening to an average of all prices. In order to make rational buying decisions, however, you should know how fast the price of one product has risen relative to the price of another product. For example, has the price of washing machines gone up faster than the price of TV sets? If the answer is yes, then the relative price of washing machines has risen and the relative price of TV sets has fallen (even though both prices, in dollar terms, may have risen over a one-, two-, or three-year period, for example).

Another way of presenting the concept of relative price is to discuss prices in terms of opportunity cost (the value of what you give up to purchase an item). Suppose you're trying to decide whether to buy a new washing machine or a new refrigerator this year. Suppose also that last year washing machines and refrigerators were exactly the same price. This year, the economy has experienced a tremendous inflation. The price of washing machines has risen 100 percent. Outrageous, you say. But what if the price of refrigerators went up 500 percent? Then the opportunity cost of buying a washing machine has dramatically fallen. Last year, buying one washing machine meant giving up one refrigerator. This year, it means giving up only one-fifth of a refrigerator.

EXHIBIT 9–5
Formula For Calculating Your Own Consumer Price Index

1. First, check your records to determine your own spending for each of the seven major CPI categories.
2. To assign personal "weights" to each item, divide each category by your total CPI spending (column B).
3. Next, call your nearest office of Bureau of Labor Statistics and ask for your city's CPI. Obtain the percentage change from the same month a year earlier for all items and for each of the seven major categories.
4. Multiply each of your own weights by the official CPI change in that category (column C). Place result in column D.
5. Add all items in column D to get your total CPI change.
6. Compare this figure with the "all items" change obtained from the BLS.

CATEGORIES	(A) AMOUNT SPENT	(B) (A) DIVIDED BY TOTAL CPI SPENDING		(C) CPI FACTOR		(D)
Food & beverages	$ ______	______	×	______	=	______
All housing (includes rent; mortgage, plus interest; property taxes; insurance; repairs & maintenance; furnishings; operations; fuel & utilities)	______	______	×	______	=	______
Clothing (purchase & care)	______	______	×	______	=	______
Medical care	______	______	×	______	=	______
Transportation (includes car ownership, operation & maintenance, public transportation)	______	______	×	______	=	______
Entertainment	______	______	×	______	=	______
All other spending	______	______	×	______	=	______
ADD ITEMS TO OBTAIN TOTAL CPI SPENDING	$ ______					______ % TOTAL (column D)

Distinguishing between Nominal and Relative Prices

When we refer to the relative price of any item, we stress the word *relative*. What is important is how expensive one good or service is compared with, or relative to, another. The relative price of apples, for example, can be compared with the price of oranges. In deciding what and how much to buy, you generally make your decision about one good or service based on its price, compared with the price of an alternative good or service.

Let's look at a common situation today in which the prices of alternative goods seem to be rising. Here are the prices given for eight-track stereo cartridges and four-track stereo cassettes in two years:

	Eight-Track Stereo Cartridge	Four-Track Stereo Cassette	Ratio Of Prices
Year One	$ 5.00	$5.00	1:1
Year Two	$10.00	$7.50	1:3/4

200

What has happened to the prices from year one to year two? The prices of both cartridges and cassettes have risen, but the relative price has changed.

In year one, cartridges and cassettes cost the same amount, but in year two the price of cartridges relative to cassettes has risen. Or, looked at the other way around, the price of cassettes relative to cartridges has decreased. In year one, the relative price of cartridges compared with cassettes was $5/$5, or 1:1. But in year two the relative price of cartridges compared with cassettes was $10/$7.50, or 1:3/4. The relative price of cassettes has fallen.

Now you can see why it is important to compare relative prices, particularly in an economy as prone to inflation as ours is today. Just because the price of a good or service rises doesn't mean it's a poor buy. You must find out whether the price of what you are interested in has risen faster or slower than the prices of other goods you wish to purchase. In other words, *you have to look at relative prices.*

AND INCOME, TOO

So far, our argument has been academic. If all prices increased but your wages or income remained the same, you really would be in trouble. Fortunately, however, annual income increases generally match or exceed price rises.

Exhibit 9–6 shows the average per capita disposable income in the United States; it has been rising at 1.5 percent a year for the last 150 years. Thus, even though prices have risen, most of us actually are better off at the end of the year because our wages or total incomes have risen even more. You may be convinced that rising prices are your undoing, but you must take stock of what your real standard of living is. If, for example, your income rose 7 percent and prices rose only 5 percent, your real standard of living has risen 2 percent, in spite of inflation. Only those whose income increases do not match or exceed the rate of inflation are truly worse off. Historically, few incomes have failed to keep up with inflation. Those who generally suffer are people on fixed incomes.

Historically, few incomes have failed to keep up with inflation. Those who generally suffer are people on fixed incomes.

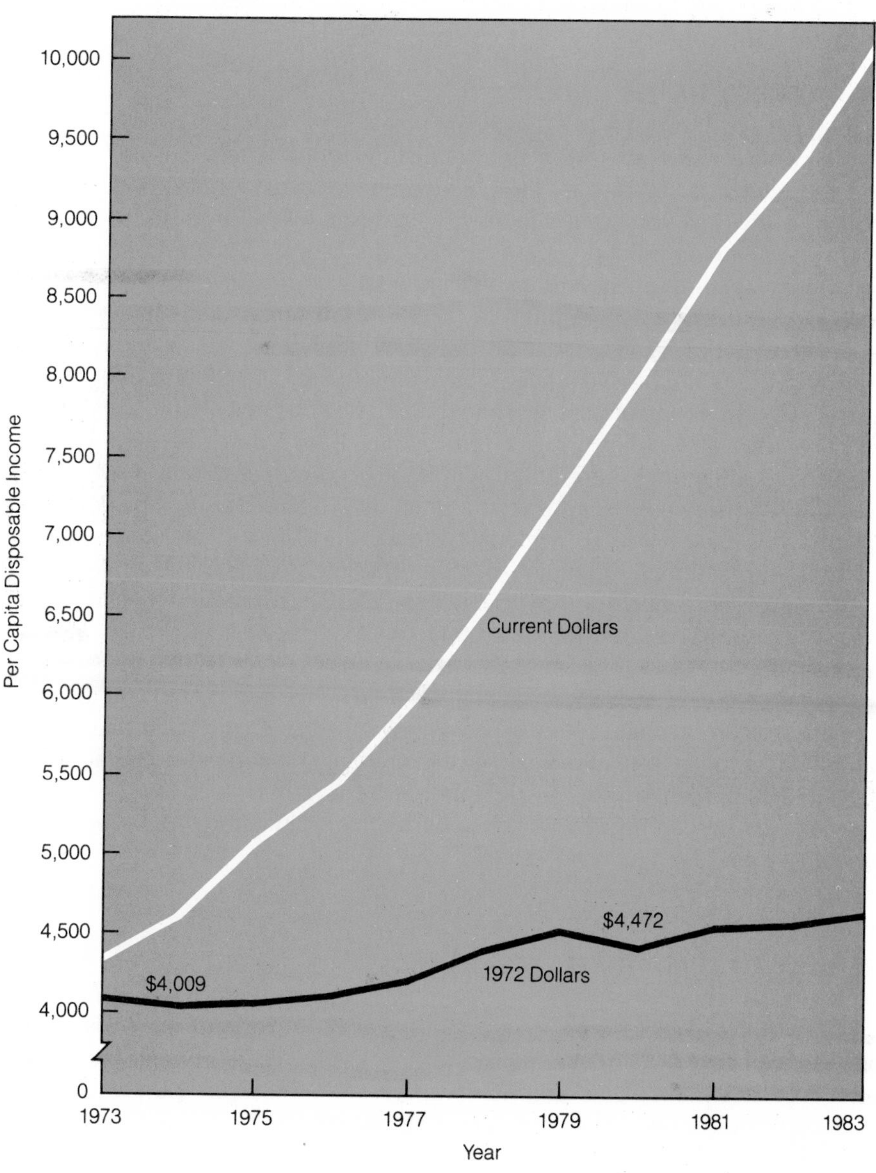

EXHIBIT 9–6
Per Capita Disposable Income, With and Without Correcting for Inflation

The colored line shows per capita disposable income without correcting for inflation. It has been going up steadily for the last decade. If we correct for inflation, however, we see that the rise is not so dramatic. In fact, correcting for inflation, per capita disposable income fell in 1974 and again in 1980, albeit only slightly in both years.

Every time you borrow money, you must pay a price for the use of that money. Whenever inflation is anticipated, creditors wish to be compensated for the cheapening of the dollars that they will be repaid.

INFLATIONARY PREMIUM An amount added to the cost of obtaining a loan to take account of the effects of inflation. If, for example, prices are rising at 5 percent a year, a dollar loaned out today will have a value of only ninety-five cents when it is received a year from now. The person who loaned that dollar will require an inflationary premium of 5 percent to take account of the decreased value of the dollar to be paid back.

ANTICIPATING INFLATION

To avoid being hurt by inflation, we must anticipate it, and we generally anticipate inflation by looking at the behavior of past prices. If we think that inflation will continue, we will act accordingly. If we have the power, we will demand higher salaries to take account of the inflation; we will realize that goods and services are going to cost more in the future; and we won't be satisfied, for example, with maintaining current levels of insurance or retirement benefits, because we know that the real value of those items will decline because of rising prices.

Remember, the real value of anything is its implicit purchasing power. As prices rise, the real value of a $50,000 insurance policy falls because $50,000 buys less and less every year.

INTEREST RATES

When we talk about interest rates, we must mention the relationship between market interest rates—that is, the ones you have to pay—and the rate of inflation. Every time you borrow money, you must pay a price for the use of that money. Whenever inflation is anticipated, creditors wish to be compensated for the cheapening of the dollars that they will be repaid. That is, creditors tack on an **inflationary premium** to take account of the depreciation in the dollars they will get back, for those dollars will buy less. For example, if you borrow $1,000 and one year later repay your creditor $1,000 plus interest and there has been no inflation at all, then the purchasing power of the principal—$1,000—is exactly what it was a year before. If, however, there has been a 10 percent inflation, your creditor will be able to purchase only $900 worth of goods and services because of that inflation: The purchasing power of that $1,000 will have fallen 10 percent. No one will want to loan money unless there is an inflationary premium in addition to the normal interest rate.

Moreover, debtors are willing to pay that inflationary premium because they know that they are going to repay their debt in depreciated dollars. If you subtract the anticipated rate of inflation from the interest rate you are charged for a loan, you get the real rate of interest—that is, the real cost to you in terms of what you are giving up in purchasing power to have command over goods and services today instead of waiting. If the rate of inflation in the United States rose to 100 percent a year, you would not be surprised, then, to see interest rates of 105 percent, if people thought that rate of inflation would remain in effect forever.

HOW TO TELL WHERE YOU STAND

How can you tell where you stand with respect to inflation? The easiest way is to try to figure out how many hours it takes you to earn enough income to buy your essentials. For example, compare the number of hours you might have to work in order to pay for a good restaurant meal with how many hours you had to work to pay for the same meal five years ago. Do the same thing for other items you buy. In all probability, most of you will find that it takes fewer hours now to purchase essentials than it did five or ten years ago. What does that mean? It means that your real standard of living may have increased, in spite of inflation. Inflation *per se* is only bad to the extent that we don't anticipate it and/or can't take account of it. Once it is fully anticipated, everything, including wages, interest rates, and investment plans, tends to adjust with it. In Israel, a country with a fairly steady rate of inflation for the last ten years, cost-of-living clauses are added on to just about all contracts. We're also starting to see this in the United States, where, in 1983, an estimated 12 million workers were covered under contracts with cost-of-living clauses.

Your timing of purchases should be based on your expected income, how much you want a good or service, whether you are willing to wait, and so on.

What Is a Cost-of-Living Clause?

A **cost-of-living,** or **escalator, clause** in a wage contract is inserted to guarantee workers that they will not be hurt by unexpected inflation. A clause may state that a worker's wages will increase 3 percent a year plus whatever percentage the Consumer Price Index rose; workers thus covered know that their real standard of living will go up 3 percent a year no matter what happens to overall prices. (Changes in a worker's overall tax that have an effect on his or her standard of living are discussed later in this chapter.) As inflation becomes a more permanent part of American economic society, you probably will see cost-of-living clauses inserted into more contracts. Social Security benefits, as well as federal pension payments, are already tied to the cost of living. Food stamp allotments are also covered by escalator clauses.

COST-OF-LIVING, OR ESCALATOR CLAUSE
A clause, usually in a labor contract, giving automatic wage increases tied in some way to cost-of-living rises in the economy. Cost of living is usually measured by the Consumer Price Index.

IF YOU KNOW PRICES ARE GOING UP, SHOULD YOU BUY NOW?

Many people think that, during inflation, all purchases for houses, stereos, cars, and the like should be made right away because prices will be higher in the future. This belief may or may not be true. If inflation is fully anticipated, your basic decision about when to purchase a house or a car does not depend on inflation itself. Your timing of purchases should be based on your expected income, how much you want a good or service, whether you are willing to wait, and so on. For example, say that you don't want to buy a car until next year, but you know the price will go up 10 percent because that has been the rate of inflation for a long time. If you buy the car this year, you most likely will borrow the money just as you would next year. Thus, for this year you will have to pay an interest rate on whatever you borrow. That interest rate will take account of the expected inflation of 10 percent, so you'll be no better off buying now than waiting until next year and paying a higher price. (Of course, this is an oversimplification. In the short term, lenders cannot always automatically pass on cost increases to borrowers. Thus, market interest rates won't always fully reflect anticipated inflation rates.)

If you think everybody is more or less able to anticipate inflation, you're not any better off buying now than waiting and paying a higher price in the future. And, as we have seen, as prices increase through inflation, income usually increases also and often even more so. In other words, the increased price of those potential purchases may be no greater relative to your income.

EXHIBIT 9–7
The Effect of Inflation on Take-Home Pay

Because of graduated income-tax rates, even families lucky enough to get raises matching the big increase in living costs wound up losing purchasing power. Here we show how a 9.4% inflation outruns a 9.4% pay raise.

	GROSS INCOME	FEDERAL INCOME TAX	EFFECTIVE RATE	AFTER-TAX INCOME IN YEAR 1 DOLLARS
Year 1	$14,000	$1,600	11.4%	$12,400
Year 2	15,316		12.3	12,164
Year 1	20,000	3,010	15.1	16,990
Year 2	21,880	3,506	16.0	16,646
Year 1	30,000	6,020	20.1	23,980
Year 2	32,820	7,035	21.4	23,361

INFLATION AND INCOME TAXES

As we will explain in Chapter 22, the United States has a progressive income tax system; that is, as your income goes up, you have to pay a higher rate of taxation. This has grave implications in a period of inflation. If, for example, all prices and wages went up every year by 20 percent, your real income wouldn't increase, and your level of living would be the same. Nonetheless, you *would* pay higher federal income taxes, because, as your *nominal* dollar income rose due to inflation, you would jump into higher income tax brackets. Hence, inflation can hurt you in that respect even if you anticipate it in all other respects. Exhibit 9–7 illustrates the effect of inflation on take-home pay. The only way out of this box is to persuade the government to express your personal exemption and the size of each tax bracket as a number of dollars times the price index. Say that prices rose by 20 percent and the personal exemption today is $1,000; when prices rise by 20 percent, it should become $1,000 plus $200, or $1,200. Each tax bracket also should be increased by 20 percent.

We also pay increased taxes due to inflation when we sell property that has increased in value. Generally, individuals have to pay taxes on what are called capital gains—the difference between the purchase price and the selling price of a good. For example, if you buy an antique car as an investment this year for $50,000 and sell it next year for $60,000, you have made a capital gain of $10,000, and you must pay income taxes on that gain.[4] But what if, during that period, all prices in the economy rose by 20 percent? Then what was your real capital gain? Since 20 percent of $50,000 is $10,000, the increase in the value of your antique car merely matched the increase in all prices. Nonetheless, Uncle Sam takes a bite out of that capital gain. So, clearly, you're worse off because of inflation.

SUMMARY

1. Prices have not always risen in the United States; in fact, they have fallen during some periods. When prices fall over any period of time, the phenomenon is called deflation.

4. Albeit at a lower rate than on ordinary income (see Chapter 22).

2. Not everyone is hurt equally by inflation, but people who hold cash are hurt by a rise in prices because that cash has a lower purchasing power. Inflation, in a sense, taxes the cash that you hold in the form of currency and checking accounts.
3. Whenever there is an unanticipated inflation, individuals on fixed incomes suffer because the purchasing power of those fixed incomes falls as inflation remains.
4. It is important to distinguish between a general rise in all prices and a specific or relative rise in the price of a commodity you are buying. Even though the prices of all goods have risen recently, some have risen at a slower rate than the average of all prices, as expressed in the Consumer Price Index.
5. If incomes didn't rise along with inflation, we would all be worse off. In the United States, where incomes have, until recently, risen at a slightly faster rate than inflation, the standard of living for Americans also has risen. The key to not getting hurt by inflation is to anticipate it.
6. Whenever inflation is anticipated, nominal interest rates will rise to take account of that inflation. In other words, an inflationary premium will be tacked on to interest rates to take account of the reduced purchasing power of the dollars paid back. In order to figure out the real rate of interest, you must subtract what you expect will be the rate of inflation over the period of the loan.
7. More and more workers are being covered by cost-of-living, or escalator, clauses, which automatically increase nominal salaries whenever there is an increase in the Consumer Price Index. In addition, workers' contracts usually are negotiated to include a real increase in wages of several percent a year.
8. With our progressive system of taxation, inflation can put individuals into higher income-tax brackets even though their *real* incomes haven't gone up. Thus, in real terms, the after-tax income falls and the individual is worse off.

QUESTIONS FOR THOUGHT AND DISCUSSION

1. Why would anybody want inflation?
2. Can inflation be all bad if our paying a higher price for something yields somebody else that higher price as increased income?
3. Do you know what a repressed inflation could be?
4. How many Americans do you think are covered by some form of cost-of-living clauses? (Hint: Social Security payments are now tied to the Consumer Price Index.)
5. Why would anybody sign a long-term contract if it had no cost-of-living clause?
6. Is it important to know the rise in absolute prices—that is, what has happened to the Consumer Price Index—or to find out what has happened to the relative prices of the things you buy?

THINGS TO DO

1. Go to the reference section of your library and look at *The Federal Reserve Bulletin, The Survey of Current Business, Business Conditions Digest,* or *The Monthly Labor Review* to find out what inflation has been during the past year or so. These government documents contain several indicators that give different types of price indexes. Does it matter which one you use?
2. Find out what has happened to the relative price of television sets, washing machines, refrigerators, and automobiles since 1970. (Hint: Find the Consumer

Price Index for all items and divide it into the price index for the four items just listed.)

SELECTED READINGS

Case, John. *Understanding Inflation*. New York: Penguin, 1982.

Friedman, Irving S. *Inflation: A Worldwide Disaster*. New York: Houghton Mifflin, 1980.

Henry, Ed. "Your Own Inflation Rate." *Money*, January 1980, pp. 84–85.

Moffitt, Donald. "Your Own Inflation Rate May Not Be As High As Official Figure: Here's How to Find Out." *The Wall Street Journal*, December 3, 1979, p. 44.

Sennholz, Hans F. *Age of Inflation*. Belmont, Mass.: Western Islands Publishing, 1979.

Wilson, George W. *Inflation: Causes, Consequences, and Cures*. Bloomington: Indiana University Press, 1982.

Consumer ISSUE F

PROTECTING YOURSELF AGAINST INFLATION

GLOSSARY

CASH HOLDINGS—The total amount of currency plus checking account balances you are keeping that are not earning a full market rate of interest.

It's not easy to protect yourself against inflation, but there are some ways you at least can improve the protection you may have already.

COMPARING PRICES WITH A COMPUTERIZED SERVICE

One way to minimize the inroads of inflation on your real purchasing power is to get the best deal possible. In particular, when you're shopping for a standard item and you know exactly the brand and type, you can take advantage of a relatively new computerized service called Comp-U-Card of America, Inc. To use the service, you first check your local stores to obtain information, either by phone or in person, about a particular product you want to buy. Then you call Comp-U-Card's toll-free number and give the operator the exact product description. He or she will scan the company's electronic listings, which are updated daily, and quote the best available price and delivery time. If you choose to buy, you supply to the company your membership and credit-card numbers. Within a few days, the order is confirmed by letter.

As an individual, you can join Comp-U-Card by paying $12; many companies, such as IBM and General Foods, make cards available to employees for fees ranging from $1.50 to $4.00. For more information, you can write directly to Comp-U-Card of America, Inc.; 733 Summer Street; Stamford, Connecticut 06901.

ADJUST YOUR LIFE INSURANCE

Because your life insurance provisions do not take account of inflation, you should adjust your policies occasionally according to the decreased purchasing power implicit in the face value of those policies. Many insurance companies are now issuing "agreements for a cost-of-living benefit," which, for a fee, allow you to increase the value of existing life insurance policies to take account of inflation. Usually the Consumer Price Index is used as a basis. Say, for example, that you have $10,000 worth of term life insurance a year, which costs you $5 per $1,000. Your total payment at the end of the year would be fifty dollars. Now, say that in one year the Consumer Price Index rises 10 percent. You would get a bill from the insurance company for five dollars. If you agreed to pay it, you would have a life insurance policy worth $11,000 in face value. You would still have the same real amount of protection, which would still cost you the same real amount, although the nominal, or dollar, payment would increase 10 percent to take account of the inflation. Whenever possible, you might wish to purchase cost-of-living benefit agreements for your insurance policies. Or, every few years, make sure you take out additional coverage to take account of inflation.

TAKING OUT LOANS

Whenever you take out any type of loan, you obviously benefit if the future inflation rate is higher than that anticipated by the creditor. But don't bet on being able to outsmart creditors; often, the interest rate you pay reflects future rates of inflation. If, on the other hand, you are fairly confident that the rate of inflation today is higher than it will be in the future, you may attempt to get variable-interest-rate loan contracts, particularly if you happen to be taking out a home mortgage. At the very minimum, you would want your mortgage to include a no-penalty-for-prepayment clause so that you could pay it off and refinance it at a lower rate if interest rates do fall. With variable interest rates, no one loses (and no one gains) because of changes in money-market interest rates that reflect changes in the rate of inflation.

RETIREMENT PLANS

Be certain that the retirement plan you take out is not the fixed-sum type, unless that sum is so large that you will be able to live on it even if inflation continues until you retire. Variable annuities for retirement and life insurance policies are generally available. These are, however, usually linked to the stock market, and the stock market, as we will see in Chapter 21, is an imperfect protector against inflation (although in the past it has not done too badly). It would be preferable to have the face value of your retirement annuity plan automatically adjust for inflation; you would, however, have to pay a higher premium each year to compensate for that adjustment. When discussing your pension plan or retirement plan with your employer or insurance agent, be sure that all these aspects are considered so you can select a plan that will protect you from high rates of inflation in the future.

YOUR WAGES

One way to ensure that you don't get caught unprepared by an unexpected rise in prices is to have an escalator clause that adjusts your wages automatically to changes in the cost of living. You may want to bargain for this individually with your employer or get your union representative (if you have one) to have an escalator clause put in the next contract.

TAXES

There is very little you can do to avoid the effects of inflation on raising your effective tax burden. One thing you can do, however, is always to vote for candidates who ask for lower taxes.

MINIMIZING CASH HOLDINGS

Inflation can also be defined as the rate of reduction in the value, or purchasing power, of cash. Therefore, the faster the rate of inflation rises, the more costly it is for you to hold cash in the form of dollar bills and checking account balances that do not pay a full market rate of interest. Hence, one way you can fight against a rising rate of inflation is to reduce your average **cash holdings.** You can do this by keeping excess cash in an interest-earning savings account (which still may not be a good deal but certainly gives you a higher rate than zero). When your money is in some sort of interest-earning account, such as a Super NOW account, you still can write a type of check against that account. Credit unions allow you to write what are called share drafts on your interest-earning credit-union account.

Finally, certain investment funds allow you to write a type of check on your investment account. We will discuss these possibilities later on.

You also can spend more time planning your expenditures so they match the receipts of your income. Thus, you won't have to carry a large amount in your checking account or in your wallet. Of course, the larger your average checking account or currency balance and the greater the rate of inflation, the more important is this consideration.

SOME WAYS TO COMBAT INFLATION THROUGH SMART BUYING

There are, of course, important buying techniques that you can apply at all times. During inflation, these techniques become even more important. You may wish to use some or all of them every time you shop.

1. Compare values. Take time to be sure you are comparing possible alternative ways to satisfy particular needs or desires, even within the same store.

2. Buy for the intended use of the product. Don't, for example, use high-quality wine for cooking purposes or fancy canned tomatoes for stew. Use dried milk solids for cooking rather than fresh milk.

3. Buy basic styles in clothing. To cut down on clothing budgets, stick to basic styles rather than high fashion.

4. Buy store-brand items. Private brands can save you from 10 to 60 percent. This is true not only for food but also for appliances. Some of Montgomery Ward's ranges are actually made by Tappan, and many of their other appliances are made by Westinghouse. J.C. Penney's Penncrest appliances are mostly made by Hotpoint, and their power tools are made by Skil. Some merchants stock private-brand liquor in order to move inventory and avoid cutting prices on their advertised brands.

5. Do not overpay for convenience. The price is usually high per unit of quantity provided when you buy additional convenience in the form of push-button containers, aerosol cans, or buttered frozen vegetables or when you buy at small convenience stores.

6. Buy in larger quantities and store.

7. Take advantage of sales throughout the year. Exhibit F–1 gives you a bargain calendar indicating when stores usually have sales.

January

bedding and towels
stationery
housewares
women's and misses' coats, suits
dryers
irons
baby gift items

February

stormwear
men's wear, especially suits
records, musical instruments
typewriters
cars
pianos
furniture

March

draperies and slipcovers

April

cleanup and fixup items
vacuum cleaners
aprons
outdoor furniture
paint, wallpaper
sleepwear
women's shoes
tires

May

outdoor furniture
garden supplies
paints
home furnishings
housewares
bicycle and car tires
sporting shoes and other sports gear
jewelry
luggage
fashion items
women's boots

June

furniture sales
sporting craft
camera gear
clothing
typewriters
men's slippers

July

refrigerators, freezers
air conditioners
white sales
woodburning stoves
fall fabrics
summer fashions
sporting items
outdoor supplies

August

freezers
fur sales
wool and fabrics

September

summer furniture specials
dishwashers
auto batteries
children's shoes
china, glassware
sporting and hunting goods

October

dryers
ranges
washers
home furnishings, furniture
auto batteries

November

radios, TVs
china, glassware, silverware
linens
jewelry
furniture

December

toys (after Christmas)
baby needs
winter sport and exercise equipment

EXHIBIT F–1
Know When to Shop

YOU CAN'T COMPLETELY PROTECT YOURSELF

The key to protecting yourself against inflation is to realize and anticipate the decline in the purchasing power of money paid to you in the future. If you think through all the exchanges you make or are going to make and include an inflationary factor, you will be ahead of the game. There is no way that you can protect yourself completely against inflation in a world where inflation has different rates that people cannot completely anticipate. If everything were written in real terms—that is, with purchasing power clauses or escalator clauses—then you wouldn't have to worry. But since not everything is—at least not yet—you should make every effort to take advantage of all available protections against inflation, such as cost-of-living benefit additions to your life insurance, cost-of-living escalator clauses in your wage contracts, and checking accounts that permit you to earn interest on unused balances. You may never like inflation, but you can learn to live with it by making sure it doesn't destroy your financial well-being, now or in the future.

SUMMARY

1. It would be advisable to adjust your life, home, and personal effects insurance to take account of inflation.
2. Any retirement plans that you participate in, such as pensions, should be set up to take account of inflation. Therefore, at least part of your retirement income should be in the form of variable annuities that will reflect increases in the stock market. In the past, the stock market has reflected inflation, although it did not do so during most of the 1970s.

3. Whenever possible, a cost-of-living clause inserted into a labor contract will minimize any negative effect that inflation could have on your standard of living.

4. During inflation, it is important to minimize the cost of holding cash by reducing the cash you hold and the balance you have in your checking account, which does not bear interest.

QUESTIONS FOR THOUGHT AND DISCUSSION

1. Why has inflation been called a tax on cash?

2. If your income goes up by 10 percent and prices do also, are you better or worse off?

3. Do all wages go up at least at the rate of inflation?

THINGS TO DO

Compute college tuition costs for the past ten years at the school you attend. The registrar's office probably can provide the information, or you can look through old catalogs. Find out the percentage increase over the period. Has it been greater or less than the change in the Consumer Price Index (which you can find in numerous government publications such as the *Monthly Labor Review*, the *Annual Economic Report of the President*, or the *Survey of Current Business*)?

SELECTED READINGS

Browne, Harry and Coxon, Terry. *Inflation-Proofing Your Investments*. New York: Warner Communications, 1982.

Burtt, George. *The Barter Way to Beat Inflation*. New York: Everest House, 1980.

Crown, George E. and Van der Wal, John. *How You Can Profit from Inflation*. New York: Van Nostrand Reinhold, 1981.

Myerson, Bess. *The Complete Consumer Book: How to Buy Wisely and Well*. New York: Simon & Schuster, 1979.

Ruff, Howard J. *Survive and Win in the Inflationary 80s*. New York: New York Times Books, 1981.

Stein, Ben and Stein, Herbert. *Money Power: How to Make Inflation Make You Rich*. New York: Avon, 1981.

CHAPTER
CONSUMING ENERGY

There used to be a time when car buyers didn't even ask about the gas mileage they could expect to get. There used to be a time when appliances were bought without any consideration of energy efficiency. . . . Those were the good old days.

CHAPTER PREVIEW

- What is going to happen to the use of energy in the future?
- What caused our first energy crisis in 1973–74?
- What is OPEC, and what has been its effect on the price of oil?
- Has the *relative* price of energy increased dramatically?
- Do Americans continue to waste energy?
- What are some alternative sources of energy?

There used to be a time when most car buyers didn't even ask about the gas mileage they could expect to get from a newly bought car. There used to be a time when the amount and quality of insulation in a house were never even discussed prior to their purchase. There used to be a time when appliances were bought without any consideration of whether they were energy efficient. It's hard to believe it now, but there was a time when the word "energy" was rarely mentioned in magazine and newspaper articles. Those were clearly the good old days. Things have changed—and changed for the worse. Since 1973, the price of energy from all sources has skyrocketed. Exhibit 10–1 shows the percent of U.S. gross national product (GNP) that goes to energy.[1] In the 1960s, final energy products accounted for a little over 9 percent of GNP. That figure remained stable until 1973 when it started shooting upward. By 1983, it had reached almost 13 percent, and the estimate for 1989 is almost 15 percent.

THE FIRST ENERGY CRISIS: 1973–1974

In the 1970s, the United States witnessed a series of crises caused by an insufficient amount of energy in various forms being made available to the consuming public. In 1973 and 1974, the energy crisis mainly affected automobile gasoline consumption and, to a lesser extent, heating oil consumption. There were also sporadic problems with electric utilities not having enough fuel for their generating systems. When these problems—which resulted from the **embargo** of crude oil shipments to the United States and other countries by the Organization of Petroleum Exporting Countries (OPEC)— arose, there was much discussion about the need to conserve energy. Many felt we were using it up at a faster rate than we could supply it.

EMBARGO
An order of a government prohibiting the departure of commercial ships from its ports.

To understand how all this happened, we must understand the formation of one of the most successful **cartels** of all times—the Organization of Petroleum

CARTEL
An agreement among a number of independent suppliers of a product to coordinate their supply decisions so that all of them make more profits. An example of a successful cartel is the Organization of Petroleum Exporting Countries (OPEC).

1. GNP is defined as the total dollar value of all final goods and services produced in the nation over a one-year period.

EXHIBIT 10–1
UP THE ENERGY SLOPE

Here we see what has happened to the percentage of GNP going for energy from 1967 through 1980 and then the predictions to 1990. In 1967, only about 8 percent of GNP went for energy. By 1989–90, almost 15 percent of our GNP will be spent on energy.

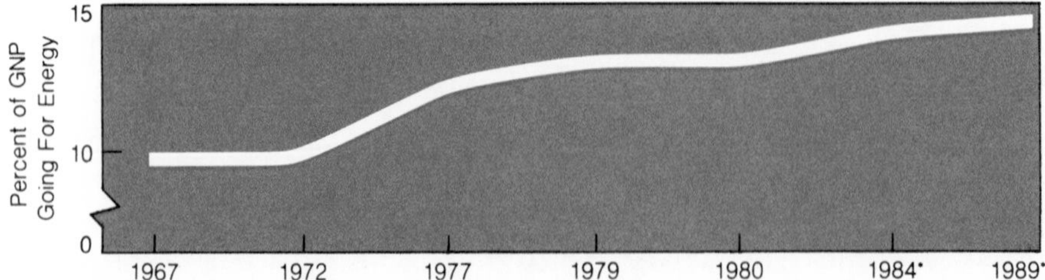

NOTE: Estimates for 1984 and 1989 are by economist Alan Greenspan.

SOURCE: *Fortune*, January 14, 1980, p. 74.

Exporting Countries. This cartel has had a relatively short but highly successful history.

A History of OPEC

In 1960, OPEC started as an organization designed to assist the oil-exporting countries. By 1970, it included Abu Dhabi, Algeria, Indonesia, Iran, Iraq, Kuwait, Libya, Nigeria, Qatar, Saudi Arabia, and Venezuela. Then a few other countries, such as Ecuador, joined the group. When OPEC came into existence, its purpose was to maximize the benefits of owning oil. During the 1960s, its success was limited because an ever-expanding supply of oil kept just ahead of demand. As demand grew, new discoveries expanded the supplies so fast that wellhead prices for crude oil actually fell slightly from 1960 to 1970. Then, in 1970 and 1971, the rate of growth of the demand for crude oil tapered off. Also in 1970, Libya, which had become a major supplier of crude oil to Western European markets, had a revolution. The successful regime cut output sharply. This was partly a political move against the oil companies whose concessions had been granted by the previous regime. Libya's cutback made sizable price increases possible in 1971. These increases were ratified by the other members in agreements drawn up in Tripoli and Teheran. Much of the success of this rise in prices was due to OPEC, but some observers contend that Libya alone was responsible.

In addition to the rising prices, there was an upsurge in demand for crude oil in the United States due to expanding technology, which required more energy consumption; improved living standards; and population increases. The United States increased its imports of crude oil from 1.5 million to 3.5 million barrels a day from 1970 to 1973.

The Yom Kippur War

But the main ingredient in OPEC's success was the outbreak of war in the Middle East in 1973. In the wake of this war, Saudi Arabia, Kuwait, and a few smaller Arab countries agreed to reduce substantially their production of crude oil, thus allowing for large price increases. The only way to raise prices, even if you're a pure monopolist, is to cut back on production and sales. Thus, OPEC could have an effective cartel arrangement only if some or all of its members cut back on production and sales. Since Saudi Arabia, which accounts for the bulk of oil production in the Middle East, did cut back greatly in 1973, the cartel arrangement worked as it has for several years. The total profits for the oil-exporting countries (and oil companies) increased dramatically as a result.

■ THE EFFECTS OF OPEC

The effects of OPEC's activities on world oil prices were dramatic. On January 1, 1973, Saudi Arabian crude oil could be purchased for $2.12 a barrel. Most of this amount—$1.52—was taken by the Saudi Arabian government. Thus, only sixty cents per barrel was left to cover private oil companies' cost of operation and profit. Within one year, the price of crude oil had risen to $7.61 per barrel; by 1980, the price had risen to $40. Exhibit 10–2 shows the OPEC average price per barrel from 1973 to 1983.

OPEC LOSES ITS GRIP

Starting in 1983, OPEC's stranglehold over the oil-importing nations seemed to be loosening. At meeting after meeting, OPEC members failed to reach a consensus on a pricing strategy or on output reductions by the major producing countries. Since every one dollar drop in the price of oil saves an industrial country about $6.5 billion, the failure of OPEC to keep the price of crude oil high in the world market was met with cheers of delight. Talk of a reduction in inflation and a windfall for oil-importing nations was heard throughout the world in 1983 and 1984.

The reason for the decline in oil prices in 1983 is twofold. On the supply side, the increasingly high price of oil brought many countries into the world production market. Exploration had been going on at a frantic pace in the North Sea, in Alaska, off Mexico and Greece, and in other places. The eventual result was that more oil was pumped in the early 1980s than ever before in the history of the world. On the demand side, however, increasing prices eventually caused consumers everywhere, and particularly in the United States, to cut back on their consumption. Exhibit 10–3 shows U.S. petroleum consumption in millions of barrels per day. The peak was reached in 1979, and it has been falling ever since. No matter how hard the members of OPEC tried, they could not fight declining world demand for their product. Again, it is virtually impossible for producers to keep the price of a product up when demand falls, unless they are willing to curtail production severely. Apparently, OPEC has not been willing to do so.

The Future Price of Gasoline

By February 1983, self-service gas stations in many parts of the country were selling regular gasoline at less than a dollar a gallon. Just a few years before,

EXHIBIT 10–2
OPEC Average Price Per Barrel, 1973–1983

SOURCE: Federal Reserve Bank of San Francisco Weekly Letter, January 11, 1980, p. 3; and American Petroleum Institute.

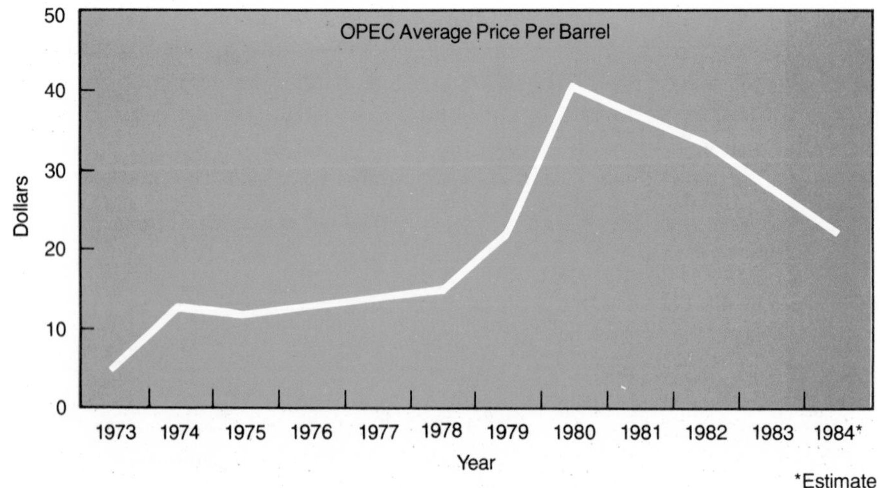

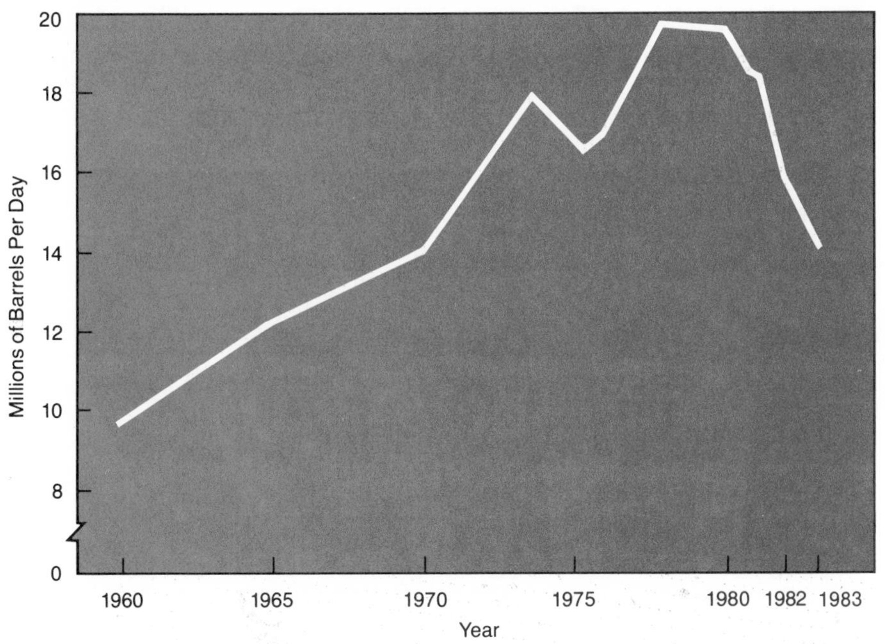

EXHIBIT 10–3
U.S. Petroleum Consumption

The U.S. reached its peak of petroleum consumption in 1979. It has been falling ever since. Increased efforts to conserve energy and the return to alternative energy sources (e.g. coal) have lessened America's need for oil.

SOURCE: Energy Information Administration

energy economists predicted that the price of gasoline would reach two dollars a gallon, but this doesn't seem likely, at least not for several years. The supply and demand of world petroleum products dictate the ultimate price of gasoline at the pump. Because so many countries have developed a substantial productive capacity for crude oil and because consumers have figured out how to conserve on petroleum products, the possibility of two-dollar-a-gallon gasoline in the foreseeable future is remote. What that means for America is obvious: Some of the goods and services we were accustomed to buying when gas was cheap may become popular again. Gas will never be as cheap as it was before, but it was less expensive in 1983 than it was in 1980. This price reduction has already resulted in a change in automobile manufacturing plans. The new age of "muscle" cars is in full swing. People are willing to pay for performance even if they sacrifice gas mileage. Why? Because the price of gas is not as high as everyone predicted it would be by the mid-1980s.

ARE WE AS BAD OFF AS WE THINK?— A STORY OF RELATIVE PRICES

Gasoline may be selling at the pump for $1.25 a gallon, your electric bill may be twice as high as it was a few years ago, and your heating bill may seem outrageous. But if you look only at the *nominal* price of your energy sources, you're making a serious error. You must compare the price of energy with the price of all other goods for a true indication of what we're losing in the energy field. The figures in Exhibit 10–4 show the ratio of the price of different energy sources to the price of all other consumer items. The charts in Exhibit 10–4 do indeed show a dramatic upsurge in the relative prices of different energy sources in 1973–74. In particular, fuel oil and coal skyrocketed and are today

The supply and demand of world petroleum products dictate the ultimate price of gasoline at the pump.

75 percent more expensive, relative to the average of all other goods, than prior to the 1973–74 energy crisis. But look at electricity in the top figure. Here we see that the relative price of electricity was falling from right after World War II to the end of the 1960s. It stayed flat until the energy crisis of 1973–74, but today it still is less than it was, relative to all other prices, prior to 1960. The price of gasoline in the bottom figure, in relative terms, is not dramatically different from the price of gasoline twenty-five years ago.

These data may surprise you, but to understand fully the true cost of anything, you must look at what you're giving up. If all other prices (including wages) have increased 100 percent and the price of gasoline also has increased 100 percent, its relative price has remained the same.

HAVE AMERICANS BEEN ENERGY PIGS?

We are constantly being bombarded with articles, slogans, political campaign platforms, and the like that tell us what "energy pigs" we have been. There has been talk about how frivolously we used air conditioning in our homes

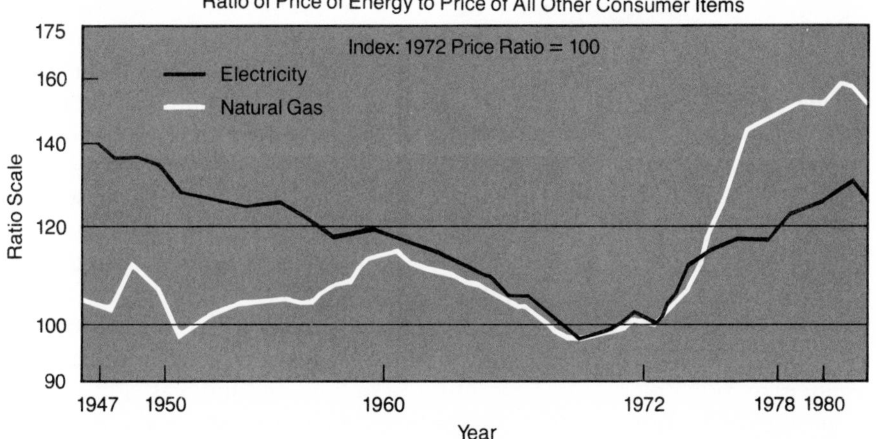

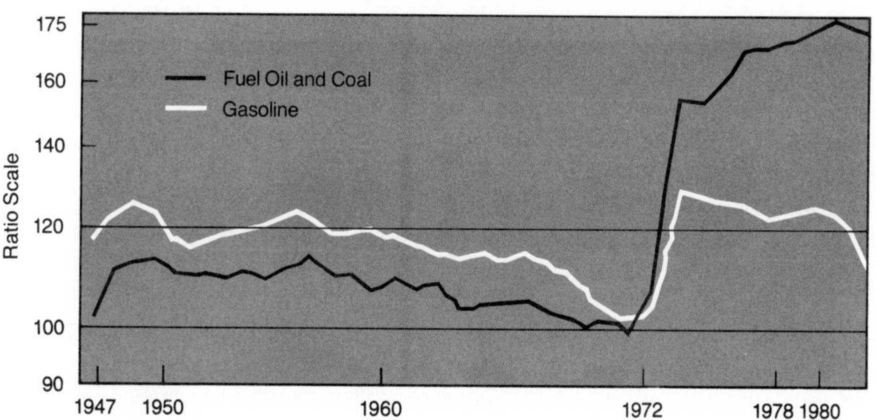

EXHIBIT 10–4
Relative Energy Price

The figures show the relative price of different forms of energy from 1947 to 1983. Notice that the relative price of electricity (top) was falling steadily until about 1972. During 1980, it was still not any higher than it was in 1960. Looking at gasoline (below), we see that the price in 1980 was about what it was, relatively speaking, in 1949.

and in our cars, how we didn't bother to insulate our homes to keep them warm in the winter and cool in the summer, how we used machines that consumed inordinate amounts of electricity to build our products. The list goes on and on.

In order to analyze that line of reasoning, we must first define what we mean by *energy waste*. When you, as a consumer, decide how to spend your income, you try not to waste it. That is to say, you try to maximize the amount of happiness and satisfaction you receive from your limited income. For you to waste your income would mean that you consumed something of value in a manner that yielded less satisfaction than if you had consumed it (or something else) in a different manner. Consider time, which is a scarce consumer resource. If you relax for two hours, do you tell yourself at the end of those two hours that you have just wasted them? You might say that, but, in effect, you've wasted them only if you were relaxing against your will—if you could have been doing another desired activity that would have yielded you a greater level of satisfaction.

What if you leave home for a trip and keep on a light that consumes electricity for which you have to pay? Is that a waste of electricity? The answer is not so clear-cut. You have to pay for the electricity, so you are giving up some other good or service that you could have purchased. What are you receiving in return? The answer may not be obvious, but the benefits could include not having to think about turning off the light, perhaps a safer house while you're away because lighted houses are less likely to be robbed, or a more cheerful house when you enter it. Are these considerations trivial? Only you, the individual consumer, can decide. No one else can tell you that you are wasting electricity when you leave on a light in an empty house, *provided that you are required to pay for the electricity.* When the annual relative price of electricity was falling (from after World War II until the early 1970s), consumers each year had to sacrifice less and less for the same unit of electricity; accordingly, they started using more electricity in ways that today, when electricity is so much more expensive, may seem frivolous and wasteful.

In retrospect, with our current knowledge of the true nature of energy supplies, perhaps we should have consumed less. Unfortunately, there was no way at that time for consumers to have this information. Consumers can only respond to the apparent cost of engaging in a consumption activity. The apparent cost—that is, the cost we actually had to pay for gasoline and electricity until 1972—was not high enough to warrant conservation of those resources. Our rate of consumption of energy had been increasing gradually but not abruptly in any one year. To prove our point, we should look at the consumption of energy in the United States in the last couple of years. Not only has it not increased, it actually has decreased, even though our population continues to grow. The data show that Americans know how to conserve energy. All they need is a signal in the form of higher relative prices.

In the past, we acted as rational consumers who responded to relatively inexpensive sources of energy. Now that energy is no longer relatively so cheap, we are changing our behavior. We are purchasing smaller engines in cars that are lighter and offer better gas mileage, we are insulating our homes more, we are seeking alternative cheaper sources of energy. We are, in a word, being more *careful* in our use of energy.

ALTERNATIVE SOURCES OF ENERGY

Since we've had so many problems with fossil-fuel sources, particularly crude oil imported from abroad, there has been a cry not only for increased energy conservation but for increased research and development and the use of alternative energy sources. Wind power, wave power, and solar power have all been considered, but they are useful to us *only if they are cost effective.*

Solar Power Demystified

To show what is meant by cost-effective alternative energy sources, let's look at solar power. On May 3, 1978, President Jimmy Carter promised renewed vigor in governmental support of solar radiation as a "clean, renewable, and economically competitive energy source." The California Energy Commission produced a pamphlet stating that "solar energy is abundant, nonpolluting, and free. It is not affected by changes in international politics or trade, or inflation at home. It is available where it is needed. It is dependable, even in winter.

And for at least the next 4 billion years, the sun will be warming the earth and providing the energy to those who take it." Sounds great, doesn't it? Why, then, aren't we using the sun for all our energy needs? The answer is because solar energy is relatively expensive. We do not yet have an inexpensive way to convert solar energy into a usable form.

The most optimistic energy engineers say that, by the time we allow for variations in atmospheric cover and clouds, the recovery efficiency of sunlight reaching the earth is only 5 to 10 percent. Thus, in order to meet the entire estimated U.S. power requirement for the year 2000, we would have to cover the equivalent of the area of the entire state of Oregon with solar collectors. That may not sound like too great an area when it is spread out across the United States, but it is also necessary to build a huge number of conversion cells. Direct conversion units contain immense quantities of cadmium, silicone, germanium, selenium, gallium, copper, arsenic, sulfur, and other elements. Thermoconversion units are made of thousands of tons of plastics, glass, and rubber. The United States imports almost two-thirds of its cadmium, and the world produces only enough to generate 180,000 megawatts of electricity—a mere 10 percent of capacity today. Additionally, consider the ecological problems resulting from covering part of the earth with solar collectors.

There has been a cry not only for increased energy conservation but for increased research and development and the use of alternative energy sources.

An Example—An Active Solar Water-Heating System

An active solar system requires not only the sun's energy but additional mechanical parts. Surprisingly enough, solar water heaters were quite prevalent in California and Florida in the 1920s. They were abandoned by the 1960s, however, because of the falling relative price of natural gas. Today, a complete solar water-heating system costs approximately $2,600. Since the sun doesn't shine constantly, it only can be relied upon 75 percent of the time. So should one pay $2,600 for a solar water-heating system? The answer depends on the energy cost of continuing with an electric or natural-gas water heater. Say that you have an electric water heater that uses 500 kilowatt hours per month and that you are paying ten cents per kilowatt hour; your monthly energy cost for hot water would be $50, or $600 per year. If you installed the solar water heater, you would save three-fourths of that, or $450. If we divide your savings of $450 into the initial cost of the solar water heater ($2,600), we get what is called payback period; it would **be equal to:**

$2,600/$450 ≑ 5.78 years.[2]

On the basis of this calculation, most people would say that the purchase of a solar water-heating system would be economically justifiable.

On the other hand, what if you were using natural gas that only cost about 30 percent of the price of electricity, or fifteen dollars per month. Your yearly cost would only be $180. Your alternative solar hot water system would save 75 percent of that, or $135 per year. The payback period would become:

$2,600/$135 = 19.26 years.

2. This calculation of a payback period is, of course, overly simplified. It doesn't take account of the interest that you could have earned had you put the $2,600 in, say, a money market mutual fund during that period.

Nuclear energy was everyone's darling in the 1960s; now it faces an uncertain future.

On purely economic grounds, you couldn't justify the capital outlay of $2,600 for a solar water-heating system if you were only paying $185 a year for natural-gas water heating.

Of course, this calculation ignores several noneconomic factors. One concerns your "insurance policy" against future increases in the price of electricity or natural gas. (Actually, you're only "insured" for 75 percent since you still have to have your regular system for days when the sun doesn't shine.) Additionally, in many instances, a solar hot-water system increases the value of your home.[3]

Gasohol: Possible Net Energy Loss

It is possible to produce alcohol from farm crops, mix it with gasoline, and create gasohol to run automobiles. Researchers at Louisiana State University in Baton Rouge, concluded, however, that more energy would be required to make gasohol than would be yielded by gasohol. LSU researchers looked at the amount of energy required to obtain alcohol from sugar cane. They added up the energy used to run the trucks, tractors, harvesters, and other machines and also to produce the fertilizer used by the farmers. Then they considered the amount of energy used to distill and process the alcohol. Other researchers (perhaps with a little more bias) from Mobil Research and Development Corporation estimated that it would require the equivalent of two to three gallons of high-grade petroleum fuel (such as gasoline) to produce enough alcohol energy to replace a gallon of gasoline. Some studies show that there is a potential for making alcohol with less energy, *provided* that the alcohol is available as a by-product, which is true in a number of cases.

Nuclear Power

Nuclear energy was everyone's darling in the 1960s; now it faces an uncertain future. Nuclear energy is used almost exclusively to produce electricity. Its major competitor today in the United States is coal. Thus, a discussion of nuclear power is really a comparison of the two fuels.

NUCLEAR POWER VERSUS COAL. The problem with nuclear power plants is that they are more expensive to build than coal-burning plants. On the other hand, nuclear power plants are cheaper to operate once they are built than are coal-powered plants. In relative terms, a new nuclear power plant costs about 50 percent more per kilowatt capacity than a coal-powered plant, but the fuel cost of nuclear power is about half the fuel cost of coal.

What seemed like a clear advantage in the 1960s is no longer the case. During that period, total generating cost per kilowatt hour, including the cost of building the plants, was about 40 percent lower for nuclear facilities than coal-fired plants. Today, given the safety problems requiring more frequent shutdowns, these figures no longer hold. In fact, the Exxon Corporation made a study in 1979 showing that the operating cost per kilowatt hour for plants built today is 5.0 cents for nuclear and 5.11 cents for coal. This certainly isn't

3. But not in all instances. Some installations are so unsightly that they decrease the market value of a house.

Stricter safety standards are being imposed on the nuclear power industry, and the cost of these standards will further erode any remaining cost advantages that nuclear power might hold over coal.

enough difference to justify the enormously greater construction costs and safety problems involved in a nuclear plant.

THE HIDDEN COSTS. There are many hidden costs of nuclear power that aren't included in these calculations. One of the most important involves waste disposal. We do not yet have a cheap and perfectly safe method of disposing of radioactive wastes, which are toxic and must be kept isolated for thousands of years. Even if we can technically dispose of nuclear wastes safely, we don't know what the cost will be in the future. In any event, the private nuclear utilities should be charged the full cost of waste disposal, but that is not yet being done. Thus, the apparent cost of nuclear power—that is, the cost charged to the consumer—is not the true cost to society.

Another cost is involved in dismantling the reactors when they end their useful life of forty years. No one knows these costs because no nuclear power plant has ever been dismantled.

THE SAFETY FACTOR. After the Three Mile Island episode in 1979, even the staunchest supporters of nuclear power started having second thoughts. Stricter safety standards are being imposed on the nuclear power industry, and the cost of these standards will further erode any remaining cost advantages that nuclear power might hold over coal.

DON'T FORGET THE HAZARDS OF COAL. Coal also presents major health and safety problems. Coal miners are exposed to danger. And air pollution from coal-fed boilers is certainly a very real public health hazard. In short, coal isn't completely devoid of hidden costs, either.

CONCLUSIONS

The most we can say about energy (its consumption and production) is that it is a rapidly changing field. Nuclear power appears to be at a dead end; nonetheless, existing nuclear plants currently provide one-eighth of all electric power. We have plenty of coal in the United States, but we can't make greater use of it until coal-using industries find ways around the pollution problems that coal creates. While solar power is growing in significance in the United States, through the year 2000 we cannot expect it to contribute more than 10 percent of U.S. energy needs. Just because one source of energy becomes expensive doesn't necessarily mean we should spend even more to find an alternative source. Perhaps the best thing we can do is to search for ways to conserve the now-expensive energy we are using. The following Consumer Issue discusses that search.

SUMMARY

1. It is estimated that, in 1967, energy took only 9 percent of GNP; in 1989, it is estimated that energy will take 14.7 percent.
2. The Organization of Petroleum Exporting Countries successfully cut back on the production of crude oil and kept prices rising from 1973 to 1983.
3. The relative prices of electricity, natural gas, fuel oil and coal, and gasoline have risen since 1973–74. But the relative prices of electricity and gasoline aren't much different that they were twenty-five years ago.
4. Americans responded to falling relative prices of electricity and gasoline throughout the 1950s and 1960s by consuming more and more of these commodities.
5. There are numerous alternative sources of energy, including solar power, windmills, wave action, and others. Solar power is cost-effective in certain states, such as Florida, and for certain specialized activities, such as hot-water heating, but it is not yet cheap enough to compete with conventional energy sources for most uses.
6. Gasohol may cost more in energy than it is worth, although in some situations it could be profitable to use.
7. Nuclear power was once considered the best future means of electricity generation in the United States; today, however, it seems as if the costs outweigh the benefits, and the growth of nuclear energy will be curtailed in the future.

QUESTIONS FOR THOUGHT AND DISCUSSION

1. Why do OPEC countries have to cut back on production in order to raise prices?
2. What is most important to you: the relative price of gasoline or the nominal price?
3. Do you believe Americans have "wasted" energy? If so, why? Do you personally waste energy? If so, how could you eliminate such waste?
4. "The sun is free." Is this a correct statement?

THINGS TO DO

1. Call a local solar water-heating company and find out the entire cost of setting up such a system. Determine for yourself whether it is cost-effective to do so. Remember to consider that you have to have a backup system for days when there isn't enough sun.
2. Calculate the relative price of gasoline today compared to ten years ago. What has happened to it?

SELECTED READINGS

"Carter Wants to Wait on Nuclear Waste." *Business World,* February 4, 1980, p. 36.

General Information on Solar Energy. Write to National Solar Heating and Cooling Information Center, Box 1607, Rockville, Maryland 20850.

Hogan, Janice. "Does Less Energy Equal Less Happiness?" *Forum,* Spring/Summer, 1981.

Miller, G. Tyler. *Energy and Environment.* Belmont, Cal.: Wadsworth Publishing Co., 1980.

Miller, Roger LeRoy. *The Economics of Energy: What Went Wrong and How We Can Fix It.* New York: William Morrow & Co., 1974.

Schurr, Sam H., project director. *Energy in America's Future: The Choices Before Us.* A study prepared for the Resources for the Future National Energy Strategies Project. Baltimore, Md.: Johns Hopkins University Press, 1979.

"A Split in OPEC: Cheaper Oil Ahead." *Newsweek,* February 7, 1983, pp. 50–53.

Consumer ISSUE  

CUTTING DOWN ENERGY COSTS

GLOSSARY

ENERGY EFFICIENT RATING (EER)—A rating system applied to all new major appliances that tells you how much it will cost to run the appliance.

This Consumer Issue examines various ways to conserve on energy. In each instance, remember the primary rule for rational consumer decision making: *Engage in an activity only up to the point where the last few dollars in cost are matched by an equal amount of benefits.* Otherwise, you'll be spending more of your resources than you're receiving in benefits.

CUTTING DOWN ON YOUR GASOLINE CONSUMPTION

1. Car pool when possible.
2. Don't buy gasoline that has an octane rating higher than is recommended by the manufacturer of your automobile.
3. Avoid stop-and-go driving.
4. Reduce the use of your air conditioner, if you have one, when driving at less than highway speeds. (At highway speeds, it is cheaper to use your air conditioner with your windows closed; open windows create so much "drag" that you use more gas than you would running the air conditioner.)
5. Turn your engine off whenever its going to be idling for more than a minute.
6. Consolidate errands in order to keep short trips to a minimum.
7. Use radial tires.
8. Don't underinflate tires.
9. Reduce car weight by keeping the trunk clear of unnecessary items.
10. Drive smoothly and steadily, maintaining as constant a speed as possible.
11. Avoid jackrabbit starts and sudden stops at intersections.

Oil company estimates of fuel savings are as follows.

1. Avoiding jackrabbit starts and driving at an easy pace reduce gas consumption by 18 percent.
2. Keeping a car's engine properly tuned reduces gas consumption by 3 percent.
3. Replacing fouled spark plugs saves 9 percent.
4. Using air conditioner sparingly saves 7 percent.
5. Maintaining proper tire inflation saves 2 percent.

If you follow all these guidelines, you could reduce your gasoline consumption by nearly 40 percent.

CUTTING DOWN ON ENERGY USE IN APPLIANCES

The operating cost of appliances is higher today than it has been for the past twenty-five years; therefore, a good way to lower fuel bills and conserve energy in your household is to use appliances efficiently. Although the following list of energy-saving tips is by no means complete, you can save many dollars a year if you apply these tips carefully to your daily activities.

Ways to Save on Energy

1. Bake several items at once when possible. Incidentally, baking is usually less expensive in the long run than cooking on top of the range because the oven shuts off for part of the baking period.

2. Defrost freezer or freezing compartments when frost is one-quarter inch think. This will increase the efficiency of your freezer.

3. Check the seals on your freezing compartment and refrigerator doors for cracks and wear. If a dollar bill placed in the door can be pulled out easily, it's time for a new seal.

4. Increase the temperature setting on your refrigerator freezer. Thirty-nine degrees is usually adequate in the food compartment, and five degrees in the freezer will keep food in good condition for about four months.

5. Minimize hot water use. Run only full loads in your washing machine, dishwasher, and dryer. This will save on both water and energy.

6. Use cold water and cold-water detergent to wash clothing that is not extremely soiled.

7. Use the lowest temperature possible when drying your laundry.

8. Eliminate the heating cycle in your dishwasher. Simply open the door at the end of the wash-and-rinse period and let the air, which is free, dry your dishes.

9. Turn the thermostat on your water heater down. Set the upper temperature at 140°, the lower at 120°.

10. Use smaller electric appliances for specialized jobs to save on electricity. For example, toast bread in a toaster, not in the oven.

11. Buy an air conditioner that has a very *high energy efficiency rating (EER),* and keep the thermostat up. Make sure the air conditioner filter is clean, and don't use the unit as an air circulator.

12. Don't leave an electric coffee maker plugged in.

13. Turn your thermostat down in the winter, and install a timer that cuts the heat off during your sleeping hours. Wear a sweater!

14. Where possible, reduce the wattage of lights or switch to fluorescent lamps.

You probably can think of other ways to save on energy. Remember, though, that reducing energy expenses often means sacrificing some convenience you now enjoy. Are you, for example, willing to forego the comforts of a warmer house in winter in order to reduce the cost of your fuel bill?

USING ENERGY LABELS WHEN YOU MAKE A CONSUMER APPLIANCE DECISION

Information on relative energy costs for various brands and models of major appliances is now available to consumers in the form of energy labels attached to new products. Information on these labels is based on tests of appliance energy use under controlled laboratory conditions designed to simulate home use. Energy-cost labeling of major appliances is mandated by the Energy Policy and Conservation Act of 1975, Title III, Part B. It is mandatory for these appliances: air conditioners, dishwashers, clothes washers and dryers, televisions, refrigerators, water heaters, humidifiers and dehumidifiers, ovens and ranges, furnaces, and heating equipment other than furnaces. Exhibit G–1 shows a typical energy-cost label. Notice that the *estimated* yearly energy cost is sixty-six dollars for this particular refrigerator. But to find out your *actual* energy cost, you need to know the cost per kilowatt hour of electricity in your area. For example, if electricity costs you ten cents per kilowatt hour, your annual cost for operating that refrigerator would be $134 a year.

REDUCING HOME HEATING AND COOLING COSTS

There are numerous ways to reduce home heating and cooling costs. One way to start is by getting a home energy audit, which is an attic-to-basement look at your house by a trained inspector. In New York and Oregon, major gas and electric companies are required to perform such audits on request. In Wisconsin, gas utilities must perform the audits on request. In New York, you can be charged a fee of up to ten dollars. Starting in 1980, the federal government required all except the smallest utilities to conduct in-home audits on request and to arrange for the installation and financing of energy-saving materials. The Department of Energy believes that some 4½ million homes per year will be audited by 1985, at a total cost of about $2 billion. Additionally, the DOE estimates that three-fourths of the homeowners who request audits will spend, to save on energy, almost $8 billion from 1983 to 1988.

Should You Switch to Solar Water Heating?

One of the few areas in which solar power is being used extensively in the home is to heat water. According to Sunset Books' *Homeowners Guide to Solar Heating*, a study in San Diego found that the life-cycle cost of a solar system was several thousand dollars less than for an electric water-heating system. This study wasn't very accurate, however, because it ignored the crucial *opportunity cost* of the initial high investment in a solar water-heating system—in many locations, anywhere from $2,400 to $3,600. In existing homes, there is already a water-heating system installed, and, in new homes, the cost of an electric system is probably one-tenth the price of a solar system. In many homes, gas is used to heat water.

When there is a subsidy from the government to do so, it does pay to install a solar water heater. The laws are changing rapidly on this, and each homeowner must check with the appropriate authorities (most easily through a tax accountant) about state and federal subsidies. Call a local distributor and installer of solar water-heating systems to get this information readily and without cost. In areas where there are federal demonstration programs, part of the capital cost of installing the system has been paid for by the government.

Should You Heat Your Home with Wood?

Something on the order of 7 to 10 million Americans are now using wood as a primary or secondary source of heat in their homes. In 1972, only 160,000 wood-burning stoves were sold; in 1978, that number skyrocketed to 1.3 million. Is home heating by wood a way to save on electricity, propane, natural gas, coal, or fuel oil? There's no easy answer, because a possible savings depends upon how much wood is available in *your* area. You can count on as many as six cords of wood being needed to heat a house for five months. In some areas, wood may be selling for $150 a cord by the time you read this book. If that's the case, you may not be so eager to trade in your gas heater for a wood-burning stove. If you do decide to change to wood, however, there are certain dangers of which you should be aware.

Dangers in Heating with Wood

1. Be aware of the fire hazard. In an effort to obtain a quick heat buildup, many wood-burning-stove users start an excessively hot, fast-burning fire. The stove and its vent

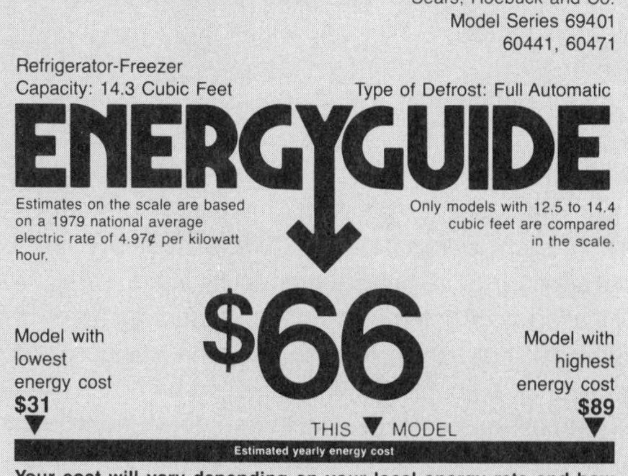

Sears, Roebuck and Co.
Model Series 69401
60441, 60471

Refrigerator-Freezer
Capacity: 14.3 Cubic Feet

Type of Defrost: Full Automatic

ENERGYGUIDE

Estimates on the scale are based on a 1979 national average electric rate of 4.97¢ per kilowatt hour.

Only models with 12.5 to 14.4 cubic feet are compared in the scale.

Model with lowest energy cost
$31

$66

THIS ▼ MODEL

Model with highest energy cost
$89

Estimated yearly energy cost

Your cost will vary depending on your local energy rate and how you use the product. This energy cost is based on U.S. Government standard tests.

How much will this model cost you to run yearly?

		Yearly cost Estimated yearly $ cost shown below
Cost per kilowatt hour	**2¢**	$27
	4¢	$53
	6¢	$80
	8¢	$107
	10¢	$134
	12¢	$160

Ask your salesperson or local utility for the energy rate (cost per kilowatt hour) in your area.

Important: Removal of this label before consumer purchase is a violation of federal law (42 U.S.C. 6302).

(Part No. 938673A)

EXHIBIT G–1
Sample Energy Label

pipe become so hot that they can ignite adjacent combustible floors or walls. Additionally, the disposal of ashes may cause a fire if they are incompletely extinguished. Special care must be taken to insulate flue pipes that connect the stove to the chimney. If a flue pipe passes through a wall, it must be insulated, or a thimble must be put around it that keeps the hot pipe away from any combustible wall materials. For information on how to install such equipment, write the National Fire Protection Association at 470 Atlantic Avenue, Boston, Massachusetts 02210. The Schraeder Company (4443 Jonestown Road, Harrisburg, Pennsylvania 17109) offers an information booklet on this subject.

2. In order to prevent your own or your neighbor's roof from catching fire, you must keep the stovepipe and chimney clean. Constant use of a wood-burning stove will cause an accumulation of creosote that can start a chimney fire. You may have to hire professional chimney cleaners to remove these deposits.

3. You must be especially aware of the danger of carbon-monoxide poisoning. This problem is unknown to many users of wood-burning stoves and often underestimated by others. For example, an unvented room heater for a mobile home must never be installed in a sleeping room. Proper ventilation is extremely important for preventing carbon-monoxide poisoning.

Finally, the installation of certain fireplaces can actually increase your heating bills. Most decorative fireplaces basically heat the air that goes up the chimney. In so doing, the fireplace extracts more heat from the home than it contributes. In modern homes, fireplace heating is inherently inefficient, and a supplemental heating stove (or stoves) is necessary.

ENERGY-SAVING HOME IMPROVEMENTS

The National Energy Conservation Policy Act of 1978 and the Energy Tax Act of 1978 both provide incentives to encourage families to make energy-saving modifications to their housing. Among these incentives are:

1. Federal income tax credits
2. Free or low-cost inspections of individual residences
3. Loans to homeowners and builders for the purchase and installation of solar equipment
4. Home weatherization grants to low-income families

The following is a list of some of the most common energy-saving home improvements, along with the government's assessment of how cost-effective they are.

1. Weather stripping and caulking. Whenever cool drafts can be felt, weather stripping and caulking are generally cost-effective. If drafts cannot be felt, these measures aren't worth the effort and money.

2. Water-heater insulation. Since a water heater is one of the major consumers of home energy, anything that can make water heating more efficient is advisable. Wrapping the outside of the water heater with a blanket of fiberglass is an extremely cost-effective, do-it-yourself measure. A one-and-a-half inch blanket of insulation can save the typical homeowner 300 kilowatts of electricity per year or twenty-five gallons of heating oil.

3. Storm doors. Typically, storm doors are not cost-effective at reducing energy consumption. Only when the consumer installs the door with an interchangeable screen and storm panels and also uses it in warm weather to reduce the use of air conditioning does it make sense, according to government experts.

4. Storm windows. In most parts of the United States, the Department of Energy believes that storm windows are cost-effective, particularly for homes heated by fossil fuels for example, oil and coal). They even seem to be cost-effective for those using electric heat; the energy savings, however, are not very significant in such cases.

5. Insulation. If no insulation is present, adding it to walls, floors, and attics may be cost-effective (with a payback period of six years or less). The Department of Energy, however, does not believe that adding to an existing level of wall insulation is cost-effective.

6. Insulating furnace ducts. This is one of the most highly cost-effective measures in most colder areas. You simply wrap the heating ducts that pass through unheated areas with insulation (similar to the way the hot-water heater is wrapped). If this measure is a do-it-yourself project, it becomes particularly cost-effective.

7. Thermostat setback device. In most areas, the Department of Energy believes that these devices are cost-effective. Note, though, that consumers can achieve the same cost savings by manually adjusting the thermostat during hours when heating or cooling is unnecessary.

CONCLUSIONS

This Consumer Issue has presented only a few ways you can conserve on energy. As modern technology changes, numerous new energy-saving devices will become available. Additionally, as the relative prices of different energy sources change, you will be forced to make decisions about conserving different types of energy in different ways. Today, newspapers and magazines, as well as TV and radio shows, are constantly presenting us with ideas about how to conserve energy. Listen, read, think, and then do something about conservation.

SUMMARY

1. In order to cut down on your automobile gas consumption, you should: use a car pool whenever possible, avoid stop-and-go driving, drive smoothly and steadily, and avoid jackrabbit starts and stops. Additionally, keeping your engine tuned and replacing fouled spark plugs can save you a considerable amount of gas.

2. There are numerous ways to cut down on energy use in appliances. Perhaps the most important are: increasing the temperature setting on your refrigerator and freezer, minimizing hot water use, turning the thermostat down on your water heater, and turning the thermostat down on your house heating unit in the winter and up in the summer.

3. When you shop for a new appliance, check energy labels that tell you the relative energy efficiency of what you are buying.

4. In some cases, it is advisable to switch to solar water heating, but you must take account of the high initial installation costs in making your calculations.

5. Heating your home with wood may reduce home heating bills, but wood fuel may be more dangerous and increase the amount of time you spend on home heating.

6. The most cost-effective home improvements you can make to save energy are: insulating your water heater, putting in storm windows, insulating furnace ducts, and installing a thermostat setback device that turns off your heating unit during the hours you're not home.

QUESTIONS FOR THOUGHT AND DISCUSSION

1. What is meant by the high capital cost of installing a solar water heater?

2. What are the benefits of car pooling? What are the costs?

3. Why weren't energy labels available on appliances ten years ago?

4. "Reduce your home heating and cooling costs, no matter what." Is that a valid statement? Analyze it.

THINGS TO DO

1. Check your living structure to find out if it is allowing warm air to escape in the winter. See if there is any cost-effective method of reducing the amount of home heating you use.

2. Write down the actual cost calculations (or show how you would calculate) to determine whether a solar water-heating unit would be cost-effective for you.

SELECTED READINGS

"Can an Interior Paint Conserve Energy?" *Consumer Reports,* February 1980, p. 65.

Hart, G. Kimball. *How to Cut Your Energy Costs: A Guide to Major Savings at Home and on the Road.* New York: Simon & Schuster, 1978.

"Heating with Wood." U.S. Department of Agriculture, Fact Sheet. Washington, D.C.: U.S. Government Printing Office, March 1981.

Information on solar energy. Lists of publications and products and installers can be obtained from the National Solar Heating and Cooling Information Center (operated for the Departments of Energy and Housing and Urban Development), P.O. Box 1607, Rockville, Maryland 20850. Call toll-free (800) 523-2929. In Pennsylvania, call toll-free (800) 462-4983.

"Saving Energy Dollars." *Consumer Reports,* October 1981, pp. 563–93.

"Solar Retrofit." National Solar Heating and Cooling Information Center, Fact Sheet No. 110 (free). Write to Office of Governmental and Public Affairs, U.S. Department of Agriculture, Washington, D.C. 20250.

"Window Design Strategies to Conserve Energy." NBS Building Science Series No. 104, available from Superintendent of Documents, U.S. Government Printing Office, Washington, D.C. 20402, Stock No. 003-003-01794-9.

CHAPTER

BANKS AND THE BANKING SYSTEM

We live in a money economy. We use currency consisting of various denominations of bills and coins, and we also use checks and their equivalent. . . . Every year, about 40 billion checks are written and processed through our banking system.

CHAPTER PREVIEW

- What is the Federal Reserve System, and how does it operate?
- What different types of checking accounts are available at depository institutions?
- What is a negotiable order of withdrawal?
- How does the cashless society affect the consumer?

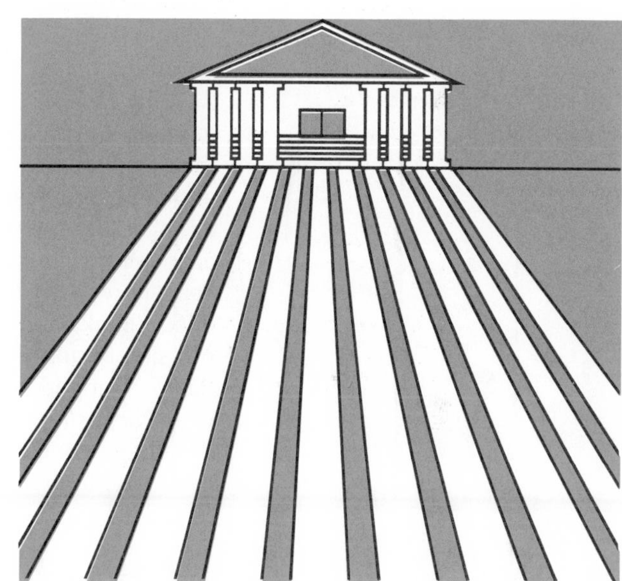

We live in a money economy. We use currency consisting of various denominations of bills and coins, and we also use checks and their equivalent. In fact, of the total amount of money outstanding in the United States, some 80 percent is in checking-account balances; every year, about 40 billion checks are written and processed through our banking system. Understanding how that system works and what services banks can offer you is, therefore, an important aspect of consumer economics. This chapter looks at the banking system as a whole, the types of checking accounts and other services that various banks offer, and the cashless society.

BANKING, ITS INSTITUTIONS, AND DEREGULATION

DEPOSITORY INSTITUTION
Any institution that can accept deposits; commercial banks, savings and loan associations, mutual savings banks, and credit unions are depository institutions.

In previous editions of this book, this chapter concerned itself only with commercial banks. The definition of a commercial bank was a financial institution that could accept checking-account deposits, otherwise known as demand deposits. For many years, commercial banks dominated the checking-account scene. That is to say, they were the only financial institutions legally allowed to let people write checks on checking-account balances. All this changed, however, in 1980 when Congress passed the historic Depository Institutions Deregulation and Monetary Control Act. The term **depository institution** was put in the title of that act for a very good reason. Commercial banks are not the only depository institutions in our nation. Rather, a host of financial institutions permit consumers to make deposits. The term depository institution, then, includes commercial banks, savings and loan associations, credit unions, and mutual savings banks. In any event, the 1980 act lifted the restrictions on all those depository institutions that had been unable to offer checking-type accounts to banking customers. Eventually, virtually all differences among depository institutions will disappear. Therefore, even though this chapter is titled "Banks and the Banking System," the information contained in it does not simply apply to those financial institutions that call themselves banks. Rather, it applies to all depository institutions. Instead of using the cumbersome words *depository institutions,* we simply will refer to them as banks throughout this chapter and the accompanying Issue.

In order to understand our banking system, it is necessary to understand the regulating agency that controls that system.

THE FEDERAL RESERVE SYSTEM

In the United States banking system, the monetary authority, or Federal Reserve System, determines the quantity of money in circulation. The Federal Reserve System was established in 1913 with the passage of the Federal Reserve Act under President Woodrow Wilson. According to its preamble, it was "an act to provide for the establishment of Federal Reserve banks, to furnish an elastic currency, to afford means of rediscounting commercial paper, to establish a more effective supervision of banking in the United States, and for other purposes."

Currently, the Federal Reserve System consists of twelve member Federal Reserve banks that have twenty-five branches, a Board of Governors consisting of seven members nominated by the president for fourteen-year terms, a Federal Open Market Committee, and other less important committees (See Exhibit 11–1).

A Clearinghouse for Checks

The Federal Reserve System has greatly simplified the clearing of checks—the method by which checks deposited in one bank are transferred to the banks on which they were written. Let's say that Mr. Smith of Chicago writes a check to the Jones family in San Francisco. When the Joneses receive the check in the mail, they deposit it in their bank. Their bank then deposits the check in the Federal Reserve Bank of San Francisco. That bank, in turn, sends it to the Federal Reserve Bank of Chicago. That Federal Reserve Bank then sends the check to Mr. Smith's bank, where the amount of the check is deducted from Mr. Smith's account. We show how this is done in Exhibit 11–2.

THE DIFFERENT TYPES OF CHECKING ACCOUNTS

1. Minimum balance
2. Free checking
3. Analysis, or transaction, plan
4. Activity, or "per check," plan
5. Package account

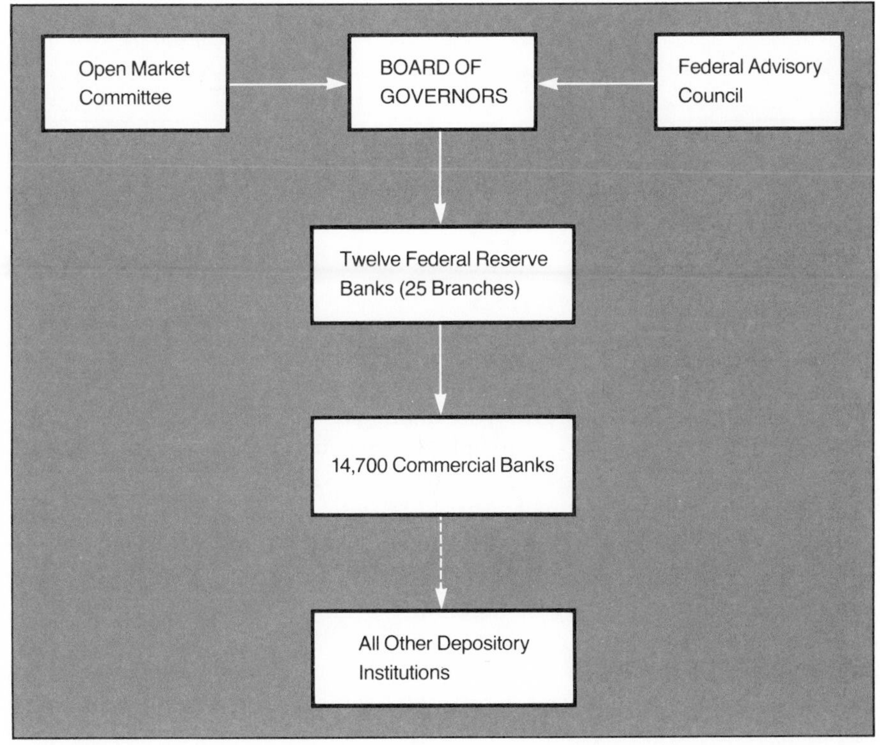

EXHIBIT 11–1
The Federal Reserve System

At the top of the system there is the Board of Governors. Then there are the 12 Federal Reserve banks, which have 25 branches throughout the country. There are almost 15,000 member commercial banks which are part of the Federal Reserve System. All other depository institutions are required to keep reserves with district Federal Reserve banks.

EXHIBIT 11–2
How a Check is Cleared

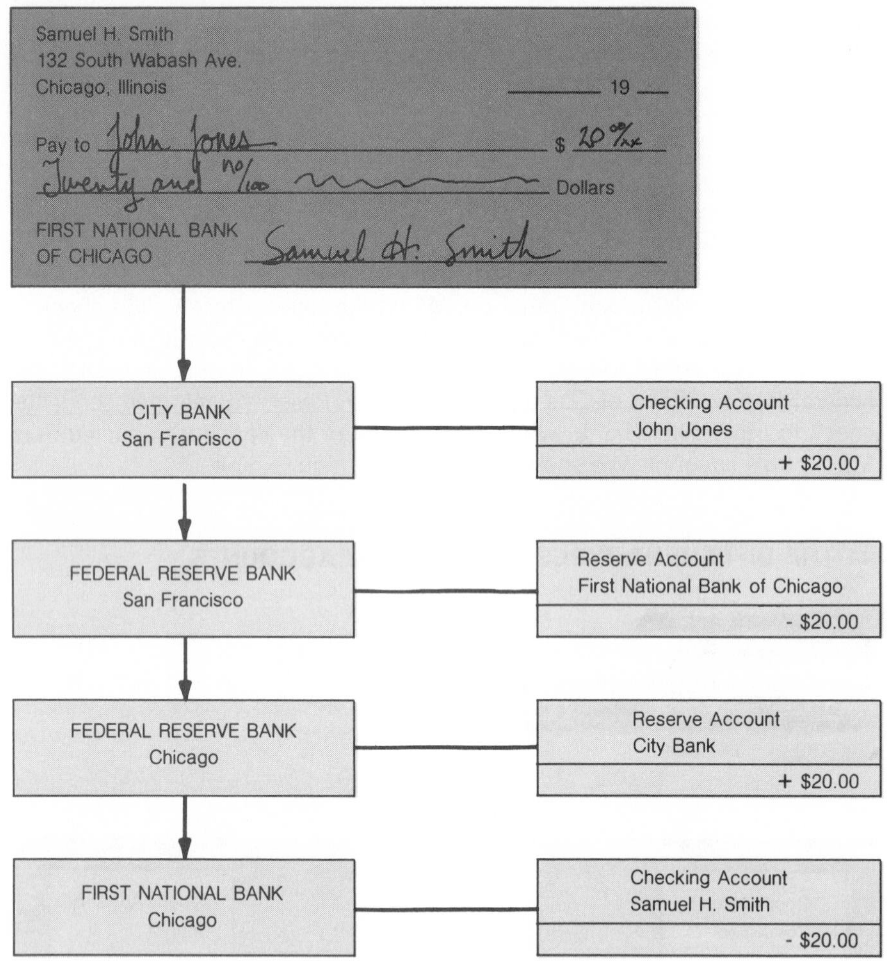

6. Overdraft account
7. NOW account
8. Super NOW account

Minimum Balance

Minimum-balance accounts give you unlimited checking at no charge per check or deposit as long as you maintain a specified balance, such as $200, $300, or $500. Whenever the account balance falls below the specified balance in any month, a service charge is usually added.

There are two methods used to determine whether or not your account has been maintained above a specified minimum balance: the minimum-balance method and the average-balance method.

MINIMUM-BALANCE METHOD. A service fee is based on the lowest balance on any day during the month. Thus, if you go below the specified balance even for one day, you will be charged a service fee.

AVERAGE-BALANCE METHOD. Balances are computed daily, then totaled at the end of the month and divided by the number of business days in the month. If your average balance falls below the minimum required balance, you are charged a service fee. On the other hand, if your average balance is above the minimum, you are not charged for service even though there may have been a number of days during which you fell below the minimum required balance. Clearly, the average-balance method is better for the consumer, especially when your deposit balance fluctuates widely during the month.

NOT REALLY A FREE ACCOUNT. Although minimum-balance checking accounts are advertised as "free," they clearly are not. If you have to keep $500 as a

At last report, the American Bankers Association estimated that only 13 percent of the nation's banks, most of them in the mid-Atlantic and New England states, offered truly free checking-account services.

minimum balance in your checking account for a one-year period, then you have lost the *potential* interest you could have earned in, say, a savings account during that time. Assume that the interest rate you could have earned in a savings account for that one-year period is 6 percent. You would have been charged implicitly, therefore, 6 percent times $500, or $30 per year, for the so-called free minimum-balance checking account.

Free Checking

This account gives you unlimited checking at no charge with no strings attached—no required minimum balance, no monthly maintenance fee, and so on. At last report, the American Bankers Association estimated that only 13 percent of the nation's banks, most of them in the mid-Atlantic and New England states, offered truly free checking-account services. Generally, banks offer free checking only to a limited number of customers—for example, to elderly persons and students. Often, smaller banks will give you free checking-account services in order to lure business away from the larger, more established banks.

Analysis, or Transaction, Plan

With this type of checking account, you are charged for every transaction you make, including deposits. At the end of the month, the total amount of transactions fees charged to you is reduced by a credit that is based on your average balance during that month. The higher the average balance you maintain, the lower the final service charge. As an example, one plan might charge you twelve cents for each check and six cents for each deposit. On the other hand, it will give you a twenty-cent credit for each $100 average balance maintained. If you average twenty checks a month plus two-and-a-half deposits a month and maintain an average balance of $100, this analysis-plan account would cost you $28.20 a year.

Activity, or "Per Check," Plan

With this type of account—often called a special checking account—your monthly fee is based on the amount of your banking activity. There are two separate charges: a flat monthly "maintenance" fee and a charge for every check written. Usually the monthly fee is fifty cents to one dollar, and the check fee is ten cents. This particular account is most suited for customers who write relatively few checks (five to ten) a month. For an individual who averages twenty checks a month, the annual cost for this account would be thirty-three dollars—if the per-month fee was seventy-five cents and the per-check fee was ten cents.

Package Plan

This combination all-in-one package has been introduced recently by many banks. Generally, you're charged a single monthly fee—probably five dollars to seven dollars—which entitles you to something called a Blue Chip, a Gold, or an Executive Account. Included may be the following services:

1. Unlimited check writing
2. Personalized checks, sometimes with your picture embossed on them or with a reproduction of a famous painting or a landscape in your area

3. Overdraft protection (If you write checks for more money than you have in your account, funds will be transferred automatically from either a credit-card account or a personalized line of credit.)
4. A safe deposit box
5. Free traveler's checks, cashier's checks, and money orders
6. Sometimes preferred interest rates on personal loans
7. Free term life insurance

One problem with overdraft accounts is that they foster a false sense of security in the customer who believes he or she has a limitless balance.

Package accounts apparently benefit only those customers who make heavy use of virtually every type of bank service. Usually, most of the services offered by package accounts are used by very few individuals who have such accounts. Statistics show that only 50 percent of package customers actually have safe deposit boxes or use the personal-loan discount offered. Moreover, a number of services attached to package accounts are offered to other customers free of charge anyway, such as free-rein lines of credit.

Overdraft Accounts

Customers who can supply satisfactory credit ratings may be able to obtain an overdraft account, where the bank automatically lends the customer money when his or her checking account balance falls below zero. Thus, instead of refusing payment on checks written on a negative balance, the bank lends the customer a specified amount and automatically deposits that amount into the account. Most plans lend a minimum of $100 and add to the account in multiples of $100. Although few banks actually will lend you the exact amount of your overdraft or negative balance, you would be better off if they did because you would pay interest only on the smaller sum.

Most overdraft accounts require that you make a special deposit at regular intervals and indicate that it is to pay off the loan. Some banks automatically deduct a part of the loan from your regular checking account after you have made deposits in it later in the month. Many overdraft accounts charge a service fee every time they add to your account. Thus, the actual interest cost on an overdraft account loan may be quite high.

One problem with overdraft accounts is that they foster a false sense of security in the customer who believes he or she has a limitless balance. Once that customer has borrowed $100, he or she tends to think it might as well be spent.

NOW Accounts

Virtually all banks offer a NOW, or **negotiable order of withdrawal**, account. In essence, you receive interest on your checking account balances provided you keep a certain minimum balance, such as $500. The interest through 1986 is regulated by the government and is currently 5¼ percent.

NEGOTIABLE ORDER OF WITHDRAWAL (NOW)
The equivalent of a check covered by a special type of interest-earning account.

Super NOW Accounts

Starting in 1983, banks have been allowed to offer **Super NOW accounts** yielding rates of interest that are governed by market conditions. For example, when Super NOW accounts started, most of them offered 8½ to 9 percent per annum interest on account balances compared to 5¼ percent interest earned on regular NOW accounts. The only catch in the deal is that the customer must keep a minimum balance in the Super NOW account of $2,500. In any

SUPER NOW ACCOUNT
A checking-type account available in most commercial banks in which market rates of interest are paid, provided that a minimum balance of $2,500 is maintained in the account.

month when the balance falls below $2,500, the interest earned for the entire month can only be equivalent to that paid on a regular NOW account.

Bank customers can earn even higher interest rates than those offered on Super NOW accounts if they are willing to engage in only six transactions a month with such an account; only three of those transactions may be in check form. These accounts are known by different names but usually have the term *money market* in the name, meaning that the interest rate earned is equivalent to what would be earned by depositing funds in a money market mutual fund (discussed in more detail in Chapter 21). Some banking customers who have large deposits keep only a small working balance in either a NOW account or a Super NOW account and the rest in an insured money market account.

A New Kind of "Banking" Account

In the 1980s, a number of brokerage firms started banking services. The first one was offered by Merrill Lynch Pierce Fenner & Smith. Their brokerage account, called Cash Management Account, or CMA, has all the 3 characteristics of a regular stock brokerage account, where stocks and bonds may be bought and sold. Such an account also allows investors to buy stocks and bonds with borrowed money. If at any time there are idle cash balances in the CMA, they are invested in a money market fund, earning market rates of interest. This is similar to having money in a NOW account or a Super NOW account at a regular depository institution.

Additionally, customers with a CMA receive books of checks and a bank credit card. For Merrill Lynch, both the checks and the credit card are issued by Bank One of Columbus in Columbus, Ohio. When you write a check, it is presented to Bank One for payment. Bank One informs Merrill Lynch, which then transfers money from your cash balance or money market fund to the bank. You also may use your credit card to charge your purchases. These, too, are presented for payment to Bank One, which again collects the funds from your Merrill Lynch account. At the end of each month, you receive a comprehensive statement detailing the transactions and status of the account.

With the advent of these kinds of stock brokerage accounts, we have moved one step closer to both nationwide banking and one-stop financial service. Clearly, the differences among financial institutions are rapidly diminishing. It is interesting to note that savings and loan associations have decided to offer brokerage services to their customers. Also, retail department stores, such as Sears, Roebuck, are offering brokerage and banking services on their premises.

STALE CHECKS

A check that is more than six months old is considered "stale." Some banks will, as a courtesy, contact their depositors before they honor a stale check; this is not required, however. Some banks will even return stale checks, indicating that they are too old, but no law requires such action. Banks are not responsible for screening stale checks, even if they are many years old. Thus, if you do not want a check to be cashed when it is presented for payment, you must put a **stop payment** on the check—that is, an order for it not to be honored.

STOP PAYMENT
An order issued by the payer to a bank not to honor a particular check when it is presented for payment.

Stop Payments

If you wish to stop a check from being collected after you have given it to someone, you can notify the bank, which will then refuse to honor it. You might issue a stop-payment order when you think a check has been lost or stolen. Some consumers order a stop payment when they realize they have been given defective merchandise.

Many banks require that you fill out a stop-payment order after you phone them. A typical stop-payment order is shown in Exhibit 11–3.

Most banks charge from three to ten dollars for each stop-payment order executed. Generally, a phone call will only stop payment on a check for fourteen days; written notice will stop payment for six months, after which time it can be renewed. Once the stop-payment order has been issued, the tellers in the bank are requested not to pay that particular check. The stop-payment information is also put on the computer in order to reject the check if another bank presents it in the bank clearing process. A stop payment can only be made on a regular check from a checking account; **cashier's** and **certified** checks cannot be stopped.

CASHIER'S CHECK
A check drawn on the bank by its own order to a designated person or institution. A cashier's check is paid for before it is obtained.

CERTIFIED CHECK
A check the bank has certified, indicating that sufficient funds are available to cover it when it is cashed.

THE CASHLESS SOCIETY

Some cities, such as Lincoln, Nebraska, and Macon and Atlanta, Georgia, are trying a system of cashless, checkless spending, and it seems to be working. What's it all about? And does it mean that money will be useless? No, it doesn't. It simply means that money will take another form. Money, as we know it, currently takes the form of cash—which consists of currency and checking-account balances—that we use as a means of storing purchasing power. Since

EXHIBIT 11–3
A Typical Stop-Payment Order

TO THE FIRST NATIONAL BANK
OF SOUTH MIAMI
SOUTH MIAMI, FLORIDA

DATE OF ORDER | ACCOUNT NUMBER

Please STOP PAYMENT on my (or our) check drawn on your bank, described as follows:

NO: DATED: PAYABLE TO: AMOUNT: $

REASON: DUPLICATE ISSUED?

THIS REQUEST IS MADE WITH THE UNDERSTANDING THAT THE BANK WILL USE REASONABLE PRECAUTION IN FOLLOWING YOUR INSTRUCTION, BUT IN CONSIDERATION OF THE ACCEPTANCE OF THIS REQUEST, IT IS EXPRESSLY AGREED THAT THE BANK WILL IN NO WAY BE LIABLE IN THE EVENT THE CHECK IS PAID, IF PAID THE SAME DAY YOUR ORDER IS RECEIVED OR IF PAID BY OVERSIGHT OR INADVERTENCE OR IF BY REASON OF SUCH PAYMENT OTHER CHECKS DRAWN BY THE UNDERSIGNED ARE RETURNED FOR INSUFFICIENT FUNDS, AND THE UNDERSIGNED FURTHER AGREES TO INDEMNIFY THE BANK AGAINST ALL EXPENSES AND COSTS THAT IT MIGHT INCUR BY REASON OF REFUSING PAYMENT ON SAID CHECK.

EXPIRATION DATE

IT IS HEREBY AGREED AND UNDERSTOOD THAT THIS ORDER WILL REMAIN IN EFFECT FOR A SIX MONTH PERIOD UNLESS OTHERWISE DIRECTED AND THE BANK WILL CHARGE $5.00 FOR EACH SIX-MONTH PERIOD OR PORTION THEREOF THAT THIS ORDER IS IN EFFECT THE BANK MAY CHARGE MY ACCOUNT WITH THIS AMOUNT

ORDER RECEIVED BY | IN PERSON | BY LETTER | SIGNATURE OF MAKER

BANK NOT LIABLE IF CHECK HAS BEEN CASHED IN THE SAME DAY THIS ORDER WAS ACCEPTED.

our receipts don't always match our expenditures, we generally keep some money in a checking-account balance or in our wallets in order to make expenditures later on each month. In the cashless, checkless society, you would still need a checking-account balance on which to draw, even though you didn't write a check and even though the transmission mechanism was semiautomatic at the beginning of each month. You would have to deposit your income checks into your account at the beginning of each month, just as you do now, although that, too, can be done automatically.

In those cities that allow cashless, checkless transactions, you still keep part of your wealth in the form of a checking-account balance, but you use it in a semiautomatic manner. When you make a purchase in a store, you merely give the merchant or salesperson a credit card, which automatically transfers money from your checking-account balance to the store's balance.

TRANSACTIONS COSTS
The costs associated with any economic activity. For example, the transactions costs involved in doing business by check include the cost of processing the check.

ELECTRONIC FUNDS TRANSFER SYSTEM (EFTS)
A system of transferring money with electronic or magnetic signals.

The cashless, checkless society is merely a means of reducing **transactions costs**. Instead of having to write out checks every month for your mortgage, your phone, your car, and your electricity, a computer does it automatically. The official banking term for computer money is **electronic funds transfer system**, or **EFTS**. There are basically three parts to an EFT system—teller machines, point-of-sale systems, and automated clearinghouses.

AUTOMATIC TELLER MACHINES (ATM). The recent EFTS development has involved teller machines, which also are called customer bank communications terminals or remote service units. They are located either on the bank's premises or in stores, such as supermarkets or drug stores. Automatic teller machines receive deposits, dispense funds from checking or savings accounts, make credit-card advances, and receive payments. The device is connected on-line to the bank's computers. Customers usually have a **debit card** or **EFT card**, which is a plastic card similar to a credit card that allows a customer to use a computer banking system. In order to make a withdrawal from an ATM, the customer uses his or her debit card in addition to punching a **personal identification number (PIN)**. The PIN protects the customer from someone else's use of a lost or stolen debit card.

DEBIT CARD (EFT Card)
A plastic card similar to a credit card that allows a consumer to use a computerized banking system.

PERSONAL IDENTIFICATION NUMBER (PIN)
A code number that is separate from an EFT card but which is needed to use an EFT card. The PIN protects the consumer from someone else's use of the lost or stolen debit card.

POINT-OF-SALE TERMINALS (POS). Such systems allow the consumer to transfer funds to merchants in order to make purchases. On-line terminals are located at check-out counters in the merchant's store. When the customer makes a purchase, his or her card is inserted into the terminal, which reads the data encoded on it. The computer at the customer's bank verifies that the card and identification code are valid and that there is enough money in the customer's account. After the purchase is made, the customer's account is debited for the amount of the purchase.

AUTOMATED CLEARINGHOUSES. Such clearinghouses are similar to actual ones now in use in which checks are cleared between banks. The main difference is that the entries made are in the form of electronic signals because no checks are used. Thus, this is a replacement system, not a system for further automating the handling of paper checks. Such systems are especially useful to businesspersons for recurrent payments, such as payroll, Social Security, or pension fund plans that come up every week or every month. The automated clearinghouse is really a glorified processing system.

This system saves you time, and it also saves the banks and companies money. It is estimated that the banking system spends over $8½ billion annually just to process 40 billion checks; obviously, if this processing can somehow be reduced, you, the consumer, will benefit. Since most of your fixed expenses for car payments, house payments, and the like are anticipated anyway, their being paid automatically isn't going to change your behavior. In the cashless, checkless society, you will get a statement at the end of every month just as you do now; in fact, you probably always will be able to phone in to find out where your finances stand. Since we all face a budget constraint in that we know we ultimately can't spend more than we make, checks and balances against overspending will have to be built into this system.

There are several serious consumer concerns over such a system.

1. Customers are unable to issue stop-payment orders on a check when there is trouble with the seller of a good or service.
2. Fewer records are available.
3. The possibility of tampering is increased, and there is less privacy.
4. There is a loss of "float," or the time between when you write a check and when the sum of the check is deducted from your account.

Will electronic money create even more problems in our supposedly hedonistic society? Perhaps, but one basic fact remains unaltered: No matter what type of credit or money system we use, each family and each individual is faced with a budget constraint. If that individual or that family engages in more impulse buying because of credit cards or electronic money systems, then less

No matter what type of credit or money system we use, each family and each individual is faced with a budget constraint.

funds will be available to purchase other items. This may mean more bankruptcies, but there is a limit to that. When one family goes bankrupt, all the creditors who won't be paid lose out as well. In other words, there is a budget constraint or scarcity problem facing the entire nation at all times. If one person spends more than he or she actually has, then someone else is going to end up with less.

Protection with Electronic Banking

REGULATION E
The set of rules issued by the Federal Reserve Board to protect users of electronic banking services.

Most of the rules governing electronic banking are included in the Electronic Funds Transfer Act of November 1978. In addition to providing a basic framework for the rights, liabilities, and responsibilities of participants in EFT systems, the Federal Reserve Board was given authority to issue rules and regulations to help implement the act. The Federal Reserve Board's implemental regulation is called **Regulation E**—Electronic Funds Transfers. While the board is still writing sections of Regulation E, the rules now in effect are quite important.

For example, anyone who finds or steals your debit card—the card that allows you to draw cash from your savings or checking account at an automatic teller—can loot your account. If, however, your card is used to steal your money, your liability is held to fifty dollars—*if* you report the card's loss to the bank within two days. (If you report the theft after two days, your liability is limited to $500.) Additionally, you are now protected against computer foulups. If the balance revealed to you in a statement or by an automatic or human teller is less than you believe it to be, the bank has only ten business days to find out who is right, unless it chooses to credit your account temporarily with the disputed amount; then it has up to forty-five days for an investigation.

SUMMARY

1. The Federal Reserve System was established in 1913 and consists of twelve member federal banks with twenty-five branches. One of the major functions of the Federal Reserve System is to serve as a clearinghouse for checks.
2. There are at least six types of checking accounts available in commercial banks: minimum balance, free, analysis or transaction, activity or "per check," package, and overdraft.
3. Pursuant to legislation passed at the end of March 1980, all banks that are federally insured, including credit unions, can offer negotiable orders of withdrawal or interest-bearing checking accounts.
4. The cashless society involves teller machines, point-of-sale systems, and automated clearinghouses.
5. Electronic funds transfer systems are covered under the Electronic Funds Transfer Act of November 1978, which gives the Federal Reserve Board authority to issue rules and regulations. Your liability is held to fifty dollars if your EFTS card is used for theft, if you report the card's loss to the bank within two days.

QUESTIONS FOR THOUGHT AND DISCUSSION

1. What is the difference between the average-balance method of computing a monthly checking-account fee and the minimum-balance method?
2. What is an overdraft account?
3. What is the difference between a certified check and a cashier's check?

4. Will an electronic funds transfer system eliminate money in our society?
5. Will an electronic funds transfer system make budgeting more difficult?

THINGS TO DO

Do a research project in your area to determine what differences exist among banks. Since the new legislation in 1980, financial institutions are becoming more and more similar. Are they still different?

SELECTED READINGS

Angell, N. *The Story of Money*. London: Stokes, 1929.

Board of Governors of the Federal Reserve System. *The Federal Reserve System: Purposes and Functions,* 5th ed. Washington, D.C., U.S. Government Printing Office, 1973. See especially Chapters 1 and 4.

Chandler, Lester and Goldfeld, Steven N., *The Economics of Money and Banking,* 8th ed. New York: Harper & Row, 1981, Chapter 7.

Hamilton, Earl G. "An Update on the Automated Clearinghouse." *Federal Reserve Bulletin* 65(7):525–531. Board of Governors of the Federal Reserve System, Division of Support Services, Washington, D.C., 1979.

Miller, Roger LeRoy. *Economics Today,* 4th ed. New York: Harper & Row, 1982. See Chapter 14, "Money and the Banking System."

Your Guide to Consumer Credit and Banking. Chicago: American Bar Association, 1980.

"What Are Your Rights When You Bank by Machine?" *Better Homes & Gardens,* February 1981.

Consumer ISSUE H

COPING WITH BANKS AND THEIR SERVICES

GLOSSARY

POSTDATE—Writing a future date on a check to try to prevent it from being cashed before that date.

SELECTING THE RIGHT ACCOUNT FOR YOU

To decide which of the eight basic types of bank accounts is most appropriate for you, you will have to do two things.

1. Figure out how many checks you write per month. If you write less than fifteen, you are a light check writer; you are average if you write fifteen to twenty-four; and you are a frequent check writer if you average more than twenty-five.
2. Determine the average amount of money you keep in a checking account over and above what you actually use. Many individuals play it close, depositing just enough to cover the checks they are going to write. Others maintain a cushion of several hundred dollars for unforeseen expenses.

Now you can decide which plan you should consider. If you write fewer than five or six checks per month, you should either put your funds into a money market mutual fund (explained in detail in Chapter 21), or, if you have more than $2,500, you should put them into a Super NOW account or an insured mutual fund account at a depository institution.

If you are a heavy check writer and if you keep a very low average balance in your account, you should shop for a bank that charges a small service fee or nothing at all for an unlimited number of transactions, provided you keep a small balance in the account. The key point to remember in finding the right bank and banking services is to shop around and to ask. Banking personnel won't always tell you right away the best deal they have to offer. It is important that you come in with the exact information about your average banking activities and then be aware of the various accounts that are available.

DEALING WITH ELECTRONIC BANKING

The EFT system was discussed in Chapter 11. Now we'll tell you how to deal with it if you choose this option.

Rule #1. Always wait for the machine's record of your transaction, and check it before you leave. Such records tell you the amount, date, and location, as well as the type of transaction. This information, on paper, allows you to verify the bank's monthly statement when you receive it. Also, if you have a dispute, it helps to have the actual receipt from the machine.
Rule #2. When you make a mistake that cannot be corrected at the machine, pick up the direct customer-service phone immediately. This same device holds true if the machine ever shortchanges you.
Rule #3. Keep all records. Put them in your wallet or purse and then collect them for reconciliation at the end of the month.
Rule #4. Transfer your machine records to a checkbook, and keep a running balance.
Rule #5. Reconcile your monthly statement, canceled checks, and machine records at the end of every month, just as you would with a regular checking account. You'll have to keep a detailed record of your machine transactions in order to do so.
Rule #6. Don't share your PIN, or secret code, for your debit card with anyone. If you have a choice, don't choose a PIN that uses your name, initials, birthdate, or

parts of your phone number, Social Security number, or EFT account number.

Rule #7. If you are dealing with an automatic teller, have anyone with you step aside so the transaction can't be observed. Do it politely or with humor, but don't take no for an answer. If someone is waiting behind you or beside you, shield your actions on the numbered keys with your free hand.

HOW TO SETTLE A COMPLAINT WITH A BANK

Because so many of our personal financial transactions filter through the banking system, it is possible that at some point an error will be made, and a dispute may arise between you and the bank. Because the error could have a long-lasting effect on your financial status and an impact on others involved in the transaction, it is important to try to settle it quickly.

As a first step, you should contact the bank directly and explain the problem, of which the bank may not even be aware. Many banks have designated employees to deal with these problems. For example, you may have deposited money that was credited to the wrong account; this deposit will fail to appear on your monthly checking-account statement. In most cases, errors and misunderstandings can be corrected at this level. If, however, you cannot resolve the dispute to your satisfaction by dealing directly with the bank, you may take your complaint to one of the agencies that regulates your bank. These are indicated in Exhibit H-1.

TYPE OF BANK	IDENTIFICATION MARKS	WHERE TO COMPLAIN
National bank	The word "national" appears in the bank's name, or the initials N.A. appear after the bank's name.	Comptroller of the Currency 490 L'Enfant Plaza East, S.W. Washington, D.C. 20219
State bank, member Federal Reserve, FDIC insured	Look for two signs at the bank: "Member, Federal Reserve System" and "Deposits Insured by Federal Deposit Insurance Corporation."	Board of Governors Federal Reserve System 20th Street & Constitution Ave., N.W. Washington, D.C. 20551
State nonmember bank or state-chartered mutual savings bank	FDIC sign will be displayed; Federal Reserve sign will not	Office of Consumer and Compliance Programs Federal Deposit Insurance Corporation 550 17th Street, N.W. Washington, D.C. 20429
Federal savings and loan association	The word "federal" appears in the name. A sign on the door or in the lobby says: "Deposits Insured by FSLIC" or "Federal Savings and Loan Insurance Corporation."	Federal Home Loan Bank Board Office of Community and Consumer Division 17th & G Streets, N.W. Washington, D.C. 20552

SOURCE: From copyrighted article in *U.S. News & World Report,* March 9, 1981.

EXHIBIT H–1
Where to File Unresolved Complaints against Your Bank

BEWARE BEFORE YOU DEPOSIT

Are all depository institutions created alike? Certainly not. Some actually are safer than others. All deposits in virtually all depository institutions are insured by an agency of the federal government, usually up to a limit of $100,000. Deposits in commercial banks that are members of the Federal Reserve System are insured up to $100,000 by the Federal Deposit Insurance Corporation (FDIC). But just because an agency of the federal government insures your deposit doesn't mean you want to take a chance on putting your money into a financial institution that may go "belly up." Sure, you'll get your deposits back up to $100,000, but it may take time. To check the financial condition of the depository institution in which you place your money, contact your local Federal Reserve bank to find out if the financial institution in which you are interested has been placed on a list of "problem banks." On June 30, 1982, for example, twenty-four of the top fifty largest savings and loan associations were considered problem banks, and some were perilously close to disaster.

WRITING CHECKS

Writing out a check is, on the surface, very easy. There are, however, certain errors you can make that can cause problems later.

a. Postdating a check. Check writers often **postdate** their checks, not knowing that banks may slip up and cash a check before its postdated date. Thus, if you postdate a check in hopes of having sufficient funds to cover it, you might end up with an overdraft anyway.

b. Making checks out to "cash." Making a check out to "cash," except when you are right in front of a bank teller's window, is not advisable. Anyone can cash checks made out that way. Thus, if you lose such a check, it is tantamount to losing currency.

c. Improperly filling out amount. It is often easy to be careless and leave spaces before and after the words and numbers indicating the amount of the check. If you do this, you risk an alteration that will increase the apparent amount of the check.

RECONCILING YOUR BANK BALANCE

Every month, you will receive a bank statement and a set of canceled checks. (You should have your deposit slips already.) It is important that you reconcile your bank balance with your checkbook or set of stubs so that you know exactly how much you have in the bank, can catch any mistakes the bank might have made, and can find out if someone has not cashed a check that you wrote.

Since you may have written checks immediately prior to the closing date on your bank statement so that checks have not been paid by the bank yet, the balance in your checkbook rarely will be exactly the same as the balance on your bank statement. Thus, you must reconcile the two by taking account of deposits you made that did not show up on your bank statement and checks you wrote that have not yet been processed.

Exhibit H–2 shows the steps to follow in reconciling your bank balance.

1. Sort your checks, either numerically or by date issued.
2. Deduct from your checkbook balance any service charges—for new checks, overdraft charges, and so on—not previously recorded.
3. Enter your bank statement balance (T). $ ______
4. After adding up all the checks outstanding that are not on your bank-balance statement, subtract the total of these unpaid checks (U) from the bank balance entered above and obtain a new balance here. $ __________ (= T − U)
5. Add up any deposits you made that did not show on your bank statement and put them here (D). $ ______
6. Now obtain your final balance by adding the unreflected deposit total (D) to the new balance you found in Step 4 (T − U). Your final balance is T − U + D.

This final balance should be the same as your checkbook balance after the service charge has been deducted.

Don't destroy your checks and the bank statement after you reconcile your bank balance. For income tax purposes, it's a good idea to keep bank statements and canceled checks for at least three years. Some individuals keep them longer in case there is a dispute with the Internal Revenue Service over federal income taxes.

SUMMARY

1. Before you decide what the best checking account is for you, you must determine how many checks you write per month and what your average checking account balance is. Then you can use the checklist in Exhibit H–1 to select a checking account.
2. One of the best deals is a free NOW account, offered currently by numerous banking and financial institutions throughout the United States.
3. When filling out checks, be sure not to postdate the check, make it out to "cash," or improperly fill out the amount.

EXHIBIT H–2
Reconciling Your Bank Statement

1. Adjust balance in checkbook for service charge and other bank charges and credits shown on bank statement not recorded in checkbook.
2. See that all deposits made by you are properly credited.
3. See that all checks enclosed in your statement are checks issued by you.
4. Check each paid check against your checkbook stubs. List all checks outstanding in space provided here.

Checks outstanding not charged to account

No.	$	
Total	$	

Bank balance shown on this statement $ ______

ADD +

Deposits not credited in this statement $ ______
$ ______
$ ______
TOTAL $ ______

SUBTRACT −
Checks outstanding $ ______

BALANCE $ ______

Should agree with your checkbook balance

QUESTIONS FOR THOUGHT AND DISCUSSION

1. Under what circumstances would you select a checking account that earned a zero rate of interest if alternative types of checking accounts offering positive interest rates were available?
2. Under what circumstances would you be willing to make out a check to cash?

THINGS TO DO

1. Determine the average amount of cash—currency and checking-account balances—you keep throughout a month. Does the sum surprise you?
2. Go shopping for a checking account. What's the best deal you can get?

SELECTED READINGS

"How Safe Are Your Savings?" *McCall's,* May 1982, p. 64.

"Lifting the Lid" (accounts with unlimited interest). *Time,* November 29, 1982, p. 65.

Marcus, A. "Checking Accounts—What's In Them for You?" *Essence,* May 1982, p. 46.

Pauly, D. "Some New Options for Nimble Savers." *Newsweek,* November 29, 1982, p. 72.

Quinn, J. B. "Playing the Savings Game." *Newsweek,* December 6, 1982, p. 121.

Quinn, J. B. "Shopping for Your Savings." *Newsweek,* April 26, 1982, p. 74.

Scherschel, P. M. "What New Bank Law Does for Consumers." *U.S. News & World Report,* October 18, 1982, p. 90.

Stern, R. L. "If You Can't Beat 'Em, Buy 'Em." *Forbes,* November 8, 1982, pp. 41–42.

CHAPTER
THE OVEREXTENDED AMERICAN

12

More than 50 percent of all Americans have outstanding installment debt at any given time. In other words, they have received money from a lender and contracted to pay back what is owed plus interest over a certain period of time.

CHAPTER PREVIEW

- How much are Americans in debt, and what are the characteristics of that debt?
- What are the various sources of credit?
- Why do individuals borrow?
- What are interest rates all about, and what is their relationship to inflation?
- Can interest rate ceilings help consumers?
- How does the Truth-in-Lending Act affect you?

In 1786, in the city of Concord, Massachusetts, the scene of one of the first battles of the Revolution, there were three times as many people in debtors' prison as there were in prison for all other crimes combined. In Worcester County, the ratio was even higher—twenty to one. Most of the prisoners were small farmers who could not pay their debts. In August of 1786, mobs of musket-bearing farmers seized county courthouses to halt the trials of debtors. Led by Daniel Shays, a captain from the Continental Army, the rebels launched an attack on the Federal Arsenal at Springfield; although they were repulsed, their rebellion continued to grow into the winter. Finally George Washington wrote to a friend:

> For God's sake, tell me what is the cause of these commotions. Do they proceed from licentiousness, British influence disseminated by the Tories, or real grievances which admit to redress? If the latter, why were they delayed until the public mind had become so agitated? If the former, why are not the powers of government tried at once?

THE INDEBTED SOCIETY

INTEREST
The cost of using someone else's money.

More than 50 percent of all Americans have outstanding *installment debt* at any given time. In other words, they have received money from a lender and contracted to pay back what is owed plus **interest** over a certain period of time, say, monthly for four years. In 1982, the median debt for families with debt was almost $7,000. For families of adults under forty-five years of age and without children, fully 85 percent had $4,000 or more of outstanding debt (excluding debt on houses). Exhibit 12–1 shows the total amount of private debt in the United States over the past few decades. It has risen to a monumental $1.9 trillion and is expected to rise even more. Of course, part of this is due to inflation and another part is due to a rising population. For a better perspective, the bottom line in Exhibit 12–1 gives the inflation-corrected per capita debt in the United States. Per capita debt in the United States is obtained by dividing the total population into that debt. It is corrected for inflation by subtracting those increases in the debt that are simply due to a rise in the Consumer Price Index.

SOURCES OF CREDIT

The numerous sources of credit for today's consumer can be divided into two general categories:

1. Sources of credit for consumer loans
2. Sources of credit for consumer sales

The first category relates to direct loans that a consumer can obtain. The second category relates to the extension of credit along with the purchase of some item, such as a stereo.

Sources of Consumer Loans

COMMERCIAL BANKS. The most obvious place to obtain credit is a commercial bank. The personal-loan departments of commercial banks make up about 50

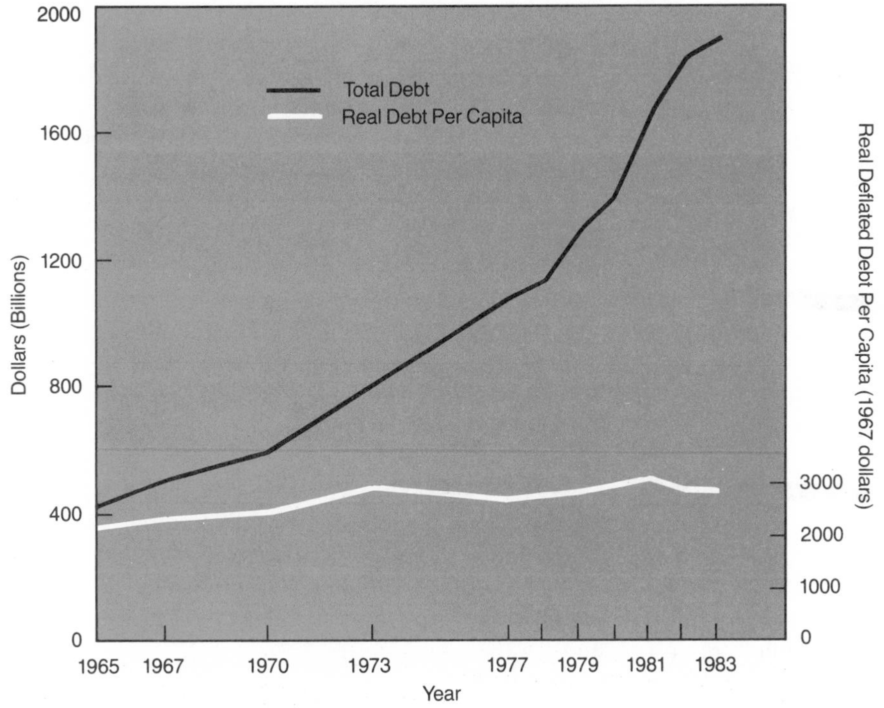

SOURCE: Federal Reserve Board of Governors.

EXHIBIT 12–1
Total Private Debt in the United States

Total private individual, noncorporate enterprise debt in the United States has been on the rise for many years and now exceeds $1 trillion. Per capita total private and noncorporate enterprise debt is expressed in 1967 dollars. That figure has more or less leveled off in the last few years as seen in the bottom line.

percent of the loans for automobile purchases, as well as about 20 percent of all loans for other consumer goods. In general, these banks are full-service commercial banks that have personal-loan departments.

CREDIT UNIONS. Credit unions are a special type of consumer cooperative agency; only members may borrow from a credit union. Teachers and workers belonging to large unions or companies often have the opportunity to join their own credit unions. Credit unions account for about 10 percent of all personal consumer credit.

SAVINGS AND LOAN ASSOCIATIONS AND MUTUAL SAVINGS BANKS. Pursuant to the 1980 Depository Institutions Deregulation and Monetary Control Act, savings and loan associations and savings banks are allowed to make some personal loans to consumers for, say, the purchase of an automobile. Right now, these sources of consumer credit are not particularly important, but they will grow in the future.

CONSUMER FINANCE COMPANIES. Consumer finance companies are small-loan companies that make small loans to consumers at relatively high rates of interest. Interest rates are typically very high because consumer finance companies cater to a higher-risk clientele. That is to say, they incur a higher risk of nonpayment on their outstanding loans than do, say, commercial banks. They must be compensated for this higher risk by receiving a higher interest rate.

Sources of Consumer Sales Credit

BANK CREDIT CARDS. Today, more than 75 percent of all families have at least one nongasoline credit card, and 25 percent have three or more. You are probably familiar with the most widely known of these—MasterCard, VISA, and Chargex. There are about 6,000 banks today that offer MasterCard and 4,000 that offer VISA. Over 300 million credit cards are in use in the United States today.

RETAIL STORES. An increasingly large number of retail outlets offer some form of credit to their customers. Virtually all major department stores, such as Sears, J. C. Penney, Marshall Fields, and Montgomery Ward, offer several types of credit arrangements to customers. These stores provide individual credit cards that are similar to MasterCard and VISA.

DENTISTS, PHYSICIANS, PLUMBERS, AND SO ON. You also can obtain consumer sales credit from your dentist, your physician, or your plumber whenever services are rendered to you and you are "billed later." After all, you have received something of value now but pay nothing in return until later, after receipt of the bill. For the most part, this type of sales credit does not carry any explicit interest charge.

LOANS ON YOUR LIFE INSURANCE

If you have a life insurance policy with a cash value (whole or straight life, usually), then you may indeed be able to obtain a relatively low-cost loan on your life insurance policy. You usually pay something less than 10 percent for a loan on the value of your policy. You cannot be turned down for a loan from your insurance company, and no questions are asked about what the money will be used for. Your credit rating has nothing to do with whether or not you get the loan. You can take as long as you wish to repay. In fact, whenever the policy becomes payable—either because it matures or the owner of it dies—any outstanding loan is deducted from the amount of the insurance claim that the company must pay. Hence, any loan you take out reduces your insurance protection.

WHY BORROW?

Why should you ever borrow money? Some of you may answer, "There's no reason you should ever borrow money. Pay cash for everything and never have debt hanging over your head." This is still the attitude throughout much of Europe, where many people are reluctant to borrow in order to purchase goods and services.

The reason most of us borrow, however, is very simple. For example, you have decided that you want to buy an automobile. Now, you're not buying an automobile *per se*; you're really buying the *services* from that automobile for each day, week, month, and year that you will have it. In fact, what is really important to you is the cost per **service flow** per period. In other words,

SERVICE FLOW
The flow of benefits received from an item that has been purchased or made. Consumer durables generally give a service flow that lasts over a period of time. For example, the service flow from a stereo may be a certain amount of satisfaction received from it every year for five years.

what does it cost you per month to operate that Ford as compared to that VW or that Toyota? What will it cost you per month or per year to buy a new car instead of keeping your old one? Cars are sometimes called **consumer durables,** as are houses, TVs, stereos, and other things that last a relatively long time. You do not consume such durable items immediately; rather, you consume the services from them over a period of time.

CONSUMER DURABLES
Goods that consumers buy that last more than a short period of time. Examples of consumer durables are stereos, television sets, cars, and houses.

Now, when you go to the movies, you consume that movie during the hour and a half or two you are there, and you also pay for that movie when you consume it. When you go out to dinner, you eat the meal and then you usually pay for it on the spot. What are you doing when you consume things and pay for them at the same time? You are timing the payment for the good or service with the rate at which you are consuming it. Why not think of this as the reason for borrowing? You want to synchronize the payments for the services you are consuming from a consumer durable, such as an automobile, with the services themselves. Therefore, you do not feel obliged to pay for the car with cash because you are going to be using it over a certain number of years. What you decide to do usually is to purchase the automobile on time. You decide to borrow. *When you borrow, then, you are merely synchronizing your cash outlay to correspond more or less with the service flow from the good you purchased.* That is why you may wish to borrow.

There are, of course, other reasons why you may wish to borrow money. They include but are not limited to:

1. Taking advantage of advertised specials when you are short of cash
2. Consolidating bills
3. Having a safeguard in emergency situations
4. Being able to shop or travel without having to carry large amounts of cash
5. Increasing *future* earning power, such as obtaining a loan to expand or to introduce a new line of merchandise
6. Attending school

Of course, most people don't explicitly think of credit in these terms. Rather, they simply reason that, because they don't have enough cash to purchase an item they want, such as a car, they must borrow.

SAVING VERSUS CREDIT BUYING

A very astute savings and loan association once ran an ad in some national magazines. The ad pointed out that if you were to save for thirty-six months and buy a car with the savings, the car would cost you, say, $5,000, and you would have had to put in the bank only $4,600, the rest being made up by the interest you received over the three years. On the other hand, pointed out the ad, if you bought the car immediately and paid for it over thirty-six months, not only would you not receive interest on your savings but you would have to pay a finance charge on the installment debt. The total price of the car might be $5,800. There is obviously a big difference between $4,600 and $5,800. The conclusion, according to the savings and loan association: It is better to save now and buy later than to buy now and go into debt.

Is anything wrong with the reasoning in that ad? First of all, the interest on your savings account is taxable by the federal government and some state

When you borrow you are merely synchronizing your cash outlay to correspond more or less with the service flow from the good you purchased.

governments, whereas the interest you pay is tax deductible. Additionally, the price of the car will rise with inflation during the three-year period. If the interest rate on your savings account does not reflect the inflation rate, the arithmetic will clearly be off. Also, a crucial point was left out: During the three years in which you saved, you would not be enjoying the services of the car or of the other things you could buy. You would be putting off your purchase for three years. Most people do not want to wait that long; they would prefer to have the services of the car immediately and pay the finance charge in order to do that. After all, the finance charge is merely a payment for using somebody

else's money so that you can consume and that other person—the saver who decided not to consume—cannot.

You have decided that the implicit utility you get per service flow of whatever you buy is greater than the interest payments you have to pay your creditor in order to get the total amount of money to buy the goods right away. No moral judgment need be passed here: It is simply a question of comparing costs and benefits. The benefit of borrowing is having purchasing power today; the cost is whatever you have to pay in finance charges. Obviously, if the cost were zero, you would borrow as much as you could because you could buy everything you wanted today and pay back whatever you owed at some later date without any penalty. In fact, the ultimate consumer probably would like to die with an infinite debt. That way, he or she could consume all he or she wanted at everybody else's expense. You must remember, though, that creditors take a dim view of this type of behavior because it means financial losses for them. When you buy something on credit with no intention of paying back that loan, there is little difference between that action and stealing. You are taking something from somebody else without intending to pay for it.

The benefits of borrowing are something that only you can decide. But the costs of borrowing are something of which we can all be made aware.

INFLATION AND INTEREST RATES

There is a very definite relationship between rising prices and high interest rates, which currently are as high as they've ever been in the history of the United States. But the relationship is not the simple one of causation that you may have been taught to expect. Contrary to popular belief, high interest rates do not and cannot, in the long run, *cause* inflation. When prices are rising, interest rates will have an inflationary premium tacked on to them. A simple example will show you why and reinforce the comments in Chapter 9.

Suppose that you are a banker who has been loaning out money at 5 percent a year for the last twenty years. Suppose also that for the last twenty years there has been no inflation. That 5 percent interest you have been charging is the *real* rate of interest you are receiving. It covers your costs and gives you a normal profit for your lending activities.

Now prices start rising at 5 percent a year, and you expect that they will rise at that rate forever. If someone comes in to borrow money, how much do you think you would want to lend at the 5 percent rate of interest that you have always charged?

Well, think about it. Say a person comes in to borrow $1,000 for a year. At the end of the year, with an inflation rate of 5 percent, the actual purchasing power of that $1,000 paid back to you will only be $950. If you ask for 5 percent, or fifty dollars in interest payments, you will be compensated only for the erosive effect of inflation on the value of the money you lend out.

Obviously, you will want to tack on an inflationary premium to the real interest rate that you had been charging when there was no inflation and none was anticipated. Hence, in periods of inflation, we find the inflationary premium tacked on everywhere. It is not surprising, then, that, during an inflationary period when prices are rising at 10 percent a year, interest rates would be 15 percent. (See Exhibit 12–2.)

EXHIBIT 12–2
The "Real" Rate of Interest

The rate of interest you are paying on a $1,000 loan for one year	15%
The (expected) rate of inflation (loss in value of money) this year	10%
The difference between the rate of interest you are paying and the loss in the value of dollars you will pay back	5%
So 5 percent is the real rate of interest you pay when you are charged 15 percent on a loan and the rate of inflation is 10 percent.	

(This example ignores tax deductions, which may reduce real interest rates even more.)

There is a very definite relationship between rising prices and high interest rates, which currently are as high as they've ever been in the history of the United States.

You, the demander of credit, or the potential debtor, should not be put off by this higher interest rate. After all, you are going to be repaying the loan in cheapened dollars—that is, dollars that have lost part of their purchasing power through inflation. In fact, some interest rates did not react very rapidly to rising inflation in the early 1970s. Credit unions, for example, were giving out automobile loans at an effective interest rate of 8 percent per annum. If the rate of inflation is 6 or 7 percent, those loans cost people only a 1 or 2 percent real rate of interest. For example, I took out a National Defense Education Act student loan while I was in college in the 1960s. The rate of interest on those loans was 3 percent. Now that I have to pay them back, I am actually *making* money because the real rate of interest on a 3 percent loan with, say, a 9 percent rate of inflation is *minus* 6 percent. That is, there is a profit of 6 percent in holding off paying those loans back. This is not the kind of deal most people get, because potential creditors generally tack on inflationary premiums whenever they think inflation is going to occur.

One thing that inflationary premiums have brought to a head is the problem with usury laws, to which we now turn.

TRUTH-IN-LENDING

The Truth-in-Lending Act, which is Title I of the Consumer Credit Protection Act of 1968, is essentially a disclosure law. Most kinds of installment debts now have to be properly labeled so that the consumer knows exactly what he or she is paying.

The congressional purpose of the act was "to insure a meaningful disclosure of credit terms so that the consumer will be able to compare more readily the various credit terms available to him and avoid the uninformed use of credit." The act, based on the consumer's right to be informed, requires that the various terms used to describe the dollar cost of credit, such as interest, points, and so on, be described and disclosed under one common label, *finance charge*. Likewise, it abolishes all the various terms used to describe the cost of credit in percentage terms, such as discount rates, add-ons, and the like, and prescribes a uniform method of computation of a single rate known as the *annual percentage rate*. As we will see, there are, however, still problems with how this rate is computed.

The original Truth-in-Lending Act did not cover credit extended to corporations, trusts, government, and partnerships; it did not apply to private loans among friends and families or to loans for business purposes or first mortgages;[1] and the extension of credit had to be for $25,000 or less, unless it was secured by real property, such as in a typical home mortgage for which no limit applies. In 1980, Congress decided that the truth-in-lending rules had become too demanding and costly for creditors and also that certain areas not covered by the act should be covered, so it instructed the Federal Reserve Board to change the rules. As of October 1, 1982, there was a slight modification that meant

1. A first mortgage is a credit instrument created to borrow the purchase price of a house. The house is the collateral for the mortgage. The fact that it is a first mortgage means that the creditor who holds the mortgage hs first claim on the house if the debtor (homeowner) defaults in payment on the mortgage.

less information must now be given to the potential borrower. Fortunately for the consumer, however, the new rules require that potential house purchasers be given an accounting of the total amount of interest they will pay over the term of the mortgage. In other words, house mortgages are no longer exempted from truth-in-lending.

WHAT IT COSTS TO BORROW

You are all well aware that borrowing costs. This shouldn't surprise you: After all, nothing is free. Why do you have to pay to borrow? Because somebody else is giving up something. What are they giving up? Purchasing power, or command over goods and services today. For other people to give up command over goods and services today, they have to be compensated, and they usually are compensated with what we call interest. Ask yourself if you would be willing to loan $100 to your friend with the loan to be paid back in ten years, with *no* interest—just the $100 to be returned. Would you do it, even if you were sure of getting the money back? Probably not. You would have to sacrifice what the $100 would have bought, while your friend enjoyed it. Most people will not make this sacrifice with no reward (and they want to be compensated for any risk of not being repaid).

It is best to think of the interest rate you pay on a loan as the price you pay the lender for the use of his or her money. What determines that price is no different from what determines the price of anything else in our economy. The various demands and supplies for credit ultimately result in some sort of interest rate being charged for the different forms of credit.

But we cannot really talk about a single interest rate or a single charge for credit. Interest rates vary according to the length of a loan, the risk involved, whether or not the debtor has put up something as **collateral** for the loan (that is, secured it), and so on. One rule is fairly certain: The greater the perceived risk involved, the more the creditor will demand in interest payments from the debtor. Don't be surprised, then, that interest rates in the economy range all the way from relatively low to relatively high. Much of that difference in interest rates has to do with the riskiness of the loan involved.

COLLATERAL
The backing that people often must put up to obtain a loan. Whatever is placed as collateral for a loan can be sold in order to repay that loan if the debtor cannot pay it off as specified in the loan agreement. For example, the collateral for a new-car loan is generally the new car itself. If the finance company does not get paid for its car loan, it can then repossess the car, sell it, and thereby attempt to pay itself.

The Truth-in-Lending Act also grants the consumer-borrower a **right of rescission** (cancellation) for certain credit contracts. (This is also called a cooling-off period.) Section 125 of the act gives the consumer three business days to rescind a credit transaction that results or may result in a lien on his or her home or on any real property that is used or expected to be used as his or her principal residence. The right of rescission is designed to allow the person additional time to reconsider using his or her residence as security for credit. This right of rescission does not, however, apply to first mortgages on homes.

RIGHT OF RESCISSION
The right to back down, or "bow out," on a contract or an agreement that has been signed. For example, before you sign an agreement to buy a set of encyclopedias, you might want to obtain a notice of cancellation that gives you the right of rescission during a three-day period.

The Truth-in-Lending Act also regulates the advertising of consumer credit. One of the primary purposes of the act's advertising requirements is to eliminate "come-on" credit ads. For example, if any one important credit term is mentioned in an advertisement—down payment or monthly payment—all other important terms also must be defined. (The real effect of this provision has been to eliminate the disclosure of *any* credit terms in most advertisements.)

A 1970 amendment to the act provides federal regulations on the use of credit cards. This amendment prohibits the unsolicited distribution of new credit cards and also establishes a maximum limit of fifty dollars on liability

It is best to think of the interest rate you pay on a loan as the price you pay the lender for the use of his or her money.

for the unauthorized use of each of such cards; that is, the owner of a lost or stolen card that has been used illegally by another person cannot be made liable for more than fifty dollars of illegal purchases.

REVOLVING CREDIT

Many credit card companies currently are imposing an annual membership fee, which is usually $18. So even if you pay your account within the billing period, you still won't receive free credit if you are required to pay a membership fee. In addition, for those people who are unable to pay off their accounts during the billing period, the creditor generally will impose a monthly finance charge of 1½ percent. The creditor computes the finance charge by multiplying the monthly rate times the "outstanding balance." This aspect of open-ended credit accounts (charge) has bothered consumers and caused trouble for the Truth-in-Lending Act. Creditors will use one of the following different techniques to compute the outstanding balance and finance charges on revolving credit accounts.

1. **Previous-balance method**—Here the creditor computes a finance charge on the previous month's balance, even if it has been paid.
2. **Average daily balance**—The finance charge is applied to the sum of the actual amounts outstanding each day during the billing period divided by the number of days in that period. Payments are credited on the exact date of payment.
3. **Adjusted-balance method**—Finance charges are assessed on the balance after deducting payments and credits.

It's important to know which method is used in assessing the finance charge you pay, because the different methods can result in quite different finance charges. For example, assume your opening balance or previous monthly balance was $300. You paid $100 on the account, which was credited on the fifteenth of the month. The monthly interest rate is quoted at 1½ percent (18% annual percentage rate). Exhibit 12–3 shows that the same monthly finance percentage rate can result in a sizeable difference in finance charges based on what the creditor considers the outstanding balance. The same monthly finance charge of 1½ percent results in three different annual rates of interest, depending on which computational method the creditor uses. The Truth-in-Lending Act requires that all revolving credit contracts and monthly bills state the "nominal annual percentage rate," which equals twelve times the monthly rate. As Exhibit 12–3 points out, however, sometimes the annual percentage rate can be misleading when comparing revolving credit accounts.

The Truth-in-Lending Act does not actually assure protection, only information. But information can be valuable, because it allows you, the consumer who is looking for credit, to shop around, to see exactly what you are paying, and to know exactly what you are getting into. Exhibit 12–4 displays a typical disclosure statement. The Truth-in-Lending Act requires that an accurate assessment of the annual percentage rate be given; it is circled for you, and that's what you should look at when you compare the price of credit from various dealers and companies. In addition, you may want to look at the finance charge, which is the total number of dollars you pay to borrow the money, whether

EXHIBIT 12–3
Computing Finance Charges Using Three Different Methods

METHOD	OPENING BALANCE	OUTSTANDING BALANCE (1)	MONTHLY INTEREST RATE (2)	FINANCE CHARGE (1) × (2)(3)
A. Previous balance	$300	$300	1.5%	$4.50
B. Adjusted balance	300	200	1.5%	3.00
C. Average daily balance	300	250	1.5%	3.75

A. Previous balance—The interest rate of .015 is multiplied times $300 to obtain the finance charge of $4.50. It is important to note that the lender gives no credit for the $100 payment received on the fifteenth when computing the outstanding balance.

B. Adjusted balance—The interest rate of .015 is multiplied times $200 to obtain the finance charge of $3.00. The creditor uses only the ending balance for the period as the oustanding balance.

C. Average daily balance—The interest rate of .015 is multiplied times $250 to obtain the finance charge of $3.75. The $250 average daily balance was calculated as follows:

Number of days	X	Balance	= Total balance
15	X	$300	$4500
15	X	200	$3000
			$7500

$$\frac{\text{Total balance}}{\text{Number of days in month (billing period)}} = \text{Average daily balance} \qquad \frac{\$7500}{30} = \$250$$

With this method, the creditor considers the average daily balance as the outstanding balance.

directly or in the form of deferred payments on a purchase. These total finance charges include all the so-called carrying charges that sometimes are tacked on to a retail installment contract, plus such things as "setup" charges and mandatory credit life insurance.[2] These all contribute to your costs of having purchasing power today instead of waiting, of having command over goods and services right now, and of taking that command away from somebody else. Expressed as a percentage of the total price, it gives your annual percentage interest rate. In some cases, it may be very, very high indeed.

ELIMINATING CREDIT DISCRIMINATION

Since October 1975, when the Equal Credit Opportunity Act went into effect, it has been illegal to discriminate on the basis of sex and marital status when granting credit. Regulations pursuant to the act issued by the Federal Reserve Board prohibit:

1. Demanding information on the credit applicant's childbearing intentions or birth-control practices.
2. Requiring cosignatures on loans when such requirements do not apply to all qualified applicants.

2. Credit life insurance is discussed in Issue Q. It usually isn't a good deal.

EXHIBIT 12–4
A Typical Disclosure Statement

ACCOUNT NUMBER				

SEARS, ROEBUCK AND CO.

DISCLOSURE STATEMENT

Sales Check No.________________ Date ____________19____

☐ Easy Payment Plan

☐ Modernizing Credit Plan

DESCRIPTION OF MERCHANDISE

OFFICE USE ONLY (Code 4 Sales)	
NO. OF MONTHS	MONTHLY PAYMENT

CASH PRICE				
CASH DOWN PAYMENT				
UNPAID BALANCE OF CASH PRICE - AMOUNT FINANCED				
FINANCE CHARGE				
DEFERRED PAYMENT PRICE				
TOTAL OF PAYMENTS – THIS SALE				

This purchase is payable in installments pursuant to my Sears Easy Payment Plan—Modernizing Credit Plan Retail Installment Contract and Security Agreement.

Beginning ____________, I will pay $ ________per month for ______months and a final monthly payment of $ ________until the amount financed and the finance charge for this purchase are fully paid.

If the **FINANCE CHARGE** exceeds $5.00, the **ANNUAL PERCENTAGE RATE** is ______ %

In accordance with my Sears Easy Payment Plan-Modernizing Credit Plan Retail Installment Contract and Security Agreement, a subsequent purchase may change the number and amount of my monthly payments, the amount of the Finance Charge and the Annual Percentage Rate of this purchase. Any such change will appear on my next monthly billing statement.

A copy of my sales check is attached hereto and incorporated by reference. Ownership of the merchandise described in such attached sales check remains in Sears until paid for in full.

If I pay in full in advance, any unearned finance charge will be rebated under the Rule of 78, after deducting a charge of $5.00.

11078-202 (F11363 WW) Rev. 12/72

3. Discouraging the applicant from applying for credit because of sex or marital status.
4. Terminating or changing the conditions of credit solely on the basis of a change in marital status.

5. Ignoring alimony and child support payments as regular income in assessing the credit worthiness of the applicant.

Basically, the Equal Credit Opportunity Act reaffirms a woman's right to get and keep credit in her own name rather than that of her husband (or of her former husband, if she is divorced). Women who wish to establish their own lines of credit are advised by bankers to do the following:

1. Open a separate checking and savings accounts in your name.
2. Start an active separate credit history, assuming you can afford it.
3. Open a charge account at a retail store. When applying, list only your own salary, not that of your spouse.
4. Apply for a bank credit card.
5. Finally, take out a small loan and repay it on time. Even if you don't need it, this would speed up the establishment of your credit reliability.

Today, a woman has the legal right to credit for her husband's credit cards. In other words, all new accounts automatically give credit references to all those on the application, including the wife.

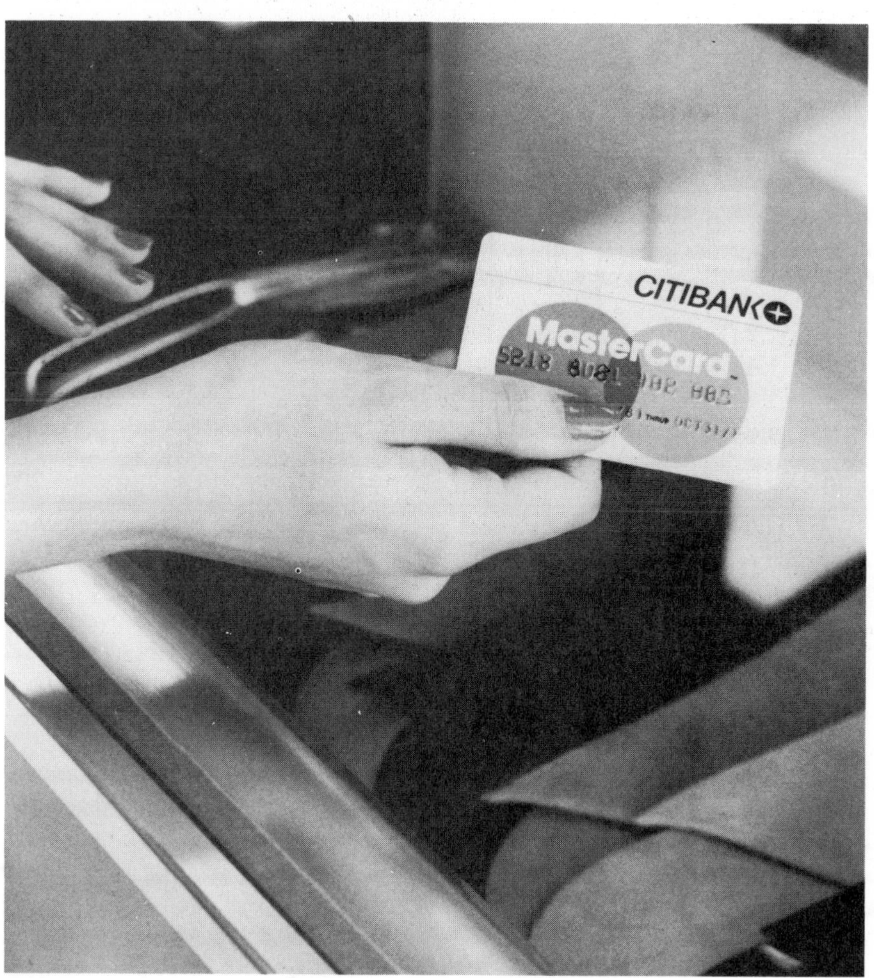

PROBLEMS WITH INSTALLMENT CONTRACTS

INSTALLMENT CONTRACT
A loan made to be repaid in specified, usually equal, amounts over a certain number of months. The contract specifies amount and method of payment.

HOLDER-IN-DUE-COURSE DOCTRINE
A doctrine that allows a third party, such as the finance company that has purchased an installment contract, to continue to receive payments even if the product is defective.

Individuals who sign **installment contracts** when they purchase furniture, appliances, and the like often have found themselves in a bind. In many cases, the merchant who sells an item on an installment contract turns around and resells that contract to a finance company. Until recently, the **holder-in-due-course doctrine** applied. Under such a doctrine, even if you were sold a defective product the holder in due course was entitled to continue to collect payments on that product, since he or she was not the original seller. When the holder-in-due-course doctrine applies, you cannot stop payment because of dissatisfaction with the product.

A new FTC rule on credit buying now gives private consumers (as opposed to commercial buyers) a defense against this practice. Installment contracts must prominently include a note that "the holder of this consumer credit contract is subject to all claims and defenses that the debtor could assert against the seller." Consider the possibility of your buying a set of encyclopedias from a door-to-door salesperson. You agree to a specified monthly payment for a certain number of years. You sign on the dotted line. The encyclopedias are delivered, and, at first, you are quite happy. Four months later, however, you discover that the binding is falling apart on 50 percent of them. You obviously have purchased a faulty product. According to the recent FTC rule, the finance company that is now in possession of the installment contract on which you are paying is just as responsible for the faulty encyclopedias as the original seller would have been.

Note that credit cards are not covered under the new FTC ruling. However, they are covered under the Fair Credit Billing Act, which eliminates the holder-in-due-course doctrine in credit-card transactions of more than fifty dollars and within 100 miles of the cardholder's home.

THE FAIR CREDIT BILLING ACT

Basically, under the rules set up pursuant to this act, you can withhold payment until the dispute over a faulty product that you purchased and paid for by credit card is resolved. It is up to the credit-card issuer, such as American Express or MasterCard, to intervene and attempt a settlement between you and the seller. You do not have unlimited rights to stop payment. You must exercise a good-faith effort to get satisfaction from the seller before you do so. The rules seem to be, however, in the consumer's favor. You don't even have to notify the credit card company that you are cutting off payment (on that item). You just wait for the company to act. However, it is probably a good idea to let the company know what you are doing. Ultimately you can be sued by the credit-card company if no agreement is reached.

Other rules were also set up in the Fair Credit Billing Act. If you think there is an error in your bill, the card company must investigate and suspend payments until it does so. You simply write to the card company within sixty days of getting the bill, briefly explaining the circumstances and why you think there is an error. It is a good idea to include copies (not the originals) of the sales slips at issue. Under the law, the company must acknowledge your letter within thirty days and resolve the dispute within ninety days. During that period, you don't have to pay the amount in dispute or any minimum payments on the amount in dispute. And, further, your creditor cannot charge you finance charges during that period for unpaid balances in dispute. It cannot even close your account; however, if it turns out that there was no error, the creditor can then attempt to collect finance charges for the entire period for which payments were not made.

> Individuals who sign installment contracts when they purchase furniture, appliances, and the like often have found themselves in a bind.

THE FAIR CREDIT REPORTING ACT

The Fair Credit Reporting Act (Title VI of the 1968 Consumer Credit Protection Act) was passed in 1970 and went into effect in 1971. Under this law, you have recourse when a credit-investigating agency gives you a bad rating. Now, when you are turned down for credit because of a bad credit rating, the company that turned you down must give you the name and address of the credit-investigating agency that was used. The same holds true for an insurance company.

The 1971 act was meant to regulate the consumer credit-reporting industry to ensure that credit-reporting agencies supply information that is equitable and fair to the consumer. The problems that led to passage of the act seem to have been the reporting of incorrect, misleading, or incomplete information, as well as one-sided versions of disputed claims. In addition, many people were concerned about the invasion of privacy involved in the distribution of such reports to those who did not really have a legitimate business need for them. These reports often contained material about a person's general reputation, personal characteristics or mode of living, and character.

The act applies not only to the usual credit bureaus and investigating concerns but also to finance companies and banks that routinely give out credit information other than that which is developed from their own transactions.

Under the rules of the law, a credit bureau must disclose to you the "nature and substance of all information" that is included under your name in its files. You also have the right to be told the sources of just about all that information. If you discover that the credit bureau has incomplete, misleading, or false information, the Fair Credit Reporting Act requires that the bureau reinvestigate any disputed information "within a reasonable period of time." Of course, the credit bureau is not necessarily going to do it, but you do have the law on your side, and you can go to court over the issue. In addition, at your request, the credit bureau must send to those companies that received a credit report in the last six months a notice of the elimination of any false information from your credit record. Finally, if the credit bureau does not correct your information, you can file a personal version concerning any disputes.

Even if you have not been rejected for credit, you still have the right to go to a credit bureau and find out what your file contains. You also have the right to ask the credit bureau to delete, correct, or investigate items you believe to be fallacious and inaccurate. The credit bureau then has the legal right to charge you for the time it spends correcting any mistakes. Also, the Fair Credit Reporting Act specifically forbids credit bureaus from sending out any adverse information that is more than seven years old. But there are important exceptions. Bankruptcy information can be sent out to your prospective creditors for a full fourteen years. And there is no time limit on any information for loans or life insurance policies of $50,000 or more or for a job application with an annual salary of $20,000 or more. That means that adverse information may be kept in your file and used indefinitely for these purposes.

FAIR DEBT COLLECTION PRACTICES ACT

In 1977, Congress passed the Fair Debt Collection Practices Act. The purpose of the act is to regulate the debt collection practices of persons who collect debts from consumers arising out of purchases that are primarily for personal, family, or household purposes. The act prohibits the following debt practices:

1. Contacting the consumer at his or her place of employment if the employer objects.
2. Contacting the consumer at inconvenient or unusual times, such as three o'clock in the morning, or contacting the consumer at all if he or she is represented by an attorney.
3. Contacting third parties other than parents, spouses, or financial advisers about the payment of a debt unless the court authorizes it.
4. Using harassment and intimidation, such as abusive language, or using false or misleading information, such as posing as a police officer.
5. Communicating with the consumer after receipt of notice that the consumer is refusing to pay the debt, except to advise the consumer of further action to be taken by the collection agency.

The enforcement of this act is the responsibility of the Federal Trade Commission. The act limits the damages and penalties that can be recovered for violation, including attorneys' fees.

SUMMARY

1. The largest nonhome consumer debt item in America is automobile loans.
2. At least 50 percent of all Americans have outstanding installment debt at any given time.
3. The sources of credit are many, including commercial banks, finance companies, consumer finance companies, credit unions, credit-card companies, and retail stores.
4. Individuals borrow in order to obtain the services of large consumer items without paying for them at one time. The installment payments can be thought of as matching the service flow from whatever was purchased, such as a house or a car.
5. Interest is the payment for using somebody else's money today. As such, it is like any other price. During inflation, interest rates must rise to take account of the rate of inflation. Hence, interest rates are relatively high when the rate of inflation is high.
6. The real rate of interest you pay on a loan is the stated rate of interest minus the rate of inflation.
7. The Truth-in-Lending Act requires that both the total finance charge and the annual percentage rate be clearly stated on a loan agreement (except on first mortgages on homes).
8. You must be careful when computing the actual percentage interest rate you will pay on an open-ended credit account. Ask specifically whether one

of the following three methods is used: previous balance, average daily balance, or adjusted balance. As you saw in Exhibit 2–3, the resultant finance charge can be much higher if, for example, the previous-balance method is used instead of the adjusted-balance method.

QUESTIONS FOR THOUGHT AND DISCUSSION

1. Why do you think the aggregate amount of debt in the United States has been growing so much? Does it have anything to do with increased incomes? Increased population? Increased price level?
2. What is the difference between credit and debt?
3. The interest rate charged by different lenders varies tremendously. Does this mean that some of them have a monopoly? If not, how can you account for the differences?
4. Does it seem fair that those who pay cash pay the same price as those who use a credit card?
5. Can you think of some very specific reasons why you would ever want to borrow money? Or ever have?
6. Is it better to save and buy? Or to buy and go into debt?
7. Do you think it is appropriate that interest rates be regulated? If your answer is yes, how does the regulation of interest rates differ from the regulation of other prices in our economy?
8. During a number of years in this decade, the rate of inflation exceeded the rate of interest that some borrowers had to pay on their loans. What does that mean about the real rate of interest those borrowers were paying?
9. Do you think the Truth-in-Lending Act has been effective? Why?
10. Can consumers figure out how they are actually being charged for their credit? What information would be helpful in addition to that which now exists?
11. If you are charged a setup fee in addition to some annual percentage rate to borrow money from a credit-card company, should that setup charge be included as part of the total finance charge? Would this raise or lower the annual percentage rate of interest?

THINGS TO DO

1. See if you can find a self-supporting adult who has *never* gone into debt. (If you find one, ask how and/or why.)
2. Make a survey in your area of the various sources of credit. Find out what the various characteristics of those sources are and what the various charges on their loans might be.
3. Pick a consumer durable good such as an automobile or an expensive stereo. Call around to find out where you could get the best loan. If there are big differences in annual interest rates charged for the loan, try to determine why.
4. Ask your neighborhood retailers who accept credit cards whether they give a discount for cash. If they do not, find out why not.
5. Ask someone who works in a savings and loan association what his or her feelings are about going into debt. See if that person thinks it is better to save and then buy, rather than to go into debt and have today.
6. Go to your reference library and find out from the *Monthly Labor Review,* the *Federal Reserve Bulletin,* the *Survey of Current Business,* or the *Business Conditions Digest* what the rate of inflation has been for the past five years. Then compare that rate of inflation with the interest rate you would have to

pay to borrow for the purchase of, say, a new car. Now calculate the real rate of interest that you would have been charged. Does that real rate of interest seem high or low? If it seems relatively low, can you figure out why it would have been so low?

7. Find out if there is a usury law in your state. Compare it to the so-called prime rate, or the rate of interest charged by banks to the lowest-risk—that is, the best—borrowers. The prime rate can be found in the *Federal Reserve Bulletin* or in the local newspaper every once in a while. Or you can call up a local banker and ask him or her what the prime rate is. If your state usury law is close to the prime rate, ask the local banker whether that has caused any problems.

8. Obtain the disclosure statements from a number of local department stores and appliance stores that offer credit. Make a comparison of the annual percentage rates listed on the forms. Then call the credit departments and find out whether they use the previous-balance, average-daily-balance, or adjusted-balance method of computing the finance charge. Now see if that will make a difference in the annual percentage rate. If it does, find out from your local field office of the Federal Trade Commission why there are such discrepancies.

SELECTED READINGS

Annual Report to Congress on Truth in Lending. Board of Governors of the Federal Reserve System (latest edition).

Buying on Time. New York State Banking Department, 2 World Trade Center, New York, New York 10047 (latest edition).

Federal Reserve Bank of New York. *Consumer Credit Terminology Handbook*. New York: Federal Reserve Bank, 1979.

Federal Reserve Board Consumer Handbook to Credit Protection Laws. Washington, D.C. Publication Services 20551.

Meyer, Martin J. *How to Turn Plastic into Gold*. New York: Farnsworth Publishing, 1974.

Consumer ISSUE I

COPING WITH THE CREDIT MAZE

GLOSSARY

ACCELERATION CLAUSE—A clause contained in numerous credit agreements whereby if one payment is missed, the entire unpaid balance becomes due, or the due date is accelerated to the immediate future.

ADD-ON CLAUSE—A clause in an installment contract that makes your earlier purchases with that firm security for the new purchase.

ASSETS—The entire property of a person, association, corporation, or estate that is applicable or subject to the payment of his or her or its debts; or the items on a balance sheet showing the book value of property owned.

BANKRUPTCY—The state of having come under the provisions of the law that entitles a person's creditors to have his or her estate administered for their benefit.

GARNISHMENT (WAGE ATTACHMENT)—A court-ordered withholding of part of your wages, the proceeds of which are used to satisfy upaid debts.

LIABILITIES—Something for which you are liable or responsible according to law or equity, especially pecuniary debts or obligations.

NET WORTH—The difference between your assets and your liabilities, or what you are actually worth. If your liabilities exceed your assets, your net worth is negative.

WHEN SHOULD YOU BORROW?

Some consumer economics books give you cut-and-dried formulas to tell you when you should borrow. It is not unusual to find a financial adviser telling consumers that they should borrow only for major purchases such as automobiles. Just about everyone who buys a house automatically assumes that it is respectable to borrow; very few of us are in a position to pay out $40,000, $50,000, $60,000 or even more for the full cost of a house. Because we know that the housing services we consume per month represent a very small part of the total price (because houses last so long), it seems meaningless to spend all that cash; instead, we take out a mortgage. The same holds for cars, especially new ones. A car is such a large expense that very few of us consider that we should pay for it in cash; 71 percent of all new automobiles are purchased on credit. After houses and automobiles, though, the reasoning gets pretty fuzzy. Is it all right to buy a stereo on credit? Some financial advisers say yes, and some say no. Is it all right to buy furniture on credit? Some advisers say yes, some say no. Of course, for clothes and food, most financial advisers are adamant about the desirability of paying cash.

A Dollar Is a Dollar Is a Dollar

When you think about it, the reasoning behind such cut-and-dried rules is pretty shaky. Gertrude Stein once wrote that a rose is a rose is a rose; and so, too, a dollar is a dollar is a dollar. What does it matter what you say your dollar is going to buy? You cannot earmark it. If you make $100 a week and you spend $10 for clothes, $50 for food and lodging, and the rest on entertainment, how do you know which dollar you used for "essentials"—food and lodging and clothes—and which dollar you used for "nonessentials"—entertainment? You don't know because you cannot tell one dollar from another. What does it matter if you say you are going to use credit to buy your

There are two rules to consider for borrowing:

The first one is: *Never overcommit yourself.*

The second one is: *Limit the times you borrow money but maximize the amounts borrowed,* because this is the way you will pay the lowest interest charges. In other words, don't borrow several small amounts at one-week intervals; wait and borrow the total amount all at once.

EXHIBIT I–1
Rules for Borrowing

clothes and pay for your entertainment with cash? It does not matter. What is important is for you to decide what percentage of your anticipated income you are willing to set aside for fixed payments to repay loans. You should care about the total commitment you have made to creditors. You want to make sure you have not overcommitted yourself. By using Exhibit I–2 you can get an idea of what may be safe for you.

WHAT IS THE MAXIMUM YOU CAN BORROW?

If you go to a bank or a credit company and ask for a loan, the loan officer probably will require you to fill out a form. On this form, you list your **liabilities** and your **assets** so that the credit officer can estimate your **net worth.** Exhibit I–3 shows a typical net-worth statement. You have to put down all your assets—whatever you own—and all your liabilities—whatever you owe. The difference is your net worth. (See Exhibit I–4). Obviously, if your net worth is negative, you will have a hard time getting a loan from anybody unless you can show that your expected income in the immediate future will be substantial.

You still do not know what your maximum credit limit is. That, of course, depends on the loan officer's assessment of your financial position. This will be a function of your net worth, your income, your relative indebtedness, and how regular your situation is. What does regularity mean? It

can mean different things to different people, but in general it means the following.

1. You have been working regularly for a long period and, therefore, have been receiving regular income.
2. Your family situation is stable.
3. You have regularly paid off your debts on time.

Or your credit worthiness can be measured by the three Cs that loan officers use as a guide to lending:

1. Capacity to pay back
2. Character
3. Capital or collateral that you own

Loan officers may appear to some of you to discriminate against people with unstable living situations—that is, those who have unstable jobs, unstable family situations, and the like. That may or may not be true, depending on your definition of discrimination. But a loan officer is supposed to make decisions that maximize the profits for his or her company. At the going interest rate, he or she may decide to eliminate people who are high risks: Loans will be refused to people who come in with records that indicate they will not pay off their debts as easily or as regularly as those people who seem more stable. If you are a credit buyer with an unstable living situation, one way you can persuade loan officers not to refuse you is to discuss your problems candidly with them and produce a past record of loan repayments that was stable in spite of your unstable situation. Or, alternatively, you could offer to pay a higher interest rate.

Nevertheless, you may sometimes be refused credit because of a bad credit rating. Once there was little you could do about this but now a new federal law offers you some recourse.

WHAT TO DO WHEN YOU ARE REFUSED CREDIT

The previous chapter discussed the Fair Credit Reporting Act of 1971. Exhibit I–5 shows what you can do to protect yourself against unfair credit reports that have caused you to be refused credit.

GIVING YOURSELF THE BEST CHANCE

How do you give yourself the best chance to get the loan you want? Make sure that you plan ahead. Credit experts suggest you do the following.

1. Write to the local credit-reporting bureaus in your area (addresses in the Yellow Pages) for information about you in their files. They ask you for a small fee, but it will be worth it. If you find any information that is missing or any mistakes, ask for corrections now.
2. If you do not have any credit history, start now by opening a checking and a savings account in your own name. Take out a small loan and repay it on time, and also attempt to get a bank credit card or a store charge account.
3. When filling out a loan application, answer *all* questions.
4. Make a copy of your loan application so that, every time you apply for a new loan, you can repeat all the same information that you have used before. Lenders usually open a new file for every new type of loan.
5. Comparison shopping is useful, but don't try to obtain the same type of loan from several lenders at the same time. Your credit record may then show a streak of applications, which will raise questions among potential lenders.
6. If a lender turns you down, try another.
7. Remember, a refusal is not permanent. You may want to try again, even with the same lender.

EXHIBIT I–2
Determining A Safe Debt Load

First, you must determine your spendable income per month. Put it down here. $ ________

Next, determine your monthly debt payments.

1. Automobile $________
2. Appliances ________
3. Cash loan ________
4. Others ________

Total $ ________

Now, determine your monthly payments as a percentage of spendable income. Then look at the following guidelines.

DEBT GUIDELINES: PAYMENTS AS A PERCENTAGE OF SPENDABLE MONTHLY INCOME.

Percentage	Current Monthly Debt Load	Can I Assume Additional Debt?
15% or less	Within safety limits	Yes.
15–20%	Right at limit	Yes, but be careful.
20–30%	Overextended	No, no, no.
Above 30%	On the verge of going under	Perish the thought!

EXHIBIT I–3

A Typical Net Worth Statement

(Personal Financial Statement) .... **OFFICE** ....

Name .... **Address** ....

Business .... **City** .... **Zip** ....

Social Security Numbers:

Borrower: .... **Spouse:** .... **Statement as of:** ....

ASSETS				LIABILITIES			
Cash on hand and in banks	....	....	....	Notes payable banks:	....	....	....
U.S. Government Securities—Schedule 1	....	....	....	Secured	....	....	....
Stocks and Bonds—Schedule 1	....	....	....	Unsecured	....	....	....
Accounts receivable	....	....	....	Notes payable other	....	....	....
Notes receivable	....	....	....	Accounts and bills payable	....	....	....
Cash surrender value life insurance	....	....	....	Accrued taxes and interest	....	....	....
Face Value $				Mortgages payable on real estate—Schedule 2	....	....	....
Real estate—Schedule 2	....	....	....	....	....	....	....
Automobiles	....	....	....	Security Agreements	....	....	....
Other assets—itemize	....	....	....	Other debts—itemize	....	....	....
....	....	....	....	....	....	....	....
....	....	....	....	....	....	....	....
....	....	....	....	....	....	....	....
....	....	....	....	....			
....	....	....	....	Total liabilities	....	....	....
....	....	....	....	Net worth	....	....	....
TOTAL ASSETS	....	....	....	TOTAL LIABILITIES AND NET WORTH	....	....	....

SOURCE OF INCOME				GENERAL INFORMATION
Salary	....	....	....	Married (name of spouse) ....
Bonus and commissions	....	....	....	Single ....
Dividends	....	....		Number of children ....
Real estate income	....	....	....	Other dependents ....
Other income	....	....	....	Are any assets pledged? ....
....	....	....	....	Defendant in any suits or legal actions? ....
....	....	....	....	Personal bank accounts carried at ....
....	....	....	....	Life insurance—face amount, company, beneficaries ....
				....
TOTAL	....	....	....	....

DO YOU HAVE A WILL? YES ___ NO ___

CONTINGENT LIABILITIES

Endorser or comaker ....

Legal claims ....

Federal Income Taxes:

1. Do you owe any Federal Tax for years prior to the current year? Yes ☐ No ☐ Amount $ ....
2. Are there any unpaid Federal Tax Assessments outstanding against you? Yes ☐ No ☐ Amount $ ....

Other ....

TYPICAL REASONS FOR REFUSAL

Bankers offer the following typical reasons why an application is refused.

1. Insufficient length of local residence
2. Insufficient income
3. Inability to verify employment
4. Excessive obligations
5. Insufficient credit history

SHOPPING FOR CREDIT

Once you have decided that you want to buy some credit—that is, you want to get some goods now and pay for them later—then you should shop around. The Truth-in-Lending Act, which requires a full statement of the annual interest rate charged, makes shopping much easier these days. This is certainly true if you are comparing revolving credit accounts: If the actual annual interest charge for one is 22½ percent, you know this is not as good a deal as another one at 18 percent.

THINGS TO WATCH FOR

Acceleration Clauses

You must be careful when you look at loan agreements because all have various contingency clauses written into them that may or may not affect you. For example, if you sign a credit agreement with an acceleration clause—meaning that the entire debt becomes due immediately if you, the borrower, fail to meet any single payment on the debt—you probably could not pay such a large sum. Obviously, if you could not meet a payment on the debt because you lacked the money, you certainly would be unable to pay off the whole loan at once. The addition of an acceleration clause in a credit agreement increases the probability that whatever you bought on credit will be repossessed.[1]

Add-on Clauses

You also should be aware of what is called an add-on clause in installment contracts, particularly when you go shopping for furniture and appliances. An add-on clause essentially makes earlier purchases security for the more recent purchase. Let's say that you buy furniture for your living room from a particular store on an installment contract. Six months later, you decice that you want new furniture for a bedroom. You return to the same store and also buy the bedroom furniture on an installment contract. If there is an add-on clause and you default on the

1. Since loans with an acceleration clause usually can be obtained at relatively lower interest rates, they still may be a good deal for people who rarely or never default on loan payments.

EXHIBIT 1–4
Determining Your Net Worth

Estimated amounts, end of this year	
ASSETS	
House (including furniture)—market value	________
Car(s)—resale value	________
Life insurance—cash value	________
Bonds, securities—market value	________
Cash on hand	________
Other (for example, stereo, cameras, savings accounts, land)	________
TOTAL ASSETS	________
LIABILITIES	________
Mortgage	________
Loans	________
Other	________
TOTAL LIABILITIES	________
NET WORTH	________
December 31, 19__	________

An annual net-worth statement may help you and/or your family to keep track of financial progress from year to year. Essentially, your net worth is an indication of how much wealth you actually own. We generally find that young people have low net worths—or even negative net worths: that is, they owe more than they own—because they are anticipating having higher income in the future. As individuals and families get further down the road, their net worth increases steadily, only to start falling again, usually when retirement age approaches and the income flow slows down or stops completely, thereby forcing the retired person or couple to draw on past accumulated savings. This very simplified statement of family net worth can be easily filled out. Just make sure you include all your assets and all your liabilities. Assets are anything you own, and liabilities are anything you owe.

If you are trying to get insurance, credit, or a job, you may be subjected to a personal investigation. Under the Fair Credit Reporting Act of 1971:

☐ The company asking for the investigation is supposed to let you know you are being investigated.

☐ You can demand the name and address of the firm hired to do the investigating.

☐ You can demand that the investigating company tell you what its report contains—except for medical information used to determine your eligibility for life insurance.

☐ You cannot require the investigators to reveal the names of neighbors or friends who supplied information.

If the investigation turns up derogatory or inaccurate material, you can:

☐ Demand a recheck.

☐ Require the investigators to take out of your file anything that is inaccurate.

☐ Require them to insert your version of the facts, if the facts remain in dispute.

☐ Sue the investigating firm for damages if negligence on its part resulted in violation of the law and caused you some loss—failure to get a job, loss of credit or insurance, or even great personal embarrassment.

☐ Require the company to cease reporting adverse information after it is seven years old—with the exception of a bankruptcy, which can remain in the file for fourteen years.

EXHIBIT I–5
What You Can Do To Protect Yourself Against Unfair Credit Reports

installment contract for the bedroom furniture, you not only can lose that furniture but all the items you purchased for the living room, even if you have paid for that furniture after making the second purchase. An example is given in Exhibit I–6.

Garnishment (Wage Attachment)

It is also possible for a court order to allow a creditor to attach, or seize, part of your property. Your bank account may be attached and used to discharge any debts, or your wages may be garnished. That is, if a judgment is made against you, your employer is required to withhold wages to pay a creditor. (If this happens, you may find it hard to keep your job or get another.)

The Federal Garnishment Law, effective July 1, 1970, is part of the Consumer Credit Protection Act. It limits the portion of an employee's wages that can be garnished. Garnishment can be no more than the lesser of the following:

1. Twenty-five percent of take-home pay, or
2. The amount by which take-home pay is in excess of thirty times the federal minimum hourly wage.

The act prohibits firms from firing an employee because of a wage garnishment.

Balloon Clause

Balloon clauses are defined as terms of an installment loan contract that require, after a period of time, a specific payment more than twice the normal installment payment. For example, a contract may indicate that $100 a month is due for eleven months; then a single payment of $600 is due in the twelfth month. If you cannot pay the $600, you either have to refinance or, possibly, lose the item purchased on credit ("interest only" loans are "balloon" loans).

THE RULE OF 78

Suppose you took out a loan for twelve months and wanted to pay it back after five months. The bank or finance company normally uses what is called *the rule of 78* to calculate what you owe in terms of the percentage of the total year's interest that would have been earned had you carried out the full contractual agreement.

If you pay off the loan after one month, then, based on the rule of 78, you will have to pay your creditor 12/78ths of the year's total interest. This is equivalent to 15.38 percent of one year's interest owed. On the other hand, the exact proportional amount of interest that you would have paid on such an installment contract for one month would equal 1/12th the year's total interest, or 8.33 percent. Notice the penalty for such an early repayment; you pay almost double the interest for that one-month loan than is stated in the installment contract.

If you keep the loan for two months and then repay it, you end up having to pay (12 + 11)/78ths, or 23/78ths of the total year's interest. Again, comparison shows that the 23/78ths equals 29.49 percent, and 2/12ths equals 16.67 percent. You almost double the effective amount of interest that you pay over what you would have paid had you kept the loan outstanding. In sum, then, using the rule of 78 to calculate early repayment results in the lender obtaining more than a strictly prorated distribution of interest.

Consider another example. If you are making an early repayment on a two-year loan with twenty-four equal installments, you would use the rule of 300.[2] If you repaid the loan after one month, you would owe 23/300ths of the total amount of interest that would have been paid over a two-year period (since there are twenty-four monthly installments). That means you would pay 8.00 percent of the total as opposed to the pro rata distribution of interest that would equal 1/24th, or 4.17 percent.

Lenders do not have to calculate what you owe in this step-by-step manner because they use prepared tables. The method used to prepare the tables, however, is similar to the process just described.

FIGURING OUT THE INTEREST RATE YOU ARE PAYING

There is a relatively simple formula to give you the approximate interest rate you actually are paying on a consumer installment loan. The formula is:

$$i = \frac{2 \cdot t \cdot C}{P\,(n + 1)}$$

where the letters have the following meaning:

- i = annual simple interest rate in decimal form
- t = how many times a year you have to pay (for example, 52 if weekly, 12 if monthly)
- C = actual dollar cost of borrowing (finance charge)
- P = the net amount borrowed
- n = the number of payments in total

Let's take an example. Assume that you apply for a loan of \$100. The finance company will give it to you for a service fee of \$10 for a one-year period, to be repaid in twelve monthly installments. You are told, therefore, that you are paying only 10 percent interest. But that really isn't what you are paying. Let's put those numbers into the preceding formula. The net amount you are receiving is \$100, so: P = \$100; C = \$10; t = 12; and n = 12. The formula becomes:

$$i = \frac{2 \times 12 \times \$10}{\$100\,(12 + 1)} = 18.46\%$$

2. Because (1 + 2 + 3 + 4 + 5 ... + 24) = 300.

EXHIBIT I–6
Example of an "Add-On" Clause

ADD-ON SALE — The Buyer agrees to the consolidation of the unpaid Time Balance (less unearned Credit Service Charge) owing under a previous Contract of the Buyer with the Principal Balance of this Contract into a new Principal Balance as follows:

1. Cash Sale Price	$ ______	
Cash Sale Price of accessories and/or services	$ ______	
	TOTAL	$ ______
2. DOWN PAYMENT		
In Cash Today	$ ______	
In Cash on Delivery	$ ______	
In Cash on	$ ______	
Trade in of	$ ______	
	TOTAL	$ ______
3. PRINCIPAL BALANCE (Difference between 1 & 2)		$ ______
4. PREVIOUS CONTRACT UNPAID TIME BALANCE	$ ______	
LESS Unearned Credit Service Charge	$ ______	
	TOTAL	$ ______
5. CONSOLIDATED NEW PRINCIPAL BALANCE (Sum of 3 & 4)		$ ______
6. COST OF LIFE INSURANCE—covering life of Buyer first-named above. (See reverse side)	NO SEPARATE CHARGE	
7. CREDIT SERVICE CHARGE ON 5		$ ______
8. NEW TIME BALANCE (Sum of 6 & 7)		$ ______

If it was a discount loan, you would receive only $90 and the formula would look like this:

$$i = \frac{2 \times 12 \times \$10}{\$90\ (12 + 1)} = 20.5\%$$

If you wish to figure out what it would cost you to borrow $1,000 for any specified period of time, look at Exhibit I–7. It shows different specified annual percentage rates for different time periods.

INTEREST RATE AND TAXES

To calculate the interest that you actually pay, you have to take account of inflation and of the taxes you save by borrowing. Interest payments and finance charges are usually tax-deductible. Every dollar of interest payments you make is one dollar less of income on which you pay taxes. That means that your tax savings would be twenty cents on each dollar if you are in the 20 percent tax bracket; if you are paying an interest rate of 10 percent and your taxable income bracket is 20 percent, the after-tax interest payment you actually are paying is only 8 percent. Obviously, the higher your tax bracket, the less it really costs you to borrow. (See Exhibit I–8.)

WHERE SHOULD YOU GO FOR A LOAN?

For some asset purchases, you immediately know where to go for a loan. If you are buying a house, you obviously don't go to your local small-loan company for a loan. Instead, you go to a savings and loan association, a commercial bank, or a mortgage trust company; or you sign a contract with the seller of the house. The real-estate agent usually helps the buyer of a house secure a loan. If you want to shop around, the easiest thing to do is to call various savings and loan associations to see what interest rates they are charging or visit those that won't reveal that information over the telephone. Consumer Issue L discusses in more detail what you should look out for when borrowing money on a house.

EXHIBIT I–7
The Cost of Financing $1,000 on the Installment Plan

PERCENTAGE RATE (ANNUAL)	LENGTH OF LOAN (MONTHS)	MONTHLY PAYMENTS	FINANCE CHARGE	TOTAL COST OF LOAN
9.25%	6	$171.19	$ 27.14	$1,027.14
	12	87.57	50.84	1,050.84
	24	45.80	99.20	1,099.20
	36	31.92	149.12	1,149.12
10.5%	6	171.81	30.86	1,030.86
	12	88.15	57.80	1,057.80
	24	46.38	113.12	1,113.12
	36	32.50	170.00	1,170.00
12%	6	172.55	35.30	1,035.30
	12	88.85	66.20	1,066.20
	24	47.07	129.68	1,129.68
	36	33.21	195.56	1,195.56
13%	6	173.04	38.24	1,038.24
	12	89.32	71.84	1,071.84
	24	47.54	140.96	1,140.96
	36	33.69	212.84	1,212.84
15%	6	174.03	44.18	1.044.18
	12	90.26	83.12	1,083.12
	24	48.49	163.76	1,163.76
	36	34.67	248.12	1,248.12
18%	6	175.53	53.18	1,053.18
	12	91.68	100.16	1,100.16
	24	49.92	198.08	1,198.08
	36	36.15	301.40	1,301.40

1. Assume your tax rate is 20 percent; that is, you must pay Uncle Sam 20 cents of the (last) dollars you earn.
2. Interest payments are tax deductible.
3. You borrow $1,000 at 15 percent; that is, you pay $150 interest.
4. But when calculating your taxes, you get to deduct that $150 from your income *before* you compute your taxes owed.
5. Hence, what you do *not* have to pay Uncle Sam is .20 × $150 = $30.
6. Your actual interest payment for that $1,000 loan is, therefore, $150 − $30 (in tax savings) = $120, or only 12 percent (instead of 15 percent) on a simple interest loan.

EXHIBIT I–8
Actual Interest Paid after Tax Deduction

To borrow for a car, again you probably won't go to the small-loan company around the corner. Rather, you should go to a credit union or a commercial bank, where the loan for a car will cost less. Note that the interest rate for a new car is usually lower than for a used car. Why? Because the car is used as collateral, and a new car is generally easier to sell than a used car. You should note also that if you buy a car that is technically brand new—that is, you would be the first owner—but you purchase it after next year's models have entered the showroom, the lending agency may consider that to be a used car and charge you the higher rate of interest.

If you want to borrow money for purchases of smaller items, a credit-union loan might be cheapest; the next best deal would be credit-card companies—MasterCard and VISA, for example.

The key to purchasing the best credit deal is to treat credit as a good or service; use the same shopping techniques for purchasing credit that you would use to purchase anything else. Your shopping shouldn't stop after you've found the best car deal, for example. You may not be getting the best deal possible if you buy the credit for the car from the dealership or its affiliate. You may do better going to your local commercial bank. But you cannot predict: You have to compare.

NOTHING IS FREE

Some companies advertise that they want to help you help yourself. They propose to consolidate all your debts into one fixed monthly payment that will be lower than the total of what you are paying now to all your creditors. Rarely, though, is this claim true; in most instances, you won't actually pay a smaller interest rate by consolidating your debts instead of paying them separately. Remember, you have already incurred any setup charges involved in taking out the various lines of credit that you want consolidated. Credit companies do nothing for free; like any other company, they won't render a service unless they make a profit on it. So if you let a credit company pay off all your existing debts and then lend you the total amount that they paid, you will have to incur the setup charge for that.

Sometimes, however, debt consolidation actually *may* save you some money. If, for example, you consolidate all your revolving credit accounts that charge you 18 percent into one 12 percent credit-union loan, you will be better off (assuming there are no early-payment penalty charges on the revolving credit accounts).

Furthermore, it may be more *convenient* for you to have all your loans consolidated into one big one. Then you only have to write one check a month instead of many. But this service will not be handed to you without charge. You may, in fact, have a smaller monthly charge, but it will be for many more months, and you ultimately will pay higher finance charges for the whole consolidation package and, thus, a higher total payment. If you detest keeping records and writing out lots of checks, you may want to incur this additional cost (and additional debt) by taking a loan consolidation.[3] As long as you realize that nobody gives you anything for free, you can make a rational choice, knowing that there are always costs for any benefits you receive. Loan consolidation certainly isn't going to pull you out of dire financial trouble; the only way out of such trouble is either to make a higher income or cut back on your current consumption so you can pay off your debts more easily. (You could, of course, sell some of your assets to pay off your debts.)

DANGER SIGNALS

If you observe any of the following, you are in danger of having overextended yourself financially.

1. You consistently postpone paying your bills or paying any given bill on a rotation basis.
2. You begin to hear from your creditors.
3. You have no savings or not enough to tide you over a financial upset.

3. But don't delude yourself into believing that you have fewer debts simply because your monthly payments are now lower.

4. You have little or no idea what your living expenses are.
5. You use a lot of credit, have charge accounts all over town and several credit cards in your wallet, and you pay only the monthly minimum on each account.
6. You don't know how much your debts total.

HOW TO KEEP FROM GOING UNDER

You can do certain things to prevent yourself and your family from getting into deeper financial trouble. Some of the following common-sense actions will be of special help.

1. Itemize your debts in detail, making sure you note the current balance, monthly payments, and dates when payments are due.
2. List the family's total net income that can be counted on every month.
3. Subtract your monthly living expenses from your net income. Don't include the payments on debts you already have. The result will be the income you would be able to spend if you had no debts. Now subtract the monthly payments you are committed to making on all your debts. If you come out with a minus figure, you are obviously living beyond your means. If you come out with a very small positive figure, you still may be living beyond your means.
4. If you think that your spending unit is, in fact, living beyond its means, you must inform your family that the money situation is tight. Tell them that you and every other spender in the family unit will have to cut expenses, such as those on recreation, food, and transportation.

CREDIT-CARD SWINDLES

You should be aware of a few ploys that dishonest individuals use to swindle credit-card holders. Sometimes, for example, a dishonest merchant will use your card to run off blank sales slips. Later he or she will fill in the amounts and forge your signature. To prevent this swindle, try not to let your credit card out of your sight. Be alert to merchants who have their card machines in a back room or where you can't watch the transaction.

The second swindle is made possible by a careless cardholder who throws away the copy of the credit receipt. The swindler, who obtains the cardholder's name and account number from the tossed receipt, is thus able to order expensive merchandise over the phone using the cardholder's identity. Since the merchandise will be delivered before the cardholder receives the bill, the swindler obtains items free of charge. To prevent this from happening to you, save copies of all your sales receipts so you can verify the accuracy of your billing statement and have proof of purchase.

SUMMARY

1. There is no definite way to decide which purchases should be bought on time and which should be bought with cash. Rather, your total outstanding debt should not exceed what you can handle.
2. You determine your safe debt load by adding up all your outstanding debt, which includes loan payments, department store payments, credit-card payments, overdue accounts on telephone and electricity, and so on. One way of determining whether this is a safe debt load is by taking 10 percent of your monthly take-home pay (that is, after taxes), and multiplying it by eighteen. If your monthly debt is greater than what is safe, you must take steps to reduce it.
3. You should estimate your net worth regularly, perhaps once a year.
4. You determine your net worth by adding up all your assets, which include the market value of your house, your car(s), your bonds, stocks, and other things. Subtract what you owe, such as your house mortgage and other loans. This gives you your net worth.
5. Keeping track of your net worth year by year gives you an idea of the financial progress you are making. If your net worth stays constant or goes down, you are spending annually more than you receive.
6. When applying for a loan, you must realize that the loan officer will look at your capacity to pay back, your character, and what collateral you can put up to back the loan.
7. When applying for a loan, put your best foot forward; either type the form or print the information clearly. And when meeting the loan officer, dress appropriately: First impressions are important.
8. If you are refused credit, the Fair Credit Reporting Act allows you to demand that the firm hired to do the credit

check tell you what its report contains, that it do a recheck, and that it insert your version of any facts in dispute.

9. When you shop for credit, shop as if you were buying any other good or service. Look for the best deal by calling around to get various offers of interest rates and monthly payments, checking to see whether an acceleration clause is in your contract, making sure all finance and setup charges are specifically stated in any contract, and recomputing the finance charge yourself—do not take the loan company's word for it.

10. Be wary of debt-consolidation schemes. They generally are expensive.

QUESTIONS FOR THOUGHT AND DISCUSSION

1. Is it important for you to determine why you are borrowing money before you borrow? Would you feel safer borrowing money to buy a durable consumer good, such as a refrigerator, TV, or stereo, rather than borrowing money for a vacation?

2. Do you think it is unfair for loan offices to delve into your character before they decide whether you are a good credit risk? Why or why not?

THINGS TO DO

1. Go to Exhibit I–2 and determine your safe debt load or the debt load of your parents. How much are you overextended or underextended? (Is it possible to be underextended in debt?)

2. Call several banks or the credit departments of various stores in your area and ask them to send you a loan application. Fill out the net-worth statement to see what your net worth is. Familiarize yourself with all the various terms. If you do not know what they mean, ask your instructor or go to a dictionary. If it is appropriate, attempt to determine your net worth for the past five years. Has it gone up or down?

3. Call or write your local field office of the Federal Trade Commission. Ask how the FTC enforces the Truth-in-Lending Act. See if their methods of enforcement have changed over the last few years.

4. Calculate the actual interest paid after your tax deduction for a typical consumer loan. Try to calculate the actual interest paid by someone who is in the 70 percent tax bracket. Is there a big difference between the two corrected interest rates?

SELECTED READINGS

"Bankruptcy Reform." *Family Economics Review*, Summer/Fall 1980.

Be Wise: Consumers' Quick Credit Guide. Washington, D.C.: U.S. Department of Agriculture, Government Printing Office, September 1972.

Before You Sign a Contract, HXT-95. Berkeley: Agricultural Extension Service, University of California.

Buying on Time, HXT-93. Berkeley: Agricultural Extension Service, University of California.

"Consumer Handbook to Credit Protection Laws." Free copy from Pubication Services, Federal Reserve Board, Washington, D.C., 20551.

"Credit Insurance: The Quiet Overcharge." *Consumer Reports*, July 1979, pp. 415–17.

Daly, M. "What to Do If You're Overextended." *Better Homes and Gardens*, November 1979, pp. 31–32.

Dunkelberg, William C. "Bankruptcy in the United States." *Family Economics Review*, Spring 1982, pp. 16–19.

Elliott, E. and Susco, W. "Debts: Who Owes What to Whom When It Comes to Credit." *Working Woman*, October 1979, p. 10.

"Getting Credit How to Score with Lenders." *Consumer Views*, Vol. X, No. 9, September 1971.

Hooper, J. B. "Good Credit Risks: What the Computer Looks For." *Good Housekeeping*, July 1979, p. 223.

Kaufman, Daniel. *How to Get Out of Debt*. Los Angeles, CA: Corwin Books, 1978.

Klein, Martin I. "How HR 8200 Alters Bankruptcy Law." *The Florida Bar Journal*, Vol. 52, No. 2, February 1979, pp. 70–82.

"Living in Debt." *Newsweek*, January 8, 1979, pp. 46–54.

"Need to Borrow? Know the New Rules." *Changing Times*, November 1982, p. 22.

Rankin, D. "How Not to Get Too Deep in Debt." *Redbook*, November 1979, p. 44.

"The Rule of 78's or What May Happen When You Pay Off a Loan Early." Available free from Department of Consumer Affairs. Federal Reserve Bank of Philadelphia, P.O. Box 66, Philadelphia, Pa. 19105.

Skousen, Mark. *The 1979 Insider's Banking and Credit Almanac*. New York: Caroline House, 1979.

"A Screwy Rule That Shortchanges Borrowers." *Changing Times,* September 1980, pp. 59–62.

"Why More People Are Going Bankrupt." *U.S. News & World Report,* November 5, 1979, p. 76.

"Why Owning a Credit Card Shouldn't Be a Family Affair." *Business Week,* January 10, 1983, p. 89.

Wishard, William R. *Credit and Borrowing in New York . . . in Illinois . . . in Texas.* New York: Caroline House, 1979.

Appendix I
Going into Personal Bankruptcy

On October 1, 1979, a new **bankruptcy** law took effect. It was the first complete revision of U.S. bankruptcy laws since 1898. Among other things, it increased the filing fee for individuals from fifty to sixty dollars, plus lawyers' fees. Remember, however, that the basic intent of the new bankruptcy law remains the same: to provide a fresh start for individuals and businesses that suffer financial failure. Basically, when you go bankrupt, the court takes all your property, sells it, splits the proceeds among the creditors, and then erases any remaining debts. Certain debts are not discharged in bankruptcy, however, including alimony and taxes and any debts incurred under false pretenses.

Exemptions

The new bankruptcy law creates a set of exemptions that may apply in your state. The court and creditors cannot take possession of these exemptions. They are as follows:

1. Your interest, up to $1,200, in a motor vehicle.
2. Your interest in a home and burial plot up to $7,500.
3. Up to $500 worth of jewelry.
4. Your interest up to $200 for any single item of clothing, appliances, animals, musical instruments, and books.
5. Any other property worth up to $400, plus any unused part of the $7,500 exemption in the equity in your house.
6. Your interest up to $750 in books or tools and implements of trade.
7. All professionally prescribed health aids.
8. Social Security, veterans benefits, unemployment compensation, alimony, child support, disability benefits, and all payments from profit sharing, annuities, and pension plans.

Note that each state may have certain variations from the Federal Bankruptcy Law. Thus, it is important to discuss your pending bankruptcy with a lawyer if you decide to go through with it.

THE NEW CHAPTER 13

Under the new bankruptcy law, you may choose a Chapter 13 repayment plan. This is basically a debt-consolidation program with legal safeguards that permits you to stretch out your payment of bills. You can develop a plan for full or even partial repayment of debts over an extended period of time. It is a meaningful alternative to full bankruptcy litigation. Any individual with regular income who owes unsecured debts of less than $100,000 or secured debts of less than $350,000 can be a Chapter 13 debtor. Under the old law, only a wage earner was eligible for such relief; the person with a small business was excluded. Now the sole proprietor of a small business can use this plan.

The new Chapter 13 continues the old law insofar as the debtor is given the exclusive right to propose a repayment plan. No creditor can force a debtor into a plan that he or she does not wish to accept. The plan may provide for repayment over a period of up to five years. It may also provide for payment of claims only out of future income or out of a combination of future income and the liquidation of some of the debtor's currently owned property. Once a Chapter 13 plan has been approved, all creditors must stop collection efforts and suspend interest and late charges on most kinds of debts. Each month, the debtor turns over a specified amount of money to a court trustee, who then dispenses it to the creditors. As long as the plan is working, the debtor may keep all of his or her assets.

One of the big benefits of a Chapter 13 plan is that you may end up paying off your debts at less than 100 cents on the dollar. If you repay at least 70 percent of your debts, you do not have to wait the usual six years until you file for bankruptcy again.

FILING FOR STRAIGHT BANKRUPTCY

If you decide a Chapter 13 plan is not for you, then you can file for straight bankruptcy. You usually will need the services of a lawyer. You must list all your debts and assets. Straight bankruptcy is the only legal way you can cancel your debts without paying them. After filing, you essentially give up all that you own (except for the exempted assets); that is, the court has control over all your assets. A trustee is named to check on those assets available for distribution to creditors. The court will return to you tools and other items necessary for you to earn your living, as well as food, clothing, basic furniture, and perhaps, but not always, your home. Exactly what you can keep varies from state to state and should be determined before you even consider declaring personal bankruptcy.

The benefit of declaring bankruptcy is that most debts are wiped out except for taxes, alimony and support payments, and the debts that others have cosigned for you (which now become their debts), plus any secured debts.

The disadvantage has already been mentioned: you no longer have control over your property. And, in addition, bankruptcy puts a black mark on your credit record. Furthermore, you can get back into debt right away. After all, you have court and lawyers' costs, which together might run to $500. And, remember, you cannot file for bankruptcy again for another six years.

CHAPTER
THE $500 BILLION STOMACH

13

In one year, the average American consumes 284.2 pounds of fluid milk and cream, 18.1 pounds of cheese, 62 pounds of poultry, 65 pounds of pork, and 91.3 pounds of sugar. . . . We are feeding a very large and hungry stomach.

CHAPTER PREVIEW

- What are some characteristics of food consumption in the United States?
- How do government inspection and labeling requirements affect the consumer?
- Specifically, what does the Fair Packaging and Labeling Act do?
- What is the difference between direct and indirect food additives and how do they affect the consumer?
- What are some attributes of good nutrition?
- Why do we use convenience foods and are they more expensive?
- What is the current status of universal product coding?

In one year, the average American consumes 284.2 pounds of fluid milk and cream, 18.1 pounds of cheese, 62 pounds of poultry, 65 pounds of pork, 83.2 pounds of fresh fruit, 103.8 pounds of fresh vegetables, and 91.3 pounds of sugar. The total amount of money spent on food products is just as staggering—an estimated almost $500 billion in 1984 alone. Americans consume more than 30 percent of the world's total agricultural output. We are feeding a very large and hungry stomach. We buy our food products at 300,000 retail stores that carry an average of 2,600 different products on their shelves at any one time. The number of brands of different types of foods—canned peas, carrots, soups, cereals—is probably many thousands when you include all the regional specialties you can buy.

FOOD AND INCOME

Even though we spend a total of $500 billion a year on food, that represents only 16 percent of GNP in the United States. Exhibit 13–1 shows that the percentage of American income spent on food consumption has actually been falling. Is this surprising? Well, it shouldn't be. Ask yourself how much more food you could buy if you doubled your income. You could certainly buy better quality, and perhaps you could eat in restaurants more often. But there is a limit, at least for most of you, and that limit is a physical one. Your stomach can hold only so much at any one sitting, and your body will maintain its weight only if you do not take in more calories than you use.

If people's expenditures for food had kept pace with their incomes over the past 150 years in the United States, we would be a nation of balloons, running into each other and having trouble sitting in chairs, driving cars, and getting on buses. While there may be some tendency for the average American to be slightly overweight, we certainly are not a nation of corpulent slobs.

EXHIBIT 13–1
Percentage of Total Income In The United States Going for Food

At the beginning of the Great Depression and for the following twenty or so years, the percentage of disposable personal income going for food remained at around 23 or 24 percent. In 1950, it started dropping, until it reached about 16 percent in 1970.

SOURCE: USDA Agricultural Economic Report No. 138, Supplement for 1971, and U.S. Department of Commerce.

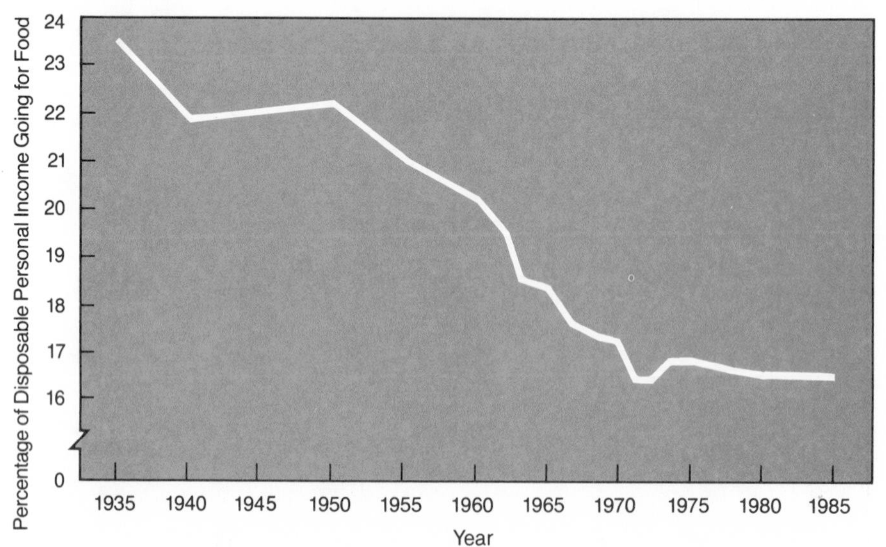

In 1856, a German statistician, Ernst Engel, made some budgetary studies of family expenditures and found that, as family incomes increased, the *percentage* spent on food decreased—not the total amount on food, of course, but the percentage. A family making $25,000 a year certainly spends more on food than a family making $10,000 a year. However, even though the richer family has an income two-and-a-half times larger than the other family's, the richer family does not spend two-and-a-half times the amount that the other family spends on food.

Engel's Law has fairly universal applicability, not only through time but across nations at any given moment. Recall our discussion of this in Chapter 8 in reference to the budgets of different families. Richer nations spend a smaller fraction of their total national income on food than do poorer nations, and we can predict that, in the United States, if we become richer, our expenditures on food will become a smaller percentage of total expenditures.

ENGEL'S LAW
A proposition, first made by Ernst Engel, that states that as a family's income rises, the proportion spent on food falls.

GOVERNMENT LABELING AND INSPECTION REQUIREMENTS

Because food is an essential part of every consumer's budget, the government has, through the years, established a system of inspection and labeling designed to aid consumers in making wiser choices about the food products we buy. You may not be aware of it, but the government is constantly inspecting meatpacking houses and various food-processing establishments to ensure that our food is processed in a clean, bacteria-free environment so we won't suffer the harmful effects that sometimes result from improper food processing. The Food and Drug Administration goes so far as to determine periodically the quantities of rodent hair, mold, and insect residue in your peanut butter! The government is also attempting to enforce fair packaging and labeling, particularly in the form of the Fair Packaging and Labeling Act of 1966. The consumer movement in the early 1960s, which resulted in this act, involved a concern over information being given to the consumer.

Fair Packaging

The law came about as a result of numerous criticisms directed at packagers. The quantity of contents were often inadequately or confusingly disclosed; there was no uniform designation of quantity by weight or fluid volume. For example, one producer would measure by ounces, while a competitor would measure by the quart or would measure by quarts and ounces combined. In addition, there was criticism of the use of presumably meaningless adjectives of exaggeration, such as "giant" or "jumbo," and the use of designations of servings, such as small, medium, and large, without any standard of reference.

The act applies to such consumer commodities as foods and drugs, devices or cosmetics that are subject to the Federal Food, Drug and Cosmetic Act, and to any other article customarily purchased for sale through retailers for consumption by individuals or for "use by individuals for purposes of personal care or in the performance of services ordinarily rendered within the household." The Federal Trade Commission at first proposed regulations that enlarged upon the term "consumer commodity" to include virtually everything. But

The consumer movement in the early 1960s, . . . involved a concern over information being given to the consumer.

when producers threatened substantial litigation if these enlarged regulations went through, the FTC instead listed fifty-two classes of products that it does not consider to be "consumer commodities" and, therefore, are not included under the Fair Packaging and Labeling Act of 1966.

The act also authorized the secretary of commerce to attempt to limit "undue" proliferation of product package sizes. If the secretary determines that an undue proliferation causes consumers to suffer an "unreasonably" impaired ability to make product comparison, then the secretary may request that manufacturers, packers, and distributors participate in the development of a *voluntary* product standard for that commodity. If no standard has been adopted within one year after such a request or if the voluntary standard adopted is not observed, the secretary of commerce is supposed to report such determination to Congress.

The act, which became effective in 1967, does not apply to tobacco, meat, poultry, and any other products already covered by federal laws. It requires, among other things, that the label of every consumer food product covered must:

1. Give the net quantity per serving and number of servings in the package.
2. Not have "too much" air space or packaging material.
3. Identify the commodity and make clear the name and place of business of the manufacturer, distributor, or packer.
4. Contain a statement in a standard location on the main display panel of the package of the net contents in units that seem appropriate for the product.

All federal efforts at fair packaging and labeling are aimed at providing consumers with a maximum amount of information so that we may make rational choices. And all such efforts may be gathered under the label "truth in packaging," or truth, plain and simple. But we have to be careful when we analyze the effects of truth-in-packaging acts passed by federal, state, or local governments. Take the case of air space in packages. If all consumers could be duped forever, the ultimate result of, say, cereal manufacturers putting their products in big boxes with quantities of air space would be that people would end up buying boxes of mostly air. Since that has not happened (at least not yet), we know that *some* consumers are informed.

Many of the informed consumers who keep producers in line are institutional buyers—governments, hospitals, day camps, day-care centers, summer camps—that buy great amounts of food and have nutritionists who make sure that the best food value is obtained. These large institutional buyers who take so much care in their food shopping are **marginal buyers.** If they find out that a particular product they have purchased is a gyp, they switch immediately; they are right on the margin between buying it and buying the second-best choice. Fortunately, there are always a number of these buyers around. In fact, one study showed that fully one-third of all shoppers are marginal shoppers; they are very price conscious, and they take time and effort to establish the validity of the claims made by all ads and labels.

MARGINAL BUYERS
Buyers who are just on the borderline between buying and not buying a product for a particular price. Marginal buyers for specific products are very concerned with price and quality of those products.

LABELING COSTS. Increased information, regulations, and other changes in labeling policies incur added costs for food manufacturers. Much of this expense is passed on to the consumer in the form of higher prices for food items. Present packaging standards can accommodate only so much information on product labels; with current demands for more thorough labeling, different standards of packaging may be necessary. The consumer should be aware that he or she will bear a good part of this expense.

Net Weight Sometimes Spells Nonsense

Even though the Fair Packaging and Labeling Act requires that the net weight of canned foods be given, it is sometimes difficult to figure out what you really are buying. You have to find out, for example, the actual eight of the fruit in a can of pears because some brands will have more syrup than others. If you do not want the syrup, then you do not care how much *it* weighs.

The Food and Drug Administration has numerous requirements for the canning industry. The usual rule of thumb is that a container must be at least 90 percent full. However, since packing liquid, such as syrup for peach halves, can be legally added, the FDA requirement isn't obviously very useful. The National Canners Association takes the position that part of the nutrients of the canned food end up in the liquids used for canning, so the liquid is part of the food product. (Many consumer economists do not, of course, agree with the canners' point of view.) Therefore, the NCA is against disclosing the drained weights on the labels of cans. But since it appears that the drained weight averages about the same percentage of labeled weight for all brands of a given product, it probably wouldn't matter. We consumers would know that we actually are paying a higher price per average drained weight, but we still would have the same selection at about the same prices we have always been paying. It could be argued, nonetheless, that what we are referring to here is an awareness issue. Why shouldn't consumers be aware of the drained weight? If you believe strongly in this issue, then you would demand that canners state drained weight instead of net weight.

USDA Grades—Another Labeling Confusion

In addition to FDA labeling requirements for canned or processed foods and meat inspection, the U.S. Department of Agriculture provides for grade marks on various meats and fresh produce. These grades are meant to guide the consumer as to the level of quality, but the labels are often misleading.

MEAT. All fresh meats, with the exception of pork, are *voluntarily* labeled as to grade. Until several years ago, the top grade available in supermarkets was "prime," followed by "choice." But new government beef-grading standards have taken effect after years of controversy and court battles. Under these new standards, some beef will qualify for a higher grade than it did before. Americans are eating leaner and leaner cuts of meat. Since the grades *prime* and *choice* for beef depend on the amount of fat marbling, fewer consumers are buying those grades for health reasons. Regulations proposed in 1982 would allow beef with less fat marbling to be labeled "choice" and "prime" by the retailer. Consumer groups are against the change because they believe it will cause beef prices to rise.

Grading for quality should not be confused with inspection. All meat sold for human consumption is inspected for wholesomeness. Grading is voluntary and is supposed to predict the eating quality of the meat. It is usually a measure of fat content or marbling. Normally, more than half the beef inspected by the USDA is also graded for quality. Of this, the USDA reports 5 percent graded prime, 78 percent graded choice, and 13 percent good. The rest is graded standard or utility and, along with most of the ungraded beef, will go into items like processed meats.

POULTRY. Poultry, which was not under federal inspection standards until the Wholesome Poultry Products Act of 1968, is now subject to USDA grading. Poultry is graded solely on physically observable characteristics, such as freezer burns, presence or absence of wing tips or other missing parts, or breaks in the skin. In other words, a grade of A on a turkey may mean that you get a tough old bird that just happens to have all its parts and suffers from no *observable* flaws. Similarly, a B bird, though technically a lesser grade, may be delicious but have a broken wing tip. Poultry grading does not guarantee quality; but you can be sure that a C rating means that the product is likely to appear physically unmarketable.

OTHER FOOD PRODUCTS. The USDA also provides for the grading of other food products, such as eggs and milk and fresh fruits and vegetables, usually those that come prepackaged. In this area particularly, the grading is often misleading. Exhibit 13–2 lists some of the grades applying to produce. As you can see, "U.S. No. 1" is not a sufficient guide to quality; in some cases, it represents

EXHIBIT 13–2
Produce Grading

The U.S. Department of Agriculture has instituted a rather complex system of product grading. For example, U.S. No. 1 is *not* the top grade for grapefruit but is for onions. For oranges from Florida, U.S. No. 1 is the third grade, the top grade being U.S. Fancy and the second grade being U.S. No. 1 Bright.

COMMODITY	TOP GRADE	SECOND GRADE	THIRD GRADE	FOURTH GRADE
Apples (all states but Washington)	U.S. Extra Fancy	U.S. Fancy	U.S. No. 1	U.S. Utility
Apples (Washington)	Washington Extra Fancy	Washington Fancy		
Grapefruit (all states but Arizona, California, and Florida)	U.S. Fancy	U.S. No. 1	U.S. No. 1 Bright	U.S. No. 1 Bronze
Grapefruit (Arizona and California)	U.S. Fancy	U.S. No. 1	U.S. No. 1	U.S. Combination
Grapefruit (Florida)	U.S. Fancy	U.S. No. 1	U.S. No. 1 Bright	U.S. No. 1 Golden
Onions	U.S. No. 1	U.S. Combination or U.S. Commercial	U.S. No. 2	
Oranges (all states but Arizona, California, and Florida)	U.S. Fancy	U.S. No. 1	U.S. No. 1 Bright	U.S. No. 1 Bronze
Oranges (Arizona and California)	U.S. Fancy	U.S. No. 1	U.S. Combination	U.S. No. 2
Oranges (Florida)	U.S. Fancy	U.S. No. 1 Bright	U.S. No. 1 Bright	U.S. No. 1 Golden
Pears (summer and fall)	U.S. No. 1	U.S. Combination	U.S. No. 2	
Pears (winter)	U.S. Extra No. 1	U.S. No. 1	U.S. Combination	U.S. No. 2
Potatoes (Note: Potatoes are also sold "unclassified," meaning ungraded.)	U.S. Extra No. 1	U.S. No. 1	U.S. Commercial	U.S. No. 2
Tomatoes (fresh)	U.S. No. 1	U.S. Combination	U.S. No. 2	U.S. No. 3

the third grade. Similarly, "U.S. No. 1 Bright" represents the second grade of oranges but the third grade of apples.

Obviously, the best way to shop for groceries is to obtain the most palatable, most nutritious foods for the least amount of money. Some guidelines for doing this are presented in the following Consumer Issue. But in order to understand some of the recent legislation involving labeling requirements, let's discuss the matter of nutrition.

NUTRITION

There is increasing evidence that nutritional levels are declining for the average American. In 1973, for example, surveys by the Food and Drug Administration showed that only 71 percent of those interviewed had even moderate knowl-

There is increasing evidence that nutritional levels are declining for the average American.

edge of their own nutrition. In 1975, similar surveys showed this percentage dropping to 65 percent. Poor diets are linked to, among other things, poor health. American sources of calories have changed dramatically over the years. In 1900, 40 percent of our caloric intake came from fruits, vegetables, and grains. Today, these products make up less than 20 percent of our total calories consumed. We have increased dramatically our intake of simple sugars, meat, and fats.

Dietary Goals

The Senate Committee on Nutrition and Human Needs issued a report in 1977, "Dietary Goals for the United States," that concluded that this country was suffering from a "wave of malnutrition." The overconsumption of fats and sugars, plus cholesterol and salt, became evident to the researchers. The goals of the report were clear-cut: increase average consumptions of fruits, vegetables, and grains and reduce consumptions of fat, cholesterol, sugar, and salt.

As a result of the report, the Senate Select Committee received a tremendous amount of pressure from agricultural groups, particularly cattle raisers. A revised second edition was published a year later, in which the recommendations became, "Decrease consumption of animal fat and choose meat, poultry, and fish which will reduce saturated fat intake." Concerning cholesterol, the new recommendation stated: "Some consideration should be given to easing the cholesterol goal for women, young children, and the elderly in order to obtain the nutritional benefits of eggs in the diet."

The Basic Four

BASIC FOUR
Four food categories needed for a nutritionally sound diet: (1) beans, nuts, and grains; (2) fruits and vegetables; (3) milk products; and (4) poultry, fish, egg, and meat products.

Many grade-school students are taught about food in terms of the **basic four:** (1) beans, nuts, and grains; (2) fruits and vegetables; (3) milk products; and (4) poultry, fish, egg, and meat products. The USDA developed the basic four groups in 1956 to be used as an easy daily food guide to maintaining a nutritionally sound diet. The USDA's basic formula, however, has been severely criticized for its failure to account for new evidence of health risks in certain food, particularly the risks associated with animal fat, cholesterol, salt, and simple sugar. The USDA is revising its "basic four" chart. The Center for Science in the Public Interest has already adjusted the basic four to what that group believes is more appropriate for today's consumer. Exhibit 13–3 reproduces its "Guide to a Balanced Diet."

FOOD ADDITIVIES

ADDITIVE
Something added to a food product to alter its quality—for example, coloring, emulsifiers.

PRESERVATIVE
A chemical substance used to preserve food from decomposition or fermentation—that is, an additive designed specifically to prevent spoiling.

More and more chemicals seem to be getting into the foods we eat. Many consumers, government officials, and nutritionists believe that such **additives** are causing health problems. Most additives are included in foodstuffs in order to improve salability and reduce marketing problems.

Direct Additives

Many chemicals are added directly to food substances as **preservatives.** For example, sodium nitrate is a red coloring agent that inhibits the growth of

EXHIBIT 13–3
Guide To a Balanced Diet

EAT:	ANYTIME	IN MODERATION	NOW AND THEN
GROUP BEANS, GRAINS, AND NUTS FOUR OR MORE SERVINGS/DAY	Barley Beans Bread & rolls (whole grain) Bulghur Lentils Oatmeal Pasta Rice Whole-grain cereal (except granola)	Granola cereals Nuts Peanut butter Soybeans White bread and cereals	
GROUP II FRUITS AND VEGETABLES FOUR OR MORE SERVINGS/DAY	All fruits and vegetables except those listed on right Unsweetened fruit juices Unsalted vegetable juices Potatoes, white or sweet	Avocado Fruits canned in syrup Salted vegetable juices Sweetened fruit juice Vegetables canned with salt	French fries Olives Pickles
GROUP III MILK PRODUCTS CHILDREN: 3 TO 4 SERVINGS OR EQUIVALENT ADULT: 2 SERVINGS (Favor ANYTIME column for additional servings.)	Buttermilk Farmer or pot cheese Lowfat cottage cheese Milk with 1% milkfat Skim-milk ricotta Skim milk	Frozen lowfat yogurt Ice milk Lowfat milk with 2% milkfat Lowfat (2%) yogurt, plain or sweetened Regular cottage cheese Part-skim mozzarella and ricotta	Hard cheese: blue, brick, camembert, cheddar Ice cream Processed cheeses Whole milk Whole-milk yogurt
GROUP IV POULTRY, FISH, EGG & MEAT PRODUCTS *TWO SERVINGS* (Favor ANYTIME column for additional servings. If a vegetarian diet is desired, nutrients in these foods can be obtained by increasing servings from Groups I & III.)	POULTRY Chicken or turkey (no skin) FISH Cod Flounder Haddock Rockfish Shellfish, except shrimp Sole Tuna, water-packed Egg whites	FISH Herring Mackerel Salmon Sardines RED MEATS Flank steak Ham* Leg of lamb* Loin of lamb* Plate beef* Round steak* Rump roast* Sirloin steak* Veal*	POULTRY & FISH Deep-fried and breaded fish or poultry RED MEATS Bacon Corned beef Ground beef Hot dogs Liver Liverwurst Pork: loin Pork: Boston butt Egg yolk or whole egg
MISCELLANEOUS NOTE: Snack foods should not be used freely, but the middle column suggests some of the better choices.	FATS (none) SNACK FOODS (none)	FATS Mayonnaise Salad oils Soft (tub) margarines SNACK FOODS Angel food cake Animal crackers Fig bars Gingerbread Ginger snaps Graham crackers	FATS Butter Cream Cream cheese Lard Sour cream SNACK FOODS Chocolate Coconut Commercial Pies, pastries, and doughnuts Potato chips Soda pop

*Trim all outside fat. "Anytime" foods contain less than 30 percent of calories from fat and are usually low in salt and sugar. Most of the "now and then" foods contain at least 50 percent of calories from fat—*and* a large amount of saturated fat. Foods to eat "in moderation" have medium amounts of total fat and low to moderate amounts of saturated fat *or* large amounts of total fat that is mostly unsaturated. Foods meeting the standards for fat but containing large amounts of salt or sugar are usually moved into a more restricted category, as are refined cereal products. For example, pickles have little fat but are so high in sodium that they fall in the "now and then" category. To cut down on salt intake, choose varieties of foods listed here that do not have added salt, such as no-salt cottage cheese, rather than the regular varieties. This guide is not appropriate for individuals needing low-salt diets.

SOURCE: Center for Science in the Public Interest, 1979.

botulism germs in hot dogs, bacon, and luncheon meats. Alone, sodium nitrate seems to be relatively safe in extremely small quantities. Nonetheless, experiments have shown that when sodium nitrate joins with naturally produced proteins called amines, the result is nitrosamines. It is believed that nitrosamines may cause cancer in humans because they have been shown to cause cancer in animals. There is clearly a trade-off here. Sodium nitrate preserves food longer; if it were banned, foods in which it is used might spoil sooner.

LONG-TERM EFFECTS. One of the major problems with food additives is their unknown long-term effects. When taken in small quantities, they appear to be safe under most circumstances. When taken over a long period of time, they may be cancer-causing (carcinogenic). Cancer may take as long as forty years to develop, so we don't know very much about such long-term effects, particularly about additives that recently have been used in foodstuffs. Also, results of laboratory testing with animals do not necessarily mean that a carcinogen for animals is the same thing as a carcinogen for humans. Saccharin is a good example. Animal tests produced evidence that the artificial sweetener is carcinogenic. On the other hand, there has been no evidence that persons using saccharin over the years have contracted cancer as a *direct* result of their saccharin intake. The so-called Delaney Clause of the 1958 Food and Drug Amendment requires, nonetheless, that any direct additive found to be carcinogenic in animals must be banned from human food. In short, "No additive shall be deemed . . . safe if it is found to induce cancer when ingested by men or animals." Cyclamates were banned in 1970 on the basis of the Delaney Clause when the artificial sweetener was found to cause bladder tumors in rats. But in 1977, when Canadian tests showed that saccharin was carcinogenic in rats, the proposed FDA ban created a public furor. Congress then voted an eighteen-month delay on banning saccharin that has since been extended. As this book goes to press, the use of saccharin in any product shipped from one state to another requires a warning:

> USE OF THIS PRODUCT MAY BE HAZARDOUS TO YOUR HEALTH. THIS PRODUCT CONTAINS SACCHARIN WHICH HAS BEEN DETERMINED TO CAUSE CANCER IN LABORATORY ANIMALS.

One of the major problems with food additives is their unknown long-term effects.

The Classification of Additives

Several government agencies have been granted authority to regulate the use of additives in products that cross interstate lines. Therefore, meat products are controlled by the U.S. Department of Agriculture, and other food products are regulated by the U.S. Food and Drug Administration. Since 1958, manufacturers of additives have been required to prove that the additives are safe for human consumption. All additives in common use prior to 1958, however, were exempted from this requirement. These additives are placed on one of two lists: Generally Recognized as Safe (GRAS), or Prior Sanction. Presumably, all the items on these lists are assumed to be safe because they have withstood the test of time. However, saccharin was on the GRAS list, and sodium nitrate was on the Prior Sanction list.

Any additives tested after 1958 either have been rejected or placed on an Approved list. Whenever an additive on the market is found to be hazardous, it is placed on a Banned list. If there are serious doubts concerning an item on the GRAS, Prior Sanction, or Approved lists, the item is placed on an Interim list.

Food Colors

The Color Additive Amendments, passed in 1960 (amending the Food, Drug and Cosmetic Act), require certification by the Food and Drug Administration of all colors made from potentially harmful chemicals. Until the food color Red No. 2 was declared unsafe and was banned in 1976, it was one of the most common food additives. There are still quite a few artificial colors used in foodstuffs for humans, even though questions about their safety still exist. For example, Red No. 3, Red No. 40, Blue No. 1, Blue No. 2, Green No. 3, Yellow No. 5, and Yellow No. 6 have been singled out by nutritionists as potentially harmful.

Indirect Additives

A potentially serious health problem arises with indirect additives, such as the chemicals used in packaging material. Polyvinyl chloride is a suspected carcinogen but is, nonetheless, used in numerous packages. The problem is that chemicals from the packaging materials leach into the covered food. The FDA regulates indirect additives by setting up tolerance levels expressed in parts per million or billion. Since it is difficult to determine what is a safe amount of any chemical substance, there are serious doubts about the value of the FDA's list.

RECOMMENDED DIETARY ALLOWANCES

RECOMMENDED DIETARY ALLOWANCES (RDAs)
A system devised by the National Academy of Sciences in which a specified daily intake of a particular vitamin and nutrient is given for infants, children, males, and females, as well as pregnant and lactating women. Not to be confused with United States Recommended Daily Allowance.

U.S. RECOMMENDED DAILY ALLOWANCE (U.S. RDA)
Related to Recommended Dietary Allowance but in a simplified form. The U.S. RDA is the maximum amount of each nutrient needed for four broad categories of the population.

In order for consumers to be able to compare the nutrient value of different foods, there must be a common measurement system. Just such a system was devised by the National Academy of Sciences. Exhibit 13–4 shows the resultant **Recommended Dietary Allowances (RDAs)** that have been established for the following groups of individuals: infants to one year old, children from one to ten, males from eleven up, females from eleven up, and pregnant and lactating women. RDAs have been determined for virtually every important nutrient needed each day by these groups of people.

United States Recommended Daily Allowance

To simplify RDAs for labeling purposes, nutritionists have condensed the RDA to the **United States Recommended Daily Allowance (U.S. RDA).** U.S. RDAs are expressed in metric measures. The U.S. RDA takes the *maximum amount* of each nutrient needed for the following categories: infants, children, children over age four and adults, and pregnant and lactating females. Additionally, the U.S. RDA uses a larger quantity than the RDA established by the National Academy of Sciences whenever evidence appears that the population is lacking in that nutrient—for example, riboflavin. Food for infants or children only uses a U.S. RDA for that age group. Other food labels have U.S. RDAs based on Group 3, children over age four and adults. Exhibit 13–5 gives that list.

Nutritional Labeling

Closely connected with U.S. RDAs is nutritional labeling, which is voluntary for all foods except those that are enriched and fortified or those for which a nutritional health claim is made. A nutrient is a chemical substance in food that performs one or more of the following functions: furnishes body fuel needed for energy, provides materials needed for the building or maintenance of body tissues, and/or supplies substances that function in the regulation of body processes. Nutritional labeling includes more than just percentages of U.S. RDAs for protein and selected vitamins and minerals. All nutritional information must contain the following:

1. Serving size
2. Servings per container
3. Caloric content or calories per serving
4. Protein content or protein (in grams and as a percentage of U.S. RDA)
5. Carbohydrate content or carbohydrate (in grams)
6. Fat content or fat (in grams)
7. Percentage of U.S. RDA of protein and selected minerals and vitamins

You can see an example of a nutritional label in Exhibit 13–6. One problem with such nutritional labels is that they don't show exact percentages of U.S. RDAs. For example, for any food containing more than 50 percent of a specified nutrient, the percentages of the U.S. RDA are listed to the nearest 10 percent. Whenever the nutrient satisfies between 10 and 50 percent of the U.S. RDA it is listed to the closest 5 percent. Amounts between 2 and 10 percent are specified as a percentage of the U.S. RDA to the closest 2 percent.

FOOD LABELING

Closely related to nutritional labeling is general food labeling. Federal law requires that every package of food, drugs, or cosmetics contains the following information on its label:

1. Name of the product
2. Name and address of the manufacturer, packager, or distributor
3. Net amount of contents or weight in pounds and ounces and in total number of ounces
4. Details of dietary characteristics, if applicable
5. Mention of whether the product contains artificial coloring, flavoring, or chemical preservatives
6. All ingredients, listed in descending order of predominance
7. Note of whether the food is an imitation and less nutritious than the product it resembles

Federal *standards of identity* have been adopted for some food products. A standard of identity is a "recipe" specifying limits of mandatory ingredients in a food. This means that the basic ingredients of these foods have been established and any item bearing that particular product label contains the standard ingredients for that product. Under these standards, companies manufacturing such items as mayonnaise and ketchup are not required to list their ingredients; however, they usually do so voluntarily.

In order for consumers to be able to compare the nutrient value of different foods, there must be a common measurement system.

THE IMPORTANCE OF FRESHNESS

We all like to buy fresh food. When we buy fruits and vegetables, we can see at a glance how old they are and whether or not they are worth the price. But when we buy canned items or processed meats and other such goods, we really cannot tell unless we open up the package or can. Few of us ever do that when we buy something wrapped in clear plastic. (It would be embarrassing if we were caught.) Because we do not know how old processed food is, government truth-in-food labeling activity has centered to some extent on food dating.

Open Dating

Food dating is not new; there is already food dating on the cans and many of the cartons you buy. For example, the top of a carton of milk usually bears the date by which the milk should be sold to ensure its subsequent freshness for home use.

Camera film has been dated for many years without government regulation; the date tells photographers how long the film will be effective. Outdated film often sells at a lower price than in-date film because the film is less likely to be good once it is out of date. The same is true, of course, with pastry items and bread. You know you can buy day-old bread and such things at certain bakeries at a lower price than fresh items. Why? Because generally the day-old food is not as good or desirable.

EXHIBIT 13–4
Recommended Dietary Allowances

(YEARS) FROM UP TO	WEIGHT (kg)	WEIGHT (lbs)	HEIGHT (in)	ENERGY (cal)	PROTEIN (g)	FAT-SOLUBLE VITAMINS			WATER-SOLUBLE VITAMINS							MINERALS						
						VITAMIN A ACTIVITY (IU)	VITAMIN D (IU)	VITAMIN E ACTIVITY (IU)	ASCORBIC ACID (mg)	FOLACIN (mg)	NIACIN (mg)	RIBOFLAVIN (mg)	THIAMIN (mg)	VITAMIN B_4 (mg)	VITAMIN B_{12} (mg)	CALCIUM (mg)	PHOSPHORUS (mg)	IODINE (mg)	IRON (mg)	MAGNESIUM (mg)	ZINC (mg)	
INFANTS																						
0.0–0.5	6	14	24	kg × 117	kg × 2.2	1400	400	4	35	50	5	0.4	0.3	0.3	0.3	360	360	240	35	10	60	3
0.5–1.0	9	20	28	kg × 108	kg × 2.0	2000	400	5	35	50	8	0.6	0.5	0.4	0.3	540	540	400	45	15	70	5
CHILDREN																						
1–3		28	34	1300	23	2000	400	7	40	100	9	0.8	0.7	0.6	1.0	900	800	800	60	15	150	10
4–6		44	44	1800	30	2500	400	9	40	200	12	1.1	0.9	0.9	1.5	800	800	800	80	10	200	10
7–10		66	54	2400	36	3300	400	10	40	300	16	1.2	1.2	1.2	2.0	800	800	800	110	10	250	10
MALES																						
11–14		97	63	2800	44	5000	400	12	45	400	18	1.5	1.4	1.6	3.0	1200	1200	1200	130	18	350	15
15–18		134	69	3000	54	5000	400	15	45	400	20	1.8	1.5	2.0	3.0	1200	1200	1200	150	18	400	15
19–22		147	69	3000	54	5000	400	15	45	400	20	1.8	1.5	2.0	3.0	1200	800	800	140	10	350	15
23–50		154	69	2700	56	5000	—	15	45	400	18	1.6	1.4	2.0	3.0	800	800	800	130	10	350	15
51 +		154	69	2400	56	5000	—	15	45	400	16	1.5	1.2	2.0	3.0	800	800	800	110	10	350	15
FEMALES																						
11–14		97	62	2400	44	4000	400	12	45	400	16	1.3	1.2	1.6	3.0	1200	1200	1200	115	18	300	15
15–18		119	65	2100	48	4000	400	12	45	400	14	1.4	1.1	2.0	3.0	1200	1200	1200	115	18	300	15
19–22		128	65	2100	46	4000	400	12	45	400	14	1.4	1.1	2.0	3.0	800	800	800	100	18	300	15
23–50		128	65	2000	46	4000	—	12	45	400	13	1.2	1.0	2.0	3.0	800	800	800	100	18	300	15
51 +		128	65	1800	46	4000	—	12	45	400	12	1.1	1.0	2.0	3.0	800	800	800	80	10	300	15
PREGNANT																						
				+300	+30	5000	400	15	60	800	+2	+0.3	+0.3	2.5	4.0	1200	1200	1200	125	18+	450	20
LACTATING																						
				+500	+20	6000	400	15	80	600	+4	+0.5	+0.3	2.5	4.0	1200	1200	1200	150	18	450	25

IU stands for International Unit.
1 kilogram (kg) = 2.2 pounds (lbs)
1 kilogram (kg) = 1,000 grams (g)
1 kilocalorie (kcal) = 1,000 calories
1 gram (g) = 1,000 milligrams (mg)
1 milligram (mg) = 1,000 micrograms (mcg)

SOURCE: Food and Drug Administration.

Nutrient	Amount	Nutrient	Amount
Protein	65 grams	Vitamin B_6	2 mg.
Vitamin A	5,000 units	Folacin	0.4 mg.
Vitamin C	60 mg.	Vitamin B_{12}	6 mcg.
Thiamin	1.5 mg.	Phosphorus	1 g.
Riboflavin	1.7 mg.	Iodine	150 mcg.
Niacin	20 mg.	Magnesium	400 mg.
Calcium	1 gram	Zinc	15 mg.
Iron	18 mg.	Copper	2 mg.
Vitamin D	400 units	Biotin	0.3 mg.
Vitamin E	30 units	Pantothenic Acid	10 mg.

SOURCE: United States Department of Agriculture and the Food and Drug Administration.

EXHIBIT 13–5
U.S. Recommended Daily Allowance

Only a few states, such as California, have made open dating mandatory; in that state, it is mandatory only for dairy products. Otherwise, open dating remains a voluntary practice. Remember that maintenance of the proper temperature for food that can spoil is just as important as the time it is kept in the store or on the shelf. In particular, maintaining the freshness of a perishable item is often more a function of the temperature at which it remains during its shelf life than how long it is on the shelf. Milk, for example, spoils rapidly at 50 degrees compared to how long it stays fresh at 35 degrees.

Many consumers are grateful for government help in requiring truth-in-labeling, truth-in-packaging, proper processing facilities, and the like. But consumers in general are increasingly dissatisfied with the government's consistent intervention in the food markets in order to keep the price of food high. You, the consumer, have been hurt by various agricultural programs designed not to help you but to help the farmer.

THE GROWING TREND TOWARD CONVENIENCE FOOD

The food industry is now providing us with buttered peas, frozen corn on the cob, stuffed baked potatoes, cheese in a spray can, complete frozen dinners, frozen tacos and so on. You name it and you can buy it already prepared. Just pop it into the oven and wait.

Why Convenience Foods?

Why are Americans buying so many convenience foods? The answer is quite simple: because our high incomes lead us to place a high value on our time. Americans are no lazier than other people. We simply are willing to pay more than others in both money and lower food quality to save time. We prefer to use our time otherwise.

One reason people like to buy convenience food is that they require almost no preparation. You need none of the pots and pans and cutting utensils of old for something that is already prepared, frozen, buttered, and ready to eat after only heating. Certain convenience foods give you less nutrient value than if you spent the time making the dish yourself. Again, that is just part of the price you pay for convenience, and you should be aware of it. People more concerned about nutritional value and those who dislike consuming large quantities of food additives shy away from convenience food, but they pay a price for that. People who always cook meals from scratch spend more time

We can make no ultimate judgment about whether convenience foods are good or bad for the American consumer.

in the kitchen than those who settle for TV dinners or canned foods.

We can make no ultimate judgment about whether convenience foods are good or bad for the American consumer. As long as you know exactly what you are getting, then you can make the choice. The following Consumer Issue on food buying shows that, looked at realistically, the cost of convenience is sometimes astronomical. If you decide that the cost is sometimes too high, you will choose foods that are not so convenient.

Not All Convenience Foods Are the Same

Perhaps it is incorrect to lump all convenience foods together. While some increase sugar in the diet, such as Tang in place of frozen orange juice, and others, such as frozen cream pies, are essentially nonfoods, others provide real convenience. Frozen fresh-cut string beans, for example, give you a reasonably fresh vegetable out of season with the time-consuming preparation job (that is, cutting and cleaning) already done.

The trend toward packaged foods is definitely on the upswing; restaurants, even some of the best ones, now have prefrozen convenience foods on their menus without your knowledge. It might surprise you to find that some parts of a thirty-five dollar meal in an expensive French restaurant are actually frozen foods. Well, you should not be surprised, because the cost of food-preparing labor in restaurants has risen so much that, to stay in business, even the best restaurants have to cut corners. And one way to do so is to buy convenience foods.

The cost of convenience is often an important factor in consumer decision making. A year-long study of 162 convenience foods was done by the Economic Research Service and the Agricultural Research Service (USDA). Of the foods studied, only 36 percent had a cost per serving lower than their home-prepared or fresh counterpart. However, consumers of these convenience foods paid a lower time "cost" in preparing them for eating.[1]

Comparing Big Macs to Home-cooked Food

McDonald's guarantees that you can buy food cheaper from them than if you prepared it yourself. But Exhibit 13–7 shows that McDonald's claims are not very accurate. The USDA shows, for example, that home-prepared hamburgers

1. Larry G. Traub and Dianne Odland, "Convenience Foods—1975 Cost Update," *Family Economics Review,* Winter 1976.

EXHIBIT 13–6
Nutritional Labeling

NUTRITION INFORMATION PER SERVING

SERVING SIZE	10¾ OZ. (305 g)
SERVINGS PER CONTAINER	1
CALORIES	140
PROTEIN (GRAMS)	4
CARBOHYDRATE (GRAMS)	24
FAT (GRAMS)	4

PERCENTAGE OF U.S. RECOMMENDED DAILY ALLOWANCES (U.S. RDA)

PROTEIN	6	RIBOFLAVIN	4
VITAMIN A	150	NIACIN	6
VITAMIN C	10	CALCIUM	6
THIAMINE	2	IRON	8

FOOD AND SOURCE	CALORIES	CALORIES FROM FAT	PROTEIN[1]	COST[2] (cents)
Hamburger:				
McDonald's	260	94	20	30
Homemade	338	125	28	24
Cheeseburger:				
McDonald's	312	128	25	38
Homemade	390	160	34	29
Big Mac				
McDonald's	546	284	40	75
Homemade	546	229	40	37
¼-lb Hamburger				
McDonald's	416	171	41	65
Homemade	468	201	43	34
Fillet of Fish				
McDonald's	416	204	24	55
Homemade	338	125	23	29
French Fries				
McDonald's	208	87	4	30
Homemade	182	69	3	13
Apple Pie				
McDonald's	260	133	3	25
Homemade	208	77	3	07
Chocolate Shake				
McDonald's	312	62	17	40
Homemade	286	123	15	15
Soft Drink				
McDonald's	104	0	([3])	20
Homemade	104	0	([3])	08

[1]Protein as percentage of U.S. Recommended Daily Allowance;
[2]Prices in Washington, D.C., area, July, 1976;
[3]Insignificant amount of nutrient present.

SOURCE: U.S. Department of Agriculture and *HELP! The Indispensable Almanac—1980*, p.237.

EXHIBIT 13–7
Comparing Big Macs to Home-Cooked Food

Although the calories and protein seem about the same for the food bought at McDonald's and that cooked at home, the estimates show that food from McDonald's costs more.

are 20 percent cheaper than McDonald's, and home-prepared apple pies are 72 percent cheaper. The USDA study, however, ignores consumers' opportunity cost—the time involved in preparing food as opposed to buying it at McDonald's. Also, there is no discussion of the cost of fuel used in going to the supermarket to buy the food, compared to the fuel used in going to McDonald's.

UNIVERSAL PRODUCT CODING (UPC)

The Universal Product Coding label shown in Exhibit 13–8 provides a system of registering purchases by means of an optical scanning device—a laser. The laser beam scans the symbol and sends information to a computer that looks up the price.

What will happen at the checkout counter in the supermarket that adopts this system? The checkout clerk will pass each item over a small window with a laser beam beneath it. The computer is sent a signal, looks up the price, and sends it to the cash register. In addition to displaying the price, the cash register will be able to print a receipt listing the price of each item by its name.

EXHIBIT 13–8
Universal Product Code (UPC)

This rectangular array of numbers and bars is appearing on more and more food packages. Called the UPC, it will be used in the automated checkout systems that supermarkets will be installing. In this example, the 24000 numerals specify a Del Monte product; the 01391 indicates that it is a can of green beans, and the zero indicates that it is a grocery product. There is a character on the extreme right side of the numbers that cannot be identified with the human eye; this character provides a signal if the code marking has been tampered with. The laser cannot read the numbers; it reads vertical bars. Two dark and two light bars of varying width have been assigned to each number.

This system may speed up the checkout process (if the same number of checkouts is maintained) and perhaps reduce the chance of human error at the checkout point and at the price labeling point.

Are there any drawbacks to this system? Consider what would happen if the computer, hooked up to each cash register in the supermarket, were to malfunction in the midst of a peak shopping hour! Then there's the controversy about whether or not prices will appear on individual items or appear simply on the shelf with the unit price. The latter arrangement makes comparison shopping very difficult indeed. For instance, if you buy a can of corn in one aisle, you probably will have forgotten its price by the time you reach the frozen-foods section; you can't therefore compare the price of frozen and canned corn unless you return to find the price of the latter.

Current Utilization

The current utilization of optical scanners in United States supermarkets has fallen far short of original predictions. By the end of 1982, according to the Food Marketing Institute, only 608 supermarkets had installed scanners. Compare the actual figure with the prediction given a few years earlier by the Scanning Manufacturers Association: 7,500 supermarkets were expected to be using scanners by the end of 1975! Additionally, scanners seem to be used only in a few major food chains concentrated in about fifteen states. Where scanners are used, consumers often have reacted negatively. The state government in California voted to *not* hand stamp prices on individual food items that used a universal product code. Los Angeles consumers reacted vociferously. The result: In L.A., prices are required on items in supermarkets.

GENERIC FOODS

Many food retailers have introduced **generic** (also called "unbranded" or "no-name") foods to their grocery shelves. These products come in "no frills" packages and contain only the product name and other essential labeling information. Since their introduction to U.S. supermarkets in 1977, sales of generic products have increased substantially, and a growing number of stores have begun to stock them. While there is little or no difference in nutritional quality between generic and national or store brands, the savings to the consumer are considerable—as much as 20 to 30 percent. The lack of advertising and lower packaging and labeling costs are passed on to the consumer.

GENERIC
The general term referring to a class of, for example, food products. Generic names are not protected by trademark registration; for example, cola is a generic name of a foodstuff.

Most stores tend to group all generic products together one section of the store to increase visibility. Since items of the same type are in different sections of the store, this may make comparison shopping a bit more difficult.

SUMMARY

1. The percentage of total U.S. income spent on food has been declining steadily since this nation began. This is characteristic of goods that are necessities as opposed to luxuries. As income rises, the percentage spent on necessities falls.
2. A German statistician named Ernst Engel made this discovery in 1856, and it is now called Engel's Law.
3. The Fair Packaging and Labeling Act became effective in 1967. It requires that the labels of most consumer products give net quantity per serving; identify the commodity; and make clear who manufactured, distributed, or packed it and where. The act authorizes the secretary of commerce to limit undue proliferation of product package sizes.
4. There are a number of so-called marginal buyers who shop carefully for many food items. They have an important effect on the price and quality of what we buy. The most obvious marginal buyers are institutions that must feed a large number of individuals.
5. The U.S. Department of Agriculture provides grades for meats, fresh produce, poultry, and other items. However, these grades can be confusing. Produce grading is especially confusing. The top grade of grapefruit in the United States is U.S. Fancy, but the top grade of pears is U.S. No. 1. In order to understand which are the top grades, turn to Exhibit 13–2.
6. Nutrition can be thought of in terms of the basic four—meat, dairy products, vegetables and fruits, and grain products.
7. Open dating of food products can be helpful not only in determining whether the product is out of date but also in determining which product should be used first.
8. There is a growing trend toward frozen convenience foods because, as Americans become richer, they are willing to pay more to save time. That is, their higher incomes lead Americans to place a higher value on their time, and they, therefore, prefer the ease of using a convenience food even though it costs them considerably more than preparing the food themselves.

QUESTIONS FOR THOUGHT AND DISCUSSION

1. Why would you expect the citizens of less-developed countries to spend a larger percentage of their incomes on food than the citizens of the United States?
2. Is it useful to look at the price index of food to figure out whether food is a "good" or "bad" deal? (Hint: How many hours does it take today to obtain enough income to buy a week's food compared to the number of hours it took fifty years ago?)
3. Is there a limit to the reduction in the percentage of disposable personal income going for food? Could it ever reach zero?
4. When you go to the supermarket to buy meat, do you look for a particular grade of meat? Does USDA grade labeling help you make wiser consumer choices?
5. Is it possible to get two identically graded cuts of meat from two different markets and have one be much better than the other?
6. Food manufacturers are adamant in their opposition to fair-packaging laws. Why should they care?
7. Do you think it would ever be possible to get food manufacturers to reverse the proliferation of product package sizes voluntarily?
8. Do you think that the net weight of canned items should exclude any liquids?
9. Why do you think food grading was introduced?
10. Do you make sure that you get the proper amounts of different types of nutrients? Why or why not? If you do, how much time does such planning take?
11. Open dating for film has been around for many, many years, yet it has only recently been used in food packaging. Why do you think it has taken so long to be used for food?
12. How much of your diet consists of convenience foods? Is that good or bad?

THINGS TO DO

1. Add up how much food you eat every week. Now add that up for the entire year. Do you eat more or less than the average for the nation?
2. Look at the latest issue of the *Monthly Labor Review* or the *Federal Reserve Bulletin* to see what the index of food prices has been in the last few years. Is there a continued upward trend?
3. At your local meat market, try to determine the differences among the various grades of meat. Ask the butcher if there is a distinct difference between the top two grades of meat and if the top grade is worth the extra money.
4. Go to the produce section of your local market. Try to figure out the U.S. Department of Agriculture labeling on the various types of apples, grapefruit, onions, oranges, and pears. Can you tell the difference between U.S. No. 1, U.S. Fancy, and U.S. Extra No. 1? Ask the grocer what he or she thinks the differences are between the various grades.
5. Write down what you have eaten in the last seven days. How closely did you stick to the recommended minimum servings of the basic four on an average daily basis?
6. The next time you go grocery shopping, find out what products use open dating. If some of the cans you purchase have numbers on them, ask the grocer what those code numbers mean. Often they refer to canning dates and other

dates that might be important in your purchase decision (although they might merely identify the packing plant).

7. Look at some of the convenience foods you buy. Try to estimate the price you are paying for convenience. Then try to figure out whether that price is relatively high or low in terms of the time you save by buying and eating the convenience food.

SELECTED READINGS

"Chemical Cuisine," an 18-by-24-inch wall poster separating food additives into ones that are safe, ones to be cautious about, and ones to avoid. Center for Science in the Public Interest, P.O. Box 3099, Washington, D.C. 20010, $1.75.

Generic Groceries—They're Cheaper, But What's in Them?" *Changing Times,* December 1978, pp. 36–38.

Greene, J. "FDA's New Code: A Clean Sweep for Food Stores." *FDA Consumer,* October 1982, pp. 12–13.

"How to Use USDA Grades in Food Buying." *Home and Garden Bulletin,* No. 196. Washington, D.C.: U.S. Department of Agriculture, Government Printing Office.

Hunter, B. T. "Food for Thought." See issues of *Consumers' Research Magazine.*

Key Nutrients, 2d ed. Washington, D.C.: Government Printing Office, 1971.

Lappe, Francis. *Diet for a Small Planet.* New York: Ballantine, 1971.

Lecos, C. "For Food Labels, Better Read = Better Fed." *FDA Consumer,* October 1982, p. 11.

Lecos, C. "RDAs: Key to Nutrition." *FDA Consumer,* November 1982, pp. 24–25.

"Peachy Idea Is Finally Ripening; Weight Labels on Canned Food." *Consumer Reports,* February 1977, p. 65.

"Technology Cuts Kitchen Costs and Drudgery." *Consumer Views,* Vol. 13, No. 4, April 1982. Published by Citibank, New York.

"What's a Marketing Order?" *Consumer Reports,* February 1982, pp. 106–107.

Consumer ISSUE J

HOW TO GET THE MOST FOR YOUR FOOD DOLLAR

GLOSSARY

COMPLEMENTARY RESOURCES—Resources that are used when purchasing or using other resources. For example, the complementary resources used in shopping are your time and often your automobile.

SUBSTITUTE RESOURCES—Those resources that can be substituted or used in place of one another. For example, a substitute resource for dollars spent on food is time used in searching for better buys in food.

UNIT PRICING—Pricing of food products expressed in a well-known unit, such as ounces or pounds.

The high cost of food may make you want to economize in food shopping. Some general ideas on how to get the best dollar value in relation to some very specific food attributes, the most important being nutrition, are given in this Consumer Issue. But you will want still more food information, because no one shops for nutritional value alone, no matter how limited the budget. You can probably satisfy all your nutritional requirements for a mere fraction of your present food spending by living on soybeans and raisins. But you are not likely to take that kind of nutritional diet seriously. If you want to see why, read on.

UNIT PRICING

In several U.S. cities, **unit pricing** of all food items is now required by law. What is unit pricing? Instead of a label on the shelf under the product indicating only the price, there now must be a label also specifying the price per convenient unit of measurement (that is, weight or liquid measure). Whereas before you needed a calculator to determine if 7 ounces of tuna fish at $1.43 is cheaper than 6½ ounces at $1.29, the store now has calculated this for you and posted the results for you to see. This makes it much easier to determine the "best buy" of any particular item. In effect, for canned goods and other prepackaged foods, you are now being told what you have always been told for meats and produce—that is, that pork chops are $2.19 per pound, but pork blades (which look nearly the same, but are slightly tougher and fattier) are $1.99 per pound. Of course, unit pricing does not account for differences in quality or personal preferences. It merely translates into comparable figures the price differences you observe in the market. In so doing, it usually makes it possible for you to capitalize on what "specials" are available. Formerly, when certain brands of canned goods were on special, they still might have cost more than the usual price of other brands not being featured. While some price differences reflect differences in quality, other differences might be due to advertising. In some cases, neither may matter to you. You may feel that canned tomatoes are canned tomatoes, and whether one brand is firmer than another does not matter since you are just going to mash them into spaghetti sauce anyway. It is when you do not prefer one particular brand over another that unit pricing is most valuable. And in all cases, it allows you to see just what you are paying for your favorites.

Shopping for Specials

Many shoppers know that one way to save money on food is to shop for specials and that the way to find specials is to look in the local newspaper. Some consumers attempting to get the best possible deals will spend time combing through supermarket ads. They will cut out the ads and go to the various supermarkets to get whatever they need that is on special. Although this method is fine for some individuals, the time you spend looking at the ads and then shopping is valuable. Also valuable is the money you spend shopping for specials—the money spent for wear and tear on your car and on the gasoline you have to consume when you go to several stores instead of one.

Unfortunately, there can be no hard and fast rules about how long you should look through newspaper ads and how many stores you should go too. Against the potential savings from buying specials at various supermarkets you must compare the anticipated costs of driving your car to those supermarkets, plus the value you place on the time involved. Hence, you know it would not be worthwhile to drive five miles to a more distant supermarket merely for its special on mustard or black peppercorns. If however, that same market had a special on meat that you could purchase for the rest of the week's meals, then it might be worth your while to go.

Generic Groceries

Generic products are no-frill items with no brand name. The label just says "laundry detergent" or "peanut butter" or "beer" or "peas." These products cost from 10 to 30 percent less than national brands. One reason they are cheaper is because simple labeling costs less. But this reduction amounts to only a few cents on every thousand units of any product. There are other ways to cut packaging costs, such as the elimination of a pop top from a soft drink. Often generic products come in only one size; that cuts down on inventory and handling costs. Since there is no brand name, there is no advertising involved. But, according to many consumer experts, the real reason generic products are priced lower is that there is lower-quality merchandise inside the can or container. Generic products are standard-grade fruits and vegetables, rather than the higher-priced extra-standard or fancy grades packed in most national brands. Nonetheless, these lower-grade generic products are basically equivalent in terms of nutrition, according to the FDA and the USDA. You might wish to use generic products when taste is not so important. As an example, consider using generic peas in a casserole but sticking with the national brand for individual servings where looks and taste are more important.

Even if you decide to buy all the available generic products, you are not going to save a fortune on your grocery bill. The reason? Only a limited number of products are available with generic labels.

Substituting One Thing for Another

From the discussion about shopping for specials, you should realize that you can substitute various resources to do a particular task. If you decide that you want to spend fewer dollars for food, you can spend more time looking for specials. In other words, you substitute your time for the food dollars that you would have spent had you not looked for specials. You have just used a **substitute resource.** When you take a car to shop at several different markets, you use a **complementary resource** in your attempt to reduce your food budget. Whenever you use a complementary resource, you have to realize that you incur a cost, even if you did not pay for it directly or immediately.

Once you understand substitution and complementarity n resource use, then you are well on your way to being a ·ational, and indeed thrifty, shopper. Some consumers ɔecome fanatical about buying food on special only. They nave lost track of means and ends. The original end in mind, of course, is to get the most value for your food dollar, taking into account all the combined resource costs involved in food shopping. While fanaticism for specials can lead to an uneconomical overuse of time, only you can decide whether that has happened to you, because only you know the value you place on your own time.

The optional use of time leads us to a discussion of when it is rational for you to purchase convenience foods that you know will cost more at the supermarket.

TO BUY OR NOT TO BUY THAT TV DINNER

Convenience foods are just that—foods made for your convenience to save you time and energy. Whether or not you like their taste is, of course, up to you, but you should be aware of the cost of convenience. For example, perhaps you have seen breaded veal steaks in the frozen-food section these days. A close look shows that there is an average of about 30 percent breading and 20 percent beef added to the veal; these are the limits permitted by the U.S. Department of Agriculture's regulations. So, all in all, those breaded veal steaks are only about 50 percent veal. If the price per pound package is, say, \$4.59, then you are paying over \$8.00 per pound for ground veal steaks with some hamburger and bread thrown in. However, if you can find the same ground veal in the market, you will find that it costs about \$3.40 a pound; ground beef is \$1.99 a pound, and readymade bread

crumbs are $1.00 a pound. That means that homemade veal steaks, made with the same ingredients as the convenience variety, would cost you $2.40 per pound.

In addition, you will find, for example, that the sugar in presweetened breakfast cereals is costing you $2.50 a pound. You will find also that you pay about twice as much per ounce for peas that are frozen in butter sauce (which contains some water) as for peas to which you add your own butter during cooking.

In some cases, you are paying as much as 100 percent or more for convenience. It is worth the price? That, of course, depends on how highly you value both your time and the taste differences between what you prepare and what the producer prepares.

American families seem to be placing more value on their time; the percentage of total food budgets spent on frozen convenience foods has risen from about 27 percent in 1955 to 35 percent in 1965 to an estimated 47 percent in 1981.

NUTRITION

According to some nutritionists, many convenience foods do not give a high amount of nutrition for their cost. We buy food for two reasons: the pleasures of eating and nutrition to keep our bodies healthy. The nutritional aspect of food is often ignored by on-the-go, busy consumers who have "more important" things to worry about. But after spending a little time determining the nutritional value of different types of food, the wise food consumer can purchase more nutrients per food dollar. One of the basic nutrients needed to maintain a healthy body is protein, and there are various inexpensive ways to obtain it.

A major source of quite inexpensive protein is peanut butter. The average protein content in most peanut-butter brands is about 15 to 20 percent, and the total protein supplied by two peanut-butter sandwiches and an eight-ounce glass of milk would be almost 75 percent of the daily protein allowance recommended for a ten-year-old by the National Academy of Sciences—National Research Council. Peanut butter is also a great source of niacin, phosphorus, and magnesium. At the same time, this meal would provide one-third the daily caloric need of a ten-year-old. Knowing the nutrient values of different foods is important for obtaining a good diet.

Are Fast-Food Meals Nutritious?

A 1975 study made by *Consumer Reports* determined that there were six nutrients commonly offered in short supply in fast-food meals. They were biotin, folacin, pantothenic acid, total vitamin A, iron, and copper. Another study was done in September 1979. By then, there were 140,000 fast-food restaurants across the country offering an amazing variety of items, including pizza, chili, tacos, hamburgers, roast beef, chicken, and fish. Since 33 percent of adults eat out every day and 28 percent of those people eat in fast-food restaurants, it was worthwhile for *Consumer Reports* to check again on the nutrient value of such food. One main finding was that fast-food entrees supply adequate amounts of protein but it appeared that there was too much sodium (salt) for the average American.

"Fast foods are not junk foods," concluded *Consumer Reports*. Any of the fast-food entrees plus French fries and a shake would provide about one-third of all the nutrients you should have in a day. But the meal would also provide more than half the calories recommended daily for a woman or child. The fast-food meal would also provide plenty of fat. And it may provide as much as 1,000 to 2,000 milligrams of sodium. For one meal, that may be too much for people on sodium-restricted diets. [Fast foods] are acceptable nutritionally when consumed judiciously, infrequently, and as part of a well-balanced diet." [1]

Exhibit J-1 shows the *Consumer Reports* results. They speak for themselves.

1. "Fast-Food Chains," *Consumer Reports*, September 1979, p. 513.

A TRIP TO THE SUPERMARKET

Before leaving this topic, consider your actual trip to the supermarket.

First of all, what kind of preparation for the trip have you made? Many shoppers prefer planning menus for the week (at least the suppers), often taking into account the meat specials that week. Generally, once the meats are decided upon, the rest of the supper menus follow rather naturally. Usually such advance meal planning encompasses a week at a time, although some shoppers prefer to do it just once every ten days.

If you have decided not to pay much attention to advertised specials and, therefore, not to read the supermarket ads in your newspapers, meal planning can often take place right in the store. You go first to the meat counter and decide what your meals will center around by looking at the specials (or even just the prices). Sometimes, especially with relatively high meat prices, you also may wish to check the prices of canned or fresh fish, eggs, or cheese and then to feature these or other meat substitutes in your meals.

Other consumers prefer to engage in a kind of "reasoned" impulse buying. In other words, they know roughly what they consume in any given week and vary only a few items each time they shop.

Comparison Shopping

In 1972, Citibank in New York sent two shoppers to supermarkets with a list of thirty-six items to buy. One shopper simply went in and bought the items without doing any comparison. The other shopper compared values. The different in total price: 30 percent! In August 1982, the same person who conducted the 1972 study repeated it. The results were amazing. The haphazard shopper's bill had shot up more than 250 percent, and even the carefully selected market basket cost 200 percent more than it had in 1972. Nonetheless, in 1982 dollars, the person who engaged in comparison shopping saved 35 percent over the haphazard shopper. In other words, there has been a slight increase in the benefits of comparison shopping.

Whether you do your food planning at home beforehand or in the supermarket, there are a few ways you might be able to save.

1. Try different brands of the same product; they can be similar in quality and nutritional value and yet may vary widely in price.

2. Large quantities are often bargains but only if they can be kept safely until they can be used up completely.

EXHIBIT J–1
Which Fast-Food Entrées Are the Most Nutritious?

	Serving size	Calories	Fat	Carbohydrates	Total sugars	Sodium	Percentage RDA* Protein	Vitamin A	Thiamin	Riboflavin	Vitamin b_6	Vitamin B_{12}	Niacin	Calcium	Phosphorus	Iron
Hamburgers																
Burger King Whopper	9 oz.	660	41 gm.	49 gm.	9 gm.	1083 mg.	57%	12%	51%	30%	19%	67%	55%	9%	29%	26%
Jack-In-The-Box Jumbo Jack	8¼	538	28	44	7	1007	61	9	56	41	13	70	57	13	29	24
McDonald's Big Mac	7½	591	33	46	6	963	59	5	52	33	13	63	55	23	44	23
Wendy's Old Fashioned	6½	413	22	29	5	708	52	8	36	26	13	83	45	8	24	27
Sandwiches																
Roy Rogers Roast Beef Sandwich	5½	356	12	34	0	610	63	5	38	29	16	37	60	2	28	23
Burger King Chopped-Beef Steak Sandwich	6¾	445	13	50	0.7	966	67	5	48	34	25	40	66	15	37	30
Hardee's Roast Beef Sandwich	4½	351	17	32	3	765	41	4	36	22	10	47	42	8	29	17
Arby's Roast Beef Sandwich	5¼	370	15	36	1	869	52	4	36	21	10	53	56	5	35	20
Fish																
Long John Silver's	7½	483	27	27	0.1	1333	72	5	17	12	16	133	24	3	46	3
Arthur Treacher's Original	5¼	439	27	27	0.3	421	46	3	11	6	10	27	18	2	32	3
McDonald's Filet-O-Fish	4½	383	18	38	3	613	35	3	39	19	6	23	25	14	27	9
Burger King Whaler	7	584	34	50	5	968	48	3	38	20	7	60	31	8	50	12
Chicken																
Kentucky Fried Chicken Snack Box	6¾	405	21	16	0	728	78	4	21	25	19	40	72	6	35	14
Arthur Treacher's Original Chicken	5½	409	23	25	0	580	57	3	12	10	24	10	87	2	33	4
Specialty entrées																
Wendy's Chili	10	266	9	29	9	1190	50	54	20	169	18	47	8	9	27	27
Pizza Hut Pizza Supreme	7¾**	506	15	64	6	1281	61	36	59	40	17	43	49	41	46	24
Jack-In-The-Box Taco	5½***	429	26	34	3	926	35	25	16	13	15	27	18	20	33	12

*Recommended Daily Allowance for an adult woman, as set by the National Academy of Sciences/National Research Council.
**One-half of a 15½-oz., 10-in Pizza Supreme Thin and Crispy. ***Two 2¾-oz. tacos.

3. Try not to shop when you are hungry. Research has shown that you are more likely to indulge in impulse buying when you are hungry.

4. Check all shelves, as lower-priced items are often placed above or below eye level. Also carefully check the value of the items placed in the center aisle or at the front of the store; they may be marked as sale items but, in fact, are being sold at regular prices.

5. Shop alone! Don't bring the family.

6. Before going to a supermarket, check store ads and featured items.

7. Take advantage of store displays that offer items at special prices.

8. Buy food in season and make it a main part of the meal when it is relatively cheap.

9. Serve fewer courses but larger portions.

10. Check unit prices on the shelf. They tell you the actual cost per count or weight.

11. Freeze bones and vegetable trimmings for stocks and soups. Once you've made a soup stock, freeze it in different-sized containers or in ice-cube trays to use as needed.

12. Whenever you can make something on your own, do so. Yogurt, for example, is easy to make and costs about one-fourth as much as the store product.

13. Combine inexpensive foods to make a balanced meal. A good example is rice and beans, which contain complementary proteins and work well nutritionally. (They're easy on your budget, too.)

14. Clip and cash in coupons for the products you use. Get a rain check for out-of-stock bargains.

15. Plan ahead so you have enough time to prepare your food. Avoid last-minute splurge shopping or restaurant meals.

16. Grow some of your own herb seasonings in windowsill pots.

SUMMARY

1. Unit pricing is required by law in many cities. When you go shopping for food, you should compare unit prices instead of trying to determine whether a 7-ounce can of tuna fish is cheaper than a 6½-ounce can when the former sells for $1.43 and the latter sells for $1.29.

2. Shopping for specials is one way to save consumer food dollars. Ads for specials generally are listed in newspapers, as well as in the markets where you shop. Be careful though: Do not drive fifteen miles just to go to a market that has salt on special. The savings you will realize on the salt will be less than the cost in extra gas (unless, of course, you are buying a ton).

3. Generally, you should compare the potential gains from shopping for specials with the potential costs, particularly in terms of your time and other complementary resources.

4. You may end up paying about twice as much per ounce for certain convenience foods, such as peas, string beans, and carrots that are frozen in butter sauce. Ask yourself if this price is too high for the extra convenience.

5. One of the basic nutrients needed to maintain a healthy body is protein, and there are various inexpensive foods that provide it, such as peanut butter, dried beans and peas, and nuts.

6. Even though American incomes are growing, the percentage of families estimated to have poor diets is rising.

7. Advance meal planning can help you shop more cost-effectively at the supermarket.

QUESTIONS FOR THOUGHT AND DISCUSSION

1. Why did it take so long for unit pricing to become more or less common in retail food markets?

2. Is it ever advisable to comb through all supermarket ads? If so, when?

3. Some nutritionists contend that TV dinners lack many basic nutrients. Others contend that they taste awful. Nonetheless, TV dinners sell very well. Why.?

4. Do you think the amount of basic nutrients should be clearly indicated on the front of every item sold in a market?

5. Why do you think meat is such an expensive food item?

6. How can you explain the fact that Americans have increasingly poor diets even though they are getting richer as a nation?

7. What is the most important aspect of your diet? Nutrition? Variety? Cost? Convenience?

THINGS TO DO

1. Check the markets in your area to see which ones engage voluntarily in unit pricing. If some do not, ask the managers why. Do you think unit pricing adds to the cost of selling food products?

2. Look at all the local newspapers for one day and compare specials on national-brand food items. What is the percentage difference from the normal price and the special price? Can you compute the extra time required to obtain the specials? If so, what would have to be the value of your time to make it worthwhile for you to make a special trip to the one store with the sale item?

3. What other resources are complementary to food shopping besides your automobile or other form of transportation? List them and estimate their yearly cost just for food shopping.

4. List all the foods you eat that could be considered convenience foods.

5. Ask a local restaurant owner about his or her food-buying habits. Ask how many of the items on the menu are prefrozen. When you go into a seafood restaurant, ask which items are fresh, fresh-frozen, or just frozen. Try to get an honest answer. Can you tell the difference between fresh and fresh-frozen seafood?

6. As an experiment, find out how much you spend on food without any advance planning, and then compare it with what you will spend on food if you carefully plan your meals ahead of time for a week. Is the difference worth the effort? (Usually it is.)

7. As a class, make a list of commonly used foods. Specify brands and amounts. Each class member should price items in three different markets and make a comparison in class.

SELECTED READINGS

Aaker, David and McElroy, Bruce. "Unit Pricing Six Years after Introduction." *Journal of Marketing,* Fall 1979.

Anderson, W. Thomas, Jr. *The Convenience-Oriented Consumer.* Austin: University of Texas, Graduate School of Business, Bureau of Business Research, 1971.

"A Beef over More Meat Making the Top Grades." *Business Week,* September 27, 1982, p. 32.

"Comparison Shopping Ten Years Later: What Does It Save on Grocery Bills?" *Consumer Views,* vol. 13, No. 10, October 1982. Published by Citibank, New York.

Cross, Jennifer. *The Supermarket Trap.* Bloomington, Ind.: Indiana University Press, 1970.

"Fast-Food Chains." *Consumer Reports,* September 1979, pp. 508–13.

"Generic Groceries—They're Cheaper, But What's in Them?" *Changing Times,* December 1978, pp. 36–38.

"Hoping to Ease Economic Punch, Many Avidly Pursue Refund Offers." *The Wall Street Journal,* October 18, 1982, p. 1.

"How to Use USDA Grades in Buying." *Home and Garden Bulletin.* No. 196. Washington, D.C.: U.S. Department of Agriculture, Government Printing Office.

CHAPTER
MORE THAN JUST KEEPING WARM

The typical American has more clothes than actually needed to provide physical protection from the cold, sun, wind, and rain. Obviously, most clothing is no longer as much a necessity as a consumer good that gives pleasure to the wearer.

CHAPTER PREVIEW

- What are some characteristics of the clothing industry?
- What determines the types of clothes we buy?
- How do clothes fit into family budget formation?
- How does durability affect the price of clothing?
- How has the Flammable Fabrics Act affected the production and sale of clothes?
- What are the federal statutes relating to the labeling of clothing products?

It is estimated that American families spent $130 billion on clothing in 1983. Together, all of us purchased $130 billion worth of shoes, pants, hats, jockey shorts, brassieres, panties, hose, suits, ties, shirts, skirts, and socks. Clothing expenditures account for between 5 and 10 percent of the typical American's total budget. Clothing is a major industry, now employing over a million workers in any one year. The fashion business, of course, occupies large amounts of advertising and media space and probably, for many people, a significant amount of mental space. There are approximately 7,000 wholesale clothing outlets, more than 90,000 retail clothing outlets, and 25,000 or more manufacturers. It is hard to tell how many manufacturers of clothing there are because so many small ones go into and out of business in any one year (or month, for that matter). In addition to all these market outlets for clothing, countless men and women make at least some of their own or their family's clothes, accounting for approximately $3.5 billion of sales in fabrics, patterns, notions, and other sewing needs.

Recent years have seen the upsurge of discount clothing stores; these stores usually have fewer salespersons and charge for such services as alterations and hemming that are "free" in nondiscount stores. In general, discount stores that offer true bargains have a smaller variety of sizes, styles, colors, qualities, and perhaps brand names. This is how they reduce their costs so that they can, in fact, sell clothes to you at a lower price than nondiscount stores.

Shopping for clothing can be time consuming. By one estimate, the typical homemaker spends 100 hours a year shopping for clothes for the family. We are, undeniably, a clothes-conscious society.

WHY SO MANY CLOTHES?

The typical American has more clothes than actually needed to provide physical protection from the cold, sun, wind, and rain. Obviously, then, most clothing is no longer so much a necessity as a consumer good that gives pleasure to the wearer.

Customs

The types of clothes we buy are often determined by customs in the community, although in the United States this is less true today than in the past. It is certainly only by custom that men wear trousers and women wear skirts. After all, in Scotland men also wear skirts; and in the United States, more and more women are wearing pants or pantsuits whenever and wherever they wish without being exposed to ridicule or discrimination. Why do men wear ties and collars while women usually do not? Again, the only explanation is custom. These customs change slowly. It took many years before fancy restaurants admitted tieless men in turtleneck sweaters.

Customs are not created in a vacuum; most are created to appease or satisfy a large segment of the population. Once customs are well established, they are hard to break, simply because the majority of the society accepts them or even enjoys them. Only when a significant and aggressive minority finds the customs disturbing are they changed.

Mental Attitude

Clothing that pleases us as wearers and that we think pleases those who see us often contributes greatly to our attitude toward our fellow humans. One of the strongest motivations of dress is preservation of the self-image of the wearer through the enhancement of the body. This is an aesthetic consideration—that is, one having to do solely with beauty. Even among primitive tribes, self-adornment is a stronger motivation than protection from the elements, or thrift, or durability. And this motivation in clothing selection has nothing to do with snobbery. It merely indicates a positive self-concept that is healthy and beneficial.

Clothing that pleases us as wearers and that we think pleases those who see us often contributes greatly to our attitude toward our fellow humans.

Values

People generally express their values, attitudes, and interests by the choices they make. To a great extent, values help determine our choice of behavior and influence much of our decision making during the course of our lives. In this sense, clothing choices make a statement about those ideas we consider important in our day-to-day living and, whether consciously or unconsciously, about the beliefs about ourselves that we would like others to share.

Our individual values, however, are closely linked to a much broader value system, one that we learn from our culture, family, friends, and our own experiences. Taken together, these values are known as a *value pattern*. This pattern includes all those things we consider important, and it helps organize them into some kind of functioning order. Clothing, then, can be said to reflect not only those values instilled in us by society but also our own individual attitudes and values.

Studies on the emphasis that we, as groups and individuals, give to clothing have found that clothing choices reveal attitudes most often related to conformity, self-expression, aesthetic satisfaction, esteem, comfort, and economy. For example, if you place a great deal of importance on conformity, you will make choices that reflect the clothing fashion of your peers. If you are more concerned with aesthetic satisfaction, you might choose clothing for its stylishness, fabric quality, or for the pleasure derived from being considered well-dressed. If you are more concerned with economy, your clothing choices will express the practicality, durability, and price of the item.

It should be noted that even though values do strongly influence clothing choices, many times values conflict, and compromises must be made. For example, a person may value conformity in dress, but his or her budget might place constraints on that desire. That latest style that everyone is wearing may be too expensive. Clearly, a compromise must be made.

Group Identification

Another aspect of clothing involves group identification. Clothing styles tell the outside world something about an individual's personality. Clothing will convey a message to others about what you do, what you believe, and what you are. In particular, clothing appearance and style may identify an individual with a particular group. Not only that but the wearing of a particular style of clothing can help create an identity for an individual.

Clothing also can be used as a form of rebellion, particularly against parental control. Teenagers often dress in a manner contrary to what is normal for the family in which they have been raised; in this way, they are telling their parents, "We are different."

CLOTHES, FAMILY HAPPINESS, AND BUDGET FORMATION

How a family dresses can sometimes enhance family satisfaction. Again, some of you may find this idea reprehensible because it puts too much weight on a material, instead of a spiritual, aspect of life. But just as variety in diet contributes to more than physical well-being, so, too, can clothing be one of the material aspects of life that contributes to self-image and self-esteem. The fact remains, for example, that parents who approve of how their children dress are often more satisfied and proud to be the heads of the family. Similarly, children as well as their parents may take great pleasure in being part of the family unit that "dresses up" to go to church on Sunday or to visit friends. But each member of the family has his or her own idea about what fashions are appropriate for himself or herself and for the others in the family. This may cause conflicts within the family or spending unit for two reasons. For one, the family's budget will, by necessity, curtail some of the clothing expenditures desired by each member. And, for another, members of the family who have clothing habits significantly different from those of other members may feel pressure to conform.

Individuality and Conformity

To avoid the problem of family conflicts about individual dressing styles, it is important that each member's individuality or "living space" not be violated. This is something that can be discussed during family councils or between individual members of the spending unit. Because clothing habits reflect each person's values and aesthetics, no set rules about dressing can be absolute for any person at any time. If one member of the spending unit wishes to rebel and buy clothes that are indeed different from everyone else's, this attempt at individuality must not only be understood but also accepted (at least in part). As with everything else, compromises will have to be made about dressing habits within a spending unit, as well as about the size of each member's clothing expenditures.

The Budget Again

Clothing enters into the budget-making decisions of every spending unit. Such decisions cannot be avoided because clothes are so important. One way to decrease the friction within the family or spending unit is to discuss each individual's desires or needs for clothes at a family council when the budget is being formed. The problems of democratic money management and the agreed-upon rules of democratic decision making within any spending unit will apply to clothing decisions also. It is best that the head or heads of the spending unit not attempt to impose his, her, or their value judgments on the other members by dictating clothing tastes and rules of fashion.

THE POWERFUL FASHION INDUSTRY

Many people accuse the clothing industry of creating obsolescence.

In the United States, the fashion industry is the fourth largest in annual sales. Understanding how fashions are decided and how they affect you, the consumer, is important for your clothing decision making. We are all aware of "high" fashion, but most of us are not direct consumers of it. However, whatever happens in the salons of Balmain, St. Laurent, or Valentino or whatever is designed by Bill Blass, Geoffrey Beene, or Ann Klein eventually has an effect on less expensive ready-to-wear clothes. Indeed, respected designers in France, the United States, and elsewhere have been designing clothes for the ready-to-wear market for the past ten years or so.

Who Dictates Fashion?

The immense size of the fashion industry and its apparent influence on our buying habits lead us back to the eternal question of consumer versus producer sovereignty. Are fashions dictated by you, the consumer, or are they dictated by the whims of producers? Nobody will ever know who truly dictates fashion, but we can consider a few salient facts. Not all fashions dictated by designers actually take hold. For example, the midiskirt failed because women refused to accept it.

Although changes in fashions cause earlier "obsolescence" than some consumers would prefer, we do have the choice of either wearing classic fashions that seldom change or of wearing old-fashioned clothes. We do not have to give in to the whims of the fashion industry. But if so many companies are able to make at least a normal profit by continually introducing new fashions, there must be consumers who demand variety in their clothing styles every year. You and I might find such changes a disagreeable waste of scarce resources. But who's to say what makes other people happy? On the other hand, even if you have decided that your clothing needs consist of replacing your one pair of jeans every six months or so, you might find that to get the same style you wore last year would mean a lot of hunting. So the success of the fashion industry might merely reflect changing availabilities of replacement articles: The fact that you now buy your jeans with flared or straight pants legs may have nothing to do with your eagerness to adopt changing styles.

If, however, people are made happy by the availability of new fashions, then it would be a value judgment to say their happiness is false. As long as we consumers are aware of the cost of purchasing fashion happiness, we certainly must have the right to decide whether we want to give up other things in order to buy fashionable clothes at a higher price than we pay for merely utilitarian clothes. Consumers may not be king, particularly with respect to fashions, but because nothing is being forced on us either, the consumer always has the choice of not being drawn into the passing fashion parade.

DURABILITY VERSUS PRICE

Many people accuse the clothing industry of creating obsolescence. That may or may not be true. But it is certain that, to have more durable goods, we generally have to pay more. All of us must decide how much durability we

want to pay for. Some manufacturers, such as Monsanto, are now "wear dating" their clothing items: A tag is attached to the garment indicating the guaranteed wear period, usually a year. Thus, the consumer can sometimes determine how much durability is being purchased.

Several years ago, a new phenomenon appeared: paper underwear, paper dresses, and other items made out of paper products that were thrown away after being used several times. This was the ultimate in planned obsolescence. But, at least in this case, the obsolescence was planned by the consumer, because those of us who bought such articles did so knowing that they would soon be thrown away. Nobody was being fooled, for the manufacturers told us explicitly how many times we could plan on wearing such a piece of clothing. Information wasn't a problem.

Why would consumers purchase such a highly nondurable piece of clothing? The answer is obvious: You need not worry about upkeep or cleaning when you know the item will be thrown away. And you can change fashions often this way, even as frequently as every day. For fashion-conscious consumers, this may seem ideal, if you are willing to pay the very high implicit price.

Durability Is Not Free

If durability were a **free good,** we could be fairly certain that producers were creating obsolescence. But durability is not a free good. You usually have to pay more for materials that last longer, and that price may be more than you wish to pay. Depending on your tastes and your budget, you may be better off buying less durable clothes and replacing them more often—especially if the cost of cleaning rises relative to other costs. Whenever the maintenance costs of an item go up relative to other costs (such as the purchase price), you have more incentive to replace the item rather than to maintain and repair it.

FREE GOOD
A good that has a supply greater than what people demand at a zero price—for example, air to burn in an auto engine.

Once you know that durability is *itself* a good, you can make more rational choices when buying clothing. You are purchasing a suit or a dress, for example, because of the service flow it yields per unit time period. Thus, if you buy a jacket that you think will last five years, you should figure out what the cost per year is; if it costs $100 but another jacket that will last only one year costs $75, the first jacket is obviously not more expensive in cost per service flow per year. You should know, also, that many durable clothes are actually cheaper than the same type retailed as a "fad." For example, there is little durability difference between a $5.99 men's polyester and cotton shirt and one for $10.99, but the fit, stitching, and finishing may be far superior in the $10.99 shirt. That may be the only difference but one for which you may be willing to pay the extra five dollars.

In your own shopping forays, remember that you should figure out the cost per year of owning a piece of clothing. It's also important to understand the maintenance costs of particular materials. A clothing label that says "dry clean only" may indicate that the item will cost you more to maintain than another item in the same line labeled "may be machine washed." This kind of information is important in figuring out the relative costs of different pieces of clothing (and also a good reason for labeling requirements).

THE TREND TOWARD LESS FLAMMABLE PRODUCTS

The U.S. government has increasingly required that children's clothing be nonflammable. In 1953, Congress passed the Flammable Fabrics Act in response to public indignation over the deaths and injuries caused by highly flammable wearing apparel. Congress enacted this particular piece of protective consumer legislation in order to prohibit "the introduction or movement in interstate commerce of articles of wearing apparel and fabrics which are so highly flammable as to be dangerous when worn by individuals. . . ." In its original form, the act was applicable only to the manufacturing and sale of a narrow range of articles susceptible to flammability—wearing apparel and fabrics to be incorporated into wearing apparel. Also, the act explicitly excluded from its control certain items of wearing apparel, such as hats, gloves, and footwear. The original version of the act, although helpful, seemed to fall short of the protection it was expected to give the consuming public. Congress had failed to include many articles that created significant hazards and had failed to permit establishment of more stringent standards of flammability.

A 1967 amendment to the act specifically prohibits the manufacture and sale of any product, fabric, or related material that fails to conform to an applicable standard or regulation. More specifically, the manufacture or sale of such a flammable product was to be considered an unfair method of competition under the Federal Trade Commission Act. In addition, the 1967 amendment repealed the specific wearing-apparel exclusion of the 1953 act. While the original act gave the Department of Commerce power only to recommend new standards and left Congress itself with the power to change the standard, the amendment gave the department the authority to determine the need for new enforceable standards of flammability. The Department of Health, Education, and Welfare (now the Department of Health and Human Services) was made responsible for providing statistical data on test injuries.

As can be imagined, this divergent responsibility for administering the act created substantial problems of coordination. In 1972, the entire responsibility for administration and enforcement of the Flammable Fabrics Act was taken from the three agencies—FTC, Department of Commerce, and HEW—and given to the newly created Consumer Product Safety Commission[1] (CPSC).

THE TREND TOWARD BETTER LABELING

The U.S. government has been quite active in improving the labeling standards of furs, wool, and textiles. Since its inception, the Federal Trade Commission has been responsible for enforcing federal statutes relating to these items.

Wool Products Labeling Act

The Wool Products Labeling Act of 1939 protects producers, manufacturers, distributors, and consumers by requiring that manufacturers' labels clearly state the type of wool and all other fibers making up 5 percent or more of the fabric content. The FTC has established the following definitions for the use of wool.

1. **Reprocessed wool.** Fibers that have been previously woven or felted into a wool product that was never used by consumers
2. **Reused wool.** Fibers taken from a used wool product and reused in another garment
3. **Virgin wool.** Wool that has never been used to make another product

The FTC is authorized to issue rules and regulations, to make inspections, and to issue **cease-and-desist orders** under the Wool Products Labeling Act.

CEASE-AND-DESIST ORDERS Legal orders from a federal agency or a judge requiring that a certain activity stop immediately. For example, the Federal Trade Commission can issue a cease-and-desist order against a fur manufacturer's deceptive labeling practice.

Fur Products Labeling Act

Passed in 1951, this act requires that fur products indicate on their labels the type of fur, the country of origin of an imported fur product, whether the fur has been dyed or tinted, and if the garment is made from scraps of fur. The act is designed to protect consumers and competitors by making it unlawful to misbrand, falsely advertise, and falsely invoice fur products. The statute was originally passed in part because of the widespread use of exotic-sounding euphemisms such as "Baltic Lion" and "Isabella Fox" for such unexotic furs as rabbit, dogskin, skunk, or alley cat. The Fur Act goes one step beyond the Wool Act in that it requires informative advertising as well as labeling of fur products.

1. See Consumer Issue A.

Textile Fiber Products Identification Act

In 1960, the FTC passed the United States Textile Fiber Products Identification Act. Under this law, *all* textile products must contain the following information on the label:

1. The generic (nontrademark) name of the fibers (such as cotton or polyester) listed in order of predominance by weight
2. The percentage of each fiber making up 5 percent or more of the product's weight
3. The name of the manufacturer
4. The country of origin of an imported fiber

Critics of the act point out that the information provided is helpful only to those consumers who understand the qualities of various clothing materials used. However, the type of fiber alone is often not sufficient indication of the wearing qualities of the garment in question. For example, yarn size in nylon products can create either one of the strongest fabrics (such as "rip-stop" nylon used in tents and sleeping bags) or one of the most fragile, such as in hosiery, with many variations in between. Finishes also can cancel out fiber characteristics or provide beneficial characteristics not available in the fiber. For example, cotton is one of the most absorbent fibers, but it can be made water-resistant, as is polished cotton. In sum, most labels containing fiber content (as provided for by the Textile Fiber Products Identification Act) are useful on clothes only to the extent that consumers have knowledge of fibers, fabrication methods, and finishes.

SYNTHETIC FABRICS

Because of the many synthetic fibers used today, it is becoming increasingly important for consumers to know more in order to be able to make intelligent purchases. Exhibit 14–1 is a partial guide to synthetic fibers used in apparel.

If you wish to have more information, you might want to order one or both of the following publications:

1. A current fiber chart from:
   Man-Made Fiber Producers Association, Inc.
   1150 17th St., N.W.
   Washington, D.C. 20036
2. Fibers and Fabrics, NBS Consumer Information, Series 1, from:
   The National Bureau of Standards
   U.S. Dept. of Commerce
   Washington, D.C. 20230

PERMANENT CARE LABELING

More informative for your clothes-buying excursions are the care instructions required by an FTC trade rule effective since 1972. This ruling specifies that all fabrics be labeled as to the laundering or dry cleaning that will be required to maintain the garment's original character. In other words, you can now assess how much time or money will be entailed in maintaining the garment

EXHIBIT 14–1
A Partial Guide to Synthetic Fibers Used in Apparel

GENERIC NAME	SELECTED BRAND NAMES	CHARACTERISTICS
Acetate and Triacetate	Acete Estron (FR = Flame resistant) Arnel	Dries rapidly. Heat sensitive; press with cool iron on wrong side. May be dry cleaned. Dissolved by organic solvents such as nail-polish remover. Abrasion resistance is poor. May be used in blends to increase flame resistance. Triacetate is more abrasion resistant and may be ironed with a moderate iron. Do not twist or stretch when wet, as both have lower strength when wet.
Rayon	Fortisan (FR = Flame resistant) Zantel	High absorbency, soft, economical. May be similar to cotton in appearance. Some finishes used on rayon may be sensitive to chlorine bleach. May be machine washable (gentle cycle) and dried at low temperatures, or hand washed and hung to dry. Avoid wringing or twisting when wet. Iron at low temperature. Follow manufacturer's directions.
Nylon	Antron Cantrece Qiana	Lightweight; exceptionally strong, durable. May be machine washed and dried. White nylon may tend to pick up other colors and soil in laundering. Wash whites separately.
Polyester	Dacron Fortrel Trevira Kodel	Lightweight, durable, colorfast. Excellent wash-and-wear characteristics. Oily soil and oil-born stains may be difficult to remove.
Acrylic	Acrilan Creslan Orlon	Soft, lightweight, bulky (low weight with high warmth). In appearance, may be similar to wool. Good colorfast qualities. Moderate abrasion resistance. May be machine washed and dried or dry cleaned. Be sure to follow manufacturer's directions for cleaning.
Modacrylic	Dynel Elura Verel	Similar to acrylics; very sensitive to heat. Uses: for deep pile coats, as simulated fur, and for wigs. Flame resistant. May be dry cleaned or machine washed and dried at low temperatures. Follow manufacturer's directions carefully.
Spandex	Lycra	Used in elastic construction, foundation garments, swimwear, suspenders. Resists deterioration from grease, oil, and perspiration and is more powerful and durable than rubber. Machine or hand wash at low temperatures.
Metallic	Lurex	Metallic fibers usually coated with plastic. Will not tarnish. Used ornamentally in apparel and home-furnishing fabrics. May be laundered or dry cleaned. Coating may melt if it becomes too hot.
Olefin	Herculon Marvess Vectra	Lightweight and durable. Heat sensitive. Primarily used for carpets but increasing usage for purses, belts, and men's knitted sportswear. Machine wash and dry at low temperature. Use a fabric softener in the final rinse. Avoid laundromat dryers and do not iron 100% olefin fabrics.
Rubber	Lastex	Used in elastic constructions such as foundation garments, waistbands, suspenders. High stretch and recovery properties. Easily damaged by grease and oil, including body oil.

you purchase. For instance, labels vary from "dry clean only" to "leather clean only" to "machine wash, warm, tumble dry"—nine different classifications in all. Some manufacturers have added even further care categories.

As confusing as this might sound, it is an acknowledgment by the FTC and textile manufacturers that fabric content is not a sufficient indicator of what you are buying. Although durability information is still not explicitly available, permanent labeling as to care instructions is certainly a great aid in purchasing clothing. These labels represent a more sophisticated version of the "drip-dry" or "wash-and-wear" categories previously in effect. It is now possible to determine just what care is necessary to maintain certain clothing; that is, you now know that you will have to iron this blouse, or incur the sometimes higher expense of dry cleaning. And the regulation does not apply solely to prefabricated garments; persons who choose to sew for their families are also being given care labels with each piece of fabric to sew into the finished garment.

Care instructions sometimes can be misleading, however, because some manufacturers use only the most conservative care instructions on their labels. Items marked "dry clean only," for example, might be safely handwashed or even machinewashed. Some garments are labeled "do not bleach" when bleaching actually would not damage the garment.

In addition, commercial dry-cleaning processes may shrink some synthetic fabrics with care instructions to "dry clean only." Home washing machines may treat clothes labeled "wash with hot water" well enough, but the much hotter water temperatures in commercial machines may damage them.

In 1976, the Federal Trade Commission proposed a revision of its care labeling rule. This proposal calls for more explicit labeling instructions and, if adopted, will require care labels to specify washing and drying methods and temperatures, use and type of bleach, and temperatures for ironing, if needed. If an item can be washed or dry cleaned, the manufacturer will have to include that information on the label. Dry-cleaning instructions will have to specify the type of solvent to be used if not all commercially available solvents are appropriate. Permanent-care labels would be required for the first time on suede and leather items, upholstered furniture, draperies, sheets, bedspreads, and so on. The rule would further require that labels be available to fabric and carpet retailers to pass on to consumers. The revision has not been completed as of this printing.

Now that you know what to look for on clothing labels and have decided what kinds of styling and durability you want, look at the following Consumer Issue to see how you can economize on your clothing purchases.

Machine wash warm, gentle cycle
Wash dark colors and prints separately
Tumble dry low setting
Remove promptly and hang
Do not use bleach on colors or prints
If touch-up is desired, use cool iron
100% NYLON
302

SUMMARY

1. Clothes are purchased for more reasons than simply physical protection. They are purchased because of custom and also because they can give the wearer a sense of well-being.
2. Different socioeconomic classes typically dress differently as a matter of class identification and to impart information to other members of society.
3. Family conflicts about individual dressing styles and clothing budgets can be resolved through democratic family decision making. Generally, it is important to compromise in terms of the individual's desire either to conform or to family dressing habits.
4. It has been said that fashions are dictated by the fashion industry. However, the flop of the midiskirt a few years ago is at least one instance of a consumers' rebellion.
5. Generally, more durable clothes are higher priced. When you're deciding which clothes to buy, take account of how long they last. Then you can compare clothes on the basis of price per year rather than total purchase price.
6. In 1953, Congress passed the Flammable Fabrics Act, which was amended in 1967. The act requires that the manufacture and sale of fabric or fabric products conform to an applicable standard or regulation. This is particularly important for children's pajamas and nightgowns.
7. Numerous acts apply to correct labeling of fabrics and fur. The Fur Act, for example, requires that the actual content of the products in question be advertised.
8. Labels indicating the appropriate care of the garment are now available to customers.

9. Current information on fibers can be obtained from the National Bureau of Standards or from the Man-Made Fiber Producers Association.

QUESTIONS FOR THOUGHT AND DISCUSSION

1. What determines how many clothes you buy each year? How much extra money do you spend on clothing for variety and style?
2. How many of your decisions about clothing are based on custom?
3. What are the prevalent clothing customs in your community?
4. Do you agree that clothing imparts information to the onlooker? Or do you think "you can't judge a book by its cover"?
5. Do you think that every member of a spending unit should be allowed to dress in his or her own way without regard to the general ideas held by the spending unit?
6. Do you think that fashion designers dictate what fashions will be or that they cater to what the public wants? What evidence do you have?
7. Have you noticed a changing attitude toward clothing in your lifetime?
8. Do you think it is fair that more durable clothes cost more than less durable clothes? Do you care about durability in your own clothing purchases?
9. Why do you think it took so long for Congress to act on flammable fabrics?
10. Why are some parents unwilling to buy flame-retardant clothing for their children? Do you think that they should be required to do so by law?

THINGS TO DO

1. Write a list of all the clothes you've bought in the last year. Also list all the clothes you no longer wear. From the first list, decide what were actual necessities and what were "frills." From the second list, decide which clothes are still serviceable. Now ask yourself how much you have spent for clothing in excess of what was actually necessary.
2. Make as long a list as you can of all our clothing habits that are based purely on custom. Why are clothing customs different in different parts of the United States and in different countries?
3. Contact a fashion designer or a fashion designer's assistant. Try to find out how decisions are made on which fashions will be selected for any particular year or season. Why do you think spring fashions are shown long before spring arrives?
4. If you are in college, try on clothes that you still have from high school. Are they still usable? That is do they cover your body and keep you warm in the winter or cool in the summer? If they are still perfectly usable, why won't you wear them?
5. Examine the labels on all the clothes you have. How helpful are they in telling you what the fabric is made of, how durable it is, how it should be washed, and so on? Can you think of better labeling that would be more helpful to you as a consumer?

SELECTED READINGS

Buck, George S. *Flammability Report.* Textile Industries, November 1971.
"Care Labeling of Wearing Apparel." *Family Economics Review,* March 1972.

Greenwood, Kathryn and Murphy, Mary F. *Fashion Innovation and Marketing.* New York: Macmillan & Co., 1978.

Jarnow, Jeannette and Judell, Beatrice. *Inside the Fashion Business,* 3d ed. New York: John Wiley & Sons, 1981.
Kefgen, Mary and Touchie-Specht, Phyllis. *Individuality in Clothing Selection and Personal Appearance,* 3d ed. New York: Macmillan & Co., 1981.
Look for That Label. Washington, D.C.: Federal Trade Commission.
Tortora, Phyllis. *Understanding Textiles,* 2d ed. New York: Macmillan & Co., 1982.
"What Fashion Changes Tell Us about the U.S." *U.S. News & World Report,* October 11, 1982.

Consumer

ISSUE K

GETTING THE MOST FOR YOUR CLOTHES SHOPPING DOLLAR

GLOSSARY

STORE BRANDS—Clothes with labels giving the store as the manufacturer. These store brands are often cheaper than national-brand clothes.

WHERE TO BUY AND HOW MUCH TO SHOP

Where you buy clothing will be dictated by your preferences in styles. Some stores differentiate themselves by catering to different tastes, by offering different qualities of goods, or by presenting a store atmosphere—in the kinds of salespersons they employ and the help they offer—different from that of other stores. Also involved, of course, is a certain amount of status: shopping at Saks Fifth Avenue implies a different self-image than does shopping at J. C. Penney.

In some stores, you will find very modish, young-looking clothes, and, in other stores, traditional styles or even old-fashioned, older-looking clothes. In any case, the style you prefer is the first consideration.

The next consideration is whether or not you should go to a discount store (if there is one in your area). Whether or not you do depends on how much you value the variety and the services that may be offered by nondiscount stores (and, of course, whether or not you feel your self-image is consistent with discount shopping). One of the services often lacking in discount stores is attentive assistance from a salesperson. Many consumers prefer not to have assistance from sales personnel, while others require constant attention. If you find a store where a salesperson is extremely knowledgeable about the durability and other characteristics of the clothes that are sold, you might be willing to pay a slightly higher price than you would in a discount establishment. The difference in price, you predict, will be more than made up for by the information you are given by the salesperson. Again, this is a choice that cannot be made for you, and it is one that you cannot figure out perfectly. You may make a mistake, but this is one method by which you become an informed shopper. You acquire information and experience as you make mistakes; next time, you will make the right decision about which kind of store to patronize.

SHOULD YOU SHOP AROUND FOR VALUES?

Whether to shop around for values is another matter of personal choice. Obviously, if you can buy the identical piece of clothing for a lower price in one store than in another and if both stores give the same amount of service in terms of alterations, allowing returns, and so on, you should buy the cheaper item. But finding the best deal involves using your time, and you must decide how valuable that time is. Also, you must decide whether you actually enjoy shopping. Some consumers detest going to store after store in search of the best deal on a particular piece of clothing. If you're one of those, you might prefer to order clothes through the mail. You are less likely to get exactly what you had in mind, but you are spared the inconvenience of walking, taking the bus or subway, or driving your car around to different stores. Many clothing outlets, particularly those for shoes and recreational equipment, offer service by mail with take-back provisions. You can also order through catalogs from Montgomery

Ward; Sears, Roebuck; J. C. Penney; Spiegel; and other stores that generally offer liberal take-back provisions. Here you save your time, but you do not get to see the article in question until it is delivered to your door. (Remember, however, that service to your door means you pay a higher price for the product; in many cases, you can arrange to pick up the items at a catalog desk in the store nearest you.)

Look at Exhibit K–1 for some hints on the best time of year to buy certain articles of clothing at sale prices.

Characteristics of Stores

There are certain characteristics of each retail clothing store that you may want to check into before you choose one. How good a reputation does the store have? Can you be certain about the quality of its products? One way to find out is to ask your neighbors or your friends. Another way is to see what percentage of its sales is to repeat customers. If you find friends and neighbors going back often to the same store, it may give good service and sell reputable products. If you have your own predetermined evaluations of particular brands, then you pick the store according to the brands it carries. How you then decide which store to go to depends upon your answers to the following questions.

1. What kind of service do you get?
2. How do you get along with the salespeople?
3. What are the take-back or exchange provisions?
4. What kinds of sales does the store have?
5. What is the refund policy for faulty merchandise or merchandise not wanted?
6. What is the store's policy on billing, past-due bills, and so on?

Most of your common-sense notions about shopping will apply here as they will whenever you spend money.

USING THE MAILS

As mentioned earlier, if you want to save shopping time, you can use the services of a mail-order firm—that is, one that sends you catalogs from which you can choose those products you intend to buy. Most catalogs also provide you with useful information, such as type of fabric, applicable warranties, and so on. This often allows for less-hurried comparative shopping at home. Moreover, if you decide to shop on credit, credit terms usually are spelled out. You may want to read the catalog first and then go to your usual clothing store to compare its merchandise with what the catalog firm had to offer. This is comparison shopping the easy way. The key, of course, is to find a reliable mail-order house, of which there are literally hundreds.

CASH OR CHARGE?

Most consumer consultants generally recommend that all clothing be purchased with cash because buying on credit costs more money. This is true for the reasons discussed in Chapter 12. If you buy on credit, you will have to pay a service charge (interest) for borrowing that money (unless you pay the bill in full before it is due). But remember the earlier discussion on the flow of services from any item. If you buy a nightgown and charge it, you can expect that it will last at least as long as the time period you might take to pay off the credit balance. In a

JANUARY

Coats (men's)
Costume and fine jewelry
Dresses
Furs
Handbags
Hats (men's)
Infant wear
Lingerie
Men's clothing
Men's shirts
Shoes (all groups)
Sportswear
Suits (men's, boy's)

FEBRUARY

Hats (women's)
Men's shirts
Sportswear

MARCH

Clothes (spring)
Coats (winter)
Hosiery
Infant wear
Shoes (boys', girls')
Skates
Ski equipment

APRIL

Coats (women's children's)
Dresses
Hats (women's)
Housecoats
Infant wear
Suits (men's, boys')

MAY

Handbags
Housecoats
Lingerie
Sportswear

JUNE

Dresses
Housecoats
Summer clothes and fabrics

JULY

Bathing suits (after July 4)
Children's clothing
Handbags
Hats (all groups)
Infant wear
Lingerie
Men's shirts
Shoes (all groups)
Sportswear
Summer clothes and fabrics

AUGUST

Back-to-school clothes
Bathing suits
Coats (all groups)
Furs
Men's clothing

SEPTEMBER

Children's clothing

OCTOBER

Back-to-school clothes
Hosiery
Housecoats

NOVEMBER

Children's clothing
Coats (women's, children's)
Dresses
Housecoats
Shoes (men's, boys')
Suits (men's, boys')

DECEMBER

Children's clothing
Coats (women's, children's)
Hats (children's)
Shoes (men's, women's)
Suits (men's, boys')

EXHIBIT K–1
When to Shop for Clothes on Sale

sense, you are then spreading out the payments for the item so that they correspond with the use of that item.

Since the purchase of clothing does not necessarily dictate that you pay cash or charge, your decision will be based on how much overall debt you want to carry, and this depends on what income you expect to make in the future, how much you value present consumption over future consumption, and what the charges will be for purchasing items on time.

Remember, though, that you are better off financially if you are allowed to charge goods for thirty, sixty, or ninety days without paying any interest. This way, you get the use of that money for that particular period, and you also get the use of the clothes you buy, with no charge for that simultaneous use. But, be sure that, in fact, there are no hidden charges for paying thirty or sixty days later. Also, see if there is a discount for paying cash. In this case, you may decide that you would rather get the cash discount because you intended to pay the bill fairly soon anyway.

BUYING PRINCIPLES

Many buying principles can be applied to clothes shopping to guarantee that you get the best deal for your money. These are as follows.

Comparison Shopping

You know you should compare values; you should look at the price of a product in one store and compare it with a similar product in another.

DURABILITY: Recall the discussion about durability in the previous chapter. That two pieces of clothing look the same does not necessarily mean they are the same: One may last longer than the other. You would not be truly comparing values if you automatically bought the cheaper item. You should find the most favorable relative cost per unit of service offered by each clothing item. And this service includes the ability to exchange it easily with the store, to get a refund if the clothing is defective, and so on.

STYLES: Quite obviously, if you choose basic or classic styles, you will have less incentive to change those styles, and, hence, your desired clothing budget may be smaller. But, of course, you give up some things—the joy of wearing highly fashionable clothes and of wearing new clothes more often.

NEEDS: You should be careful to buy clothes that, as some consumer economists say, "fit your needs." Only you can come close to knowing what your true needs are. And you should avoid becoming a bargain fanatic; that is, do not buy everything on sale just because it is on sale. Instead, take an inventory of the items you have and decide where you really have a deficiency in your clothing stock. (See Exhibit K–2.)

Remember that you generally can save up to 25 percent on many clothing items if you buy **store brands** instead of national brands. If you're not committed always to buy brand names, you can save quite a lot (depending, of course, on the quality of the house brand).

CARE: You should decide before buying how much time and money you are able to give to clothing care. Be sure to check labels for care instructions; dry cleaning can be an expensive alternative to hand or machine washing, but sometimes it is mandatory in the proper care of certain fabrics.

IF YOUR CLOTHES ARE DAMAGED AT THE CLEANERS

Dry cleaning is a necessity for many clothes, and sometimes a dry cleaner will unintentionally damage an article of clothing. What should you do if this happens? Either go to the retailer where the garment was purchased, or to the cleaner, and ask that the garment be sent to the International Fabricare Institute (the successor to the American Institute of Laundering and National Institute of Dry Cleaning) in Joliet, Illinois. Its Research Center and Dry Cleaning Analysis Laboratory are located at 12251 Tech Road, Silver Springs, Maryland 20904. The lab charges six dollars to analyze the textile and determine what ruined it. Typically, if the retailer is at fault in selling a defective item, he or she will replace it or reimburse you. If the dry cleaner is at fault, he or she will do the same. Some retailers, such as Sears, J. C. Penney, and Montgomery Ward, have their own testing labs to test damaged garments.

If you don't obtain satisfaction, you should contact the manufacturer or the Better Business Bureau in your area.

SUMMARY

1. Clothing shopping begins with a decision about what type of clothes to buy and in what price range. These two determinations will considerably narrow your range of possible retail stores in which you will shop.
2. When shopping for clothes, you should take into account the time and use of other complementary resources involved.
3. When making a decision about where to shop, check the reputation of a store. You can find this out from friends who have shopped there before, as well as by learning which brand names are carried in that store.
4. Check out the kind of service you will get before you make a purchase. What are the take-back guarantees and exchange provisions?
5. You can use the mail to save shopping time. Get catalogs from Sears, Montgomery Ward, Spiegel, and other companies to find out specific facts about the clothes you wish to buy. Then use that information for purposes of comparison when you shop in the retail stores in your area.
6. Whether you pay cash or charge your clothing purchases should depend upon the total amount of debt you are already handling, not on the particular purchase made. Go back to Exhibit I–2 to find out if you have a safe debt load. Make sure you do not exceed it just because you are partial to a particular article of clothing.
7. Durability is an important quality of any piece of clothing you purchase. Try to compare clothing articles by their cost per year. That means you have to know the durability and also the cost of maintaining the particular piece of clothing.
8. If you buy highly stylish clothes, remember that styles will change more often for you than if you buy more classic styles. You pay for stylishness.
9. Purchasing store-brand items instead of national-brand names may save you up to 25 percent.

QUESTIONS FOR THOUGHT AND DISCUSSION

1. How often do you shop for durability?
2. Do you want salespersons to offer help in a clothing store? Or would you rather pay a lower price and shop at a discount store?
3. How much time do you spend shopping for clothes? Do you spend more or less time trying to find good

EXHIBIT K–2
Figuring Out Your Clothing Needs

1. What do you have already?
2. What clothes are required by:
   a. your job or school?
   b. your social life?
   c. your recreational activities?
3. How many changes of clothes do you require to meet your minimum standards of:
   a. cleanliness?
   b. variety?
   c. social status?
4. How do your answers to questions one through three square with the income you can spend?

clothing buys than you do good food buys? If you do, is this rational? Why?

4. Is it a sign of laziness to order articles of clothing through the mail? For whom would this be the most appropriate consumer behavior?

5. What determines your clothing needs? Do you think about them often?

6. Do you think that males looking for clothes spend more, less or the same amount of time as females?

THINGS TO DO

1. Make a clothing inventory. Write down how often each item has to be replaced. Try to determine whether you replace the item more often than is absolutely necessary. If so, why do you do that?

2. Order some of the major mail-order catalogs. After you've received them, compare the clothing in each with the prices in each. If there are significant differences, can you determine why? Now try to establish whether your local retailers sell the same items at the same price. If there is a significant difference, ask your local retailers why.

3. Order the two guides to fibers mentioned in the last chapter. Compare them with our partial guide to synthetic fibers. See how up-to-date this guide is compared to what you received in the mail. Why do you think the characteristics of certain fabrics may change over time?

SELECTED READINGS

Buying Clothes for Your Family, HXT-N. Berkeley: Agricultural Extension Service, University of California, 1970.

Gallagher, D. "Are We What We Wear?" *Mademoiselle*, November 1981, p. 78.

Harroo, L. R. "How to Maintain a Healthy Wardrobe." *Essence*, March 1, 1980, pp. 42–43.

"Little Ways to Make Clothes Last Longer." *Good Housekeeping*, April 1980, p. 190.

"Newest Shopping Options." *Vogue*, June 1981, p. 136.

Removing Stains from Fabrics, HG-62. Washington, D.C.: U.S. Department of Agriculture, Superintendent of Documents, 1972.

"Stretching Today's Fashion Dollar." *Consumers' Research Magazine*, October 1981, pp. 14–18.

U.S. Department of Agriculture, Agricultural Research Service. "Dry Cleaning Leather," *Agricultural Research*, Vol. 25, No. 9, 1977, pp. 13–19.

"What Garment Care Labels Don't Tell You." *Changing Times*, December 1980, p. 40.

CHAPTER

PUTTING A ROOF OVER YOUR HEAD

Housing is just like clothes or food: Once we pass a certain minimum level, the rest depends on our tastes and preferences. And our tastes and preferences must be put into line with the reality of our limited budget.

CHAPTER PREVIEW

- What is the nature of the housing industry?
- What different types of dwellings do we live in?
- What are the advantages of renting? of buying?
- What has the federal government done to cope with the housing problem?
- Why is housing so expensive?
- What are some of the problems with the moving industry?
- What are the sociocultural influences of owning land?

If you happen to be an Eskimo living in the Yukon Territory, putting a roof over your head is complicated but not impossible: You make an igloo. If you happen to live in the bush country of Tanzania, putting a roof over your head takes some time, but eventually your thatch hut will be just what you need. If you were a pioneer settling on some cleared land in the Old West, putting a roof over your head would have meant building a log cabin.

Today, by way of contrast, if you are Mr. and Mrs. Superwealthy, deciding on a new roof over your head may involve $30,000 in architect's fees, $200,000 for a plot of land (not too small, of course), and perhaps another $300,000 for quite a nice house. If, on the other hand, you are the average new-home buyer, you have a three-bedroom house with 1,300 square feet of floor space that, with its land, had a market value of $85,000 in 1983.

Housing is a necessity, even for the poorest of humans, but we know that the types of housing services that people seem to "need" vary drastically from region to region, from suburb to suburb, and from person to person. The variety of houses that you can purchase seems almost infinite. And the price range that you have to look at is also large. Housing is just like clothes or food: Once we pass a certain minimum level, the rest depends on our tastes and preferences. And our tastes and preferences must be put into line with the reality of our limited budgets.

Early Americans must have had just as many fanciful ideas about how they would like to live as we have. But today, some of us—in fact, most of us—live like kings compared to earlier Americans. Why is that? Simply because we are all richer. Each year for the last 150 years, our real incomes have gone up at about 1½ percent per capita. And we have spent an increasing proportion of our budgets on housing services, mainly because most of us really do like to cater to our fancies. We like the good life, and that includes a spacious house with unique features.

THE HOUSING INDUSTRY

There are now more than 55 million single-family dwelling units in the United States. There are at least 22 million apartments and another 9 million mobile homes. In almost any one year, more than 1 million new houses are being built, and between 3½ million and 5 million families buy homes.

Americans also like to add on to existing houses, as evidenced by the $20 billion we spend every year for add-ons, improvements, and maintenance. The number of houses in the United States has been rising at the rate of about 2½ percent a year for the last thirty years.

However, these figures sometimes can be deceiving. A truer picture of our circumstances might emerge by measuring the additional services we are getting from the rising housing stock. It is one thing for 1 million one-bedroom apartments to be built, and it is quite another to have 1 million new four-bedroom houses. After all, why do we buy houses or mobile homes or buy or rent apartments? We buy or rent them for the services they yield, just as we buy clothes or cars or anything else that lasts. When we buy a house, we expect to reap an implicit rate of return in the form of housing services over a number of years; thus, it is important not to confuse the existing stock of housing and the *flow* of services from that stock.

What we are buying is not simply the house itself but the pleasure we derive from living in it month in and month out. And that pleasure is a function of the house's size, the convenience it offers, how pretty the view is, what the neighborhood is like, and everything else that can contribute to our happiness when we are home. Generally, the reason that there is "no place like home" is that all of us try to make our homes as special as possible so that we get maximum utility, or service, from them. It is important, then, to realize that when a consumer buys a $120,000 house, that consumer receives a larger flow of services per month than if he or she had bought a $60,000 house.

People who have their own houses built incur tremendous money and time costs, worry, and stress. Why do they do it? Many of them incur all those costs so they can specify the exact house that will maximize the utility and pleasure they get from the roof over their head.

In 1984, it is estimated that there is well over $7 billion worth of cooperative housing in the United States, serving more than 450,000 families.

Different Types of Roofs

We mentioned before that it is important to distinguish between the different levels of housing services that are being added to our housing stock. Everybody is familiar with the single-family dwellings, but fewer people are as familiar with multiple-family dwellings, such as duplexes, high-rise apartments, and so-called tenements. Additionally, in the United States we have seen an increase in the number of available condominiums, cooperatives, and townhouses. The single-family detached dwelling, the most popular type of residence in the United States, is also the most expensive way to live in terms of energy, use of resources, and time for maintenance.

COOPERATIVES. In a building of **cooperative** apartments, each dweller owns a **pro rata** (proportionate) share of a nonprofit corporation that holds a legal right to that building. In addition, a member of a cooperative:

1. Leases the individual unit he or she occupies.
2. Accepts financial responsibility for his or her own payments and, in addition, accepts responsibility for increases in assessments if one or more members fail to make their payments.
3. Pays a monthly assessment to cover maintenance, service, taxes, and mortgage for the entire building.
4. Votes to elect a board of directors.
5. Must obtain approval from the corporation before remodeling, selling, renting, or changing his or her unit.

COOPERATIVE
An apartment building or complex in which each owner owns a proportionate share of a nonprofit corporation that holds a legal right to the building. Each owner must obtain approval from the other members of the co-op before extensive remodeling, selling, or renting.

PRO RATA
Proportionately, according to some exactly calculable factor.

Much cooperative housing has been produced for middle-income families, although recently it has become more popular with higher-income families in such places as New York City. In 1984, it is estimated that there is well over $7 billion worth of cooperative housing in the United States, serving more than 450,000 families.

Cooperative housing grew slowly until 1950, when legislation was passed that allowed the Federal Housing Administration (FHA) to insure the mortgages of cooperative housing units. Today, numerous business organizations design, finance, contract for construction, and then sell cooperative housing projects to prospective member-residents. In many cases, after the cooperative unit is sold, another profit-making organization can be hired to manage the entire unit.

Co-ops themselves are nonprofit organizations and are, therefore, owned and operated solely for the benefit of the members. The FHA estimates that the cost of living in a cooperative apartment is about 20 percent less than renting a comparable apartment from a private landlord. It is interesting to speculate how this 20 percent differential could continue to exist. Perhaps it does because, for one thing, maintenance costs would be lower in the co-op since owner-members generally take better care of their apartments than renters do. The fact that co-ops are nonprofit organizations and other apartments are profit-making ventures definitely contributes to the 20 percent price differential. Also, fuller occupancy and lower turnover would contribute to lower operating costs. Furthermore, owner-members can claim income-tax deductions that are not available to renters.

Members in cooperative units have a right to sell their particular unit when they decide to move. They recoup any difference between what they owe on their mortgage and what the resale price of their unit is. In general, the co-op itself has the first option to buy the apartment that is put up for sale. In most cases, if the apartment is to be sold to someone else, the members of the cooperative must approve the sale.

CONDOMINIUM
An apartment house or complex in which each living unit is individually owned and where each owner receives a deed allowing him or her to sell, mortgage, or exchange the unit independently of the owners of the other units in the building.

CONDOMINIUMS. In **condominiums**, which represent a newer type of ownership than the cooperative,[1] the apartment dweller has the legal title to the apartment that he or she owns. A condominium owner, however:

1. Does have joint ownership interest in the common areas and facilities in the building, such as swimming pools and tennis courts.
2. Must arrange his or her own mortgage and pay taxes individually on his or her unit.
3. Must make separate payments for building maintenance and services.
4. Does not accept financial responsibility for other people's units or their share of the overall operating expenses.
5. Votes to elect a board of managers that supervises the property.
6. Has the right to refinance, sell, or remodel his or her own unit.

Condominiums have become especially popular in resort areas where the owners do not live year-round. In 1972, 25 percent of all new housing units constructed were condominiums, and by 1984 it was estimated to be up to 29 percent.

Some housing experts contend that because condominiums have certain advantages over cooperative units, we should see a continued growth in condominiums relative to co-ops. In many situations, owners who want to sell their condominium apartments are under fewer restrictions than are owners of co-op units. The condominium can be sold without the approval of a board of directors. With a condominium, if the owner of a unit defaults on a payment, it affects only his or her own mortgage. In the case of a cooperative unit, any owner who defaults causes the other co-op members to chip in to cover what

1. Although the condo concept is very old (such arrangements existed in ancient Rome and medieval Europe), in this country legal obstacles impeded its growth until 1961, when the Federal Housing Administration was authorized to insure condominium mortgages.

has been defaulted. Condominium owners usually are free to rent or lease their units to anyone.

Tax Advantages

All the various tax advantages of owning a home also apply to condominiums and cooperatives. Basically, all local taxes and interest on the mortgage for the prorated share in the cooperative and the entire share for the condominium unit are deductible from income before taxes are paid. Because this benefit is not directly available to renters, it is one reason a number of people prefer to own condominiums or join a cooperative instead of renting an apartment, even though an apartment in a cooperative or condominium looks the same and gives the same types of housing services.

Condo Conversions

One of the most dramatic phenomena to hit the housing industry is the wave of condominium conversions throughout the country. Literally thousands of apartment buildings and complexes are being turned into condominiums every few months. The situation is so serious in terms of how it affects renters that many localities and states have either passed or are considering passing legislation to slow down this growth of condo conversions. Although renters often are given first choice at buying the unit they currently are renting, many (if not most) of them are unable to come up with the necessary down payment to make the purchase, or they cannot obtain financing. Why are so many apartments being converted to condominiums? There seem to be at least three possible answers.

—**The profitability of owning rental housing has fallen dramatically in the last ten years.** The movement for tenant rights has prevented landlords from easily evicting nonpaying renters and from recouping any damages that renters cause to apartment buildings. Additionally, legally imposed rent control—maximum rental rates—reduces the profitability of owning and managing rental units.

—**Stricter building codes, particularly with respect to energy-conservation requirements mandated by the Department of Housing and Urban Development, make conversions less expensive than building new buildings.** Many of the energy-conservation requirements for building materials and methods do not apply to existing structures. In short, it is cheaper to convert existing apartment complexes to condominiums than it is to build condominiums from scratch.

—**As more and more people find themselves taxed more heavily, particularly by the federal government, they seek ways to reduce their taxes.** All local taxes and interest on a mortgage are deductible from income before taxes are paid, so many renters can no longer afford to remain renters; they must buy a living unit in order to receive the tax advantages that now seem more necessary for many Americans. In short, the demand for condominiums is growing more rapidly than the demand for rental units.

For whatever reasons, condo conversions seem to be here to stay. Whether we can solve the immense problems for renters forced out of their units remains to be seen.

One of the most dramatic phenomena to hit the housing industry is the wave of condominium conversions throughout the country.

Townhouses

A **townhouse** is a regular house with a front and back yard but with common sidewalls. The obvious advantage of a townhouse is economy, for its construction permits savings on the cost of land, insulation, windows, foundation, roof, and walls. Some townhouses are sold as condominiums. One main problem with such housing units may be lack of adequate soundproofing as a result of shared walls and the proximity of neighbors.

RENTING A PLACE TO LIVE

TOWNHOUSES
Houses that share common sidewalls with other houses.

Until recently, it was common for renters to be looked down upon as people who were unable to manage their money correctly. The proof, of course, was a lack of home ownership. But this attitude has been changing, and today many people rent apartments by choice even though they could easily buy their own homes.

There are several reasons some individuals wish to rent rather than buy.

1. Renters have greater mobility than those who own homes.
2. No down payment is involved; nor is a credit check necessary for securing a mortgage. (But there may be a breakage or cleaning deposit.)
3. Renters are freed from the maintenance tasks and depreciation that homeowners must face.
4. The exact cost of purchasing housing services can be figured easily for the period of the lease.
5. Renters don't have to worry about property values because they don't own the property.
6. It is easier to avoid excessive spending on home improvements.
7. Future housing needs in terms of the size of a family do not have to be estimated carefully.
8. Renters can take time to become familiar with a new community before investing in a house.
9. Common recreation facilities may be insured.
10. There is no loss of interest on investment of savings.
11. There is no liability of ownership.

Some apartments are rented on a month-to-month basis with the rent paid in advance. The renter or tenant automatically has the right to live in the apartment for the next month. In this type of tenant/landlord relationship, the contract may be terminated on thirty days' written notice. Given the proper thirty-day notice, the rent can be raised at any time, or the tenant can be asked to leave. There are advantages and disadvantages to this short-term contract. On the one hand, renters can move when they wish without giving a long advance notice. But, on the other hand, there is the uncertainty of possibly being asked to leave on short notice or of finding the rent raised sooner than had been anticipated.

LEASE
A contract by which one conveys real estate for a specified period of time and usually for a specified rent; and the act of such conveyance or the term for which it is made.

Alternatively, renters may obtain a **lease**. This is simply a long-term contract that binds both landlord and tenant to specified terms. The lease, which is usually for one year, generally requires two months' rent in advance and perhaps one month's rent as a cleaning, breakage, or security deposit.

As with any contract, you should be aware of all provisions of the lease. Most leases tend to protect landlords more than tenants. We discuss this important topic in Consumer Issue M on how to rent a place to live.

Until recently, it was common for renters to be looked down upon as people who were unable to manage their money correctly.

The Advantages of Buying Rather than Renting

Some of the advantages of renting instead of buying a place to live have been pointed out. Here are a few of the advantages of buying a housing unit.

1. You can remodel your home or make it into anything you want.
2. A home offers an investment option that historically has been a good hedge against inflation.
3. Home ownership causes you to save because part of your monthly payments creates equity interest in the housing unit.
4. Owning a home gives you the tax benefits of being able to deduct interest payments and property taxes from your income before paying taxes.
5. Home ownership allows you to save on taxes by "doing it yourself."

The best way to understand the last point is to consider a numerical example. Suppose that your house needs repainting. You get a number of bids for the labor, averaging $2,000. How much do you have to earn to get $2,000 *after taxes*? That, of course, depends on what your **marginal tax rate** is. If your marginal tax rate is 50 percent, then you would have to earn $4,000 in order to have $2,000 to pay someone to paint your house. If you decided to do it yourself, you would, in effect, be working for yourself but not declaring the income that you earned—that is, the $2,000 worth of services you performed rather than paying someone else. So, instead of spending your time working to earn $4,000, of which $2,000 goes to Uncle Sam and $2,000 to the house painter, you paint the house yourself and avoid any taxes at all because, as yet, the Internal Revenue Service does not require you to estimate the market value of do-it-yourself services performed around the house.

MARGINAL TAX RATE
The last tax bracket that a taxpayer finds himself or herself in after figuring out how much is owed to the government. In our progressive tax system, tax rates go up as income goes up but only on the last, or marginal, amount of income. Your marginal tax bracket could range anywhere from 0 to 50 percent.

Calculating Whether to Rent or Buy

The editors of *Changing Times* published some interesting data that should aid individuals who are faced with a decision of whether to buy or rent a place to live.[2] How much rent can you pay and still come out ahead of buying? That's a hard question to answer because monthly outlays for rent aren't directly comparable to those for homeownership. As a homeowner, you get tax breaks that vary with your income and a chance for profit when you sell. Thus, it's possible to lay out more each month than a renter does and still come out ahead in the long run. But remember, as an owner you'd have to pay for maintenance, property taxes, and other expenses that usually are included in rent.

Taking such variables into account is a complicated job that might well be assigned to a computer. And that is just what Professor Michael S. Johnson of Cornell University has done. What follows is an example of the kind of rent-or-buy analysis Johnson's computer programs can produce. The figures show break-even rents for an $80,000 home being considered for purchase by a

2. Adapted from *Changing Times,* November 1981, pp. 31–32.

married couple with three tax exemptions. In this instance, the couple would find their income on the left, then read across to the column headed by the number of years they would expect to live in the home. The figure there shows how much rent they can pay before they'd be better off buying.

Notice that the higher their income, the more advantageous it is for this couple to buy. That's because people in higher tax brackets benefit more from the deductions associated with ownership. Note also that the break-even figure declines the longer the couple owns the home. This is due to the additional time available for price appreciation and for amortizing the costs of buying and selling.

Because income and time of ownership are only two of several variables in the decision, Johnson had to make some assumptions about the rest. Among them are these: (1) Both rents and house prices rise by 8 percent a year; (2) the purchase is financed with a twenty-five year, fixed-rate mortgage at 15 percent; (3) homeownership costs include 1.5 percent of the home's market value for annual maintenance, 0.5 percent a year for insurance, $125 a month initially for utilities (increasing 10 percent per year), and 2 percent of initial market value annually for property taxes; (4) closing costs are assumed to be 4 percent of purchase price for buyers and 8 percent for sellers; (5) the money to be used for the down payment could earn 14 percent a year if invested elsewhere. Exhibit 15–1 illustrates Johnson's findings.

Johnson's program also enables you to derive break-even rents that show the maximum amounts you can spend on rent before it makes more sense to buy. Johnson has found that homeownership often proves advantageous for married people earning more than $30,000. Single people, with their higher tax rates, tend to benefit even more.

For seven dollars, Johnson will calculate rent-or-buy analyses for individual cases. You can supply your own assumptions or use standard averages employed by Johnson. For information and the forms needed to order an analysis, write to Housing Analysis, care of Professor Michael S. Johnson, Department of Consumer Economics and Housing, MVR Hall, Cornell University, Ithaca, New York 14853.

In the last decade, individuals who have purchased their own houses have made extremely high rates of return.

INVESTING IN A HOUSE

Since it is fairly certain that the population will continue to grow for some time, pressures on land prices also will continue to exist. Does this mean that you should invest in a house with land around it because you are certain that it will increase in value?

If you consider your housing purchase an investment, you are not *guaranteed* that you will make any more than if you had invested in something else. The reason is fairly simple. Because it's a fact that the value of land has risen over time as populations increased, many people take that into account when they try to purchase land or houses, and the price of land is consequently bid higher. If something is so obvious that you and I know about it, how can we expect to make a killing on it? If we think we can, we are fooling ourselves. Buying a house may or may not be a good investment, but do not expect to get rich simply because you bought a big house with plenty of land. The price you paid for that house probably reflected everybody else's anticipation of rising land values. In the last decade, however, individuals who have purchased their own houses have made extremely high rates of return, higher than they

EXHIBIT 15–1
When Does It Make Sense to Buy?

Initial monthly break-even rents for a couple with three tax exemptions contemplating buying an $80,000 home and owning it for the periods indicated.

INCOME	1 YEAR	2 YEARS	3 YEARS	4 YEARS	5 YEARS	10 YEARS
$20,000	$1,454	$1,066	$936	$870	$830	$748
30,000	1,382	997	869	805	767	694
40,000	1,279	897	772	712	676	615
50,000	1,210	830	707	647	614	559
60,000	1,189	809	686	627	593	539

could have made in virtually any other investment except precious metals, antiques, and diamonds. Although there is no guarantee that such high rates of return on housing will continue into the future, many people still want to buy instead of rent, and many of their compelling reasons have to do with special tax advantages.

THE TAX GAME

Did you know that if you buy a house and borrow the money to pay for it, all the interest payments that you pay to the bank or mortgage company can be deducted from your income before you pay taxes? This may not mean much to you if you're not in a very high tax bracket, but it will make a big difference when you get up into a higher one.

For example, suppose you bought a $100,000 house and were somehow able to borrow the entire $100,000. Let's say that the interest you paid every year on that $100,000 came to $12,000. You would be able to deduct that $12,000 from your income before you paid taxes on it. If you were in the 50 percent tax bracket, you would get a tax savings of $16,000; the interest on your loan would, in effect, be costing you only $6,000. Now you know why, as people get into higher income-tax brackets, it generally pays to buy a house instead of renting.

Unfortunately, the benefit from this implicit subsidy is directly proportional to your marginal tax bracket, which, of course, is directly proportional to how much you make. Since poor people are poor because they make little money, they are not in a high marginal tax bracket. Thus, even if a poor person deducts all the interest payments on his or her house, the implicit tax savings will be small, if there is one at all. This interest rate subsidy to homeowners has not been very helpful to lower-income people.

Taxes and housing are related in another way. If you buy or build a house for $40,000 and sell it ten years later for $80,000, you have made $40,000. You will be taxed on that sum, for it is a **capital gain**.[3] However, if you buy another house of equal or higher value within two years, you pay no capital gains taxes at all until much later. Additionally, you are allowed one exclusion from the payment of capital gains on the sale of your own residence after you reach the age of fifty-five. Currently, you can exclude up to $125,000 of capital gains (profits) on the sale of your personal residence once you reach that age.

CAPITAL GAIN
An increase in the value of something you own. Generally you experience a capital gain when you sell something you own, such as a house or a stock. You compute your capital gain by subtracting the price you paid for whatever you are selling from the price you receive when you sell it.

HOUSING AND EDUCATION

Most education from kindergarten through twelfth grade is provided by public school systems. Because these public school systems are at least in part financed by property taxes, it is not unusual to find superior school systems in areas where property values are high and where the total property taxes collected are usually large. Of course, there need not be this relationship between property tax revenues and quality of education, but it is sufficiently common to consider it when buying a house (or even when deciding where to rent). In other words, when you buy a house, you are also buying a complementary

3. Capital gains tax rates are generally lower than normal personal income tax rates.

good—education for any younger children you have. In areas that have better elementary (or "primary"), junior, and senior high schools, the housing prices may be correspondingly higher. Note that this is true so long as children are not bused out of their neighborhood to another part of town. Also note that if you have no school-age children, you are still required to pay property taxes.

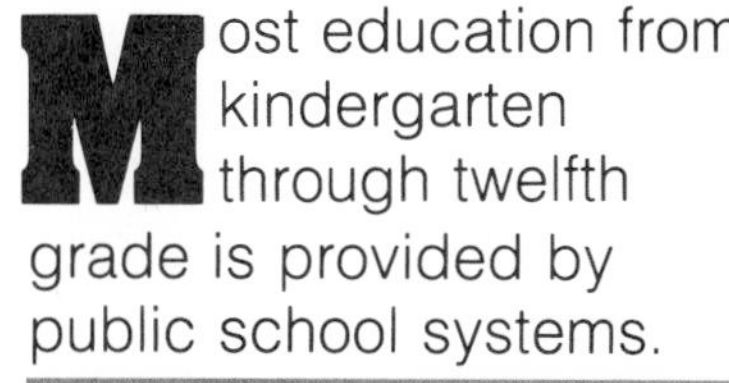
Most education from kindergarten through twelfth grade is provided by public school systems.

As parents, we have some choice in the quality of our children's schooling even without sending them to private schools, but only if we are willing to move to where we feel there are better schools. The quality of schools is obviously a strong selling point for some suburban areas. You need only drive around with a real-estate agent in Scarsdale, New York, or in Beverly Hills or Palo Alto, California, where the public schools are considered above average and where the real-estate agent will certainly let you know about them to know that good schools are a selling point.

HOUSES DO NOT LAST FOREVER

Remember, when you buy a house, you are not buying the house for itself but for the services that it yields, and the way to get a constant level of services from a given house is by maintaining it. Houses have a tendency to fall apart just like anything else you own, and repairing them can sometimes be expensive. It will be shown that the average increases in craftsmen's wages are among the highest in the nation. The same is true for the wages of persons who come to fix your sprinkler system, your clogged drain, your leaking roof, or your broken furnace. Because the maintenance expenses on a house can be extremely important, you should figure out how much it will cost to keep up. If you have a home with a large front or back lawn and much shrubbery, you know that you will have high maintenance expenses for the grounds. You or someone else in your family must do the work, or you must hire a gardener. In either case, you pay more for your housing services—but, of course, you get more in aesthetic pleasure. You have to plan to repaint most houses every few years. If your home has carpets, they have to be cleaned professionally every once in a while and eventually replaced.

All maintenance costs should be included in the costs per year of having any particular house. After all, you are buying a service flow for, say, a year at a time, and you should not ignore some of the very important costs of obtaining those services.

OBTAINING A MORTGAGE

MORTGAGE
A loan for a house, co-op, or condominium apartment.

Unless you are really cash rich, you will have to pay for a good part of your house by taking out a **mortgage,** which is a loan that a bank or trust company makes on a house. In some states, you hold the title to the house; in others, the mortgagee does. In nine states plus the District of Columbia, a special arrangement is made whereby the borrower (mortgagor) deeds the property to a trustee—a third party—on behalf of the lender (mortgagee). The trustee then deeds the property back to the borrower when the loan is repaid. If the payments are not made, the trustee can deed the property to the lender or dispose of it by auction, depending on the individual state's law. As the mortgagor, you

Conventional loans can be arranged on just about any terms satisfactory to both parties.

make payments on the mortgage until it is paid off. More than 90 percent of all people who buy homes do so with a mortgage loan.

Sources of Mortgages

There are basically four sources of mortgage money, the most important being savings and loan associations, which account for almost 50 percent of all home loans made. The second most important are mortgage companies, which account for somewhere around 20 percent. Commercial banks follow, and mutual savings banks make some mortgage loans, particularly in the East. There is a whole category we'll call "other," which includes pension funds, mortgage pools, insurance companies, mortgage investment trusts, and state and local credit agencies. Only under special circumstances can you get a mortgage loan from one of these institutions.

THE KINDS OF MORTGAGES

There are basically three kinds of mortgages. Although you may not be eligible for two of them, all three are available from the same sources: commercial banks, savings banks, mortgage banks, savings and loan associations, and insurance companies.

Conventional Mortgages

Most conventional mortgages run for twenty to thirty years. In recent years, however, savings and loan associations have been reluctant to write mortgages for thirty years; in fact, some of them are charging higher interest rates for mortgages that last so long. Naturally, the rate of interest charged is determined by conditions in the credit market. Interest rates in the past few years have been at record highs or close to them. This should not, however, be a surprise when you consider the high inflation rates of recent years. The mortgagee's interest rate has to take account of any expected loss in the purchasing power of the dollars that will be paid back to it in the future.

With a conventional mortgage loan, the money that the lender risks is secured only by the value of the mortgaged property and the financial integrity of the borrower. To protect the investment from the start, the conventional lender, such as a savings and loan association, ordinarily requires a down payment of anywhere from 5 to 25 percent of the value of the property, depending on market conditions. Some private insurers will protect lenders against loss on at least a certain portion of the loan. When such extra security is provided, the lender may go to a higher loan figure. The borrower, of course, pays the cost of the insurance.

If you make a very large down payment, thus lowering the risk of lending, the lender may be willing to grant you a slightly lower interest rate, perhaps a fraction of a percent below the prevailing local rate.

Conventional loans can be arranged on just about any terms satisfactory to both parties. Different lenders favor different arrangements, which means it will pay you to shop around. And because most borrowers pay off their mortgages well before maturity, it is wise to look around for liberal conditions on prepayment; you will not want to pay a penalty if you wish to prepay.

Veterans Administration Mortgages

These loans can be obtained only by qualified veterans or their widows. The interest rate charged is administered rather than determined strictly by the forces of supply and demand in the money market. The VA loan is guaranteed rather than insured. That is, the government simply promises that, on an approved loan, it will repay up to a certain amount or a certain percent, say, 60 percent. The borrower has no insurance premium to pay.

Loans with nothing down are possible under the VA program, often for amounts up to $100,000 and for up to thirty years. However, you cannot get a loan on a VA-financed house for more than the VA appraisal of its current market value; nor can you mortgage it for longer than the VA estimate of its remaining economic life. All VA loans can be prepaid without penalty. Recently, VA loans have become available for second mortgages and for mobile homes.

Although the Veterans Administration makes some mortgage loans directly to veterans—usually in rural areas where lenders are not making guaranteed loans—in all other circumstances, a would-be borrower should go to the usual sources of mortgage money, such as a savings and loan association, a mutual savings bank in states where they exist, commercial banks, and mortgage companies. It is particularly useful to check with the bank, savings and loan, or mutual savings bank where you happen to be a saver or depositor. If they have a history of your past records, they probably will be more accommodating to you.

FHA Mortgages

The Federal Housing Administration issues insurance covering the entire amount of an FHA loan. This added security enables qualified borrowers to obtain a much more generous loan in relation to the value of the property than they could obtain with an uninsured loan. Of course, to the borrower, a bigger loan means a smaller down payment.

Generally, it is possible to borrow 97 percent of the first $25,000 of the appraised value of an approved home that you intend to live in yourself, plus 95 percent on the balance over $25,000, up to a maximum loan of $67,500. The maximum interest rate that can be charged usually has been below market interest rates. But you also have to pay a ½ percent premium for the insurance, and a 1 percent origination fee (for the work of drawing up the papers) is also permitted. The loan can be for as long as thirty-five years, not to exceed three-fourths of what the FHA estimates is the remaining economic life of the dwelling. There are no penalties for prepayment.

You can apply for an FHA-insured mortgage loan just as you would apply for any other loan. The lender—be it a savings and loan association, mortgage company, or commercial bank—will supply you with the necessary forms and help you complete them. If willing to make the loan, the lender will notify the FHA of your loan application. The FHA, in turn, will assign an approved private

In the late 1970s, a number of more flexible payment arrangements were established for home buyers.

appraiser to whom the loan application is sent. When the appraisal has been completed, the application will be forwarded to the FHA for review, approval, and commitment.

Although the FHA has no arbitrary rules with respect to age or income, these factors are considered for their possible effect on your ability to repay the loan over the period of the mortgage.

The FHA also sponsors a subsidy program for low- and moderate-income families. In this program, down payments can be as low as several hundred dollars and interest as low as a couple of percentage points.

The big difference between FHA loans and so-called conventional loans is that the FHA interest is not determined strictly by market conditions but is set at an arbitrary rate by the Secretary of Housing and Urban Development. Usually, the secretary tries to fix a rate below the lowest prevailing market rate; this practice has been associated with a questionable "point" system.

WHAT ABOUT POINTS?

DISCOUNT POINTS
Additional charges added to a mortgage that effectively raise the rate of interest you pay.

Sometimes you may be asked to pay **discount points.** This is merely a device to raise the effective interest rate you pay on a mortgage. This often occurs whenever there are restrictions on the legal interest rate you can be charged for your mortgage loan. You may think this unfair, but if you are faced with the possibility of either paying the discount points or not getting the loan at all, you may decide to pay the implicitly higher interest rate. A point is a charge of 1 percent of the amount of a loan. Typically, two points are charged for each one-fourth of 1 percent difference between the rate available on conventional mortgages and the ceiling rate on FHA and VA mortgages. Points also are charged on conventional mortgages in several states, such as Florida and California. Basically, this amounts to prepaid interest. This charge may be assessed against the buyer, or the seller, or both. To see how a discount point system works, say you have to pay four discount points on a $25,000 loan; that means that you get a loan of $25,000 minus 4 percent of $25,000, or only $24,000. However, you pay interest on the full $25,000. Obviously, the interest rate you pay on $25,000 understates the actual interest you pay because you get only $24,000. Some states have laws against discount points, and FHA and VA have restrictions on buyers paying points (so they are charged to the seller but ultimately tend to be passed on to the borrower in the form of a higher price).

ALTERNATIVE MORTGAGE ARRANGEMENTS

In the late 1970s, a number of more flexible payment arrangements were established for home buyers. Exhibit 15–2 describes five different types of mortgages: graduated payment, variable rate, rollover, price-level adjusted, and reverse annuity. Exhibit 15–3 is an example of monthly payments for a standard mortgage, as well as payments under the provisions of a variable-interest-rate mortgage, a five-year rollover mortgage, and two types of graduated payment mortgages. An example of a price-level-adjusted mortgage, where the outstanding balance and monthly payments change according to fluctuations in the price level, can't be shown because we don't know what the price levels will be in the next few years.

Notice that the interest charges under a flexible plan are somewhat higher than under a conventional plan. That's because you don't begin to pay back the principal until six years after you take out the mortgage loan. Essentially, then, you have the loan for a longer period.

Limitations on Flexible-Payment Schedules

Flexible payments are limited to mortgages on single-family, owner-occupied homes. The down payment for any home subject to flexible payments may be as low as 5 percent of its price. Older people, perhaps those nearing retirement, also can take advantage of flexible mortgages given through savings and loan associations. A flexible mortgage here, however, would be the reverse of the preceding example—higher monthly payments during the first few years decreasing with time when the home buyer might be living on a fixed retirement

EXHIBIT 15–2
Five Kinds of Mortgages

TYPE OF MORTGAGE AND HOW IT WORKS	PROS AND CONS	WHO BENEFITS
Graduated-payment mortgage. Monthly payments are arranged to start out low but increase later, perhaps in a series of steps at specified intervals. The term of the loan and the interest rate remain unchanged.	The main object is to make buying easier in the beginning. Initial payments have to be balanced by larger payments later. One disadvantage: Possible "negative amortization" in the early years, which means that, for a time, your debt grows instead of diminishing.	Mainly first-time home buyers, who have had a hard time becoming homeowners but can reasonably look forward to higher earnings that will enable them to afford the bigger payments coming later.
Variable-rate mortgage. Instead of a fixed interest rate, this loan carries an interest rate that may change within limits—up or down—from time to time during the life of the loan, reflecting changes in market rates for money.	Because the size of the payments you'll have to make in the future is uncertain, this loan is a bit of a gamble. If money rates go down in the future, your payments will go down. But if rates go up, so will your payments.	Helps lenders keep their flow of funds in step with changing conditions, and this, in turn, could make home loans easier to come by when money is tight. You may get fractionally lower interest at first or other inducements to make future uncertainties more palatable.
Rollover mortgage. The rate of interest and the size of the monthly payment are fixed, but the whole loan—including principal, rate of interest, and term—is renegotiated, or rolled over, at stated intervals, usually every three to five years.	If interest rates go up, you can expect to be charged more when you renegotiate. But you'll also have the opportunity to adjust other aspects of the loan, such as term and principal. Or you can pay off the outstanding balance without penalty. Renegotiation is guaranteed.	Lenders, for the same reason variable-rate loans are good for them. Benefits to borrowers are as shown for variable-rate loans, with this plus: Periodic renegotiation gives you a chance to rearrange the loan to suit your changing needs without all the expense of refinancing.
Price-level-adjusted mortgage. The interest rate remains fixed, but the outstanding balance and monthly payments change according to fluctuations in a specified price index.	If interest cost is your big worry, this plan at least ties down the percentage rate. All else remains uncertain, including how much you'll have to pay in total and each month.	If this plan gets you a loan when you can get one no other way, then it helps you. Otherwise it mainly helps lenders. Not likely to become popular with borrowers.
Reverse-annuity mortgage. You take out a loan secured by the accumulated equity in your house. The money is used to purchase an annuity that provides monthly income to you. You continue to live in the house. Its sale pays off the loan.	This is not a plan for putting money *into* a house. It's a plan for taking money *out*. It converts an existing frozen asset into current income that you can use without giving up your house.	Homeowners, principally older and retired people who have paid for or substantially paid for their homes but need additional current income to live on.

EXHIBIT 15–3
A Standard Mortgage with Four Alternatives

Here are figures for a 30-year, 9% loan for $30,000.

				GRADUATED PAYMENTS	
MONTHLY PAYMENTS	Standard Mortgage	Variable Interest	Five-Year Rollover	Five-Year, 7½% Increase	3% Increase
Year 1	$ 241	$ 241	$ 241	$ 182	$ 200
2	241	252	241	196	206
3	241	263	241	211	212
4	241	273	241	226	219
5	241	284	241	244	226
6	241	294	292	262	233
11	241	294	292	262	270
OUTSTANDING BALANCE					
Year 1	$29,795	$ 29,795	$ 29,795	$30,533	$30,304
2	29,570	29,592	29,570	30,945	30,562
3	29,326	29,389	29,326	31,212	30,765
4	29,057	29,184	29,057	31,306	30,908
5	28,764	28,976	28,764	31,197	30,983
10	26,828	27,618	27,416	29,098	29,975
TOTAL PAID					
Year 1	$ 2,896	$ 2,896	$ 2,896	$ 2,188	$ 2,408
2	5,793	5,922	5,793	4,540	4,888
3	8,690	9,075	8,690	7,070	7,443
4	11,586	12,356	11,586	9,788	10,075
5	14,483	15,764	14,483	12,710	12,785
10	28,969	33,435	32,026	28,419	27,607
30	86,900	104,122	102,197	91,254	92,335

Adapted from *Changing Times*, May 1978, pp. 21–22.

income that is lower than his or her actual income when the mortgage was taken out.

The Increase in Rollover Home Loans

In 1980, the Federal Home Loan Bank Board—the regulatory agency for chartered savings and loan associations—approved rollover mortgages for these financial institutions. Since then there has been an overwhelming increase in renegotiable home loans. Such mortgages already predominated in Canada by 1980, and it was only a matter of time before they gained popularity in the United States. Mortgage interest rates jumped by as much as 7 percentage points in a two-year period, greatly benefiting lucky holders of fixed-payment mortgages but badly cutting into the profitability of savings and loan associations in particular. Lenders simply said they couldn't continue to offer the standard mortgage of yesteryear. To be sure, the upsurge in rollover mortgages has brought serious opposition from consumer groups that argue that home loans with interest rates that can be increased hurt the elderly and others on fixed incomes.

Shared-Appreciation Mortgages

Perhaps the most radical idea in house-purchase financing in the 1980s has been the shared-appreciation mortgage. The lender, such as a savings and loan association, agrees to make a mortgage loan at a lower-than-market rate of interest. In exchange for the lower rate, the lender receives a share of the appreciated value of the house when it is sold.

Consider an example. A house buyer wishes to obtain a $75,000 mortgage on a $100,000 house. A savings and loan association may agree to lend the $75,000 at five percentage points lower than the going mortgage rate of interest. In exchange, the lender has a claim on a one-third share of the appreciated value of the house. If the house is sold ten years later for $200,000, the increased value is $100,000. The lender would receive one-third of that, or $33,333.33.

Shared-appreciation mortgages were sold on a large scale starting in 1980 by Coast Federal Savings and Loan Association in Sarasota, Florida, and Advance Mortgage Corporation, a mortgage banking firm based in Detroit. The attraction of a low rate of interest on the mortgage is obvious, but there are drawbacks. Subject to Internal Revenue Service rulings, the overall tax savings for the borrower may be less than if he or she had chosen a conventional mortgage with a higher rate of interest. There is also a problem with valuation of home improvements; if, indeed, the lender has a claim on one-third of the increased value even if some of that appreciation is due to the homeowner's own improvements, there is less incentive to make those improvements.

Perhaps the most radical idea in house-purchase financing in the 1980s has been the shared-appreciation mortgage.

CREATIVE FINANCING. The term *creative financing* is currently used to describe loans provided by a source other than the traditional lenders or those with contract features that make them more attractive to the mortgagees. Exhibit 15–4 is an example of some of these innovative methods of financing a home.

Because interest rates on existing mortgages are usually lower than current interest rates, *mortgage assumptions* are attractive to potential buyers. However, there are usually two problems associated with assuming an existing mortgage.

1. FHA and VA loans can be assumed at the same rate by a new borrower, but conventional loans might contain a *due-on-sale clause,* which states that the balance of the loan must be paid when the home is sold. Since the enforceability of the due-on-sale clause has been upheld by a 1982 Supreme Court ruling, assumption of conventional mortgages containing the clause will be difficult.
2. Even if the existing loan can be assumed, it might be for such a small amount that the borrower will have to arrange a second mortgage or come up with a larger down payment.

Perhaps the easiest and least expensive way to finance the purchase of an existing home is by the use of a mortgage assumption with the seller holding a *second mortgage* (called a *purchase money mortgage*) for the balance of the purchase price. The terms and conditions of the arrangement can be tailored to fit the financial requirements of both the buyer and the seller. The main obstacle to this type of arrangement is finding a seller who doesn't immediately need to take his or her *equity* in cash from the sale of the residence. Your real-estate agent should be able to help you in your search for this type of financing.

MAKING THE MOVE

Ours is a mobile society. One in five U.S. families moves once every year; among people twenty-five to thirty-four years old who have gone to college, almost 38 percent move every year. The average American moves twelve times in his or her lifetime. The decision to move often comes from a desire to change location, to go to a place with a better school system, or to be in a different climate. Sometimes a move is forced on a family by a job commitment. Whatever the reason, you may find when you have to move that you have too many personal possessions to be moved in your Chevy or Volkswagen. Either you

EXHIBIT 15–4
Creative Financing Has Its Pitfalls

Land contract. The buyer doesn't get title to the property until the loan is paid off. A land contract is sometimes thought of as a way to get around a due-on-sale clause in a mortgage. However, the standard due-on-sale clause used by most home mortgage lenders covers land contracts as well as sales.

Lease-purchase option. The buyer rents the property until he either moves out or exercises his option to buy it. This can be a profitable arrangement if the option price turns out to be less than the market value of the house when the option is exercised. A disadvantage is that lease payments are not tax-deductible. And a lease option is not a way to circumvent a due-on-sale clause because most such clauses say the loan must be paid off if the owner gives anyone a lease that contains an option to purchase the property.

Ground lease. The buyer buys the house but leases the ground under it. This arrangement requires a lower down payment for a mortgage because the value of the land is not financed. Usually the lease contains an option to buy within a few years. A ground lease can help make a mortgage affordable, but lease payments aren't deductible, and not owning the land may make the house harder to sell.

Wraparound mortgage. Suppose the seller has an assumable mortgage with a below-market interest rate: a five-year-old $33,000, 9 percent loan now paid down to $31,631 with twenty-five years left to go. He sells you the house for $70,000, and you make 20 percent down payment of $14,000. A lender (who could be the seller) gives you a wraparound mortgage in the amount of $56,000 at 11 percent for twenty-five years.

You make a monthly payment of $548.86 on the $56,000 loan. The lender in turn makes the $265.53 payment for you on the original loan, which you have assumed. The lender pockets the $283.53 difference. Because, in effect, he lent you only $24,369 ($56,000 minus $31,631), his return is about 14 percent ($283.33 × 12 ÷ $24,369), not the 11 percent for the wraparound.

In many cases, real-estate agents have suggested that home sellers offer to be the wraparound lenders for potential buyers. However, the purported advantages of such an arrangement could be an illusion. The seller could get exactly the same return by letting the buyer assume or buy the property subject to the first mortgage and by taking back a second mortgage with an interest rate equal to the return he'd get using a wraparound. The seller's return and the buyer's total payments would be exactly the same either way.

Balloon payment. In a balloon-payment loan contract, a borrower agrees to make a lump-sum payment of the loan balance at the end of a certain period, typically two to ten years. In the meantime, periodic payments are set up as if the loan were going to run for much longer. This arrangement keeps current payments down and gives the borrower an opportunity to sell the property or refinance the loan before the balloon comes due.

rent a truck or you call in a professional mover. Even in the best of circumstances and with the best movers to help you, you are not in for a picnic. Moving at its worst can be a total disaster, causing an incredible amount of stress. The next Consumer Issue gives some pointers on how to choose a moving company, what to prepare for, and how to make things easier for yourself. Do not expect too much, however. Moving is never easy.

You also must include in the cost of a move the time and energy that you'll expend. All costs taken together must be considered before a final decision concerning relocation is made. Professional moves are expensive, but the do-it-yourself price isn't exactly peanuts, especially if you have rented a truck that gets only five to eight miles per gallon of gasoline. If the move is a long one and if another vehicle also must be driven, the expenses mount quickly.

There are many problems in the moving industry, some of which can never be solved. Many of them, however, are the result of government-business relationships that do not seem to benefit the consumer at all. Moving is an industry regulated by the Interstate Commerce Commission, an agency set up in 1887 to regulate some of the abusive practices of railroads. Since then, the ICC has increasingly taken over regulation of all forms of transportation, including moving. As a result, at one and the same time you have a friend and a foe. You have a friend because many ICC regulations are designed to benefit you; in addition, if something goes wrong and you think you have been cheated, you can complain to the ICC, and you often will get a redress of your grievances. On the other hand, you have a very definite foe, because the ICC frequently does things at the behest of the industry to help the industry and not the consumer.

The stifling of competition, with the help of the regulatory agencies involved, is not unknown in this industry. For example, if a large moving company wants to do business in a state where it does not yet have a license, hearings are held to find out whether the company should be allowed to service that state. Generally, there are no reasons to prevent such competition because we, the consumers, will benefit from it ultimately through better service and/or lower prices. However, because the movers already servicing that state will lose some of their business to new competition, they fight to prevent the competition.

How they do it is interesting. A hearing is held in which the competitors find people who have been moved by the company wishing to gain entrance into the state. The people selected are those who had problems in their moves. The competitors pay the travel expenses for them to come to the hearings to complain. But the company that wants to move into the new state fights back. It pays the travel expenses for satisfied individuals it has moved to testify in its favor. This battle of sob stories versus glowing reports seems little better than a hearing at which gasoline is poured over a plastic pipe and set on fire to demonstrate the danger of the pipe. But consumers should expect such behavior, because special-interest producer groups always look out for their own, and not for general, interests.

No matter what kind of housing services you intend to purchase, you should have some idea of the best way to buy and sell a house, how to evaluate a rental, what to do when you make the move, and how to insure it all. These topics will be discussed in the following Consumer Issues.

The average American moves twelve times in his or her lifetime.

SUMMARY

1. Americans purchase many different types of housing services, including single-family houses, apartments, condominiums or cooperatives, mobile homes and townhouses.

2. Individuals purchase or rent a house or apartment in order to obtain the flow of services from that particular asset.

3. Cooperatives and condominiums are becoming increasingly popular types of ownership arrangements. The co-op is a nonprofit corporation that is owned and operated solely for the benefit of its members (the individuals who own residences in the building). A co-op owner can sell his or her unit, but the other members of the co-op must approve the sale.

4. The owner of a condominium has title to the unit he or she occupies and has fewer restrictions than the co-op owner. For example, the condominium owner can rent or lease the unit to anyone.

5. Renting is an attractive alternative to buying because there is greater freedom of mobility, no down payment, and no maintenance tasks, and the exact cost can be figured out easily.

6. An investment in a house does not guarantee a higher-than-normal rate of return on your investment.

7. If at all possible, you may wish to obtain a Veterans Administration mortgage or a Federal Housing Administration insured mortgage. Ask your real-estate agent or the banks you have contacted about these possibilities.

8. You also may wish to take part in a flexible-mortgage-payment plan whereby you pay a lower amount during the first five years and a higher amount from then on. You may have to pay a higher interest rate on a flexible-payment schedule, however.

9. All real-estate taxes and interest payments on mortgages for houses are deductible from your federal income taxes.

10. Your choice of housing may determine your children's education because public school systems are financed in part by property taxes that depend on the value of the property in the area around the school.

11. The moving industry is regulated by the Interstate Commerce Commission, which has set regulations that benefit you when you make a move, but it has also allowed for the elimination of much competition in the moving industry.

QUESTIONS FOR THOUGHT AND DISCUSSION

1. Why do you think housing is such a special commodity?

2. When somebody tells you he's going to buy a $70,000 house, does that sound like a lot of money? (What is the average price of a new house today?)

3. Is it better to buy or rent a house?

4. If you had to live in either a co-op or a condominium, which would you choose? Why?

5. Do the tax advantages of owning a home benefit everyone equally? (Hint: What about our progressive tax system?)

6. Why has there been a change in the attitude toward renting versus home owning?

7. If you buy a house for $50,000 in 1978 and sell it for $75,000 in 1985, are you better off? (Be careful: What about inflation?)

8. Which is the best kind of mortgage: conventional, VA, or FHA?

9. Do discount points seem unfair?

10. If you are certain that a cleaning deposit for a rented apartment or a house

actually will end up being a cleaning fee, has your effective rent been raised or lowered?

THINGS TO DO

1. If you are living in a house or you know someone who is, try to determine the exact cost per month of living in it. Make sure you include the maintenance costs, the opportunity cost of the difference between the value of the house and the mortgage (sometimes called the equity in the house), the interest on the mortgage, and so on. When you have calculated a monthly figure, search around your neighborhood to find out what sort of apartment or house you could rent for that amount. Is buying obviously a better deal than renting?
2. Send away for literature on the numerous condominiums that are advertised in travel and housing sections of Sunday newspapers. See what advantages there are to buying a condominium rather than a co-op or other dwelling unit. Do you find advantages that were not listed in the text? What are they?
3. Call a real-estate agent and ask where the best housing investments should be. If the agent tells you that land on the water or land with a view is always a good investment, ask why.
4. Can you see how decisions about what kind of car to buy resemble decisions about what kind of house to buy when you consider maintenance problems?
5. Find out how property taxes are figured in your area and how the money is spent.
6. Call up the local office of HUD or FHA. Ask what special government help can be provided if you decide to buy a house. Find out what the income limitations are. In other words, does the special help apply only to poor people, or does it also benefit middle-income people?

SELECTED READINGS

Aaron, Henry J. *Shelter and Subsidies: Who Benefits from Federal Housing Policies?* Washington, D.C.: The Brookings Institution, 1972.

Edwards, Carolyn S. "Alternative Mortgage Instruments." *Family Economics Review,* No. 4, 1982, pp. 1–18.

Federal Trade Commission. *The Mortgage Money Guide: Creative Financing for Home Buyers.* Federal Trade Commission, Sixth and Pennsylvania Ave., N.W., Washington, D.C. 20580 (free).

Fredlind, Daniel R. *Residential Mobility and Home Purchases.* Lexington, Mass.: Lexington Books, 1974.

"Housing Yourself in the Eighties: Can You Afford a Mortgage?" *Consumer Reports,* July 1981, pp. 400–405.

"Housing Yourself in the Eighties: How Can Sellers Help?" *Consumer Reports* July 1981, pp. 405–406.

Mader, Chris. *The Dow Jones-Irwin Guide to Real Estate Investing,* rev. ed. New York: Dow Jones-Irwin, 1982.

McLean, Andrew James. *Real Estate: The Ultimate Handbook.* New York: Contemporary Books, 1981.

Perl, Lila. *The House You Want.* New York: David McKay Co., 1965.

Rothenberg, Henry. *What You Should Know about Condominiums.* Radnor, Penn.: Chilton Book Co., 1974.

Seiders, David F. "Changing Patterns of Housing Finance." *Federal Reserve Bulletin,* Vol. 67, No. 6, 1981, pp. 461–74.

Consumer ISSUE L

BUYING, SELLING, AND INSURING A PLACE TO LIVE

GLOSSARY

BASIC FORM POLICY—Homeowner insurance policy that covers eleven risks.

BROAD FORM POLICY—Homeowner policy that covers eighteen risks.

COMPREHENSIVE FORM POLICY—Homeowner policy that covers all risks except usually flood, war, and nuclear attack.

EARNEST MONEY—Sometimes called a deposit on a contract or an offer to purchase a house. It is the amount of money you put up to show that you are serious about the offer your are making to buy a house. Generally you sign an earnest agreement or a contract that specifies the purchase price you are willing to pay for the house in question. If the owner selling the house signs, then generally you are committed to purchase the house; if you back down, you can lose the entire earnest money, or deposit.

REAL PROPERTY—Property in physical structures and in land.

TITLE—The physical representation of your legal ownership to a house. The title is sometimes called the deed.

TITLE INSURANCE—Insurance that you pay for when you buy a house so you can be assured that the title or legal ownership to the house is free and clear. If, for example, you purchase a house and pay for title insurance and six months later the builder who put in a new bathroom sues you because the former owners did not pay for the work, the title insurance company may be forced to come up with the money.

The American dream seems to be that each of us will own his or her own home. Let us assume that you share that dream. When you decide to buy a house, you should figure out how much you can safely spend.

HOW MUCH CAN YOU AFFORD?

It is very easy to get carried away with buying housing services. A nice house is something that makes you and your family feel good and probably proud. But a nice house may also mean many unanticipated financial headaches. To make a sound decision, you first should calculate the level of your *dependable* monthly income. In other words, if you happen to be making lots of extra money this year, to count that as a permanent situation may get you into trouble. Be conservative.

Next, you must figure out your monthly housing expenses. This includes your payments on a mortgage, insurance premiums, taxes, costs of maintenance repairs, heating, air conditioning, electricity, telephone, water, sewage and so on. Your mortgage payments may be higher than you think. Exhibit L–1 can be used to estimate monthly payments on different sized mortgages. Remember that this is just the amount you would have to pay on the loan. In addition, you would be paying insurance and taxes. Exhibit L–2 presents a chart you can use to calculate the monthly costs of owning your home.

Remember, you can rarely finance 100 percent of the cost of the house. You may have to pay up to one-fifth or more of the purchase price as a down payment. In addition, there are closing costs. Exhibit L–3 gives rules for estimating how much housing you can afford. It tells you, for example, that the purchase price divided by your annual income should come to 2.5 or less. Another helpful

MORTGAGE LOAN (FOR 30 YEARS)	MONTHLY PAYMENT OF PRINCIPAL AND INTEREST AT: 8%	10%	12%	14%	16%	18%
$ 30,000	$220.13	$263.28	$ 308.59	$ 355.47	$ 403.43	$ 452.13
40,000	293.51	351.03	411.45	473.95	537.91	602.84
50,000	366.89	438.79	514.31	592.44	672.38	753.55
60,000	440.26	526.55	617.17	710.93	806.86	904.26
70,000	513.64	614.31	720.03	829.42	941.33	1,054.96
80,000	587.02	702.06	822.90	947.90	1,075.81	1,205.67
90,000	660.39	789.82	925.76	1,066.39	1,210.29	1,356.38
100,000	733.77	877.58	1,028.62	1,184.88	1,344.76	1,507.09

EXHIBIT L–1
Monthly Mortgage Costs

rule of thumb is that you should not spend more than one-third of your take-home pay for housing payments. These are only rough rules, but they do serve as a guide. If you were to buy a $75,000 house on a yearly income of $12,000 you'd be asking for trouble. After housing expenses, food, and transportation, you would have no money left over for desired recreation, medical bills, clothing, or saving.

New versus Used

As with the purchase of almost any goods that last a long time, you can choose between an older house and a new house. The new ones are advertised in the home section of your weekly newspaper. In some years, as many as 2 million new housing units are built in the United States. On the other hand, an older or secondhand house might make as much sense or more for you than a new one. Of course, you must be more careful about future maintenance problems with an older home, but using an inspection service ahead of time can help you anticipate such problems. Many older houses have the advantage of being on landscaped property. Often they provide more space for the same money than a new house does.

WHEN TO USE A REAL-ESTATE AGENT

You can start a housing search by first looking in the classified section of a newspaper. This will require much time, telephoning, and traveling to see houses that might interest you. If you are casually looking for a house, this may be the best way to do it. Generally you will save a real-estate agent's commission if the people advertising are selling the house themselves. However, the majority of ads are placed by real-estate companies, so you end up paying the brokerage fee even if you find the house through the newspaper. If you decide to use an agent, first call several of them, tell them what you want, and have them show you a few houses. You will find out very soon how serious each broker is about servicing you. You will also find out whether he or she understands your tastes and preferences and can, therefore, effectively help you search for a house. If you know individuals in the area who have used agents, find out which ones have given satisfactory service. It will be helpful if you have a good idea of what your housing needs are and what you specifically do and do not want.

What Does an Agent Do?

Essentially, agents provide buyers and sellers of houses with information. Information, remember, is a costly resource. This is particularly true with such a nonstandard product as a house. Every house is different from every other, and it is difficult to get buyers and sellers together for such nonstandard products. Generally, for standard products, or even for nonstandard products that do not cost very much, there are no agents. But in the housing market, the reverse is true. A house is the largest purchase any family will make, and it involves something that is, so far, completely nonstandardized. The agent, then, saves you information costs by engaging in the search procedure for you and for the seller. He or she becomes a specialist in matching up the wants of buyers with the products offered by sellers.

Questions to Ask Any Agent Who Is Going to Sell Your House

1. What specific services will the agent provide for the fee paid?
2. Will the real-estate agency give you an estimate of the market value of your house?

3. Does the agency advise you on how to improve your property to make it more salable?
4. Will your house be listed in a multiple-listing-service directory, and, if so, will the agency cooperate with other brokers?
5. Will the agency advertise and hold an open house for other agents?
6. Will the real-estate agency help you in the price negotiations and the paper work required to close any deal?

How Much Will You Pay?

For selling a house, most agents charge a fixed fee that is paid, at least nominally, by the seller. But do not be fooled about how fixed this fee is. In times of bad housing markets, you can bargain with an agent over a house you think you want to buy. You can stipulate, for example, that you will buy the house if a refrigerator, a stove, or some such thing is supplied. Or, in a good market, the seller can do the same thing; the seller will agree to pay the fixed commission but over a seven-year period. Essentially, this means that the commission will be worthless to the agent and cost the seller of the house less. Such arrangements are against the rules of brokerage societies, but that shouldn't worry you. The very fact that agents have fixed commissions is against present antitrust laws. If real-estate agents can break the Sherman Antitrust Act, then, in your own best interests, you can try to persuade them to break their own rules governing fixed commission rates.

Using Alternative Agents

An alternative or cut-rate agent (broker) often will charge a flat fee rather than a commission of 6 or 7 percent. Some

HOUSING EXPENSES PER MONTH	CURRENT	FUTURE
Mortgage payments	________	________
Property taxes	________	________
Insurance	________	________
Heating oil	________	________
Gas, electricity, water, telephone, sewage	________	________
Yard care, trash pickup, etc.	________	________
Savings fund for repairs, remodeling, and maintenance	________	________
Other	________	________
Total	________	________

EXHIBIT L–2
Checklist for Figuring Total Housing Expenses

fees are as low as $300 to $350. The cut-rate broker usually will advise the seller about advertising and will line up prospective buyers. Unlike a regular agent, however, the alternative broker does not normally show the house to the prospective buyers. That is the job of the seller. In many areas, cut-rate brokers offer exactly the same services as regular agents, but, instead of charging 6 or 7 percent, they charge only 1 to 5 percent, sometimes depending on how long it takes to sell the house.

Two examples of alternative brokers are Alanta-based Home Sellers Center, Inc., with almost 100 flat-fee franchises on the eastern seaboard, and For Sale by Owners, Inc., a company based in Tucson, Arizona, with 80 franchises.

HOW TO BARGAIN

Most Americans are unaccustomed to bargaining because goods and services are sold at set prices. But buying a house is a different situation. The asking price generally is not the final sale price. If you are unaccustomed to bargaining for a house or you feel uncomfortable doing it, you can let a real-estate agent do it for you.

You might get a general idea of how much profit the seller is trying to make by finding out what was paid for the house before. You can look at the deed to the house which is a public document, at the office of the county clerk or county registrar of deeds. You can find out what the house costs by looking at the federal tax stamps affixed to the deed when the ownership was transferred. For example, if the stamps cost $1.10 for every $1,000 and a deed has $33 worth of stamps, the owner paid $30,000. (Don't forget the impact of inflation on the pricing during the years since the person purchased the house.)

Many times, sellers do not expect to get the prices they are asking on their houses. They set a price that they think may be, say, 5 or 10 percent more than the price they will finally receive. It is up to you to find out how far they will go in discounting that list price. You can start out by asking the real-estate agent whether he or she thinks the price is "firm." Because the broker's commission is a percentage of the sale price, the higher the price, the more the agent benefits but not if it means waiting months or years for a sale. The broker's desire to get that commission as soon as possible is an incentive to arrange a mutually agreeable price so that a deal will be made. Note, though, that it is probably best to assume that the broker works for the seller and represents the seller's interests rather than the buyer's. You may want to bargain, for example, on a $75,000 list price, for, say, $69,000 plus the refrigerator, freezer, washer, and dryer that are already in the house. This sort of bargaining happens all the time. You should not accept the list price just because you think you want the house. Although that price may be the lowest you can get it for, it may not be. You know only if you bargain; and if you are unwilling to do it yourself, ask the agent to do it. The agent may ultimately decide to take a lower (implicit) commission rate in order to seal the deal. The first stage of sealing the deal is signing a written earnest or binder agreement.[4] But before this is done, certain basic, common-sense precautions must be taken.

BEFORE YOU SIGN ANYTHING

Before you sign anything, make sure you are getting a house that is structurally sound. Pay an expert to go over everything in the house that could cause problems—wiring, frame, plumbing, sewage, and so on. Often, you can get this done for $25 or $50, but for more expensive houses you will have to pay $100 to $200. It is money well invested unless you are an expert at figuring out what can go wrong with the house just by looking at it. Look at the listings under "building inspection service" or "home inspection service" in your telephone directory Yellow Pages. Again, these companies are selling the same thing that a broker is selling—information. Such information can save you hundreds, if not thousands, of dollars in repairs you would later discover had to be made. Often, if structural faults in a house can be shown by a building

4. The earnest or binder agreement may also be called a sales or purchase contract.

Most savings and loan association officers will use the rules stated here to determine how much housing you can afford. Rule 1 states that the purchase price of the house should not exceed 2½ times your yearly after-tax income. Rule 2 states that your monthly mortgage payment should be no more than ⅓ of your total monthly income. Rule 3 indicates that most savings and loan associations will not loan you more than 95 percent of the purchase price of your house; generally, the maximum is closer to 80 percent (in some cases, even as low as 65 percent).

Rule 1. $\frac{\text{Price}}{\text{Income}} \leq 2.5$

Rule 2. $\frac{\text{Mortgage payment}}{\text{Monthly income}} < 33\frac{1}{3}\%$

Rule 3. $\frac{\text{Loan amount}}{\text{Value}} < 95\%$ (usually around 80%)

SOURCE: The United States Saving and Loan League.

EXHIBIT L–3
A Guide To How Much Housing You Can Afford

inspector, you can have the seller of the house agree to pay for the repairs even after you take over the house itself. Or this can be a point in bargaining: The price that you agreed on can be reduced by the amount of the repair costs.

WHAT HAPPENS WHEN YOU DECIDE TO BUY?

Generally, when you have decided to buy a house, you make an offer and put it in writing. You also must put up **earnest money** or deposit binder money. The earnest agreement or binder states in some detail your exact offering price for the house and lists any other things that normally are not included with a house but are to be included in this deal, such as a washer or dryer. Within a specified time period, the seller of the house either accepts or rejects the earnest agreement or binder. If the seller accepts and you try to back down, the earnest money you put up, which may be several thousand dollars, is legally no longer yours. But sometimes you can get it back even when you decide against the house after signing the agreement. In any earnest agreement, it is often wise to add an escape clause if you are unsure about getting financing. Put in a statement such as, "This earnest agreement is contingent upon the buyer's obtaining financing from a bank for [X thousand] dollars." Remember, the earnest agreement (called an "offer" in California) is *your* proposal. Put in what *you* want. Let the seller change it; then you review it.

If the earnest or binder agreement has been accepted, then a contract of sale is drawn up. This is sometimes called the sales contract, conditional sales contract, or a purchase contract. Usually the signing of a contract of sale is accompanied by a deposit, which may be 10 percent of the purchase price paid to the seller. Often the buyer merely adds to the existing earnest money to bring it up to the desired amount.

The deposit may be put into an escrow account or a trusteed savings account that earns interest from the time it is paid to the seller to the time the buyer takes possession of the house. When any substantial sum is involved, it is, of course, advantageous to the buyer to have the deposit put into a trusteed savings account with the interest accruing to the buyer rather than the seller. This is particularly advantageous if there is a large time difference between the signing of the conditional sales contract and the actual date of possession of the house.

CLOSING COSTS

Exhibit L–5 indicates the typical closing costs on a $70,000 house. Quite a bit of money, isn't it? Closing costs can end up being 3 to 4 percent of the total purchase price, and that is money that you have to produce "up front," in addition to your down payment. That means you have to have cash for closing costs. Exhibit L–6 shows a form you can use to figure costs when you plan to buy a house.

TITLE SEARCH AND INSURANCE

Often when you purchase something as large as a house, you must be sure that you really own it, that no one with a prior claim can dispute your **title** to the land and structure. Any one of the following four methods of search can inform you if you do in fact have title, free and clear, to the property.

1. An abstract. Usually a lawyer or title guarantee company will trace the history of the ownership of the property. The resulting document is called an abstract, and it will indicate whether any claims are still outstanding. Note, however, that the abstract, no matter how lengthy it might be, does not guarantee that you have the title. Nonetheless, if the search has been careful, it provides reassurance.

2. Certificate of title. In some areas of the country, this is used in place of an abstract. An attorney merely certifies that all the records affecting the property have been looked at, and, in the opinion of the attorney, there are no claims on it. Note, however, that the attorney is not guaranteeing his or her opinion and cannot be liable if some obscure claim does arise in the future.

3. Torrens certificate. This is a certificate issued by a governmental unit giving evidence of title to **real property.** It is used mainly in large cities. You can get it faster, and it usually is safer than an abstract or certificate of title. An official recorder or registrar issues a certificate stating ownership and allowing anyone who has prior claim on the real property to sue. If no suit develops, then a court will order the registrar to record the title in your name; a certificate to this effect will be issued.

4. Title insurance. A title-guarantee company will search extensively through the records pertaining to the property you wish to buy. When it is satisfied that there are no prior claims to that property, it will write an insurance policy for you, the new owner. The insurance policy guarantees that if any defects arise in the title, the title company itself will defend for the owner and pay all legal expenses involved. Note that this may sound better than it actually is. Title insurance generally does not cover governmental actions that could restrict use or ownership of the property you just bought. Often title insurance excludes mechanics' liens not recorded with the proper official agency when the policy was issued. In other words, if work was done on the house and not paid for by the former owner, it is possible, even with title insurance, that you could end up paying for that work. You should always ask the seller for a copy of paid bills for any obviously recent repairs or additions to the home.

EXHIBIT L–4
Home Buyer's (Or Renter's) Guide,
Or How to Decipher What the Ads Say

Convenient to shopping:	bathroom window overlooks the local A&P parking lot
Family room:	unfinished basement with 1 60-watt bulb
$200 to heat:	$640 to heat
Desirable corner:	corner
Entrance foyer:	door
Only 10 minutes from . . .	only 45 minutes from . . .
Many extras . . .	recent owners have left behind half-used bar of soap, numerous rags and coat hangers, and three switches connected to nothing
Immaculate:	the walls in the kitchen are not quite as filthy as the grease rack at Sam's Standard Station
Piazza:	porch
Gleaming bathroom:	bathroom
Comfortable:	very small
Cozy:	even smaller
Cute:	itsy bitsy
Victorian:	many drafts
Colonial:	built prior to the first Eisenhower administration
Gracious colonial:	forget it—too expensive
Leisure home:	enter only during July and August
Make an offer:	say something funny

Service charge:	on 75% or 80% loan = 1½% on 90% or 95% loan = 2% to 2½%
Title insurance:	on 75% or 80% = $25,000 on 90% or 95% = $100 to $200
Recording fee:	about $15
Insurance on home in case of fire:	about ¼% of sale price
The bank also collects the taxes on the house.	
Credit report:	$50
Appraisal:	$75 to $100 (on VA and FHA $50)
TOTAL CLOSING COSTS:	3% to 4% of house value

EXHIBIT L–5
Typical Closing Costs on a $70,000 Home

The service or setup charge on a mortgage usually varies from 1½ to 2½ percent, the lower figure being applied to a loan that is 75 to 80 percent of the purchase price of a house. If, for example, you put a down payment of 20 percent ($14,000) on a $70,000 house, you would have to pay a setup or service charge of 1½ percent of $56,000, or $840. Title insurance would range from $100 to $200. A recording fee would be another $15; other costs make the total closing costs 3 to 4 percent of the value of the house, or, for a $70,000 house, about $2,100 to $2,800.

THE REAL ESTATE SETTLEMENT PROCEDURES ACT

A recent law requires that all closing costs be specifically outlined to you before you buy a home. Under the 1976 revisions of the Real Estate Settlement Procedures Act, when you borrow money to pay for a house:

1. The lender must send you, within three business days after you apply for a mortgage loan, a booklet prepared by the U.S. Department of Housing and Urban Development outlining your rights and explaining settlement procedures and costs.
2. The lender must give you, the applicant, within that three-day period an estimate of most of the settlement costs.
3. The lender must clearly identify individuals or firms that he or she may require you to use for legal or other services, including title insurance and search.
4. If your loan is approved, the lender must provide you with a truth-in-lending statement showing the annual interest rate on the mortgage loan.
5. Lenders, title insurers, and others involved in the real-estate transaction cannot pay kickbacks for referrals.

For further details about RESPA regulations, you may write the Assistant Secretary for Consumer Affairs and Regulatory Functions, Real Estate Practices Division, Department of Housing and Urban Development, Room 4100, Washington, D.C. 20410.

If You Decide to Have a House Built

Some consumers decide to have a house built especially for them. Although this book cannot cover the process in detail, here are some tips.

1. Know the builder.
2. Call a consumer agency such as the Better Business Bureau to find out if any complaints have been lodged against the builder.
3. Get a detailed written contract. Do not rely on a verbal agreement. For added assurance, have a real-estate lawyer inspect the sales contract.
4. Ask for a warranty, such as the Ten-Year Plan offered by the National Association of Home Builders or the Homeowners Warranty Corporation.
5. Hire an inspector.
6. Follow through on any defects; that is, have the builder correct them immediately.
7. Keep accurate records of all correspondence with the builder as well as receipts for repair work, motel bills, or other costs you had to incur because the builder didn't clear up problems. You may need these if legal action is necessary.

MORTGAGE TALK

When you shop for a mortgage, you should know the language of the mortgage trade.

1. Prepayment privilege. You can prepay the mortgage before the maturity date without penalty. This is something you might do later on if interest rates in the economy fall below what you actually are paying. You would pay the mortgage off by refinancing it at a lower interest charge.
2. Package mortgage. This mortgage covers the cost of all household equipment as well as the house itself. You might try to get this if you do not have the cash to buy furniture and you think you can get a lower interest charge through a mortgage company than through other credit sources. (Some finance experts advise against this because you pay interest on the money for the equipment long after you have used it up.)
3. Open-end mortgage. This mortgage allows you to borrow more money in the future without rewriting the mortgage. With an open-end mortgage, you can add on to the house or repair it and have the mortgage company pay these new bills. The mortgage company then charges

you a larger monthly payment or increases the life span of your loan.

INSURING YOUR HOME

Types of Insurance Policies

There are basically two types of insurance policies you might buy for a home.

1. A standard fire insurance policy that protects the homeowner against fire and lightning, plus damage from water and smoke caused by the fire and fire department. If you pay a little bit more, the coverage can be extended to protect you against damage caused by hail, windstorms, and explosions.

2. A homeowner's policy that provides protection against a number of risks under a single policy, allowing you to save over what you would pay if you bought each policy separately. It covers both the house and its contents. In addition to standard fire policy coverage, liability coverage can also be obtained.

Different Types of Policy Coverage

1. Property coverage includes garage, house, and other private buildings on your lot; personal possessions and property whether at home or while you are traveling or at work; and additional living expenses paid to you if you could not live in your home because of a fire or flood.

2. There are basically three types of liability coverage: (a) personal liability in case someone is injured on your property or you damage someone else's property and are at fault; (b) medical payments for injury to others who are on your property; and (c) coverage for the property of others that you or a number of your family damages.

Forms of Homeowner's Policies

There are a number of forms of homeowner's policies, each covering more risks than the other. Exhibit L–7 shows what each is like. As you can see, the **basic form** covers eleven risks, the **broad form** covers eighteen risks, and the **comprehensive form** covers those risks and all other perils, except those listed at the bottom of the chart.

EXHIBIT L–6
An Estimate of Cost and Cash Requirements for Purchasing a House

Loan Amount $______	Purchase Price	$______
ESTIMATED COSTS		
Service Charge		$______
Title Insurance		______
Recording Fee		______
Due Seller for ______ Taxes		______
Fire Insurance Premium		______
Interest from ______ to ______		______
Tax Registration		______
Allowed toward ______ Taxes		______
Assessments		______
Credit Report		______
Escrow Fee		______
Appraisal Fee		______
TOTAL		$______*
		______
ESTIMATED CASH REQUIREMENTS		
Down Payment	$______	
Estimated Cash	$______	
Subtotal	$______	
Less Earnest Money	$______	
TOTAL	$______	
ESTIMATED MONTHLY PAYMENT AT ____% FOR ____ YEARS		
Principal & Interest		$______
Taxes		______
Insurance		______
Mortgage Life Insurance		______
Mortgage Disability Insurance		______
TOTAL		$______

*Plus reimbursement to seller for unused fuel oil

Adding a Personal-Articles Floater Policy

You may wish to pay a slightly higher premium to insure specific personal articles such as specific cameras, musical instruments, works of art, and jewelry. This is done under a personal-articles floater addition to your homeowner's policy. You will be asked to submit a list of those items and an affadavit giving their current market value. When you insure under a floater, you have provided all-risk insurance and, therefore, can omit the covered property from your fire and theft policies.

Personal-Effects Floater Policy

You also can take out a personal-effects floater policy to cover personal items when you are traveling. In most

EXHIBIT L–7
Guide To Package Policies For Homeowners

These are the principal features of the standard types of homeowner's insurance policies.
The amount of insurance provided for specific categories, such as personal property and comprehensive personal liability, can usually be increased by paying an additional premium.
The special limits of liability refer to the maximum amounts the policy will pay for the types of property listed in the notes. Usually, jewelry, furs, boats, and other items subject to special limits have to be insured separately to obtain greater coverage.

	BASIC FORM HOMEOWNERS HO-1	BROAD FORM HOMEOWNERS HO-2	SPECIAL FORM HOMEOWNERS HO-3	COMPREHENSIVE FORM HOMEOWNERS HO-5	(FOR CONDOMINUM OWNERS) HO-6
PERILS COVERED (see key next page)	perils 1–11	perils 1–18	perils 1–18 on personal property except glass breakage; all risks, except those specifically excluded, on buildings	all risks, except those specifically excluded	perils 1–18, except glass breakage
STANDARD AMOUNT OF INSURANCE ON:					
house, attached structures	based on property value; minimum $8,000	based on property value; minimum $8,000	based on property value; minimum $8,000	based on property value; minimum $15,000	$1,000 on owner's additions and alterations to unit
detached structures	10% of amount of insurance on house	10% of amount of insurance on house	10% of amount of insurance on house	10% of amount of insurance on house	no coverage
trees, shrubs, and plants	5% of amount of insurance on house; $250 maximum per item	5% of amount of insurance on house; $250 maximum per item	5% of amount of insurance on house; $250 maximum per item	5% of amount of insurance on house; $250 maximum per item	10% of personal property insurance; $250 maximum per item
personal property on premises	50% of insurance on house	50% of insurance on house	50% of insurance on house	50% of insurance on house	based on value of property, minimum $4,000
personal property away from premises	10% of personal property insurance (minimum $1,000)	10% of personal property insurance (minimum $1,000)	10% of personal property insurance (minimum $1,000)	50% of insurance on house	10% of personal property insurance (minimum $1,000)
additional living expense	10% of insurance on house	20% of insurance on house	20% of insurance on house	20% of insurance on house	40% of personal property insurance
SPECIAL LIMITS OF LIABILITY*	standard	standard	standard	standard	standard

EXHIBIT L–7
Guide To Package Policies For Homeowners (Continued)

KEY TO PERILS COVERED:

1. fire, lightning
2. damage to property removed from premises endangered by fire
3. windstorm, hail
4. explosion
5. riots
6. damage by aircraft
7. damage by vehicles not owned or operated by people covered by policy
8. damage from smoke
9. vandalism, malicious mischief
10. glass breakage
11. theft
12. falling objects
13. weight of ice, snow, sleet
14. collapse of building or any part of building
15. bursting, cracking, burning, or bulging of a steam or hot-water-heating system or of appliances for heating water
16. leakage or overflow of water or steam from a plumbing, heating, or air-conditioning system
17. freezing of plumbing, heating, or air-conditioning systems or domestic appliances
18. injury to electrical appliances, devices, fixtures, and wiring (excluding tubes, transistors, and similar electronic components) from short circuits or other accidentally generated currents

*Special limits of liability: Money, bullion, numismatic property, bank notes—$100; securities, bills, deeds, tickets, etc.—$500; manuscripts—$1,000; jewelry, furs—$500 for theft; boats, including trailers and equipment—$500; trailers—$500.

SOURCE: Adapted from New Jersey Insurance Department, *A Shopper's Guide to Homeowners Insurance*, 1977.

cases, a personal-effects floater isn't necessary because your regular homeowner's insurance covers you. Because a personal-effects floater covers only the articles when they are taken off your property, you still need insurance for them when they are on your property. The policy does not cover theft from an unattended automobile unless there is evidence of a forced entry. In general, even when there is evidence of forced entry, the company's liability is limited to 10 percent of the amount of insurance and to not more than $250 for all property in any one loss. You can have this restriction removed from the policy upon payment of an additional premium.

Flood Insurance

You will notice that even a comprehensive homeowner's insurance policy does not cover floods. If you live in an area that may have flooding due to hurricanes and the like, it is advisable to purchase federally subsidized (that is, by all federal taxpayers) flood insurance. You must live in an area designated eligible by the Federal Insurance Administrator of the U.S. Department of Housing and Urban Development. Your insurance agent will be able to tell you if you are eligible.

HOW MUCH INSURANCE SHOULD YOU HAVE?

You should have 80 percent of the total value of your house insured—that is, 80 percent of its replacement value. If you have at least that much coverage, you can collect the full replacement cost, not the depreciated value, of any damaged property (up to the limits of the policy). For example, say your ten-year-old roof is damaged in a fire, and it costs $2,500 to replace it. If you have at least 80 percent coverage on your house, your insurance company must pay you the full amount of the roof damage, whereas if your house is covered for less than 80 percent of replacement, you will get less. Specifically, you will be paid only that portion of the loss equal to the amount of insurance in force divided by 80 percent of replacement cost of the entire house times the loss on the roof. If your house would cost $60,000 to replace and you have only $30,000 of insurance, then on your roof damage of $2,500, you will be paid:

$$\frac{\$30{,}000}{\$48{,}000} \times \$2{,}500 = \$1{,}563$$

A little explanation of this formula is in order. The fraction consists of the actual amount of insurance that you had on your structure ($30,000) divided by the amount of insurance you would have to have had to cover 80 percent of the replacement value, or .8 × $60,000 = $48,000.

You need not insure your house for the full replacement value for two reasons: The land has a value that would not be destroyed in a fire or flood, and even if the house were totally burned down, the foundation, sidewalks, driveway, and such things would still be standing. If you are living in a house you bought many years ago, the cost of replacement may be much more than you think. In the last chapter we discussed the phenomenal increase in construction costs; take that into account when you purchase homeowner's insurance. You may want to have an arrangement with your insurance company whereby the value of your insurance is increased 10 percent every year or two to keep pace with construction increases. Avoid being left in the cold if your house burns down.

Accurate Appraisal of Replacement Cost

You may wish, or be required by the lender, to use the services of a professional appraiser in order to get an accurate replacement value of your house. You will have to pay from $50 to $200 to do so if you have someone come out to look it over. You can find appraisers in your Yellow Pages. You can also fill out a form and pay a lot less if you use the services of companies such as GAB Business Services, Inc., 1101 State Road, Princeton, New Jersey 08540 (telephone 800-621-2306). Write or call for a GAB valurate and return it with a small fee. You will get back an appraisal based on your local labor materials cost. American Appraisal Associates, Inc., of Milwaukee, Wisconsin, provides a similar service but only through certain insurance agents. You can ask your local insurance agent to evaluate the house; or, if you know a local home builder, he or she may be able to help you out. Your banker might also be of help.

HOW TO SAVE ON INSURANCE

There are a number of ways you may be able to reduce your insurance premium.

1. Increase the deductible.
2. Pay your premiums on a three-year basis rather than a one-year basis.
3. Install fire extinguishers throughout the house and fire-alarm systems.
4. Move to a low-crime area where you can obtain less expensive theft insurance.
5. Purchase a package policy rather than separate policies for different perils.

PREPAYING INSURANCE AND TAXES

Most mortgage sellers require the mortgagor—that is, the homeowner—to prepay taxes and insurance as part of the monthly house payments. If a savings and loan association is the mortgagee, a special reserve account is set up within the savings and loan association, and home insurance and taxes are paid from it every year. This way the mortgagee does not have to worry about foreclosure on the house because of unpaid taxes or problems if the house burns down and is not insured. The special reserve account that you must pay into monthly may not earn interest for you. Rather, the holder of that account uses it to earn interest for the mortgaging institution.

NEW HOME WARRANTIES

In 1974, the National Association of Home Builders (NAHB) established a consumer protection feature called Homeowner's Warranty, or HOW. HOW covers major structural defects on a home for a ten-year period so that subsequent buyers are automatically protected. HOW policies cannot be purchased on the open market; only an active HOW member-builder can sell one along with the house that he or she has built. The builder pays a one-time fee and passes it along to the buyer. Premium costs range from $2.20 to $5.00 per $1,000 of a home's selling price. The premium depends on the location of the house.

HOW covers the home in a three-step plan.

1. During the first year, HOW builders guarantee their new homes to be free from defects in workmanship and materials, major structural defects, and flaws in the electrical, plumbing, heating, cooling, ventilating, and mechanical systems.
2. During the second year, the HOW builder guarantees the same items, with the exception of workmanship and materials.
3. For the remaining eight years, the owner is insured against all major structural defects.

Whenever a builder refuses to abide by the terms of the warranty within the first two years (or if the builder goes out of business), the insurance takes over and covers the cost of all authorized repairs after the owner pays the first $250. Historically, over half the claims paid out by HOW have occurred during the initial two-year period.

Remodeler's Warranties

The Homeowner's Warranty Corporation also makes available a five-year warranty program for remodelers. This plan, introduced in January 1983, guarantees remodeling work done by registered HOW contractors. The coverage is similar to that found in the HOW package for new homes, except that the homeowner pays the first $100. Premiums on this remodeler's warranty program depend on the project's price. A $175 premium is charged for the first $5,000 of the contract price, plus an additional $3.50 for each $1,000 thereafter.

Buying Repair Insurance

An increasing number of used-home buyers purchase warranties or insurance against defects in the home. These contracts protect new owners against such things as defective plumbing and wiring and sometimes appliance, roofing, and structural defects. Such warranties have been available to buyers of new homes for several years; they are issued through builders affiliated with the National Association of Home Builders. Some plans give protection against major structural defects for up to ten years.

For $150 to $300 per year, buyers of used homes can obtain similar coverage. One of the largest warranty providers is American Home Shield Corporation based in Dublin, California. It offers its program through over 2,000 agents in California, New Jersey, Florida, Arizona, and Texas. The basic yearly fee is around $200; however, homeowners must pay a $20 fee for each service call. Certified Homes Corporation, based in Columbia, Maryland, offers warranties in sixteen major areas, mainly in the northeast. It gives an eighteen-month contract but only to homes found in good condition after the inspection. It is estimated that 2 million used homes will be covered by such warranties by the end of this decade. It might be worthwhile for you to check out the availability of such insurance policies in your area.

MAKING THE MOVE

If you are moving from one part of the country to another, you can employ the services of moving consultants. But generally this will be useful only if you are in an upper income bracket. Otherwise, your time may be worth less than a moving consultant's time.

Although the government regulates movers, you cannot necessarily be certain of a guaranteed move. Some regulations apply to the moving industry, and you should be aware of those that may affect you directly.

1. The moving van must come on the promised day. The company can be fined up to $500 if it fails to do so.
2. The price estimates must be based on the moving company's actual physical inspection of whatever you ask it to move.
3. Well in advance of the actual moving day, a mover must give you, the customer, an *order for service,* which states the estimated price of the move and the mutually agreed-upon pickup and delivery dates.
4. The shipment must be delivered and all services performed on payment of the estimated amount plus no more than 10 percent additional in the case of an underestimate. You have fifteen working days to pay any amount over 110 percent of the written estimate.

How to Pick a Mover

Picking a mover is tricky because, even within one moving company, there is extreme variability in quality of service. The level of complaints seems to be about the same for each of the largest firms: North American Van, United, Bekins, Allied and Aero Mayflower. Different cost estimates from several companies aren't particularly meaningful because the ICC has made sure that the industry charges about the same price for weight and mileage.

Don't Cut Time Corners

Do not try to postpone your move to the very last minute. Make sure the movers come a few days before you have to vacate your house. Sometimes movers do not come to your old house on time, and that may spell disaster if you are supposed to leave the day the mover has been scheduled to come. You can get by without your furniture for a day or two, but what will you do if you have to stay around after you were supposed to vacate the premises?

Appliances

Since you must pay extra to have appliances prepared for moving, call your regular repair services and have their technicians do it. Also have them explain what must be done to put things back into service later on.

Watch Out!

When the movers are loading your belongings, make sure you see a copy of the inventory form and look at what they mark to describe the condition of your furniture. Code letters indicate scratched, marred, gouged, cracked, soiled, and so on. If you think the mover's description is exaggerated, make sure it is changed, or threaten to call the whole thing off. If the description of damage to your furniture is exaggerated before it leaves your home, then you will have no recourse for a damage payment if your furniture is damaged in transit. Because a full 25 percent of all moves end in some dispute over damages, this is an important point. The ICC suggests that you personally observe the weighing of the empty truck, its loading, its reweighing, and its unloading. When your furniture is finally delivered, be there. You also should personally check off the items on your inventory sheet as they are unloaded. Do not sign an inventory sheet, no matter what the driver says, until you've had time to discover all damage and all loss.

Making a Claim

There's a good chance you will want to make a claim for lost, broken, or damaged items. There is generally a claims bureau in most cities, and somebody will be sent out to estimate damage or to take things to be repaired. Under a 1972 ICC rule, the van line on an interstate move is "absolutely responsible for all acts or omissions" of its agents. If you fail to get satisfaction, call the nearest Interstate Commerce Commission office. If that also fails, write to the Director of the Bureau of Operations, Interstate Commerce Commission, Washington, D.C. 20423. If you think you have been badly abused, you may want to go to small claims court, which we discussed in Consumer Issue B.

An Alternative

If you have some extra time and some friends to help and if you want to save some money and avoid fights with movers, you can always rent a truck from U-Haul, U-Drive, or various other companies. Remember, though, you must count the time and fatigue costs of this particular moving method. Because the cost of moving yourself is directly related to the income you forego or the implicit value you put on the leisure time lost in doing the moving, you may find moving yourself the most economical way. People who are students during the school year and do not have summer jobs, for example, have a very low opportunity cost and, therefore, may wish to take advantage of this situation by renting a U-Haul. On the other hand, it would not make sense for a high-income executive to spend two weeks driving a truck across the United States in order to save moving expenses.

Problems with Self-moving

If you decide to move yourself, be aware of a number of possible problems.

1. You may not have any experience loading a trailer. The weight must be distributed evenly in the vehicle to prevent the trailer from jackknifing.
2. Be sure to place large, heavy items on the bottom, and fill open spaces with small items. If you can, strap down your items.
3. Be careful of back strain, a frequent result of self-moving.
4. Be wary of inexperienced helpers; don't overestimate either their abilities or their strength.
5. Realize that, unless your insurance is in effect, you will not be covered during the move.
6. Be wary of the emotional and physical stress involved in being your own mover. Take it easy!
7. Be sure you have someone to help you unload at your destination. Paying for casual labor can be expensive—in money and damaged goods.

SUMMARY

1. A general rule of thumb in determining how much housing you can afford is no more than about two-and-a-half times your annual income.
2. If you are buying or selling a house, you probably will find the services of a real-estate agent helpful. However, remember that those services will cost you.
3. A real-estate agent essentially brings together the buyers and sellers. He or she is, therefore, a provider of information.
4. If you are selling a house, try to bargain with potential agents on the commission they will charge you. You can bargain about when you will pay the commission (because a commission paid over a five-year period is less costly to you than a commission paid immediately upon the sale of the house) and certain other details of the sale. Shop around for an agent, just as you would shop around for anything else.
5. When you are buying a house, it is best to work with an agent who understands your needs and does not attempt to get you into a house that you do not want. You can also bargain with agents when you are buying a house. If, for example, you are ready to make a purchase, you may ask the agent to do such things as buy you a refrigerator and stove if he or she wants you to purchase the house, actually split the commission with you (where that is legal), put a new carpet in, or have the house painted at the agent's expense.
6. You can let the agent do the bargaining for you if bargaining makes you uncomfortable.

7. When bargaining on a house, never let the seller know that you are excited about the purchase. In fact, the seller should not learn anything about you at all. It is best to have an agent do your bargaining; your emotions cannot get involved, and you should not "show your hand."

8. It is usually advisable for you to have a building-inspection service come out to the home you wish to buy before you make any offer whatsoever. Look in your Yellow Pages for such services. If you are truly concerned, have more than one inspection service look at the house.

9. When figuring out the cost of a house, remember that you must take into account the closing costs, which can run as high as 3 or 4 percent of the purchase price of the house. This money must be in cash, as must the down payment on that house. Generally, you must purchase some form of title insurance in order to obtain a mortgage. However, if you are in doubt, hire your own lawyer to do the title search.

10. Shop around for a mortgage just as you shop for anything else. Seek out the best deal in terms of the down payment required, the annual percentage interest rate charged, and whether or not there is a penalty for early prepayment in case you decide to sell the house after a few years.

11. Make sure that you obtain sufficient insurance on your house so that at least 80 percent of its value is covered. Shop around for housing insurance, making sure you check out each company's policies with respect to how much they will pay you for personal furnishings lost in a fire, for alternative housing if you are forced to leave your home because of a fire, and so on.

12. Moving can be a traumatic experience. You can avoid some of the traumas by taking several steps. Plan well in advance, work out all the details with the potential mover, set your actual moving day for several days before you must leave your house or apartment, take a complete inventory of what you are shipping, check the mover's log to make sure that more defects in your furniture are not recorded than actually exist, and do not expect perfection. You may wish to try some of the smaller movers. Many consumers indicate that they receive better service from other than the top five large moving firms.

QUESTIONS FOR THOUGHT AND DISCUSSION

1. Do you think that a mortgage rate of 15½ percent is high? Why?

2. Why would you want to borrow on a mortgage for thirty years instead of fifteen years?

3. Would you prefer to buy a new or a used house? Why?

4. Can you think of any other features of a house you should look at in addition to the ten listed in the text?

5. Do you think real-estate brokers charge too much?

6. Would you ever pay more than the asking price for a house?

7. Which type of title insurance do you think is best?

8. Why do you think mortgage companies require you to prepay insurance and taxes?

9. Is it always best to repair everything that goes wrong in a house?

THINGS TO DO

1. Call several savings and loan associations to find out what their interest rate is on a twenty-year, $60,000 mortgage on an $80,000 house. If you find significant differences, ask why.

2. Drive around different residential areas in your town. Try to figure out why one area is more expensive than another.

3. Look in the Yellow Pages under real-estate agents and see what some of the large ads say. Try to figure out whether it is possible for one agent to do a better job than another.

4. Obtain a typical contract or earnest agreement from an agent in your area. Go over the details with the agent to find out whether the agreement is more beneficial to the buyer or to the seller. (Actually, it should be most beneficial to the agent.)

5. Get a copy of a typical mortgage agreement from a savings and loan association. Try to read (and understand) the small print.

SELECTED READINGS

Casey, Douglas. *The Complete Real Estate Adviser*. New York: Pocket Books, 1981.

Financing for Home Purchases and Home Improvements: A Guide to Financing Costs and Home Buying Ability. Washington, D.C.: Federal Housing Administration (latest edition).

Heatter, Justin W. *Buying a Condominium*, rev. ed. New York: Atheneum, 1982.

Home-Buyer's Checklist. National Homebuyers and Homeowners Association, 1225 19th Street, N.W., Washington, D.C. 20036 (latest edition).

The Home Buyer's Estimated Monthly Housing Costs. Superintendent of Documents, U.S. Government Printing

Office, Washington, D.C. 20402, $1.75, Stock No. 023-000-00319-8.

"How HOW Is Doing Now." *Changing Times*, February 1983, pp. 70–72.

Huges, Allen. *A Home of Your Own for the Least Cash: New Alternatives*. New York: Acropolis Books, 1982.

Kass, B. J. and Sakie, H. *Condominium Owner's Handbook*. 152 18th Street, N.W., Washington, D.C. 20036.

Questions and Answers on Guaranteed and Direct Loans for Veterans. Washington, D.C.: Veterans Administration, 1982.

Temple, Douglas. *Creative Home Financing: You Can Buy a House, Condo, or Co-op in Today's Market*. New York: Coward, McCann & Geoghegan, 1982.

Watkins, Arthur M. *How Much House Can You Afford?* New York Life Insurance Company, Box 10, Madison Square Station, New York, New York 10010.

Wise Home Buying. U.S. Department of Housing and Urban Development, October, 1978, HUD-267-H(8), U.S. Department of Housing and Urban Development, Washington, D.C. 20410.

Consumer

ISSUE M

RENTING A PLACE TO LIVE

GLOSSARY

RESIDENCE CONTENTS BROAD FORM—A renter's insurance policy that covers possessions against eighteen risks. It includes additional living expenses and liability coverage in case someone is injured in the apartment or house you are renting.

If you have decided that you wish to rent, you are faced with at least four problems:

1. Obtaining information on rental units available
2. Making sure you get the right rental unit for you
3. Making sure the contract or lease is appropriate
4. Knowing what to do when you have valid complaints after you have rented the housing unit

INFORMATION ABOUT RENTAL UNITS

There are basically four ways you can obtain information about potential rental units. They are:

1. Ads in the local newspapers
2. Listing agencies
3. "For Rent" signs in front of apartment buildings and houses
4. Friends and acquaintances

A source of information that prospective renters may not be aware of is rental-information agencies that go by the name of Rentex, Apartment Hunt, and so on. Basically, you pay a fee—between twenty and fifty dollars—which usually gives you the right to an unlimited number of searches through the files of the agency. In principle, these files are updated and give you information that will save you time and keep you from fruitless inspections of apartments that are not suitable for you. For example, if you definitely want to keep a pet in your apartment, many vacant rental units can be eliminated immediately because they do not allow pets on the premises. If you have small children, this also may be a factor to consider; many apartments do not allow children at all.

Consumers' experiences with rental-listing agencies are mixed. Some report that the listings are up-to-date and accurate. However, the majority contend that inaccurate listings caused them to waste more time than if they had simply responded to ads in the newspaper.

A number of rental-listing agencies practice a form of "bait and switch." They put a listing in the classified-ad sections of local newspapers for an extremely advantageous rental unit. When you call the agency, you are told that you must pay an advance fee for an "exclusive" list of available houses and apartments. When you ask for the address of the "too-good-to-be-true" rental unit listed in the newspaper, you are told that that one has been rented, "but we have lots of other listings." Unlike real-estate brokers, who receive a commission *after* they have found you a place to live, rental-listing agencies do not refund fees if you do not find a rental through their listings. It is not surprising that the New York Better Business Bureau issued a press release a few years ago indicating that "all advance fee rental agencies [are] not in the public interest." Some states have outlawed them.

MAKING THE RIGHT CHOICE

When looking for a rental unit, it is often helpful to carry a checklist with you to make comparisons. That way, you will not sign a lease on an apartment or house only to discover that you had forgotten to inquire about an essential attribute of the rental unit that you now find doesn't exist. Exhibit M–1 is just a partial checklist. You can make up your own and add important factors that you desire.

THE THORNY PROBLEM OF SECURITY DEPOSITS

It is virtually impossible to rent any type of housing unit without leaving a "refundable" security (cleaning or breakage) deposit, usually equal to one month's rent. The deposit is supposed to be returned to you if you leave the apartment in an "appropriate" condition. Landlords argue that they need security deposits because they often find damage caused by tenants.

Not even the majority of states have laws regulating security deposits. You can look at deposits in either of two ways. You are never going to get it back; thus divide the number of months you are going to live in the rental unit into the security deposit to come up with the "surcharge" you are actually paying per month.[5] Or, you can attempt from the beginning to have a strong case in favor of getting the money back. To do that, consider the following.

1. Go through the apartment with the manager or owner the day you move in, marking down every single indication

5. But that doesn't mean you should give up. If you do, though, at least register your complaint with the appropriate agency so that some record exists.

EXHIBIT M–1
Shopping for an Apartment

	APARTMENT A	APARTMENT B	APARTMENT C	APARTMENT D
Monthly rent (including all expenses that you have to pay directly, such as utilities, recreational fees, parking fees, etc.)				
Size of security or cleaning deposit				
Are pets allowed?				
Is there a manager or superintendent on the premises at all times?				
Garbage-disposal facilities?				
Laundry equipment available on the premises?				
Is the laundry room safe?				
When can the laundry room be used?				
Is there a lobby?				
Is there a doorman?				
Will you have direct access to your unit?				
If there is an elevator, what is its condition?				
Is the apartment close to public transportation if you need it?				
Is it close to food stores?				
Entertainment?				
Other shopping?				
Are there sufficient electrical outlets?				
Are carpets and drapes included?				
Is there enough closet space?				
Are there safe and clearly marked fire exits?				
Are the tenants around you the ones you want to live near (children, singles, retired, etc.)?				

of wear and tear or damage that already exists. Make sure you have a copy of that set of notations; sign it yourself, and have the landlord who is with you sign it. Better yet, have it notarized. In some cases, it might be better to live in the apartment a few days to find out in more detail what doesn't work. This is particularly true if you have rented a furnished apartment or house.

2. Retain copies of all bills for improvements, repairs, or cleaning that you had done as evidence that you carefully maintained the unit.

3. Take fairly detailed snapshots showing the condition of the apartment when you moved in and when you leave. Have them developed by a company that puts the date on the picture.

4. If the building you live in is sold, obtain a letter from the former owner explaining who is holding the security deposit money.

5. Find out what your local regulations are. If they require that the apartment be "broom cleaned," sweep up the apartment and then show the job to the superintendent or the manager.

6. If you follow these five suggestions, you will be ready to go to court if your deposit is not refunded. When you are clearly prepared, most landlords will return your security deposit.

MAKING SURE THE LEASE IS OKAY

Most standard form leases seem to put everything in favor of the landlord (who usually provides it!). There are a number of clauses that you may want to attempt to delete.

Clauses to Avoid

CONFESSION OF JUDGMENT. If your lease has this provision, your landlord's lawyer has the legal right to go to court and plead guilty for you in the event that the landlord thinks his or her rights have been violated—that is, that the property has been damaged or the terms of the lease have not been met. If you sign a lease that has a confession-of-judgment provision, you are admitting guilt before committing any act. Such a clause is, in fact, illegal in some states.

WAIVER OF TORT LIABILITY. If this provision is in your lease, you have given up in advance the right to sue the landlord if, in fact, you suffer injury or damage because of your landlord's negligence. (If such a clause is illegal in your state and you sign it, it will not hold up in court anyway.)

ARBITRARY CLAUSES. These are any clauses that give the landlord the ability to cancel the lease because he or she is dissatisfied with your behavior. Some leases include clauses that:

1. Forbid immoral behavior.
2. Forbid hanging pictures on the wall.
3. Forbid you to have overnight guests. (This is usually done by requiring that the apartment be occupied only by the tenant and members of the tenant's immediate family.)
4. Forbid you to assign or sublease.
5. Allow the landlord to cancel the lease and hold you liable for rent for the balance of the lease if you are one day late.
6. Allow the landlord to enter your apartment when you are not there.
7. Make you liable for all repairs.
8. Make you obey rules that have not yet been written.

Clauses to Add to Your Lease

1. If the person renting the unit to you says that it comes with dishwasher, disposal unit, and air conditioner, make the lease specifically list these items.

2. If you have been promised the use of a recreation room, a gymnasium, a parking lot, or a swimming pool, make sure that the lease says so specifically. Also, have it indicate whether or not you must pay extra for the use of those facilities.

3. If the landlord has promised to have the apartment painted, have this indicated in the lease. If you wish to be able to choose the color, also have that in the lease.

4. In certain cases, you may be able to negotiate a right to premature cancellation if you are transferred to another job. Usually, however, you must negotiate the amount you pay the landlord for exercising this privilege. Ideally, it will be less than the security deposit.

5. If you wish to have any fixtures, shelves, furnishings, and so on that you install become your property when you leave the premises, specify this in the lease.

What to Do When You Have Trouble with Your Landlord

If you believe that you have been unfairly treated by your landlord, there are several steps you can take. If you are acting alone in your complaint, you can do the following.

1. Explicitly indicate what your grievance is, such as uncomfortably low (or high) temperatures, a stopped-up sewage system, a continuously leaking toilet, a refrigerator whose freezing compartment doesn't work, and so on.

2. Make a number of copies of the complaint list. Mail one to the manager or owner and one to the housing inspector (if one comes to your complex), and keep one for yourself. If there is an organized tenants group in your area, send a copy to it. You can find out if there is a local group by writing the National Tenants Organization, 425 Thirteenth Street N.W., Washington, D.C. 20005.

3. Whenever you contact the agency that administers the housing code in your area, request a visit from a housing inspector who will certify the validity of your complaint.

Withholding Rent

If the complaints you have are serious enough, you may, in some states, have the legal right to withhold part or all of your rent. Approximately half the states allow the tenant to deduct repairs from the rent; they also provide for not paying any rent when the dwelling is uninhabitable. Many states also have procedures for rent strikes that can be done legally. Note that if you repair and deduct from your rent the cost of repairs, there may be a limit to how much money can be used. In many states, the limit is half a month's rent or $100, whichever is greater. In Massachusetts, the limit is two months' rent; in New Jersey, there is no fixed maximum.

A Final Alternative

If your rental situation is truly disagreeable, you might consider looking for another apartment where you won't have similar problems. When one manufacturer's product does not satisfy you, you often turn to a competitor. The same principle could be applied to rental units.

MAKING SURE YOU HAVE INSURANCE

Homeowners are not the only ones who can get an insurance policy to cover loss through fire, theft, and the like. While it is true that the landlord or owner of your building is liable for damage to the building and for injuries occurring in common areas, such as the lobby or hallway, you are responsible for protecting the inside of your dwelling, and you are liable for accidents that occur there. Renters' insurance, called **residence contents broad form**, is a policy that covers personal possessions against the risks described in the previous Consumer Issue. It includes additional living expenses and liability coverage.

Before you look for a rental policy, make a detailed inventory of your possessions. Decide on the coverage you want and then do some comparison shopping.

Note that household possessions are sometimes insured for half their value. Everything, including linens and plants, should be listed in your inventory. The inventory list must be kept in a safe place away from the dwelling, and a copy should be given to your insurance agent.

A general policy for, say, $5,000 of property insurance and $50,000 of liability coverage probably will run less than $100 a year, depending on where you live.

If you are in a high-crime area and cannot find commercially available insurance, then you can apply through the Federal Crime Insurance Program and the Fair Access to Insurance Requirements (FAIR) Plan. The former covers loss by burglary; the latter covers fire, vandalism, and windstorms. Neither plan gives you liability coverage. Ask a commercial insurance agent in your area where you can obtain information on policies available through these programs or write HUD, Washington, D.C., for an informative booklet.

SUMMARY

1. Information about rental units can be obtained from newspaper ads, listing agencies, "for rent" signs on apartment buildings and houses, and friends and acquaintances.
2. When comparing apartments, a fairly sophisticated checklist can be used to make a more objective survey.
3. If you desire to have your security (cleaning or breakage) deposit returned to you when you vacate a rented unit, you must take certain precautions, such as going through the unit with a manager or landlord the day you move in and checking off all damage that has already occurred. You also may want to retain copies of bills for improvement repairs and cleaning and take snapshots of the condition of the apartment when you moved into it.
4. When signing a standard form lease, avoid confession of judgment and waiver of tort liability and all arbitrary clauses.
5. Grievances with managers or owners can be handled through a housing agency in your city or an organized tenants association.
6. Insurance can be purchased through a residence contents broad form policy.

QUESTIONS FOR THOUGHT AND DISCUSSION

1. Do you think that rental listing agencies should be illegal?
2. When would it be appropriate not to use a checklist to make comparisons among potential rental units that you are looking at?
3. Why do you think certain apartment owners consistently are able to keep security deposits?
4. Do you think a confession-of-judgment clause should always be illegal?

THINGS TO DO

1. Obtain a standard form lease contract. Find out how many arbitrary clauses are inserted. Is there a confession of judgment and a waiver of tort liability?
2. Find out if there is a tenants' organization in your neighborhood by writing the National Tenants Organization, 425 Thirteenth Street N.W., Washington, D.C. 20005.
3. Obtain literature from your local tenants' organization (if one exists). Is that organization attacking some of the problems mentioned in this Consumer Issue?

SELECTED READINGS

Clubb, M. W. "Lease to Buy." *Mother Earth News,* September/October 1982, p. 140.
Dreier, P. "Renters' Revolt." *Progressive,* September 1982, pp. 16–17.

"Housing Yourself in the Eighties: Should You Buy or Rent?" *Consumer Reports*, July 1981, pp. 393–99.

"How to Read a Lease." *Consumer Reports*, October 1974, pp. 707–11.

"Learn to Spot the Traps in a Lease." *Changing Times*, January 1980, pp. 17–18.

Tilling, T. "Reasons for Renting." *Parents*, September 1982, pp. 41–42.

CHAPTER
THE APPLIANCE SOCIETY

In 1970, virtually no one had calculators, drip coffee makers, or hand-held hair dryers. Now, over 99 percent of U.S. homes have calculators and almost one-third have drip coffee makers and hand-held hair dryers.

CHAPTER PREVIEW

- What is a consumer durable?
- How do you decide when to buy an appliance?
- Should appliances be bought on credit?
- What types of warranties are available?

Once we've bought or rented a place to live, our next concern is to equip that dwelling with an array of appliances designed to make life easier, cleaner, more entertaining, more economical, and, in some cases, more complicated. We call this category of items **consumer durable goods,** because they should have a lifetime of several years or more. They include washers, dryers, television sets, stereos, freezers, refrigerators, ranges, vacuum cleaners, sewing machines, dishwashers, trash compactors, water-softening equipment, water heaters, and floor polishers. To get an idea of how durable appliances are, look at Exhibit 16–1, which shows the life expectancy of various appliances.

CONSUMER DURABLE GOODS
Consumer goods that have a lifetime that exceeds one year—for example, washers, dryers, refrigerators, stereos.

The following chapter treats another consumer durable—the automobile—and Chapter 23 looks at recreational equipment, such as campers, trailers, and boats. All such consumer durable goods have the following characteristics:

1. They yield a service flow over their useful lifetime.
2. The purchase price does not represent the price that is actually paid for one year's service flow. The purchase price is greater.
3. Their purchase is often financed on credit.
4. They wear out or depreciate.
5. They must be cared for and repaired.
6. They often are replaced when no longer usable.
7. They may be covered by some form of property insurance.
8. They represent a status symbol.

The ownership of appliances, particularly small appliances, has grown dramatically in the last decade. Just look at Exhibit 16–2, which shows the growth in consumer appliances from 1970 to 1983. In 1970, virtually no one had calculators, drip coffee makers, or hand-held hair dryers. Thirteen years later, over 99 percent of U.S. homes had calculators and almost one-third had drip coffee makers and hand-held hair dryers.

THE SAVING ASPECT OF BUYING EQUIPMENT

As we just pointed out, the purchase price of a consumer durable good, such as a washing machine, exceeds the actual price of one year's service flow. For example, if a washing machine costs $400 but is expected to last ten years, then, in the most simplified case, the service flow per year costs approximately $40. If you pay cash for the washing machine, you would consume only $40 of the original $400 and would save the rest. The purchase price of a washing machine, then, is part consumption and part saving. Consider that there is an implicit income stream equal to the flow of services to be received from the washing machine during each of the following nine years. We value it at approximately $40 a year; thus, after the expenditure of the $400 purchase price, $360 are left over as savings that will be consumed at the rate of $40 per year for nine more years.

Another way of looking at it is to compare the cost of home laundering to the cost of using a commercial laundromat. If it would cost an additional forty dollars a year in both extra time and expense to use the laundromat, then, in fact, owning a washing machine constitutes a "savings" of forty dollars per year (disregarding such expenses as repair costs).

EXHIBIT 16–1
Life Expectancy of Various Appliances

Gas clothes dryer	13 years
Electric clothes dryer	14 years
Clothes washer	11 years
Dishwasher	11 years
Freezer	20 years
Gas range	13 years
Electric range	12 years
Refrigerator	15 years
Black-and-white television	11 years
Color television	12 years

SOURCE: Department of Agriculture

Thus, when making spending decisions on consumer durable goods, it is important to determine how much of that spending is actual consumption for the year in which the purchase is made and how much is actual saving for future years. This is true for houses, washing machines, cars, and any other consumer durable good.

DECIDING ON WHEN TO BUY EQUIPMENT

In many respects, a consumer durable good is just like a machine that a business buys. Businesses are able to reach decisions on the profitability of investing in different types of business equipment, and we can use a similar analysis to determine whether or not a new piece of consumer equipment should be purchased. That is, when and how much should you invest in new furniture, a new washing machine, a new refrigerator, or a new dryer?

We do this by looking at the costs and then the benefits of the purchase of a consumer durable item. Let's think in terms of all costs and all benefits being expressed in dollars per year. Consider a hypothetical example in which you are debating the advisability of purchasing a freezer in order to store food purchased on sale in larger quantities for a longer period of time.

The Cost Side of the Picture

The cost side of any durable good will, at a minimum, include: depreciation, operating costs, repairs, and interest, not to mention the *time* costs spent on repairs.

1. **Depreciation.** Let's take a simple example in which the freezer has a ten-year life period, at the end of which it has a zero value and must be scrapped. Its full purchase price is $500; the average annual depreciation will be $50 a year. Actually, this is an understatement of depreciation in the first year and an overstatement of what it is in the later years of the useful life of the freezer. It would be virtually impossible to sell it an the end of one year for $450. Just as with automobiles (discussed in Chapter 17), equipment in the home depreciates more the first year than in subsequent years. We'll ignore that fact for the moment.
2. **Operating costs.** Most durable goods, and particularly a freezer, use some form of energy. In this case, it is electricity. Energy guides are now available for freezers, refrigerators, room air conditioners, and so on. Energy consumption of each unit is now required to be part of the consumer literature given with the sale of such appliances. Therefore, it is easy for you to estimate what it will cost you per year to operate a particular appliance. For simplicity's sake, let's assume that this cost will be sixty dollars per year.
3. **Repairs.** A freezer probably will have to be serviced occasionally over the ten-year period. You might even buy a service contract that would explicitly require a payment of so much per year in exchange for complete coverage of all replacement of parts and labor. Let's say that would cost, on average, thirty dollars per year (either for directly paid repairs or for a service contract).
4. **Interest.** If the $500 for the freezer has to be borrowed, then an explicit interest payment must be made. On the other hand, if you have $500 in your

EXHIBIT 16–2
Growth in Consumer Appliance Ownership

Calculators, drip coffee makers, and hand-held hair dryers were owned by an insignificant percentage of households in 1970. Their ownership skyrocketed thirteen years later.

APPLIANCE	1970	1983
Calculators	—	98.9%
Clothes dryers	44.6%	63.0%
Clothes washers	62.1%	77.1%
Dishwashers	26.5%	51.0%
Drip coffee makers (on a stand)	—	32.0%
Hair dryers (hand-held)	—	37.4%
Home freezers	31.2%	47.8%
Room air conditioners	40.6%	56.2%
Television (black & white)	98.7%	99.9%
Television (color)	42.5%	88.4%

SOURCE: Adapted from *Merchandising Magazine*.

savings account and withdraw it, you are paying an *implicit* interest rate equal to the interest foregone on that $500. Let's say that the $500 is in an account yielding 8 percent per year. Interest of 8 percent times $500 equals $40 a year in lost interest (ignoring compounding).

5. **Total costs.** We find, then, that the total annual cost, on average, of service from the freezer is:

Depreciation	$ 50
Operating costs	60
Repairs	35
Foregone interest	40
TOTAL	$185

Now we'll turn to the benefit side.

Benefits

The benefits of having a freezer include, but are not limited to, reduction in food bills, convenience, reduced food spoilage, and less time and gas spent on shopping trips.

1. **Reduction in food bills.** Depending on the size of the freezer, the owner can take advantage of sales on meat, frozen fruit juices, frozen vegetables, ice cream, fish, poultry, and a few other items that can be frozen and stored. Also, the freezer allows the owner to grow large quantities of food at home and put them "under wraps" for a long time. Finally, some foods can be bought in bulk at reduced per-unit prices—for example, a side of beef. Let's assume that over a one-year period, this saves the owner $110.
2. **Convenience.** It is certainly more convenient to pop into the laundry room or the garage and remove a few steaks for dinner than to go to the market. It is difficult to put a dollar figure on the value of this convenience, but if you value such convenience very highly, then this will be an important benefit factor.
3. **Less time and gas spent on shopping trips.** If you can spend less time going shopping by doing it less often because of the freezer, then we can place a value on your saved time.[1] This is the *opportunity cost* we talked about in Consumer Issue C. Again, it is difficult to talk in terms of what this opportunity cost is without knowing specifically your alternatives and the value you place on them. However, we can get a monetary handle on the reduction in gas costs and automobile expenses in general by looking at the price of an average trip to the grocery store. Let's assume that the total saved in opportunity costs and reduced automobile expenses is fifty-five dollars a year.
4. **Other benefits.** These benefits will include less spoilage of food and the like.
5. **Total benefits.** We can add up the total benefits as follows.

Reduced food bill	$110
Convenience	?
Reduced time and automobile expenses	55
Other	?
TOTAL	$165 + ? = ?

If those items for which we entered a question mark had a combined value of more than five dollars, we would have to say that the benefits outweigh the costs for this particular durable good.

THE QUESTION OF BUYING ON CREDIT

When we considered one of the costs of buying a consumer durable good, we mentioned that many items are purchased on time through the credit market. What should the wise consumer do when deciding upon how to finance the

1. This is complementary resource saving, a topic discussed earlier.

The *reason* you are borrowing money has little to do with whether or not you *should* borrow it.

purchase of a new washer or dryer or freezer? That is basically a question that we answered in Chapter 12 and in Consumer Issue I. The *reason* you are borrowing money has little to do with whether or not you *should* borrow it. What is important is that you maintain a safe debt load. Just because you are able to obtain relatively easy financing for a new washer or dryer does not automatically mean that you should buy it on credit. If doing so will put you over your estimated safe debt load, then you definitely should not buy on credit. If you cannot afford a new washer or dryer at that particular time, then you will have to make do with what you have. That may mean going to a laundromat, but it will also mean staying out of financial difficulties and having greater peace of mind.

It really isn't correct to say that paying cash is the least expensive method of payment because you pay no finance charges. When you purchase a consumer durable good on credit, you are buying two separate items. One is the durable good, such as the washer or dryer; the other is the use of someone else's money for a specified period of time. In both cases, a cost is involved: In the latter, it is interest; in the former, it is the purchase price or annual average price per year of useful life of the equipment. As in all cases when purchasing credit, you must use the same shopping techniques you would use to buy anything. We have covered these techniques already in Chapter 12 and in Consumer Issue I.

COPING WITH FAULTY EQUIPMENT

Sometimes consumer durables may be defective and need repair or replacement. Of course, we are all used to buying products for which there is a statement attached attesting to a "money back guarantee" or "full satisfaction guaranteed." But such guarantees often aren't worth much more than the paper on which they were printed. Warranties on equipment have traditionally been varied in scope and applicability. Consumers often have not known what was really being guaranteed and what was not. According to the President's Task Force report on appliance warranties and service:

> The majority of the major appliance warranties currently in use contain exceptions and exclusions which are unfair to the purchaser and which are unnecessary from the standpoint of protecting the manufacturer from unjustified claims or excessive liability.

Early in the 1970s, the Federal Trade Commission observed that automobile warranties given by car manufacturers and dealers were not "adequate." A survey by an appliance industry organization, the Major Appliance Consumer Action Panel (MACAP), revealed that many warranties did not state the name and address of the warrantor, did not mention the product or part covered, did not indicate the length of the warranty, and did not indicate what the warrantor would actually do and who would pay for it. Instead, they presented the coverage in "legalese" that would be difficult for the average consumer to understand.

The New Warranty Act

Much of this has been changed by legislation. The Magnuson-Moss Warranty—Federal Trade Commission Improvement Act of 1975 closed many of the loopholes that manufacturers had included in their warranties. The act does not require that a manufacturer provide a written warranty or a guarantee, but if a warranty is offered, it has to comply with the following legal provisions.

1. Any warranty on a product that costs fifteen dollars or more must include a simple, complete, and conspicuous statement of the following: name and address of warrantor, a description of what is covered and for how much, a step-by-step procedure for placing warranty claims, an explanation of how disputes between the parties will be settled, and the warranty's duration. This must be available to the consumer as prepurchase information.
2. Manufacturers cannot require as a condition of the warranty that the buyer of the product use it only in connection with other products or services that are identified by brand or corporate name. In other words, the maker of a flashlight cannot require that the purchaser use only Duracell batteries in that flashlight for the warranty to be effective.

Full versus Limited Warranties

If a warranty meets minimum federal standards, it can be designated a **full warranty.** If it doesn't, it must be designated explicitly as a **limited warranty.** Under a full warranty, the consumer merely informs the warrantor that the product is defective, does not work properly, or doesn't conform to the written warranty. The warrantor must then fix the product within a reasonable time and without any charge whatsoever. In fact, in order to obtain the designation "full warranty," the warrantor must pay the consumer for all incidental expenses if there are unreasonable delays or other problems in getting the warranty honored.

FULL WARRANTY
A warranty under which the consumer merely informs the warrantor that the product is defective or doesn't work correctly. Then the warrantor must fix or replace the product within a reasonable amount of time without charge.

LIMITED WARRANTY
Other than full warranty.

Further, the Federal Trade Commission now has the power to set a limit on the number of unsuccessful repair attempts possible under a full warranty. If, after a reasonable number of repairs, the product is still defective, the customer can choose between a refund or a replacement. The replacement must be made free of charge. If the refund option is chosen, the warrantor can deduct an amount for "reasonable depreciation based on actual use."

Full warranties apply to both initial purchasers and to those who buy the product secondhand during the warranty period.

Settling Disputes

Under the new law, consumers who are unsatisfied with what the warrantor has done for them must try an informal settlement procedure first. Then, if still dissatisfied, the consumer may sue and is entitled to recovery of purchase costs, damages, and attorneys' fees if the suit is won.

If many consumers feel they have been victimized by a fraudulent warranty, they may engage in a federal class action suit. At least 100 consumers with a minimum claim of $25 each must be involved, and the total amount in controversy must be at least $50,000.

IMPLIED WARRANTIES

Up to this point, we have been discussing what are considered *express warranties* because they are *expressly* pointed out in some written document, such as on a label or a card enclosed with an instruction booklet for a consumer durable. There are also several types of *implied warranties* that the law derives by implication or inference from the nature of the transaction. No implied warranties are covered under the Magnuson-Moss Warranty Act. They are created according to the Uniform Commercial Code, which is the code of law governing sales of items in the United States. There are basically two types of implied warranties: one of merchantability, the other of fitness.

Implied Warranty of Merchantability

IMPLIED WARRANTY OF MERCHANTABILITY
An implicit promise by the seller that an item is reasonably fit for the general purpose for which it is sold.

An **implied warranty of merchantability** arises in every sale of goods made by a merchant who deals in goods of the kind sold. Thus, a retailer of ski equipment makes an implied warranty of merchantability every time he or she sells a pair of skis, but a neighbor selling skis at a garage sale does not.

Goods that are merchantable are "reasonably fit for the ordinary purposes for which such goods are used." They must be of at least average, fair, or medium-grade quality—not the finest quality and not the worst. The quality must be comparable to quality that will pass without objection in the trade or market for goods of the same description. Some examples of nonmerchantable goods include: light bulbs that explode when switched on, pajamas that burst into flames upon slight contact with a stove burner, high-heeled shoes that break under normal use, or shotgun shells that explode prematurely.

The implied warranty of merchantability imposes *absolute* liability for the safe performance of their product upon merchants when dealing in their line of goods. It makes no difference that the merchant might not have known of a defect or could not have discovered it.

Implied Warranty of Fitness

IMPLIED WARRANTY OF FITNESS
An implicit warranty of fitness for a particular purpose, meaning that the seller guarantees the product for the specific purpose for which a buyer will use the goods, when the seller is offering his or her skill and judgment as to suitable selection of the right products.

There is an **implied warranty of fitness** for a particular purpose whenever any seller (merchant or nonmerchant) knows the particular purpose for which a buyer will use the goods *and* knows that the buyer has relied upon the seller's skill and judgment to select suitable goods.

A "particular purpose of the buyer" differs from the concept of merchantability. Goods can be *merchantable* but still not fit the buyer's particular purpose. For example, house paints suitable for ordinary walls are not suitable for painting stucco walls. A contract can include both a warranty of merchantability *and* a warranty of fitness for a particular purpose that relates to the specific use or special situation in which a buyer intends to use the goods. For example, a seller recommends a particular pair of shoes, *knowing* that a customer is looking for mountain-climbing shoes. The buyer purchases the shoes *relying* on the seller's judgment. If the shoes are found to be suitable only for walking, and not for mountain climbing, the seller has breached the warranty of fitness for a particular purpose.

A seller does not need "actual knowledge" of the buyer's particular purpose. It is sufficient if a seller "has reason to know" the purpose. However, the buyer must have relied upon the seller's skill or judgment in selecting or furnishing suitable goods in order for an implied warranty to be created. For example, Judy Josephs buys a shortwave radio from Sam's Electronics, telling the salesperson that she wants a set strong enough to pick up Radio Luxembourg. Sam's Electronics sells Judy Josephs a Model XYZ set. The set works, but it will not pick up Radio Luxembourg. Judy Josephs wants her money back. Here, since Sam's Electroncis is guilty of a breach of implied warranty of fitness for the buyer's particular purpose, Judy Josephs will be able to recover. The salesperson knew specifically that she wanted a set that would pick up Radio Luxembourg. Furthermore, Judy Josephs relied upon the salesperson to furnish a radio that would fulfill this purpose. Sam's Electronics did not do so. Therefore, the warranty was breached.

Rarely does something good come about free of charge.

THE COST SIDE OF IMPROVED WARRANTIES

Rarely does something good come about free of charge. Certainly, improved warranties and expanded product liability are appreciated by aggrieved consumers, but benefits will be paid for by all consumers as a group. Consider just the product liability side of the question.

Manufacturers are now liable for many injuries that consumers suffer when using their products, unlike a number of years ago. Injured consumers can now collect for pain and suffering and the like if it is due to a faulty product; this is true even in some cases where the consumer was using the product in an inappropriate manner. Manufacturers now are faced with an increasing number of liability suits. From 1970 to 1977, the number of product liability claims jumped almost 45 percent, according to the Insurance Services Office, a national insurance rating and advisory organization. The average loss per claim in the United States had jumped 250 percent in that same time period.

Manufacturers have attempted to protect themselves from such claims by increasing the amount of liability insurance that they purchase. Such insurance policies protect manufacturers from damage claims filed by users of the manufacturer's product. But, as liability claims have increased in both number and size, so, too, have the insurance costs of such manufacturers. The average member of the National Machine Tool Builders Association paid $71,000 for product liability in 1976, as opposed to $10,000 in 1970. It is clear that these increased costs that manufacturers must sustain are and will continue to be passed on to the consuming public. That means that the prices of the equipment that you buy will be higher because of your ability to get larger awards if you are injured when using the product. Moreover, manufacturers will be more inclined to provide safer and higher-quality products in order to avoid more costly lawsuits because of someone being injured by a defective product. But that means that equipment will, therefore, have a higher price tag because of the expenses involved in making that equipment safer and of higher quality. We can surmise that the consumer will be faced with a smaller array of options to choose from in the equipment market in terms of quality. Lower-quality and less-safe products gradually will disappear. For many consumers, such a change is beneficial. They prefer to pay a higher price for a safer product and to not have to worry about avoiding less-safe products. Low-income persons, however, may not feel they can afford the more expensive item.

TWO SYSTEMS OF PRODUCT LIABILITY—A PROPOSAL

Consumers who don't think they are getting a fair deal because of increased product liability say that they don't want to pay the higher price for the higher-quality product but would prefer to buy the lower-quality product and have more income to spend on other items. One possible way to satisfy both those who want safer products and those who do not is to allow manufacturers to set up two types of product-liability systems. The first type would basically be a no-fault system in which, no matter what happened, the consumer who purchased the product would be fully reimbursed for pain, suffering, lost income, inconvenience, and the like due to the use of the manufacturer's product. This would be similar to a full warranty. The consumer would have to pay extra for this full-liability aspect of the product. The same product also would be offered with no liability, or very little. In other words, it would be extremely difficult for the consumer to sue the manufacturer if that consumer had opted for this liability system. However, those consumers would not have to pay the higher price. They could buy the product at a "bargain" price, knowing full well that they could not sue very easily if they suffered injury using the product.

Is such a system workable? We don't know. But we do know that such a system would give consumers the choice of either paying or not paying for full product liability. Today, if current trends continue in the courts, all consumers will be required to pay the higher price of full product liability, even if they don't want to.

SUMMARY

1. Consumers purchase consumer durables that often yield a service flow over a lifetime, are often financed on credit, wear out, and must be cared for and replaced.
2. The purchase of a consumer durable involves part consumption and part saving because the durable, by definition, does not wear out immediately. In order to make rational decisions when buying equipment, consumers must undertake a cost-benefit analysis.
3. Costs of a durable good include, at a minimum, depreciation, operating costs, repairs, and foregone interest.
4. Whether or not credit should be used to purchase a durable good depends on whether a safe debt load has been reached.
5. Legislation passed in 1975 tightened the definition of warranty that manufacturers can use. Improved warranties, however, will lead to higher-priced goods and perhaps a reduced-quality array.
6. The Uniform Commercial Code stipulates that every good sold by a merchant (a person dealing in those same kinds of goods) has an implied warranty of merchantability. Additionally, any person who sells a good for a specific purpose gives an implied warranty of fitness for that specific purpose.

QUESTIONS FOR THOUGHT AND DISCUSSION

1. Why is the purchase of a stereo a form of saving?
2. Is there any special reason individuals associate buying consumer durable goods with buying on credit?
3. Why must we consider interest if we purchase a consumer durable with cash?
4. Do you think it is possible for manufacturers to offer better warranties without raising the price of the product?

THINGS TO DO

1. Look at the warranties of any consumer products that you have recently purchased or are about to purchase. Do any of them give full warranties? If they are limited warranties, under what conditions can you have the product repaired or replaced?
2. Calculate the amount of saving that went into the purchase of a durable good that you now own. (Hint: Figure out how many years it will last.)

SELECTED READINGS

"Adding Insult to Injury: The Drive to Change the Product-Liability Laws." *Consumer Reports,* July 1978, pp. 412–16.

Clarkson, Kenneth W. *et al. West's Business Law,* 2nd. ed. St. Paul, Minn.: West Publishing Co., 1983, Chapters 20 and 21.

Consumer Research Center. *The Product Liability Controversy: A Handbook for Consumers.* Washington, D.C.: Consumer Federation of America, 1979.

"The Failure of Product Recalls." *Consumer Reports,* January 1981, pp. 45–48.

Gerner, Jennifer and Bryant, Keith. "Appliance Warranties as a Market Signal?" *The Journal of Consumer Affairs,* Summer 1981.

Marr, Janet. "The Magnuson-Moss Warranty Act." *Family Economics Review,* Summer 1978, pp. 307.

Tippett, Kathryn S. "Service Life of Appliances by Selected Household Characteristics." *Family Economics Review,* Summer 1978, pp. 7–10.

Consumer ISSUE  

BUYING AND SERVICING YOUR CONSUMER DURABLES

GLOSSARY

SERVICE CONTRACT—For an annual fee, the appliance owner receives a contract allowing for all repairs to be made without further payments.

Every household must constantly make decisions about buying, repairing, and replacing consumer durable items. A college student may merely rent most items, along with an apartment or a dormitory room. That is to say, basic household furnishings are paid for in the monthly or school-year payment for rent. Single persons just out of college or a young couple starting a household together will have a large number of purchase decisions to make, particularly when they move into their first house.

PLANNING IS IMPORTANT

Different consumer durables last for different periods of time. They must, therefore, be replaced at different periods of time. For example, the average replacement age of a washing machine is ten years; a dryer, fourteen years; ranges, freezers, and refrigerators, fifteen years. These figures will change, depending roughly on how well the item is taken care of, its initial quality, and the frequency of its use. For example, a washing machine will last longer in a family where there are no children because it will not be used as often.

Given that major appliances have a limited life, you must plan for potential future use, not just for what may be needed for the next year or so. For example, a couple setting up a household and planning to have children may consider purchasing larger-capacity refrigerators and ranges in anticipation of having more mouths to feed in a few years. The same would be true for a washing machine. It may be more expensive to buy a small clothes washer now and have to replace it with a larger-capacity one three years from now when there is another person in the family.

Operating Costs

When making plans for the purchase and use of major equipment, operating costs must also be considered. Such costs can be estimated for the near future but not for the distant future because of the rapidly changing energy scene. Consumer Issue G gave some tips on how to save energy costs. Here, let us consider whether you should choose to have gas or electric appliances. Of course, those individuals who live in areas in the United States that do not offer natural gas to residents don't have a choice. Liquid propane that is delivered directly to the house and stored in large cylinders can be used as a substitute. To make a rational choice between gas and electric major appliances, you must consider the following factors:

1. The relative cost of gas and electricity in your area
2. The difference in the initial cost of the appliance, depending on whether it is for gas or electric energy sources
3. The availability of the alternative energy sources in your area in the future

4. Comparative costs of installing either type of equipment
5. Your preferences

In order to determine how much major and minor appliances will cost you per year, you can use Exhibit N–1, which gives an estimate of the average wattage per appliance, the average hours used per year, the average kilowatt hours used per year, and the yearly cost at an estimated 7.10 cents per kilowatt. That figure is the estimated national average residential charge based on figures from the Department of Energy.

Servicing Costs

In making a spending plan for durable goods, you must also consider what servicing costs will be. This can be done easily in the case of major appliances that have specific full warranties for one, two, or three years. It can also be calculated easily if you decide to purchase a service contract each year after the full warranty has terminated.

Filling Out the Spending Plan

Exhibit N–2 presents a possible spending plan for you to fill out. Some people like to plan one year ahead; others, two; and others, three. The planning period really is a function of how rapidly you believe your economic situation is going to change. The faster you think it will change, the shorter your planning period should be.

If the total cost of the household equipment that you plan to buy or replace during the planning period exceeds the amount of money that you anticipate you will have available, then obviously you must change your plans. You can postpone or eliminate purchases; you also can look for substitutes. If, initially, you cannot afford a new washing machine, then you can use laundromats. If you desire a larger-capacity refrigerator but cannot afford one,

APPLIANCE	AVERAGE WATTAGE	AVERAGE HOURS USED PER YEAR	AVERAGE KILOWATT HOURS USED PER YEAR	YEARLY COST AT 7.10¢ PER KILOWATT HOUR	YOUR COST
Air-conditioner (window)	1,566	750	1,175	$ 83.43	$______
Blender	386	39	15	1.07	______
Clothes dryer	4,856	204	993	70.50	______
Coffee maker	894	119	106	7.53	______
Deep fryer	1,448	57	83	5.89	______
Fan (attic)	370	786	291	20.66	______
Fan (circulating)	88	489	43	3.05	______
Freezer (frostless, 15 cubic feet)	440	4,002	1,761	125.03	______
Frying pan	1,196	157	188	13.35	______
Hair dryer	381	37	14	.99	______
Heater (portable)	1,322	133	176	12.50	______
Iron	1,008	143	144	10.22	______
Mixer	127	102	13	.92	______
Oven (microwave)	1,500	200	300	21.30	______
Oven (self-cleaning)	4,800	239	1,147	81.44	______
Radio/phonograph	109	1,000	109	7.74	______
Range	8,200	128	1,050	74.55	______
Refrigerator (frostless, 14 cubic feet)	326	3,448	1,124	79.80	______
Refrigerator/freezer (14 cubic feet)	615	2,947	1,812	128.65	______
Roaster	1,333	154	205	14.56	______
Sewing Machine	75	147	11	.78	______
Toaster	1,146	34	39	2.77	______
TV (black & white, solid state)	55	1,500	83	5.89	______
TV (color, solid state)	200	1,500	300	21.30	______
Vacuum cleaner	630	73	46	3.27	______
Washing machine (automatic)*	521	198	103	7.31	______
Waste disposer	445	67	30	2.13	______
Water heater	4,474	1,075	4,810	341.51	______

*Not including water heating

EXHIBIT N–1
Cost of Operating Selected Major and Minor Appliances per Year

you will substitute your time, effort, and the use of your car in going to the store more often.

BUYING TIPS

Although it would be difficult in a few pages to present all the different principles that relate specifically to buying each available major and minor appliance—as well as giving characteristics of different types of rugs, furniture, and bedding—we can present a few general principles that might help you make decisions on consumer durables.

1. **Before you begin checking various stores, check consumer information publications,** such as *Consumer Reports* or *Consumers' Research Magazine.* Also ask your friends about their experiences with various dealers and appliance brands.
2. **Do comparison shopping at all times.**
3. **Attempt to compare prices based on a constant quality unit of the consumer durable.** In other words, take into account the service offered by different dealers, the convenience of their locations, and so on when comparing prices.
4. **Read and understand all contracts before signing.** Know what your obligations are.
5. **Do not "overspend" your time in comparison shopping.** Checking two or three reliable dealers may be sufficient.

6. Check guarantees and warranties before purchasing the item. Make sure you understand what they mean. Any points that are not clear should be clarified by the seller (preferably in writing).

7. Use a shopping list and keep it practical. Include all relevant information that will help you make a wise choice. For example, if you are going to look for a carpet, know the room size, and bring along a sample of the paint and fabrics in the room to coordinate with the carpet color. Or ask the store owner if you can take some samples with you to see how they look in your home.

8. Consider how the item will be used before you make your choice. Don't spend money, for example, on a highly durable carpet that will be in a room used only occasionally.

9. Consider which features of the durable good are most important to you. If you truly dislike cleaning an oven, then a self-cleaning one is important, even though its operating costs may be quite high.

10. Remember that quality and price often, but not always, go hand in hand. Thus, you may seek out a lower-quality durable good if the item is necessary and you don't think you can afford the higher quality, or if the item is for temporary or limited use.

Bargains in Shopping

Scanning the classified ads in a newspaper is sometimes a good way to find essentially new items at drastically reduced prices. When you're in the market for a major appliance, browse through the classified section of your newspaper. You may be amazed to find just what you want—at bargain prices.

There are also many other places to purchase secondhand items, including auctions, flea markets, garage sales, and secondhand stores. Anyone interested in this method of saving money should read Suzanne Wymelenberg's and Douglas Matthews's book,

EXHIBIT N–2
Consumer Durable Spending Plan for the Period _______ to _______

PURCHASES OF CONSUMER DURABLES	ESTIMATED COSTS	DATE OF ANTICIPATED PURCHASES	AMOUNT OF MONEY TO ACCUMULATE EACH PLANNING PERIOD
Washer	________	________	________
Dryer	________	________	________
Refrigerator	________	________	________
Freezer	________	________	________
Range	________	________	________
Oven	________	________	________
Dishwasher	________	________	________
Trash compactor	________	________	________
Vacuum cleaner	________	________	________
Carpets (list each room separately)	________	________	________
Furniture (list each room separately)	________	________	________
Blender	________	________	________
Toaster	________	________	________
TV	________	________	________
Stereo	________	________	________
Other consumer durables	________	________	________
COST OF OPERATION AND SERVICING	**ESTIMATED COST**	**ESTIMATED FREQUENCY**	**AMOUNT OF MONEY TO ACCUMULATE EACH PLANNING PERIOD**
Washer	________	________	________
Dryer	________	________	________
Other	________	________	________

Total amount of money available to spend for purchase and servicing of consumer durables during planning period: ________

Secondhand Is Better (Arbor House, 1975). Secondhand stores are often listed in the Yellow Pages under specific categories, such as furniture. You usually get a wider selection at a secondhand store than can be found at a garage sale or in the classified ads.

Shopping for Safety

Safety may be one of the most important aspects of any product you buy; thus, it is important for you to consider the safety features of any consumer durable on your shopping list. In Exhibit N–3 you can check off the safety features that are available for the items you wish to buy.

SERVICING YOUR CONSUMER DURABLES

Virtually all consumer durable goods require some type of servicing and care throughout their useful life. In fact, homeowners can attest that the more appliances there are in the household, the more time and money they must spend having them repaired.

The Pros and Cons of a Service Contract

Whenever a new appliance is purchased—particularly a washer, dryer, freezer, refrigerator, and, to a lesser extent, stereo equipment—it is possible to purchase a **service contract** that covers all parts and labor for a specified period after the full or limited warranty runs out. For example, if you purchase a refrigerator from J. C. Penney or from Sears, the store will offer you a full service contract for a specified amount of time. In a sense, a service contract is really a purchase of insurance. You pay a predetermined amount of money each year in order to avoid the possibility of having to pay a larger amount on costly repairs. You are betting that you would have paid a larger amount in repairs than the service contract actually costs. The seller of the service contract is betting that, on average, for all the individuals who purchase such contracts, the repairs will cost less than the total amount collected. Clearly, on the average, the seller of service contracts must be right because the seller must make a profit on that venture. Does that mean that you always lose out by purchasing such a contract? No, you don't. That would be equivalent to saying that you lose out on a life insurance policy unless you die prematurely. If a service contract is regarded as insurance, then buying it makes sense for individuals who do not want to face the prospect of unusually large repair bills at any time during the year.

There is another positive aspect to purchasing a service contract. You may decide to have smaller, less important repairs performed more frequently under a service contract than you would if you had to pay each time you called the serviceperson. In so doing, you may extend the useful life of the appliance, thereby delaying the need to replace that appliance.

Money magazine does not believe that service contracts on many appliances are warranted.[2] They suggest that you base your decision on whether to buy a service contract on the first year's performance of the appliance. Refrigerators, freezers, and clothes dryers have very low repair frequency rates during the second through fifth years. Unless you bought a lemon, which should be obvious during the first year, the money on a service contract for any of these appliances is probably unwarranted. The same holds for a central furnace until it is several years old.

EXHIBIT N–3
A Safety Checklist for New and Used Appliances

☑ **1.** When door or cover is open, washer, dryer, dishwasher, or microwave range automatically stops.

☑ **2.** The "off" controls are clearly indicated.

☑ **3.** Both stationary and portable appliances have three-pronged grounding electric plugs, particularly those to be used outdoors or in damp places (not necessary, however, on toasters and open-coil heating units).

☑ **4.** Trash compactors and self-cleaning ovens have safety locks so they cannot be opened during operation.

☑ **5.** Refrigerators, dryers, and freezers have doors that can be pushed open from inside so that children cannot be trapped.

☑ **6.** Control knobs are beyond the reach of small children.

THE COST OF A SERVICE CONTRACT. Exhibit N–4 gives the annual cost by year of service contracts for a TV and a washer. In addition, there is a total cost over the six-year period. As the exhibit shows, the annual cost rises as the unit becomes older. When looked at over a six-year period, the total service contract costs seem quite out of proportion to the cost of the appliance. Thus, one might conclude that a service contract is best suited for individuals who do not take care of their appliances.

BEFORE YOU CALL A SERVICEPERSON. Because service calls are costly, you should go through the following checklist to see if you can solve the problem yourself and not have to pay someone else to repair your appliance.

2. "Unwarranted Appliance Service Contracts." *Money*, February 1977, p. 62.

APPLIANCE	ANNUAL COST BY YEAR OF OWNERSHIP 1 and 2*	3	4	5	6	TOTAL COST FOR SIX YEARS
Clothes washer	$45	$45	$49	$50	$ 58	$247
Color TV	58	71	81	89	102	401

*Cost of coverage for years 1 and 2 were added together because many service contracts handle them this way. This simply means that part or all of the first year's coverage is reflected in the warranty.

EXHIBIT N–4
Cost Per Year of Service Contract over a Six-Year Period

1. Make sure that you have read carefully and followed all the manufacturer's instructions. In many instruction booklets for durable goods, there is a troubleshooter's checklist that may help you solve your problem very simply. Many wasted dollars are spent on service calls just to have the serviceperson unplug the drain in a self-defrosting refrigerator, even though the owner could have done it very easily with the help of the instruction booklet.
2. Check fuses or circuit breakers.
3. Make sure gas, water, or electric connections have been turned on correctly.

If all else fails, call the serviceperson and give the model number of your appliance (taken from the nameplate). This often avoids paying for two service calls: one to see what was wrong and the second to bring a part that could have been in the serviceperson's truck to begin with.

WHAT TO DO WHEN YOU HAVE A COMPLAINT

If you have a complaint about a consumer durable that has not been satisfied by the seller of that good, you may wish to contact the company that manufactured or distributed the product. A polite letter telling what has happened and what you want the company to do about it usually will bring some action. Address your letter to the customer relations department; be sure that you make a copy of your letter and that you enclose *copies* of sales slips, guarantees, agreements, cancelled checks, receipts, or contracts. Never mail the originals! Send your complaint either by certified or registered mail, return receipt requested.

If you still do not receive satisfaction, you may wish to contact one of the following private organizations.

1. Appliances: Major Appliance Consumer Action Panel (MACAP). See Exhibit N–5. You can call Westinghouse at (800) 245-0600 and Whirlpool at (800) 253-1301. For other manufacturers, write the Consumer Relations Department at the address given on the model and serial number plate or in the instruction manual. (If you have lost your appliance instruction manual, write American Home Appliance Manufacturers at the same address as MACAP, or call (312) 984-5800.)
2. Carpets and rugs: Carpet and Rug Industry Consumer Action Panel (CRICAP), Box 1568, Dalton, Georgia 30720.
3. Furniture: Furniture Industry Consumer Advisory Panel, P.O. 951, High Point, North Carolina 27261. Phone: (919) 885-5065. If you still do not receive satisfaction, you may wish to contact your state's Consumer Protection Agency, which was listed in Consumer Issue A.

SUMMARY

1. Because major appliances have a limited life, it is useful to set up a household plan to determine needed purchases and replacement.

EXHIBIT N–5
The Right Way to Complain

If you have a problem that you haven't been able to solve locally, write or call the manufacturer, giving all details. If that doesn't resolve the difficulty, write or call collect MACAP, 20 N. Wacker Dr., Chicago, Illinois 60606, telephone (312) 236-3175.

Include the following information:

☐ Your name, address, and telephone number
☐ Type of appliance, brand, model, serial number
☐ Date of purchase
☐ Dealer's name and address and service agent's name and address if different from dealer's
☐ Clear, concise description of the problem and service performed to date

MACAP cautions that it is important to keep receipts of repairs even when a service call is under warranty. The receipts may be required to prove an appliance needed excessive repairs and should be replaced.

2. When making plans for purchases, consider operating costs. These are a function of the relative costs of gas and electricity, initial cost of appliance, and installation costs.
3. Service contracts are available on most appliances. Experts recommend, however, that they are not necessarily a good deal for refrigerators, freezers, and clothes dryers, which traditionally don't require many repairs.
4. Complaints about appliances may be lodged with the Major Appliance Consumer Action Panel, the Carpet and Rug Industry Consumer Action Panel, and the Furniture Industry Consumer Advisory Panel.

QUESTIONS FOR THOUGHT AND DISCUSSION

1. Should you be concerned about a potential energy "crisis"?
2. When would it be advisable to purchase a service contract on a major or minor appliance?
3. Most items listed in the safety checklist in Exhibit N–3 are required by law. When would you want to use such a checklist?

THINGS TO DO

1. Write MACAP to obtain information on how successful that organization has been.
2. Take the safety checklist, Exhibit N–3, with you to an appliance store. Are there any particular brands of appliances that do not conform to that checklist? Ask the salesperson if he or she knows why.

SELECTED READINGS

"Do-it-yourself Sources for Appliance Parts." *Workbench,* January/February, 1980, pp. 124–29.

Handbook of Buying Issue. Consumers' Research Magazine, October 1980.

"Quick Fixes for Small Appliance Problems," *Popular Mechanics,* August 1979, pp. 98–99.

Rush, A. "Appliance Repairs: How to Make Sure You Get What You Pay For." *McCalls,* February 1980.

"Shopping Tips: Automatic Washers and Dryers." *Changing Times,* April 1977.

Consumer ISSUE 10

BUYING A HOME PERSONAL COMPUTER

GLOSSARY

CENTRAL PROCESSING UNIT (CPU)—The heart of the computer, it is composed of several sections and directs the activities of the computer.

DISK DRIVE—The mechanical device used to rotate a disk during data transmission.

MICROPROCESSOR—The central processing unit of a microcomputer, it fits on a small silicone chip.

OPERATING SYSTEM—A collection of programs designed to permit a computer system to manage itself.

OUTPUT—The information that comes from the computer as a result of processing.

PRINTER—The device that produces hard copy computer output.

REGISTER—An internal computer component used for temporary storage.

SOFTWARE—Programs used to direct the computer in problem solving.

No one needs to be told that the age of the computer is upon us. The number and kinds available, and the uses to which personal home computers can be put, are already staggering. It is estimated that, within the next two to three decades, the personal home computer will become as common as the television set. Computers have been around for a long time, but small, so-called microcomputers for home use are relatively new to the consumer scene. It all started back in 1980 when Steve Jobs and Stephen Wozniak made a home model in their garage and started selling it. So began the Apple revolution. The Apple computer is the second biggest-selling microcomputer in the world, although the number of competitors is growing at an astounding rate.

WHAT A COMPUTER CONSISTS OF

At the heart of every microcomputer is what is called the **microprocessor.** This microprocessor controls the memory and the input and **output** of the computer. In a microcomputer, the microprocessor is small enough to fit on a fingertip. Larger model computers have what is called a **central processing unit (CPU)** that serves the same function. Along with the microprocessor is a set of **registers.** These registers are devices that receive, hold, and transfer information quickly. They are designed for temporary storage. Microcomputers have fewer registers than large computers, and they are slower.

Actually, there are many other differences between microcomputers and the larger model computers. But from the consumer point of view, the major difference is cost. Microcomputers are designed for one person or one task, so the **operating system** is less complex. Nonetheless, microcomputers are powerful in proportion to their size. To fully understand the power of the current group of personal computers, consider that, in the 1960s, the International Business Machines (IBM) 360 Model 30, which was the big computer that most universities, hospitals, and government agencies used, required an air-conditioned room about eighteen feet square. In the 1960s, it cost $280,000, which in today's dollars would be at least equivalent to $600,000. IBM's desk-top personal computer today costs about $4,000 to $5,000. It is not much bigger than a typewriter, and it performs about as many functions and at a faster speed than the big, mainframe IBM computer of the 1960s.

SOFTWARE TELLS IT ALL

The previous discussion focused on hardware, or the actual physical parts of the microcomputer. But no matter how sophisticated the hardware is, it is useless without appropriate software. **Software** is the general term used for all the programs that tell the computer what to do. One of the major questions that the prospective buyer of a microcomputer must ask is: "What software is available for me?" In other words, if you are buying a personal computer to help in your business decision making, as well as to prepare federal income-tax returns, you must make sure that there is software compatible with your hardware that will carry out those tasks. Otherwise, unless you are a very sophisticated programmer yourself, you will have difficulty using your microcomputer. This leads you to the first step in choosing your personal computer: You have to analyze your software requirements. After you do this, you can select a model that is compatible with your software needs.

WHERE TO BUY YOUR COMPUTER

There are numerous places to purchase computers today. In many large cities, Xerox and IBM have retail stores in which their own computers, as well as those of other manufacturers, are sold. Radio Shack sells only its own computers, but it has a very extensive line of both hardware and software. Sears is now selling the IBM personal computer. Many lower-priced models of personal computers manufactured by Commodore, Atari, Texas Instruments, and Timex can be found in large retail outlets, such as K-Mart. Finally, there are specialty stores, such as Computerland, where a large number of computers are available and where a trained sales staff can give you demonstrations and explain to you the various features of the different computers.

You can buy virtually anything relating to microcomputing through the mail at a substantial discount. Just check out what's available in one of the numerous computer magazines, such as *Byte* or *Personal Computing*. When purchasing by mail, however, service may be a problem. If you pay a higher price and purchase your item at a local store, you may be able to take it back and get quick turnaround repair service or a replacement for defective products. But mail-order houses do not support the products they sell; they are simply shipping outfits that can tell you where to send your product when something goes wrong.

SHOULD YOU BE PRICE CONSCIOUS?

Most consumers are very price conscious about major purchases. When you are buying your first microcomputer, you should be also. However, the lowest-priced microcomputers usually have very little support or service. Thus, in the long run, you could spend more. Timex, for example, sells a small personal computer for less than $100. If you are serious about using a microcomputer for your work or as a word processor later on, it wouldn't be wise to purchase a Timex. Basically, you have to look at your present software needs and those you anticipate having in the future.

In order to have maximum capability for future software needs, you should purchase a microcomputer that at least can support the so-called CP/M operating system. This is a universal language translator common throughout most of the United States. It is actually an industry standard. More software is available for the CP/M operating system than for any other operating system in the world. The Apple IIe computer, for example, can support the CP/M operating system with the purchase of some additional equipment.

Another key factor in determining what you should buy is the amount of internal memory, i.e., memory built right into the machine itself. For example, most programs that are at all sophisticated require quite a bit of internal memory.

OTHER KEY FEATURES TO CONSIDER

Do you want to play games in color and also have color graphics? If so, then you'll want to buy a personal computer that has color display capabilities. The Atari 800, for example, has 256 different colors in it.

The keyboard is another sensitive issue. Most offer standard touch-sensitive keys. The Atari, on the other hand, offers a pressure-sensitive keyboard. Additionally, if you decide you want to use your personal computer as a word processor, then you have to make sure that the keyboard is sufficiently sophisticated to make word processing easy for you.

It is no longer worthwhile to purchase a personal computer that uses cassettes in order to generate

programs or store information. Purchase only a personal computer that has disk-drive capabilities for external storage. Most personal computers use a 5½-inch **disk drive.** You simply purchase so-called mini-floppy disks and insert them. Finally, the **printer** may be an important aspect of your purchase. If you only want the computer for business output or fun and games, then you shouldn't worry too much about the quality or the speed of the printer. If, however, you eventually want to use your microcomputer as a word processor, then you have to decide whether you want letter-quality printing. Letter-quality printing used to cost quite a bit, but recently letter-quality printers have been advertised by mail-order houses for less than $700.

BEFORE YOU SIGN THAT CONTRACT

Be careful what you sign when you buy your first microcomputer system. Don't sign any contract that disclaims your implied warranty rights. Also, make sure that you include in the contract a clause stating that you are not a computer expert; you are, therfore, relying on the expertise of the salesperson to recommend the right computer for your specific problems. (A warranty of fitness for a particular purpose is discussed in Chapter 16.)

SUMMARY

1. It is estimated that, within the next two to three decades, the personal home computer will be as common as the household television set. The number and kinds of computers, and the uses to which they can now be put, are already numerous.

2. At the heart of every microcomputer is the microprocessor, which controls the memory and the input and output of the computer. The central processing unit in a larger-model computer serves the same function. This is called the hardware system of the computer.

3. Because microcomputers are designed for individual use, their operating system is less complex than for a larger computer. Nonetheless, they are powerful in proportion to their size.

4. Software is the general term used for all programs that tell the computer what to do. Analyzing your software requirements is the first step in choosing a personal computer. After you do this, you can select a model that is compatible with your software needs.

5. Computers can be purchased from a variety of sellers: retail stores, specialty stores, mail-order houses, and so on. You usually can purchase computer-related materials from a mail-order house at a discount. You should, however, be aware that service may be a problem if you do so. Specialty stores usually offer a variety of computers and materials and employ trained sales personnel who can provide demonstrations and offer other important information to you.

6. While there are several differences between microcomputers and the larger models, from the consumer standpoint the major difference is cost. Although it is important to be price conscious when purchasing your first computer, it should be noted that the lower-priced models usually have very little support or service. In the long run, then, you may end up paying more than if you purchased an intermediate- or higher-priced model. When purchasing a computer, always keep in mind your current and future software needs.

7. For maximum capability for future software needs, you should buy a microcomputer that can support the CP/M operating system. The CP/M system is the universal language translator most common throughout the United States.

8. The amount of internal memory available in a computer is a key factor in determining the model you should buy. The keyboard is another feature to consider. In addition, if you want to have color graphics, you must buy a model with color display capabilities.

9. Purchase only a computer that has disk-drive capabilities for external storage.

10. The printer may be an important aspect of your computer purchase. If you plan to use your computer as a word processor, for example, you have to decide whether you want letter-quality printing. Printing speed is also a determinant.

11. When signing the contract for your computer purchase, be sure it does not contain disclaimers of your implied warranty rights. Also include in the contract a clause stating that you are not a computer expert and that you are relying on the expertise of the salesperson in purchasing a particular model for your purposes.

QUESTIONS FOR THOUGHT AND DISCUSSION

1. What are some ways personal computers can be used in the home today?

2. How do you think their use will be expanded in years to come? Give specific examples.

THINGS TO DO

1. If you know someone who has a home computer, ask if you can have a demonstration. What does the individual use the computer for primarily? Is he or she satisfied with the model purchased? What kind of training and service is available?

2. Visit several stores that sell computers. Get information about the various models and prices, the training offered, and the service available. What do you think would be a good choice for your purposes?

3. Check various computer magazines and compare the information you found in retail stores with what a mail-order company offers in the way of computer sales and service.

SELECTED READINGS

"The Coming Shakeout in Personal Computers." *Business Week,* November 22, 1982, pp. 72–75.

Davis, J. and Goldstein, W. "Books on Computers—A Current Checklist." *Publishers Weekly,* November 12, 1982, pp. 29–31.

Hawkins, W. J. "The Boom Is on in New Personal Computers." *Popular Science,* November 1982, p. 93.

Hedberg, A. "Choosing the Best Computer for You." *Money,* November 1982, pp. 68–70.

"Home Computers." *Money,* November 1982, p. 75.

Horwitz, S. "The Computer/Video Blitz." *Harpers Bazaar,* December 1982, p. 156.

Perry, R. L. "Using a Computer Store." *Mechanics Illustrated,* April 1982, p. 37.

Stone, A. "A Home Computer Primer." *Natural History,* November 1982, p. 84.

Thomas, D. "A Home-Style Computer." *Macleans*, October 11, 1982, pp. 57–58.

Toong, H-M. D. and Gupta, A. "Personal Computers." *Scientific American*, December 1982, pp. 86–88.

Veit, S. "Computer Clones." *Computer Electronics*, November 1982, pp. 64–65.

Veit, S. "Computer Hotline." *Computer Electronics*, November 1982, pp. 102–103.

CHAPTER
GETTING THERE BY CAR IS HALF THE WORRY

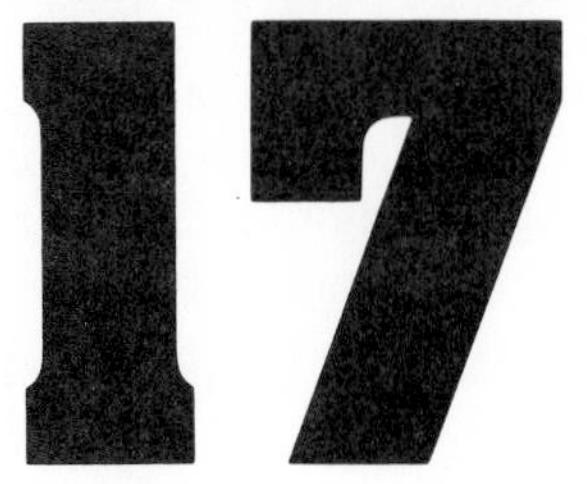

The twentieth century in America might well be called the Age of the Automobile. From a modest beginning at the turn of the century . . . right up to the beginning of the 1980s, the automobile has been a pervasive part of American life.

CHAPTER PREVIEW

- How much do we spend on transportation?
- What are the safety aspects of automobiles?
- How do safety standards affect the cost of a car?
- What are some characteristics of the automobile repair industry?
- What are some characteristics of the automobile insurance industry?
- Is no-fault insurance a good deal?

The twentieth century in America might well be called the Age of the Automobile. From a modest beginning at the turn of the century, when a few courageous souls drove around in Stutz Bearcats, Hupmobiles, and Model Ts, until the time Henry Ford developed low-cost mass-production techniques to put out an $870 "Tin Lizzie," right up to the beginning of the 1980s, when fully 88 percent of all American families owned cars, the automobile has been a pervasive part of American life.

THE CAR'S POSITION IN THE OVERALL ECONOMY

Even though it appears that automobiles are still one of the most important parts of the U.S. economy, spending on new and used cars as a percentage of the gross national product has been falling. In 1955, it reached about 5.3 percent. In 1983, the estimated spending on new and used cars was a mere 3 percent of the GNP. But that doesn't mean the automobile is going to be replaced.

WE SPEND A LOT ON CARS

In the United States today, there are over 100 million cars. The number of new cars turned out by the factories every year sometimes exceeds 7 million. Money spent on purchasing automobiles, on automobile repairs, and on other related expenses accounts for 12 percent of total income in the United States. The automobile industry itself is also huge. One out of every six people in the United States is in some way concerned with automobiles, whether it be as a factory worker in Detroit or as an employee of a company making spare parts or servicing cars. The notion beind the statement that "whatever is good for General Motors is good for America" could derive from the sheer numbers of people involved in automobile-related employment. By 1982, 80 percent of all commuters using vehicles to get to work used an automobile or truck as their major mode of transportation. Only 19 percent used public transportation, and 1 percent used other means. Additionally, of those workers using an automobile or truck, more than three-fourths drove alone. Indeed, workers show a trend toward using less public transportation. From 1970 to 1976, the percentage of workers using public transportation declined from 24 to 19 percent. (However, since 1976, the rapid rise in gasoline prices has caused this trend to turn around slightly: About 21 percent of workers used public transportation in 1980.)

FOUR-WHEELED COFFINS

Some have depicted the automobile as a four-wheeled rolling coffin, because approximately 30,000 Americans are killed every year in vehicle accidents, and 2 million others are injured. The economic cost of the injuries, deaths, and property damage exceeds $60 billion annually. Then there is the cost of pain and suffering, both for those involved in the accidents and for their loved ones. We can put no dollar figure on this tragic aspect of private transportation.

Many highway deaths could have been avoided had the drivers been more careful. But, according to some observers, many others could have been avoided if additional safety features were required on automobiles. In 1958, the Ford Motor Company tried to sell additional safety features to the American car-buying public, but sales declined, and Ford lost money. Finally, after the exposé by Ralph Nader in his book *Unsafe at Any Speed,* Congress passed the Motor Vehicle Safety Act of 1966, the basis of most current safety requirements on automobiles.

Some of the requirements imposed on car manufacturers by the National Highway Traffic Safety Administration have been:

1. Dual braking systems
2. Nonprotruding interior appliances
3. Over-the-shoulder safety belts in the front seat
4. Head restraints on all front seats
5. Seat-belt warning systems and ignition interlocks
6. Collapsible, impact-absorbing arm rests
7. Impact-absorbing instrument panels

Automobile safety devices raise the costs of automobiles. You, the consumer, pay for that safety directly out of your pocket.

The Cost of Safety

Automobile safety devices raise the costs of automobiles. You, the consumer, pay for that safety directly out of your pocket. But, of course, you get a benefit—a safer mode of transportation. It is not known, however, whether the total amount of automobile safety on the highway has dramatically risen because of the safety standards. After all, some people react to the higher relative cost of automobiles by not buying new cars as frequently as before. And the older the car, the higher the probability of a mechanical failure that could cause an accident. The average age of cars being driven on the highway today has risen as the costs of new cars have increased because of the required safety devices.

Alternatives Available

Alternatives are available that might reduce the number of accidents and injuries on the highway. Although their availability does not necessarily make these alternatives *preferable,* they still are worth thinking about.

At least half of all U.S. highway deaths are, in one way or another, related to drinking. Perhaps 50 percent of the 10,000 or so pedestrians killed every year are drunk, and 50 percent of the drivers involved in fatal highway accidents are legally drunk. In many states, to be legally drunk means a driver must have had the equivalent of three martinis on an empty stomach. Thus, many instances of poor driver judgment may be related to alcohol-induced slowness of mind and reflexes.

One alternative to the solutions already tried for increasing highway safety involves reducing the number of drunks on the road. This would mean, for example, much higher fines and stiffer jail sentences. In Sweden, for example, where there is an alcoholism problem, accidents caused by drunk driving are relatively few because the costs of being caught driving drunk are tremendous—jail and huge fines. Any time people get drunk in Sweden, they either stay where they are, they let somebody else drive, or they call a taxi or take a bus. With stiff enough fines in the United States, the same thing could be true here. Generally, though, we have been extremely lenient with drunk drivers, no matter what they do on the road. You can find people with four and five drunk-driving arrests on their records still driving. Generally, only when they kill or maim somebody do they realize their mistake. And, even then, they eventually may be drunk on the road again.

There is a reversal in that trend, however. We are now seeing stiffer penalties for drunk driving and more stringent classifications as to when a person may be considered "legally drunk." For example, California, Arizona, Wisconsin, Texas, and Florida have, in the last several years, stiffened dramatically their drunk-driving laws. Although accurate statistics are not yet available, at first blush it appears that the new, stiffer penalties for drunk driving have, in those states, reduced the number of accidents caused by drunk drivers. Presumably, other states will follow suit in relatively short order as they see the benefits resulting from getting tough with drunk drivers.

Another way of preventing fatalities and injuries resulting from accidents is to cut down on the number of road hazards and increase the ease with which people can drive safely. This would require breakaway signs, energy-absorbing materials at off ramps and around bridge abutments, and so on. Some experts have estimated that we could save more lives by investing in better roads than by paying billions of dollars a year in additional costs for safer cars. Also, sturdier cars that are more likely to withstand accidents use up more resources and take more gas to drive—further costs of safety.

THE PRIVATE COST OF DRIVING

The cost of driving a car involves more than making a monthly payment, although that is part of it. The **private costs** of driving include such things as wear and tear, repairs, gas and oil, insurance, and taxes, in addition to whatever payments are made and whatever the implicit cost is if you paid cash. (Remember the discussion in Chapter 15 about whether to buy or rent.) Exhibit 17-1 shows the estimated cost of operating an automobile as given by the American Automobile Association. It ultimately costs about 19.4 cents to 30.9 cents a mile to run a car. Repairs on cars can be quite expensive. And, in addition, you have an information problem about whether or not you are being asked to pay for more than you need when your car breaks down.

PRIVATE COSTS
The costs that are incurred by an individual and no one else. The private costs of driving a car, for example, include depreciation, gas, insurance, and so on.

The Repair Industry

The automobile repair industry is immense. There are at least 100,000 mechanics' garages in the United States, as well as 200,000 gas stations that also give repair service. In total, we probably spend $50 billion a year on automobile repairs. The labor costs for auto repairs have increased rapidly in the last few years. Obviously, it is important that you find a reputable repair shop for your car. If you know of none, ask your friends and acquaintances where they have received good repair work. Because repeat customers generally are going to be treated better, it is also advisable to take your car back to the same garage if you are satisfied. The task of finding a competent mechanic is not easy. Studies have shown that the same minor repair can cost anywhere from $50 to $300. There is also a problem with respect to overpriced "crash" parts of cars; some cars that have been involved in accidents may cost more to repair after the crash than they actually are worth.

Some consumer economists believe that preventive maintenance avoids large repair bills. This is true, but you must take account of the maintenance costs themselves. In the long run, it may be cheaper not to keep your car in perfect condition but, rather, to let some things (other than brakes, tires, and safety-related parts) wear out and replace them only when they do or to trade in your car every few years. Some state governments buy fleets of cars that they do no servicing on at all for a year and then trade in. This seems to be cheaper than trying to maintain the cars; as the price of repair services rises, this practice will become still cheaper by comparison. Thus, you have two choices: You

EXHIBIT 17–1
Cost of Operating an Automobile

TYPE OF CAR	**LOW-COST AREA** SMALL TOWNS, RURAL LOCATIONS	**HIGH-COST AREA** LARGE METROPOLITAN AREAS
Subcompact (4 cylinder)	19.4¢/mile	22.8¢/mile
Compact (6 cylinder)	22.5¢/mile	26.7¢/mile
Intermediate (6 cylinder)	24.6¢/mile	28.5¢/mile
Standard (8 cylinder)	26.8¢/mile	30.9¢/mile

SOURCE: *Your Driving Costs*, 1982 ed. American Automobile Association, 8111 Gatehouse Road, Falls Church, Virginia 22047.

In total, we probably spend $50 billion a year on automobile repairs.

can buy a car that you expect to keep for only a short period of time, or buy a car that has a reputation for very low service requirements. Each year, the April issue of *Consumer Reports* recounts its readers' experiences with the repair needs of different makes and years of cars. This is an important aid when you try to assess the annual cost of operating an automobile.

Individuals who purchase automobiles often are unaware of the necessity of regular servicing. Furthermore, many automobile drivers could, if they wanted to, save considerable dollars by learning a minimal number of maintenance techniques. Numerous adult education classes in auto mechanics are available in high schools, community colleges, and elsewhere throughout the country.

Anybody seriously concerned with reducing repair costs would be advised to take one of these classes.

When you buy a car, one of the first things you must think about is insuring yourself against theft, fire, liability, medical expenses, and damage.

Getting Good Repairs

Every car owner faces the problem of having his or her car repaired. Finding a good repair shop or an honest mechanic may be a difficult job in your area. There are currently two private programs being developed to certify reliable workmanship on cars—one for mechanics and one for garages.

Certifying Mechanics

The National Institute for Automotive Service Excellence began certifying mechanics in 1972. In order to be certified by the institute, a mechanic must pass a written examination and have at least two years of experience in the area being tested. There are now over 94,000 certified automotive mechanics in one or more of eight categories, including automatic transmission, manual transmission and rear axle, front-end brakes, electrical system, engine repair, heating and air conditioning, and engine tune-up. Additionally, there are about 17,200 mechanics who have mastered all eight tests and have been certified as "general mechanics" by the institute. If you are interested in seeking the services of a certified mechanic, contact the National Institute for Automotive Service Excellence, 1825 K Street N.W., Washington, D.C. 20006. For a small fee, they will send you a list of certified mechanics and their locations.

Certifying Garages

There is a growing network of reputable service stations identified and thoroughly tested by the Automobile Association of America through its approved Auto Repair Services Program. This first nationwide attempt to identify good repair shops started in 1977 and now includes more than 2,000 garages in twenty-four states. Any shop seeking approval from the AAA is inspected. The tools, the mechanics' qualifications, and the repair bays are examined. Then the AAA questions customers about how satisfied they are with the repair service.

You do not have to join the AAA to take advantage of the program. Just look for the red, white, and blue sign with the AAA symbol and the words "Approved Auto Repair." You can call your local affiliated auto club for the names of approved shops in your area. Alternatively, you can write to AAA headquarters, 8111 Gatehouse Road, Falls Church, Virginia 22047.

THE AUTOMOBILE INSURANCE INDUSTRY

When you buy a car, one of the first things you must think about is insuring yourself against theft, fire, liability, medical expenses, and damage. Very few people drive without automobile insurance. Whether most people have adequate insurance is another matter, and we will discuss what is adequate in the following Consumer Issue.

The insurance industry is highly regulated. Every state has an insurance commissioner who passes judgment on the rates charged by various insurance companies. Although there is a tendency for any regulated industry to have several regulations that stifle competition, the automobile insurance industry remains competitive in many situations. It is not unusual for different prices to be charged for the same amount of insurance. But prices can be misleading because different insurance companies offer different qualities of service. One company may be less willing to pay off claims than another; one may have an insurance adjuster at your house immediately if you have a small accident; another may never send one out, leaving you to do the adjusting yourself. Although insurance costs are not consistently related to quality of service, they are consistently differentiated among different classes of drivers.

Why? Simply because the probability that an accident will occur is different for these different classes. Competition among the various insurance companies has forced each one of them to find out which classes of drivers are safer than others and to offer those classes lower rates. For example, because statistics tell us that single males from the ages of sixteen to twenty-five have the highest accident record of all drivers, these drivers pay a much higher price for auto insurance. And because statistics tell us that female drivers have fewer accidents overall than male drivers, women in a family often pay lower insurance rates for cars that they use exclusively.

Look at Exhibit 17–2, which shows the percentage of drivers in each age group that had accidents in 1979, according to the National Safety Council. We see that the under-twenty-five age group had more than twice the number of accidents than the middle age groups and significantly more than the twenty-five-to-thirty-four and 75-and-over age groups. That's why young drivers are charged more for automobile insurance.

Insurance rates also depend on the following variables:

1. The car you drive
2. Where you drive
3. What the car is used for
4. Marital status
5. Occupation
6. Safety record

NO-FAULT INSURANCE, PROS AND CONS

NO-FAULT AUTO INSURANCE
A system of auto insurance whereby, no matter who is at fault, the individual is paid by his or her insurance company for a certain amount of medical costs and for the damage to the car.

No-fault auto insurance is "an idea whose time has come." Some policy-makers believe, however, that the place for no-fault action is at the state, not the federal, level. Labor and consumer groups, however, were dissatisfied with the pace of state action and the lobbying tactics of no-fault opponents. Therefore, pressure was brought upon the Senate and the House to institute a federal plan. Supporters of such a plan indicate that, over a period of time, it will save motorists a billion dollars a year in auto insurance premiums. Under a no-fault insurance system, your insurance company does not first have to decide whose fault the accident was before payments are made to you for medical expenses due to injuries sustained in the accident. In a traditional liability-based fault system, a determination must be made as to who caused an accident. The insurer of the party deemed "at fault" then pays the bills of the other party—medical, automobile repairs, lost earnings, and, in some cases, pain and suffering.

No-fault insurance is not a new idea. Almost all other insurance is already no-fault. For example, when you purchase life insurance (unless you die by suicide shortly thereafter), the life insurance company pays without asking about fault. The same is true of fire and homeowner's insurance, as well as health and accident insurance. If you break an ankle and are covered under a medical plan, the insurer does not ask you whose fault it was before your medical bills are paid.

Original proponents of no-fault auto insurance believed that the system would soon be adopted by all states in the union; however, as of 1979, only fifteen states had converted to "pure" no-fault. They were Colorado, Connecticut, Florida, Georgia, Hawaii, Kansas, Kentucky, Massachusetts, Michigan, Minnesota, New Jersey, New York, North Dakota, Pennsylvania, and Utah. Another eight states had passed some modified form of no-fault automobile insurance. In some no-fault states, the no-fault laws apply only to bodily injuries. Property-damage claims are then settled by the standard liability and collision sections of automobile insurance policies, as they have been in the past.

If you live in a no-fault state, that does not mean you cannot sue the other party in the case of an automobile accident. Generally, you have to satisfy certain "threshold" criteria before you are allowed to sue for pain and suffering, inconvenience, lost wages, and deprivation of the company of a spouse. The medical threshold level ranges from a few hundred dollars up to a couple thousand dollars in the no-fault states. In other states, all that is required is that you suffer serious injury or permanent disfigurement before being allowed to sue.

EXHIBIT 17–2
Percentage of Drivers in Each Age Group Who Had Accidents in 1979

UNDER 25	25–34	35–44	45–54
36%	23%	16%	14%

55–64	65–74	75 AND OVER
14%	15%	24%

SOURCE: National Safety Council

Reducing Legal Fees

Originators of the no-fault system pointed out that only forty-four cents of each premium dollar in fault-based insurance went toward paying the injured parties in an automobile accident. Much of the remaining fifty-six cents of each premium dollar went to the cost of litigation—to lawyers. Proponents of no-fault insurance reasoned, and still do, that such a system would dramatically reduce the amount of needless expenditures on legal fees, particularly when minor injuries were involved.

SHOULD YOU BUY AND HOLD?

More than half of all Americans buy a new car every two to three years, on average. Individuals buy new cars because they seek status gratification, or because they want to avoid "buying someone else's troubles." A new car does give a one- to three-year warranty to cover repair costs. Nonetheless, the wise automobile shopper can save thousands of dollars by buying a used car instead of a new car, and these thousands of dollars in savings can more than offset repair bills on the used car. Consider also that most new-car bugs have been

More than half of all Americans buy a new car every two to three years, on average.

worked out during the first year of ownership, thereby saving the used-car buyer those time-consuming (but warranty-covered) trips back to the dealer.

Hertz Rent-A-Car Corporation recently conducted a study demonstrating the savings available to the purchaser of a two- to three-year-old car. Exhibit 17–3 compares the savings over a new-car model based on the age of a used car. Both the price of the car and the average operating expense over a three-year period were calculated. The greatest percentage savings is realized when buying a two- to three-year-old used car. It doesn't make much sense to buy a car that is four to seven years old.

THE SOCIAL COSTS OF DRIVING

SOCIAL COSTS
The costs of an action that society bears. Social costs include both private costs and costs that the individual does not bear. For example, the social costs of driving a car include the private costs plus any pollution or congestion caused by that automobile.

When you get into your car and fire it up, you incur, in addition to the private costs, the **social costs** of driving. You are all aware of them, particularly if you live in Los Angeles, New York, or Washington, D.C. One of the biggest social costs of driving has been air pollution. That engine does not just pull your car around. It also emits by-products that, when added together, do little good for your lungs or mine. In some places, they can do so much harm that many people refuse to live there. Pollution from automobile exhaust contributes 60 percent to total pollution in the major U.S. cities today. This is, of course, why the federal government as well as individual states have started regulating the pollution output of automobile engines. And this is also why standard automobile engines with pollution-abatement equipment do not run the way those you drove five years ago did. It has not been easy to eliminate the harmful by-products of internal combustion.

Thus, you, the individual driver, are being forced to take account of the social cost you impose on the rest of society in the form of pollution. When you are forced to purchase automobile engines that have pollution-abatement equipment, you pay directly in the form of a higher purchase price and indirectly in the form of reduced power and higher gas consumption.

Private automobile transportation involves other social costs that are equally obvious. One of them is congestion. Congestion on bridges, highways, and in inner cities is a problem of social concern, even though private individuals, at least until now, were not forced to pay the full price of driving their cars. That price includes making other people late for work or making them spend more time in their own cars. In other words, by the mere fact that you get on a crowded bridge, you slow down everybody else somewhat. When you add up the value of everybody else's time, you see that you impose a pretty high cost. And the same is true of every other person on that bridge.

The obvious solution is to make people pay the full cost of their driving by charging them more. Many will decide to cross the bridge at other than rush-hours or to go to work in car pools. Someday, we may arrive at a full costing solution. In the meantime, we build highways, freeways, expressways, bridges, underpasses, overpasses, parking lots—ad nauseam—until, if we keep on this way, eventually the landscape will be one massive automobile metropolis. Many people are clamoring for a change in this trend; they want mass transit. Unfortunately, mass transit on a large scale seems to be far in the future.

EXHIBIT 17–3
Cost Savings of Used Versus New Cars

AGE OF USED CAR AT PURCHASE	PERCENT SAVINGS OVER COST OF NEW CAR OVER THREE YEARS
1 year	10%
2 years	30%
3 years	48%
4 years	51%
5 years	52%
6 years	53%
7 years	53%

SUMMARY

1. Fully 88 percent of all American families own cars.
2. Highway deaths number around 30,000 a year, and property damage caused by the automobile exceeds $60 billion.
3. The National Safety Administration sets standards for the production of new cars. The cost of increased safety is not insignificant.
4. An alternative to making a car safer is to make the highway safer by eliminating drunk drivers.
5. The automobile repair industry is indeed huge in the United States, accounting for perhaps $50 billion in consumer expenditures a year. Preventive maintenance is important in eliminating large repair bills; however, some preventive maintenance may be more costly than it is worth, particularly if you do not plan to keep your car very long.
6. The automobile insurance industry is regulated, but there is enough competition for you to benefit from shopping around.
7. No-fault insurance eliminates the liability-based system that had previously been in effect. Essentially, if you have no-fault insurance, your insurance company pays you in case of an accident, no matter who was at fault.
8. Buying a two- to three-year-old car can mean substantial savings.
9. The social costs of driving include the pollution, noise, and congestion caused by automobiles.

QUESTIONS FOR THOUGHT AND DISCUSSION

1. Why do you think Americans spend so much for automobiles?
2. Automobiles in America are much larger than in Europe. Why?
3. Even though they are told that speed kills, American drivers continue to drive as fast or faster than the speed limit on highways. Why?
4. Can you distinguish between those safety features in a car that benefit only the occupants of a car and those that benefit so-called third parties?
5. Why does safety cost? Why has the automobile industry not provided a perfectly safe car?
6. Do you think it would be difficult to keep drunk drivers off the road?
7. What costs do you, or would you, take into account when purchasing a car?
8. Do you think no-fault insurance is "fair"?
9. What has Congress been doing to reduce the social costs of driving?

THINGS TO DO

1. Write to the Federal Highway Safety Administration for a listing of safety requirements on cars. Which ones do you think are appropriate or inappropriate?
2. A few years ago, a safety requirement was suggested that would oblige automobile manufacturers to relocate gasoline tanks and protect them from crashes in order to avoid fire. The Ford Motor Company asserted that the requirement would raise the price of each car by $11.20 and estimated that there were only 600 to 700 auto-fire deaths annually. Ford concluded that the new safety standard would not be worth the price. Assume that 10 million cars are produced a year. What is the total cost of this new safety feature? If the

Ford Motor Company is right about the number of auto-fire deaths annually, what is the implicit value placed on human life? Is it too high or too low?

3. Find out what the growth rate of bicycle and motorcycle sales has been in the past decade. Has this growth rate exceeded the growth rate of automobile sales? Can you think of reasons to support your findings?

4. Write to your state's insurance commissioner for information on how the commissioner protects you from insurance companies.

5. Contact an independent insurance adjuster and talk to him or her about his or her work. How are claims handled? What are the most prevalent types of accidents in your area? How should you file a claim?

6. Write to the Federal Highway Administration in Washington, D.C., asking for its estimate of the current cost per mile for operating a subcompact, compact, and standard-size car. Compare it with the figures in Exhibit 17–1. Now, in percentages, figure out the relative costs. Is it now more or less expensive in operating cost per mile to have a standard-size car compared to a compact?

7. Find out from the National Highway Traffic Safety Administration what safety equipment this year's cars had to have. With this knowledge, would you feel safer in a newer car? How much would you be willing to pay for this additional safety?

SELECTED READINGS

"Auto Insurance: Good Drivers Are More Equal." *Nation's Business,* November 1979, p. 112.

Borgeson, L. "Women and Cars." *Vogue,* October 1982, p. 220.

Chandler, J. "How to Get Your Car Repaired Honestly" *Mechanics Illustrated,* December 1982, p. 49.

Costs of Owning an Automobile. Washington, D.C.: U.S. Department of Transportation, Federal Highway Administration (latest edition).

Flanagan, W. G. "Where Are the Tire Kickers?" *Forbes,* November 22, 1982, p. 228.

Nader, Ralph, *et al. The Lemon Book.* Ottawa, Ill.: Caroline House Publications, 1980.

Nader, Ralph. *Unsafe at Any Speed: The Designed-in Dangers of the American Automobile.* New York: Grossman Publishers, 1972.

O'Connell, Jeffrey. *The Injury Industry and the Remedy of No-Fault Auto Insurance.* Washington D.C.: Consumers Union, Commerce Clearing House, 1971.

Olson, S. "Prospects for the Automobile: Sputtering Toward the Twenty-first Century." *Futurist,* February 1980, pp. 27–29.

Smith, K. "Insurance Safety Studies Disputed." *Motor Trend,* October 1982, p. 28.

Sullivan, P. "Getting a Good Deal on a New Car." *Essence,* November 1982, p. 120.

U.S. Department of Transportation. *The Car Book: A Consumer's Guide to Car Buying.* Washington, D.C.: U.S. Government Printing Office, 1981.

U.S. Department of Transportation. *Common Sense in Buying a New Car.* Washington, D.C.: U.S. Government Printing Office, 1978.

"What You Should Know before Buying Auto Parts." *Popular Mechanics,* October, 1982, pp. 137–38.

Your Driving Costs. Falls Church, Va.: American Automobile Association (latest edition).

Consumer ISSUE   P

BUYING TRANSPORTATION

GLOSSARY

ASSIGNED RISK—A person seeking automobile insurance who has been refused coverage. That person is assigned to an insurance company that is a member of the assigned-risk pool in that person's state.

LIABILITY INSURANCE—Insurance that covers suits against the insured for such damages as injury or death to other drivers or passengers, property damage, and the like. It is insurance for those damages for which the driver can be held liable.

UMBRELLA POLICY—A type of supplemental insurance policy that can extend normal automobile liability limits to $1 million or more for a relatively small premium.

ZERO DEDUCTIBLE—In the collision part of an automobile insurance policy, the provision that the insured pays nothing for any repair to damage on the car due to an accident that is the fault of the insured. Zero deductible is, of course, more expensive than a $50 or $100 deductible policy.

SHOULD YOU BUY A NEW OR A USED CAR?

When most of us go out to purchase transportation, we are tempted to buy something new. There are certainly good reasons for buying a new car instead of a used one. A new car has never been owned by someone else; therefore, you have to worry only about how you will treat it during its first few years, not about how it was treated beforehand. A new car may be safer, it may run more smoothly, it may be more stylish—although today these various aspects are not as subject to annual changes as they were in the past.

You may choose a new car simply because you like to have new things. Be aware, however, of the price you are paying for that new car; a full-sized domestic car may automatically depreciate about $1,000 when you take it off the dealer's showroom floor.

Nevertheless, in some cases, when you buy a new car, you get the benefit of an extremely desirable warranty. American Motors, for example, had the following warranty for its 1983 automobiles: twelve months or 12,000 miles on the complete car, from windshield-wiper blades to complete engine overhaul if needed; tires are not included. (See Exhibit P–1.) Volkswagen has a warranty that gives you 12,000 miles (or one year) of servicing on any parts that might need replacement, plus one year or 20,000 miles on the internal parts of the engine and transmission; and, under prescribed conditions, Volkswagen will tow your car to the nearest dealer or give you a rental car if yours has to be kept overnight for warranty repairs.

THE FINANCIAL BENEFITS OF LEASING A NEW CAR

Many individuals no longer buy a new car. Rather, they lease one from a new-car dealer for a two-to-four year period. In some cases, leasing for three years is cheaper than buying and selling or trading in the average car. Hertz Corporation's Car Leasing Division contends that over 60 percent of all new cars in California are leased or rented. Nationally, one in every four cars is now leased, as compared to one in twenty-five some fifteen years ago. In the typical thirty-six-month (closed-end) lease, you pay a specified monthly figure for the use of the car. You take care of it as if it were personally owned. At the end of three years, you walk away from it. In many larger cities, the auto insurance included in your leasing agreement is

When you buy a new 1983 AMC automobile from an authorized AMC dealer, American Motors Corporation* warrants to you that for 12 months or 12,000 miles (20 000 km)** from the date of delivery or first use, whichever comes first, it will, except for tires, pay for the repair or replacement of any part it supplies which proves defective in material or workmanship.

All we require is that the automobile be properly maintained and cared for under normal use and service in the fifty United States or Canada and that warranty repairs or replacement be made by an authorized AMC dealer.

Except for other written warranties issued by American Motors applicable to AMC automobiles, no other warranty is given or authorized by American Motors. American Motors shall not be liable for loss of use of automobile, loss of time, inconvenience or other incidental or consequential damages. Some states and provinces do not allow limitation or exclusion of incidental or consequential damages so the above exclusion and limitation may not apply to you. This warranty gives you specific legal rights and you may also have other rights which vary from state to state or province to province.

*In Canada: American Motors (Canada) Inc.
**In Canada: 20 000 km

Reprinted with permission of American Motors Corporation.

EXHIBIT P–1
1983 AMC Full 12-Month/12,000-Mile New Automobile Warranty

sold to you at a lower rate than if you had bought it on your own for a privately owned car.

For many individuals, an important advantage of leasing a car is the convenience of accounting for the business use of a car. If you use your car 50 percent of the time for business, you simply figure that 50 percent of your annual lease cost is deductible from your income before you pay taxes.

THE FIRST STEPS

If you've decided to purchase a car, then your first step might be to conduct a type of market research. This would involve quizzing relatives and friends on their experiences with different cars. Additionally, you could start doing research by reading such magazines as *Car and Driver*, *Road and Track*, and other auto-enthusiast periodicals. Finally, you can leaf through issues of *Consumer Reports* that give test results for various new cars. At the same time, you must establish the amount of money you are going to spend. This will determine whether you seek a new car or a used car, what size car, what luxury class, and what options you will be able to afford.

IF YOU DECIDE TO BUY A NEW CAR

If you decide to buy a new car, you'll have to decide where to buy it, which one to buy, and what accessories to purchase.

The Dealer

1. Location. Where to buy depends on a number of factors, the most important being how far the dealer is from your job or home. After all, you must take the car in for servicing, and a new car, no matter how good it is, is going to have at least a few problems in the beginning. If you value time and convenience highly and if you can conveniently leave your car off at the dealer and walk to work or walk back home, you will be ahead of the game.
2. Dealer service facilities and personnel. To find out about the dealer's service facilities and personnel, ask specific questions about them, such as: What does the dealer do to make service easier for customers? What are the size and reputation of the service department? How long is service work guaranteed—no days, thirty days, or ninety days? How much electronic diagnostic equipment does the shop have? Are there provisions for replacement transportation while your car is in for service? When is the service department open? All these questions are important and should not be treated lightly because, as we all know, cars, whether they be new or used, require servicing.
3. Dealer reputation. Talk to customers who have bought from the dealer and have used his or her service department to find out how satisfied they are. Or, better yet, take your present car in for servicing and see how satisfied you are with the service department. (This is important for both new and used-car purchases.)
4. The deal offered. Obviously, the deal offered is of utmost importance in all the preceding considerations. You may be willing to pay a *slightly* higher price at a specific dealer you like very much and who has a good reputation for service. Shopping around is, of course, a necessary step for most people when they buy a car.

GETTING THE BEST DEAL ON A NEW CAR

There are differences in price for the same car with the same accessories, depending on the dealer you buy from and depending on your bargaining skills. However, remember that the difference in price for the same car will never be great, particularly for the lower-priced subcompacts and compacts. Thus, it will not be worth

your while to go to twenty-five dealers to bargain on a particular car. In fact, one study showed that, after contacting three dealers, the probability of getting a better deal was very small.

You can obtain dealer cost and a list price on all cars and options from auto guides sold at newstands, such as the December issue of *Changing Times,* and in some paperback books, such as Edmund's and Car/Puter's Autofacts. Or you can fill out a form on which you list the car and all the options you want to buy and send it to Car/Puter International, Inc., 1603 Bushwick Avenue, Brooklyn, New York 11207. For a small fee, you will receive a computer printout showing dealer cost and list price for that car with all its options. Dealer markups vary from 17 to 25 percent, depending on whether the car is a subcompact, compact, intermediate, or full-sized model. Luxury cars, such as Cadillacs and Lincoln Continentals, have a markup of 25 percent. When we speak of markup here, we are referring to the difference between what the dealer pays for a car and what is shown on the sticker pasted to the car window.

Shopping by Phone

Although many dealers refuse to give out prices over the telephone and others will only give you the sticker price, there are some, especially foreign-car dealers, who will tell you exactly what your final cost will be. In fact, if you are assertive enough over the telephone, sometimes you can negotiate a deal without ever visiting the showroom. Consider the following tactic. Call the dealer and ask to speak to a salesperson. Immediately indicate that you were just disappointed by a competing dealer who had "low-balled" you. That is, you had been quoted one price, and then the salesperson upped that figure when you were just about to close the deal. Telling the salesperson this over the phone right away alerts him or her that you have shopped around, are serious, and won't accept a higher-than-stated price. When the salesperson on the phone suggests a particular figure for the car you want with the options you want, ask him or her if that is the best possible offer. In many cases, the salesperson will be forced to be honest with you and probably will offer you a lower price just to get you into the showroom.

Using a Buying Service

If you want to skip all of the haggling and frustrations associated with bargaining for a new car, you may wish to use a buying service, which is simply an intermediary that offers the car from $125 to $500 above factory cost, depending on the basic price and the size of the car. You buy the car from a regular dealer but at a guaranteed price. Warranties, rebates, and service are the same. Those who do not favor car-buying services contend that, since the buyer does not usually select the dealer, the service after the sale may be less dependable, more inconvenient, and more costly than had the car buyer chosen the dealer.

Here is a list of the four leading car-buying services in the United States.

1. United Auto Brokers, Inc., 1603 Bushwick Avenue, Brooklyn, New York 11207.
2. Nationwide Auto Brokers, Inc., 17517 West Ten Mile Road, Southfield, Michigan 48075.
3. Motor Club Auto Buying Service, 14411 West Eight Mile Road, Detroit, Michigan 48235.
4. American-wide Auto Buying Service, Inc., 2507 David Broderick Tower, Detroit, Michigan 48226.

Each of these brokers has computerized pricing, which, for a small fee, will tell you exactly what the dealer paid at the factory for the car you want. Additionally, if you wish to order a car from these services, most can be purchased for $125 to $300 over wholesale price.

What Type of Car to Buy?

Deciding on what new car to buy depends at least in part on how much money you want to spend. You should figure out the exact yearly out-of-pocket costs you will incur for different price ranges and then decide what you are willing to pay. Remember, many times when you go up the ladder of car prices, you are not buying any more safety or speed but only styling, prestige, and so on. Be aware of the price you are paying for these qualities.

You also should be aware of the various operating costs of the new cars you are considering. Compacts are cheaper to run than full-sized cars, but they hold fewer people comfortably and less baggage, and they give you less protection in a big crash.

Options

The options you should choose also depend upon your tastes relative to your income. Some options are wise to take, even if you don't want them. It would be ridiculous to try to get a stick shift on a Cadillac because, when you want to sell it, few people would want to buy it. You also should consider things like power steering and power brakes on larger cars because, without these features, large cars are very hard to sell (and very hard to drive and park while you own them).

Tires are an important feature on any car and something on which you won't want to compromise. Radial tires seem to offer the most protection, the safest handling, and sometimes the longest life. Today, many new cars come with radials; if the car of your choice comes without them, you should consider immediately trading in the standard tires for radials.

Another accessory you definitely should consider is a rear-window defogger. Most cars now have them as standard equipment, but some do not. If you live in a cold climate, the extra thirty to sixty dollars are well spent; on cold mornings, a defogger improves rear-window visibility. Of course, the assumption is that you are willing to pay for safety; only you can decide whether you are.

Air conditioning may seem like a luxury to many people, but it is very difficult to resell a car in Sun Belt states without it. Therefore, in those states where it is hot much of the year, air conditioning should be considered a necessity.

Exhibit P–2 gives you a chart you can fill in to compare the actual cost of four different types of cars you may want to buy with different options.

List Price	Car #1	Car #2	Car #3	Car #4
OPTIONS				
Power steering and brakes				
Automatic transmission				
Nonstandard engine				
Air conditioning				
Rear-window defogger				
Special radio/tape deck				
Limited slip differential				
White-wall tires				
Tinted glass				
Vinyl roof				
Tires—radial, oversized, or snow				
Speed control				
Fuel economy indicator				
Other				
Freight charges				
Federal excise tax				
Dealer service charge				
State sales tax				
State registration and licensing fees				
TOTAL COST				
Subtract trade-in or down payment				
TOTAL AMOUNT TO BE PAID TO DEALER				

EXHIBIT P–2
Price Comparison Chart

TRADING IN YOUR WHEELS

When you trade in your old car, you can be fairly certain you will get no more than the standard trade-in price listed by the National Automobile Dealers Association in its *Official Used Car Guide,* or "blue book." It might be a good idea for you to look up this information yourself. Your bank usually has a copy.

Here is an area where private sellers are just as guilty of irresponsibility as dealers. How often have you heard of friends trying to trade in an old clunker with many things wrong with it? Usually, they assure the dealer that the old clunker is running perfectly.

It is generally a good idea to bargain on your trade-in *after* you have completed the new-car sale with the dealer. Then you won't have to deal with what is called the "high-ball" gimmick. The salesperson will quote you a price for your used car as a trade-in that exceeds by $200, $300, or even $500 its blue-book value. Presumably, you might be deluded into thinking that you are getting a bargain; however, the additional price you receive for your trade-in will merely be included somewhere else in the price of the new car. You can assume that you will get the wholesale price of the car as a trade-in if it is in good condition. You can also attempt to sell the used car yourself, but remember that you must incur the time and hassle costs of doing so (for example, changing the title, taking care of sales taxes, and so on).

IF YOU BUY A USED CAR

If you decide to buy a used car, there are a number of things you must think about. Because you do not know how any given car was treated by its previous owner, you must be especially careful about its condition. One way to make certain that nothing major will go wrong is to have an independent mechanic check the car over before you commit yourself to buying it. You may be charged for this, just as you will be charged by a building inspector who checks out a house you want to buy. You are buying information from the mechanic, information that may save you hundreds of dollars in the future. The mechanic may point out that the transmission is about to go, that the gaskets leak, and so on. You may wish to take the car to an electronic diagnostic center that will charge from fifteen to fifty dollars to electronically analyze all major aspects of the car you intend to buy. Generally, these centers do not repair work. However, their technicians usually can indicate what it will cost to have the used car repaired if anything shows up in their diagnosis.

Another way of insuring yourself against major repair expenses is by working with used-car dealers who have written warranties on their products. Sometimes you have to pay for such a warranty, and sometimes its price is merely included in the price of the used car. You are buying a type of insurance that costs you a little in the beginning but reduces the probability that you will pay out a lot in the future. Very rarely, a used car may still be covered by the manufacturer's one-year, 12,000 mile or two-year, 24,000-mile warranty. Because such a used car is worth more to you than those without warranties, you will be willing to pay more.

One thing you can check out yourself is whether a used car has been in a major accident. Look for mismatched colors in the paint and for ripples, bumps, and grainy surfaces on the bodywork. These will indicate extensive repainting and, therefore, extensive repairs. Such discoveries may not dissuade you from wanting to buy the car, but they should persuade you to have some shop testing done by an independent mechanic.

There are numerous ways to examine a prospective used-car purchase. The section on buying a used car in any annual *Consumer Reports Buying Guide* gives you more than a dozen on-the-lot tests and eight to ten driving tests you can do yourself. It also tells you approximately what each repair job will cost if you notice something wrong. However, because nothing can duplicate a shop test by a good mechanic, this step is highly recommended unless you have an extremely good warranty with the deal. You also might be able to get a helpful brochure from your local consumer-affairs office. If you are purchasing a used car from a dealer, ask the dealer if he or she will give you the name and address of the car's previous owner. Then query this person on possible problems, defects, or advantages of the car.

WHEN THOSE NEW-CAR REPAIRS GO WRONG

When the former director of the Office of Consumer Affairs, Virginia Knauer, was in office, she told a meeting of automobile dealers: "Every month, complaints about automobiles head the list of problems that consumers write to me about." In order to counter the problems that customers have with dealers and with repair people, an organization named AUTOCAP was formed.

How Does It Work?

Say you are dissatisfied with the car you just bought from a dealer. You call a toll-free number in your state and register your complaint. You are immediately mailed a form on which to detail your problem. When you return the form to AUTOCAP headquarters, the dealer involved is notified by mail and urged to work out the problem with you. If this fails, the matter goes before AUTOCAP for arbitration. The arbitrating panel consists of four dealers and three public members.

It is a painless job to arrive at a "just" settlement when a dealer and a customer can agree. Obviously, the panel is not a court of last resort; it has no enforcement powers and relies on dealer cooperation to handle complaints satisfactorily. But, according to Connecticut car dealer and panel head, Richard D. Wagoner, dealer cooperation has been excellent: Only two dealers had balked in the first year of operation.

When Things Get Sticky

When the going gets sticky on a matter of warranty or car performance, AUTOCAP goes directly to factory representatives. So far, the results have been satisfying; manufacturers have cooperated in all respects.

And if you, the customer, feel that you did not get fair treatment at AUTOCAP's hands, you can go to the state motor vehicle agency or take private legal action. The following automobile-dealer organizations are operating AUTOCAP under sponsorship of the National Automobile Dealers Association as this book goes to press:

Kentucky Automobile Dealers Association, P.O. Box 498, Frankfort, Kentucky 40601.

Metropolitan Denver Automobile Dealers Association, 70 West 6th Ave., Denver, Colorado 80122.

Automotive Trade Association of National Capital Area, 8401 Connecticut Ave., Chevy Chase, Maryland 20015.

Central Florida Dealer Association, 1350 Orange Ave., Winter Park, Florida 32789.

Idaho Automobile Dealers Association, 2230 Main St., Boise, Idaho 83706.

Greater Louisville Automobile Dealers Association, 332 W. Broadway, Louisville, Kentucky 40202.

Cleveland Automobile Dealers Association, 310 Lakeside Ave., West, Cleveland, Ohio 44113.

Oklahoma Automobile Dealers Association, 1601 City National Bank Tower, Oklahoma City, Oklahoma 73102.

Oregon Automobile Dealers Association, P.O. Box 14460, Portland, Oregon 97214.

Utah Automobile Dealers Association, Newhouse Hotel, Salt Lake City, Utah 84101.

Louisiana Automobile Dealers Association, 201 Lafayette St., Baton Rouge, Louisiana 70821.

Indianapolis Automobile Trade Association, 822 North Illinois, Indianapolis, Indiana 46204.

Connecticut Automotive Trade Association, 18 N. Main St., West Hartford, Connecticut 06103.

The four largest domestic automobile producers have offices to handle customer complaints when dealers are unable or unwilling to clear up troubles with your new car. You can write to the following offices directly:

American Motors Corporation, Owner Relations Manager, 14250 Plymouth Road, Detroit, Michigan 48232.

Chrysler Corporation, Your Man in Detroit, Box 1086, Detroit, Michigan 48231.

Ford Customer Service Division, Owner Relations Department, Park Lane Tower West, 1 Park Lane Boulevard, Dearborn, Michigan 48126.

General Motors Corporation, Owner Relations Manager, 3044 West Grand Boulevard, Detroit, Michigan 48202.

If you wish to find out about an older car having a possible safety defect, you can call the Auto Safety Hotline at the National Highway Traffic Administration in Washington, D.C. The hotline exists to exchange information about auto safety defects between the public and the government. You can report problems you have had with cars in order to help others, as well as finding out about defects in a car you might own or wish to own. The hotline operator can tell you if a used car you are attempting to purchase has ever been included in a recall campaign by the manufacturer. The number to call is (800) 424-9393. You also can check to see if the used car you bought was fixed after being recalled by the manufacturer for a defect; this would eliminate the risk of driving a car with a known safety problem that wasn't fixed when it should have been.

FINANCING THAT PURCHASE

A new or used car is usually such a major purchase that at least part of it has to be financed by credit. Do not automatically accept the credit that the dealer offers you when you decide to buy a car. Shop around for credit just as you shop around for anything else. Fortunately for you, the Truth-in-Lending Act of 1968 requires every lender to disclose the total finance charge and actual annual interest rate to be paid. Thus, the credit offered you by the dealer can be compared to the credit offered you by competing sources, such as banks and finance companies. Remember, if you default on your car payment, your car may be repossessed. This is a real possibility: In some states, finance companies can take your car away from you without a judicial hearing. Do not buy a car that is more expensive than you know you can afford.

Where to Borrow for a Car

There are numerous sources for automobile loans: life insurance policies, savings and loan or commercial bank passbook savings accounts, credit unions, commercial banks, auto insurance companies, and auto dealers themselves.

Life insurance loans are possible if you have a whole life policy[1] that has been in effect for at least a few years. It willl have accumulated cash value, and you can borrow up to that amount from the company. The maximum annual percentage rate for a life insurance loan is often limited to 8 percent by law. The only problem with taking such a loan is that it reduces the amount of life insurance you have in effect.

A passbook loan is available if you have a savings account. The bank or savings and loan association may lend as much as 90 percent of the amount on deposit. The bank will freeze enough to cover the unpaid balance on a loan, but the entire account will continue to earn interest.

Generally, credit unions offer the most beneficial rates on automobile loans; so if you are a member of one or can

1. See Chapter 19 for explanation.

become a member without too much trouble, find out what you will be charged there.

Banks are the second most commonly used source of automobile financing, after the auto dealers themselves. What your local banker will charge you depends on your credit rating, the amount of down payment or trade-in value on the car you are buying, and the general state of the economy.

Auto insurance companies sometimes issue car loans through a bank or through their own subsidiaries. To find out if your auto insurance company does this, call your agent.

You will find that if you go to a small-loan company or to a dealer, you will pay the highest annual percentage fee for an auto loan.

What Length of Loan to Take Out

Most consumer experts recommend that automobile loans be taken out for the shortest period possible. They point out that you end up paying a relatively high interest charge when you take out a three- or four-year car loan. Additionally, you end up having a hefty balance to pay when you are ready to trade in your car before the end of four years.

Does that mean that you should not take out a four-year auto loan? No, not necessarily. You really are asking a question about how much you should be in debt; the fact that it concerns an automobile is irrelevant. If you think you would be uncomfortable having a debt outstanding for four years, then that may be a reason to opt for a shorter time period. However, if you do so, you must use more of your discretionary fund to pay off the automobile loan's monthly payment, and you will, therefore, have less to spend on other items during that period. The fact that it costs you in additional charges to keep an auto loan outstanding longer should not be surprising. You are asking to use someone else's money for a longer period. If you think that you can borrow at a lower rate using something other than an automobile as collateral, then it would be more costly to take out a four-year auto loan. As with all borrowing decisions, you must balance the benefits of having more cash available for other purchases against the increased cost for borrowing more or for borrowing for a longer period of time.

GETTING AN ADEQUATE AMOUNT OF INSURANCE

An important step when buying an automobile is making sure you have adequate automobile insurance. Of the many kinds of coverage you can purchase, the most important is liability insurance.

LIABILITY INSURANCE. This insurance covers bodily injury liability and property damage. **Liability insurance** pays when the policyholder is at fault to another person. Liability limits are usually described by a series of three numbers, such as 25/50/5, which means that the policy will pay a maximum of $25,000 for bodily injury to one person, a maximum of $50,000 for bodily injury to more than one person, and a maximum of $5,000 for property damage in one occurrence. Most insurance companies offer liability up to $300,000 and sometimes $500,000. The cost of additional liabiity coverage is relatively small. It is wise to consider taking out a much larger limit than you would ordinarily expect to need, because awards in personal injury suits against automobile drivers who are proved negligent are sometimes astronomical. Some dependents of automobile accident victims have been successful in suing for $1 million or more. Exhibit P–4

EXHIBIT P–3
What Your Car Loan Will Cost Per $1,000 Borrowed

	ONE YEAR		TWO YEARS		THREE YEARS		FOUR YEARS	
ANNUAL PERCENTAGE INTEREST	MONTHLY PAYMENT	TOTAL FINANCE CHARGE	MONTHLY PAYMENT	TOTAL FINANCE CHARGE	MONTHLY PAYMENT	TOTAL FINANCE CHARGE	MONTHLY PAYMENT	TOTAL FINANCE CHARGE
12	89	66	47	130	33	196	26	264
13	89	72	48	141	34	213	27	288
14	90	78	48	152	34	231	27	312
15	90	80	49	176	35	260	28	344
16	91	92	49	176	35	260	28	344
17	91	92	50	200	36	296	29	392

NOTE: Figures have been rounded to nearest dollar.

EXHIBIT P–4
Automobile Financial Responsibility/Compulsory Limits

There may have been changes in some states since these data were published. For the latest information, check your own state department of motor vehicles or your auto-insurance agent.

STATE	LIABILITY LIMITS*
Alabama	10/20/5
Alaska	25/50/10
Arizona	15/30/10
Arkansas	25/50/15
California	15/30/5
Colorado	15/30/5
Connecticut	20/40/5
Delaware	10/20/5
District of Columbia	10/20/5
Florida	10/20/5
Georgia	10/20/5
Hawaii	25/unlimited/10
Idaho	10/20/5
Illinois	15/30/10
Indiana	25/50/10
Iowa	15/30/10
Kansas	25/50/10
Kentucky	10/20/5
Louisiana	5/10/1
Maine	20/40/10
Maryland	20/40/10
Massachusetts	10/20/5
Michigan	20/40/10
Minnesota	25/50/10
Mississippi	10/20/5
Missouri	25/50/10
Montana	25/50/5
Nebraska	15/30/10
Nevada	15/30/10
New Hampshire	25/50/25
New Jersey	15/30/5
New Mexico	15/30/5
New York	10/20/5[1]
North Carolina	25/50/10
North Dakota	25/50/10
Ohio	12.5/25/7.5
Oklahoma	10/20/10
Oregon	15/30/5
Pennsylvania	15/30/5
Rhode Island	25/50/10
South Carolina	15/30/5
South Dakota	15/30/10
Tennessee	10/20/5
Texas	10/20/5
Utah	20/40/10
Vermont	20/40/10
Virginia	25/50/10
Washington	25/50/10
West Virginia	20/40/10
Wisconsin	15/30/10
Wyoming	10/20/5
CANADA	
Alberta	$100,000 inclusive**
British Columbia	$100,000 inclusive**
Manitoba	$50,000 inclusive**
New Brunswick	$100,000 inclusive**
Newfoundland	$75,000 inclusive**
Northwest Territories	$50,000 inclusive**
Nova Scotia	$100,000 inclusive**
Ontario	$200,000 inclusive**
Prince Edward Island	$100,000 inclusive**
Quebec	$50,000 property damage[2]
Saskatchewan	$100,000 inclusive**
Yukon	$75,000 inclusive**

* The first two figures refer to bodily injury liability limits and the third figure to property damage liability. For example, 10/20/5 means coverage up to $20,000 for all persons injured in an accident, subject to a limit of $10,000 for one individual; and $5,000 coverage for property damage.

** "Inclusive" means that the amount of liability insurance shown is available to settle either bodily insurance or property damage claims—or both.

[1]50/100 in cases of wrongful death.

[2]Quebec has a complete no-fault system for bodily injury claims, scaled down for non-residents in proportion to their degree of fault. The $50,000 limit relates to liability for damage to property in Quebec and to liability for bodily injury and property damage outside Quebec.

SOURCE: *Insurance Facts*, 1981–82 edition, Insurance Information Institute, 110 William Street, New York, NY.

shows the minimum bodily-injury liability limits and property-damage liability coverage you must have in the different states and in the different provinces of Canada.

People who aren't satisfied with the maximum liability limits offered by regular automobile insurance coverage can purchase a separate amount of coverage under a policy usually known as an **umbrella** policy. Umbrella limits sometimes go as high as $5 million.

MEDICAL PAYMENTS. Medical payments on an auto insurance policy will cover hospital and medical bills and, sometimes, funeral expenses (for those in your car). Medical payment insurance pays regardless of who is at fault in an accident. Usually you can buy $2,000 to $5,000 for around $10 or $15 a year. Some policies allow you to buy medical payment insurance for your passengers. For you personally, however, you may not want to buy medical payment insurance through your auto insurance policy if you have sufficient medical coverage through, say, a group policy at your place of employment.

COLLISION. This type of insurance covers damage to your car in any type of collision not covered by another insured driver at fault. It is usually not advisable to purchase full coverage (otherwise known as **zero deductible**) on collision. The price per year is quite high because it is likely that, in any one year, small repair jobs will be required and will be costly. Most people take out $50 or $100 deductible coverage, which costs about one-quarter the price of zero deductible.

COMPREHENSIVE. Comprehensive auto insurance covers for loss, damage, or anything on your car destroyed by fire, hurricane, hail, or just about all other causes, including vandalism. It is separate from collision insurance. Full comprehensive insurance is quite expensive. Again, a $50 or $100 deductible is usually preferable.

UNINSURED MOTORIST. This type of coverage insures the driver and passengers against injury by any driver who has no insurance at all or by a hit-and-run driver. Many states require that it be in all insurance policies sold to drivers. The risk is small, so the premium is relatively small.

ACCIDENTAL DEATH BENEFITS. Sometimes called double indemnity, this coverage provides a lump sum to named beneficiaries if you happen to die in an automobile accident. Although it generally costs very little, it may not be desired if you feel you have already purchased a sufficient amount of life insurance.

How to Shop for Insurance

Shopping for automobile insurance is usually easier than shopping for a car. You may want to look first to your local credit union or to some special insurance source available to you if you are a member of certain organizations. Sometimes companies get special rates for their employees. If you are a government employee, you can often get special types of automobile insurance from a government employees' insurance company. However, when comparing insurance companies, remember that you also should look at the service they give. You can shop for insurance by figuring out the exact policy you want, including liability, uninsured motorist, medical, collision, comprehensive, and perhaps towing, with the specific limits you want; then get a written statement from several insurance companies' agents. Insurance premiums can vary by 50 percent or more, depending on what company you select.

The insurance agent you work with is also important. If one in your area has a reputation for being fair and knowledgeable, you may want to take suggestions from that person. Again, you are being sold information as part of the package. (You also may be buying "clout" if you are dealing with a company agent rather than a broker for many different companies.)

There are basically two types of policies: family and special. Generally, when you ask for an insurance quote, you will be quoted for a family automobile policy. It includes liability, comprehensive, collision, uninsured motorist, and medical in the amount you specify. A cheaper, but more restricted, type of policy is deemed special. It is restricted to better-than-average drivers and combines bodily injury and property damage liability, accidental death, and uninsured motorist protection. So, instead of offering you separate amounts on those items, a lump-sum maximum is given per accident. If that maximum is, say, $100,000, then compensation to any one person, to a group of people, or for property damage will not exceed $100,000. In most cases under a special policy, medical payment insurance pays only the difference between what the medical bill is and what your health insurance pays. In other words, you cannot collect the full amount from both policies. Finally, under a special policy, you purchase collision and comprehensive insurance separately. Also, you may be able to get safe-driver policies, reductions if you have taken driver training, and so on. You should discuss all these possibilities with prospective insurance agents.

Exhibit P–5 will help you compare insurance policies. When calling around to get insurance, you can fill in the chart and compare policies.

For a perhaps outdated rating on automobile insurance companies, look at the July 1977 issue of *Consumer Reports* (Part II of a three-part series on auto insurance).

Problems of Insuring Young Drivers

Parents do not have to be told how expensive it is to insure a young driver in a family, particularly if that driver is a male. There are ways of reducing such auto insurance expenses, however. One way is to limit the son's or daughter's driving to occasional use of the family car. "Occasional use" is defined by most insurance companies as using the car less than 50 percent of the time. That means if the car is used for going out on weekends or occasionally to school, then the young driver qualifies for the lower rate. However, if the car is used every day for driving to school, then the lower rate does not apply. Some companies give discounts if the driver has a B or better average in school, and there are discounts for compact or subcompact cars. A driver's education course will also qualify some students for an auto insurance discount.

How to Lower Your Insurance Rates

The following are some tips on lowering your automobile insurance rates.

1. Don't buy coverage that you don't need, such as collision and comprehensive insurance on an older car. For example, if you have a five-year-old car whose blue-book value is relatively low, you may not want to bother with collision insurance because you never collect more than blue-book value (and damage may be more than the car is worth).

2. See if a special policy is suitable for your needs, rather than a more expensive family automobile insurance policy.

3. Avoid high-performance or expensive cars for which auto insurance is much higher.

4. Take a higher deductible on collision and comprehensive insurance. Remember, the higher the deductible, the lower the premium.

5. See if you qualify for a discount for not smoking, not drinking, belonging to a car pool, having an accident-free record for the past three years or more, having a car with heavy bumpers or a passive restraint system, driving a compact car, or keeping your mileage low each year.

6. Don't use your car for work if you can obtain other transportation.

7. Don't duplicate insurance. If you have a comprehensive health and accident insurance policy, then you don't need medical coverage in your automobile insurance plan.

8. Pay your insurance premium for the full period rather than in installments. (Note, however, that you lose the use of that money during the time period.)

9. Any time your situation changes, notify your company. Do this when your estimated yearly mileage drops, when you join a car pool, when a driver of your car moves away from home, and so on.

EXHIBIT P–5
Comparing Auto Insurance Companies

KIND OF COVERAGE	LIMITS DESIRED	COMPANY A	COMPANY B	COMPANY C
1. Liability:				
Bodily injury	$ ______ /person, $ ______ /accident	______	______	______
Property damage	$______ /accident	______	______	______
2. Physical damage:				
Compensation for total lost	blue-book wholesale price	______	______	______
Collision	$______ /deductible	______	______	______
3. Medical payments	$______ /person	______	______	______
4. Uninsured motorist	$______ /person, $______ /accident	______	______	______
5. Accidental death benefits	$______	______	______	______
6. Towing	$______	______	______	______
7. Comprehensive	$______ /deductible	______	______	______
8. Other	$______	______	______	______
ANNUAL TOTAL		______	______	______

WHEN YOU ARE REFUSED INSURANCE

Sometimes, because of a bad driving record, you will be refused liability coverage by an automobile insurance company. When this happens, you become an **assigned risk**. You must first certify that you have attempted within the past sixty days to obtain insurance in the state in which you reside. A pool of insurance companies (or sometimes the state) will then assign you to a specific company in the pool for a period of three years. At the end of three years, you can apply for reassignment, provided you are still unable to purchase insurance outside the pool.

If you are an assigned risk, you can purchase only the legal minimum amount of insurance in your state. In most cases, you will pay a much higher premium for the same amount of coverage than someone who is not an assigned risk.

SUMMARY

1. When looking for a new car dealer, consider location, dealer service facilities and personnel, dealer reputation, and the deal offered.
2. Because new cars generally have problems that you will want the dealer to take care of, the proximity of the dealer and his or her willingness to handle such warranty problems are important considerations when deciding where to buy a new car.
3. Deciding on the size of a car should involve not only purchase cost but running costs, as well as ride smoothness, acceleration, availability of options, and handling.
4. The purchase of a used car requires as much shopping as for a new car, or more, for the mechanical condition of the car is now in question. If you wish to have a warranty, purchase a used car from a dealer offering a one-month or 300-mile warranty. However, you will have to pay a higher price for that benefit.
5. Shop for automobile financing just as you shop for any other product. Shop on the basis of the down payment required, setup charges, actual finance charge, and actual annual interest, as well as the number of months required to pay. Remember, the sooner you pay off the loan, the less interest you pay. On the other hand, if your payments are high relative to your income, you will have less money for other purchases.
6. There is a minimum insurance required to drive an automobile in all states. However, it is generally quite cheap to purchase additional coverage. For example, it may cost you only $3 more a year to increase your liability from $50,000 to $150,000.
7. Shop for automobile insurance systematically, asking each company its price for a standard policy, such as $25,000 for bodily injury to one person, a maximum of $50,000 bodily injury to more than one person, and a maximum of $5,000 for property, plus $10,000 medical payments, plus $100 deductible collision, full comprehensive and uninsured motorist coverage. After you have received the different bids on such a policy, find out the payoff procedures in case of an accident. Does the company have a claims department? How well is it set up? How fast will it operate? How soon can you get a loaner car in case of an accident?

QUESTIONS FOR THOUGHT AND DISCUSSION

1. For a few years, one car company had a 50,000-mile or five-year warranty on the drive train of its new automobiles. This warranty is no longer available. Why do you think it was discontinued?
2. Why do you think some automobile companies have longer warranty periods than others?
3. Many automobiles are obviously less safe than others. Why do you think people knowingly drive such unsafe cars?
4. Do you think that the most important factor in deciding which car to buy is the amount of gasoline it consumes?
5. In 1973 and 1974, large American cars stopped selling well. Do you know why?
6. Would you prefer to take out an automobile loan for twenty-four months or forty-eight months?
7. What is the most important safety feature a car can have?
8. Would it ever be considered rational not to carry automobile insurance?

THINGS TO DO

1. Even if you are not in the market for a new car, try shopping for one over the phone. Pick a particular make, body style, and set of accessories. Call five different new-car dealers in your area. See if you can get an actual quote on the phone. Are there any big differences among the quotes you get. You will be surprised at how little the quotes vary.
2. Make a list of the various new-car warranties available for cars such as Ford, Chevrolet, Oldsmobile, Volkswagen, Volvo, and Mercedes. See if the more expensive cars have a better warranty.

3. Go to the library and get the latest December *Annual Buying Guide* of *Consumer Reports*. Look at the section on buying a used car. Could you perform the eight to ten on-the-lot tests given in that section? Have you ever tried the driving tests given in that section when you were looking for a used car?

4. Find out whether your area has a local office of AUTOCAP, which is under National Automobile Dealer Association sponsorship. See what AUTOCAP in your area has done.

SELECTED READINGS

Aerospace Education Foundation. *The Safe Driving Handbook*. New York: Grossett & Dunlap, 1970.

"Buying a New Car: How to Drive Home a Bargain." *Changing Times*, October 1981.

Consumer Action Auto Insurance Guide. San Francisco, Calif.: San Francisco Consumer Action, 26 Seventh Street, San Francisco 94103.

Garretson, K. "How to Keep Car Repair Bills in Line." *Better Homes and Gardens*, February 1980, pp. 77–78.

"Good Reasons for Buying an Old Car." *Changing Times*, September 1981.

"How to Shop for a Car Loan." *Consumer Reports*, July 1979, pp. 418–19.

"Managing Your Auto Insurance." A three-part series in June, July, and August *Consumer Reports*, 1977.

"Ways to Save Gasoline and Money in Your Driving." *Consumers' Research Magazine*, January 1980, pp. 26–29.

CHAPTER
THE HEALTH CARE DILEMMA

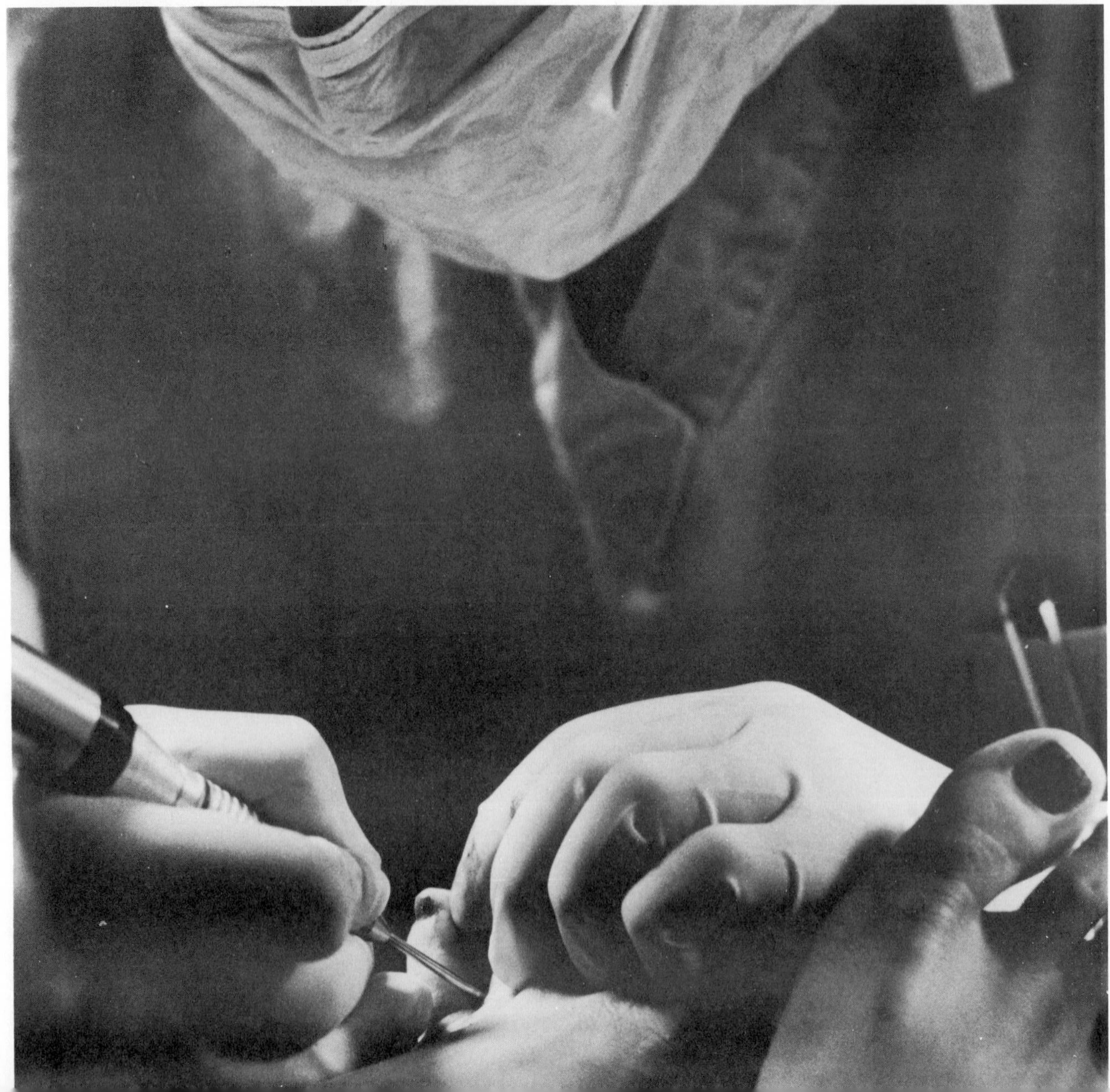

The lack of adequate health care for large segments of the American population has been long decried by presidents, laypersons, and even doctors. . . . and the cost of medical services has risen at a faster rate than the overall Consumer Price Index.

CHAPTER PREVIEW

- What has Medicare to do with the high cost of medical services?
- Why are there relatively few medical doctors in the United States?
- What are the restrictions on entry into the medical-care industry?
- How does the American Medical Association fit into all this?
- What has the Food and Drug Administration done to protect the consumer from injurious drugs?
- What has the restriction on advertising drug prices to consumers done to the cost of drugs?
- What is group health service all about?
- What are HMOs?

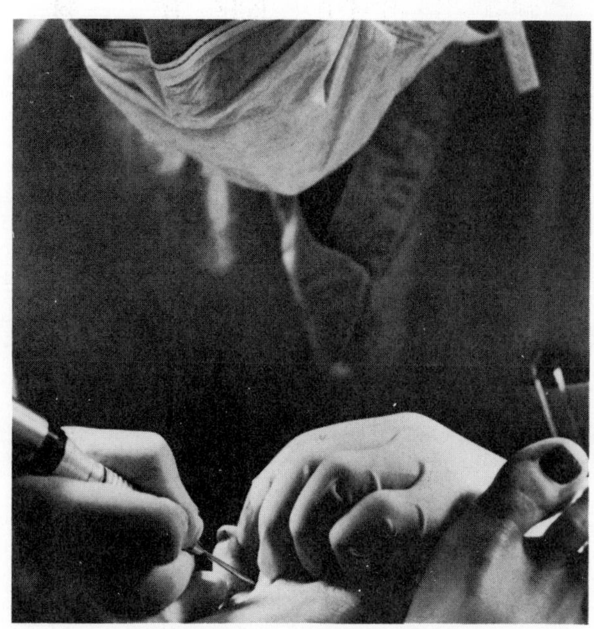

The woeful lack of adequate health care for large segments of the American population has been long decried by members of Congress, presidents, laypersons, and even doctors. There have been many suggested solutions to our health-care crisis, some of which have been enacted in the form of Medicare and Medicaid. But even before those programs went into effect, politicians started demanding more comprehensive medical care insurance.

In addition to the problems of inadequate supplies of medical care, concerned legislators and citizens could not help noticing the spiraling costs of obtaining what medical care is available. The cost of medical services has risen at a faster rate than the overall Consumer Price Index. Thus, not only is health care more expensive than it was, but its *relative* price is rising; it is more expensive in relation to other services than it once was.

MEDICAL-CARE EXPENDITURES

The expenditures for medical care in the United States have increased dramatically in the last four or five decades. We spent only $4 billion on medical care in 1929. We increased our spending to $40 billion by 1965. It is well over $300 billion today. In 1929, expenditures for medical care represented 4 percent of total national spending, but today's expenditures represent nearly 10 percent. We can say, therefore, that as real incomes rise, Americans demand not just more medical care but more than is in proportion to the rise in incomes.

More Spending Doesn't Mean Better Health

In spite of the enormous sums of money Americans spend on health care, the Surgeon General has reported that "our 700 percent increase in health spending has not yielded the striking improvement over the last twenty years that we might have hoped for." Despite all the money poured into health care, U.S. citizens are nowhere near the healthiest in the world. For example:

1. Twenty-six other countries have a lower death rate from heart ailments.
2. Eleven other countries do a better job of keeping babies alive during the first years of life.
3. Fourteen other countries have a higher life expectancy for men, and six others have a higher life expectancy for women.

The Surgeon General contends that the reason for this anomaly is that too little time, money, and effort have been spent on *preventive medicine*. Half the U.S. deaths are attributed to unhealthy behavior or life style, 20 percent to environmental factors, 20 percent to human biological factors, and, surprisingly, only 10 percent to inadequate health care.

WHY DOES MEDICAL CARE COST SO MUCH?

Nobody expects medical care to be free. After all, it uses resources, and resources themselves are never free. But many people have wondered why medical-care costs have been going up so much faster than all other costs.

This has happened for several reasons. The first has to do with the increases in demand brought about by government programs.

When Medicare Started

Prior to Medicare—"free" medical care for the aged—congressional estimates of what that program would cost were many times less than what the actual cost turned out to be. When Medicare was instituted, the actual price of health-care services to many people was drastically lowered. In some cases, the price was reduced to zero. As the price fell, the quantity demanded rose so much that the available supply of medical-care services was taxed beyond capacity. The only thing that could give was the price, and it gave. Hospital room charges have skyrocketed since the imposition of Medicare. But Medicare alone has not caused drastic increases in medical prices.

Insurance Framework

Approximately 80 million Americans are covered by some form of private medical insurance, most of which pays a certain part of hospital expenses. Herein lies the problem. Insurance rarely covers **outpatient service**; rather, it covers only **inpatient service.** Individuals covered by insurance, therefore, have an incentive to go to the hospital to be taken care of by their private doctors. And their private doctors have an incentive to send them to the hospital in order to collect the insurance payments, knowing full well that fewer patients would be able to pay for the services performed in their doctors' offices because they would not then be covered by insurance. Additionally, insurance plans generally have very little control over the number of tests and examinations that are performed on patients. Hospitals have an incentive, therefore, to use the most exotic techniques possible and doctors to order them, knowing full well that patients will have a large percentage of the costs reimbursed by insurance companies. The problem is that patients covered under insurance do not pay the *direct* costs of the medical care they receive in a hospital. Hence, they demand much more than they otherwise would. This increase in quantity demanded causes hospital expenses to go up, if all other things are held constant.

OUTPATIENT SERVICES
The services of doctors and/or hospitals that do not involve the individual remaining as a registered patient in the hospital.

INPATIENT SERVICES
Services rendered to an individual by doctors and/or a hospital while the patient remains in the hospital for at least one night.

Additionally, there seems to be a tendency in some communities to build too many hospitals. Perhaps the lure of those insurance dollars causes this phenomenon. In any event, the result is, somewhat amazingly, hospitals with a high percentage of empty beds. In order to recoup all their overhead costs, these hospitals end up charging higher prices than they would if they were fully utilized. Additionally, hospitals attempt to compete for patients and doctors. One way to do this is to order all the latest equipment, which translates into higher costs because this equipment is so expensive.

Other Reasons

There is an increased sophistication in the medical field, most notably in the areas of diagnosis, surgery, drug treatment, and physical therapy. Along with this increased specialization has come the supposed need to visit two or more specialized doctors, rather than one as in the past. This, of course, raises the

Individuals are suing their doctors and hospitals more than ever before, and juries frequently are awarding larger amounts.

cost of medical care. Additionally, we are getting better services than before. Many hospitals now have complete staffing around the clock and use much more sophisticated equipment. All of this costs more. Recently an even more important phenomenon, malpractice insurance expenses, has caused medical costs to rise.

MALPRACTICE

Individuals are suing their doctors and hospitals more than ever before, and juries frequently are awarding larger amounts. The result? Skyrocketing malpractice insurance costs. Just look at a few examples. In 1972, Baylor University Medical Center in Dallas, Texas, paid $11,000 for malpractice insurance; in 1976, the bill was $1.5 million! In 1974, Mt. Sinai Hospital Medical Center in Chicago paid $281,000 for $6 million in malpractice insurance; in 1976, the same insurance companies wanted $3 million to provide the $6 million in coverage. Had the hospital paid the premium sought by the insurance companies, the daily cost of malpractice insurance to the patient would have gone from seven to twenty-two dollars per day. A number of hospitals have stopped paying regular insurance companies for such coverage. Instead, they are self-insuring; that is, they set aside a certain sum of money each month in a reserve account to cover any claims against them in malpractice lawsuits. Unfortunately, this means that some hospitals could conceivably go out of business if an extraordinarily large malpractice suit were won by a former patient.

We also find that hospitals may protect themselves from additional malpractice suits by engaging in excessive testing and prolonged stays in intensive-care units after surgery. This adds to medical-care costs.

Some concerned individuals have suggested that the government step in to offer malpractice insurance to hospitals that do not feel they can afford the escalating rates. However, this would mean that hospitals could then force the general taxpayer to cover any of their mistakes. In the future, there may be other solutions to the malpractice-insurance problem.

THE SHORT SUPPLY OF MEDICAL CARE

Medical care consists of a number of items, including but not limited to the services of physicians, nurses, and hospital staff; hospital facilities; maintenance of the facilities; and medications and drugs. What determines the supply of the most important item (at least up until now)—physicians' services—in the total medical care package?

The Production of Medical Doctors

In 1978–79, 34,969 people took the Medical College Admissions Test (MCAT); only 16,527 were accepted into medical schools. Applicants to the Harvard Medical School run to almost 3,500, but the class size remains at fewer than 150. Some students apply to as many as ten different medical schools and, when turned down, reapply two or three times. Moreover, probably two or three times as many students do not bother to apply because they know the odds are against them. Why is there such a large discrepancy between those who want to go to medical school and those who are accepted? If you compare the number of students who wish to attend law school with the number of students who actually go, the discrepancy is much smaller than that for medical school. Obviously, the number of medical schools in the United States is severely restricted, as is the number of entrants into those schools.

Restrictions

In principle, restriction on the number of medical schools is due to state licensing requirements that universally prohibit proprietary medical schools (schools run for profit). Also, it is difficult for a university that does not have

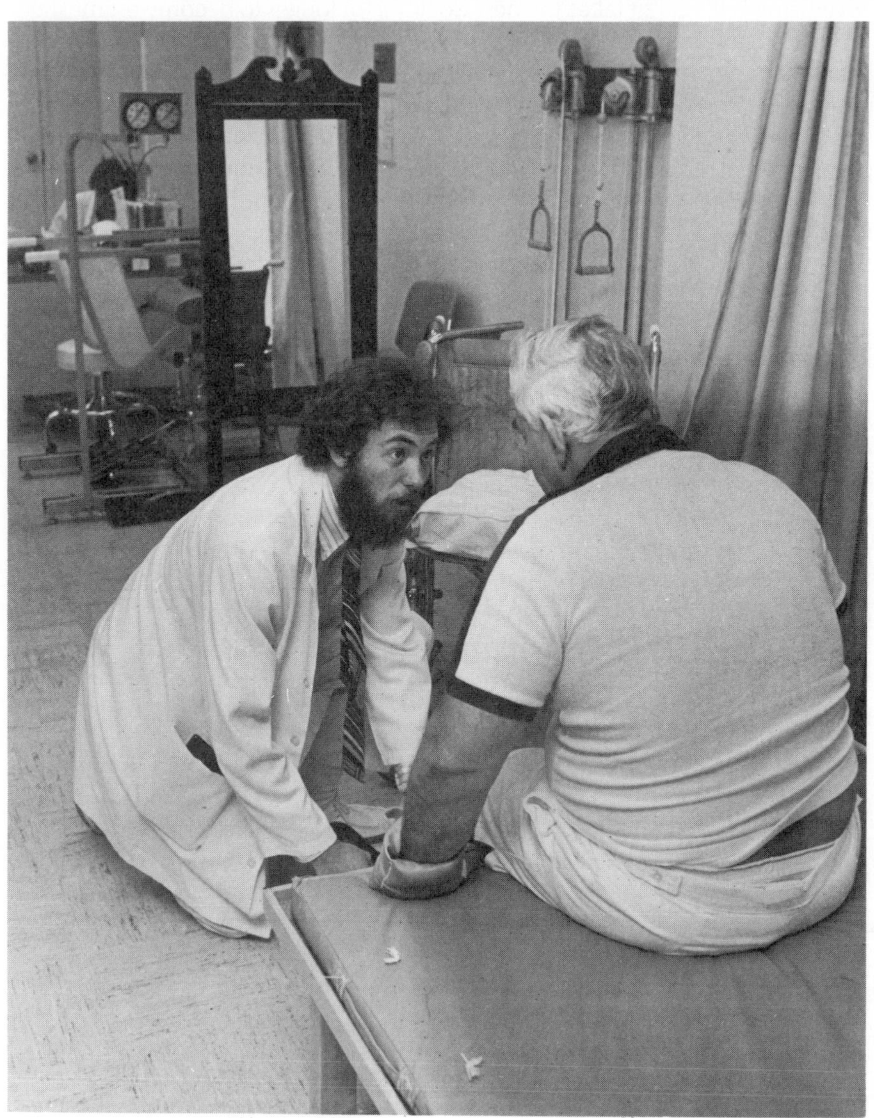

a medical school to start one. A university can start a graduate department of Romance languages without asking permission of any agencies or boards, just as it can start a law school without asking anybody. However, unless the medical school is accredited by the state, the graduates are not even allowed to take the licensing exam required for practicing medicine.[1]

Doctors and Advertising

Until recently, it was virtually impossible for any doctor to advertise. Various county medical associations had restrictions against medical advertising. According to physicians' codes, advertising was unethical; basically, though, these codes were an attempt to limit competition among doctors. Additionally, the ban on advertising benefited established doctors and hurt new doctors. The best way for a new doctor to become known would be to advertise. If advertising is illegal, it takes the new doctor a lot longer to become established.

The Federal Trade Commission, however, has changed physicians' codes. In an attack against restrictions on advertising in both the legal and the medical professions, the Federal Trade Commission pointed out that both the notions of free speech and free competition require that advertising be allowed in all professions. In the future, you undoubtedly will see more physicians telling you, in newspaper ads, on TV, and on the radio, about their services. Ultimately, the consumer will benefit by such advertising: Studies have shown that advertising does lead to less price variation and a lower average price for similar services and products in situations where the advertising is mainly informative. In the case of physicians and lawyers, most advertising has been informative, telling us about location, services, and price.

The Future Supply

The current shortage of physicians has been estimated to be 50,000. However, recent rates of medical-school graduation and the addition of foreign-trained physicians who are immigrating to the United States will eliminate this shortage. In addition, Congress has enacted a number of programs to increase the supply of medical personnel. For example, in 1971 the Comprehensive Manpower Training Act and the Nurse Training Act were passed; $3 billion was provided for this purpose. Actually, some researchers believed that "there [was] a distinct possibility of excess capacity in medical schools and a surplus of physicians by the late 1970s." [2]

In 1980, the Department of Health and Human Services presented President Carter and the Congress with a report about physician requirements for the 1990s. The report predicted that, during the final decade of this century, physician requirements for the United States would range between 553,000

1. Licensing of doctors is now done under the requirements of the National Board of Medical Examiners. Among the national requirements are two years of college, four years of medical school with a final examination, and an internship.

2. Charles T. Stewart, Jr., and Corazon M. Siddayao, *Increasing the Supply of Medical Personnel: Needs and Alternatives*. Washington, D.C.: American Enterprise Institute for Public Policy Research, 1972, p. 66. This seems to be what is happening in certain urban areas. However, a shortage of doctors is still apparent in most rural areas in the United States.

and 596,000. The supply of doctors, on the other hand, is expected to exceed 600,000. Thus, HEW believes that we will see a surplus of medical doctors in America by 1990, if not before. It also foresees a slight oversupply of dentists by 1990. The government agency attributes the growth of licensed physicians to expansion of training facilities and enrollments with the federal government's support. As a result of the report, the Carter administration continued its efforts to reduce or cut off completely federal-aid grants to health-professions schools and eliminate assistance for starting new schools.[3]

DRUG REGULATION

The **ethical-drug industry** has always presented problems to regulators and consumers, particularly in the area of information. Even the drug companies often do not know the effectiveness or the side effects of a drug. Doctors rarely take the time to get exact information on all the drugs they prescribe, and drug companies have not always carefully screened the drugs they have sold. The largest regulator of drugs in the United States is the federal Food and Drug Administration (FDA).

ETHICAL DRUG INDUSTRY
The industry that produces the drugs that are sold by prescription only. Patent drugs, on the other hand, are sold over the counter without prescriptions.

Drug regulation is a difficult task. Consumers spend more than $21 billion a year for drugs, of which about $11 billion worth are sold only by prescription. Drugs save many lives and reduce suffering caused by many illnesses. More than 90 percent of the prescriptions written today are for drugs that did not even exist thirty years ago.

What the FDA Does

Since the Kefauver-Harris Amendment to the 1938 Food, Drug and Cosmetic Act passed in 1962, the FDA has required drug companies to follow quite detailed, extremely lengthy procedures before approval can be given for a new drug. A drug company may spend years completing these steps before it can get approval for a new drug.

The Benefits and Costs of FDA Requirements

If aspirin had to meet the current FDA requirements for drug certification, it would fail to pass muster. Do you know why? Because it is not known why it works, and it is known to have side effects if taken in too large a quantity. Certainly aspirin would at least require a prescription if it were under current rulings. Now ask yourself this: Do you think it should be dispensed only by prescription? Do you think it should be taken off the market because nobody knows how it works? We are certain that taking too much of it can give you duodenal ulcers and kidney dysfunction. If you believe it should be taken off the market, then you will agree with the spirit of the 1962 Kefauver-Harris Amendment. If you have doubts, then read on.

3. Department of Health, Education and Welfare, "A Report to the President and Congress of the Status of Health Professions Personnel in the United States." Superintendent of Documents, U.S. Government Printing Office, 1980.

If aspirin had to meet the current FDA requirements for drug certification, it would fail to pass muster.

A study was done by Dr. Sam Peltzman a few years ago. Among the costs of the 1962 FDA amendment, he found that the entry rate of new drugs into the market had slowed considerably. His conclusions were the following:

> The 1962 Drug Amendment sought to reduce consumer waste on ineffective drugs. This goal appears to have been attained, but the costs in the process seem clearly to have outweighed the benefits. It was shown [in the study] that the amendments have produced a substantial decline in drug innovation since 1962.
>
> The net effect of the amendment on consumers, then, is comparable to their being taxed something between 5 and 10 percent on their . . . drug purchases.[4]

As with all legislation, consumers have to weigh the costs against the benefits in deciding where they stand. The benefits of preventing certain drugs from entering the market are that no one suffers the side effects. The costs are those just mentioned. Dr. Peltzman believes the costs outweigh the benefits, but you may interpret his data differently.

Restrictions in Pharmaceutical Sales

Did you know that only 5 percent of prescriptions are compounded by the pharmacist? The other 95 percent the druggist fills by dropping pills into bottles and/or by merely typing the patient's and doctor's names and dosage instructions on the pharmacy's label, which is then pasted on a bottle supplied by the manufacturer. Why, then, does it cost so much to get drugs? One reason has been the restriction of price competition among druggists: It is not considered "ethical" to advertise prescription drug prices. Thirty-seven states had expressly prohibited drug-price advertising for many years. In many cases, druggists would claim that professional ethics prevented them from discussing on the phone what they charged for filling a prescription or what their prescriptions cost.

Pharmacy practices came to light in 1972 when the federal Price Commission then in existence was going to require that retailers display base prices of their best-selling drugs. The American Pharmaceutical Association claimed that this would be a police-state method of holding down prices. Unfortunately for us, the consumers, the Price Commission backed down; it did not require the posting of prices. Instead, pharmacies were told they could provide consumers with the standard list of wholesale drug prices and the store's professional fee or markup for filling a prescription.

Because most druggists did not post prescription prices, it was (and still may be) more difficult for us to shop around for pharmaceutical bargains than it is to shop for other goods. It was not surprising, then, that a 1967 AMA study in Chicago showed price differentials of 1,200 percent for exactly the same drug! The U.S. Justice Department drew the obvious, logical conclusion:

> Differentials such as these can only exist when they are unknown to potential customers; for a given choice, most consumers would refuse to pay 10 or 12 times the going price for a drug available elsewhere. The cost to the public of the lack of price competition is enormous.

In 1976, the magazine *Money* priced three of the ten most prescribed drugs in four stores in five cities. *Money* found as much as a 406 percent difference

4. Sam Peltzman, "An Evaluation of Consumer Protection Legislation: The 1962 Drug Amendments," *Journal of Political Economy*, 81 (September/October 1973): 1089–1090.

in the price for a given drug. The results were as follows (price on a per-pill basis):

DRUG	LOWEST PRICE	HIGHEST PRICE	SPREAD
Valium (5 mg.)	8.9¢	23.2¢	161%
Darvon Compound-65	7.6¢	19.8¢	161%
Tetracycline (250 mg.)	4.9¢	24.8¢	406%

The price of the drug that is not trademarked is much less, but only about 10 percent of all new drug prescriptions are written with the generic name of the drug.

The Supreme Court Intervenes

The 1976, a landmark case for consumers was handed down by the U.S. Supreme Court. A consumer activist, Lynn Jordan of Virginia, decided to do something about not being able to shop around for the lowest-priced prescription drugs because a Virginia law banned prescription-drug price advertising. She, along with the consumer council she headed in the Virginia State AFL-CIO, sued and won.[5] It has been ruled unconstitutional for states to forbid pharmacies to advertise prices for prescription drugs, even though statute or pharmacy-board regulations prohibit it. According to Justice Harry A. Blackmun, "Advertising, however tasteless and excessive it sometimes may seem, is nonetheless dissemination of information as to who is producing and selling what product for what reason and at what price." If consumers are to make more intelligent marketplace decisions, they need the "free flow of commercial information," according to Blackmun and the Court.

Even before the Supreme Court decision, some states had gone further and actually required the posting of drug prices. Since January 1, 1974, New York State pharmacists have had to post the price and name of the 150 most frequently prescribed drugs. Boston, since 1971, has required the posting of the 100 most frequently prescribed drugs and their prices. California, Minnesota, New Hampshire, and Texas have followed suit. The Food and Drug Administration, toward the end of 1973, decided to help standardize pricing information to be given to consumers. It said that it would prescribe the format to be used for the posting and advertising of prescription-drug prices.

Generic versus Brand-Name Drugs

Prescriptions for drugs can either be written in terms of the drug's generic name or its brand or trademark name. The price of the drug that is not trademarked is much less, but only about 10 percent of all new drug prescriptions are written with the generic name of the drug. Why do doctors often prescribe expensive brand-name drugs? It may be that physicians become accustomed to certain proven drugs and automatically prescribe them. It may even be because physicians are courted by drug companies that give them free golf balls, free dinners, and the like. In most states, a druggist is required to make no substitution when filling out a prescription that mentions a brand name. However, one study of a penicillin drug called Ampicillin, its generic name, showed that even though 53 percent of the prescriptions had that name on them, 98 percent of the sales were for major brand names. When you consider that the brand-

5. *Virginia Pharmacy Board* vs. *The Virginia Consumer Council,* 425 U.S. 748 (1976).

The Food and Drug Administration believes strongly that there is no significant difference in quality between the generic and brand-name products tested.

name price is usually two to four times more expensive than the lowest generic price, you can see what this does to health-care costs.[6]

The Food and Drug Administration believes strongly that there is no significant difference in quality between the generic and brand-name products tested. Nonetheless, there are strong proponents of brand-name drugs. They believe that generic drugs are not as effective as brand-name drugs; they measure effectiveness by the amount of active medication that is absorbed from the intestine into the bloodstream.

ALTERNATIVE HEALTH-CARE SYSTEMS

The traditional health-care system has been the standard "fee for service" between doctor and private patient. But, in recent decades, alternatives to this system have become numerous. Although we lack the space to go into all of them, we will discuss group health and HMOs (Health Maintenance Organizations).

Group Health Service

A group health service is basically a hospital incorporating all aspects of health-care services in which doctors work for a salary, not for a fee. You become a member of a group-health-care plan by paying a specific fee determined by the number of members in your family. All group-health services are then provided without charge, except for certain drugs. In some plans, you can pick your own doctors from among those on staff; in others, you cannot. Group-health plans stress preventive medicine. The AMA has fought against prepaid medical plans such as Kaiser, Group Health Cooperative of Puget Sound, Health Insurance Plan (HIP) of New York, and Ross Loos. With these medical plans, everybody is charged the same price for the same service. All plans are prepaid, and the charges are not a function of subscribers' incomes. There is no way to **price discriminate** as there is with the typical "fee-for-service" method of payment that most physicians use.

PRICE DISCRIMINATION
Charging different people different prices for the same item.

The AMA has used various tactics to discourage doctors from participating in group-health plans. Many doctors have been expelled from their county medical associations and, therefore, can practice specialties only with the group-health plan hospital. But the AMA has not always succeeded in squelching budding medical establishments that promote competition with private physicians and do not price discriminate. For its efforts, the AMA has been prosecuted under the Sherman Antitrust Act in Washington, D.C., and under other state antitrust acts.

HMOs

Toward the end of 1974, many Americans were asked by their employers whether they wanted to drop group health insurance in favor of prepaid medical

6. Brand-name prescription drugs may cost thirty times more than their generic counterparts.

care. Those employees who chose that particular option became members of an HMO, or Health Maintenance Organization.

HMOs range from group-practice setups like clinics with such extras as specialists, affiliated hospitals, and dentists to individual-practice foundations in which doctors continue to practice in their own offices but take HMO patients in exchange for a share of the premium.

Employees were given this opportunity to switch from group health to prepaid medical care by a provision in the Health Maintenance Organization Act of 1973. Under the law, any company of twenty-five or more workers that has some sort of group-health-insurance plan must negotiate a group HMO contract and offer it to employees, provided that there is a qualified HMO in the area and only if the employer is first contacted by an HMO organizer. The legislation requires HMOs to accept individual members as well as groups of employees.

The list of basic services that must be covered by the monthly premium includes: hospital and physical care, including maternity; X rays and laboratory tests; preventive health services, including regular checkups; birth-control services; alcoholism and drug-abuse treatment; and, for children only, dental checkups and eyeglass examinations.

HMOs are often slightly more expensive than the typical health insurance program. Proponents of HMO legislation, however, point out that the higher premium cost is more than made up for in savings in out-of-pocket medical expenses. HMOs save considerable money on hospitalization, largely by treating people in the doctor's office instead of sending them to the hospital.

There are now approximately 212 HMOs in the United States. The largest operate entire hospitals with hundreds of physicians, nurses, and technicians. The smallest have a few staff members plus internists, pediatricians, and obstetricians. When you need the services of some other specialist, the HMO usually will send you to one and foot the bill.

Critics of our current health-care delivery system point out that less than one-half of one percent of the billions of dollars we spend each year is spent on health education.

Pros and Cons of HMOs

There are many critics of HMOs. In particular, they criticize the impersonal nature of HMOs, stating that they operate on a quick turnover, assembly-line basis, and members cannot choose just any doctor, but only one from the list of qualified HMO doctors. On the other hand, advocates of HMOs say that because the worry of paying for each visit to the doctor is removed, people tend to seek treatment earlier, cutting down the chances of a serious disease. Statistically, we see that HMO members are sent to hospitals 30 to 60 percent less often than nonmembers. Thus, it has been argued (but not proved) that HMO members are absent from their jobs less frequently.

HEALTH EDUCATION

Critics of our current health-care delivery system point out that less than one-half of one percent of the billions of dollars we spend each year is spent on health education. Thus, it might be possible to improve the health of Americans without driving up costs if more individuals were taught to maintain their health. This would mean more time, effort, and money allotted to health education from preschool all the way through college. It would mean offering more health-maintenance courses throughout the country. It would mean having hospitals spend time with patients who are recuperating, teaching them the do's and don't's of proper health care.

There appears to be a significant trend toward more self-help in the health-education area. The "wellness" movement in America encourages individuals to take strides on their own to prevent medical problems. The number of books on the shelves today on how to stay healthy, how to eat properly, and how to exercise is indeed astounding, relative to the number available, say, ten years ago. Undoubtedly, this trend will continue for many years as Americans find that they can, on their own, stay healthy and lower their own medical expenses.

SUMMARY

1. The relative price of health-care services has been rising. In particular, hospital costs have gone up dramatically in the last few years.
2. Medicare, which drastically lowered the price of health-care services to many aged people, as well as insurance schemes that do not show the consumer the direct costs of medical care, have caused the demand for medical-care services to rise dramatically.
3. One reason medical services have always been so costly is that the number of medical doctors in the United States is restricted.
4. The relatively high cost of medical care has caused many consumers to perform self-diagnosis and self-treatment.
5. The federal Food and Drug Administration regulates the ethical-drug industry in the United States. A 1962 amendment to the Food, Drug and Cosmetic Act has significantly lengthened the time it takes for a drug company to get a new drug certified as safe.
6. Until recently, prescription-drug prices in almost all states were not posted and, in fact, could not be posted according to the rules of pharmaceutical associations. This had the effect of reducing competition among pharmacies and increasing prices to consumers for prescription drugs.
7. Alternative health-care systems, such as group health and health maintenance organizations, are proliferating in the United States.

QUESTIONS FOR THOUGHT AND DISCUSSION

1. Do you think it is fair that health-care services can rise in price?
2. Should health-care services be a right and not a privilege?
3. What is the difference between health-care services and other services performed in our economy?
4. Why would insurance schemes increase the demand for hospital services?
5. Do you think more patent drugs should be sold by prescription only? Or do you think more prescription drugs should be sold without a prescription?
6. What is the argument in favor of restricting advertising of prescription-drug prices?
7. What is the argument against that restriction?
8. Do you think the future will see more group-health-care facilities or fewer?

THINGS TO DO

1. Discuss the arguments concerning medical costs or the short supply of medical care with someone in the medical profession. Are the opinions of the textbook author and the person you spoke to the same? If so, elaborate. If not, how do they differ? What would account for these differences?
2. Ask a medical doctor you know why practicing physicians are not recertified periodically.
3. Call up several pharmacies in your area to find out the price of fifty capsules of 250 mgs. of tetracycline. If they will not give you the price on the phone, ask why not. See if there is much difference among the prices quoted. If there is, ask why.

SELECTED READINGS

Annas, George J. *The Rights of Hospital Patients.* New York: Avon Books, 1979.

Berliner, H. S. and Salmon, J. W. "America's Inadequate Preventive Health Care Policy." *USA Today,* January 1980, pp. 39–41.

Bronson, G. "Checking Your Medical Policy's Health." *Money,* September 1982, pp. 72–74.

Cutting Prices: A Guide to Washington Area Surgeons' Fees. Washington, D.C.: Health Research Group, Dept. 241, 2000 F Street, N.W., Suite 708, Washington, D.C. 20036.

"Drugs on the Market." *Consumers' Research Magazine,* May 1982, pp. 21–24.

"Evaluating Your Medical Benefits." *Business Week,* August 30, 1982, pp. 88–89.

"Excess Marks the Spot" (FDA Regulations). *Time,* September 27, 1982, p. 83.

First Facts about Drugs. FDA Fact Sheet 1712–0122. Washington, D.C.: Consumer Product Information, 1970.

Getting Yours: A Consumer's Guide to Obtaining Your Medical Record. Washington, D.C.: Health Research Group, Dept. M-R, 2000 F Street, N.W., Suite 708, Washington, D.C. 20036. Send $2 and a large, self-addressed, stamped envelope.

"Hidden Costs of Drug Safety: FDA's Regulations Effect on Drug Industry Research Projects." *Business Week,* February 21, 1977, p. 80.

"The HMO Approach to Health Care." *Consumer Reports,* May 1982, pp. 246–48.

Rubenstein, R. "Wellness Is All." *Psychology Today,* October 1982, pp. 28–34.

"Today's Leading Health Hazards." *Futurist,* August 1982, pp. 8–13.

"Why Malpractice Rates Are Taking Off Again: Medical Malpractices." *Business Week,* November 12, 1979, pp. 39–41.

Consumer ISSUE 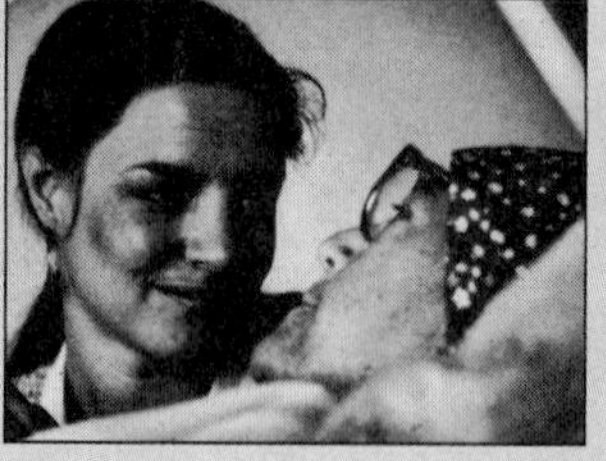 

HOW TO KEEP YOUR MEDICAL COSTS DOWN

GLOSSSARY

COINSURANCE—A joint assumption of the financial risk, usually between you, the insured, and your insurance company. You are a coinsurer with the insurance company if you are required to pay a certain portion of your medical bills.

DEDUCTIBLE—The amount you have to pay in medical bills before your insurance policy takes effect.

LIMITATION—Upper limit on payment of a health insurance policy; for example, it covers 120 days and then you begin to pay.

MAJOR MEDICAL—The type of medical insurance that covers only major medical costs. A major medical policy might, for example, pay 80 percent of all bills in excess of $500 a year.

WAITING PERIOD—The period during which an insurance policy is not in effect or for which you will be paid nothing on the policy. For example, if there is a waiting period of thirty days under a particular policy, you may have to be disabled for thirty days before a payment is made to you for loss of earnings.

HOW TO KEEP YOUR MEDICAL COSTS DOWN

There is no way you can eliminate completely the costs of medical care for you and your dependents. However, you can insure yourself against at least extraordinary costs and, if you see fit, against all normal medical-care expenditures throughout the year. In this Consumer Issue, we will give the pros and cons of different types of medical insurance coverage, including an explanation of how Medicare and Medicaid affect you.

KEEPING HEALTHY

One of the best insurance policies against excessive medical costs is a consistent, comprehensive program of keeping fit. All of us know what we *should* do, but many of use have a tendency to let ourselves become run down, hypertensive, overweight, and so on. This is not the place to go into detail about preventive care of the human body, but we will briefly discuss three steps you can take toward health—and away from the doctor's office.

1. Good diet. This means getting all the minimum amounts of vitamins and nutrients in a regular basis and in the right quantities. The right quantity is usually such that you do not become overweight or, for some persons, too underweight. Good diet does not require a high income; as we pointed out in Chapter 12, even people with low incomes can obtain a nutritious diet if they are willing to sacrifice variety.

2. Adequate exercise. Medical people are fairly convinced that if you exercise, you feel better, sleep better, and are less prone to serious cardiovascular illnesses. Again, this does not require money; for example, jogging is free (but does require a *time* cost).

3. Moderation of foreign substances. There is much less agreement on this point than on the others, but many experts believe that you should not abuse your mind and body with such drugs as nicotine, alcohol, hallucinogens, "uppers," "downers," and the like. They also counsel against becoming dependent upon patent medicine;

hypochondria can lead to an overuse of medicines that may eventually cause serious bodily damage.

Prescription Drugs by Mail

When you are required to take prescription drugs, there is one way to shop around for the lowest price, particularly for drugs that you must take on a regular basis. There are discount mail-order houses throughout the United States with prices averaging 20 to 25 percent below chain-store prices. Here are three large mail-order drug firms.

1. The National Retired Teachers Association/American Association of Retired Persons, 1224 24th St., N.W., Washington, D.C. 20037. You must be a member: To become one, you must be a retired teacher or over fifty-five. There are eight regional centers offering mail-order and walk-in service.
2. Pharmaceutical Services, 127 West Markey Road, Belton, Missouri 64102. If you are a member of the National Education Association, you get an additional 10 percent discount.
3. Getz Prescription Company, 916 Walnut Street, Kansas City, Missouri 64199.

TYPES OF MEDICAL INSURANCE

There are five basic categories of medical service for which health insurance can be purchased. No doubt you can find other categories for special problems.

Hospital Expenses

Experts believe that over 90 percent of persons in the United States are now protected under some voluntary programs that will cover at least part of medical-care costs arising from illness or accident. Hospital-expense protection provides benefits toward full or partial payment of room, board, and services any time you are in a hospital. Usually it includes use of operating room, lab, Xrays, medicines, and incidental care. Almost all insurance companies that issue any sort of total health insurance package will issue hospital-expense insurance.

Surgical Insurance

Almost all Americans who have some sort of hospital insurance also have surgical insurance that pays for the services of a surgeon. Generally, a fee schedule fixes the maximum amount **limitation.** Exhibit Q–1 gives an example. Any excess over the stipulated maximum must be paid either by another type of insurance policy or out of your own pocket. The higher the maximum limits for surgery, the higher the cost of the insurance; you must decide what risk you want to take. Typically, health insurers will pay for a second opinion on surgery. This often cuts down on unneeded surgery and has been quite effective in reducing medical-care costs in America.

Regular Medical Protection

This type of protection pays for visits to the doctor's office, as well as all Xray, diagnostic, and laboratory expenses related to such visits. There is generally a maximum number of calls allowable for each sickness and also a one-call deductible. In many cases, when your family is covered under your medical insurance policy, only you, the subscriber, are covered under regular medical insurance provisions. Your spouse and your children are covered only in case of accidents. This type may cost you more in annual premiums than you would pay to the doctor in an average year.

Major Medical

What happens in the event of a very serious or prolonged illness or a terrible automobile accident requiring $50,000 worth of medical expenses? If you do not have **major medical** insurance, you are faced with a financial disaster that may take years to pull out of. Major medical insurance takes over where all basic health plans just discussed stop. Over 85 million Americans are now covered under these policies. The maximum coverage ranges from $5,000 to $50,000 and, in some cases, to a quarter of a million dollars. This maximum may apply to one illness or to the total of many illnesses during a policy year.

EXHIBIT Q–1
Typical Surgical Insurance Benefits

Procedure	Benefit
Appendectomy	$ 500
Gallbladder removal	720
Hernia repair	450
Tonsillectomy	350
Thyroid removal	900
Benign tumor	400
Prostate gland removal	550
Fracture, closed reduction of femur	550
Fracture, closed reduction of rib	200
Brain tumor	4,000
Intervertebral disc removal	1,600
Kidney removal	2,000
Eardrum incision	200
Boil, incision	100

Major medical is cheaper if you have a basic policy, but you can often buy it alone. Under a major medical plan, after a specific **deductible,** say, $100 to $1,000, the insurance company will reimburse you for 80 or 90 percent of all your medical expenses for a single illness up to the maximum amount for which you have contracted. This feature, called a **coinsurance** clause, requires you, the policyholder, to pay 10 or 20 percent of the total bill. Note that even though you end up paying part of your bill when there is a coinsurance clause, you might be better off with such insurance in times of rapidly rising medical costs. If you are covered by a fixed schedule of rates, you end up paying a larger and larger difference if those rates do not go up as medical costs rise. Coinsurance, on the other hand, means that you pay only a certain percentage, say, 20 percent, of the rising medical rates; the insurance company pays the rest. Most major medical coverage is sold under group plans as part of a comprehensive medical insurance scheme. Exhibit Q–2 gives an example of a major medical policy.

Disability Insurance

Almost 80 million persons are covered by this form of insurance that guarantees you benefits if you can no longer work because of accident or illness. Such insurance compensates you for lost wages. Sometimes this is called salary-continuation insurance. Under many policies, you can expect to get 50 to 65 percent of your normal earnings if you are making average wages. Because the probability that illness will prevent you from working increases with your age, it is a good idea to get a noncancellable policy that offers you protection through your entire working life. Such a policy will be more expensive, of course. Many policies have a **waiting period**—that is, a period following your disability during which you receive no payments. The longer the waiting period, the less you have to pay for this type of insurance. When you buy health and disability insurance, be sure you find out how long the waiting period is. A one-year waiting period may render the policy useless to you except for permanent injuries. That may not be what you want; you may want the policy to go into effect thirty days after an accident or the onset of an illness.

Since 1976, many companies have changed one aspect of salary continuation insurance: They no longer insure occupations but, rather, the income stream, thus attempting to motivate the person to obtain some other gainful employment without missing out on insurance benefits. This focuses attention away from disability and toward rehabilitation.

One thing to watch out for with disability policies is their participation limits. These limits will indicate, for example, that if other disability income coverage, such as Social Security or workers' compensation, is in force during any given period of disability, the amount of coverage will be reduced; the total payments to the disabled will not be more than, say, 60 or 80 percent of the disabled's former gross salary. You must be aware of these participation limits if you have several disability insurance policies. You may be paying for benefits you can never collect.

EXHIBIT Q–2
Example of How Major Medical Coverage Operates

Policy coverage:	
Policy limit	$500,000
Deductible	$100 per year
Coinsurance	90%
Medical costs:	
Hospital Expenses:	
A. Room and Board—$500.00 per day for 20 days	$10,000
B. Miscellaneous Medical Expenses (Xray, lab fees, etc.)	4,500
C. Surgical Expense	3,000
Total Expense	$17,500
Less Deductible	100
	$16,500
Coinsurance	.9
Paid by Major Medical	$14,850
Paid by Insured	$ 1,650

OTHER TYPES OF INSURANCE

Dental Insurance

Although few insurance policies cover dental work, such coverage is becoming an increasingly important part of all health insurance policies. Because it is generally provided only on a group basis, if you are not part of a group—such as a large company, government agency, labor union, and so on—you may be unable to buy dental insurance.

There has been quite a dramatic rise in the number of persons with dental expense protection. In 1967, 2.3 million people were covered under dental insurance plans. By 1981, 27 million people were protected by some form of dental insurance. The largest providers of that protection were private insurance companies that insured 20 million persons under regular dental plans. Blue Cross-Blue Shield covered 2.8 million individuals; the remainder were covered by Dental Service Corporation and union welfare funds.

Most dental insurance is a standard prepayment plan that covers 80 percent of the cost of treatment after some sort of deductible, such as $50 or $100. There is a fairly low maximum that can be paid in any one year, usually $600 to $1,000. Exhibit Q–3 shows hypothetical fixed allowances for different dental treatments.

Mental Health Insurance

Although most health insurance does not cover the cost of mental-health care, some plans are being considered. Several unions already have coverage for psychiatric services, as well as treatment for alcoholism.

WHERE SHOULD YOU GO FOR HEALTH INSURANCE?

A variety of organizations will sell you health insurance. The largest are Blue Cross and Blue Shield; the next largest are the commercial insurance companies. In addition, there are labor-union plans, community-organization plans, and consumer cooperatives, as well as group-health plans, one of which may be available in your locality.

Blue Cross and Blue Shield

Formed in 1929 by a group of Dallas schoolteachers, Blue Cross had a membership of over 500,000 by 1938. Today it has about 80,000,000 members with almost eighty Blue Cross plans throughout the nation.

Blue Shield, on the other hand, was established in 1946 by the coordinators of the Associated Medical Care Plans. Blue Shield, originally sponsored by the AMA, is sometimes known as the Doctors' Plan because Blue Shield subscribers can choose the doctor of their choice. While Blue Cross is concerned primarily with hospital insurance, Blue Shield is concerned with surgical and general medical.

Of all those who have any kind of insurance for hospital care, over 40 percent participate in one of the seventy-four autonomous Blue Cross plans. Many Blue Cross group policies offer a 120-day plan that gives you full hospital protection for 120 days in a semiprivate room. Obviously, you save money if you can participate in a group Blue Cross plan. If you are not already aware of the possibility of joining a group plan, ask your employer, your fraternal organization, or any other organization of which you may be a member. Somewhere you ought to be able to get group coverage.

Many people take out Blue Shield as well as Blue Cross because Blue Shield covers the cost of physicians' services. Blue Shield plans contract with participating physicians to accept payment according to a preplanned fee schedule. If you select a physican who does not participate in the plan, Blue Shield gives you a cash refund up to a set amount on a given fee schedule; you make your own financial arrangements with that doctor. You can plan on paying a monthly rate of between thirty dollars and fifty dollars for family coverage, particularly if you are involved in a combination Blue Cross-Blue Shield arrangement.

In addition to Blue Cross-Blue Shield, there are almost 1,000 nonaffiliated health insurance plans from which to choose. All are independent of both Blue Cross-Blue Shield and insurance companies. However, these numerous plans cover only 5 percent of all persons receiving health-care insurance. Among the most significant independent organizations are the various group-health plans that you and your family can participate in for a fixed fee irrespective of your income.

Group-Health Plans

As a member of a group-health plan, you receive health care from a group-health hospital where doctors are paid a salary (that is, their income is not based on the number of operations they do or the number of patients they see). Although there are numerous group-health plans in existence today, almost 95 percent of the total number of subscribers to these plans belong to the largest nine. One of the largest is the Kaiser Permanente Medical Care Program. It has approximately 3.7 million members in seven separate health plans and operates in California, Oregon, Hawaii, Washington, Colorado, and Ohio. In June 1979, a joint venture called Kaiser/Prudential Health Plan was formed, serving the Dallas-Fort Worth area.

The cost for a group-health plan varies. In 1980, for example, Kaiser Permanente members in northern California (the largest region served) paid $31.76 per

EXHIBIT Q–3
Typical Dental Insurance Benefits

Cleaning	$ 20
Xray	30
Extraction	30
Silicate filling	25
Removable space maintainer	90
Anesthesia	35
Crowns, porcelain	180
Maxillary dentures	380

month for an individual plan and up to $91.22 per month for a family of three or more for the most popular group-health plan. Benefits for this particular plan include unlimited hospitalization and physicians' services in the hospital, with no additional charge for maternity coverage. Outpatient benefits include unlimited doctor office visits, covering periodic checkups, allergy tests, lab and Xray, and speech and occupational therapy at either no charge or a maximum of one dollar per visit. Prescription drugs are provided at no charge in the hospital and at nonmember rates as an outpatient, unless the group elects to prepay for outpatient drugs as a special benefit. In other words, prepaid outpatient drugs are optional and will add to the monthly premium.

THE PROS AND CONS OF GROUP HEALTH. According to a 1967 report of the National Advisory Commission on Health Manpower, the quality of many group-health plans was equal to the medical care available in most communities; and members' medical-care costs were at least 20 to 30 percent less than those obtained elsewhere. Cost is controlled mainly by eliminating unnecessary health care, particularly hospitalization. Because partner doctors generally get a year-end bonus, depending on the difference between total revenues and total costs, they have an incentive to prevent illnesses before they become serious enough to require hospitalization. It is not unusual to find highly computerized testing services that check for fifty to 100 possible medical ills and make a permanent medical history.

Detractors of group-health care maintain that, because the doctors are essentially profit sharers, they will stint on needed hospitalization. Moreover, many patients complain about the impossibility of seeing the same doctor every time. There also may be long waits for certain medical procedures.

SHOULD YOU JOIN AN HMO?

The last chapter indicated that health maintenance organizations (HMOs) are popping up all around the country. These medical clinics practice preventive medicine. If you work for a company with twenty-five or more workers, your employer must offer you HMO membership as an alternative to any existing health-care program the company might have. If you join, you pay a monthly fee slightly higher than a conventional health-care insurance premium. However, if you compare the total out-of-pocket health care expenses, many HMOs offer a savings. One survey showed that you end up spending 10 to 40 percent less. That is because most conventional insurance policies require you to pay a deductible, such as the first $100 of physicians' fees for office visits. If you want more information on HMOs, contact your employer or look in the Yellow Pages of your phone book under "Health Maintenance Organizations."

WHEN YOU GET OLDER

When you get older, you may not have to bother about a private medical-care insurance plan. You may be satisfied with Medicare benefits, although you might want supplemental health insurance as well to cover some aspects of medical care for which those public plans do not provide.

The Medicare program became effective July 1, 1966. It was an addition to the Social Security Act and has been amended a number of times. Twenty-five million persons are eligible for the hospital insurance provided under the Medicare program. Insurance companies and Blue Cross-Blue Shield participate in the Medicare program as fiscal intermediaries for the government. Medicaid is slightly different than Medicare. Under Title 19 of the Social Security Act, the states may expand with federal matching funds their public assistance to persons, regardless of age, whose income is insufficient to pay for health care. The Medicaid program became effective January 1, 1966.

Medicare consists of two parts. Part A is compulsory hospitilization insurance and is financed by contributions from employees and employers. Part B is a voluntary medical insurance program designed to help pay for physicians' services and some medical services and supplies not covered by the hospital part of Medicare. Part B is financed by monthly premiums shared equally by those who choose this protection and the federal government.

Medicare Part A

The hospital insurance plan pays most of the cost of service in a hospital or skilled nursing facility for covered people sixty-five years or older.[7] This includes the cost of

7. Under the 1972 amendments to the Social Security Act, individuals under the age of 65 are extended Medicare coverage if they require hemodialysis or renal transplantation for chronic renal disease and if they are currently fully insured or entitled to monthly Social Security benefits or are the spouses or dependent children of such insured or entitled individuals. Medicare protection is also extended to people 18 years old and over who are receiving Social Security or Railroad Retirement monthly benefits based on disability and who have been entitled to such benefits for at least 24 consecutive months.

regular nursing services, a semiprivate room, meals, inpatient drugs and supplies, laboratory tests, Xray and other radiology services, hospital costs for anesthesia services, use of appliances and equipment, and rehabilitation services. There is, however, a hospital deductible amount that is "intended to make the Medicare beneficiary responsible for expenses equivalent to the average costs of one hospital day." As of 1983, this deductible was $304 per hospital benefit period (defined as a period of illness not interrupted for more than ninety days). In other words, if a particular period of illness lasts for more than eighteen days and if the person is then well for forty-five days and then ill again (that is, requiring hospitalization or confinement to a skilled nursing facility), the first and second illnesses would have occurred in the same benefit period. If the person were well for seventy-five days, then the new hospitalization would constitute another benefit period and again be subject to the $304 hospital deductible amount.

Under this program, any illness must commence with a hospital stay of at least three days if skilled nursing facilities are to be covered. After the hospital stay, any referral to a skilled nursing facility must commence within thirty days (except where a problem arises regarding space availability and so on). Medicare helps pay for up to 100 days in a participating facility during each benefit period. Medicare recipients are subject to deductible amounts that depend on the length of illness.

Subsequent to either a hospital stay or a covered nursing facility stay, individuals may be eligible for home health benefits, including occupational therapy, part-time services of home health aides, medical social services, and medical supplies and appliances. There is no limit to the number of home health visits.

As of November 1, 1983, Medicare began to help pay for hospice care for terminally ill beneficiaries with a life expectancy of six months or less. Covered hospice care includes nursing services, therapies, medical social services, homemaker-health aide services, short-term inpatient care, outpatient drugs for pain relief, and respite care. Special benefit periods, daily coinsurance amounts, and coverage requirements apply.

All the benefits of Part A require treatment in participating health-care facilities. (Most facilities do participate.) And the law further specifies that the various dollar amounts charged to recipients, such as the $304 deductible and daily amounts, are subject to annual review. By the time you read this, the figures may have changed substantially. In no case, does Part A cover doctors' services, but Part B does.

Medicare Part B

This supplementary medical insurance plan helps pay for the cost of doctors' services, as well as other medical costs, for participants over age sixty-five. There is a charge, however, which was $12.20 per month in 1983. Applicants for hospital insurance (Part A) automatically will be enrolled for Part B medical insurance unless otherwise indicated.

Essentially, the federal government pays two-thirds of the cost of the medical insurance, and the beneficiary pays the rest. The amount the beneficiary pays is reviewed annually to ensure that it is in keeping with current medical costs. Recently, however, changes in the law have provided that monthly payments cannot increase beyond the percentage increase in general Social Security benefits, so the government may end up paying for more of the coverage in the future.

The medical insurance program helps pay for the following:

1. Doctors' fees in a hospital, office, or home for surgery and other services
2. Home visits
3. Xrays, surgical dressings, diagnostic services
4. Drugs administered by a doctor or nurse as part of treatment
5. Doctors' services for lab, Xrays, and other services (covered 100 percent for bed patients in a hospital; covered as other benefits if not).
6. Limited services of chiropractors, ambulances, some physical therapy coverage (with a payment limitation), services of certain practitioners, such as Christian Scientists and naturopaths.

Under no circumstances should you believe that the supplementary medical insurance under Medicare pays for the full costs of any of the preceding services (with the single exception of doctors' lab and Xray services). First, there is a seventy-five dollar deductible every year. After that, you pay 20 percent, and the insurance plan pays 80 percent, just as with major medical insurance. And the medical insurance does not cover routine checkups, eye examinations, hearing examinations, glasses or hearing aids, immunizations, routine dental care, self-administered prescription drugs, or the first three pints of blood received in any given year.

Medicaid

Medicaid, an addition to Medicare, is health care for the needy, regardless of age. Because it is state administered, the particulars vary from state to state. Those in need under the age of sixty-five will find that Medicaid in some states is very generous and, in others, practically nonexistent.

COVERING THE GAPS IN MEDICARE INSURANCE

Medicare is paying less and less of total medical bills for older people. There are a number of alternative supplements that older persons can rely upon to fill in these gaps. In fact, there is a group of insurance policies called Medigap that is designed as supplemental insurance to fill some, but never all, the gaps in Medicare's coverage. Annual premiums range from about $75 to over $300, depending on the extent of benefits. Blue Cross and Blue Shield sell Medigap policies; other sellers of Medigap policies are insurance companies and associations for retired persons, such as the National Council of Senior Citizens and the American Association of Retired Persons, in conjunction with the National Retired Teachers Association.

The worst of the Medigap policies purport to provide nursing-home coverage. Typically, they do not really do so. They pay only when the beneficiary has been hospitalized recently and is entering a nursing home because of the same illness. Additionally, some will pay only if the home is a Medicare-certified "skilled nursing facility." In many parts of the country, these homes are nonexistent, so the policies are worthless.

WATCH OUT FOR CANCER INSURANCE

The latest rage in medical insurance is cancer insurance. Insurance experts call it "trading on fear." This insurance has been available for more than two decades, but only recently has it become popular. Over 15 million Americans have this coverage, a big jump from 2 million in 1974. The attractive part of a cancer insurance policy is that the premiums seem low, often less than $150 a year for a family. Additionally, no physical exam is required, and the policies can be renewed for life.

One in four Americans does get cancer. But that means three out of four do not. If you look at the actuarial benefits of having a cancer insurance policy, it appears to be frightfully expensive. Additionally, most cancer policies fail to disclose significant major exclusions. Investigators in Massachusetts, for example, concluded that policies sold in that state paid only 30 percent of cancer costs. The General Accounting Office reports that cancer policies pay back as little as nineteen cents in benefits out of every premium dollar. Money spent on cancer insurance would be better spent on improving your broad health-care coverage.

CUTTING MEDICAL COSTS—SOME POINTERS

1. Find more information on how to stay healthy. Develop rules and follow them.
2. Have a family physician diagnose your complaints and refer you to a specialist only when one is necessary.
3. When looking for a doctor, get several names from a local hospital or medical society. Telephone each doctor and ask for a list of fees and methods of practice.
4. Pick your doctor before you get sick. Also, schedule physical exams on a regular basis.
5. If you have a choice, pick your hospital. Avoid being admitted on a Friday if your problem won't be dealt with until Monday and there's no real reason for you to be there.
6. See if hospital tests before surgery can be done on an outpatient basis to avoid unnecessary room and board charges.
7. Explore the alternative of outpatient surgery.
8. Cut prescription costs by asking your doctor to specify the generic name of the drug.
9. Shop around for presciption-drug prices. Many pharmacists will now give prices over the telephone. If you are going to be using a medicine over a long period of time, buy the pills in larger quantities.
10. Make sure your insurance coverage is adequate and that all members of your family are covered.
11. If possible, opt for a policy with a larger deductible, particularly if you and your family are not bothered by numerous minor illnesses.
12. Obtain group protection, as opposed to individual or family policies, if you can.
13. If you, and not your employer, pay your own premiums, pay quarterly or annually, rather than monthly.
14. Occasionally compare your health insurance policy with alternatives to see if you are still getting the best deal.
15. Read some recent books on medical care, such as *The Medicine Show*, by the editors of *Consumer Reports; The Consumer's Guide to Successful Surgery* by Dr. Seymour Isenberg and Dr. L. M. Elting (New York: St. Martins Press); and *The Peoples' Hospital Book* by Dr. Ronald Gots and Arthur Kaufman (New York: Crown).
16. You might want to look at a publication produced by the Washington Center for the Study of Services called *Washington Consumers' Checkbook Health*, available from Suite 303, 1910 K Street N.W., Washington, D.C. 20006.
17. If you are going to have surgery, get a second opinion. The Department of Health and Human Services maintains a twenty-four-hour hotline for anyone who wants a second opinion on surgery. Phone (800) 325-6400 or, in Missouri, (800) 342-6600. You will be given the number of the nearest of the 162 referral centers. For additional information on surgery, write Surgery, Department of Health and Human Services, Washington, D.C. 20201.

SUMMARY

1. One of the best ways to reduce health-care costs is to remain healthy. Eat a good diet, get adequate exercise, and use foreign substances in moderation.
2. Medical insurance can provide payment for hospital expenses, disability, surgery, and regular medical protection, such as routine office calls.
3. In addition, major medical insurance will cover up to 90 percent of large medical expenses, sometimes up to $500,000.
4. Medical insurance can be purchased through your job, through various group plans, and individually, from such companies as Blue Cross-Blue Shield or commercial insurance agencies. Call several insurance brokers to find out what policies are available.
5. The largest health insurer today is Blue Cross-Blue Shield.
6. As an alternative, a group-health-care plan may be appropriate. Generally it is cheaper than buying insurance either individually or through your place of employment. Group-health services often pay for almost all medical expenses incurred except dental expenses. To find out about group-health care in your area, check with any large employer that offers a variety of health options to its

employees. Or write any of the large group-health plans, such as Group Health Cooperative of Puget Sound or H.I.P. in New York City; most major group-health plans have a policy of easy transfer among each other, so they are likely to maintain a listing of other similar programs.

7. Medicare is a hospital insurance plan that pays most of the cost of service in a hospital or skilled nursing facility for covered individuals sixty-five years of age and older. If this is something you are concerned about, call your Social Security office to get the exact coverage that would be available for you. There are Social Security offices in just about every major city in the United States. Or you can write the Social Security Administration, Washington, D.C., for this information.

8. Older people may wish to take advantage of supplementary medical care insurance provided by Medicare Part B.

QUESTIONS FOR THOUGHT AND DISCUSSION

1. Teenagers tend to ignore nutrition; they also tend to suffer few illnesses. Why?

2. Do you think the medical insurance industry should be more strictly regulated in terms of the premiums it charges individual members?

3. Why is it cheaper to be a member of a group insurance plan than to subscribe individually?

4. When would it be worthwhile to purchase a major medical policy with a large limit—say, $250,000?

5. Do you think group health is a workable concept?

6. Do you prefer to go to just one doctor for all your complaints, or do you like to see a variety of doctors? Would this influence your answer to question 5?

7. Medicare costs much more than individual recipients put in. Who pays for the difference?

THINGS TO DO

1. Obtain the payment schedules for at least two medical insurance plans and compare the two. If they are vastly different in coverage and payment, does this difference correspond to a distinct difference in the premiums that must be paid? If not, what is the reason for the difference?

2. Find out about dental insurance in your area. Can you figure out why it has taken so long for dental insurance to catch on?

3. Order some of the free booklets from Blue Cross-Blue Shield. Read through them to see if the information there indicates why medical costs have been rising so rapidly.

4. Compare the coverage and payment schedule for a private insurance plan such as Blue Cross-Blue Shield with what would be covered under Medicare Part A and Medicare Part B. Which is a better deal?

SELECTED READINGS

Blodgett, R. "Health Insurance: Are You Covered?" *McCalls,* November 1982, p. 80.

Clark, M., *et al.* "Premium on Fear." (Cancer insurance.) *Newsweek,* December 19, 1979, p. 86.

Duncan, S. J. "What's Next on Health Cost Control?" *Nation's Business,* November 1982, pp. 22–24.

Handbook of Nonprescription Drugs. Washington, D.C.: American Pharmaceutical Association, 2215 Constitution Avenue, N.W., Washington, D.C. 20037. Published every two years. Contains details on more than thirty types of products.

Herman, Tom. "When Medicare Stops: Here Are Guidelines for Buying Supplementary Health Insurance." *The Wall Street Journal,* June 18, 1979, p. 40.

Holcomb, B. "What About an HMO?" *Health,* October 1982, p. 46.

"How to Pay Less for Prescription Drugs." *Consumer Reports,* January 1975,

Long, James W. *The Essential Guide to Prescription Drugs.* New York: Harper & Row, 1977.

Medicare and Health Insurance for Older People. Long Beach, Calif.: AARP/NRTA, Dept. M-H, P.O. Box 2400, Long Beach, 90801.

"Policies That Cover What Medicare Doesn't." *Changing Times,* September 1982, p. 66.

APPENDIX II
Providing for the Ultimate Expense

We all know the cliché that nothing is certain except death and taxes. We will discuss taxes in a later chapter; here, let us briefly examine alternatives to the typical expensive American funeral.

Funerals are indeed big business. The National Funeral Directors Association represents some 14,000 of the 27,000 funeral directors in the nation. The funeral industry as a whole is probably in for some economic difficulties in the future: the death rate is going down, and, obviously, the funeral market is limited by the death rate. Because more than 25,000 funeral homes must share fewer than 20 million deaths annually, the average number of funerals for each funeral home is not very large—around eighty a year. Over 60 percent of funeral homes average only one funeral a week. On the other end of the scale is Forest Lawn Memorial Park in Los Angeles, which averages more than 5,000 funerals a year.

The funeral industry has been facing increasing costs, not only for equipment, such as coffins and hearses, but also for labor. It is not surprising that the estimated price of a typical burial has been rising, nor that the funeral industry has become more competitive.

Prefinanced Plans

The Federal Trade Commission has accused a number of funeral directors of pressuring people to sign up for prefinanced burial and funeral plans. Of course, there is nothing wrong with planning ahead, but you must be careful that the commission paid to a salesperson who signs you up for a burial ahead of time is not excessive.

In 1983, the estimated total cost for a typical funeral service was approximately $2,400. If you wish to provide for much less expensive funeral outlays for yourself or your family, purchase *A Manual of Simple Burial* by Ernest Morgan[1], which describes alternatives to traditional funerals and explains what memorial societies, organ banks, and so on are.

For example, the Continental Association of Funeral and Memorial Socieites, of which there are over 100 members, will arrange for a dignified but economical burial service for a member of your family. The societies may arrange with a local firm for a cremation without embalming that can cost less than $200.

Notice that there is a difference between prearrangement and prefinancing. You can make prearrangement with all types of funeral services, but you don't necessarily have to get involved in prefinancing. Indeed, you must be careful of prefinancing plans, because implicitly you are allowing a funeral-home owner or director to keep your money, interest-free, until you die or until a loved one for whom you are prefinancing a burial plan dies.

1. Burnsville, N.C.: The Celo Press.

In addition to prearranging burial services, you might wish to obtain a uniform donor card on which you specify that you are donating your body or parts of your body to medical research. You can obtain one from a local teaching hospital.

THE CONSUMER IS AT A DISADVANTAGE

In no other area does the consumer seem to be at a greater disadvantage. This is due in great measure to the following facts.

1. Lack of knowledge. For many years there has been relatively little or no advertising in the funeral business, so the consumer has no idea about the range of prices and qualities of burial services.
2. Lack of experience. Clearly, most consumers lack experience in taking care of burial arrangements for a loved one. This lack of experience means that a naive consumer can be victimized by an unscrupulous funeral director.
3. Emotional state. When a loved one dies, it is difficult to be rational about what is an appropriate burial. Again, some unscrupulous funeral directors will play on the emotional state of grieving relatives.

What You Must Do When Arranging for a Funeral

1. Take care of the immediate needs of the bereaved.
2. Contact the funeral director and the clergyperson preferred by the family.
3. Notify the attorney who cared for the affairs of the deceased.
4. Secure personal data and any special requests or instructions of the deceased affecting the funeral services; contact the local newspaper for the obituary.
5. Make the necessary arrangement with a cemetery.
6. Cooperate with the funeral director and attorney in securing forms for filing claims with insurance companies, banks, fraternal groups, veterans or military organizations, governmental offices, and others.

KEEPING FUNERAL COSTS UNDER CONTROL

Once you have decided on a funeral director, obtain a written statement of the charges for the funeral arrangements. The statement should contain the following:

1. Services, including merchandise selected, and the total price
2. The supplemental items of service or merchandise requested and the price of each item
3. The terms of payment

Casket A coffin or box of any material that holds the deceased.

Columbarium A building or wall for above-ground accommodation of cremated remains.

Cremation The reduction of human remains by means of heat. The remains are commonly called ashes and weigh between six and eight pounds.

Crematorium An establishment in which cremation takes place.

Crypt A concrete chamber in a mausoleum into which a casket is placed. The chamber is slightly larger than the casket.

Disposition Final placement or disposal of a dead person.

Double-depth grave One grave space that accommodates two caskets, one on top of the other.

Embalming Temporary preservation of the deceased by means of chemicals.

Entombment Opening and closing of a crypt, including the placement and seating of a casket within.

Grave liner A concrete container into which a casket or urn is placed for ground burial. Its function is to prevent the ground from settling.

Honorarium Payment (as to the clergy) for professional services.

Inurnment Opening and closing of a niche, including the placement and sealing of an urn within.

Mausoleum Building or wall for above-ground accommodation of a casket.

Niche A chamber in a columbarium into which an urn is placed.

Opening and closing Preparing a grave space for ground burial—that is, digging a grave, placing a casket or urn within, and covering it over.

Side-by-side grave A double or companion grave space that accommodates two caskets adjacently.

Urn A container for cremated remains.

Urn garden An area in a cemetery for ground burial of cremated remains.

Vault An elaborate container into which a casket is placed for ground burial. It serves to prevent ground settling and also helps slow the deterioration of the casket.

SOURCE: *The Price of Death*. Consumer Survey Handbook 3. Seattle Regional Office, Federal Trade Commission.

EXHIBIT Q–4
Glossary For Funeral Services

4. The items for which the funeral director will advance his or her cash, such as flowers, long-distance calls, and so on.

Funeral directors often quote a single amount for "standard" services. These include the casket and the use of the funeral home facilities and a hearse. However, they do not include the cemetery plot (which could have been chosen earlier), the burial or cremation fees, and such items as flowers, obituary notices, and the clergyperson's honorarium.

In addition to the type of funeral service, you will have to decide on at least the following four items: casket, cemetery space, grave, and cremation. Strangely, several states require a casket even though the family has decided that the loved one will be cremated. Even in states where it is not required by law, a funeral director may nonetheless tell the consumer that a casket is necessary. This must be verified ahead of time.

After the funeral, a number of legal items have to be dealt with. They are covered in more detail in Consumer Issue W.

SELECTED READINGS

Bowman, Leroy. *The American Funeral*. Washington, D.C.: Public Affairs Press, 1959.

Harmer, Ruth Mulsey. *The High Cost of Dying*. New York: Collier, Macmillan, 1963.

Mitford, Jessica. *The American Way of Death*. New York: Simon & Schuster, 1978. (Reprint of 1963 edition with updated section.)

"Planning a Funeral at a Fair Price." *Changing Times*, September 1980, pp. 31–32.

CHAPTER

OTHER FORMS OF PROTECTION

LIFE INSURANCE AND SOCIAL SECURITY

19

The average American wants a sense of security more than just about anything else in his or her life. The responsibility for providing family economic security may be assumed by family, employers, charitable institutions, or the government.

CHAPTER PREVIEW

- What are the principles behind life insurance?
- What are the different types of life insurance?
- How does whole life compare with term insurance?
- What are the different types of living and death benefits, and how can they be received?
- What are annuities, and why would you want one?
- What is Social Security all about, and what are its defects?

We have discussed home insurance, liability, automobile insurance, and medical insurance at some length. These are basically forms of protection or income security. Now we'll discuss two additional forms of protection—life insurance and Social Security.

SECURITY

A sense of security is important for most families. In fact, psychologists contend that the average American wants a sense of security more than just about anything else in his or her life. Some of the major hazards to *financial* security are listed here, along with the ways Americans provide for these hazards.

1. **Illness:** health and medical insurance, savings account for emergencies, Medicare, Medicaid;
2. **Accident:** accident insurance, savings account, state workers' compensation, Social Security, aid to the disabled, veterans' benefits;
3. **Unemployment:** savings fund for such an emergency, unemployment compensation;
4. **Old age:** private retirement pension plans, savings account, annuities, Social Security old age insurance;
5. **Premature death:** survivors' insurance under the Social Security Act, life insurance, workers' compensation, savings, investments;
6. **Desertion, divorce:** savings, investments, aid to families with dependent children; and
7. **Unexpected, catastrophic expenses:** health insurance, property insurance, liability insurance.

The responsibility for providing family economic security may be assumed by the family, relatives of the family, charitable institutions, employers, or the government. Until recently, financial security was provided primarily by the first three, but now employers and the government are assuming some responsibility for this kind of protection.

PREMATURE DEATHS

The mortality rate in the United States has been on the decline for many years, as it has been in the rest of the world. People are suffering from fewer fatal diseases than they used to and are living longer, as can be seen in Exhibit 19–1. Nonetheless, every year there are at least 300,000 premature deaths. In many cases, a premature death can lead to financial hardship for dependents. When a person who is responsible for a household and children dies, those responsibilities must be met somehow. This can bring financial hardship to a family unit. The same is obviously true when the major wage earner dies. Both cases call for financial protection against the burden imposed by such a premature death. Therefore, it is not unusual to find an extremely large life insurance industry in the United States.

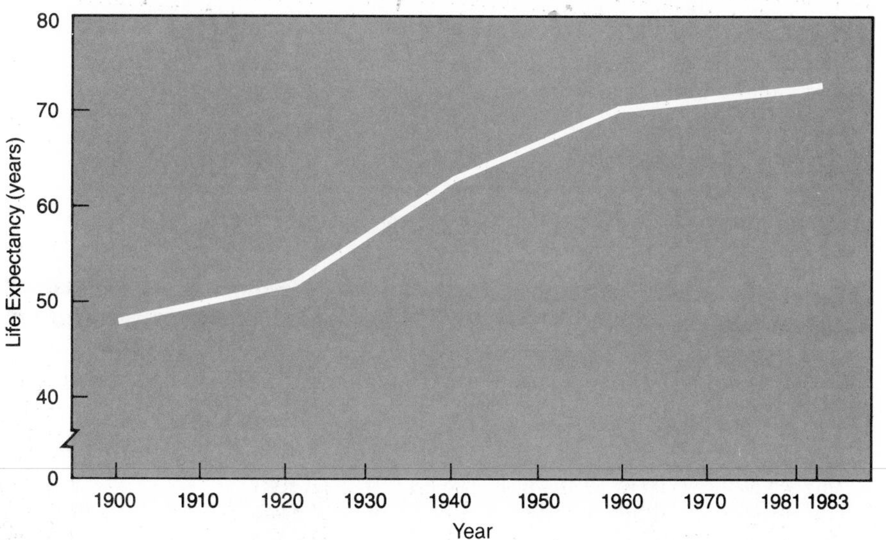

EXHIBIT 19–1
Life Expectancy

At the start of the twentieth century, the average American at birth could expect to live a little more than forty-seven years. By the middle of the century, this number had jumped to almost seventy.

SOURCE: *Historical Statistics of the United States*, U.S. Bureau of the Census, p. 25, and the U.S. Department of Commerce.

SELLING LIFE INSURANCE

The life insurance industry in the United States has grown rapidly. In 1900, there were a mere eighty-four life insurance companies selling some 14 million policies with a total face value of only $7.5 billion. By the beginning of the 1960s, there were some 1,441 companies selling 282 million policies, with a face value of $10,200 of life insurance per family. By the beginning of the 1980s, there were 1,800 companies. In 1982, the average American family had $39,000 in life insurance or a total of $15 trillion. Over 90 percent of all wife-husband families have life insurance. It represents 85 percent of the assets that males leave at their deaths. The average U.S. household spends over $1,000 a year to insure its family members and their possessions. Employment in the insurance industry also has been growing. In the last thirty years, it has increased from 600,000 to 1.78 million. We can expect that the industry will continue to grow as the American economy grows.

UNDERWRITER
The company that stands behind the face value of any insurance policy. The underwriter signs its name to an insurance policy, thereby becoming answerable for a designated loss or damage on consideration of receiving a premium payment.

HISTORY OF INSURANCE

The first recorded life insurance policy was written in June 1536 in London's Old Drury Ale House. A group of marine **underwriters** agreed to insure the life of William Gybbons to the grand sum of $2,000. This coverage was obtained for an eighty-dollar **premium.** (Unfortunately for the underwriters, he died a few days before the policy was to run out.) And so it was that life insurance became a sideline for marine underwriters. Then, in 1692, the Society for the Equitable Assurance of Lives and Survivorship began issuing policies covering a person for his or her lifetime. Old Equitable, as it became known, continues in existence today. In North America, the first corporation

PREMIUM
The payment that must be made to the insurance company to keep an insurance policy in effect. Premiums usually are paid quarterly, semiannually, or annually.

to insure lives was the Presbyterian Ministers' Fund, started in Philadelphia in 1759. By 1800, there were only 160 life insurance policies in force in the United States. Only after the Civil War did the industry begin to flourish.

PRINCIPLES BEHIND LIFE INSURANCE—RISK POOLING

Life insurance is just like any other type of insurance: If the risk is spread among a large enough number of people, the premiums that have to be paid will be small compared to the coverage offered. In any particular age group, only a very small number will die in any one year. If a large percentage of this age group pays premiums to a life insurance company in exchange for a benefit payment in case of premature death, there will be a sufficient amount of money to pay off the survivors of those few who die.

Given a long enough time for collection of data about the group and about the particular disaster—in this case, premature death—insurance companies can predict with great accuracy the total number of premature deaths in any one year. They then can estimate the total payout they will incur if they insure the group; hence, they can predict the rates for each member of the group in order to meet this payout, plus a profit for the company.

Insurance, then, involves the pooling of a large number of risks. Indeed, the principle of insurance is simply the principle of risk pooling. Insurance is used to protect against large losses. Life insurance companies are not gambling on when a particular person will die prematurely. Rather, life insurance companies use statistics for large groups of individuals to calculate the total amount of risk for the group and insure against that.

THE DIFFERENT TYPES OF LIFE INSURANCE

Although the insurance principles just outlined are simple to grasp, the variety of insurance programs you can purchase are indeed many and complex. In this chapter, we outline the basic types of life insurance policies. The Consumer Issue following this chapter offers some ideas to help you determine your own life insurance needs and some recommendations about the appropriate type of insurance for you.

Life insurance falls basically into two types—term and whole life—but there is also a variety of others that we will discuss.

WHOLE LIFE INSURANCE
Insurance that has both death and living benefits. That is, part of your premium is put into a type of savings account.

TERM INSURANCE
Life insurance that is for a specified term (period of time) and has only a death benefit; it is a form of pure insurance with no savings aspect.

THE TWO BASIC TYPES OF INSURANCE

Whole life insurance combines protection with a savings plan, whereas **term insurance** offers pure protection. Whole life is also called straight life, ordinary life, or cash-value insurance; these are merely different names for the same type of life insurance.

TERM INSURANCE

Premiums for term insurance, unlike those for whole life, commonly increase at the end of each term, such as every five years, if you wish to keep the same face value on your insurance policy. The increased premium reflects the rising probability of death as age increases. Thus, it will cost you relatively little to buy term life insurance when you are twenty-five years old, but, by the time you are sixty, your premiums will have risen dramatically. However, by that time, you probably won't want as much term insurance because your children will be well on the way to financial independence, and you will have built up other forms of financial resources for any dependents you still have. That means that you can reduce the premium burden by reducing the amount of insurance carried to protect your family.

An important point to note here is that term insurance is one way for a young, growing family to have more insurance at an *affordable price* than it could have with the more expensive types of insurance. This occurs at a time in the life cycle when adequate insurance is needed most, but family income is

The principle of insurance is simply the principle of risk pooling.

UNIFORM DECREASING TERM INSURANCE
A term insurance policy on which the premiums are uniform throughout its life, but the face value of the policy declines.

normally relatively low. Families often choose **uniform decreasing term insurance,** which has a level premium but a decreasing face value. A similar type of policy is called a home protection plan. It is decreasing term insurance that decreases at *approximately* the same rate that the outstanding amount of money owed on a house declines as payments are made on the mortgage. Thus, when a home protection policy is taken out for a face value equal to the amount of the mortgage on the home, the home can be paid off with the insurance benefits if the breadwinner dies any time during the life of the mortgage.

Renewability

Standard term insurance is often labeled one-year term or five-year term because those are the intervals, or terms, between premium increases. Other periods are also available. A term policy is *renewable* if the coverage can be continued at the end of each period merely by payment of the increased premium without the need for a medical examination. The renewability feature must, of necessity, add to the cost of the policy, but if you wish to preserve your insurability despite any changes in your health, you certainly would want to pay the extra costs for this feature. Term policies are commonly renewable until the policyholder reaches some age of retirement, such as sixty-five or seventy. All coverage then stops.

In one sense, the premiums for any term policy are constant for the life of the policy, but since most term policies are written with a one-year or five-year "life," the constancy of premium is not too meaningful. The premium is truly constant throughout a long period of time only with decreasing term insurance, in which the face value falls every year.

Convertibility

Often, riders can be attached to term policies that give you the privilege of converting them to other than pure insurance without the necessity of a medical examination. You pay for this additional feature, however. If you have a convertible term policy, you can convert it to whole life without any problems. The main reason you might want to convert is to continue your coverage after you pass the age of sixty-five or seventy. After converting the policy, you would pay whole life premiums based on your age at the time of conversion. Most insurance experts believe that these two features—convertibility and renewability—should be purchased. They give you much flexibility at a not inappropriate additional cost.

Exhibit 19–2 shows the costs of $50,000 of one-year renewable term insurance for a male thirty-five years of age. If this man keeps $50,000 of term insurance until age sixty-five, he will pay in a total of $17,893. He will have no cash value in the policy, as he would in a whole life policy.

WHOLE LIFE INSURANCE

Whole life insurance accounts for a little less than half the total value of all life insurance in force in the United States. The average payoff value of such policies is around $15,000. Life insurance salespersons will almost always try to sell you a whole life policy because it is more profitable for them and their company. (It has been estimated that a salesperson earns about nine times more selling the same amount of whole life than he or she does selling term insurance.)

Whole life insurance accounts for a little less than half the total value of all life insurance in force in the United States.

Premiums

Whole life premiums generally remain the same throughout the life of a policy. As a result, the policyholder pays more in each of the early years than is necessary to cover the company's risk in later years. Exhibit 19–3 gives an example of a $10,000 ordinary life insurance policy with an annual level premium of $222.70 for a male thirty-five years of age. In the first year, $205.50 of the $222.70 goes to the insurance company to cover insurance costs, and $17.20 goes to the **cash value** for the purchaser of the policy. By the sixth year, the deposit to cash value is greater than the level annual premium and stays greater throughout the life of this particular policy. You can see in the summary of this policy that by the twentieth year—that is, when your poliyholder is fifty-five years old—there is a total cash value in that policy of $5,608.97, after having paid in $4,454.

CASH VALUE
Applied to whole life policies only, it represents the amount of "savings" built up in the policy and available to the living policyholder, either to borrow against or to receive if the policy is canceled.

The cash value of a whole life insurance policy certainly is not the same thing as a savings account. Insurance industry people often promote whole life as an insurance policy combined with a savings plan, but it is definitely not that if you die. The cash reserve is not a separate item given to your named **beneficiary** as a separate payment. Rather, it is included in the face amount of the policy. Thus, looking at Exhibit 19–3 again, let us assume you have paid in for ten years. Your total cash value is shown to be $2,053.48. What if you die at the end of ten years? You have a $10,000 ordinary life policy, and your named beneficiary gets $10,000, not $10,000 plus your cash value of $2,053.48.

BENEFICIARY
The designated person or persons for any insurance policy. In a life insurance policy, the beneficiary is the person who receives the benefits when the insured dies.

Owners of whole life policies often take comfort from the fact that their premiums are level and, therefore, represent one of the few costs that do not go up with inflation. (However, the real value of the policy, as well as the premiums, declines as the buying power of a dollar falls.) True, the cost is relatively high to begin with, but it gets no higher. The exact level of premiums that you would pay for a $10,000 ordinary life insurance policy, as represented in Exhibit 19–3, depends on your age when you buy the policy; the younger

EXHIBIT 19–2
A Typical $50,000 Yearly Renewable Term Policy, Male, Age Thirty-Five

YEAR	ANNUAL PREMIUM	YEAR	ANNUAL PREMIUM
1	$ 165.50	11	$ 312.50
2	172.50	12	339.00
3	181.00	13	368.00
4	192.00	14	400.00
5	204.50	15	435.00
6	219.00	16	473.50
7	235.00	17	515.50
8	252.00	18	560.50
9	270.50	19	609.50
10	290.50	20	642.50
20th Year Total	$6,838.50	Total at Age 65	$17,893.00

EXHIBIT 19–3
Composition of Cash Value and Operating Charges in Twenty-Year Ordinary Life Premiums

$10,000 ORDINARY LIFE
Dividends* to Purchase Paid-up Additions
Annual Premium: $222.70 Male: Age 35

YEAR	DEPOSIT TO CASH VALUE	DEPOSIT TO INSURANCE	TOTAL CASH VALUE
1	$ 17.20	$205.50-	$ 17.20
2	179.71	42.99	196.91
3	190.43	32.27	387.34
4	201.97	20.73	589.31
5	213.47	9.23	802.78
6	225.43	2.73-	1,028.21
7	237.14	14.44-	1,265.35
8	250.35	27.65-	1,515.70
9	262.61	39.91-	1,778.31
10	275.17	52.47-	2,053.48
11	270.17	47.47-	2,323.65
12	282.60	59.90-	2,606.25
13	294.64	71.94-	2,900.89
14	306.82	84.12-	3,207.71
15	320.64	97.94-	3,528.35
16	333.21	110.51-	3,861.56
17	346.11	123.41-	4,207.67
18	360.95	138.25-	4,568.62
19	376.12	153.42-	4,944.74
20	391.60	168.90-	5,336.34

	SUMMARY 20TH YEAR	AT AGE 65
Total Cash Value	$5,608.97*	$10,566.83†
Total Deposits	$4,454.00	$ 6,681.00
Net Gain	$1,154.97	$ 3,885.83

*Dividends are neither estimates nor guarantees, but are based on the current dividend scale.
†Includes terminal dividend.

you are, the less it will be because the company expects to collect premiums from you for many years. The older you are, the greater it is.

As we will see when we compare whole life with term insurance (already discussed), whole life is relatively expensive because it is a form of financial investment as well as an insurance protection. The investment feature is known as its "cash value." In Exhibit 19–3, the cash value at the end of twenty years was in excess of $5,000; at age sixty-five, it was actually in excess of the face value of the policy. You can, of course, cancel a whole life policy at any time you choose and be paid the amount of cash value it has built in. Individuals sometimes "cash in" a whole life policy at the time of their retirement when the cash value can be taken out either as a lump sum or in installments called annuities, which are discussed later in this chapter. These are the so-called living benefits of a whole life policy.

LIVING BENEFITS
Benefits paid on a whole life insurance policy while the person is living. Living benefits include fixed and variable annuities.

Living Benefits

Living benefits are the opposite of death benefits. The death benefit of a life insurance policy is obviously the insurance you have purchased. The living benefit, on the other hand, includes the possibility of converting an ordinary policy to some sort of lump-sum payment or retirement income. In any one year, up to 60 percent of all insurance company payments are in the form of these so-called living benefits.

Note that the level premium for a whole life policy is paid throughout the life of the policyholder—unless you reach the ripe old age of, say, 95 or 100.

Borrowing on Your Cash Value

One feature of a whole life insurance policy is that you can borrow on its cash value any time you want. The interest rate on such loans is relatively favorable. However, if you should die while the loan is outstanding, the sum paid to your beneficiary is reduced by the amount of the loan. In any event, the borrowing power given to you in a cash value of a whole life insurance policy can be considered a type of cushion against financial emergencies. However, if you ever have to drop a whole life insurance policy because you are unable to pay the premiums or because you need its cash value, you most certainly will take a loss. And, of course, you will give up the insurance protection.

When You Reach Retirement Age

When you reach retirement age, you can discontinue premium payments on a whole life policy and choose to do one of the following:

1. Get protection for the rest of your life, but at a lower value.
2. Get full protection, but for a definite number of years in the future.
3. Get a cash settlement that gives back whatever savings and dividends that have not been used to pay off the insurance company for excessive costs it has incurred for your particular age group.
4. Convert the whole life policy into an annuity where a specified amount of income is given each year for a certain number of years.

Death Benefits

In most life insurance policies, you specify a beneficiary who receives the death benefits of that policy. If you buy a $10,000 ordinary life policy and do not borrow any money on it, your beneficiary will receive $10,000 when you die. However, certain options can be used for settling a life insurance policy. Before you purchase any insurance policy, you should discuss the particular settlement terms that are available with the underwriter of that insurance. Generally, there are four optional settlement plans:

—**Plan 1:** Lump-sum payment.
—**Plan 2:** The face value of the insurance policy is retained by the insurance company, but a small interest payment is made to the beneficiary for a certain number of years or for life. At the end of a period, the principal is then paid to the children or according to the terms in the contract.
—**Plan 3:** The face value is paid to the beneficiary in the form of installments, either annually, semiannually, quarterly, or monthly. The company makes regular payments of equal amounts until the fund is used up. In the meantime, the company adds interest on the money remaining to be paid out. There are two types of options here. Each payment is for a specific amount where the payments are spread out over a specific time period. If each payment is made

for a specific amount, then the length of time during which the payment will be made depends on the amount of income payment, the face value of the policy, and the rate of interest guaranteed on the policy. If payments are spread out over a given time period, then the amount of each payment depends on the number of years the income is to be paid, the face value of your policy, and the rate of interest guaranteed on the policy.

— **Plan 4:** Regular life income is paid to the beneficiary. The insurance company guarantees a specified number of payments or payments that will total the face value of the policy. If the beneficiary dies before the guaranteed payments have been made, the remainder goes to the estate of the beneficiary or as directed in the contract. This is sometimes called an annuity plan.

In sum, whole, straight, or ordinary life insurance gives you pure insurance plus forced savings and, hence, the possibility of retirement income, as can be seen in Exhibit 19–4. You can instead buy pure insurance—that is, term

EXHIBIT 19–4
How Whole Life Insurance Works to Provide Both Savings and Protection

Here you see a typical whole life insurance policy for a thirty-five-year-old male with a face value of $50,000. Its "cash value" is represented by the bold line; cash value and dividends accumulate throughout the life of the policy. The annual level premium is $1,073.50.

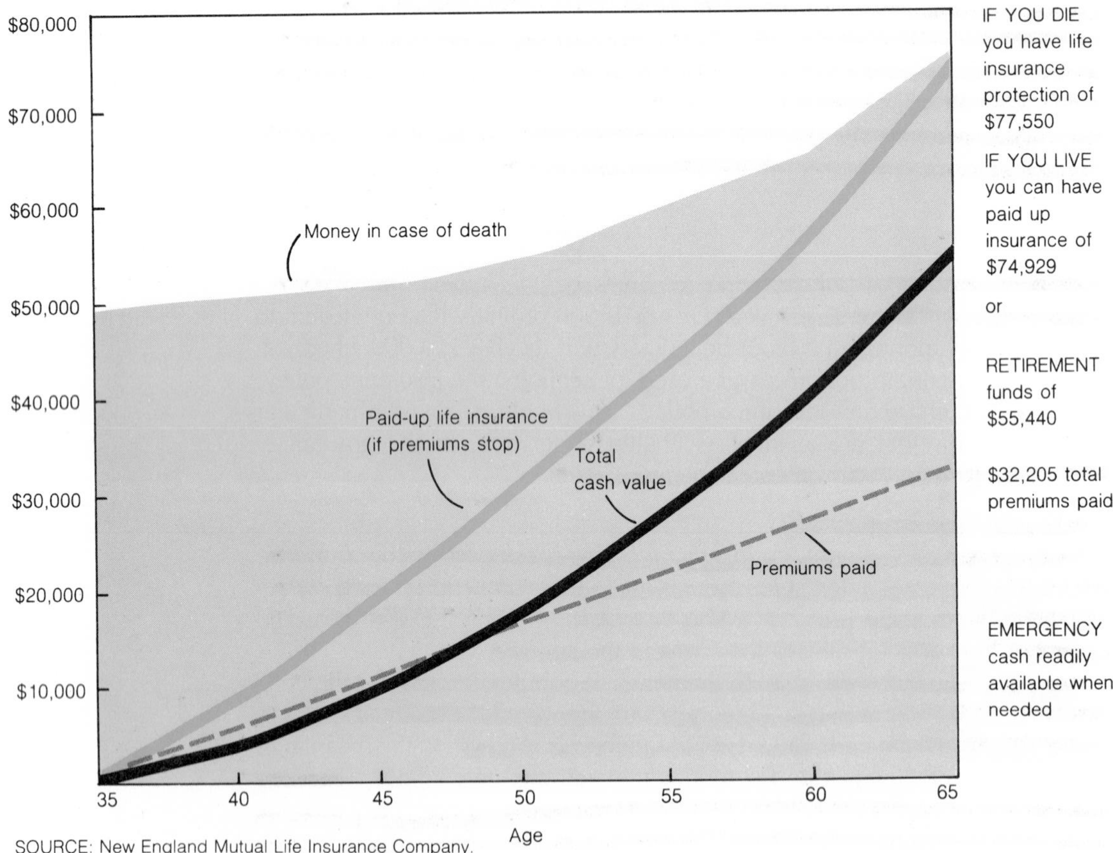

SOURCE: New England Mutual Life Insurance Company.

insurance—at a lower cost than whole life. You can invest the difference in your own saving and retirement plans and perhaps be better off (or, at least, no worse off) if you can get a higher rate of return on your savings than the insurance company offers. The latest research suggests that whole life can be a sensible long-term investment for those who could otherwise expect their own investments to earn only about 4 percent *after taxes.* But if, on your investments, you can make 5 percent or more after taxes, whole life may not be the type of policy for you. For a summary of the different insurance plans we have talked about, look at Exhibit 19–5.

UNIVERSAL LIFE INSURANCE

A new type of insurance policy, which combines some aspects of term insurance and some aspects of whole life insurance, is called universal life. Every payment, usually called a "contribution," involves two deductions made by the issuing life insurance company. The first one is a charge for term insurance protection; the second is for company expenses and profit. The money that remains after these deductions earns interest for the policyholder at a rate determined by the company. The interest-earning money in the policy is called

EXHIBIT 19–5
Summary of Insurance Plans

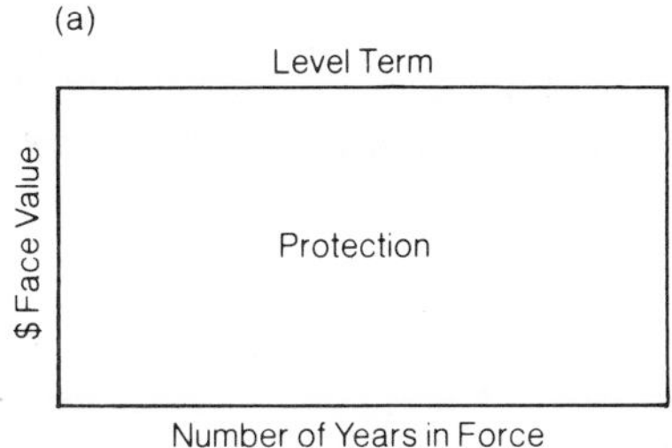

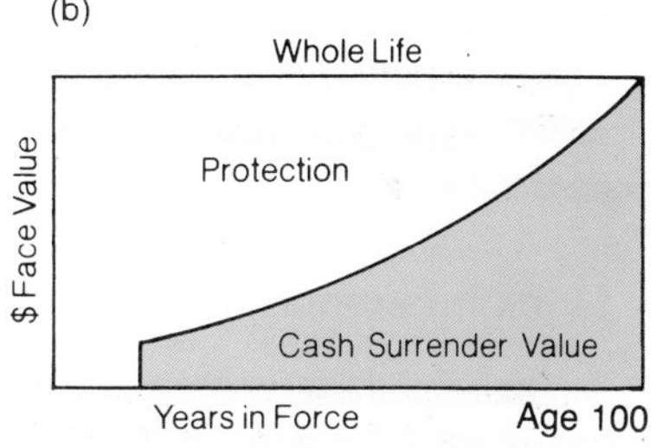

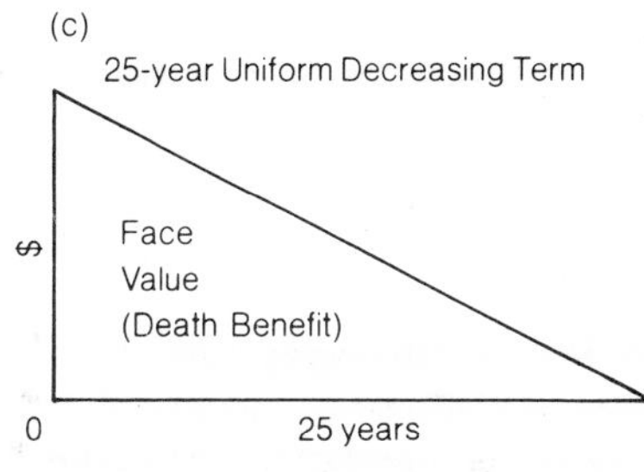

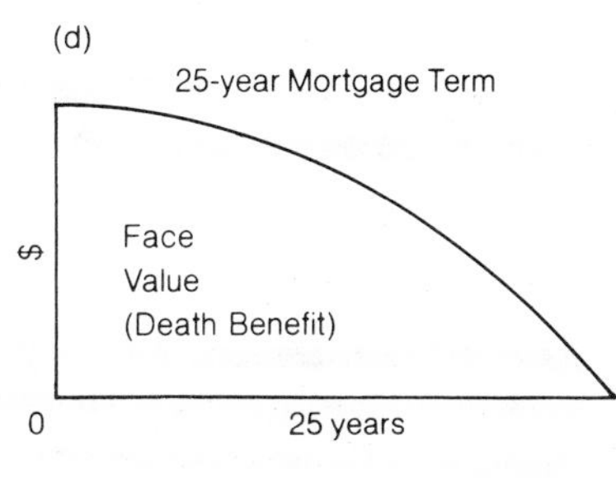

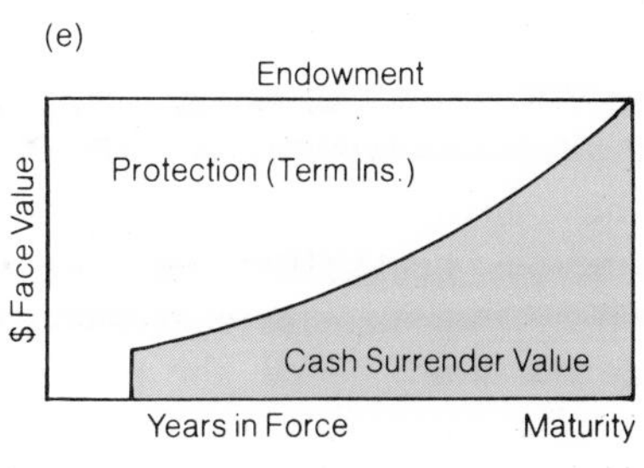

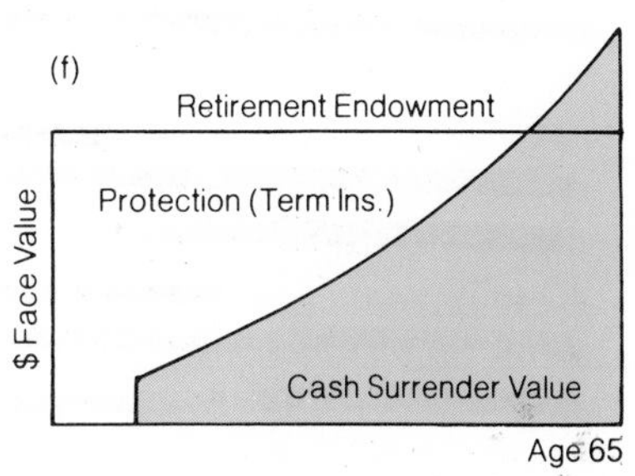

A new type of insurance policy, which combines some aspects of term insurance and some aspects of whole life insurance, is called universal life.

the policy's *cash value*, but that term does not mean the same thing as it does for a traditional whole life insurance policy. With a universal life policy, the cash value grows at a variable interest rate rather than at a predetermined rate.

Consider Exhibit 19–6, which gives an example of a universal life policy issued by the Kemper Investor Life Insurance Company in Chicago. This particular policy, called "Real Life I," offers level coverage, level premiums, and, when this example was provided by the company, a 12 percent tax-free cash accumulation. A number of other companies, including Hartford Life Insurance Company, E. F. Hutton Life Insurance Company, the Life Insurance Company of Virginia, and TransAmerica Occidental Life, offer universal life policies.

There are two major advantages of universal life insurance over whole life insurance. The first one is a complete disclosure of the fees that the insurance companies take out for managing the policy. The other is that the interest rate earned on the cash value, at least for now, seems to be higher than for traditional whole life policies. Simply stated, universal life insurance is a term insurance package with an investment fund. As with any package arrangement, you have to ask yourself whether you can get a better deal by purchasing the components separately. In other words, you must decide whether you should buy the best term insurance policy you can find and then find the best investment.

TYPES OF INSURANCE COMPANIES AND THEIR POLICIES

There are basically two types of insurance companies—stock and mutual. These companies generally issue two types of policies—participating and nonparticipating.

Stock Insurance Companies

A stock insurance company is owned by stockholders. They take the risk and the loss and are entitled to any profit. Stock companies sell life insurance rates, which are kept as low as possible because of competition. If they are set too low, the stockholders take a loss; if they are more than sufficient, the stockholders obtain a profit. Most property and casualty insurance policies are written by stock companies.

Mutual Insurance Companies

A mutual insurance company is a cooperative association that persons establish to insure their own lives. There are no stockholders. General mutual company rates are set high enough to cover all contingencies. Most life and health insurance policies are written by mutual companies.

PARTICIPATING POLICIES. Because a mutual company has to take account of all cost increases during the year, it generally sets rates that will cover all costs plus any extraordinary ones. At the end of the year, it will figure what its costs actually were and refund to its participating members—those who are insured—a pro rata share of the difference. This refund, generally called a dividend, is a partial return of your insurance premium; hence, the premium charged you by a mutual company offering a participating policy is generally (although not always) an overstatement of your actual net cost per year because you get a refund or dividend at the end of the year.

NONPARTICIPATING POLICIES. Stock companies generally issue nonparticipating policies. You receive no refund or dividend at the end of the year; thus, the premiums you pay represent the actual cost of your policy.

Other Ways to Purchase Life Insurance Policies

In addition to life insurance that you buy as an individual, you also may be eligible for certain other types of life insurance policies that generally are offered to you at more attractive rates.

GROUP INSURANCE. Group insurance is usually term insurance written under a master policy that is issued to either a sponsoring association or an employer. Some types of group insurance are currently offered to employees of universities and large businesses, to members of athletic associations and professional associations, and the like. Per $1,000 of protection, the cost of group insurance is generally lower than individually obtained insurance for many reasons but primarily because of the lower selling and lower bookkeeping costs. The selling costs are lower because the employer or sponsoring group does all the selling; there is no commission to be paid to a selling agent. And the bookkeeping costs are lower because, again, the employer or the association may do all the bookkeeping. Generally, no medical examination is required for members of the group unless they want to take out an abnormally large amount of group insurance. Today, there are perhaps 400,000 master group life insurance policies outstanding in the United States.

INDUSTRIAL INSURANCE. This type of insurance involves weekly premiums—usually costing ten, twenty, or fifty cents—which are collected at the home by an insurance agent. This is a debit system of insurance whereby the company debits (charges) its agents a certain sum based on the premiums the agents are expected to collect on their assigned route. Because the system was first used to sell insurance to early industrial workers in England, it is called industrial

EXHIBIT 19–6
Kemper Investor Life Insurance Company's Real Life I $100,000 Policy

AGE*	ANNUAL PREMIUM	CASH VALUE /10 YEARS	CASH VALUE /20 YEARS
20	$ 173	$ 805	$ 3,454
30	264	2,384	7,987
35	371	3,562	11,310
40	532	5,087	15,532
45	753	7,192	20,775
50	1,070	9,831	26,813
55	1,467	13,063	34,175
60	2,023	16,716	42,158
65	2,816	20,553	49,900

*Discount three years for female rate.

life insurance. The insurance agent visits the home and writes a receipt for these small sums. Industrial policies are written for small face values, usually $500 or no more than $2,000. Surprisingly, there are 85 million industrial policies in force today. The average death payment is, of course, small, so the percentage of the total amount of life insurance in force is small. Industrial insurance is extremely expensive; the premium per $1,000 of coverage is typically higher than virtually any other type of insurance coverage.

Recently, insurance companies have started to sell monthly debit ordinary life insurance, basically the same thing as industrial life insurance but with monthly, rather than weekly, payments. More recently, some companies have lumped industrial insurance and monthly debit ordinary under the name "home service insurance." No matter what it is called, this type of insurance generally is not a good deal.

SAVINGS BANK INSURANCE. As of the late 1970s, only three states offered savings bank insurance: New York, Connecticut, and Massachusetts. You must either live or work in those states in order to purchase the insurance. The rates are quite low because, again, there are no selling costs. You go directly to the savings bank to buy the insurance. Generally, savings bank life insurance gives you a better deal than other forms of life insurance, but, of course, you do not get the benefits of any information that salespersons from other commercial companies might be able to give you.

CREDIT LIFE INSURANCE. If you take out a loan, in many cases you may be forced to buy insurance, in the amount of the loan, on your life. The reason is simple: Without such insurance, if you die with part of the loan outstanding, the creditor may have trouble collecting it. But if the creditor is named the beneficiary in the life insurance policy you are required to take out as part of the loan, then he or she is assured payment of any remaining amounts due. Today, there are almost 100 million credit life insurance policies outstanding. The average amount per policy is small, perhaps $1,300. Credit life insurance may seem inexpensive, but it isn't. It typically makes sense only for a person fifty years old or more who lives in a state with a low maximum rate and then only if an existing insurance program is inadequate. It might, for example, be better than nothing for a person with a health problem who cannot be insured. Most consumers, however, are better off simply upgrading their basic insurance portfolio. Thus, be careful: Your creditor may, in fact, be abusing his or her right to force you to take insurance. Check to see that the rate you are actually paying is commensurate with other group policy rates. If it is not, then the difference you pay should be added to the total finance charge in order for you to figure out the true percentage rate of interest you are paying on the loan.

SOME SPECIALIZED INSURANCE POLICIES

A variety of companies offers a number of special life policies. They include combination plans and variable life insurance policies. Every year, new ones are added and old ones modified. Only a lengthy talk with an insurance agent could give you all the latest, most complete descriptions.

Combination Plans

A number of companies are offering plans that combine different types of insurance.

FAMILY PLAN. This insurance plan is a combination of some term insurance and some whole life insurance. Under the family plan, every member of the family has some insurance; newborns are automatically covered so many days after birth.

FAMILY INCOME PLAN. This combination term insurance and whole life insurance policy is designed to provide supplemental income to the family should the breadwinner die prematurely. In a typical twenty-year family income policy plan, if the policyholder dies, his or her beneficiary might receive $10 per month for each $1,000 of the term portion of the policy during the balance of the twenty years. Then, at the end of the twentieth year, the beneficiary would receive the face value of the whole life portion of the policy, either in a lump sum or in monthly installments. There is a variation of this policy called the family maintenance plan; with such a plan, the monthly payments continue for a full twenty-year period *after* the insured dies.

EXTRA PROTECTION POLICY. This policy also combines term and whole life insurance in double, triple, and even quadruple amounts. A triple protection policy, for example, gives, for each $1,000 of whole life insurance, $2,000 of term insurance. The term insurance usually continues until age sixty or sixty-five and then expires; however, the whole life portion of the policy remains in force. Insurance experts point out that these policies give less protection for the extra premium dollar than the family policies previously mentioned. However, the extra protection continues for a longer time.

A variety of companies offers a number of special life policies. They include combination plans and variable life insurance policies.

Modified Life Policies

Modified life plans generally are sold to newly married couples and young, single professionals just starting out. For the first three to five years, the policy is term insurance. It then converts automatically to whole life protection at a higher premium. In the trade, it is called Mod 3 and Mod 5.

Adjustable Life Insurance

One of the newest insurance policies available, adjustable life, presumably offers insurance plans adjusted to each customer's needs and budget. First offered by Minnesota Mutual Life Insurance Company in 1971, it differs from conventional life policies in two ways: You can switch back and forth between whole life and term coverage, and you can change the amount of insurance protection. Basically, you can increase coverage as much as you please if you can pass a medical examination or present evidence of insurability. You can adjust for inflation once every three years by adjusting your coverage and the premium, if you keep the same policy. You can also buy a guaranteed-insurability rider at an extra cost.

OPTIONS AND CLAUSES

Of the plethora of clauses and options that can be added to whole life and term insurance policies, we will describe six.

1. **Guaranteed insurability option.** This option, sold with whole life policies, allows the policyholder to purchase additional insurance at specified ages and amounts without having to meet medical qualifications.
2. **Automatic premium loan option.** With this provision, the insurer automatically will pay any premium that is not paid when due. The premium then becomes a loan against the cash value of the policy. This option will continue until a total of the automatic loans is equal to the cash value; then the policy is terminated.
3. **Convertibility.** A clause or option applied to term insurance policies that allows you to switch the policy to whole life or endowment at standard premium rates regardless of any change in your health.
4. **Accidental death or double indemnity.** An additional sum that is paid to your beneficiary if you die as the result of an accident. Because it usually doubles the face amount of the policy, it is called double indemnity.
5. **Incontestability.** Most policies have a clause that prohibits the company from challenging statements made in your application after two years if you should die; thus, even if you made false statements, it cannot nullify the policy after a stated period.
6. **Guaranteed renewability.** A clause typically applied to renewable term insurance, requiring that the insurance company renew the term policy for a specified number of term periods, even if there has been a significant change in the health of the insured.

ANNUITIES

ANNUITY
An amount payable to the owner of the policy yearly or at other regular intervals. Also, the right to receive or the obligation to pay such an amount.

Unlike life insurance, an **annuity** is issued on a bet that you will not live. An annuity pays the policyholder for living; it generally provides for periodic payment of a fixed sum, either yearly, monthly, or weekly. Certain kinds of annuities provide for partial retirement income and, therefore, eliminate the need to pay, for example, large life insurance premiums as in the level payment plan previously discussed. Annuities can provide safe retirement income in a relatively easy manner (you cannot readily spend your savings) and can also provide tax advantages by deferring income-tax payments until a later date, when most individuals are in a lower marginal tax bracket. There are several types of annuities, among them the relatively new variable annuities.

Variable Annuities

Under this type of annuity, you can either pay small sums into a plan over a period of years or pay a large sum shortly before retirement to provide retirement income. This is the only type of annuity that may be "inflation-proof," as the sum you receive on a fixed regular basis is not in itself fixed; it varies with the stock market return, for the money you pay in is invested in the stock market. Your payments depend on the market value of the common stocks in your account.

Variable annuities often yield a greater return than fixed annuities. Of course, this is due in part to the greater risk involved, because, if the stock market declines during the period, you are collecting against your variable annuity. The amount you receive in payments also depends upon the vagaries of the stock market.

Unlike life insurance, an annuity is issued on a bet that you will not live.

Fixed Annuities

The most common type of annuity is a fixed annuity. The advantages of fixed-dollar annuities generally given by insurance experts are that they provide you with freedom from investment worry and protection against a financial depression. Fixed annuities are of two general kinds, named according to when the income is to start.

1. **Deferred life annuity:** This type of fixed annuity is most often purchased a number of years before retirement age, either by making annual premium payments over a number of years or by paying a lump sum some years before the annuity income would begin. Either way, payment is made some years before the date on which you desire income to begin.
2. **Immediate annuity:** This type of fixed annuity is usually purchased just before retirement, often in place of or in exchange for a level payment whole life policy. Its premium must be paid in a single lump sum.

Whether you choose a deferred or an immediate annuity, there are several kinds of payments from which to choose.

1. **Straight life:** You are guaranteed a fixed income for life, but all payments cease at your death. (In this case, the company providing the annuity is clearly betting on your death.)
2. **Temporary:** You are guaranteed a specified income for a certain length of time only.
3. **Installments certain:** You are guaranteed income for the remainder of your life; in addition, you are guaranteed payments for a certain period—say, ten or twenty years—even if you do not live that long. If you die before the end of the guaranteed period, your beneficiary collects. If you live longer than the guaranteed period, you still receive income, because this payment plan guarantees that period in addition to income for the length of your life.
4. **Installment refund:** In this case, you are again guaranteed payments for life. In addition, rather than a guarantee for a specific period, your heirs are guaranteed installment payments until such time as the balance on what you paid is returned.
5. **Cash refund:** This plan is similar to the installment refund, except that, at your death, the balance is paid to your heirs in a lump sum.
6. **Joint and survivorship:** Two or more persons (usually husband and wife) are guaranteed an income for life as long as either is living. This type of payment plan most clearly eliminates the need for life insurance.

It should be noted that annuities are a relatively expensive investment; that is, they often yield a relatively low rate of return. Exhibit 19–7 shows some average costs of annuities, and Exhibit 19–8 indicates how annuities compare with other types of investments. As with whole life insurance, an important factor to consider when thinking about annuities is how well you could invest

EXHIBIT 19–7
Comparison of Costs of Two Kinds of Annuities

IMMEDIATE SINGLE PREMIUM ANNUITY (Income to Begin at Once)

AGE		MONTHLY INCOME PER $1,000			COST OF $10 OF MONTHLY INCOME		
MALE	FEMALE	STRAIGHT LIFE	10 YEARS CERTAIN	INSTALLMENT REFUND	STRAIGHT LIFE	10 YEARS CERTAIN	INSTALLMENT REFUND
50	55	$4.93	$4.88	$4.73	$2,030	$2,050	$2,110
55	60	5.51	5.41	5.20	1,838	1,847	1,920
60	65	6.30	6.08	5.81	1,605	1,644	1,721
65	70	7.36	6.87	6.56	1,375	1,455	1,524
70	75	8.80	7.73	7.50	1,145	1,293	1,331

DEFERRED ANNUAL PREMIUM ANNUITY (For Men Age 65 When It Starts*)

	MONTHLY INCOME PER $100 A YEAR PURCHASE			COST PER YEAR OF $10 OF MONTHLY INCOME		
AGE AT ISSUE	STRAIGHT LIFE	10 YEARS CERTAIN	INSTALLMENT REFUND	STRAIGHT LIFE	10 YEARS CERTAIN	INSTALLMENT REFUND
30	$33.17	$31.33	$30.38	$ 30.15	$ 31.92	$ 32.92
35	26.49	25.01	24.50	37.75	39.98	40.82
40	20.57	19.42	19.03	48.61	51.49	52.55
45	15.34	14.49	14.20	65.19	69.01	70.42
50	10.71	10.12	9.92	93.37	98.81	100.81
55	6.62	6.26	6.13	151.06	159.74	163.13

*A woman would receive 15 to 20 percent less in annuity income per $100 of annual premium than a man of comparable age at issue.

in alternative income-producing assets, and this includes considering the forced savings nature of annuities. In most cases, younger persons should invest in some form of life insurance before considering annuities. And it is perhaps best to diversify your investments anyway; there is no ideal investment designed to meet every individual's needs.[1]

INVOLUNTARY BENEFIT PROGRAMS—THE CASE OF SOCIAL SECURITY

During the depths of the Depression, the nation realized that numerous people had not provided for themselves in case of emergencies. It was also realized that a large percentage of the elderly population that could not rely on its children for support became destitute. In an effort to prevent a recurrence of so much pain and suffering by elderly people, Congress passed the Social Security Act of 1935. By January 1940, when the first monthly benefit started, only 22,000 people received payments. Today, however, well over 90 percent of people sixty-five or older are receiving Social Security benefits or *could* receive them if they were not still working. Today, over 16 percent of the population is receiving all or part of its income from the Social Security Admin-

1. There is, however, a tax advantage to annuities that is important to high-income individuals in high marginal tax brackets. The interest credited to annuity cash values is not taxable as income until you begin to receive your annuity income. Generally, this income annuity is obtained during the retirement years when you will be in a lower tax bracket.

istration. If U.S. population growth continues to slow down, the average age of the population will continue to rise. Hence, the total number of people eligible for and receiving Social Security will increase as a percentage of the total population. Exhibit 19–9 shows the past and projected percentage of the population sixty-five and over.

We've called this section "Involuntary Benefit Programs" because you and I, with few exceptions, have no choice. If we work, we must participate in the Social Security program. Self-employed people had been able to avoid it, but today they must pay self-employment Social Security taxes if they do not work for someone else. If you work for someone else, your employer must file Social Security taxes for you if you earn over fifty dollars in any quarter. Of the people earning money in the United States, those who contribute to Social Security make up fully 95 percent. Why Social Security has been made obligatory is sometimes difficult to determine. Supporters of the program say that it is to ensure that all older Americans have at least a basic living income and, therefore, will not need welfare payments.

The Provisions of the Social Security Act

The Social Security Act provides benefits for old-age retirement, survivors, disability, and hospital insurance. It is, therefore, sometimes called the **OASDHI.** It is essentially an **income transfer** program, financed out of compulsory payroll taxes levied on both employers and employees: Those who are employed transfer income to those who are unemployed. You pay for Social Security while working and receive the old-age benefits after retirement. The benefit payments usually are made to those reaching retirement age. Also, when the insured worker dies, benefits accrue to his or her survivors. Special benefits provide for disabled workers. Additionally, Social Security now provides for Medicare, which was outlined in Consumer Issue Q.

The Social Security Act of 1935 also provided for the establishment of an unemployment insurance system. Unemployment insurance is not really a federally operated program. Rather, it is left to the states to establish and operate such programs. Although all fifty states have these programs, they vary widely

OASDHI
Old Age, Survivors, Disability, and Hospital Insurance. Usually, the government name for Social Security insurance.

INCOME TRANSFER
A transfer of income from some individuals in the economy to other individuals. This is generally done by way of the government. It is a transfer in the sense that no current services are rendered by the recipients. Unemployment insurance, for example, is an income transfer to unemployed individuals.

EXHIBIT 19–8
Comparison of Annuity against Savings or Investment

COST OF AN ANNUITY			RETURNS ON INVESTING OR SAVING THE SAME AMOUNT TO YIELD $100 A MONTH TO LIVE ON		
Purchaser:	Life expectancy:	$100 a month guaranteed for life costs:	You can live on dividends or interest only if your money earns:	With lower earnings, you can tap both interest and principal, and your money will last:	And if still living, your life expectancy will then be:
A woman age 62	19½ years (49% live at least 20 years)	$17,300	7%	At 3%, 19 years At 4%, 22 years	At 81, 9 years At 84, 7½ years
A man age 65	14½ years (27% live at least 20 years)	$13,750	8¾%	At 3%, 14 years At 4%, 16 years	At 79, 7½ years At 81, 7 years

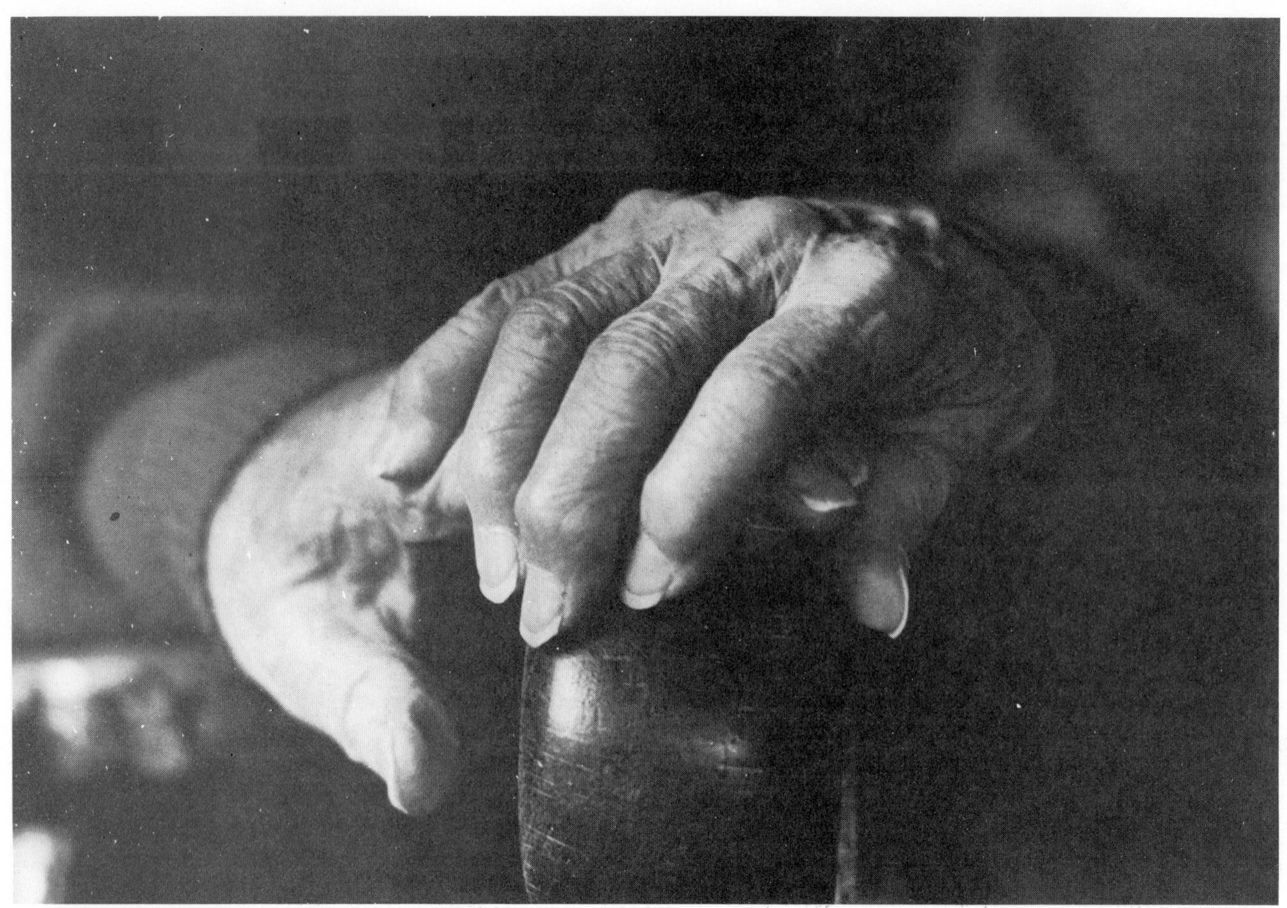

in the extent and the amount of payments made. Programs are basically financed by taxes on employers; these taxes average about 2 percent of total payroll. A worker who finds himself or herself unemployed may become eligible for benefit payments. The size of these payments and the number of weeks they can be received vary from state to state. Currently, about 80 million workers are covered by unemployment compensation.

BASIC BENEFITS OF SOCIAL SECURITY

In the following Consumer Issue, you will learn where to get information with which to figure, tentatively, the benefits that you are allowed under Social Security. (The predictions must be tentative because Congress frequently changes the benefits.) Essentially, Social Security is a form of life insurance. Every time you have a child, the maximum life insurance benefit of Social Security is automatically restored, and its term is automatically increased to a potential twenty-one years. Here is what you can expect from Social Security:

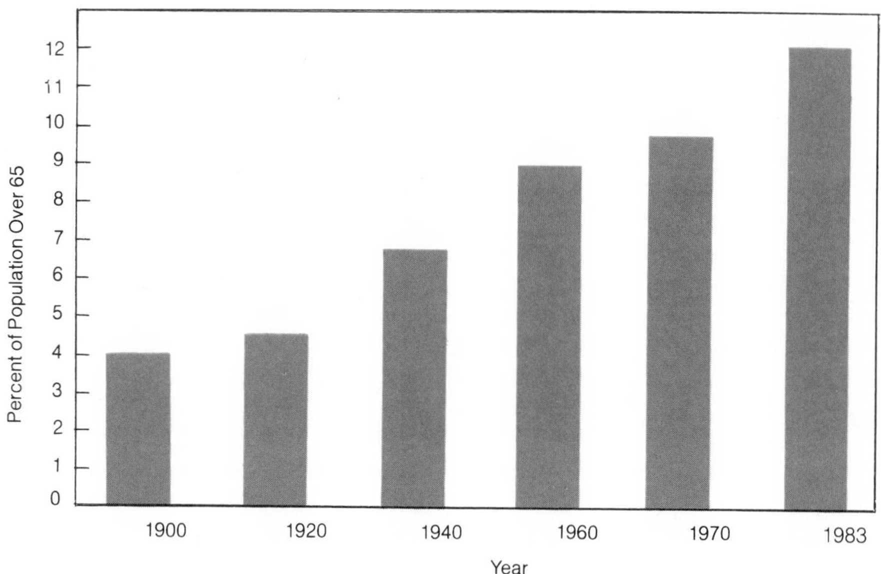

EXHIBIT 19–9
U.S. Population over Age Sixty-Five

1. Medicare payments in the future
2. If you should die, payments to your beneficiary
3. If you should die, payments to your children until they have completed college
4. Payments to you or your dependents if you are totally disabled and unable to work
5. A retirement annuity—that is, a payment of a certain amount of money every month after you retire until you die (This payment, however, is legislated by Congress and can be changed by Congress.)
6. If you die, a modest lump-sum payment, presumably to take care of burial expenses

Whenever you figure out your insurance needs, you must consult the basic coverage that you have on your Social Security. You will learn how to do that in the following Consumer Issue.

PROBLEMS WITH SOCIAL SECURITY

A number of respected researchers have reached some pretty depressing conclusions about Social Security. In the first place, you have to remember that Social Security is not really an insurance policy in the sense that you are guaranteed a certain amount of money. Your beneficiaries get that amount of money only if you die, just as with a regular insurance policy; but, if you live, you get retirement payments that are a function not of how much money you have put in but, rather, of what Congress legislates. Future Congresses may not be as kind as past Congresses, so you may find yourself with a very small retirement income if you rely on Social Security.

A number of respected researchers have reached some pretty depressing conclusions about Social Security.

HOW SOCIAL SECURITY IS PAID

In theory, Social Security is supported by a tax on the employee's income that is matched by the employer. However, you must realize that generally you, the employee, pay for much of the program because your wages could be that much higher if the employer did not have to contribute. The combined Social Security and Medicare tax for 1983 was set at 6.7 percent of the worker's income with an equal amount paid by the employer. This tax was applied only to the first $35,700 earned a year.[2] After that, it was no longer applicable. Hence, the Social Security contribution, otherwise known as a payroll tax, is highly regressive. (It is indicated on your payroll receipt as FICA—Federal Insurance Contributions Act.) Note, though, that benefits are proportionally greater for low-income earners than high-income earners, partially compensating for the regressive nature of the tax. The tax rates, moreover, have been increasing rapidly, more than doubling since 1967. Nonetheless, few seem to have seen the regressive nature of this particular income tax and the fact that, for the majority of taxpayers, it is greater than the income taxes they pay.

THE LATEST SOCIAL SECURITY REFORM

Every few years Congress decides to reform the Social Security system in order to "save" it. The latest reform was passed in 1983. The reform means only one thing: Get out your pocketbooks. Here are some of the important changes:

1. Employers will pay an increased rate of 7 percent in 1984. The rate for both employers and employers and employees goes up to the following:

1985–7.05 percent
1986–7.15 percent
1988–7.51 percent
1990–7.65 percent

2. Self-employed individuals will pay a higher tax, equal to 11.3 percent in 1984 and 13.3 percent by 1990.
3. Social Security benefits will be taxed. If half a person's benefits plus all of their income adds up to more than $25,000 ($32,000 for couples filing jointly), as much as one-fourth of the benefits would be owed in taxes. That means that people have to save more for retirement.

IF YOU WORK AFTER SIXTY-FIVE, YOU MAY NOT GET PAID

The Social Security Act, as it currently stands, penalizes you tremendously if you decide to remain working past the retirement age (sixty-five), for you can earn only $6,600, after which your Social Security check is reduced. If your earned income exceeds that figure, Social Security benefits are reduced one dollar for every two dollars above the exempt amount. "Earned" here means income that is made as a wage earner, not as dividends, interest, or pensions.

2. By law, this tax base automatically rises whenever the rate of inflation reaches specified levels.

If you decide to invest a lot of money, you can be making millions of dollars and still get full Social Security. But if you decide to be hard worker and continue getting wages, you may lose all your Social Security payments if you earn, for example, $9,000 a year. It is conceivable that you could work till the age of seventy and never get one penny in benefits from Social Security, even though you were forced to pay in your entire working life. Your decision to work after age sixty-five certainly will be influenced by this highly regressive taxation system. We say "taxation system" because you are obviously taxed if, for every dollar you earn, you lose fifty cents in Social Security benefits. That sounds like a tax rate of 50 percent, does it not? (That is in addition to taxes that you pay already, such as Social Security and income taxes). This seems a bit steep since, under the federal personal income-tax system, the 50 percent marginal tax rate does not apply to individuals unless they make incomes of well over $30,000. But for people over sixty-five, this 50 percent rate started at $6,600 in 1983, and for those between sixty-two and sixty-five, it started at $14,920. This earning limitation is eliminated after age seventy.

The Social Security Act, as it currently stands, penalizes you tremendously if you decide to remain working past the retirement age (sixty-five).

This is one aspect of the Social Security program that many observers feel is quite unfair, because it penalizes older people for working. Professor Carolyn Shaw Bell of Wellesley College also points out that the Social Security system is not insurance but, rather, a transfer. People who are working pay Social Security taxes. People who get Social Security benefits receive the income that is taxed away. Essentially, it is a subsidy from younger workers to older, retired people. There is also a transer from those who continue to work after age sixty-five to their peers who do not work. At the beginning of this decade, for example, there were 3 million people over age sixty-five in the labor force, a full 22 percent of older men and 10 percent of older women. These 3 million people, according to Professor Shaw Bell, are "unjustly hemmed in between bleak job market prospects on the one hand, and the necessity, on the other, of paying out of their meager earnings to support not only themselves but others of their own age." That is to say, of course, that these 3 million people who are working are continuing to pay Social Security taxes.

Under the latest Social Security reform, passed in 1983, the penalty for working after the age of 65 will be reduced. Starting in 1990, people will have to surrender only $1 of benefits for every $3 they earn over $10,000 or so (the exact cutoff won't be known until 1990). However, those who work past the age of 70 will continue to lose no benefits, whatever their earnings.

THERE WILL ALWAYS BE A PROBLEM WITH SOCIAL SECURITY

No matter what Congress does, there will always be a problem with our Social Security system. Whenever the government sets up a system that is not actuarially sound, that system will eventually be in trouble. As long as Congress continues to increase benefits, while at the same time the labor force grows less rapidly than the number of retirees, financial strain will hit the system. Every bailout that Congress has passed for Social Security has been one that was supposed to last for 20 or 30 years. Yet within several years the system is in financial trouble again. What you can be certain of is that, if you are under the age of 40, your retirement benefits from Social Security will not be as good a deal as they have been for those who have already retired and for those who are over the age of forty. Therefore, plan on providing for more of your own retirement.

SUMMARY

1. The major hazards to financial security are illness, accident, unemployment, old age, premature death of the person providing financial support, desertion, divorce, and unexpected catastrophic expenses.
2. Life insurance can take many forms, the most popular being term and whole life.
3. Term insurance is generally for a five-year period, after which time a higher premium must be paid to obtain the same face value in insurance because the probability of death has increased as the individual becomes older.
4. Whole, straight, or ordinary life insurance involves pure protection in addition to a savings plan whereby part of your premiums are put into investments that return interest to the policyholder. At any time, a whole life policyholder has a cash value in his or her policy.
5. Whole life insurance has living benefits. You can, for example, borrow on your cash value; you can get protection for the rest of your life at retirement; you can get a cash settlement; and you can convert your whole life policy to a stream of income—called an annuity—over a certain period of time.
6. There are two types of insurance companies: stock and mutual.
7. Mutual insurance companies generally issue participating policies, whereas stock insurance companies issue nonparticipating policies.
8. Death benefits can be paid to your beneficiaries in a lump sum equal to the face value, or as interest on the face value of the insurance policy plus principal at the end of a specific period, or in installments until the face value has been paid.
9. There are a number of specialized life insurance policies, such as a family plan and a family income plan.
10. An annuity can be obtained from an insurance company to provide income for retirement or for some other purpose. There are fixed annuities and variable annuities, the latter making a payout depending on the rate of return in the stock market; the former has a fixed payout because only fixed income investments, such as bonds, are purchased by the company issuing the annuity.
11. Social Security is a form of social insurance in the United States. It provides for living and death benefits.
12. However, Social Security is not an insurance policy in the normal sense of the word. Basically, contributions to Social Security are merely transfers of income from those who work to those who do not work.
13. Social Security taxes are paid both by the employer and the employee. However, in the economy as a whole, employees receive salaries that are lowered by the amount that employees must pay to Social Security. After all, that payment is a cost of hiring employees.
14. Under current law, individuals from ages sixty-five to seventy-two who work often lose benefits from Social Security because their incomes are too high. In addition, they continue to pay Social Security taxes.

QUESTIONS FOR THOUGHT AND DISCUSSION

1. Who do you think should have life insurance?
2. Why would an insurance salesperson try to sell you a whole life policy?
3. Why is a life insurance premium cheaper for college students than for older adults?
4. When would it be worthwhile to borrow on the cash value of a whole life insurance policy?
5. Do you know anybody who would be a good candidate for limited payment whole life insurance? Would you ever be a good candidate?
6. Why would someone choose decreasing term insurance with a constant premium rather than level term insurance with an increasing premium?
7. When do you think it would be appropriate to have a convertibility feature in your term insurance policy? That is, when do you think it would be advantageous to pay the extra price to have the option of changing your term insurance to whole life insurance?
8. Why do you think group insurance is cheaper than individually written insurance?
9. If you had the choice, would you choose a variable or a fixed annuity?
10. Do you think Social Security is a good deal?

THINGS TO DO

1. Try to determine whether life insurance companies make a higher profit than other companies in the United States.
2. Phone several life insurance agents in your area and ask what the premium cost is of a $10,000 straight or whole life insurance policy. Is there great variation?
3. Check newspaper ads for mail-order life insurance policies. In light of the analysis presented in this chapter, how do you interpret the claims made?
4. Select two nationally prominent politicians and compare their stands on Social Security measures. Credit your sources of information.

SELECTED READINGS

American Council of Life Insurance. *Life Insurance Fact Book.* Washington, D.C.: American Council of Life Insurance (published yearly).

Annuities from the Buyer's Point of View. American Institute for Economic Research, Economic Education Bulletin, Vol. X, No. 7, August 1970.

"Credit Insurance: The Quiet Overcharge." *Consumer Reports,* July 1979, pp. 415–17.

Federal Trade Commission. *Staff Report on Life Insurance Costs Disclosure.* Washington, D.C.: U.S. Government Printing Office, 1979.

Greene, Mark, R., and Swadener, Paul. *Insurance Insights.* Cincinnati, Ohio: Southwestern Publishing Company, 1974.

"Life Insurance—A Special Report." A two-part series in *Consumer Reports,* February 1980, pp. 79–107, and March 1980, pp. 163–86.

Life Insurance Fact Book. Washington, D.C.: American Council of Life Insurance, 1850 K Street, N.W., Washington, D.C. 20060 (published annually).

"Life-Insurance Regulation: What's Needed?" *Consumer Reports,* March 1980, pp. 187–88.

Oehlbeck, Trace. *The Consumer's Guide to Life Insurance.* New York: Pyramid Books, 1975.

Spielman, Peter, and Zelman, Aaron. *The Life Insurance Conspiracy.* New York: Simon & Schuster, 1979.

"Universal-life Insurance." *Consumer Reports,* January 1982, pp. 42–44.

U.S. Department of Health and Human Services. *Your Social Security.* Washington, D.C.: U.S. Government Printing Office, 1980.

Welker, Ernest P., editor. *Life Insurance from the Buyer's Point of View.* American Institute for Economic Research, Economic Education Bulletin, Vol. XX, No. 7, July 1980.

Consumer ISSUE R

HOW TO MEET YOUR INSURANCE NEEDS

GLOSSARY

INTEREST-ADJUSTED COST (IAC)—An insurance cost index that takes account of dividends, interest, and earnings of the policy.

Before you figure out how much insurance you should buy, what type it should be, and where you should get it, first consider who should be insured in your family. You have to take into account the Social Security benefits you have coming, and that sometimes is not easy. You then have to look at the actual economic (or financial) dependency that anybody has on a particular member of a spending unit. If you are a single college student, for example, it is usually not recommended that you have any insurance at all (unless you want to use it as a forced savings mechanism or as insurance against becoming medically uninsurable later on in life). By the same token, it is usually absurd for a family to insure its children unless the children contribute a substantial amount to the family income. If one of them dies, the family's earning power generally will not fall. This is not necessarily true for a homemaker, however, who frequently contributes to the family earnings stream by employment outside the home, as well as implicity through the value of services rendered to the family. In this case, the family unit may want to take out an insurance policy on the homemaker's life. The basic wage earner should, of course, be the one with the most insurance because, if he or she dies prematurely, the *spending unit* will suffer the greatest loss.

SOME INSURANCE BUYING RULES

Insurance is another item competing for your consumer dollar, just as is a new bicycle, a new car, or a new house. When you make an expenditure on life insurance, you obtain a certain amount of satisfaction in knowing that your dependents will be financially secure in the event of your premature death. Note, however, that there are other possible uses of these same funds that also yield satisfaction; thus, there is no pat answer or formula that will tell you exactly how much insurance is best for you.

1. Identify the major risks that you and your family reasonably face; insure them according to the *potential* loss they can produce.
2. Insure big losses, not small ones.
3. Never buy an insurance policy until you have compared at least two companies (and perhaps more), not only on the costs but on the terms of coverage. Use the **interest-adjusted cost** figure for comparison.
4. Limit your losses and control your risks through preventive measures.
5. *Buy* insurance; don't have it sold to you.

ARE YOU UNDERINSURED?

There is a good chance that you are underinsured if anybody depends on you for even part of his or her livelihood. If, however, you live alone or are young and unmarried, or even are married but your spouse also contributes to the family kitty, then you may not need

much (if any) life insurance. If you are married and have children, or a spouse who depends on you for at least part of his or her income, then you probably should have some form of life insurance. You should first realize that Social Security is the basis of all your protection needs, assuming you are covered by Social Security. You will have to find out from your local Social Security office exactly what kinds of benefits your dependents have coming in case of your death.

An assumption will be made in this Consumer Issue that you yourself should make when trying to figure out your insurance needs: Assume that you drop dead tomorrow. How much would be left to your dependents, in what form, and over what period? This is not an easy thing to figure out, so plan on spending some time at it. You may want to work it out with an insurance agent, but you can probably do it on your own.

FIGURING OUT YOUR SOCIAL SECURITY

The first thing you should do is write the Social Security Administration. Give the representative your Social Security number and the name on your Social Security card, and ask for a current report of your account. You can request a statement of your earnings every year. It is best to do it at least once every three years because there is a time limit on correcting errors. You can obtain a "Request for Statement of Earnings" card like the one pictured in Exhibit R–1. After you have received this, take it to your local Social Security office and request the following facts:

1. Survivors' benefits for a spouse and one child under eighteen
2. Survivor's benefits for a child eighteen through twenty-one as a full-time unmarried student

3. Survivors' benefits for a spouse and two or more children under eighteen
4. Maximum family payment allowed
5. Widow's or widower's pension benefits starting at sixty-two; widow's pension benefits starting at sixty
6. Total disability benefits for the wage earner, spouse, and two or more children
7. Total disability benefits for wage earner, spouse, and one child

The Social Security Administration will gladly send you a booklet that will help you figure this all out yourself. Or you can write directly to the Superintendent of Documents, Washington, D.C., requesting a copy of the U.S. Department of Health and Human Services publication, *Estimating Your Social Security Retirement Check* (SSA) 05-10070, January 1983. Exhibit R–2 gives a schedule of benefits that were available as of 1982.

You should be wary of books claiming to give you information on how to obtain Social Security benefits that you thought were unavailable. You might see an ad that proclaims, "Ten million people whose average age is thirty are collecting Social Security benefits today." That statement is true, but it refers to young blind people, disabled workers, and dependent survivors who get Social Security checks. You can get all the information you need to know from your nearest Social Security office. Don't waste your money on a book claiming to make you rich off the system.

Now that you have this information, you can figure out the financial condition of your family. Go back to page 234 and see how a net-worth statement is calculated when you apply for a loan. Figuring out your net-worth gives you a starting point. The average net worth of American families in the United States is estimated at $25,000.

You now have two major details of your financial situation in case you have dependents and die tomorrow: Social Security payments to your dependents and a net worth that is left to them. Now you must figure out a monthly income goal for a spouse and children under eighteen, a lump-sum education-fund goal for each child, a monthly retirement income goal for a widow or widower starting at age sixty-two, and a monthly income goal, if any, for a widow or widower between childrearing and retirement. This latter is optional, depending on whether or not the family wants the widow or widower to have to work.

FIGURING OUT HOW MUCH INSURANCE TO BUY

Neither you nor anyone else can estimate *exactly* how much life insurance you should buy. That depends not only on all the factors already mentioned but also on how "safe" you want to be. After all, buying insurance means that part of your income can no longer be used for other purchases. You have to decide how much you want to give up in order to be "fully" insured. Nonetheless, you can get a general idea of how much life insurance you need by using a method developed by financial counselors at the First National City Banks in New York (Citibank). Citibank's economists, personnel, and insurance specialists have calculated that a family can

EXHIBIT R–1
Request for Statement of Earnings Card

REQUEST FOR STATEMENT OF EARNINGS

SOCIAL SECURITY NUMBER → [ ][ ][ ]

DATE OF BIRTH → MONTH | DAY | YEAR

Please send a statement of my Social Security earnings to:

NAME (MISS, MRS., MR.) ____________________

STREET & NUMBER ____________________

CITY & STATE ____________________ ZIP CODE __________

Print Name and Address In Ink Or Use Typewriter

SIGN YOUR NAME HERE (DO NOT PRINT) ____________________

Sign your own name only. Under the law, information in your social security record is confidential and anyone who signs another person's name can be prosecuted. If you have changed your name from that shown on your social security card, please copy your name below exactly as it appears on your card.

EXHIBIT R–2
Social Security Benefits

Monthly retirement benefits for workers who reached the age of sixty-two before 1979 (effective June 1982).

FOR WORKERS		FOR DEPENDENTS				
AVERAGE YEARLY EARNINGS	WORKER AT 65	SPOUSE[1] AT 65 OR CHILD	AT 64	AT 63	AT 62	FAMILY[2] BENEFITS
$ 1,200	235	117	107	98	88	353
2,000	305	152	140	127	114	459
2,600	345	172	158	143	129	517
3,000	377	188	173	157	141	577
3,400	405	202	185	168	151	652
4,000	444	222	203	185	166	759
4,400	476	238	218	198	178	844
4,800	504	252	231	210	189	919
5,200	530	265	242	220	198	994
5,600	556	278	254	231	208	1,030
6,000	582	291	267	242	218	1,068
6,400	608	304	278	253	228	1,106
6,800	636	318	291	265	238	1,143
7,200	669	334	306	278	250	1,183
7,600	698	349	320	291	261	1,222
8,000	724	362	331	301	271	1,267
8,400	739	369	338	308	277	1,294
8,800	757	378	347	315	284	1,325
9,200	774	387	354	322	290	1,354
9,600	787	393	360	328	295	1,377
10,000	802	401	367	334	300	1,403
10,400	817	408	374	340	306	1,430
10,800	830	415	380	345	311	1,452
11,400	851	425	390	354	319	1,490

[1]If a person is eligible for both a worker's benefit and a spouse's benefit, the check actually payable is limited to the larger of the two.
[2]The maximum amount payable to a family is generally reached when a worker and two family members are eligible.

maintain its standard of living with an after-tax income of 75 percent of its current after-tax income should the breadwinner die. Citibank believes that, if a family winds up with less than 60 percent of the pre-death level of after-tax income, its living standard will be seriously lowered. Thus, in Exhibit R–3 there are net-income-replacement columns labeled 75 percent and 60 percent: These are the target net after-tax income-replacement levels that insurance should provide. The Multiples of Salary Chart basically tells you how many times your current gross salary you should own in life insurance to provide 75 or 60 percent of your current after-tax income for your family should you die. The chart assumes that your family will also receive Social Security benefits. In figuring out the chart, Citibank's staff assumed that insurance proceeds would be invested to produce, after inflation, a rate of return of 5 percent a year. Moreover, it is assumed that the principal from the insurance policy gradually would be eaten up, so it would disappear by the time of the surviving spouse's death.

Take an example. If your spouse is twenty-five years old, your gross earnings are $9,000 a year, and you wish to provide him or her with 60 percent of your after-tax income if you were to die, you need to have in force three times your gross earnings, or $27,000 worth of life insurance. This figure may seem low, but it takes into account the higher Social Security benefit that a younger spouse would obtain.

NOW THAT YOU'VE FIGURED OUT HOW MUCH, WHAT SHOULD YOU BUY?

Say that you calculate that you need $50,000 worth of life insurance. Which type should you purchase? A number of life insurance plans were just presented, the most important being term, whole life, universal life, and endowment. All but term insurance include some element of saving. Thus, you are not only buying pure insurance; you also are investing and getting a rate of return. Your decision whether to buy pure insurance or to buy savings will determine the payments you must make to the insurance company. The cheapest way to buy insurance is, of course, to buy term because you buy only protection. If you already have a satisfactory savings program, you may not wish to save additional sums with an insurance company. Many insurance experts agree that the cheapest insurance you can buy is term; if you want additional saving features, you will get a higher rate of return by going to sources other than insurance companies.

Consumers' Union points out, as do several other research organizations, that if purchasing whole life insurance is compared with buying term and investing the difference—that is, the difference between the whole life premium and the lower term premium—the combination of term and other investments will yield a larger sum of money at the end of any period. A critic of this conclusion, Herbert S. Denenberg, contends that this comparison is true only if you manage to get somewhere around a 6 percent rate of return on your savings (over a longer period of time) if you invest them yourself. He contends that, if you expect to get only 4 percent, you are better off buying whole life.[3] We will see in the following chapters on saving and investing that it is quite difficult *not* to get 6 percent on savings in a variety of ways. Therefore, we will stick to the conclusion that your best bet is to buy term insurance and not to involve an insurance company in your savings plan.

However, insurance salespersons have numerous arguments as to why you should buy whole life, not term, insurance. They will say that whole life is a bargain, or even "free," because you eventually get back much or all of your money. Note, however, that if you die, your beneficiary will get only the face value on the policy, not the additional cash value. Salespersons use the cash-value aspect of whole life to tout its desirability over term insurance. Because term has no cash value, salespeople will tell you that buying it is "just throwing money down the

3. Herbert S. Denenberg, "Consumers Union: No Help for Insurance Shoppers." *Business and Society Review*, No. 6 (Summer 1973), pp. 107–108.

EXHIBIT R–3

The Multiples of Salary Chart (For Net Income Replacement)

To calculate the amount of life insurance needed for either net-replacement level, multiply your present gross salary by the number under that level.

If your gross income or spouse's age fall between the figures shown, take an average between the multiples for nearest salaries and ages.

Social Security benefits will be part of both levels.

If personal liquid assets (savings, predictable inheritance, retirement plan, investment, etc.) equal one year of gross salary or less, use them as part of the fund for the small-emergency reserve and final expenses. If they equal more than one year, subtract that extra amount from the insurance needed to replace income.

People with no personal assets who can't afford the 75 percent level might try for at least 60 percent. The average family would then face some lowering in level of living but wouldn't be financially devastated.

	PRESENT AGE OF SPOUSE							
YOUR PRESENT GROSS EARNINGS	25 YEARS*		35 YEARS*		45 YEARS*		55 YEARS†	
	75%	60%	75%	60%	75%	60%	75%	60%
$ 7,500	4.0	3.0	5.5	4.0	7.5	5.5	6.5	4.5
9,000	4.0	3.0	5.5	4.0	7.5	5.5	6.5	4.5
15,000	4.5	3.0	6.5	4.5	8.0	6.0	7.0	5.5
23,500	6.5	4.5	8.0	5.5	8.5	6.5	7.5	5.5
30,000	7.5	5.0	8.0	6.0	8.5	6.5	7.0	5.5
40,000	7.5	5.0	8.0	6.0	8.0	6.0	7.0	5.5
65,000	7.5	5.5	7.5	6.0	7.5	5.0	6.5	5.0

*Assuming federal income taxes for a family of four (two children). There are four exemptions and the standard—or 15 percent itemized—deductions. State and local taxes are disregarded.

†Assuming you have only two exemptions. (Any children are now grown.)

Reprinted by permission of First National City Bank, New York.

drain." This "down the drain" argument ignores the fact that the term premiums are lower than whole life premiums in the early years. For a man twenty-five years old, whole life premiums in the early years may cost three to four times more than term premiums.

Life Insurance Sold on Campus

Insurance agents have become familiar figures on many campuses, where they sometimes contact students four to six times a year. The insurance agent approaches a premium-paying problem of the poor student by offering to finance on credit the first annual premium and even the second, with a loan to be paid off perhaps five years later. This student policyholder typically signs a policy assignment form, which makes the insurance company the first beneficiary if the student dies. Thus, the insurance company will make sure that it can collect the unpaid premium and interest. Generally, buying insurance as a college student is not advisable because most college student do not have dependents.

Additionally, the cost of campus life insurance is extremely high compared to policies available to the general public. Thus, if a college student has to be insured, he or she should look at a standard life insurance policy, either term or whole life.

What If You Need Someone to Force You to Save?

If you like the idea of having forced savings, then buying whole life insurance may be the way to do it. You'll feel compelled to pay the insurance premiums, and you know that part of the premium goes to a savings plan. The lower rate of return on savings left with an insurance company is compensated for by the fact that you have any savings at all, savings that you would not have had otherwise because you find it difficult, if not impossible, to save.

You do have other options. In some instances, you can have your employer credit union take out a payroll deduction every month to put in your credit union account. You can also have your employer take out a certain amount of money each month for U.S. Savings Bonds. In both instances, you will have more liquidity if you need it than if an insurance company had been doing your "forced saving" for you. (But if you don't trust yourself, you may prefer less liquidity.)

If Your Income Is High

As another argument for whole life over term, some insurance agents point out that, for individuals in extremely high income brackets, it may be better to buy whole life insurance, borrow on that insurance to pay the premiums, and be able to deduct the interest payments on the borrowing from ordinary income so that taxes do not have to be paid.

SOME ADDITIONAL CONSIDERATIONS

A fact that we have not yet mentioned about a permanent or whole life insurance policy contract is that it is essentially a piece of property and has certain characteristics that are perhaps unique. Under current law, provided that the permanent insurance plan is set up properly, it can accumulate income, tax free: Dividends as well as interest on cash value are not taxable as current income. Essentially, then, you get a higher return than is actually shown in your life insurance savings plan because you are not paying a tax on the savings you are accumulating. Remember, if you have a regular savings account, you have to pay federal and sometimes state income tax on the interest earnings of that account.

Another fact that may or may not be important for most individuals is that death benefits on ordinary or straight life insurance policies usually go to age 100; except in very rare cases, there is always going to be a death benefit.

TAKE ADVANTAGE OF GROUP PLANS

Whenever you can take advantage of group term insurance plans, you probably should do so to take care of at least part of your life insurance needs. For reasons mentioned in the previous chapter, group insurance is generally cheaper than individually issued insurance (unless you happen to be significantly younger than the average age of the group).

SHOPPING AROUND FOR INSURANCE

It generally is unwise to buy insurance from the first insurance salesperson who knocks on your door. Because large sums of money may be involved, it is usually advisable to look over several plans. Be aware, however, that life insurance policies are incredibly complex. Seek out a knowledgeable insurance salesperson who represents a large number of companies and who can explain clearly the benefits of each program and the average annual costs per $1,000 of five-year renewable term insurance. A good source of information on comparative life insurance costs can be found in a series of studies presented in *Consumer Reports* (see the February and March issues of 1980). Consumers' Union presents the basic facts on the types of policies available and compares different companies on the basis of a sophisticated index—the interest-adjusted cost index—that takes account of dividends, interest, and earnings on the policies. Not everyone can buy insurance from some of the companies listed. For example, only teachers and staff members in schools, universities, and educational or scientific institutions can buy insurance from Teachers Insurance and Annuity Association of America, one of the lowest-cost insurance policies available. If you work or live in Massachusetts, New York, or Connecticut, you can take advantage of extremely low-cost, five-year renewable term insurance available from mutual savings banks.

SOME WAYS TO CUT INSURANCE COSTS

1. Don't carry insurance on children. Either save the premiums or use them to buy additional term insurance for yourself.
2. Consider term as opposed to whole life insurance.
3. If you don't smoke or drink, try to find insurance companies that give discounts to nonsmokers or nondrinkers. See if you fit into a preferred-risk category.
4. Attempt to buy insurance on group plans through your employer or any organization of which you are a member.
5. Pay your premiums annually instead of quarterly or monthly.
6. If you have a participating policy, don't let your dividends or refunds accumulate on deposit with the insurance company at a lower rate than the money could earn at a savings institution.

SUMMARY

1. In deciding whom to insure, base your decision upon who depends on whom and what financial stress would be undergone when an individual dies prematurely.
2. Information about the basic benefits you are allowed under Social Security can be obtained from the Social Security Administration, Washington, D.C., or your local Social Security office.
3. Basic insurance buying rules are: Identify and insure major risks according to potential loss, insure big rather than small losses, and always compare at least two companies on costs and terms of coverage.
4. If you want a forced savings plan, then you may wish to purchase whole life insurance. However, if you can save on your own, you generally will do better by purchasing lower-cost term insurance and putting the difference in high (long-run) income-yielding assets, such as long-term savings certificates, the stock market, and so on.
5. Shopping for insurance requires the same skills as shopping for any other customer product. Information is the key. You may wish to consult *Consumer Reports'* special issues in 1980, which rate life insurance companies by their respective costs.

QUESTIONS FOR THOUGHT AND DISCUSSION

1. Can you think of any reason why children should have life insurance?
2. Can you think of any reason why a college student should purchase life insurance?
3. Are you underinsured?
4. Are you overinsured?
5. If you are relatively young, is it possible for you to figure out what Social Security will pay you on retirement?
6. Who should buy term insurance as opposed to whole life?

THINGS TO DO

1. Try to determine whether you are overinsured or underinsured. If you are underinsured, go to the next project.
2. Call at least two (preferably three or four) insurance agents. Take the time to sit down with each of them to discuss your insurance needs. Find out what their recommendations are for an adequate amount of insurance. Ask why they are not suggesting you purchase term or decreasing term insurance.
3. Take a look at the special reports in the 1980 issues of *Consumer Reports*. If you already have insurance, see where your insurance company rates relative to others. Would it be worthwhile for you to change policies?

SELECTED READINGS

"An Array of New Products to Woo the Policyholder." *Business Week*, January 3, 1982, p. 126.
Carter, Malcolm. "How Much Life Insurance Do You Really Need?" *Money*, April 1982, pp. 133–42.
Halverson, R. P. "Term versus Whole Life Insurance." *Working Woman*, December 1982, p. 40.
Hildreth, J. M. "Changes to Expect in Social Security." *U.S. News & World Report*, January 3, 1983, p. 61.
"Life Insurance: A Special Two-Part Report." *Consumer Reports*, February/March 1980.
"What Will Social Security Do for Your Survivors?" *Consumer Reports*, February 1980, p. 82.

CHAPTER
SAVING

20

Almost two-thirds of all American families have savings accounts, and over 35 million Americans have stocks and bonds. The total amount of saving in the United States in any one year may exceed $160 billion.

CHAPTER PREVIEW

- How much do Americans save every year?
- Why do people save, and what determines how much they save?
- What is the nature of compound interest?
- What are the various types of savings institutions?

SAVING
The act of not consuming or not spending your money income to obtain current satisfaction. Saving is an act that you engage in over time in order to have more wealth to consume in the future.

Almost two-thirds of all American families have savings accounts, and over 35 million Americans have stocks or bonds. The total amount of **saving** in the United States in any one year may exceed $160 billion for the rest of the 1980s. We see in Exhibit 20–1 the amount of saving over time in the United States.

THE TENDENCY TO SAVE

The tendency to save in the United States has existed ever since the country started. The relationship between consumption and personal disposable income over the last three-fourths of this century has been almost constant. This implies that what Americans do *not* consume—that is, save—is about 7 to 9 percent of their income year in and year out.

WHY SAVE AT ALL?

When most people think of saving, they immediately think of saving for some special item, such as a down payment on a new house, a vacation next summer, a new car, or a TV. But there is another way to look at saving and that is to take a long-term view.

The reason you may want to save is either to leave a large estate to your heirs or to provide for yourself and your family during periods when your income is abnormally low, such as when you might be disabled or after you retire. You can look at saving, then, as a way to spread your consumption over your lifetime so that it remains smooth even when your income fluctuates or sometimes falls to zero, especially after you retire. Even if you are very, very

EXHIBIT 20–1
Personal Savings in the United States for the Last Twenty-Five Years

Personal savings have been going up at fairly steady rates for the last quarter of a century. Note, however, that part of this increase in savings is due to inflation, because we have not corrected for it in this chart.

SOURCE: U.S. Department of Commerce.

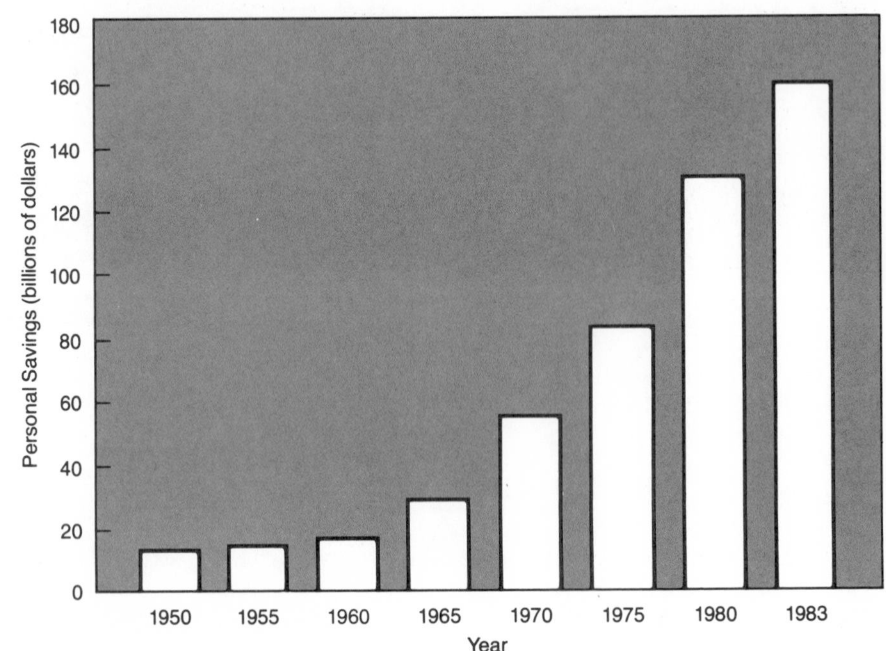

poor and just barely making a living, you know that, some time in the future, you will no longer be able to work. Either you will reach mandatory retirement or you will become so unproductive that nobody will hire you. Your income stream will be cut off. Unless there are children, a benevolent government, or private charities that will take care of you, you will face starvation unless you have accumulated savings.

Therefore, you must decide today how much of your current income you want to set aside for those retirement years. Unless you literally will starve if you reduce your current level of consumption by even a very small amount, you probably will attempt to save a part of your income. Most people would rather reduce current consumption by a small amount to ensure at least minimal support after they can no longer work. Were they not to reduce their current consumption at all, they might face certain starvation as soon as their income stream stopped.

Thus, saving is a method by which individuals can achieve an optimal consumption stream throughout their expected lifetime—"optimal" not meaning adequate or necessary but, rather, the most desirable from the individual's point of view. If you face the constraint of a very low income for all your life, in most cases you still would want to provide some savings to live on when you no longer can work.

Even if you are very, very poor and just barely making a living, you know that, some time in the future, you will no longer be able to work.

WHAT DETERMINES HOW MUCH YOU SAVE?

If you want to save something for that proverbial rainy day, what determines the amount you save? We can offer a few ideas here. Obviously, the more money you can make on your savings, the more you will want to save (if nothing else changes). In other words, if a savings and loan association offered to give you 50 percent interest a year on your deposits, you probably would want to save more than you do now at an interest rate of less than 10 percent. Look at it this way: We save in order to be able to consume more in the future. When we put a dollar in a savings account today, we expect to be able to buy more than a dollar's worth of goods in the future. Consider a numerical example. Assume that there is no inflation. You want to buy an FM tuner for your stereo system. It costs $100 (and, because there is no inflation, it will cost $100 next year also). If a bank offered you a savings deposit that yielded a 100 percent rate of interest per year, you could deposit a mere $50 today, take out $100 next year, and buy your FM tuner. But what if that bank offered you only 1 percent interest? You would have to put in about $99 today in order to have $100 next year to buy the FM tuner. A 100-percent yield on your savings account would certainly encourage you to save for future purchases more than a 1-percent yield would.

Saving, Inflation, and Taxes

In the preceding example, we left out inflation, and we also left out taxes. Today, rates of inflation are high. Clearly, what you are interested in as a saver is the real rate of return of putting your money into a savings account. If the bank offers you a 10-percent rate of interest and the rate of inflation is also 10 percent, your real return from saving is zero. Actually, it's *negative,* because

Today, with the present tax system and rate of inflation, there is little incentive to save.

taxes have not been included. Many people have to pay taxes on the interest income they earn from their savings. If you are earning a 10-percent rate with 10-percent inflation and you have to pay a 20-percent tax rate on what your savings earn, you'd have only 8 percent interest before inflation. With inflation at 10 percent, you would be earning minus 2 percent. If you take account of inflation and taxes, often the real return on a savings account (and on other savings instruments) is negative. That means that you have less real after-tax purchasing power at the end of a year than at the beginning, and, in the meantime, you don't have the use of the money income you put in the savings account.

Sound like a raw deal? It is. And it's one reason Americans are now saving at a lower *percentage* rate than they have in years. The solution? Besides reducing the rate of inflation, the government could exempt from taxes all interest income below $5,000 per year. This would offer people an incentive to save more. Today, with the present tax system and rate of inflation, there is little incentive to save but lots of incentive to spend.

Other Determinants of the Rate of Saving

Of course, to decide whether to save, or how much to save, you consider more than the interest rate on your savings; you also consider the value you place on consumption today as opposed to consumption tomorrow. Obviously, when you put off spending $100, you do not get the pleasure from whatever you might have spent it on: You have to wait. If you are impatient, even a high interest rate on savings may not induce you to save much. Those of you who are not so impatient about consuming may save more.

Another major determinant of how much of your current income you think you should save is the variability of your income. For example, people who have stable incomes from secure government employment generally save a smaller percentage of their income than do people who are in business for themselves. Obviously, the more variable your income, the more likely you are to have years when your income is lower than usual. Hence, during years when it is higher than usual, you generally will save more.

Moreover, how much you will save depends on how much future retirement income you decide you should have and on how much you earn. To fully understand how much you will have in the future, you must understand compound interest. Obviously, if you earned no interest at all, your total savings at the end of a specified period—say, thirty years—would be exactly what you put in. But that is not what usually happens; you should earn interest on whatever you save.

THE NATURE OF COMPOUND INTEREST

If you decide to save by not consuming all your income, you can invest what you save. You can put it in the stock market, or you can buy bonds—that is, lend money to businesses. You also could put it in your own business. In any event, you might expect to make a profit or interest every year in the future for a certain period of time. To figure out how much you will have at the end of any specified time period, you have to compound your savings, using a specified interest rate. Say you put $100 in a savings and loan association that yields 5 percent per year. At the end of one year, you have $105. At the end of two years, you have $105 plus 5 percent of $105, or $5.25, which gives you a total of $110.25. This same compounding occurs the third year, the fourth year, and so on.

The Power of Compounding

The power of **compound interest** is truly amazing. Exhibit 20–2 shows one dollar compounded every year for fifty years at different interest rates. At an interest rate of 8 percent, $1 will return $46.90 at the end of fifty years. Thus, if you inherited a modest $20,000 when you were twenty years old and put it in an investment that paid 8 percent compounded annually, at seventy years of age you would have $938,000. It's not so hard to understand how some people become millionaires! It usually does not take much in brains or business acumen to get an 8 percent rate of return in the long run. Somebody who had

COMPOUND INTEREST
Interest that earns interest. For example, if you put a dollar in a savings account that earns 5 percent each year and you leave the interest in, it is compounded. At the end of the first year, you would get 5 cents interest; at the end of the second year, you would get interest of 5 percent times $1.05, or a compound interest of 5.25 cents.

EXHIBIT 20–2
One Dollar Compounded at Different Interest Rates

Here is shown the value of the dollar at the end of a specified period after it has been compounded at a specified interest rate. For example, if you took $1 today and invested it at 5 percent, it would yield $1.05 at the end of the year. At the end of ten years, it would be equal to $1.63, and, at the end of fifty years, it would be equal to $11.50.
In this table, interest is compounded once a year at the end of every year. There are other ways of compounding interest, such as semiannually (once every six months), daily, and continuously. The actual compound factor in this exhibit would have to be altered for each compounding scheme. Clearly, the more frequently a given interest percentage is compounded, the larger the return after a given period of time.

YEAR	3%	4%	5%	6%	8%	10%	20%	YEAR
1	1.03	1.04	1.05	1.06	1.08	1.10	1.20	1
2	1.06	1.08	1.10	1.12	1.17	1.21	1.44	2
3	1.09	1.12	1.16	1.19	1.26	1.33	1.73	3
4	1.13	1.17	1.22	1.26	1.36	1.46	2.07	4
5	1.16	1.22	1.28	1.34	1.47	1.61	2.49	5
6	1.19	1.27	1.34	1.41	1.59	1.77	2.99	6
7	1.23	1.32	1.41	1.50	1.71	1.94	3.58	7
8	1.27	1.37	1.48	1.59	1.85	2.14	4.30	8
9	1.30	1.42	1.55	1.68	2.00	2.35	5.16	9
10	1.34	1.48	1.63	1.79	2.16	2.59	6.19	10
11	1.38	1.54	1.71	1.89	2.33	2.85	7.43	11
12	1.43	1.60	1.80	2.01	2.52	3.13	8.92	12
13	1.47	1.67	1.89	2.13	2.72	3.45	10.70	13
14	1.51	1.73	1.98	2.26	2.94	3.79	12.80	14
15	1.56	1.80	2.08	2.39	3.17	4.17	15.40	15
16	1.60	1.87	2.18	2.54	3.43	4.59	18.50	16
17	1.65	1.95	2.29	2.69	3.70	5.05	22.50	17
18	1.70	2.03	2.41	2.85	4.00	5.55	26.60	18
19	1.75	2.11	2.53	3.02	4.32	6.11	31.90	19
20	1.81	2.19	2.65	3.20	4.66	6.72	38.30	20
25	2.09	2.67	3.39	4.29	6.85	10.80	95.40	25
30	2.43	3.24	4.32	5.74	10.00	17.40	237.00	30
40	3.26	4.80	7.04	10.30	21.70	45.30	1,470.00	40
50	4.38	7.11	11.50	18.40	46.90	117.00	9,100.00	50

invested in the stock market fifty years ago would have received much more than 8 percent. There are a number of people around who inherit moderate amounts of money when they are young. If this money is put in the stock market and left there to compound itself, it grows to quite unbelievable amounts after thirty to forty years. Hence, we should be careful about assuming the astuteness of elderly millionaires; they could have been very conservative, having done nothing with the money they inherited except putting it in the stock market and leaving it there. No business sense would be needed at all, and the person could easily become a millionaire by the age of sixty-five.

To fully demonstrate the power of compound interest, consider what would have happened to the twenty-four dollars that the Dutch paid for Manhattan in 1626 if it had been invested at 6 percent a year. Look at Exhibit 20–2 and see that, at the end of fifty years, $1 becomes $18.40. The time period from 1626 to 1976 is 350 years, or 7 × 50. Thus, to find out the value of that $24, do the following computation: $24 × 18.4^7$, or $24 × 18.4 × 18.4 × 18.4 × 18.4 × 18.4 × 18.4 × 18.4. This equals $1,783,704,664.

In Exhibit 20–3, you can see what $1,000 will compound to in ten years at different interest rates and also what would happen if you deposited $1,000 a year, each year, for ten years. Exhibit 20–4 shows an example of the difference between compound and simple interest.

TIME DEPOSITS

TIME DEPOSIT
Another term for a savings account in a commercial bank. It is so called because, in theory, you must wait a certain amount of time after you have given notice of your desire to withdraw part or all of your savings. However, this requirement is generally not exercised by the bank.

One of the major outlets for savings dollars in the United States is **time deposits.** Time deposits are defined as savings instruments that, in principle, cannot be turned into cash until a specified amount of time has passed after the request for cash is made. Additionally, the money usually must remain on deposit for a specified period of time in order for it to earn interest. The most common types of time deposits are savings accounts in commercial banks, savings and loan associations, and credit unions.

LIQUID ASSET
An asset (something that you own and that has value) that can be easily turned into cash. Cash is the most liquid asset. Houses are certainly much less liquid.

A major virtue of time deposits is their liquidity. A **liquid asset** is one that readily can be turned into buying power. Even though, in principle, you must wait a specified period of time before a time deposit can be turned into buying power, in practice, institutions offering time deposits rarely, if ever, require such a waiting period. Hence, the owners of time deposits can turn those time deposits into buying power rapidly.

Why Use Time Deposits?

Time deposits are a popular form of savings for personal investment for the following reasons.

PRINCIPAL
A capital sum, to be distinguished from interest. A bond has a capital sum of, say, $1,000 and pays $100 interest a year. Its principal is $1,000.

SAFE INVESTMENT. Since most time deposits up to $100,000 are insured in one way or another, the owner is virtually guaranteed that the **principal** will never be lost. Moreover, the value of the time deposit does not fluctuate as does, for example, the value of stocks purchased. The interest paid on time deposits is certain, and there is rarely, if ever, a default (nonpayment).

EXHIBIT 20–3
How Compound Interest Helps You Build a Nest Egg

$1,000 accumulates in 10 Years

Interest Rate (compounded annually)	4	4½	5	5½	6	6½	7	8
$1,000 accumulates in 10 Years	$1,480	$1,553	$1,629	$1,708	$1,791	$1,877	$1,967	$2,159

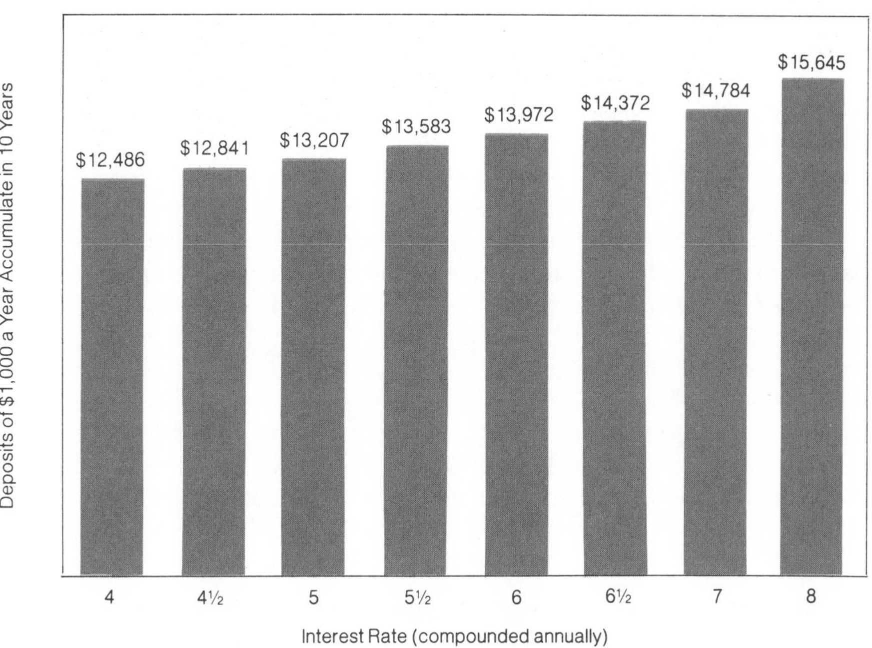

USE AS A TEMPORARY INVESTMENT OUTLET. Because it is easy to "get in and out" of time deposits, many individuals use them to accumulate funds to transfer to another investment or to purchase a consumer durable good.

SAVING FOR EMERGENCIES. Since time deposits are highly liquid, the individual owner can liquidate them for immediate buying power to cover unexpected doctor bills, casualty losses, or other emergencies.

EXHIBIT 20–4
The Difference between Compound and Simple Interest

At 5 percent simple interest, 1¢ becomes in 1980 approximately $1 if it is invested at the birth of Christ.

On the other hand, 1,984 years later, the 1¢ invested at 5 percent compounded annual interest grows to about $9,464 followed by 36 zeros!

Disadvantages of Time Deposits

LOWER RATE OF RETURN. A major disadvantage of time deposits is their relatively low rate of return. Note, though, that one reason the rate of return on time deposits is so low is that the risk of losing your money is also low. It is usually difficult, if not impossible, to obtain a higher rate of return without incurring greater risk. Or it is usually difficult to obtain a higher rate of return without purchasing investment assets, which certainly are less liquid than time deposits.

THE VARIETY OF TIME DEPOSITS AVAILABLE TO YOU

During the 1980s, a virtual plethora of savings instruments became available to the average saver. These instruments are being offered by commercial banks and the so-called thrifts—savings and loan associations, mutual savings banks, and credit unions—as well as certain brokerage houses and even retail stores, such as Sears. By the time you read this text, even more savings instruments may be offered by the various financial institutions in the United States.

You'll have to be careful in determining exactly what the options are because banks and thrifts give their **small-scale certificates of deposit** exclusive-sounding names, such as Money Maker, Tax-miser Fund, and so on. But these small-scale certificates of deposit, or savings certificates, have similar characteristics. Here are some of the best known.

SMALL-SCALE CD
A small-denomination certificate of deposit issued in an amount ranging from $25 to $1,000. It cannot be cashed in before a specified time. If it is cashed in before maturity, there is an interest-reduction penalty.

PASSBOOK SAVINGS ACCOUNTS. With such accounts, banks and thrifts give you a passbook in which your deposits and withdrawals are entered. Actually, some banks no longer have passbooks because all transactions are computerized.

Here are some of the possible savings accounts you can open.

1. **Individual.** Owned by only one person, either an adult or a minor
2. **Joint.** Usually owned by two persons, most often a husband and wife
3. **Voluntary trust.** Can be opened by an adult in trust for a child or another person and is controlled by the trustee during his or her life (After the trustee's death, it is payable to the person named as beneficiary. Note, though, that the trustee can change the beneficiary at any time.)
4. **Custodial.** Similar to a trust account except that it is irrevocable and becomes the property of the minor for whom it was opened
5. **Landlord trust.** An account made for the benefit of tenants whose lease security deposits must be placed in such accounts
6. **Fiduciary.** Accounts opened by the administrators of an estate or a guardian for a minor or an incompetent person

During the 1980s, a virtual plethora of savings instruments became available to the average saver.

CLUB ACCOUNTS. There are several special types of savings accounts that enable customers to save for a special goal. Chanukah, Christmas, and vacation club accounts allow you to accumulate savings usually by depositing a fixed amount for fifty weeks. Often little or no interest is paid on these accounts, but they give you an incentive to save. If the bank does offer interest, you don't receive it unless you keep your money on deposit for a requisite number of months.

BONUS SAVINGS ACCOUNTS. These passbook-type accounts pay a slightly higher interest rate if a minimum required balance is maintained and/or a minimum holding period is used. The bonus-type account reverts to a regular account if any of the stipulations are violated.

SEVEN- TO THIRTY-ONE-DAY CERTIFICATE. This savings certificate requires a $2,500 minimum. The interest is tied to the rate paid by the U.S. government on ninety-one-day Treasury bills.

NINETY-ONE-DAY CERTIFICATE. This small-scale certificate of deposit requires a minimum $2,500 investment. Typically, it pays slightly more than the seven- to thirty-one-day rate.

SIX-MONTH CD. This is the normal, or standard, CD. This particular savings certificate's interest rate is pegged to the six-month Treasury bill rate offered by the U.S. government. The minimum investment is $2,500.

THE SEVEN- TO THIRTY-ONE-DAY, NINETY-ONE-DAY, AND SIX-MONTH SAVINGS CERTIFICATES. If you must obtain cash before the end of the specified maturity date, you pay a penalty. For the seven- to thirty-one-day account and the ninety-one-day account, you lose all interest for early withdrawal. For the six-month savings certificate account, you lose three months' interest for early withdrawal. Obviously, these savings certificates are not appropriate if you think you will need cash before the end of the maturity date.

SMALL SAVERS CERTIFICATES. These small savers certificates are attractive because they require a minimum deposit, which is determined by the institution that offers them. Originally, they were for thirty months; now they are for eighteen months. The yield on them is equivalent to the eighteen-month Treasury yield offered by the U.S. government.

LONGER-TERM CERTIFICATES OF DEPOSIT. All financial institutions can offer longer-term certificates of deposit at rates that may be set at any level by the offering institution. Typically, the saver negotiates a rate with his or her banker prior to making the commitment for a long-term certificate of deposit. The trade-off here is a higher yield for a small deposit versus a very lengthy maturity. In other words, your money is tied up for a longer time and not available for emergencies unless you are willing to pay a substantial penalty for early withdrawal.

FLOATING-RATE DEPOSIT ACCOUNTS

Banks and thrifts now offer a variety of floating-rate deposit accounts. These differ from time deposits in that there is no fixed date of maturity. Often, however, you are not guaranteed a particular interest rate for more than a very short period of time. We already talked about two such accounts in the chapter on banking.

NOW and Super NOW Accounts

It is possible to obtain a relatively low but guaranteed rate of interest on your checking account balance by opening a NOW checking account. If you have $2,500 or more, you can open a Super NOW account and obtain an interest rate that is considerably higher than NOW account interest rates. One major benefit of NOW and Super NOW accounts is that they are insured by an agency of the federal government, either the Federal Deposit Insurance Corporation (FDIC) for banks, the Federal Savings and Loan Insurance Corporation (FSLIC) for savings and loans, or the National Credit Union Administration (NCUA) for credit unions, up to a maximum of $100,000.

Money Market Accounts

Virtually all banks and thrifts offer some form of money market account. Here you can obtain the highest interest rates possible at a thrift or bank and still have some flexibility. That is to say, you can, without penalty, make six transactions a month of which three may be withdrawals. The minimum deposit in such an account is $2,500. You will earn an interest rate approximately equal to the interest rate available on money market accounts offered by nonfinancial institutions. The big difference is that your money market account in a bank or thrift is insured by one of the previously mentioned agencies of the federal government. Flexibility, high interest yields, and insurance make these accounts attractive to many savers.

The average rate of saving in the United States has remained around 7 to 9 percent.

U.S. GOVERNMENT SAVINGS BONDS

You also can buy savings instruments from the U.S. government. The most popular among small savers are Series EE bonds and Series HH bonds.

Series EE Bonds

The minimum denomination for an EE bond is $50; the maximum amount you can invest in EE bonds in a single year is $15,000. The maturity date for these bonds is nine years. Right now, any EE bond purchased and held for at least five years will pay you a variable rate equal to 85 percent of whatever the yield on five-year U.S. government Treasury securities averages over your holding. For example, if the rate on the Treasury's five-year securities averages 14 percent, your bond would earn nearly 12 percent. If there is a steep drop in interest rates, however, you are protected. The minimum guaranteed yield on EE bonds is 7.5 percent. You must keep in mind the five-year restriction when you consider cashing in a bond, however. You can get the variable rate only if the bond is held for five years or more.

Series HH Bonds

These bonds are issued in denominations ranging from $500 to $10,000, and they pay 7½ percent over a ten-year maturity. You obtain the interest via a Treasury check twice a year. At the bond's maturity, you also get exactly what you paid for them. The annual cash purchase limitation on series HH bonds is $20,000 face value. There is an interest penalty on HH bonds that are redeemed before the ten-year maturity period is up.

HOW MUCH TO SAVE?

This chapter has explained why people save and described some popular saving outlets. In the following chapter, we will discuss other areas where savings dollars can go, such as stocks, bonds, art work, real estate, and the like. Remember, any money that is saved or invested is income that is not spent in the current year. Thus, every individual and family faces the decision of how much current income should be set aside for future consumption. The average rate of saving in the United States has remained around 7 to 9 percent. Therefore, you might want to save the average or, say, 9 percent.

No fixed rules can be made for everyone, however. When you're young, your rate of saving may be negative; that is, you may borrow in addition to spending all your year's income. When you're older, your rate of saving may hit the national average or even be greater. Then, of course, when you retire, your rate of saving may become negative again as you consume the fruits of your past saving.

SUMMARY

1. Individuals save in order to provide for income during periods when their earning capacity falls, such as during sickness or after retirement. In addition to the rate of return or interest you obtain from your savings, the variability of your income also will determine how much you save. The higher the interest paid and the higher the variability of your income, the more you will save.
2. In our competitive society, very few things come free of charge. Hence, any investment deal in which you become involved cannot guarantee you a higher-than-normal rate of return unless substantial risk—that is, a high chance of losing everything—is involved.
3. When trying to figure out how much total savings you will have accumulated after a certain length of time and number of deposits, you should consult a compound interest table such as the one presented in Exhibit 20–2. If, for example, your savings were invested at an average yield of 8 percent, at the end of twenty years every dollar invested will have grown to $4.66.
4. A wide variety of savings instruments is now available to the average saver. Among these are passbook savings accounts, club accounts, bonus savings accounts, various small-scale certificates of deposits, and large-scale certificates of deposit. These accounts usually require specified minimum balances and/or have fixed maturity dates and interest rates.
5. Banks and thrifts also offer floating-rate deposit accounts, which have no fixed maturity dates. Often, however, these accounts do not guarantee the saver fixed interest rates for long periods. NOW, Super NOW, and money market accounts are examples of floating-rate accounts that require minimum balances (usually $2,500) and are insured by agencies of the federal government.
6. The federal government also offers savings instruments. The most popular are the Series EE bond and the Series HH bond. The minimum denomination for a Series EE bond is $50, with a maturity date of nine years and a maximum annual investment of $15,000. Series HH bonds are issued in denominations ranging from $500 to $10,000 and pay 7½ percent over a ten-year maturity. The maximum annual investment is $20,000.

QUESTIONS FOR THOUGHT AND DISCUSSION

1. "Poor people barely have enough to survive on and, therefore, cannot save anything for a rainy day." Do you agree or disagree?
2. What determines how much you save?
3. Would it make a difference whether the interest on your savings were compounded daily, weekly, semi-annually, or annually? If so, what is the difference?
4. Why do you have to worry about the rate of inflation when you invest your savings?
5. What is the maximum yield you can obtain today from putting your money in a savings and loan association? Is that yield greater than the rate of inflation? Are you taxed on the interest you receive?

THINGS TO DO

1. Try to figure out what percentage of your income you save. Remember that the purchase of a so-called consumer durable, such as a television set, a stereo, a house, or a car, is a form of saving because you receive implicit income from that consumer durable for a long period of time. The income you receive is the satisfaction you obtain from the durable.
2. Assume that, by the time you retire at age sixty-five, you want to have $100,000 saved up. Also assume that you can earn 10 percent per year on your savings. Determine from Exhibit 20–2 how much you have to put in the bank today to have $100,000 at age sixty-five at a 10 percent rate of return.

SELECTED READINGS

Credit Union Statistics. National Credit Union Administration, 2025 M Street, N.W., Washington, D.C. 20456 (latest edition).

Credit Union Yearbook. Credit Union National Association, 1616 Sherman Avenue, Madison, Wisconsin 53701 (latest edition).

Egan, Jack. "The Run for Your Money: Bank Money-Market Accounts." *New York Magazine*, December 20, 1982, pp. 15–19.

Harris, Marlys. "The Best Place for Your Cash Now." *Money*, February 1983, pp. 100–04.

Quinn, Jane Bryant. "Shopping for Your Savings." *Newsweek*, April 26, 1982, p. 74.

Savings and Loan Fact Book. U.S. Savings and Loan League, 221 North LaSalle Street, Chicago, Illinois 60601 (latest edition).

"Savings Bonds—Do They Make Sense Now?" *Changing Times*, April 1980, pp. 35–38.

Weiss, Martin D. "What to Do with Your Savings." *Consumer's Digest*, March/April 1981.

"Where to Put Your Savings Now." *U.S. News & World Report*, August 16, 1982, pp. 60–62.

Your Insured Deposit. Federal Deposit Insurance Corporation, 550 Seventeenth Street, N.W., Washington, D.C. 20429.

Consumer ISSUES

HOW TO SAVE

DIFFERENT WAYS TO SAVE

Americans, on average, save relatively little of their disposable income. Many U.S. families don't save at all. The need to save, however, remains the same for everyone. Saving offers two advantages that are important for your basic financial security. First of all, savings are liquid: You can go to the bank or thrift institution in which you have deposited your savings and get cash out immediately. Secondly, savings are safe. Savings consist of safe deposits in insured accounts; regardless of what's happening to the economy, you can always be sure that your insured savings are safe. Therefore, it behooves you to save. Here are some ways to do so.

Get into the Habit

Some people make saving a habit. That is to say, they pay themselves first by having a certain percentage taken out of each paycheck before anything is spent. Mark and Joanne Skousen, in their excellent new book *Never Say Budget,*[1] call this the 10-percent solution. They state that everyone, no matter how poor, can always figure out a way to save 10 percent of disposable income *before* any purchases are made. They point out that 10 percent is always easy to figure, that it is affordable, that it is regular, and that it hedges against inflation.

For nonsavers, saving comes last and usually not at all. In order to be a saver, saving must come first.

Using Refunds

Another way to save is to use all refunds as part of your savings. Have more taken out of your check as federal government withholding than you know you're actually going to have to pay in taxes. Then put the refund at the end of the year in your savings plan. If you work for a company and get reimbursed for your business expenses, put those refunds in your savings plan. And if you get reimbursed by your medical insurance plan for medical payments you've already made, put those reimbursements in your savings plan, too.

Filling Up That Coin Jar

The coin play is a family ritual that dates back at least to when milk was delivered in bottles. A milk bottle or some other glass jar kept in a kitchen or a closet can be used for saving coins. When it is full, the bank will provide you with coin wrappers in which you can separate the various coins. Every night, every family member can empty his or her pockets and change purses of coins to put in the coin jar. It may not seem like much, but an extra twenty or thirty dollars a month in savings can add up, particularly if those savings are put into some of the interest-earning savings instruments we just discussed.

Using the Debt-to-Credit Switch

Most people incur installment debt. Fortunately, most installment debt has an end; that is, when you've made the last payment on your car or stereo, you make no others. However, a good saver will continue making that same payment, but rather than sending it to the finance company, he or she will put in into the savings plan.

Kicking-the-Habit Plan

One way to make saving a habit is to kick another habit. For example, suppose you are a smoker who spends, say

1. Mark and Joanne Skousen, *Never Say Budget! How to Put Money in the Bank and Still Have Freedom to Spend.* Available from Mark Skousen, P.O. Box 611, Merrifield, Virginia 22116.

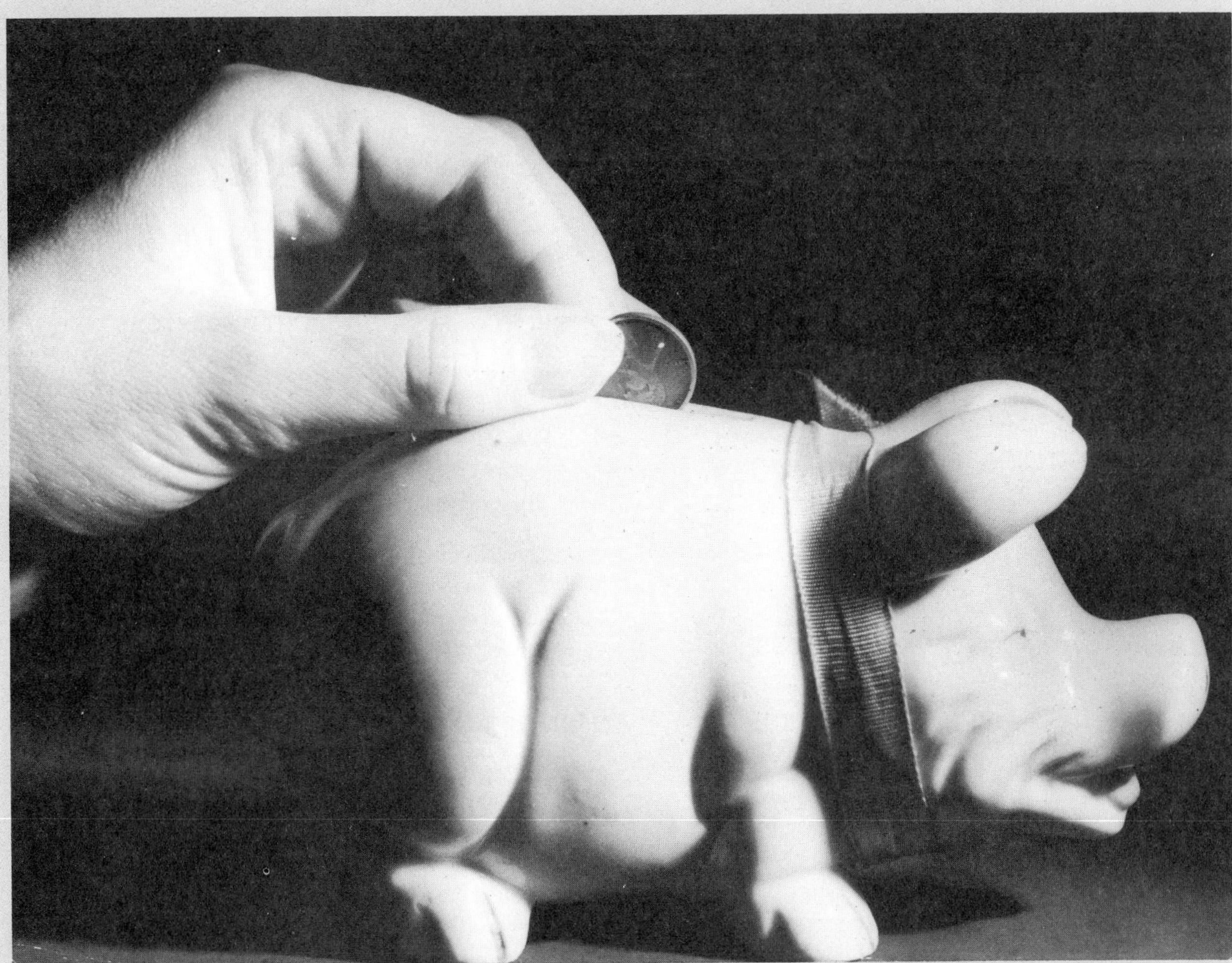

fifteen dollars a week on cigarettes. If you can kick the smoking habit, you can now make a habit of putting that money into your savings plan.

Let's say that you have another habit—having a morning coffee break. If you kick the habit of drinking coffee each morning on your break, you don't have to spend that amount of money on coffee anymore. You can put the unspent money into your savings plan.

IS YOUR DEPOSIT INSURED?

When shopping among various time deposit institutions, you must find out if your deposit will be insured. In most savings banks and commercial banks, your deposit will be insured by the Federal Deposit Insurance Corporation (FDIC). Deposits in savings and loan associations are most often insured by the Federal Savings and Loan Insurance Corporation (FSLIC). Credit union deposits are usually insured by the National Credit Union Administration. (NCUA), which supervises the National Credit Union Shareholder's Insurance Fund.

As of 1980, each depositor is protected to an upper limit of $100,000 should the covered savings institution fail. It is important to understand just how this $100,000 protection limits your potential loss.

Applies to a Single Depositor

The $100,000 protection applies to the total number of accounts a single depositor has under his or her name within a single bank. Thus, if you were to have a $56,000 savings account in one bank and also $50,000 in a checking account, you would be insured up to $100,000, not $106,000. If you have accounts in the same name in a main office and in one or more branches of the insured bank, the accounts are added together to determine your insurance.

Splitting Your Funds among Banks and Accounts

If you have so much of your savings in time deposits that you reach the maximum limitation on insurability, you can either split your funds among a number of banks or split your funds among a number of accounts. For example, if you are married, you can have an account, your spouse can have an account, and you both can have a joint account. Thus, your maximum insurability as a unit is increased to $300,000. If you have children, you can set up guardian or trustee accounts that are insured separately.

SUMMARY

1. Savings offer two factors important to your financial security: liquidity and safety.
2. There are several approaches to saving: (1) you can make saving a habit by deducting a specified amount from your paycheck before purchases are made; (2) you can put all refunds (for example, tax refunds, insurance reimbursements) into your savings plan; (3) you can save coins in a coin jar and then deposit it; (4) if you have paid off an installment debt, you can continue deducting the same amount and deposit it in your savings plan; and (5) you can take the money spent on an unwanted habit (for example, smoking cigarettes) and put it in your savings plan.
3. The Federal Deposit Insurance Corporation (FDIC) insures deposits in commercial and savings banks.
4. The Federal Savings and Loan Insurance Corporation (FSLIC) insures deposits in savings and loan associations.
5. The National Credit Union Association (NCUA), using the National Credit Union Shareholders' Insurance Fund, insures credit union deposits.
6. Most insured deposits have a limit of $100,000 in protection.
7. It is possible to split up your funds among different banks and accounts in order to insure all your time deposits.

QUESTIONS FOR THOUGHT AND DISCUSSION

1. How is saving important to your financial security?
2. Besides those recommendations listed in this Issue, what other practical methods for saving can you suggest?

THINGS TO DO

Make a directory of alternative savings outlets that you might be able to use, assuming you had, say, $1,000 to put away for a rainy day. Write down the advantages and disadvantages of each. Which one would you pick?

SELECTED READINGS

Personal Money Management. American Bankers' Association, 1120 Connecticut Avenue, N.W., Washington, D.C. 20036 (latest edition).

Quinn, Jane Bryant. "Those Misleading Bank Ads." *Newsweek,* January 31, 1983, p. 60.

"The Safety of Your Savings." *U.S. News & World Report,* May 12, 1980, p. 74.

"Saving: How to Pay Yourself First." *Consumer Views,* Vol. X, No. 11, November 1979.

Skousen, Mark and Joanne. *Never Say Budget!* P.O. Box 611, Merrifield, Virginia 22116, 1983.

"What Will Your Bank Think of Next?" *Changing Times,* January 1983, pp. 62–63.

CHAPTER
INVESTING

There's an unfortunate fact to which we have alluded time and again. You cannot get anything free. If you go into an investment deal with the idea that you'll make a killing, you may be sure that the risk you are undertaking is relatively high.

CHAPTER PREVIEW

- How are risk and rate of return related?
- What's the difference between preferred and common stocks?
- Can people get rich quick in the stock market?
- Why is a pension plan important?

THE SIMPLE FACTS ABOUT INVESTING

There are many things you can do with your accumulated savings. You can keep all or part of them in cash, which earns no interest at all and, in fact, loses value at the rate of inflation. You can put them into a savings account that gives a relatively low rate of interest but is extremely secure. You can invest your money in shares of stocks of various corporations. You can invest your money in U.S. Savings Bonds, which yield a relatively low rate of interest. You can purchase land. You can purchase consumer durable goods, such as cars, houses, and stereos, that yield a stream of services over their lifetime. In other words, you can do an infinite number of things with your savings. What you *should* do depends upon your goals; what your goals are will tell you how much risk you want to take.

There is an unfortunate fact to which we have alluded time and again: You cannot get anything free. If you go into an investment deal with the idea that you'll make a killing, you may be sure that the risk you are undertaking is relatively high.

RISK AND RATE OF RETURN

The higher the prospective rate of return you expect to get on any investment, the higher the risk you take. That is why, if you are offered a "deal" that you are told will make you 50 percent a year, you may be certain that the risk of losing everything is pretty high. On the other hand, if you take your savings and invest them in a savings and loan association, you may make only 9 percent a year, but you don't risk losing your entire savings.

A better way to understand why you cannot get a high rate of return without taking a high risk is to understand why no particular investment deal is necessarily any better than any other, at least unless you have some pretty specialized information. Let us explain this by taking a specific example—making money on the stock market. But, first, we need a few facts.

STOCK MARKET
An organized market where shares of ownership in businesses are traded. These shares generally are called stocks. The largest stock market in the United States is the New York Stock Exchange; the second largest is the American Stock Exchange.

COMMON STOCK
A common stock is a legal claim to the profits of a company. For each share owned, the common-stock owner generally has the right to one vote on such questions as merging with another company or electing a new board of directors.

EQUITY
A legal claim to the profits of a company. This is another name for stock, generally called common stock.

Some Facts about the Stock Market

The **stock market** is the general term used for all transactions that involve the buying and selling of shares of stocks issued by companies. These stocks are pieces of paper giving the owner the right to a certain portion of the assets of the company issuing the security. Most stock is **common stock,** also called **equity.** Say a company wishes to expand its operation. It can obtain the money capital for expansion by putting up part of the ownership of the company for sale. It does this by offering stock, usually common stock, for sale. If a company worth $1 million wants $200,000, it may sell stock. Suppose you alone own the company, and you arbitrarily state that there are 100,000 shares of stock that you own completely; you would then have to put out on the market about 20,000 shares of your stock, which you would sell at ten dollars a share. You would get the $200,000 for expansion, and the people who paid the money would receive 20,000 shares of your stock. They would have claim to one-fifth of whatever the company earned as profits.

There are many different submarkets within the stock market. At the top of the ladder are the big ones: the New York Stock Exchange and the American Stock Exchange. Measured by dollar value, about 65 percent of all stock transactions are carried out at the New York and the American. There are also regional stock exchanges throughout the country, as well as the national over-the-counter market and regional over-the-counter markets. These markets are somewhat less organized than the New York, American, and regional exchanges. Stocks on over-the-counter markets are usually not traded as often as those on the big exchanges. Stocks in companies that are small and less well known than bigger companies are usually traded on the over-the-counter market. More than 50,000 different stocks are bought and sold on the over-the-counter market.

Preferred Stocks and Bonds

Preferred stock is a fancy name for what is simply the debt of a company. It is called "preferred" because, in the event of distributable earnings or in the event the company goes out of business, the holders of that stock have a preferred claim against the company prior to that of the common stockholders. That is, whatever assets can be retrieved are distributed first among preferred stockholders after bondholders have been paid. A preferred stock is actually a type of bond that can be defined very simply. A **bond** is basically an I.O.U. or promissory note of a corporation, usually issued in multiples of $1,000. A bond is evidence of a debt in which the issuing company usually promises to pay the bondholders a specified amount of interest for a specified length of time and then to repay the loan on the expiration date. In every case, a bond represents debt: Its holder is a creditor of the corporation and not a part owner, as is the shareholder or stockholder. So you can see that preferred stock is merely a bond, except that failure to pay the interest or dividend on preferred stock does not legally allow the preferred stockholder to sue the company. The preferred stockholder simply has preference to the earnings, if any, for payment of interest before any dividends can be paid to the common stockholders. Sometimes the preferred stock is "cumulative": If any arrears of unpaid dividends (or interest) accumulate, the common stockholders cannot take any dividends until the preferred stockholders have been paid for the missing years.

PREFERRED STOCK
A type of debt obligation similar to a bond that a company sells to investors. Preferred stocks pay a specified dividend every year (or at some other interval). If the company goes bankrupt, preferred stockholders have the right to collect on their investment before common stockholders obtain any of the liquidated assets of the bankrupt company.

BONDS
A type of debt that a business or a government issues to investors. A bond represents a promise to pay a certain amount of money (called interest) each year. At the end of a specified amount of time, the principal on the bond is repaid to the bondholder.

Capital Gains and Losses

Preferred stock may also be *convertible,* which means that the preferred stockholder has the option to exchange—that is, convert—it into common stock at a present exchange rate. There are also such things as convertible bonds that can be exchanged for common stock at some present exchange rate.

Stock can go up and down in price. If you buy a stock at ten dollars and sell it at fifteen dollars, you make a **capital gain** equal to five dollars for every share you bought and then sold at the higher price. That is called an appreciation in the price of your stock, which you realized as a capital gain when you sold it. If the value of your stock falls and you sell it at a loss, you have suffered a **capital loss** because of the depreciation in the market value of your stock. Some, but not all, stocks pay dividends. (Dividends are paid by checks

CAPITAL GAIN
The difference between the buying and the selling price of something you own when the selling price is higher than the buying price.

CAPITAL LOSS
The difference between the buying and the selling price of something you own when the selling price is lower than the buying price.

EXHIBIT 21–1
Comparison of Stocks And Bonds

STOCKS	BONDS
1. Represent ownership (except preferred stocks)	**1.** Represent owned debt
2. Have no fixed dividend rate (including preferred stocks)	**2.** Require interest be paid, whether or not any profit is earned
3. Allow holders to elect a board of directors, which, in turn, controls the corporation (except holders of preferred stock)	**3.** Usually entail no voice in or control over management
4. Have no maturity date; the corporation does not usually repay the stockholder	**4.** Have a maturity date when the holder is to be repaid the face value
5. Are issued by all business corporations (and are purchased by stockholders)	**5.** Need not be issued by corporations
6. Allow holders to have a claim against the property and income of the corporation after all creditors' claims have been met	**6.** Give to bondholders a prior claim against the property and income of the corporation that must be met before the claims of stockholders

mailed to the stockholders.) Normally, when you buy a stock that has never paid a dividend, you expect to make money on your investment by an increase in the value of the stock. That is, if the company is making profits but not giving out dividends, it must be reinvesting those profits. A reinvestment in itself could pay off in the future by higher profits. The value of the stock would then be bid up in the market. Your profit would be in the form of a capital gain rather than dividend payments.

Most individuals pay lower federal income taxes on capital gains than they do on dividends. Dividends are taxed at ordinary income rates, whereas capital gains are taxed at lower rates. Normally, one only pays taxes on 60 percent of long-term capital gains (assets that are held for more than one year before sold). Therefore, it is often preferable to obtain capital gains rather than current dividends.

WHAT AFFECTS THE PRICE OF A STOCK?

Some observers believe that individual psychological or subjective feelings are all that affect the price of a stock. If people think a stock will be worth more in the future, they will bid the price up. If they think it will be worth less in the future, the price will fall. However, that is not a very satisfactory theory. Usually psychological feelings are based upon the expected stream of profits that the company will make in the future. Past profits may be important in formulating a prediction of future profits. However, past profits are bygones, and bygones are forever bygones. A company could lose money for ten years and then make profits for the next fifteen.

If a company hires a new management team that has a reputation for turning losing companies into winning ones, people in the stock market might expect profits to turn around and rise. If a company has a record number of sales orders for future months, one might expect profits to go up. Whenever profits are expected to rise, we typically find a rise in the value of the stock. That is, people bid up the price of the stock. Any information about future profits should be valuable in assessing how a stock's price will react.

Some observers believe that individual psychological or subjective feelings are all that affect the price of a stock.

MAKING MONEY IN THE STOCK MARKET

You probably have heard of the infamous J. P. Morgan, who supposedly made his fortune by manipulating the stock market. You also have probably heard of persons becoming millionaires overnight by making astute investments in securities. You may even have a parent who talks at length about the stock market, reads the *Wall Street Journal* and the financial page of the local newspaper, and comments about the prices of various stocks going up or down. If

The broker is *not* the one you should ask about which particular stock to buy. *The broker is no more likely to be right than you are.*

you listen to someone who "follows the market," making money *seems* as easy as calling up your stockbroker for the latest hot tips.

Getting Advice on the Market

Look in your Yellow Pages under "Stock and Bond Brokers," pick a phone number at random, and call it. Ask to speak with a registered representative or an account executive (in the old days, called "customers' men") and talk to this broker as if you had, say, $10,000 to invest. Ask him or her for advice. You probably will be asked what your goals are. Do you want income from your investment? Do you want growth in your investment? Do you want to take a chance? Do you want to be safe? After you tell the broker the strategy you wish to pursue, you will be told the best stocks to buy. If you ask the broker what he or she thinks the market in general will be doing over the next few months, you are bound to hear an opinion—and an authoritative one, at that. After all, if you want to know what to do with your garden, you ask the person who runs the local nursery. If you want to know about your car, you ask your local mechanic. That is, you generally seek out specialists in your field of interest. Why not seek out a specialist, then, when you are interested in making money?

A broker is a specialist, one from whom you can get much useful information. A broker can tell you all about the stock market and can give you quotes on all the different stocks—that is, what their prices are and how many of them were sold in the last few days and what the history of the prices has been. You can be told about the various types of securities you can buy—stocks listed on the big exchanges like the New York and the American, over-the-counter stocks that are sold only in very restricted sections of the country, preferred stocks, bonds, convertible debentures, puts, calls, warrants, and so on and on. A stockbroker is the person you should ask concerning all these different avenues of investment.

But the broker is *not* the one you should ask about which particular stock to buy. *The broker is no more likely to be right than you are.* You might even select the stocks to purchase by throwing a dart at a list of stocks on the New York Stock Exchange. If you are shocked by this revelation, consider that the stock market is the most highly competitive market in the world, and information costs there are perhaps the lowest of any market in existence.

Public Information

Information flows rapidly in the stock market. If you read in the *Wall Street Journal* that International Chemical and Nuclear (ICN) has just discovered a cure for cancer, do you think you should rush out and buy ICN stock? You might, but you will be no better off than if you had bought any other stock. By the time you read about ICN's discovery (which will mean increased profits in the future for the company), thousands and thousands of other people already will have read it. A rule that you should apply, and one that will be explained several times in this chapter, is that *public information does not yield an above-normal profit or rate of return*. Once information about a company's profitability is generally known, that information has a zero value for predicting the future price of the stock. So if you read about a new discovery by Kodak that is going to make immense profits in the future, by the time you go to buy Kodak stock, its price will have already been bid up by people who found out that information before you did. It's a harsh but simple fact that you just can't make a killing by learning about things that a lot of other people already know.

Hot Tips

What about the hot tips your broker might have? First of all, it's highly unlikely that the tips will be true **inside information.** After all, if it were really inside information, why would it be given to you? Why would the broker not take advantage of it, get rich quick, and quit being a stockbroker? The broker's information might have come from the brokerage's research department. Almost all stock brokerage companies have large research staffs that investigate different industries, different companies, and the future of the general economy. These research departments issue research statements on different companies and industries in the economy, recommending which stocks are underpriced and, therefore, should be bought. *The value of this research information to you as an investor is zero.* You will do no better by following the advice of research branches of your stock brokerage company than you will be randomly selecting stocks—particularly stocks listed on the New York and American Stock Exchanges. Nevertheless, the amount of research on those companies that is completed by firms, individuals, organizations, governments, and so on is indeed staggering. Because information flows so freely, by the time you receive the results of research on a particular company, you can be sure that thousands and thousands of other people already have found out. And because so many brokerage firms employ research analysts, you can be sure that there are numerous analysts investigating every single company that has shares for sale in the open stock market.

INSIDE INFORMATION
Information about a company's financial situation that is obtained before the public obtains it. True inside information is usually known only by corporate officials or other insiders.

The Random Walk

Recall from your high-school physics course the study of Brownian motion of molecules. The molecules jumped around randomly, and there was simply no way to predict where one would jump next. This is exactly what happens when something follows a random walk: It goes in directions that are totally unrelated to past directions. If something follows a random walk, no amount of past information is useful for predicting what will happen in the future. The stock market would be expected to exhibit a random walk merely because it is so highly competitive and because information flows so freely. Examining past prices on the market as a whole or on individual stocks would not be expected to yield any useful information as to prices in the future. Years and years of academic research on the stock market have left little doubt that the stock market is, indeed, a random walk. (If you find out otherwise, you may be able to get rich very quickly.)

A stock is not like a dog—which is to say, it will not eventually come home to its former price. Indeed, because a stock does not know where its home is and does not have a mind or a purpose, what has happened to that stock in the past does not matter. You can find no usable information by examining past stock prices. Or, according to Nobel Prize winning economist Paul Samuelson:

A stock is not like a dog—which is to say, it will not eventually come home to its former price.

Even the best investors seem to find it hard to do better than comprehensive common-stock averages, or better on the average than random selection among stocks of comparable variability.[1]

What about Investment Plans?

Investment plans and sophisticated investment counselors are numerous. In their advertising, they guarantee you the highest possible rate of return on your stock dollars. A typical piece of advertising might show, for example, the average rate of return for investing in all the stocks on the New York Stock Exchange. An investment counselor would show you that his stock portfolio makes 15 percent a year, rather than the average 8 percent, by buying all stocks together. However, these investment counselors usually neglect to point out that the 15 percent rate of return does not take account of the investment counseling fees or the trading costs—that is, brokers' commissions—for buying and selling stocks. Investment services usually do a lot of trading: They go in and out of the market—buying today, selling tomorrow. Each time someone buys a stock or sells a stock, that person pays a commission to the broker. Thus, the more trading your investment counselor does for your account, the more trading costs you incur. In fact, in almost all cases that have been thoroughly examined, investments made through counselors do no better than the general market averages because any special profits they make are eaten up by brokerage fees and their own counseling fees. Thus, you would be better off just paying brokerage fees and not using the services of an investment counselor.

MUTUAL FUNDS

MUTUAL FUND
A fund that purchases the stocks of other companies. If you buy a share in a mutual fund, you are, in essence, buying shares in all the companies in which the mutual fund invests. The only business of a mutual fund is buying other companies' stocks.

This fact was confirmed in a study of **mutual funds.** Mutual funds take the money of many investors and buy and sell large blocks of stock; the investors get dividends or appreciation on their shares of the mutual fund. The mutual fund, then, is a company that invests in other companies but does not sell any physical product of its own. You can buy shares in mutual funds just as you can buy shares in General Motors. The study of mutual funds concluded that mutuals that did the least amount of trading made the highest profits, an expected result if you understand the competitive nature of the stock market.

The Two Types of Mutual Funds

A mutual fund or investment trust is principally either of two types: the *closed end* or the *open end*. Shares in closed-end investment trusts (mutual funds), some of which are listed on the New York Stock Exchange, are readily transferable in the open market and are bought and sold like other shares. These companies are called closed end. Open-end funds sell their own new shares to investors, stand ready to buy back their old shares, and are not listed on

1. Paul Samuelson, *The Bell Journal of Economics and Management Science,* 4 (Autumn 1973): pp. 369–74.

the stock exchange. Open-end funds are so called because they issue more shares as people want them.

The only commission you pay to buy closed-end mutual funds is the standard commission you would pay on the purchase of any stock. There are two types of open-end mutual funds, a no-load and a load. The **no-load mutual fund** charges no setup or loading charge for you to get into the fund, while the load mutual fund charges you about 8 percent to get into the fund. Both may charge a yearly management fee. The salesperson or stockbroker who sells you an open-end mutual fund with a loading charge usually keeps most of that charge as commission. Mutual-fund experts divide open-end and closed-end funds into the following categories:

NO-LOAD MUTUAL FUND
A mutual fund that has no service charge for buying its shares.

1. **Income funds.** These funds attempt to achieve high yields by concentrating on high-divided common stocks or bonds or a combination
2. **Balance funds.** To minimize risk, these funds hold common stocks and a certain proportion of bonds and preferred stocks
3. **Maximum capital gains funds—dividend income incidental.** These are often aggressively managed and take higher-than-average risks by buying into little-known companies
4. **Long-term growth funds—income secondary.** Fund managers go after larger, more seasoned, higher-quality growth stocks that do not generate dividends
5. **Specialized funds.** Funds that restrict themselves to certain types of securities, such as gold-mining stocks

In addition, there are the following types of closed-end funds:

1. **Real-estate funds.** Otherwise known as REITs, or real-estate investment trusts. These are of two types—a mortgage trust, which borrows money from banks and relends it at a higher rate to builders and developers, and an equity trust, which owns income-producing property.
2. **Dual-purpose funds.**Types of closed-end funds that sell two classes of stock—income shares and capital shares. The first group of purchasers receive all the fund's net income; the second group participates only in capital gains.

MONEY MARKET MUTUAL FUNDS

Perhaps the most well-known mutual fund today is a *money market mutual fund*. We have already made reference to such funds when we talked about saving instruments. Banks and thrifts offer money market accounts insured up to $100,000. Alternatively, there are literally hundreds of uninsured but very safe money market mutual funds available to the same investor. The name money market comes from the fact that all proceeds are invested in relatively short-term money market instruments, such as Treasury bills, commercial paper sold by reputable corporations, and other short-term debt instruments. There are actually three types of money market funds:

1. **Government funds.** These invest only in U.S. Treasury obligations and those of other federal agencies
2. **General-purpose funds.** These invest in banks and corporations, as well as in government obligations

3. **Tax-exempt funds.** These invest in obligations of state and municipal governments whose interest payments are not taxable by the federal government. Typically, investors earn smaller dividends, but the tax-free advantage of these kinds is appealing to those investors in higher marginal tax brackets

Most money market mutual funds allow check-writing privileges and telephone transfers. However, there are restrictions. For example, checks may have to be for $500 or more in certain funds. The big disadvantage of money market mutual funds to the small saver is that they are not insured by an agency of the federal government. The advantage is that they often offer higher interest rates than those offered by commercial banks and thrift institutions. As with all investments, those money market mutual funds that offer higher interest rates than others do involve the investor in a slightly higher risk. For in order for certain mutual funds to make relatively higher rates of interest, they must invest the proceeds in slightly riskier assets, such as debt obligations of longer maturity and debt obligations issued by corporations that do not have the highest possible security ratings.

Is There No Way to Get Rich Quick?

The general conclusion to be reached from our analysis of the stock market is that all the investing schemes everybody talks about are really quite useless for getting rich quickly. That does not mean, of course, that some people will not get rich by using them. Luck has much to do with making money in the stock market—just as it does with winning at poker or craps. If you do make money with your particular scheme, it does not mean you are extra smart, a better investor, or a prophet. You may just be lucky. You may, however, make more than a normal rate of return on your invested capital if you spend a tremendous amount of time searching out areas of unknown profit potential. But then you are spending resources—your own time, for example. Your fantastic profits can be considered as payment for the time you spent—the value of your opportunity cost—analyzing the stock market and different companies.

The question still remains: How can you make money? You know that you can make a normal rate of return merely by throwing a dart at the listing of stocks on the New York Stock Exchange. Pick eight stocks, for example, and just keep buying them with your investment dollars. Never sell until you need money for retirement. Over the long run, you will probably make around an 8 to 15 percent rate of return. On the other hand, you might want to pick particular stocks if you have inside information or information that is better than the tips anybody else has. In such a case, you stand to gain more than you would by picking stocks randomly. Also, if you think you can somehow evaluate public information better than anybody else can, you may want to do more than select random stocks. But before you decide whether you can evaluate better than others, you had better think seriously about how many others there are in the world. The stock industry is huge. Why do you think you can evaluate public information better than everybody else?

OTHER SUREFIRE SCHEMES

By now, you ought to be quite suspicious about any special investment deals that become available. Because there is so much competition in the investment markets and because you, as a single consumer, are not likely to be smarter than any of the experts around, you should consider every single investment as a trade-off between risk and rate of return (and also liquidity). The higher the potential rate of return, the higher the risk. There is no reason why you should expect to do better than average unless you have some special information.

All the investing schemes everybody talks about are really quite useless for getting rich quickly.

Real Estate

Will Rogers once said, "It's easy to make money: just figure out where people are going and then buy the land before they get there." Obviously, if Will Rogers was aware of this truism, all the experts knew it, too. What do you think happens when it is known where people will be going? That information will be used by others, who will thereby bid up the price of land in the places where people are going. Only if you think you have such information ahead of everyone else can you expect to make a higher-than-normal rate of return in any type of land investment.

Do not be taken in by such statements as, "land is always a safe investment." The value of land can fall like the value of anything else. The fact that the overall price of land has been going up for a long time does not mean that you will make more than what you could make, say, investing money in a savings and loan association. Although, on average,you might make more in land, on average, you also take a greater risk because land deals frequently fall through completely.

You can think of a thousand and one other investment opportunities to which the same logic applies. Just remember that you do not get something for nothing; any time you do something with your savings, you are going to be subjected to the rigors of a competitive marketplace. Only special information is valuable. Otherwise, you will get no more, on average, than you could get investing your dollars in a huge variety of alternatives.

PENSIONS AND RETIREMENT PLANS

If you are involuntarily or voluntarily covered by a retirement of a pension plan, you are saving because that plan is, in fact, a savings plan. Moreover, if you have anything other than term insurance, you are also saving, because the cash value of whole or ordinary insurance can be turned into a retirement annuity.

Setting Up Your Own Pension Plan

For many people, one of the smartest ways to save is to set up a personal pension plan. It is beneficial to save via an individual retirement plan because you do not pay taxes on the allowed amount of savings put into the plan or on the interest and dividends the plan generates until you take the money out, usually at retirement. In effect, you are being given an interest-free loan from the government that earns interest itself on which you can defer taxes for many years and pay them, usually, when you are in a lower tax bracket. The benefit of putting away, say, $1,500 a year in a tax-free retirement plan is directly proportional to your marginal tax rate. If you were in the 50 percent tax bracket, for example, you would have paid Uncle Sam $750 in taxes, had you not put the money in the plan instead. When you put the $1,500 in the approved plan, you earn interest on the total amount however many years it is in effect, and then pay taxes only as you take money out of the plan on a retirement basis. There are basically two plans available to individuals who are self-employed or whose employers do not provide pension plans.

Keogh Plans

The Keogh Act of 1972 was passed in order to help self-employed individuals set up their own pension plans. Modified by the Employment Retirement Income Security Act of 1974, a Keogh Plan retirement program originally allowed a maximum investment of $7,500 per year, and the plan had to be administered by a bank or other third party. Starting in 1981, the contribution level climbed to $30,000 or 15 percent of your income. Additionally, you can be the trustee of your own Keogh Plan. You are penalized if you take the money out of the plan before you are 59½ years old, unless you are totally disabled. You must take money out of the plan when you reach 70½, even if you have not retired and still have current income. Many insurance companies, mutual funds, and banks have developed master plans that simplify the establishment of a Keogh fund.

Individual Retirement Accounts

A relatively newer retirement system is the Individual Retirement Account (IRA). You may contribute to an IRA and deduct on your tax return up to $2,000 each year. Each year's contributions can be made in one lump sum or installments. If you have a nonworking spouse, you may have a spousal IRA and deposit an additional $250 per year for a combined total of $2,250 annually. Working couples may contribute a combined total of $4,000 annually.

In principle, no contributions can be made to an IRA in any year in which money currently is being put into another pension program that qualifies for tax advantages; however, your existing IRA can continue and earn further taxes or dividends and interest. Like the Keogh Plan, you must withdraw from the plan when you reach 70½, and you pay a penalty on funds withdrawn before age 59½ (regular income taxes plus a 10 percent penalty). You can manage your own IRA, deciding which investments to make and not to make; however, a number of banks have set up IRAs to ease the recordkeeping problems of management.

SUMMARY

1. In the stock market, shares of American businesses are bought and sold just about every weekday throughout the year. When you buy and sell stocks, you may either sell them for more than you paid and experience a capital gain or sell them for less than you paid and experience a capital loss.
2. When you buy a share in a company, there is no guarantee that you will receive dividends or that you will make any particular rate of interest on your investment. However, if you loan money to the company—that is, buy one of its bonds—you are guaranteed, as long as the company does not go bankrupt, a specified dollar interest payment every year and a specified principal payment

when the bond matures or when the bond's life runs out. It is important to purchase bonds only if the interest rate paid at least compensates you for inflation that you anticipate.

3. It is generally a waste of time to consult stock market analysts in deciding which stocks to buy for your investment portfolio. The stock market is one of the most highly competitive markets in the world, and any useful information is immediately used by those who perceive it. Thus, the price of a stock represents all the information (properly discounted) that exists about the company, the industry,or the economy as a whole.

4. Stockbrokers can be helpful in explaining how the stock market works, the different types of securities you can buy, and so on.

5. Do not be taken in by so-called investment plans that purport to guarantee you a higher-than-normal rate of return in the stock market. Generally, these investment plans consume any above-normal rates of return in the fees they charge you or the commissions you must pay to buy and sell stocks often.

6. Mutual funds may be an easy answer to your investing problems, for they purchase a wide variety of stocks. It is generally advisable to buy into a no-load mutual fund that has no sales charges. Also, it may be possible to buy into mutual funds that purchase a nearly random selection of stocks and, therefore, do not have any management expenses. These mutual funds eventually will be offered to you at a lower management fee than those currently in existence.

7. All schemes to make you richer should be investigated thoroughly, for, on average, they rarely guarantee you a higher-than-normal rate of return unless you accept a higher amount of risk. For example, even though the amount of land is fixed and the population is growing, real estate is not always a good investment. Here's an example of public information having zero value as a guide to where to invest your accumulated savings. The same would be true for any arguments telling you that the best investments are antiques, oil and gas wells, old paintings, cans of food, and so on.

QUESTIONS FOR THOUGHT AND DISCUSSION

1. "Risk and rate of return are positively related." Do you agree with that statement? Why or why not?
2. Which do you think are a better investment—stocks or bonds?
3. Do you think stockbrokers have more information about which stocks to buy than you have?
4. What is the value of public information?
5. Do you think the small investor should be given special treatment by the stock exchanges and brokerage houses?
6. "The stock market is the backbone of American capitalism." Comment.
7. Do you believe in the so-called random-walk theory of stock prices?
8. Why do you think there were no mutual funds in existence years ago?
9. The value of land has always gone up. If that's true, why don't investors put all their money in land?

THINGS TO DO

1. Call an antique dealer and ask about the investment opportunities in antiques. What's the rate of return on investing in antiques. Is this rate of return

higher or lower than what you could expect if you put your money in a savings and loan association?

2. If you live in one of the large cities that has a stock exchange, visit it. You will be able to see a competitive market in action. Also, you can usually pick up information on stock markets and how they work. Call a brokerage firm in your area to ask if there is a national or regional exchange nearby.

3. Look at the financial page of any newspaper. Find out what all the various financial quotations actually mean, either from your instructor or from a stockbroker.

4. List the steps you would follow in purchasing a stock on the New York Stock Exchange.

SELECTED READINGS

Baruch, Hurd. *Wall Street: Security Risk.* London: Acropolis Books, 1972.

Donoghue, William E. *William E. Donoghue's Complete Money Market Guide.* New York: Bantam Books, 1982.

Dorfman, John, ed. *Stock Market Sourcebook.* New York: Doubleday, 1982.

Fabozzi, Frank J., and Zarb, Frank G., eds. *Handbook of Financial Markets: Securities, Options, and Futures.* New York: Dow Jones-Irwin, 1981.

Friend, Irwin; Blume, Marshall; and Crockett, Jean. *Mutual Fund and Other Institutional Investors: A New Perspective.* New York: McGraw-Hill, 1970.

Gup, Benton E. *The Basics of Investing.* New York: John Wiley, 1979.

"How to Judge Money-Market Funds." *Consumer Reports,* January 1983, pp. 30–34.

Lorie, James H., and Hamilton, Mary T. *The Stock Market.* Homewood, Ill.: Richard D. Irwin, 1973.

"Markets and Investments." See issues of *Business Week.*

Sloan, Alan. "Buying Bonds for Riskier Times." *Money,* April 1982, pp. 86–94.

Understanding Bonds and Preferred Stocks. New York Stock Exchange, 11 Wall Street, New York, New York 10005.

Wiesenberger, Arthur. *Investment Companies.* New York: Arthur Wiesenberger & Company (published annually).

"Will You Ever Collect a Pension?" *Consumer Reports,* March 1982, pp. 124–30.

Consumer ISSUE T

HOW TO BE A RATIONAL INVESTOR

GLOSSARY

LIQUIDITY—The "moneyness" that an investment has. The most liquid asset you can own is, of course, cash.

MUNICIPAL BONDS—Bonds sold by government agencies, such as cities. The distinguishing feature of these bonds is that the interest income from them is nontaxable.

REAL RATE OF RETURN—The rate of return received on any investment after the effect of inflation has been taken into account.

TAX EXEMPT—Investments that yield income that is tax exempt. Generally, tax exempts are municipal bonds with an interest rate that is not taxed by the U.S. government.

THIRD MARKET—A network of traders who bypass the major stock exchanges.

As you noted in the preceding discussion, the various schemes you could follow to get rich quickly in the stock market are useless because the stock market is so highly competitive. That is true for just about every investment opportunity into which you could put your savings. Nonetheless, you must do something with your savings if you want to insure yourself against inflation. In Consumer Issue F you received some specific tips on how to deal with inflation, but some of them bear repeating here.

INFLATION AND THE INTEREST RATE

You should make sure that the **real rate of return** on your investments is at least positive. For example, you should not be content with buying a Series EE Savings Bond from the U.S. government at 8 percent interest if the rate of inflation is also 8 percent. If you do such a thing, your real rate of return will be *negative,* because you have to pay taxes on those earnings. In a period of uncertainty about the future rate of inflation, you probably should invest at least some of your savings in mutual funds that buy only short-term debt. Thus, you'll get essentially the same interest rate that the big money market people—through pension plans, trust departments, etc.—get.

Picking a Broker

If you decide to buy stocks, you usually can do so only through a broker. But if you use the random-walk theory, you will need the broker only to execute your orders—that is, to buy and sell stocks. You won't want him or her to give you any advice at all about which stocks to buy and which to sell or when to leave and enter the market. You may, therefore, wish to use the services of a discount brokerage firm. Exhibit T–1 shows an ad for a cut-rate brokerage firm. To do business with a discount broker, you telephone your order in to a trader who buys or sells the stocks you want and later confirms the trade, usually by mail. Most discount brokers have a toll-free 800 number. Within five business days after the transaction, you must either send a check for the securities you bought or deliver the stock certificates of the securities you sold. New customers to discount brokerage firms usually are required to put down part or all of the cash to make their first buy order or to furnish stock certificates before their first sell order. Most discounters have a minimum fee, ranging from $15 to $35 per transaction,

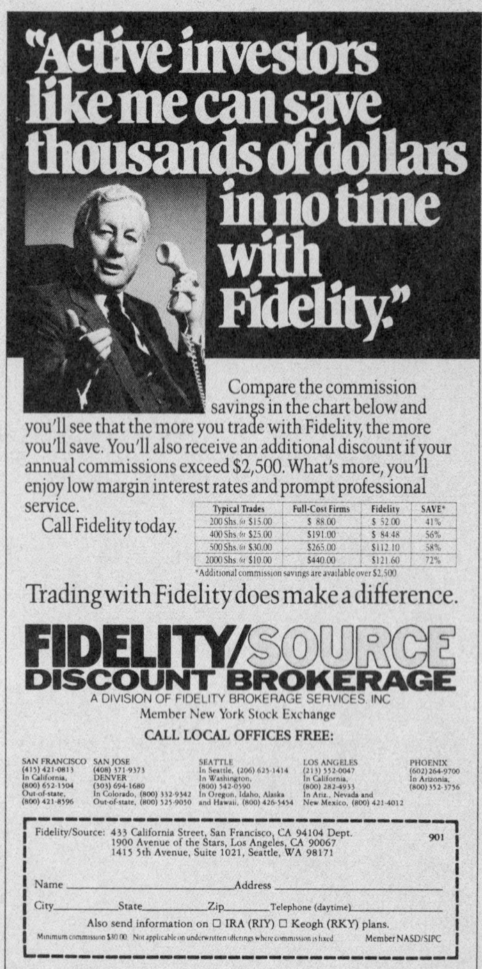

EXHIBIT T–1
Cut-Rate Brokerage Fees

which tends to discourage orders of under $1,000. Most discounters figure their commission based on the old fixed-rate, New York Stock Exchange schedule.

Most discounters have a two-tiered pricing plan. There is a higher commission rate for trades on major stock exchanges, a lower one for trades on the **third market.** The third market is a network of traders who bypass the major stock exchanges.

In any event, you should pick a broker who meets your needs. If, as many people do, you like having a broker call you often with hot tips, then you want to get an outgoing one who will keep in close touch. But if you value your time and aren't particularly interested in the stock market *per se,* then just call any broker in the book, let it be known that you never want to be called, and that all you want is for your orders to be executed. Because there is a penalty in the form of a higher service charge for smaller orders, wait until you have enough saved to order your shares of stocks in blocks of 100 or more.

If you want to know more about the ins and outs of the stock market, there are hundreds of books to consult. Most will give you different schemes, but if you believe what you read in the previous chapter, you will ignore them. Probably, the most widely read and most informative book on the stock market is *How to Buy Stocks,* by Louis Engel, available (sometimes free) from Merrill Lynch, Pierce, Fenner and Smith, Inc., and also from Bantam Books.

Full Cash Management

A number of major stock-brokerage firms and banks are offering full, or one-stop, financial management. Merrill Lynch first unveiled its cash management account in 1977. For an annual fee of fifty dollars, you receive the services of a broker on commission who handles your stock buying and selling. In your cash management account, any uninvested sum over $1,000 is swept into a money market mutual fund; amounts under $1,000 are swept weekly into a money market account. You have the choice of three short-term funds: government, conventional, and tax exempt. You get a checking account and a VISA debit card. You also get credit on the stock securities you hold. Citibank in New York offers similar services and, in addition, has automatic teller machines. For many who wish to invest in the stock market and have a checking account as well as a credit card, the one-stop financial services offered by brokerage firms and banks are certainly something to consider.

READING QUOTATIONS ON THE NEW YORK STOCK EXCHANGE

By far the most well-known public market is the New York Stock Exchange. As with all other stock exchanges, at the beginning of each trading day shares of stock open at the same price at which they closed the day before. At the end of each day, each stock has a closing price. This is the information that newspapers report. The example that follows of the stocks traded on the New York Stock Exchange is from a typical newspaper financial page. American Stock Exchange quotations are often given in most newspapers, too. Major newspapers throughout the country will also carry regional or local stock exchange listings.

In a listing, each company's name is printed in an abbreviated form. For example, in the listing shown in Exhibit T–2, *IntPaper* means International Paper. Often, other letters will appear next to the name of the company. For example, the letters *Pf* means that preferred stock is being quoted in that row. Prices are listed in dollars and fractions of a dollar; for example, the figure 34¾ means $34.75.

READING QUOTATIONS OF OVER-THE-COUNTER MARKET TRANSACTIONS

There is no actual stock exchange in the over-the-counter market. Rather, dealers in specified stocks stand ready to buy and sell at a specified bid and ask price. In other words, dealers in over-the-counter securities carry inventories of those securities. The information about over-the-counter listed securities varies slightly from that given for shares in companies traded on the New York and American Stock Exchanges. Over-the-counter quotations normally list the highest bid and the lowest ask price among dealers at the end of each trading day. Exhibit T–3 shows a partial list of over-the-counter market transactions with explanations of each column.

WHAT ABOUT BONDS?

Bonds are an alternative to stocks that many people invest in for savings. However, unanticipated inflation can make bonds a bad deal. This is particularly true, of course, for low-interest U.S. Savings Bonds, but it may also be true for any other type of bond—federal, state, and municipal government, plus corporate—that is *long term* and has an interest rate that fails to reflect fully the decreasing purchasing power of the dollars you loaned the people who gave you the bond. Remember, if you expect the inflation rate to be 10 percent a year and you buy a long-term bond that yields 11 percent, you will make only a 1

A	B	C	D	E	F	G	H	I	J	K
HIGH	LOW	STOCK	DIV.	YLD. %	P-E RATIO	SALES IN 100S	HIGH	LOW	CLOSE	NET CHANGE
57¼	39½	Interco	2.88	6.6	6	313	43½	42⅞	48⅜	+⅝
45	29	Intrik	2.60	9.0	4	3	29⅛	28⅞	28⅞	−⅜
16	10¼	IntAlum	.60	5.8	8	37	10⅝	10⅜	10⅜	+⅛
65¼	48⅜	IBM	3.44	5.8	10	5874	59⅝	58⅝	59	+⅜
22⅜	17½	IntFlav	1	5.3	10	440	19¼	18½	18¾	...
21⅛	4¾	IntHarv		..	..	311	5⅝	5⅜	5⅝	+⅛
53½	25¾	IntMin	2.60	9.5	4	448	28	27¼	27½	−¼
24	17½	IntMulti	1.48	6.3	6	47	23⅞	23⅜	23⅝	+½
51½	33	IntPaper	2.40	7.0	3	859	34¾	34	34⅛	+⅛

These stocks and prices are excerpted from a page in the *Wall Street Journal*. Definitions of the abbreviations used and explanations of the columns are as follows:

A High: This is the highest price paid for the stock during the last fifty-two weeks. Stock prices are usually quoted in ⅛ at a point (12½¢) per share or multiple thereof.

B Low: This is the lowest price paid for the stock during the last fifty-two weeks.

C Stock: This is the name of the company, usually abbreviated.

D Div.: This is the annual dividend based on the most recent quarterly or semiannual distribution.

E Yld.%: This is the annual dividend amount divided by the closing price of the stock.

F P-E Ratio: This is the ratio found by dividing the closing price by the most recent twelve months' earnings per share.

G Sales in 100s: This is the number of round lots (100 shares each) sold that day. The odd lots, which are less than 100 shares each, are not listed.

H High: This is the highest price for the stock on this trading day.

I Low: This is the lowest price paid for the stock on this trading day.

J Close: This is the price of the stock at the end of the trading day.

K Net Change: This is the difference between the closing price of the stock on this trading day and the closing price of the stock on the previous trading day.

EXHIBIT T–2
Partial List of New York Stock Exchange Composite Transactions

percent rate of return in real terms (ignoring taxes!).

In effect, bonds are fixed income-bearing types of investments. You buy a bond, and it yields you a specific annual return in dollars that can be translated into an interest yield. In other words, if you buy a bond that yields you $100 a year and it cost you $1,000, you receive a 10 percent rate of return; if it cost you only $500, you get a 20 percent rate of return. Generally, as with all investments, the higher the rate of return, the higher the risk that the issuer of the bond will not be able to pay interest—or will not be able to pay at all.

If you decide to buy any bonds at all, make sure you go through a broker who knows what he or she is doing in the bond market. Tell the broker how much risk you are willing to take and when you want the bonds to mature. You can buy bonds that mature in 1990, 2000, 2010, or in six months, if you want. Bonds are issued by the U.S. government, and by corporations. For some people, there is an advantage to buying local municipal bonds.

Reading Bond Market Quotations

Bonds normally have a face value of $1,000, but they can sell for more or less than that amount. In other words, they sell at a premium or a discount from their face value. Prices for bonds are listed as a percentage of their face value. A figure of 79⅝, for example, means that a $1,000 bond is selling for $796.25.

Exhibit T–4 is a listing of sample bond quotes from the New York Bond Exchange. Actually, the majority of bonds, including all tax-exempt bonds, are traded in the over-the-counter market. Listings of over-the-counter bond transactions are similar to those for over-the-counter stocks in that the listing will include a bid and ask price.

Often, there will be more than one listing of bonds for a particular company; this simply means that the company has different bond issues, each maturing at a different date or having different characteristics.

Tax-Exempt Bonds

Municipal bonds generally are **tax exempt;** that is, the interest you earn on those bonds is not taxed by the federal government, and, in some cases, it is not taxed by state governments either. Nevertheless, these bonds are not always a special deal. Unless you are in a higher income-tax bracket—in fact, unless you are in about the 42 percent or higher income-tax bracket—tax-exempt bonds offer you no advantages over nonexempt bonds. Because the bond market is highly competitive and everybody knows the advantages of not having to pay taxes on interest from these municipal bonds, their price is, therefore, bid up so that only people in the higher tax brackets get any special benefit. In fact, if you were in the 14 percent tax bracket and you bought a tax-exempt bond, you would be worse off than if you bought nonexempt bonds because the effective yield would be so low.

To decide whether a tax-exempt bond is worth buying, you first determine how the yield compares with the rate you can earn on another investment that is not tax exempt. Exhibit T–5 shows the yield in your particular tax bracket. Say that you are in the $20,200 to $24,600 bracket and the tax-exempt yield is 6.0 percent; that would be equivalent to an 8.33 percent rate of return from some other investment that did not have this special tax advantage. On the other hand, if you were in the $35,200-to-$45,800 bracket, the 6.0 percent would be equivalent to 10.53 percent of taxable interest. (State taxes are not figured in this exhibit because the rates and rules governing taxability of municipal bonds vary widely.)

Tax-exempt bonds are usually available in both $1,000 and $5,000 denominations. Unfortunately, most of the newer bonds are being issued in $5,000 denominations, so small investors cannot purchase them directly. However, you can buy shares in tax-exempt bond mutual funds instead of buying the bonds themselves. Exhibit T–6 gives you a sample of tax-free mutual funds that also allow you to write checks for $500 or more against their accounts. (The Fidelity Limited Term Municipal Fund has a minimum of $1,000 per check, however.)

Financial Backing Differs

Note that tax-exempt bonds are classified not only according to the organizations that issue them—states, territories, cities, towns, villages, counties, local public housing authorities, port authorities, water districts, school districts—but also according to the sources of funds that the issuing organizations can utilize to pay interest and principal. As an example, *general obligation* tax-exempt bonds are backed by the full credit, and ordinarily by the full taxing power, of the state or municipality. On the other hand, *revenue* tax-exempt bonds are backed only by revenues from a specific activity, such as a water-supply system or a toll road. In addition, bonds are rated according to their riskiness, ranging from very risky to not risky at all. Owners of bonds issued by New York City

EXHIBIT T–3
Partial List of Over-the-Counter Markets Transactions

A	B	C	D	E	F
STOCK	DIV.	SALES 100S	BID	ASKED	NET CHG.
Antares Oil Cp.	. . .	37	1¼	1½	. . .
Apogee Ent	12	72	15⅜	15⅝	+ ⅛
Apple Comptr	. . .	3881	16¼	16⅜	− ¼
Arden Group	. . .	43	3⅜	3½	+ ⅜

A Stock: The name of the company.
B Div.: The expected annual dividend.
C Sales 100s: The number of round lots sold that day.
D Bid: The price at which one dealer is willing to buy the stock from another dealer. Actual prices paid by investors may be higher as the securities are marked down for a retail bid.
E Asked: The price at which one dealer is willing to sell the stock to another dealer.
F Net Chg.: The change in the last bid price from the previous day. For example, Apple Computer closed at $16¼ bid today down ¼ point from the previous day's closing bid of 16½.

A	B	C	D	E	F	G	H
BONDS		CUR. YLD.	VOL.	HIGH	LOW	CLOSE	NET CHG.
A Airl	11s88	14.	11	79⅝	79⅝	79⅝	−1½
A Airl	5¼ 98	CV	341	57	53	53	−2
A Brnd	5⅞ 92	11.	5	55⅞	55⅞	55⅞	. . .
A Can	6s97	13.	2	45⅝	45⅝	45⅝	− ½
An Mot	6s88	CV	5	55	53	55	+2
A Sug	4.3s93	10.	1	50⅝	50⅝	50⅝	− ⅜
ATT	2⅞s87	4.2	25	69	68½	69	+ ½
ATT	13¼ 91	14.	234	96¾	96¼	96¾	+ ⅛
Anhr	9s05	CV	15	124	124	124	−2

A Name of the company.
B Coupon or nominal interest rate of the bond and its due or maturity date.
C Current yield, or the coupon rate divided by the current selling price. Where "cv" appears, the bond is convertible into the company's stock. The price of the conversion is not given, however. Rather, a *Standard and Poor's* or a *Moody's Bond Book* or the financial statement of the corporation will give such information.
D Number of bonds sold.
E Highest selling price of the bond that trading day. (Corporate bonds are quoted in ⅛ points. A bond selling at 79⅝ has a price of $796.25)
F Lowest price paid for that bond that trading day.
G Closing price.
H Net change from the previous trading day's closing price.

EXHIBIT T–4
Reading Bond Quotes

found out all too painfully that tax-exempt municipals may not be such a good deal. You have to be wary about them, as you do about all investments.

BOND RATINGS. You can check several sources to find out about the financial stability of the issuing organization for any bonds you wish to buy. Specifically, you can go to a library to look at *Moody's Bond Record*, where bonds are rated from the highest grade Aaa to the lowest grade C (speculative in a high degree).

REAL-ESTATE DEALS

Of course, by now you will be suspicious of any "special" high-yield real-estate deals. But you should not necessarily rule out real estate as a possible investment for your savings, as long as you avoid being taken in by real-estate schemes—particularly those introduced by door-to-door salespeople or mail ads. If you have any interest in land in the middle of Arizona or Texas or Florida, investigate before you invest. Generally, you are locked into those deals for many, many years before you can get out any money at all; that is, they are extremely *illiquid*. Moreover, the selling charges may be incredibly high, and many of them border on being frauds. If you do decide to go into real estate, remember that rate of return is positively related to risk; the higher the potential rate of return that someone offers you on a real-estate deal, the higher the risk you are going to take. Just as long as you are aware of that, you won't be duped.

ALL THAT IS GOLD DOES NOT GLITTER

What about investing in precious metals? Isn't it a certain thing? The answer is unequivocally no. People who bought gold in 1980 when it reached around $800 an ounce probably weren't too happy when it fell to $400 an ounce a few months later. To be sure, the price of gold has gone up over time. But that does not mean that you are guaranteed a high rate of return forever. The price of silver also went up. In fact, in 1977 it was selling for $4.41 an ounce, and, during the first couple of months of 1980, it went up to $40 an ounce, but then the price dropped back down to $10 an ounce. Some people made a killing; some people lost a fortune. The price of platinum was $155 an ounce in 1977 and reached $800 an ounce in 1980.

You should not construe these examples to mean that investment in precious metals is not advised. It is. A well-diversified investor is the best investor around.

Diversification means that you, as an investor with savings dollars, should indeed have a certain percentage of your investments in precious metals, such as South African gold Krugerrands or Canadian gold maple-leaf coins, pre-1965 U.S. silver coins, and a variety of other precious metals. But do not think that you are guaranteed a high rate of return. Nothing is intrinsically a sound investment at all times for all people.

VARIETY IS THE SPICE OF INVESTMENT

It is generally advisable to seek variety in your savings plans for several reasons. First, not all your savings should be in illiquid assets. If you have a disaster that requires money quickly, you would like to have some cash or savings-account reserve that you can take out immediately without losing anything. Remember, however, that you pay a cost for keeping cash—the cost of the rate of inflation that shrinks the purchasing power of those dollars.

The second reason to vary your savings is that you can reduce your overall risk by having a large variety of different investment assets. There are no fixed rules to follow, although many investment counselors have their own. They might suggest you keep a certain fraction of your assets in cash, a certain fraction in a savings account, and so on. But there is no scientific rule or reason behind such advice. You must decide yourself how much **liquidity** you want, how much risk you want to take, how many long-term investments you want, and how many short-term investments you want.

Remember, as you increase the variety of risks you have in your investment portfolio, you lower the overall risk involved in that whole portfolio, but you also lower the overall rate of return you will receive. You may want to gamble as part of your investment program. You may want to buy, for example, penny stocks that sometimes jump tremendously in value. You may want to buy stocks on local over-the-counter markets that have a high variability and sometimes really hit. But you certainly should not put all your eggs in this basket because, if you lose, you will have nothing. At the other end of the spectrum, you could be absolutely safe by keeping everything in a savings account; but because you would be unable to make a higher rate of return, you probably don't want to do that, either. Remember, successful investment does not mean making a killing. It means avoiding losses that deprive you

EXHIBIT T–5

The After-Tax Return on Tax-Exempt Municipal Bonds

Here are yields that, after federal income taxes, would equal the first column at the left. As an example, if you were filing a joint return and had taxable income on from $24,600 to $29,900, a tax-exempt yield of, say, 7 percent would be equivalent to a taxable yield of 10.29 percent.

	TAXABLE INCOME IN THOUSANDS—JOINT RETURN (% TAX BRACKET)									
TAX-EXEMPT YIELDS IN PERCENT	$20.2 to $24.6 (28)	$24.6 to $29.9 (32)	$29.9 to $35.2 (37)	$35.2 to $45.8 (43)	$45.8 to $85.5 (49)	$60.0 to $85.6 (54)	$85.6 to $109.4 (59)	$109.4 to $162.4 (64)	$162.4 to $215.4 (68)	Over $215.4 (70)
4.0	5.56	5.88	6.35	7.02	7.84	8.70	9.76	11.11	12.50	13.33
4.5	6.25	6.62	7.14	7.89	8.82	9.78	10.98	12.50	14.06	15.00
5.0	6.94	7.35	7.94	8.77	9.80	10.87	12.20	13.89	15.63	16.67
5.5	7.64	8.09	8.73	9.65	10.78	11.96	13.41	15.28	17.19	18.33
6.0	8.33	8.82	9.52	10.53	11.76	13.04	14.63	16.67	18.75	20.00
6.5	9.03	9.56	10.32	11.40	12.75	14.13	15.85	18.06	20.31	21.67
7.0	9.72	10.29	11.11	12.28	13.73	15.22	17.07	19.44	21.88	23.33
7.5	10.42	11.03	11.90	13.16	14.71	16.30	18.29	20.83	23.44	25.00
8.0	11.11	11.76	12.70	14.04	15.69	17.39	19.51	22.22	25.00	26.67
8.5	11.81	12.50	13.49	14.91	16.67	18.48	20.73	23.61	26.56	28.33
9.0	12.50	13.24	14.29	15.79	17.65	19.57	21.95	25.00	28.13	30.00
9.5	13.19	13.97	15.08	16.67	18.63	20.65	23.17	26.39	29.69	31.67
10.0	13.89	14.71	15.87	17.54	19.61	21.74	24.39	27.78	31.25	33.33

EXHIBIT T–6

Tax-Free Mutual Funds with Check-Writing Privileges

Here is information on eight different tax-free municipal funds that allow you to write checks for a minimum of $500 ($1,000 for Fidelity Limited Term Municipals). This information was accurate as of 1980 but may be slightly different today.

	TYPE OF PORTFOLIO	SMALLEST OPENING INVESTMENT
Warwick High-Yield Municipal Bond Fund Box 1100, Drummer's Lane, Valley Forge, Pa. 19482 800-523-7910; in Pennsylvania, 800-362-7688	Long-term; medium- and lower-rated bonds	$ 3,000
Warwick Long-Term Municipal Bond Fund	High-rated bonds	$ 3,000
Federated Tax-Free Income Fund 421 Seventh Ave., Pittsburgh, Pa. 15219 800-245-2423; in Pennsylvania, 412-288-1948 collect	Long-term; high- and medium-rated bonds	$ 1,000
Warwick Intermediate-Term Municipal Bond Fund	Average maturity of seven to twelve years; high- and medium-rated bonds	$ 3,000
Rowe Price Tax-Free Income Fund 100 E. Pratt St., Baltimore, Md. 21202 800-638-1527; in Maryland, 301-547-2000 collect	Long-term; high- and medium-rated bonds	$ 1,000
Chancellor Tax-Exempt Daily Income Fund 100 Gold St., New York, N.Y. 10038 800-221-5168; in New York, 212-791-4654 collect	Short-term; high- and medium-rated notes and bonds	$ 2,500
Fidelity Limited Term Municipals 82 Devonshire St., Boston, Mass. 02109 800-225-6190; in Massachusetts, 617-726-0650 collect	Average maturity of less than twelve years; high-rated bonds	$10,000
Warwick Short-Term Municipal Bond Fund	High-rated notes and bonds	$ 3,000

of retirement savings and, at the same time, you will get a normal rate of return on those savings. Any other goals you choose may cost you.

Now take a look at Exhibit T–7 for a summary of some investment outlets. And then "let the buyer beware."

SUMMARY

1. To ascertain the rate of return from any investment, subtract the rate of inflation from the interest rate you receive on your investment to get some notion of the real rate of return.

2. It is advisable to diversify your investments: Have some in cash, some in a savings account, some in the stock market, some in bonds, and some in mutual funds that buy only short-term government securities or certificates of deposit and bankers acceptances.

3. It pays to shop around for the best deal in terms of the commission you must pay to purchase stocks: Different brokerage firms have different rates.

4. Unless you are making enough income to be in a relatively high income-tax bracket, it is not worthwhile for you to purchase tax-exempt municipal bonds.

5. Be wary of real-estate deals, particularly those touted by door-to-door salespersons or mail advertising announcements. You never get something for nothing. No investment deal can truly offer you a higher-than-normal or competitive rate of return unless you are willing to take a greater risk.

QUESTIONS FOR THOUGHT AND DISCUSSION

1. Why do you think so many people have bought U.S. Savings Bonds?

2. The rate of return on the stock market is basically the rate of return to American business. So long as American business continues to make a rate of return of around 10 percent, so, too, should investors in the stock market. Do you agree or disagree?

3. Why do you think you can obtain so much free research from various brokerage houses?

4. What do you think determines the price of a stock?

5. What is the difference between a corporate bond and a government bond?

6. Why do you think the interest earned on municipal bonds is not taxed by the federal government?

7. Why is there so much diversity of opinion about what are appropriate investments?

THINGS TO DO

1. List any investments you have (or would like to have), and figure out which ones provide a hedge against inflation. Figure out what your average yearly rate of return is (or would be) on those investments.

2. Find the Consumer Price Index increase for last year; that is, find out what the rate of inflation was then. Then compute the real rates of return on Series EE Savings Bonds, savings accounts, and any other investment on which you have information. Can you explain how some

EXHIBIT T–7
Various Investment Outlets

This exhibit shows the various investment outlets, ranging from cash to Treasury bills. Column 1 lists how well your principal is protected. Column 2 lists how good these particular investments have been as a hedge against inflation. Column 3 lists average rates of return in the late 1970s. Column 4 indicates how well you can expect that return to continue year in and year out. Column 5 indicates what kind of transactions costs are involved in getting in and out of the particular types of investments. Column 6 indicates whether or not you have a liquid asset. And column 7 gives you your chances for long-term growth.

INVESTMENT	(1) PRINCIPAL	(2) INFLATION	(3) RATE OF RETURN %	(4) CERTAINTY OF CONTINUED RETURN	(5) LOW CHARGES OR FEES	(6) LIQUIDITY UNDER ALL CONDITIONS	(7) CHANCE FOR LONG-TERM GROWTH
Cash	Exc.	Poor	0	—	—	Exc.	None
Life insurance	Exc.	Poor	5(a)	Exc.	Fair	Exc.	Poor
United States savings bonds	Exc.	Poor	5–9 7.5–9	Exc.	Exc.	Exc.	Poor
Savings account in commercial bank*	Exc.	Poor	6(b)	Exc.	Exc.	Exc.	Poor
Bank savings certificates	Exc.	Poor	(c)	Exc.	Exc.	Exc.	Poor
Mutual savings bank*	Exc.	Poor	6(b)	Exc.	Exc.	Exc.	Poor
Federal savings & loan assoc.*	Exc.	Poor	6(b)	Exc.	Exc.	Good	Poor
Credit union	Exc.	Poor	7(d)	Good	Good	Good	Poor
Corporate bonds	Good	Poor	11	Exc.	Good	Good	Poor
Corporate stocks	Fair	Exc.	3½–8	Good	Good	Good	Good
High-grade preferred stocks	Good	Poor	7½–9	Good	Good	Good	Poor
Convertible bonds	Good	Good	3–4½, 5–9	Good	Good	Good	Good
Investment companies (mutual funds)	Fair	Exc.	9–11	Good	Poor	Good	Good
Real-estate mortgages (as investments)	Fair	Poor	11–12	Fair	Poor	Poor	Poor
Unimproved real estate	Fair	Good	—	Poor	Poor	Poor	Good
Short-term money market funds	Exc.	Good	8–12	Poor	Good	Exc.	Poor
Treasury bills	Exc.	Good	10–16	Good	Good	Exc.	Poor

*Insured up to $100,000 by FDIC or FHLIC.
(a) Depends on your tax bracket.
(b) Will be allowed to move up to market interest rates by 1986.
(c) Rates are changing constantly.
(d) Industry average.
SOURCE: Adapted from "What to Do with Your Savings," *Changing Times.*

real rates of return are actually negative? Why would any investor leave money in such an investment?

3. Ask a stockbroker to send you information on mutual funds in the United States. Find out the characteristics of growth funds versus income funds versus high-risk funds versus low-risk funds. How would you decide which mutual fund to buy? Find out the difference between load and no-load mutual funds. Why would anybody want to pay the sales commission to buy a load fund as opposed to a no-load fund?

4. Look at the next-to-the-last page of the *Wall Street Journal,* which shows the Dow Jones Industrial Average. Can you see any pattern in what has happened to the average price of stocks?

5. Find out the latest rates for purchasing less than $2,000 worth of stock. Try to determine why some investment brokerage houses charge less than others.

6. Read a book on the stock market, such as *How to Buy Stocks* by Louis Engel. Now read a book on how to get rich quickly in the stock market. What is the difference in the information obtained from these two books? How valuable is the information from the second book?

7. Find out from a stockbroker or a local financial service what the interest rate is for tax-exempt municipal bonds. Does that interest exceed the rate of inflation?

SELECTED READINGS

American Research Council. *Your Investments.* New York: McGraw-Hill (latest edition).

Blamer, Thomas, and Shulman, Richard. *Dow 3,000.* New York: Simon & Schuster, 1982.

Chestnutt, George A., Jr. *Stock Market Analysis: Facts and Principles.* Greenwich, Conn.: Chestnutt Corporation (latest edition).

Curran, John J. "Rival Managers for Your Cash." *Fortune,* January 24, 1983, pp. 107–10.

Dorfman, John. *Family Investment Guide.* New York: Atheneum, 1981.

Encyclopedia of Stock Market Techniques. Larchmont, New York: Investors Intelligence, Inc. (latest edition).

Engel, Louis. *How to Buy Stocks—A Guide to Successful Investing.* New York: Bantam Books, 1975. A free copy may be obtained upon request from Merrill Lynch, Inc., 1 Liberty Plaza, New York, New York 10006.

"Forbes Mutual Fund Survey." Issued annually in the August 15 issue of *Forbes.*

Holt, Robert Lawrence. *The Complete Book of Bonds: How to Buy and Sell Profitably.* New York: Harcourt Brace Jovanovich, 1981.

Mamis, Justin. *How to Buy: An Insider's Guide to Making Money on the Stock Market.* New York: Farrar, Straus & Giroux, 1982.

Rolo, Charles J. *Gaining on the Market: Your Complete Guide to Investment Strategy.* Boston: Little, Brown, 1982.

Rosenberg, Claude N. *Stock Market Primer.* New York: Warner Communications, 1982.

Sosnoff, M. T. "Market Trends." See issues of *Forbes.*

Taylor, Tom. *Get Rich on the Obvious: How to Turn Your Everyday Observations into Stock Market Profits.* New York: Harcourt Brace Jovanovich, 1982.

Woy, James B., ed. *Investment Information: A Detailed Guide to Selected Sources,* Management Guides Series, No. 19. Detroit, Mich.: Gale Research Company (latest edition).

CHAPTER
PAYING FOR GOVERNMENT

22

The government provides numerous goods and services, such as a court system, police, firefighters, public schools, public libraries, and myriad programs . . . Governments do not run on thin air, however; they have to be financed.

CHAPTER PREVIEW

- What are the different theories that justify taxation?
- What type of tax system do we have in the United States?
- How important is the federal personal income tax as a source of government revenues?
- What is the history of our progressive tax system?
- What are tax "loopholes" all about?
- How do special interest groups affect what the government does with our tax dollars?

The government provides numerous goods and services, such as a court system, police, firefighters, public schools, public libraries, and myriad other programs to help specific groups in the nation. Governments do not run on thin air, however; they have to be financed. And the only way a government can be financed is by having you, the consumer, give up part of your income to it. You have to do it now to the tune of about 42 percent of every dollar you make. Just look at Exhibit 22–1. Here you see how long the average American has to work for the government in order to pay all of government's expenses. In 1983, the Tax Foundation of Washington, D.C., estimated that the average American worked from the first of the year until May 15, the date the Tax Foundation has dubbed "Tax Freedom Day." In other words, the average American must work until May 15 to pay for government. Then, after that date, the average American starts working for him- or herself. Much of that money, of course, is returned to you in the form of transfers, such as Social Security, unemployment compensation, and the like; but at least 24 percent is for direct expenditures by governments. Government is big business. We will give you a few ideas on how you can expect governments to behave based on some simple economic principles that you apply to your own day-to-day decision making. Before we do that, however, let us look at various methods of taxation and some of the principles behind them.

THE WHYS AND HOWS OF TAXATION

Governments—federal, state, and local—have various methods of taxation at their disposal. The best known, of course, is the federal personal income tax, which generates almost 45 percent of all taxes collected by Uncle Sam. At the state and local levels, personal income taxes are not as popular; property taxes make up the bulk of the taxes collected. In addition to these taxes, there are corporate income taxes, sales taxes, excise taxes, inheritance taxes, and gift taxes, not all of which can be investigated in detail here.

EXHIBIT 22–1
Tax Freedom Day

Government spending during the past fifty years has created a situation in which the average American works until May 15 for the government. The Tax Foundation has dubbed this day for Tax Freedom Day.

SOURCE: Tax Foundation, Inc., Washington, D.C.

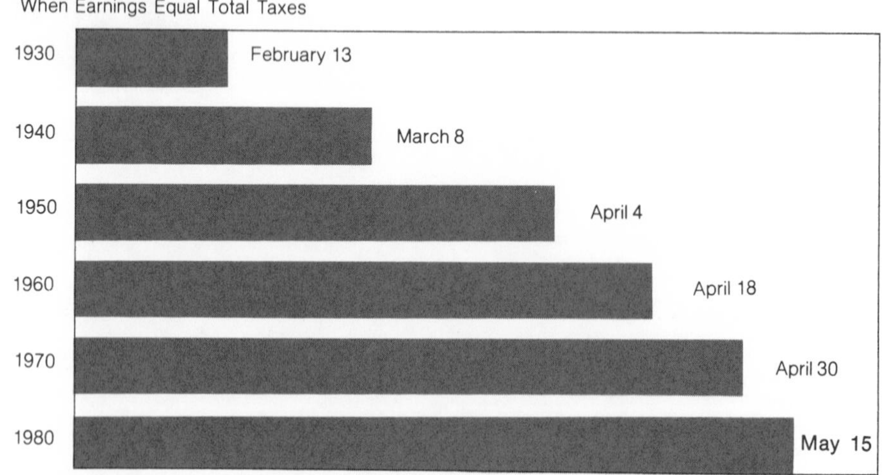

FIRST, A LITTLE THEORY

Naturally, everybody would prefer a tax that someone else pays. Because we all think that way, no tax could be devised that everyone would favor. Economists and philosophers have come up with alternative justifications for different ways of taxing. The three most often discussed principles of taxation are: benefits, ability to pay, and sacrifice.

The Benefit Principle

One widely accepted doctrine of taxation is the *benefit principle.* According to this principle, people should be taxed in proportion to the benefits they receive from government services. The more they benefit, the more they should pay; if they benefit little, they should pay little. This principle of taxation has problems in application, however. First of all, how do we determine the value people place on the goods and services the government provides? Can we ask them? If people think that others will pay their way, they will claim, upon being asked, that they receive no value from government services. For example, they will tell the interviewer they are unwilling to pay for national defense because they do not want any of it, it is of no value to them. This is the **free-rider problem.** We all want to be free riders if we think we can get away with it. If you think everybody else will pay for what you want, then most likely you will gladly let them do so. The problem is schematized in Exhibit 22–2. How much national defense will you benefit from if you agree to pay and everyone else also pays? $90,000,000,100. How much will there be if you do not pay but everyone else does pay? $90,000,000,000. If you think everyone else will pay, would you not be tempted to get a free ride?

One way out of this dilemma is to assure that the higher a person's income, the more services he or she receives and, therefore, the more value he or she gets from goods and services provided by the government. If we assume that people receive increases in government services that are *proportional* to their incomes, then we can use this benefit doctrine to justify proportional taxation.

FREE-RIDER PROBLEM
With certain types of goods and services, individuals attempt to get a "free ride" by not paying for what they use. For example, many persons, if asked how much they were willing to pay for national defense, would say "nothing," hoping that others would pay.

PROPORTIONAL TAXATION
A system of taxation in which the rate of taxation is uniform regardless of income size. For example, proportional taxation of 20 percent would take 20 percent of an income of $100 and also 20 percent of an income of $1 million.

PROGRESSIVE TAXATION
A taxing system in which the more your income increases, the higher your tax bracket becomes. In a progressive system, you pay a higher rate on the last dollar you earn than on the first dollar you earn.

AVERAGE TAX RATE
Simply the total amount of taxes you pay divided by your income.

PROPORTIONAL TAXATION. **Proportional taxation** is merely a system by which taxpayers pay a fixed percentage of every dollar of income. When their incomes increase, the taxes they pay increase. If the proportional tax rate is 20 percent, you pay twenty cents in taxes out of every dollar you earn. If you earn $1,000, you pay $200 in taxes; if you earn $1 million, you pay $200,000 in taxes.

PROGRESSIVE TAXATION. At this point, we should contrast proportional taxes with **progressive taxation.** If a tax is progressive, the more you earn, the more you pay in taxes, as with the proportional system; but, in addition, the *percentage* taken out of each additional dollar earned rises. In the terminology of marginal and average, we can describe progressiveness as a system by which the marginal tax rate goes up.[1] (So does the **average tax rate,** but not as much.) In the example illustrated in Exhibit 22–3, the first $100 of income is taxed at 10 percent, the next $100 at 20 percent, and the third $100 at 30 percent.

1. We first looked at marginal tax rates when discussing the tax benefits of home ownership in Chapter 15.

We all want to be free riders if we think we can get away with it.

REGRESSIVE TAXATION
Unlike progressive taxation, a system in which your tax rate falls as you earn more and more income.

The average rate is always equal to or less than the marginal rate with a progressive tax system. With a proportional system, the marginal tax rate is always the same, and it equals the average tax rate.

Can the benefit principle of taxation be used to justify progressiveness? Yes, it can. The only additional assumptions needed are: (a) the *value* people obtain from increased goods and services provided by the government goes up faster than their income, and/or (b) the *amount* of government goods and services received goes up faster than income. The benefit principle alone, without one of these two assumptions, cannot be used to justify progressive taxation.

REGRESSIVE TAXATION. As you can imagine, **regressive taxation** is the opposite of progressive taxation. A regressive tax system takes away a smaller and smaller additional percentage as income rises. The marginal rate falls and is usually below the average rate. As an example, imagine that all revenues of the government were obtained from a 99 percent tax on food. Because we know that the percentage of income spent on food falls as the total income rises, we also know that the percentage of total income that would be paid in taxes under such a system would likewise fall as income rises. It would be a regressive system.

Social Security taxes are a good example of a regressive system. The individual contributor paid 6.7 percent on income up to a maximum level, which, in 1983, was $35,700. A person making twice that amount, $75,000, paid exactly the same Social Security taxes; thus, that person's average tax rate for Social Security fell to one-half of 6.7 percent, or only 3.35 percent. As income goes up past the maximum level, the average Social Security tax falls.

The Ability-to-Pay Doctrine

The second principle of taxation considers people's ability to pay. It states that those who are able to pay more taxes *should* pay more taxes. Obviously, people who make more money generally should be able to pay higher taxes. But do we make them pay taxes that go hand in hand with income (a proportional system)? Or do we make them pay taxes that increase, but at a rate that is not in proportion to their incomes (a regressive system)? To answer these questions, we must decide whether their ability to pay rises faster than, in proportion to, or slower than their incomes. Whatever assumption we make determines whether we use a progressive, proportional, or regressive tax sys-

EXHIBIT 22–2
Scoreboard for National Defense

A free rider will gladly let everyone else pay for him or her. If you don't pay your share of national defense but everyone else does pay, there still will be $90,000,000,000 available for the country's defense. Whether you pay or not seems to make very little difference.

	If you pay	If you do not pay
If everyone else pays	$90,000,000,100	$90,000,000,000
If no one else pays	$100	$0.00

INCOME	MARGINAL RATE	TAX	AVERAGE RATE
$100	10%	$10	$\frac{\$10}{\$100} = 10\%$
$200	20%	$10 + $20 = $30	$\frac{\$30}{\$200} = 15\%$
$300	30%	$10 + $20 + $30 = $60	$\frac{\$60}{\$300} = 20\%$

EXHIBIT 22–3
A Progressive Tax System
The percentage of tax taken out of each additional dollar earned goes up; that is, the marginal tax rate increases progressively.

tem. The ability-to-pay doctrine would lead us to recommend progressiveness only if we assume that ability to pay rises more rapidly than income.

The Sacrifice Doctrine

The third principle of taxation holds that the sacrifices people make to pay their taxes should be equitable. It is generally assumed that the sacrifices people make when paying taxes to the government become smaller as their incomes become larger. When a $100 tax is paid, a millionaire is surely sacrificing less than a person who earns only $1,000 a year. The pleasure that the milllionaire gives up for that last $100 is less than the pleasure the other person gives up for that last $100. Again, we are faced with the problem of determining how fast satisfaction from income rises as income itself rises, and this involves a value judgment. If the satisfaction from income rises at a rate that is more than, equal to, or less than in proportion to income, we will end up justifying a system of progressive, proportional, or regressive taxes, respectively.

THE PERSONAL FEDERAL INCOME TAX

You are probably aware that the personal income tax system in the United States is progressive. Exhibit 22–4 shows part of the 1984 tax schedule. Notice that, as income rises, the marginal tax rate rises. The rate applicable to the previous lumps of income stays the same, however. Many students think that, if you are in the 50 percent tax bracket, you pay 50 percent of all your income to the federal government. But that is not the case. You may pay 50 percent of your income to the government on your last (marginal) $15,000 earned; however, income made before that last bracket is taxed at progressively lower and lower rates. As we see in Exhibit 22–5, personal income taxes account for almost 45 percent of all federal revenues. They should not be taken lightly.

HOW OUR PROGRESSIVE SYSTEM CAME INTO BEING

The Constitution gives Congress the authority "to lay and collect taxes, duties, imports and excises. . . ." No reference was made to an income tax at the time the Constitution was drafted. But, in 1894, the Wilson-Gorman Tariff Act provided for individual income taxes of 2 percent on incomes above $4,000. The country knew about income taxes from the period during the Civil War, when $4.4 million of such taxes were collected. Nonetheless, the concept of

EXHIBIT 22–4

Federal Personal Income Tax for a Childless Couple, 1984

This exhibit shows the different income brackets and the marginal tax rates along with the average tax rates. As you can see, the marginal tax rates go up to a maximum of 50 percent. On income from "services," the maximum is 50 percent. All wages are considered service income, but interest on bonds or dividends from stock is not.

NET INCOME BEFORE EXEMPTIONS (BUT AFTER DEDUCTIONS)	PERSONAL INCOME TAX	AVERAGE TAX RATE (5)	MARGINAL TAX RATE (5)
Below $ 3,400	$ 0	0	0
5,500	231	4.2	11
7,600	483	6.4	12
11,900	1,085	9.1	14
16,000	1,741	10.9	16
20,200	2,497	12.3	18
24,600	3,465	14.0	22
29,900	4,790	16.0	25
35,200	6,274	17.8	28
45,800	9,772	21.3	33
60,000	15,168	25.3	38
85,600	25,920	30.3	42
109,400	36,630	33.5	45
162,400	62,600	38.6	49
Over 162,400	—	—	50

income taxation set forth by the Wilson-Gorman Tariff Act was violently challenged and had to be settled by a Supreme Court decision in 1895. Finally, in 1913, the Sixteenth Amendment was passed. The amendment reads as follows:

> **AUTHORIZING INCOME TAXES.** The Congress shall have power to lay and collect taxes on incomes, from whatever source derived, without apportionment among the several states, and without regard to any census or enumeration.

Section 2 of the Underwood-Simmons Tariff Act of 1913 provided for a 1 percent rate on taxable income with an exemption of $3,000 plus $1,000 more to a married head of household. Notice the concept of exempting the first several thousand dollars of income from taxes. Today, we have personal exemptions equal to $1,000 for every member of the family. A single person is allowed a $1,000 exemption, whereas the head of a family with a spouse and three children is allowed a $5,000 exemption.

The Underwood-Simmons Tariff Act also provided for a surtax that was levied progressively on income over $20,000 with a maximum total tax rate of 7 percent on income over $500,000. These taxes may seem paltry in comparison with today's rates, but they were considered quite large in those times. The concept of progressiveness was first introduced in 1913 and met with considerable debate, which raged for several years thereafter. Today, there is no doubt that progressiveness is here to stay, at least in principle. However, the apparently progressive nature of our personal income-tax system has declined somewhat in recent years. Up to 1961, the maximum tax rate was a whopping 91 percent. Today, it is only 50 percent.

LOOPHOLES

Our progressive tax schedule does not bear a very close relationship to what actually happens in the United States. Everybody knows that there are many **loopholes** in our tax laws. Attempts to close these loopholes have been resisted by those most strongly affected. When the 1969 Tax Reform Act was finally put into law, it had been altered with so many amendments that even attorneys and accountants had difficulty figuring out how to use it. Cynics renamed the 1969 legislation the "Lawyers' and Accountants' Relief Act;" it was certain that these professionals would see a great increase in the business of helping mere mortals figure out how to complete their tax forms.

LOOPHOLES
Legal methods by which your tax liabilities can be reduced.

Tax shelters or loopholes are devices that allow individuals in high-income brackets to take advantage on their personal income-tax returns of various business incentives, such as accelerated depreciation, the deduction of intangible oil-drilling expenses, capital gains preferential rates, and so on.

Individuals who benefit from tax loopholes are certainly partial to them. Additionally, Congress creates numerous tax loopholes in order to encourage specific types of activities. As an example, consider all the energy tax credits that are available now for individuals who engage in energy-conserving construction on their homes and office buildings. These may be properly labeled tax loopholes, but they also encourage Americans to conserve precious energy.

Prior to the 1976 Tax Reform Act, it was relatively easy for a group of, say, dentists to form a partnership to drill an oil well. From that moment on, they were able to pay for part or even all of their investment by deducting a combination of these special incentives just mentioned against their dental incomes. By merely giving up dollars that otherwise would go in taxes, or at least so it seems, they had a chance to bring in a well and strike it rich.

Using similar reasoning, many, many people have invested in tax shelters or loopholes. In 1965, partnerships in the major tax-shelter industries of livestock, real estate, petroleum, and natural gas reported $900 million in net losses and $1.4 billion in net profits. By 1971, losses were $4.2 billion, and profits were only $2.4 billion. The reason for this growth is quite obvious: The once sparsely populated upper-income brackets (say, 40 percent or 50 percent and up), where people start to look seriously for tax shelters have become increasingly crowded as inflationary forces and rising real incomes have begun to move much larger numbers of people into such high levels of taxable income.

The Tax Reform Act of 1976 sharply curtailed the number of loopholes that high-income individuals could enjoy. It eliminated the possibility of writing off a larger sum than one actually had invested in some project, such as cattle raising or oil drilling. It also increased taxes that had to be paid on any income that previously was sheltered from income taxes. It is fairly certain that the impact of the 1976 Act will be to reduce the size of the tax-shelter industry.

EXHIBIT 22–5
Federal Revenues Accounted for by Personal Income Taxes
During the Depression, individual income taxes accounted for less than 20 percent of federal revenues. Now, however, individual income taxes account for almost 45 percent of federal revenues. The importance of the personal income tax has increased.

FISCAL YEAR	% OF FEDERAL REVENUES ACCOUNTED FOR BY PERSONAL INCOME TAXES
1940	15.5
1944	39.5
1950	40.7
1955	45.1
1960	45.6
1965	43.8
1969	44.9
1971	43.0
1974	42.3
1976	44.6
1979	44.8
1982	44.6

SOURCE: U.S. Department of the Treasury.

Capital Gains

One of the biggest loopholes is personal-income taxation has concerned capital-gains rates. A capital gain is defined as the difference between the buying

Our progressive tax schedule does not bear a very close relationship to what actually happens in the United States.

and selling price of a capital asset, such as a stock, a bond, or a house. If you buy a share of Silver Syndicate Mining stock for thirteen dollars and, being a financial wizard, are able to sell it for sixty-seven dollars, your capital gains are fifty-four dollars. In the past, capital gains have been taxed at one-half a person's marginal tax rate, up to a maximum of only 25 percent. Recently, however, there have been changes in the tax laws so that capital gains are not treated so favorably. In order to qualify for the lower capital-gains rate, most assets must be owned for at least twelve months. Over the years, special interest groups have succeeded in getting more and more of their income classified as capital gains. Today, for example, the following types of income are eligible for preferential capital-gains-tax treatment: patent royalties, oil exploration and cattle raising.

THE IMPACT OF HIGHER TAX RATES ON THE WAY PEOPLE WORK AND PLAY

As inflation pushes more and more people into higher and higher tax brackets, they find themselves faced with a difficult dilemma—the more they make, the more the government takes from them. It is not surprising, then, that individuals have responded by altering some of their behavior patterns and also by seeking ways to avoid higher and higher taxes. We will look briefly at four such relatively new phenomena. They have to do with barter, do-it-yourself activities, buying consumer durables, and leisure.

The New Barter Society

Barter has existed in America at least since Peter Miniut convinced the Indians to trade Manhattan Island for some blankets and beads in 1626.[2] However, barter is an expensive way of making exchanges. It is much more rational to use money as a medium of exchange. Nonetheless, barter has recurred in recent years and not for the reasons you might think. It has little to do with the higher cost of living or inflation in general. Rather, it can basically be considered as a way to avoid paying income taxes.

Take a simple example. A dentist needs approximately $1,000 worth of legal services to set up a new pension plan; a lawyer needs approximately $1,000 worth of gold inlays to replace silver fillings. Assume that both are in the 50 percent tax bracket; thus, if they individually went out and purchased the needed services, each would have to earn $2,000 in order to have $1,000 after taxes to pay for those services. If, on the other hand, they make a trade—bartering legal services for dental care—no taxes will be paid if the deal is kept from the IRS. They each will save $1,000 in taxes but will end up with exactly the same amount of services they wished to buy in the first place.

The IRS is aware of the new barter society and looks at it with a wary eye. Of course, barter arrangements are difficult for the IRS to track down when people don't declare them. The law on this matter is clear, however: You are supposed to declare income realized in any form.

There is a growing number of barter groups throughout the nation. Useful Services Exchange is a nonprofit clearinghouse in Reston, Virginia. Learning Exchange in Evanston, Illinois, probably has 50,000 participants by now. Vacation Exchange Club (which we look at in Consumer Issue V) allows people to barter houses for their vacation time, as does Holiday Home Bureau. United Trade Club in San Jose, California, has almost 2,000 members, including doctors and lawyers. The Business Owners' Exchange in Minneapolis has about 500 members, including lawyers, dentists, and CPAs. For a $150 fee, members can trade their professional services, as well as cars, boats, and so on. The Business Owners' Exchange issues checks that look like commercial bank checks and sends members monthly statements listing sales and purchases, although no real money is exchanged.

2. Many historians believe that Minuit got ripped off by the Indians since they didn't even own Manhattan Island.

As inflation pushes more and more people into higher and higher tax brackets, they find themselves faced with a difficult dilemma—the more they make, the more the government takes from them.

Do-It-Yourself Activities

We already explained the tax advantages to the homeowner of do-it-yourself activities in Chapter 15. To repeat, rather than earning income that is taxable to hire someone to repair or maintain your home, you can provide the services yourself, not declare those do-it-yourself services as income, and avoid paying taxes. Consider a numerical example. You are in the 50 percent tax bracket. You have to have a room painted and the best price you can get from a professional painter is $500. You must earn $1,000 in order to have $500 after taxes to pay the painter. On the other hand, if you paint the room, yourself, you are not taxed on the implicit income you are earning—that is, the income from painting the room. If, for example, you give up only $750 worth of your time (before taxes), you will be better off by $250 (before taxes).

The do-it-yourself population has increased dramatically in the United States, in part because of rising repair and construction costs, but also because individuals have been put into higher tax brackets, thus making it more beneficial for them to avoid taxes in this manner.

Buying Consumer Durables

The less well-known effect of the high tax rate is the increased incentive for individuals to buy more consumer durable goods, such as boats, tennis courts, bigger homes, and sophisticated music systems, as opposed to their saving and investing more money in normal outlets. Consider a numerical example. A family wishing to save $10,000 has a large number of normal options for those savings: a savings and loan association account, a mutual fund, and so on. Let's assume that it can obtain a return before taxes of 10 percent per annum. Let's also assume that this family is in a 50 percent tax bracket; thus, its after-tax rate of return on that $10,000 saving will be only 5 percent, or $500 a year. Now consider that it has the option of having a tennis court installed for $10,000. A tennis court is a consumer durable item; it is a form of investment because it yields a stream of (implicit) income in the future in the form of the pleasure derived from playing tennis on it. Let us say that, in order to duplicate the services from a tennis court on its property, the family would have to fork over $1,000 a year to a private club around the corner. Thus, the implicit income stream or yield on the investment in the tennis court is approximately $1,000 a year. However, that income is not reported to the IRS. According to current IRS rulings and tax statutes, the implicit income or service flow from owner-used consumer durable goods, such as tennis courts, is nontaxable. The rate of return, then, of investing in a tennis court will be higher for this family than investing in bonds, for example.

Looked at in this manner, it is not surprising that individuals are buying more and bigger boats, more tennis courts, more expensive stereos, more luxury cars, and larger houses. This is particularly true for high-income individuals who face high tax rates.

The Leisure World

Finally, one of the easiest and perhaps most pleasureful ways to avoid paying income taxes is to work less and, therefore, earn less income. Taking a longer vacation, choosing a job with fewer hours, quitting a second job, or retiring at an earlier age—these are all ways individuals can reduce their tax burden. Essentially, they substitute taxable income with leisure, which is a form of implicit income and is, as yet, nontaxed. We can predict that, as more individuals are pushed into higher income-tax brackets, work effort will fall accordingly.

One of the easiest and perhaps most pleasureful ways to avoid paying income taxes is to work less and, therefore, earn less income.

SPECIAL INTEREST GROUPS

When we analyze the behavior of businesspeople, we generally assume that they will do whatever is in their own best interests. Of course, there are exceptions, but it is best not to count on them. If we look at individual economic behavior, we generally are correct in assuming that people act in their own best interests and not necessarily in the best interests of society. This is not to say that people are inherently bad; it's just human nature. If we take these same ideas about human behavior and apply them to how politicians and government officials will act, we realize that it will not be in *their* best interests to look out *only* for the general welfare. You and I as consumers are a diffuse group made up of millions and millions of people with millions and millions of different tastes, wants, and needs. How could politicians satisfy all of us? Impossible, right? They can, however, satisfy **special interest groups.** That's what our political system is all about: Special interest groups have very defined, clear-cut interests in specific pieces of government legislation. Because they can see the direct benefit and measure it in dollars and cents, they know how much it is worth for them to spend in order to get that legislation passed. If we were to analyze the legislation now on the books, we would find that most of it is indeed sponsored by special interest groups and, in fact, benefits special interest groups only.

SPECIAL INTEREST GROUPS Groups in society that have a special interest in common. Special interest groups generally attempt to influence government legislation to benefit their own particular groups.

When it was discovered, for example, that various milk associations contributed perhaps $2 million to the reelection campaign of President Nixon, it was also discovered that, just before this contribution was given, milk-support prices were raised, benefitting the dairy industry by about $600 million. This kind of behavior is exactly what you would expect, because special interest groups are going to look out for their own interests; and if it means influencing government actions, that is what they will do. As long as you are aware of this, then you, as a citizen, can guard against it by considering carefully all propositions and referenda on which you are asked to vote. If you first ask the question, "What special interest group is this legislation for?," and then see if, in fact, it benefits you, you will be on your way to a good analysis. If, however, you start reading the slogans attached to the proposed or passed legislation, you are going to get lost in contradictory and often meaningless arguments. The same is true if you want to decide whether or not to vote for a particular incumbent candidate. You can look at his or her legislative record and find out to which special interest groups he or she has catered. This does not mean, however, that you as an individual will not benefit by special interest legislation. We showed, for example, that usury laws will benefit all those people with very good credit ratings who will continue to get credit at the lower interest rate. If you happen to be a plumber, you obviously are going to benefit

When we analyze the behavior of businesspeople, we generally assume that they will do whatever is in their own best interests.

from very strict building codes that require sophisticated plumbing for all new houses.

Nor should it surprise you that regulatory agencies in general end up working on behalf of the regulated firms instead of on behalf of you, the consumer. Consumers generally know nothing about the industry in question because the technical details are too complicated, and it would not be worth their while to learn anything about them. However, the firms themselves know the most about their own industry and have the most incentive to influence the regulators. Hence, few are shocked to find out that the Interstate Commerce Commission has worked in the past to preserve non-competition in the transportation industry. It should not surprise you that the Civil Aeronautics Board fought tooth and nail against competition in the airline industry for many years. It should not surprise you that just about all regulatory agencies act to dampen, instead of encourage, competition. You, the consumer, generally lose out by this government/business marriage. However, in some cases you may win. It is up to you to decide, by analyzing the benefits and the costs of different types of regulatory activities.

CAN WE IMPROVE OUR TAX SYSTEM?

Those of you who have tried to fill out a federal income-tax form know that our tax system is incredibly complicated. When one U.S. president's life-long valet asked him to help out with his taxes, the president could not because they were too complicated to figure out. It is estimated that the cost of filling out forms, measured in people's time, is somewhere between $5 billion and $15 billion a year! Additionally, there is all the money spent on accountants and lawyers. Why has all this happened? Just as you would expect, because of special interest groups getting special benefits for themselves and thus further complicating our tax laws.

One reason special interest groups find it worthwhile to attempt to get special legislation that reduces their tax burden is the high progressive income-tax rate. The higher the rate you pay, the greater incentive you have to find a loophole or, as a member of a group with other people in the same situation, to influence tax legislation to benefit your group. If all taxes were only 2 percent, nobody would try very hard to find loopholes. But if you are in the 50 percent tax bracket, you had better believe it is worthwhile to find one. Every dollar of income you can have declared nontaxable nets you 50 cents in cash, for that is the tax you do not have to pay. With the incredible numbers of loopholes and complexities, our so-called progressive tax system really is not progressive at all, or at least not very. Given this fact, there are some obvious tax reforms that could benefit the majority of Americans. When we talk here about tax reform, we certainly do not mean the kind that goes through Congress every few years. The tax reform act passed in 1969 benefitted only lawyers and accountants and just about everybody else lost. As we already pointed out, another tax reform act was passed in 1976 that eliminated many of the loopholes, but it is so complicated that, again, mainly and accountants have benefitted. Another tax reform act was passed in 1981 and yet another in 1982.

The only meaningful way to talk about tax reform is to forget about all special interest groups and do something drastic but simple, such as the following proposal I have put forth for a number of years now.

1. Eliminate all deductions except an absolute minimum number of bona fide business expenses.
2. Increase the exemption to say, the poverty line of income, meaning that the first $3,000 or $4,000 of income is not taxed at all.
3. Establish a uniform 15 to 20 percent proportionate tax rate on all income, no matter where it is from and no matter who earns it.

This is certainly drastic compared with what we now have. Notice, however, that the tax rate of 15 to 20 percent is lower than the actual taxes paid as a percentage of total income right now in the United States. How could this be? If you eliminate the high, complicated progressive tax system, you eliminate people's wasted efforts to avoid taxes. There would be a proportionately higher degree of work effort and higher national income on which to base our taxes. That is how we actually could lower the overall tax rate and still get as much revenue as we now get.

Believe it or not, many rich people would be against lowering tax rates because they know that, with all the existing loopholes, they pay very few taxes anyway. Some pay much less than 15 to 20 percent of their total income.

Simplifying the tax system could avoid so many complications, perhaps make life so much easier for all of us, reduce the incentive for any of us to cheat, and increase the amount of work many of us want to do, because our tax rates would be lower. Because we do not have a progressive tax system anyway, it is ridiculous to argue against a uniform nonprogressive tax system on the basis of the "need" for "soaking the rich." We do, in reality, get them to pay a high percentage of their income in taxes anyway.

Unfortunately, you and I still have to suffer. Pure tax reform is a long way off. Until then, it behooves you to know the ins and outs of tax reporting and tax payments. There is nothing wrong with your taking advantage of every single legal way to reduce the taxes you owe your government. You have a right to spend what is legally yours. After all, you earned it.

SUMMARY

1. The three best-known principles of taxation are the benefits principle, the ability-to-pay principle, and the sacrifice principle.
2. In both the benefits and ability-to-pay principles, an additional assumption is necessary to justify a system of progressive taxation in which progressively more is taken away from those who earn higher incomes. This additional assumption is that benefits and the ability to pay increase *more* than in proportion to income.
3. In a progressive tax system, you pay a higher tax rate only on the last dollars earned. For example, someone in the 50 percent tax bracket in our progressive tax system does *not* pay 50 percent of all income in taxes; rather that person pays 50 percent on the last tax bracket amount of income only.
4. The personal federal income tax, the most important source of government revenues in this country, accounts for about 45 percent of all federal revenues.

5. Tax loopholes or shelters are usually available only for higher-income earners. In other words, the benefit of a tax loophole is directly proportional to your marginal tax bracket. And unless you are making a high income, your marginal tax bracket isn't very high.
6. Capital-gains tax rates are usually lower than tax rates on income. That is why it is beneficial to have any of your income received as a capital gain.
7. In analyzing any prospective government legislation, you must realize that it probably has been influenced by special interest groups. Therefore, informed voters must analyze the legislation to see who will benefit and who will pay. Very little legislation proposed and supported by special interest groups is made with the general welfare in mind. In fact, most of this legislation by necessity must hurt the consumer. Many restrictions on economic activities are of this nature, as are the subsidies legislated for particular industrial and agricultural groups in our society.
8. It would be possible to improve our complicated tax system by eliminating all loopholes, instituting a large exemption, and using a flat proportional tax of 15 to 20 percent.
9. Individuals are now avoiding taxes by bartering goods and services, taking more leisure, engaging in more do-it-yourself activities, and purchasing more consumer durable goods whose implicit income stream is not taxed.

QUESTIONS FOR THOUGHT AND DISCUSSION

1. Why do you think the concept of progressive taxation is so popular in the United States?
2. Which aspect of government expenditures do you think is most important for your own well-being?
3. Which principle of taxation do you think best justifies progressive taxation?
4. Would you prefer to have most taxes collected from individuals or from corporations?
5. How do tax loopholes hurt or help you as a consumer?
6. Do you think tax loopholes should exist?
7. Why has our progressive tax system failed to eliminate income differences in the United States since World War II?
8. Is there any way to prevent special interest groups from affecting government legislation?

THINGS TO DO

1. Get a copy of next year's individual income-tax schedule from your local office of the Internal Revenue Service. Compare it with one from ten years ago. Is there any difference?
2. Call a local stockbroker and ask if he or she has any recommendations about tax shelters. Have the stockbroker send you copies of information on any tax shelters for sale. Do you think they would be beneficial to you if you were making $5,000 a year? $50,000 a year? $500,000 a year?

SELECTED READINGS

"Any Chance for a Flat Rate Income Tax?" *Changing Times,* August 1982, p. 8.

Drake, K. "How the States Are Cutting and Sometimes Raising Taxation." *Money,* February 1980, pp. 54–55.

Dunn, D. H. "The Paperwork—and Worse—Facing High-Bracket Taxpayers." *Business Week,* December 6, 1982, p. 111.

"Federal Taxes Going Up." *Consumers' Research Magazine,* November 1982, pp. 15–18.

Flanagan, William. "Give Me Shelter." *Esquire,* January 1980, pp. 11–12.

"A Loss of Faith in the Progressive Tax." *Business Week,* September 6, 1982, p. 15.

Meyer, P. S. "Tax Shelters That Never Leak." *Forbes,* November 22, 1982, p. 244.

Mohs, M. "Rendering unto God Instead of Caesar." *Money,* February 1980, pp. 56–58.

People and Taxes. Washington, D.C.: Ralph Nader's Research Group (monthly newspaper).

Stern, Phillip M. *The Rape of the Taxpayer.* New York: Random House, 1973.

Your Federal Income Tax. Washington, D.C.: Superintendent of Documents (published annually).

Consumer ISSUE U

EASING YOUR TAX BURDEN

GLOSSARY

ZERO BRACKET AMOUNT (ZBA)—That amount of income not subject to federal personal income taxes.

Supreme Court Judge Learned Hand once said, "Anyone may so arrange his affairs that his taxes shall be as low as possible; he is not bound to choose that pattern which will best pay the Treasury; there is not even a patriotic duty to increase one's taxes." In other words, you have every right as a taxpayer to minimize the taxes you pay. In this short Consumer Issue, it will be impossible to give you a complete course in how to ease your tax burden. If you are really interested in getting all the details, you might want to buy one of the various tax books, such as Lasser's *Tax Guide*, H&R Block's *Income Tax Workbook*, or The Research Institute of America's *Individual Tax Return Guide*, all of which are published yearly. You can also get *Your Federal Income Tax* free from the Internal Revenue Service in your area. You can get numerous booklets from the Internal Revenue Service for every imaginable loophole for which you might be eligible. If that is not enough for you, you can buy the services of sophisticated tax lawyers or certified public accountants.

THE DO'S AND DON'TS OF HIRING TAX HELP

There are literally hundreds of thousands of individuals who sell their services as tax-return preparers. Many of them work out of national franchises that advertise heavily. As tax laws become more complicated, the tax-preparation business is bound to grow. To avoid deception in buying these services, follow these rules.

1. Be wary of tax preparers who promise to give you a check for your refund immediately. The preparer is probably offering you a loan on which you will pay interest.

2. Never sign a blank return.

3. Never sign a return prepared in pencil; it can be changed later.

4. Never allow your refund check to be mailed to the preparer.

5. Be wary of tax advisors who "guarantee" refunds, who want a percentage of the refund, or who supposedly "know all the angles."

6. Avoid a tax preparer who advises you to overstate deductions, omit income, or claim fictitious dependents.

7. Make sure the tax preparer signs the return he or she prepares and includes his or her address and tax identification number. (You, however, are legally responsible for virtually all errors on your return, no matter who fills it out, unless there is a blatant case of fraud brought against the tax preparer.)

8. Be wary of preparers who claim they will make good any amounts due because of a mistake on your return. Usually the preparer means that he or she will pay the penalty charge, for the tax money due must come from you.

9. Find out the educational background of the preparer. Has that person a degree in accounting?

10. Use only preparers who have permanent addresses so you will have no difficulty finding that person a few months later if problems develop.

TAKING THE ZBA

If you have no expenses that qualify as legitimate deductions, you merely take the **zero bracket amount, or ZBA,** as a deduction. The government allows a flat $2,300 for single persons and a flat $3,400 for married persons filing joint returns as a standard deduction. Thus, a minimum tax rate of 11 percent is applied to the first dollars over the ZBA.

RECORDKEEPING

But if your legitimate deductions are greater than the ZBA, you must keep good records to support those deductions and to take advantage of all the benefits in the tax laws. If the IRS conducts a tax audit and you cannot adequately substantiate the deductions you have taken on your tax returns, they will be disallowed, and you may have to pay a penalty or, at a bare minimum, interest on the taxes that are now overdue. You have to keep supporting documents for at least three years after the date your return was filed, or for at least three years from the date your tax was paid, whichever occurred later. In fact, it is a good idea to keep them even longer, just in case you want to be sure of what you did, although they cannot legally be subpoenaed by the IRS after three years unless fraud is involved.

What Kinds of Records

Remember, when in doubt, keep a record. You should have records for all medical expenses, for all business expenses, for all taxes paid—everything that could possibly be used to reduce your effective tax burden. The best way to keep records, of course, is to write checks. If you do any amount of business for which the expenses are tax deductible, you also should keep a complete diary of those expenses. If you move because of a job change, you are allowed to deduct moving expenses; make sure you have records for all of those. When you sell your house, keep a record of that transaction.

The best way to keep records, of course, is to do it regularly. Every month when you go through your check stubs to balance your statement, separate the checks into individual envelopes labeled for business expenses, telephone, medical expenses, and so on. If, in fact, you can prove that you use part of your home as a place of business, then you must keep records on all the expenses on your house; rental or mortgage payments, heating bills, light bills, telephone bills, electricity bills. Again, the best way to do this is to pay everything by check. The next best way is to keep a receipt for everything you pay for in cash. Here is where charge cards are also useful. You get a receipt every time a charge is made on your card; if it is a receipt for a tax-deductible item, it will be useful for recordkeeping purposes.

Other Pointers on Recordkeeping

Here are some other pointers that will help you, come tax-paying time.

1. Always identify your sources of income.
2. Keep adequate records in order to take advantage of capital gain and loss provisions. This would apply to the purchase and sale of any asset, such as stocks and bonds.
3. Make sure you explain to yourself on a piece of paper all the items reported in an income-tax return, so you will be ready in case of an audit.
4. You must keep records indefinitely on the purchase, sale, and expenses of remodeling a home. Eventually you may have to pay capital-gains taxes when you sell a house and don't buy a new one—say, when you retire.[3] In order to reduce those capital-gains taxes, you must be able to prove that you spent money in remodeling or adding to your house.
5. Retain copies of your filed tax returns as part of your records. They can help you prepare future returns, particularly if you engage in income averaging, a method used to reduce your taxes.

What If You Are Uncertain?

Whenever you are uncertain about the acceptability of the deduction, you might consider taking a chance. Many of the deductions are subject to interpretation by the IRS; that is, they are ambiguous, and, if you are audited, you stand as good a chance of winning your case as not winning it. At the most, because this action does not involve fraud or anything illegal, you pay only an interest-rate penalty on the taxes due. At least until 1983, that interest rate was somewhat less than the rate of inflation, so you really did not lose out by owing the government money for back taxes. However, it might prove inconvenient to pay any interest fine in one lump sum. You have to keep that in mind, too.

If, in fact, you do not think you have many deductions at all, it is generally not worth your while to agonize over your tax form. That is, you take a standard ZBA deduction, fill in the rest of the lines, and pay your taxes. That way you do not have to keep any records except those of the income you made. That certainly simplifies life, but it may not ease your tax burden. It only eases your tax work.

MINIMIZING YOUR TAXES

Exhibit U–1 lists possible deductions you can use to help reduce your federal income taxes. You, of course, may find others in some of the many excellent guides to filling out your tax forms. But, remember, it certainly is not worthwhile for you to spend weeks filling out tax forms in order to save a mere twenty-five dollars. You must figure out at what point you should *stop* trying to reduce your tax burden. This, of course, is a function of your marginal tax bracket. If you are in the 14 percent bracket, every extra dollar you can find as a legal deduction saves you only fourteen cents. If it takes you an extra hour to find $10 more of deductions, the benefit to you of those $10 of deductions is only $1.40. Is your time worth more than $1.40 an hour?

AMERICANS ARE HONEST

Americans in general are very honest. The IRS estimates that fully 95 percent pay their lawful due to the government. Being honest, though, does not prevent you from taking advantage of what is legally your right. That is, you can be very honest and report all income but, at the

3. Currently, though, you are exempted from taxes on the first $100,000 of such gains if you are over fifty-five.

Accounting and auditing expenses paid for preparation of tax returns Alterations and repairs on business or income-producing property Attending conventions Attorneys' fees in connection with your trade or employment Automobile expenses incurred during business trips, trips for charitable organizations, and trips for medical care Automobile expenses if used for your business, pro-rated Automobile license(s) Business expenses of employees in excess amounts received as reimbursements Campaign contributions Charitable contributions (cannot exceed 50 percent of your income)	Child-care expenses (This now applies to divorced and separated people, as well as couples where one is a full-time worker and the other is either part-time, going to school full-time, or looking for a job. There is a maximum tax credit of $720, $1,440 for two or more children. These amounts decrease as your adjusted gross income increases.) Condominium owners' interest and realty taxes Depreciation of property used in business Dues for professional societies and organized labor unions Educational expenses if required to maintain your employment or professional standards	Fees paid to secure employment Home office (This is only for individuals who have a separate place used only as an office and also a place where the individual receives clients. It was greatly restricted by the 1976 Tax Reform Act.) General sales taxes (state and local) Income tax, state and city Interest you paid or finance charges for any loans or retail installment contracts Medical expenses in excess of 3 percent of adjusted gross income Moving expenses Property taxes Safe deposit box expenses

EXHIBIT U–1
Possible Income Deductions That Can Lower Your Tax Liability

same time, make sure that you take all legitimate deductions. You owe that to yourself and to your family.

HOW TO AVOID A TAX AUDIT

Most, if not all, taxpayers wish to avoid being audited by the IRS. It is time-consuming, often traumatic, and may cost you more tax dollars. Thus, astute taxpayers try to minimize the chances of being audited when they fill out their returns. Exhibit U–2 shows the percentage of individual returns that are audited, depending on income and whether deductions are itemized. If you fill out a simple Form 1040A with no itemized deductions and your income is less than $10,000, there are seven chances out of a thousand that your return will be audited.

What Prompts an Audit?

The most common reason for an audit concerns unallowable deductions—deducting normal living expenses, for example. In fiscal 1981, 71 percent of all Internal Revenue Service Center audits were made for this reason.

Audits also are made when an individual who is not qualified to do so uses head-of-household tax tables. For example, two formerly married individuals with joint custody of their children can't both claim to be the head of the household.

Individuals are also audited because:

1. Savings and loan associations, employers, and Social Security wage reports revealed information that did not agree with the tax return.
2. More than one return was filed under the same Social Security number.
3. There was a discrepancy between the state income-tax return reported by state tax agencies and the federal income-tax return.
4. The wrong tax table was used.
5. There were computation errors.

Beating the Computer

A large number of audits are triggered by computer scoring on audit potentials. The computer scores depend on the size of itemized deductions. If you claim a specific deduction that is much greater than the average for your income class, you can be almost certain of being audited. Exhibit U–3 shows the figures for the average amount of deductions based on returns. These averages do not give you the right to deduct the specified amounts. You are allowed to claim only actual payments for taxes, contributions, interest, and so on. On the other hand, if your deductions are significantly less than the average, that may mean you are overlooking something (or are healthy and, perhaps, frugal).

NONBUSINESS INCOME	FIELD OR OFFICE AUDIT
Under $10,000	Standard deduction, or ZBA, is used, 0.7 percent (7 out of 1,000)
Under $10,000	Itemized deductions are claimed, 4.3 percent (43 out of 1,000)
$10,000–$50,000	2.5 percent (25 out of 1,000)
$50,000 and up	12.4 percent (124 out of 1,000)

EXHIBIT U–2
Percentage of Audited Individual Returns

Backing Up Your Deductions

The computer, of course, can't support material that you present for deductions, but the human classifiers at the IRS will spot it. If, for example, you have extremely high medical expenses one year, make a separate schedule of them and attach copies of all the bills to your return. This will assist the classifier and perhaps save you a trip to the local field office. On the other hand, it's inappropriate to overdo the extra schedules. To reduce your chances of being audited, verify, when you file, anything that might stand out and raise questions.

Human classifiers can quickly spot inconsistencies, so avoid them if possible. Your income after deductions must be enough to buy such essentials as food and clothing, so don't overdo the deductions. And employee or business expenses must be appropriate for your occupation.

HOW TO SURVIVE A TAX AUDIT

Should you receive in the mail a note from the IRS that says, "We are examining your federal income tax return for the above year(s) and we find we need additional information to verify your correct tax," don't despair. Many individuals are audited randomly, even though their returns seem to be in order. Prior to your scheduled audit, remember that personal attitude helps in a successful negotiation with the auditor. Therefore, you should:

1. **Be prepared.** Know the facts in your case and, if possible, the law relating to the specific deductions being questioned.
2. **Be businesslike.** Answer the letter from the IRS promptly and help the agent dispose of major issues quickly during the initial interview.
3. **Be cooperative.** Answer all questions, but do not volunteer unsolicited information, unless, of course, the agent has overlooked something that could alter things in your favor.

Using Those Records

When you are audited, you realize how important recordkeeping is. An IRS auditor has the right to disallow completely unsubstantiated itemized deductions or to reduce them to what he or she might consider "reasonable." When you are asked to verify specific itemized deductions, provide only the information relating to those deductions, and provide it as completely as possible. You don't want to give the impression that you are hiding something.

For most individuals who are audited, negotiations with the IRS agent proceed smoothly. Once an agreement is reached, you will sign a form stating that you will pay the taxes you owe. See Exhibit U–4 for ten do's and don'ts when you get called in for an audit.

If You Disagree with the Agent

If you don't agree with the agent's proposal, you can take your dispute to a higher IRS level, either a district

EXHIBIT U–3
Average Deductions Claimed on Adjusted Gross Income (1981)

ADJUSTED GROSS INCOME	MEDICAL, DENTAL	STATE, LOCAL TAXES	CONTRI-BUTIONS	INTEREST	CASUALTY, THEFT
$ 10,000–$ 12,000	$1,413	$ 1,056	$ 678	$ 2,523	$2,149
12,000–$ 16,000	1,235	1,233	$ 670	2,519	1,655
16,000–$ 20,000	938	1,414	659	2,685	830
20,000–$ 25,000	756	1,718	670	2,887	1,186
25,000–$ 30,000	672	1,983	697	3,122	1,043
30,000–$ 40,000	605	2,496	834	3,483	806
40,000–$ 50,000	553	3,211	1,079	4,282	891
50,000–$ 75,000	676	4,400	1,567	5,586	1,126
75,000–$100,000	859	6,637	2,512	8,312	1,003
100,000–$200,000	1,260	10,013	4,807	12,170	2,182

Here are some hints from tax advisor Paul N. Strassels on how to act if the IRS calls you in for an audit.

Do dress the way you normally do for business—whether in a finely tailored suit or in jeans. But don't flaunt wealth with expensive jewelry.

Do act natural—but if you can't help being visibly jittery, then tell the auditor you're nervous.

Do take the audit seriously. Don't joke about it with the auditor or be flip in your answers.

Do bring along a tax advisor, and let him do the talking whenever you can.

Don't antagonize the auditor by being late.

Don't volunteer information, be chatty, or go to lunch with the auditor.

Don't walk in without any records—or try to overload the auditor with material. It can backfire on you.

Don't rush the auditor or allow yourself to be rushed.

Don't try for sympathy, plead that "everyone does it," or lash out at taxes in general. It's a waste of time.

Don't underestimate the auditor or be shocked if "he" is a she.

SOURCE: *U.S News & World Report*, March 24, 1980, p. 81; and Paul N. Strassels (with Robert Wool), *All You Need to Know about the IRS* (New York: Random House, 1979).

EXHIBIT U-4
Ten Do's and Don'ts

conference or an appellate division conference. Or you can ask that a ninety-day letter be issued and postpone settlement negotiations until it is issued.

Generally, when the amount in dispute is more than $2,500, a district conference is in order. If you aren't satisfied with the outcome of the district conference, you can go to the appellate division of the IRS.

The Next Step Is Tax Court

If you are still not satisfied, you can request a date in the tax court. If your dispute involves no more than $1,500 in additional taxes for any one year, you can go to the small-tax-case division of tax court. In these courts, tax cases are settled informally and as quickly as possible.

Small-Tax-Case Division

There are no formal rules of evidence or formal written opinion in this court. Consequently, there is no need for detailed findings of opinions and fact. Each case in the small-tax-case division is heard by commissioners rather than judges. You, the dissatisfied taxpayer, can petition the court; that is, you can represent yourself, so you don't need the expensive services of an attorney.

Your chances of obtaining a decision in your favor are quite good. Latest data indicate that 72 percent of all cases were decided at least partially in favor of the taxpayer.

SUMMARY

1. Tax guides, such as Lasser's *Tax Guide* or H&R Block's *Income Tax Workbook*, are helpful for individuals who prepare their own returns. A number of these guides become available in most bookstores throughout the country at the beginning of the year.

2. If you have complicated tax problems, it is best to seek the advice of a certified public accountant and/or a tax lawyer. However, weigh the costs with the potential benefits; good tax advice does not come cheap.

3. If, in fact, you do not anticipate being able to deduct a large number of items from your income before you pay taxes, it may be economical for you to use the standard ZBA deduction and a short form for filing your taxes.

4. If you decide to fill out a long form, you must have a record for everything you decide is a legitimate deduction.

5. The easiest way to keep records is to write checks for everything. Note, however, that, in many cases, you must substantiate those checks with receipts.

6. If you decide to take business expenses, you must keep a diary of expenses for which you do not obtain receipts, such as meals with business colleagues.

7. Whenever you are uncertain about the legitimacy of a deduction, it is best to decide in your own favor; generally, deductions are subject to the interpretation of the IRS agent who might audit your returns, and his or her interpretation could be the same as yours.

8. Your local office of the Internal Revenue Service will send you many free booklets explaining all facets of our taxing system. Additionally, for small fees you can have some of the more complete tax guides written by the IRS sent to you directly. If there is no local IRS office nearby, write the nearest major city for these booklets.

QUESTIONS FOR THOUGHT AND DISCUSSION

1. When would it not pay to keep meticulous records for tax purposes?

2. When is it definitely a waste of time to have a CPA fill out your tax returns?
3. What is the cost to you of deducting an expense from your income before paying taxes if a tax audit determines that the deduction is not legitimate?
4. "It is cheaper to give things to charity than to sell them." How could this be true?

THINGS TO DO

1. Send away for free booklets from the Internal Revenue Service. See if you can find information that will be useful for your own tax planning.
2. Try to find out from the IRS what percentage of taxpayers are audited every year.
3. Buy one of the best-selling tax guides. Read through it to see if you can get a general feeling for how our tax system works. Do you think we have a complicated system or not?
4. Write down a list of reforms you think would make ours a better system.

SELECTED READINGS

How to Prepare Your Personal Income Tax Return. Englewood Cliffs, N.J.: Prentice-Hall (published annually).

Jakobs, Vernon, and Schoeneman, Charles W., *The Taxpayer's Audit Survival Manual.* Wilmington, Delaware: Enterprise Publishing, 1982 (725 Market St.; Wilmington, Delaware 19801).

Lasser, J. K. *Your Income Tax.* New York: Simon and Schuster (published annually).

Ober, Stuart. *Everybody's Guide to Tax Shelters: How to Avoid Taxes Like a Millionaire.* New York, Dial Press, 1982.

Price, M. R. *In This Corner, the IRS.* New York: Dell, 1981.

Schnepper, James. *How to Pay Zero Taxes: Over One Hundred Ways to Reduce Your Taxes—to Nothing!* Reading, Mass.: Addison-Wesley, 1982.

Sprouse, Mary L. *How to Survive a Tax Audit.* Baltimore: Penguin Books, 1982.

Steiner, Barry, and Kennedy, David W. *Perfectly Legal 275 Foolproof Methods for Paying Less Taxes.* New York: Warner, 1982.

CHAPTER
LEISURE, RECREATION, AND TRAVEL

23

America has been called the consumer society, but another name that might be equally applicable is the leisure society. . . . The average American puts in not much more than thirty-five hours a week, at best.

CHAPTER REVIEW

- What are the complements of leisure activities?
- How have Americans used their increased leisure time?
- What is the true cost of owning a recreational vehicle?
- How you do obtain information on possible leisure activities?

America has been called the consumer society, but another name that might be equally applicable is the leisure society. We see in Exhibit 23–1 the dramatic reduction in the number of hours worked per week for the average wage earner in the United States for the last 120 years. It wasn't that many years ago when individuals actually worked seven days a week, ten hours a day. There still may be those who work that long and even more, although the average American puts in not much more than thirty-five hours a week fifty weeks a year, at best. That means that there are more hours available in which recreational activities can be pursued.

SUBSTITUTES AND COMPLEMENTS

SUBSTITUTE
Something that can be used or done in place of something else.

Lesiure time activities or leisure time per se is a **substitute** for something else—work time. Given that there is a time constraint in everyone's existence, the more you work, the less time you have for leisure. Hence, a decision to have more leisure time is necessarily also a decision to work less and, therefore, to have less money income. That means that, as a nation, we have chosen to substitute leisure for money income. If the average workweek in the United States were fifty hours a week, individuals could take home more money income but would have less time to themselves for leisure activity.

COMPLEMENT
Something that is used along with something else, such as recreational equipment used during leisure time.

Increased leisure time has brought with it the increased expenditure of consumer dollars on recreational activities. Exhibit 23–2 shows the dramatic rise in recreational expenditures as a percent of gross national product. This is occurring because recreational equipment and services are **complements** to leisure time. They are used together. If individuals have more leisure time and wish to spend it skiing, playing tennis, playing golf, or taking photographs, they will purchase the complementary items associated with those activities. We can predict, therefore, that, as we become a more leisure-oriented society, expenditures on recreation will be an increasing part of total consumer spending.

EXHIBIT 23–1
Hours Worked Over Time

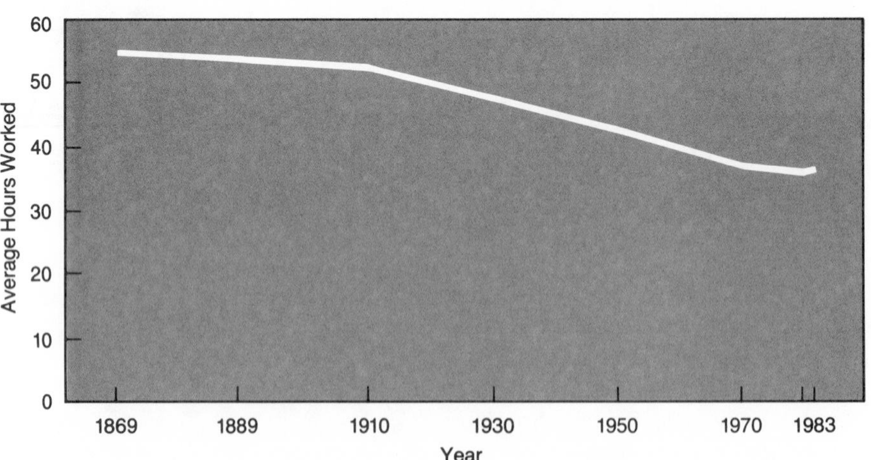

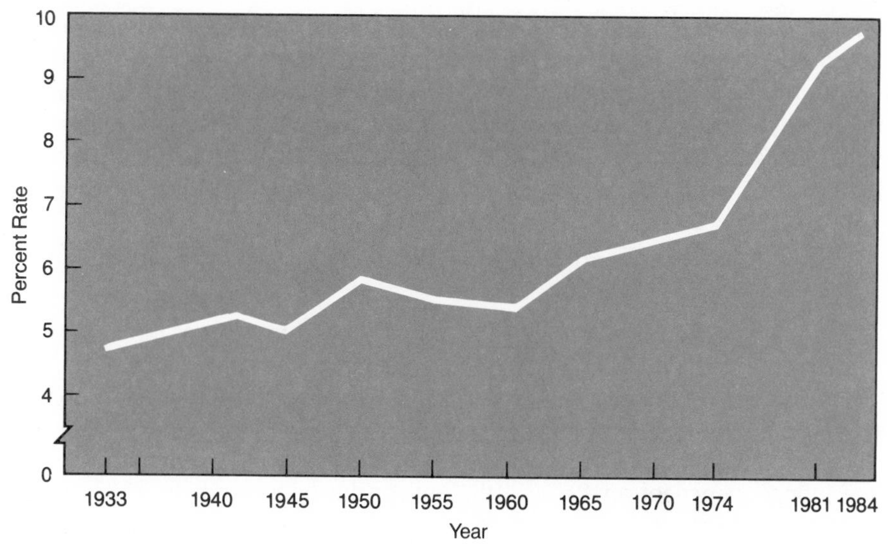

EXHIBIT 23–2
Percent of Personal Consumption Expenditures Devoted to Recreation

Back in 1933, only 4.7 percent of present consumption expenditures were devoted to recreation. This percent has been rising ever since, today reaching 9 percent or more. (The 1984 figure is an estimate.)

Vacations

In 1874, the average American worked 338 days out of every year. Today, the average American works only 240 days. The number of legal holidays and the amount of paid vacation time have increased dramatically in the last century. Vacations have become a part of every American's life style. However, we still have a way to go to catch up with some of our European counterparts. Even though Americans have been richer than, for example, people living in France, we have not yet fully accepted the idea of everyone taking one month's vacation every summer. Traditionally, in France, all factories close down during the month of August, when residents of urban areas flock to resorts. To avoid crowding at these resort areas, some French people now take their vacations in July or September. Two weeks has been the standard vacation time for Americans for a number of years, although that is changing slowly. It appears that we have preferred to take our vacation time in smaller doses—four-day weekends and the like—as opposed to taking it all at once in the middle of the summer.

Expanding leisure time and expanding vacations go hand in hand. We can, therefore, predict that planning vacations will become an increasingly important part of family decision making.

Reducing the Number of Days Worked

In the beginning of the 1970s, many sociologists and labor-market experts predicted that there would be an end to the five-day workweek, just as there was an end to the seven-day and then the six-day workweek. They pointed out that more and more workers were going to be willing to work ten hours a day for four days, rather than eight hours a day for five days. A number of companies actually attempted an experiment by offering their workers the four-

In 1874, the average American worked 338 days out of every year. Today, the average American works only 240 days.

day, nine-hour-per-day workweek. Some of them still have it, and their workers are satisfied; others found that they did not like having an extra full day to fill up during the working part of the year. Thus, we might predict that, rather than taking longer weekends, workers are going to opt for regular workweeks with longer vacations, so they get all their leisure activity in an uninterrupted period.

Vacations and RVs

Expanding vacation opportunities for Americans led to a boom in the sales of recreational vehicles (RVs). The trend flattened out abruptly, however, and even sank during the energy crisis of 1973–74. After that, the trend boomed again until 1979–80, when the relative price of gasoline started to skyrocket. Even when higher gasoline prices were posted, numerous Americans preferred the independence of an RV and the call of the open road. In 1983, when gasoline prices started falling and economy was in a recession, RV sales started to increase.

A family faces an interesting consumer decision-making problem when it contemplates the purchase of a new or used RV, which is a consumer durable (discussed in Chapter 16 and Consumer Issue N). It is similar to the decision to buy an automobile, which was discussed in Chapter 17 and Consumer Issue P. In other words, a cost/benefit analysis must be done in order to determine whether it is appropriate to buy a recreational vehicle. There are a number of very expensive aspects of RVs to be considered.

RVS ARE LEFT IDLE MUCH OF THE TIME. The important difference between an RV and many home appliances or the family automobile is that the RV is used only during vacation times or long weekends. Generally, it is too bulky and consumes too much gas to be used as a second car by a family. Thus, the "down" time may be so considerable as to make an investment in an RV quite uneconomical. Consider the extreme case when an RV sits in the driveway depreciating for fifty weeks out of the year and is then used for the family's annual two-week vacation in the woods. The benefits of owning that RV consist of the service flow during a two-week period, rather than a fifty-two week period. It is possible to count as part of the service flow the pleasure of seeing the RV in the driveway for the remaining fifty weeks, but, for most people, that pleasure is not tremendously valuable.

DEPRECIATION AND OPPORTUNITY COST. The RV depreciates whether it is being used or not, just like an automobile or a stereo or a refrigerator. During the first year, the depreciation is the greatest; thus, the purchase of a new RV means that the new owner will find that the RV's resale value may be lowered 25 percent or more one year hence. This is a true and actual cost of owning that RV for its first year and must be included in the cost/benefit calculations.

Equally important, particularly given that the RV will not be used very much during the year, is the opportunity cost of owning it. We talked about opportunity cost in Consumer Issue C when we referred to the time parents must spend raising children. We also talked about opportunity cost when we discussed doing a cost/benefit analysis before making a decision to buy an appliance (see Chapter 16). When deciding to purchase an RV for $16,000, the prospective owner must realize that, even if he or she pays cash for that RV, there is an implicit interest charge every year. That $16,000 could earn interest in a money market mutual fund at, say, 10 percent per year. Thus, the opportunity cost of owning the RV for the first year is going to be $1,600. Of course, the opportunity cost becomes explicit if the $16,000 had to be borrowed at some specific interest rate. Instead of opportunity cost, we call it interest on the loan, but it is actually giving you the same information.

Consumers' Research Magazine compared the benefits of vacationing with an RV to using a car and staying in hotels. For thirty-four days of vacation, a motor home in 1976 (costs would be considerably more today) averaged $102.18 a day compared to using an automobile and a motel, which would cost $48.94 a day. *Consumer's Research Magazine* contended that you would have to be on the road eighty-six days a year to make a recreational vehicle pay.

INSURANCE. A new type of policy for insuring recreational vehicles provides the standard liability and physical damage coverage that are provided in the typical automobile policy. Furthermore, it provides for additional living expenses and miscellaneous personal-property coverage if you lose the use of your recreational vehicle during a trip.

THE ALTERNATIVES TO OWNING RECREATIONAL EQUIPMENT OR PROPERTY

The discussion about an RV is important because it highlights the expenses involved in purchasing that vehicle. The same is true for any other item that is purchased and used only infrequently. The owner incurs depreciation and opportunity costs irrespective of how much the item is used; thus, it may not make sense to own an RV, or SCUBA equipment, or a vacation home. As an alternative, the wise consumer might consider renting whatever is needed. It is possible, for example, to rent a recreational vehicle for two weeks, three weeks, or a month, provided that it is reserved ahead of time.

It is increasingly easier for Americans to rent not only RVs but full camping and backpacking equipment, SCUBA equipment, golfing equipment, boats, skiing equipment, and the like. Whenever you desire to use recreational equipment for short periods of time, the alternative of renting it should be considered. When making your calculation, don't be shocked at the high rental rate per day or per week; rather, compare that seemingly high rental rate with the implicit cost you would incur if you decided to purchase the equipment on your own.

There are disadvantages to renting. You have to plan in advance to make sure that you will be able to obtain the item. Often, you have to put down a deposit that you will lose if you change your mind. Further, you cannot customize the rented piece of equipment as you would if you owned it. And we can't forget pride in ownership: Individuals get value from actually owning something that they can take care of personally and show off as their own. may turn out to be the most important reason for some individuals to buy their own recreational equipment rather than rent it.

Another Possibility—Resort Time Sharing

One of the newest methods for supposedly reducing vacation costs is resort time sharing. You buy the use of a resort facility for a specified period of time each year. You can swap your time with someone else's time, however. Most time shares involve a week or two in condominiums in prime vacation areas. In the United States, there are approximately 2,000 condominium developments that allow time shares. Resort time sharing is a European idea recently introduced in the United States. Prices vary, depending on the resort and the facilities, as well as on the unit you are purchasing. A typical two-bedroom condominium may sell for $6,000 to $9,000 (although off-season rates can be 50 percent less). Additionally, you probably will end up paying $100 or more per month for maintenance fees.

There are two ways to strike a time-share deal: One is by purchasing 1/52 interest (for one week) in the real estate; the other is simply to buy the right to use the place without having any ownership interest. The latter method is obviously going to be cheaper, but then you do not benefit from any increased value in the vacation property. For further information, write to American Land Development Association, Resort Time-Sharing Council, 1000 16th Street, N.W., Washington, D.C. 20036.

Careful analysis of time-sharing arrangements does not usually yield favorable results. That is to say, most time-sharing arrangements only make sense if you think the property will appreciate considerably in the future. While that may have been an accurate assumption in the 1970s and early 1980s, property appreciation recently has been much less than in the past decade. That means if you opt for time sharing, you may end up spending a large amount of money for what you could simply rent at a much lower rate. Furthermore, you won't get the benefit of a big capital gain when you turn around and sell your share of the condominium unit a few years hence.

One of the newest methods for supposedly reducing vacation costs is resort time sharing.

MAKING TIME FOR RECREATION

Recreation permits you to refresh your body and your mind after work through activity and play. It means literally "to be recreated." In a sense, we can distinguish between recreation and simply leisure, or free time. When you are engaged in recreation, you actually are pursuing a diverting activity. True, recreational activity involves free choice: You can say to yourself, "This is what I like to do," rather than, "This is what I have to do."

Never Finding Time for Recreation

Some individuals never seem to find time for recreation. When they are not working on a job for pay, they are engaged in doing tasks around the house. This may be the way an individual has to lead his or her life; however, for those who never seem to have time for recreation and feel guilty about it, then time must be found. Work always will expand to fit the time allowed; thus, unless a positive approach is taken to *develop* more time for recreational activities, it never will be found.

The Value of Increased Recreation

Sociologists and psychologists contend that, when recreation is freely chosen, it allows the individual to get in touch with him- or herself, to find out and respond to his or her own personal needs and desires. Moreover, recreational activities that are undertaken with family and friends increase the bonds between the individual and those around him or her.

Thinking about Necessary Recreation

Perhaps the best way to determine your particular recreational needs is to start thinking—about yourself, your free time, the costs involved, and your alternatives.

THINKING ABOUT YOURSELF. If you can take time out to try to discover what your interests really are, you also may discover what types of recreation will be best for you. Does playing tennis really not satisfy you? Is it because you really don't want to engage in such a highly competitive sport? If so, then maybe something else less competitive would be better for you. Do you really need time away from everyone else? If so, then perhaps you should switch from sports in which you participate with others to activities you can do by yourself, such as birdwatching, fishing, or nature photography.

Recreation permits you to refresh your body and your mind after work through activity and play. It means literally "to be recreated."

THINKING REALISTICALLY ABOUT YOUR LEISURE TIME. Are you ever going to get three weeks away from your job to take that course in mountain climbing you've dreamed about? If you are being unrealistic in your dreams and you know it's never going to happen, then perhaps your energies would be better directed toward some other recreational activity that you actually can fit into your available free time. Do you really like to read but keep telling yourself that you need a large block of time in order to do so? Why not try to read just a chapter a night of a novel you have always wanted to savor. You might be amazed at how much you can do recreationally if you do it in very small time slots. A basic principle is to fit in the recreation you want in the time slots available, rather than wishing you had more leisure time or leisure time in different amounts than you are now able to arrange.

THINKING ABOUT RECREATIONAL EXPENSES. You must continue to be realistic in terms of the recreation you desire, for much recreation requires expenses on complementary items. To become an avid skier may require more than just relatively inexpensive rented equipment. To do serious photography may require a complete darkroom at a price that exceeds your budget. You may have to substitute. There are numerous recreational activities that do not require any out-of-pocket expenses. Seeing free movies at the library or checking out books doesn't cost a cent. In fact, in many major cities, there are free activities provided by different groups every weekend and often during the week.

THE RANGE OF RECREATIONAL ACTIVITIES

It would be impossible to list the numerous recreational activities that are available to any individual in any part of the country. Exhibit 23–3 points out the activities that are most popular in the United States with respect to those that are physically demanding, those that take place outdoors, those that are creative, and those that are done at home.

Getting Information on Recreation

It's easy to get information on various recreational activities. The problem is sorting out all the possibilities! In most cities, newspapers list many recreational activities and the whereabouts of clubs that can be contacted. YMCAs and YWCAs offer a plethora of recreational options. Local colleges and universities can be a source of possibilities. Bulletin boards can be consulted. Parks in your area probably have recreation programs throughout the year, both for yourself and other members of your family.

Your local library will undoubtedly have numerous sections on different types of sports, arts, and so on. You can learn about thousands of possibilities with just a small investment of your time.

At the largest newsstand in your area, you will find magazines dedicated to numerous recreational activities, from gardening to rock collecting to model airplanes to boating to sewing.

YOU NEED INFORMATION TO BUY WISELY

If you decide to buy something to be used as part of your recreational program, you should apply the same buying principles as with anything else. You first want to acquire as much information as is reasonable for the purchase you are making. This can be done by asking friends and colleagues if they have any information on where to buy what you need, what brand you should buy, what quality, and so on. Another way you can get information about something you might want to buy is to first rent it, use it awhile, and then make a decision. Individuals who are trying to decide which brand of skis to purchase, for example, sometimes rent different brands and decide after having used each brand a day or two. Are you thinking about buying a recreational vehicle? Rent one first to see if it's really for you. Renting can be not only a convenient way to use an expensive piece of equipment but also a way to obtain information about the advisability of owning it.

EXHIBIT 23–3
The Most Popular Recreational Activities in the U.S.

FITNESS ACTIVITIES	OUTDOOR ACTIVITIES
Badminton	Birdwatching
Bicycling	Boating
Bowling	Camping
Calisthenics	Fishing
Hocky	Gardening
Jogging	Hiking
Skating	Hunting
Skiing	Picnics
Softball	Windsurfing
Swimming	
Tennis	
Volleyball	
Windsurfing	
CREATIVE ACTIVITIES	**HOME ACTIVITIES**
Acting	Collecting stamps
Dancing	Shells
Jewelrymaking	Antique bottles
Playing musical instruments	Games—cards, Scrabble
Needlework	Gourmet cooking
Painting	Reading
Pottery	Indoor Gardening
Refinishing furniture and houses	
Sewing	
Singing	
Writing	

Your Yellow Pages can also offer a wealth of information about where products are available. The salespeople in the stores you go to will certainly have information that will help you.

SUMMARY

1. Leisure and money income (that is, work) are substitutes.
2. Time and leisure activities are complements.
3. Hours worked by the average American have fallen from what they were 100 years ago. We have bought more leisure. As more Americans have purchased more leisure, they also have purchased more complementary products, such as recreational vehicles and sporting equipment.
4. Purchasing any consumer durable good involves looking at opportunity cost and depreciation. An RV that is used only two weeks a year may be much more expensive to own than to rent for those two weeks.
5. Information can be obtained readily on a vast range of recreational activities from YMCAs, YWCAs, local colleges and universities, parks, libraries, and so on.

QUESTIONS FOR THOUGHT AND DISCUSSION

1. Why do you think that hours worked have leveled off over the last fifteen years in the United States?
2. Would rich people tend to take longer vacations than poor people? (Hint: Remember opportunity costs).

3. If the price of tennis rackets and tennis balls fell, do you think people would play more tennis?
4. Why do Americans now engage in more physical recreational activity?

THINGS TO DO

1. Go to your local or college library and find the section on sports activities. Do you find any books on activities that were unknown by your parents when they were your age?
2. Visit a local recreational-vehicle sales lot. Ask the salesperson to explain to you the full cost per year of owning an RV. Did he or she include the opportunity cost of the down payment you would have to provide in order to obtain a loan for the RV?

SELECTED READINGS

Green, F. G. "RVs—The Cost of Ownership." *Consumers' Research Magazine,* May 1979, pp. 16–19.

"Mobile Homes and RVs." *Consumers' Research Magazine,* October 1976, pp. 144–45.

Owen, John D. '"Work Weeks and Leisure: An Analysis of Trends 1948–1975." *Monthly Labor Review,* August 1976, p. 3.

"Recreational Vehicles." See issues of *Outdoor Life.*

Sutton, H. "80s Traveler: His Life and Future Times." *Saturday Review,* January 5, 1980, pp. 20–24.

"Swap Houses for a Cheap Vacation." *Changing Times,* April 1979, pp. 39–41.

Consumer ISSUE  

BEFORE YOU SPEND YOUR VACATION DOLLAR

GETTING INFORMATION ON POSSIBLE VACATIONS

It would be impossible to list all the available information sources on vacations. As we become a more vacation-conscious society, we also find that there are more and more sources of information on what type of vacation we should take. Here are just a few suggestions.

1. In the travel section of your local library or a large bookstore in your area, you will find books for every possible type of vacation you might want to take, from inexpensive camping trips to grand tours of Europe. For many years now, individuals traveling on a limited budget have been using the budget-travel books put out by Eric Frommer (Simon and Schuster, publishers). You will find, however, that those books can't seem to keep up with inflation in this country and elsewhere, so you usually have to add 10 to 20 percent to all the prices listed to determine what you actually will pay.
2. Write to tourist offices throughout the world for travel information. Every country has a tourist office and will provide information free of charge. If you live in a large city, you can look in the Yellow Pages under "Tourist Information" and "Consulates and Other Foreign Government Representatives." A telephone call will usually result in a wealth of free information via the mail.
3. If you are planning any camping trips, you can write the U.S. National Park Service, Department of the Interior, 18th and East Streets, Washington, D.C. 20240.
4. Each state has a Tourist Information Bureau. Write directly to obtain needed information.
5. If you are a member of the American Automobile Association, you can obtain travel guides on the United States, Canada, Mexico, and elsewhere.
6. Airlines often have free or low-cost information on traveling to various parts of the world.
7. Read the travel section in your local newspaper to find out about alternative travel ideas.
8. Subscribe to a travel magazine, such as *Travel and Leisure*.
9. Check your local bus depot and/or railway station for information on low-cost tickets that are good for travel anywhere for a set period of time.

Using a Travel Agent

You can also get information, brochures, and suggestions from a travel agent in your area. More importantly perhaps, a travel agent can take care of all your reservations for transportation, lodging, and tours. You can expect a travel agent to do the following for you:

1. Have all schedules and costs of planes, trains, and boats.
2. Provide you with details on group arrangements and tours.
3. Provide you with the dates of special events and festivals.
4. Provide you with motel-hotel room rates and availability.
5. Help you obtain a passport and/or visa and tell you which shots you might need to have.
6. Make reservations for you for tours, planes, trains, motels, hotels, and special events.
7. Tell you how rates vary, depending upon the seasons.
8. Give you advice on tipping customs, clothing, and restaurants.

9. Make up a tour for you and/or your family that fits your tastes, interests, and available budget. In the travel trade, this is called an independent inclusive tour.

How You Pay a Travel Agent

Generally, the travel agent is paid for his or her services via commissions paid by airlines, hotels, and restaurants. In other words, you are not directly billed, but you implicitly pay for the agent's services when you pay your plane, train, and hotel bills. However, you may expect to be charged for any extras, such as certain reservations in foreign hotels, reticketing, and long-distance telephone calls and telegrams.

How to Pick a Travel Agent

Friends can be the greatest source of information about a good travel agent. The company you work for may use a specific agent; this might be advantageous to you because the agent will want to maintain good relations with the company and, therefore, may give you some special service. You may wish to speak with travel agents who are members of the American Society of Travel Agents; any agency displaying the ASTA symbol has been in business at least three years and meets certain financial and ethical standards set up by the ASTA.

In order to get the most out of the travel agent you choose, you must make him or her aware of your budget and your tastes and preferences. Let the agent know if you prefer a formal or a very relaxed atmosphere. That way he or she will be able to book you in the appropriate type of restaurant. The more the agent gets to know you personally, the better the services he or she can render.

IF YOU DECIDE TO DO IT ALONE

Do-it-yourself vacation planning is not all that difficult, particularly if you have a definite idea of where, when, and how you are going to travel.

Transportation Reservations

All airlines have booking offices with agents who can help them with fares and schedules over the telephone. You can reserve tickets and pick them up at the airport, charging them to one of your credit cards. If you decide to use the rail system in the United States, you can call Amtrak; the toll-free number throughout the United States for reservations and information is (800) 342-2520. If you plan to go by rail into Canada, contact the Canadian National Railways, 630 Fifth Avenue, New York, New York 10020 or the Canadian Pacific Railways, 581 Fifth Avenue, New York, New York 10017.

If you desire to go by bus, contact either your local Greyhound or Continental Trailways office, or write them at the New York Port Authority Bus Terminal at 8th Avenue and 41st Street, New York, New York 10014.

If you are planning to drive in the United States or elsewhere, you can obtain maps from gas stations; the Mobil Guides are especially useful. If you plan to drive in a foreign country, you should obtain information about international drivers' licenses and international automobile registration by writing or calling the American Automobile Association, 28 East 78th Street, New York, New York 10021. It is important to check whether your automobile insurance will cover you everywhere you plan to visit. If you are planning to go into Canada, your insurance company must provide you with a Canadian nonresident interprovince motor-vehicle-liability-insurance card. In Mexico, United States insurance isn't usually valid for more than forty-eight hours after entry. The point is, settle your car insurance problems *before you leave home*.

If you plan a day-by-day itinerary, you can write in advance for hotel/motel reservations. Most major chains of motels have toll-free numbers that can be found in your Yellow Pages. If you are planning a trip with your family, find out which hotels/motels offer "family plans." Often, for a small fee or nothing at all, a motel will give you an extra bed in your room, thus saving you the charge of two rooms.

CUTTING VACATION COSTS

Proper planning and a willingness to cut some corners may save you a significant amount of money. Here are some suggestions for cutting vacation costs. A travel agent or some of the many budget travel books may present others.

1. Take vacations off season. Sometimes rates are 50 percent less in hotels during the off-season months. A European holiday in October is considerably less expensive than in July. Not only are hotels cheaper but so,

too, are plane fares. A travel agent or airline representative can give you the exact differences between high season and off season. Thus, timing becomes crucial to saving money on vacations. You might even consider splitting your vacation into two holidays, taking advantage of bargain rates at the beginning and end of each season.

2. Take advantage of airfare bargains. Ask if there is a special "K" class with no meal on the flight you wish to take. Find out if there are any special tour fares. Some may require that you purchase a minimum amount of ground accommodations, but the saving can be well worth your while. Charter flights are often quite a bargain, these must be planned in advance, however, and some of them leave many hours after they are scheduled to depart, thus imposing much discomfort on families waiting for the flight. If you have small children, this may be an important factor for you in deciding against a charter flight. Also, consider the fact that charter flights are usually sold by the seat, regardless of the person's age. Thus, if you are traveling with small children, you will be charged the full charter-flight fare for each of them. Compare this with a regularly scheduled airline that might offer significant savings for children under twelve.

3. Look into "stopover" possibilities on your travel arrangements. Sometimes, for a small additional charge, you may be able to visit several cities at once.

4. Try to go where the crowds are not. Head away from the jammed resorts; go to the more remote and less well-known areas.

5. Get a copy of the *Traveler's Directory* from 51-02 39th Avenue, Woodside, New York 11277. It provides a listing for the United States and abroad of hundreds of people and places that will put you up for free, provided that you offer the same hospitality to others. You also must offer a "donation" of several dollars for the book.

6. If you are a student, obtain an international student identity card from the Council on International Educational Exchange, 777 United Nations Plaza, New York, New York 10017. Many hotels, restaurants, theatres, and museums will give you reduced rates.

7. Consider a Eurail pass in Europe, which gives you unlimited first-class rail travel. It must be purchased in the United States; ask your travel agent or write Eurail Pass, c/o French National Railroad, 610 Fifth Avenue, New York, New York 10020.

8. In the United States, consider a similar type of pass offered by the major bus companies. Greyhound has an Ameripass, and Continental Trailways has an Eaglepass.

9. If you decide on a vacation tour, shop around. When comparing prices, make sure you compare tours that provide similar services. Do you pay for porters and tour guides? Do you pay for theater tickets? What is included and what isn't? What type of accommodations will you get?

10. Hosteling is possible. Throughout the world, there is a network of youth hostels that are inexpensive dormitory-style accommodations. Fees in the United States range from $2.50 to $4.50 per day for lodging. In other countries, the fees are lower. In almost fifty countries, there are 4,500 hostels available. For information on trips and applications for youth-hostel passes, write American Youth Hostels, AYH National Campus, Delaplane, Virginia.

11. Consider camping as an alternative to hotels. Look at Rand-McNally's *Guidebook for Campgrounds* in which some 16,000 United States and Canadian campgrounds are listed. If you plan to stay in national parks throughout the country, the purchase of a Golden Eagle Passport will save money. Write the U.S. Superintendent of Documents, Washington, D.C. 20402, for the following brochures: *Camping in the National Park System, Boating in the National Park System,* and *Fishing in the National Park System.*

12. You can write some private organizations, too. The Sierra Club, 1050 Mills Tower, 220 Bush Street, San Francisco, California 94104; American River Touring Association, 1016 Jackson Street, Oakland, California 94607; and Wilderness Society, Western Regional Office, 4260 Evans Avenue, Denver, Colorado 80222 will provide you with timely camping information.

13. If you are driving your car, try to find hotels that do not charge for overnight parking.

14. Consider older, downtown hotels that have had to reduce their rates in recent years to compete with airport and suburban hotels and motels.

15. Consider house-swapping. Several clubs have been established to help you obtain inexpensive lodging in another part of the country or the world. Write Holiday Home Exchange Bureau, Inc., P.O. Box 555, Grants, New Mexico 87020 or Vacation Exchange Club, Inc., 350 Broadway, New York, New York 10013. These clubs' annual directories list individuals interested in exchanging homes. There is a brief explanation of the home and facilities.

IF YOU DECIDE TO RENT A CAR

Often it's convenient to rent a car on vacations. All national car-rental agencies have toll-free numbers that you can call for information and reservations; these agencies will be listed in your Yellow Pages. Here are some pointers on how to get the most out of your rental dollar.

1. See if there is an additional drop fee if you leave the car in another city.

2. Reserve the car at least a week in advance to avoid last-minute disappointments in selection and the necessity of renting a larger, more expensive car than you had desired.

3. Find out if you are eligible for a discount. There are discounts given to executives, employees of educational institutions, and so on. It is relatively easy to obtain a discount.

4. Sometimes in major airports in other countries, it is possible to bargain with the various rental agencies that are lined up as you leave the baggage checkout counter.

5. Find out what happens if the car is returned late. Are you allowed a few hours' grace period?

6. Verify that the mileage written on your contract is the mileage on the rental car's odometer.

7. Check the insurance coverage. Often, your own insurance will not cover rental cars, particularly in foreign countries. It may be worthwhile to pay the extra daily fee to have full comprehensive insurance so even minor accidents aren't worrisome.

8. If your health and medical insurance covers all accidents, it isn't worthwhile to pay for extra medical coverage when you rent a car.

9. See if car rental can be included in a fly-drive package plan. It may be much cheaper that way.

10. Avoid renting a car at the airport. Rates from car-rental agencies that will come to pick you up are often significantly lower than rentals in many airports.
11. If you are planning an extended stay in Europe, consider a longer-term lease arrangement with a European company or a self-buy agreement, where the car is bought back at the end of the vacation. It is no longer true that purchasing a car in another country saves you enough money to make it worthwhile. When you add insurance costs, shipping fees, and the amount of time you have to wait for the car to be delivered from Europe, you don't really save much, if anything.
12. Rent the smallest car that is convenient for you and your family.
13. Inquire about alternative rental arrangements. Most companies have special excursion plans.

USING CREDIT CARDS

Even if you decide that you do not want to borrow in order to go on vacation, it still may be advisable for you to have several major credit cards. These provide positive identification when renting an automobile and can be used for the deposit. The bills will constitute an accurate record of all hotel, plane, train, and restaurant expenses. The use of credit cards avoids the necessity of carrying large amounts of cash, purchasing large amounts of travelers' checks and keeping track of them, or attempting to use personal checks when you travel.

Many major credit cards provide an instant-cash service in case you run out of money. American Express, for example, has set up machines in major airports from which you can purchase travelers checks using your American Express card.

Whether or not it is advisable to go into debt to take a vacation depends upon your own particular financial situation. What is important is that you do not exceed your safe *debt limit* by taking a vacation. Some people go into debt to take a vacation and, as a result, are unable to replace an old washing machine or get a new refrigerator. At the time they make the decision, they believe it is more important to take a restful and/or exciting vacation so they will feel better the rest of the year. Looking forward to a vacation may provide a necessary inducement to undertake tasks that might otherwise be avoided. Vacations are, for some people, just as important as having enough to eat, warm clothes, and a roof over their heads.

SUMMARY

1. Information on possible vacations can be obtained from travel books, national tourist offices, the U.S. National Park Service, state tourist information bureaus, the American Automobile Association, major airlines, travel sections of local newspapers, and travel magazines.
2. A travel agent can provide you with all schedules, details on group arrangements and tours, dates of special events and festivals, passport and visa details, and so on. Travel agents are paid by the companies for which they sell tickets or book reservations. You do not pay agents directly.
3. Ways to reduce travel costs include taking vacations off season, taking advantage of airfare bargains, going to uncrowded resorts, using student discounts when possible, taking bus tours, and houseswapping.

QUESTIONS FOR THOUGHT AND DISCUSSION

1. Look at the suggestions in this Issue for reducing travel costs. What benefits do you lose if you follow any of these suggestions?
2. How do travel agents make their income? Why would you ever want to use a travel agent?
3. Why do students get special discounts if they have student ID cards?

THINGS TO DO

If you have never done so, visit a travel agency to see what types of information are available.

SELECTED READINGS

Giesiking, H. "How to Make the Most of Your Vacation Time." *Travel Holiday,* March 1982, pp. 111–12.
Walzer, M. "Time Off." *Harpers,* December 1982, p. 26.
"Where to Go." See issues of *Outdoor Life.*
"The World at Cut Rates." *Time,* November 8, 1982, p. 55.

CHAPTER
RETIREMENT AND THE GOLDEN YEARS

An increased percentage of our population is now 65 or over. Because we are approaching zero population growth, we no longer will be a nation of young people, a nation as enamoured of the youth culture as we used to be.

CHAPTER PREVIEW

- What percentage of the population is over sixty-five?
- Should there be mandatory retirement at any specified age?
- Is there any trend toward early retirement?
- What are the financial risks of early retirement?

One major change in our society is the increased percentage of the population that is sixty-five or over. Because we are approaching zero population growth, we no longer will be a nation of young people, a nation as enamored of the youth culture as we used to be. We gradually will see a reversal in the trend to younger and younger presidents of major corporations, universities, and foundations. We will become more like such countries as France, where Americans are surprised by the large number of "old" people. Today, the median age of the population is thirty, and 11½ percent of the population is sixty-five or over. In the year 2000, the figure will have risen to 12½ percent.

Thus, the problems of aging and retirement are going to become increasingly important for this nation. Geriatric problems—problems of the aged—take three different forms.

1. We must individually face the problems of our own aging and retirement.
2. Often, we must face the problems of the aging of our parents.
3. From a societal point of view, we may wish to consider policy changes to improve the cultural and economic lot of the aged.

THE PLIGHT OF THE ELDERLY TODAY

In the beginning of the 1980s, there were 24.2 million individuals sixty-five or over. Of these, 3⅔ million officially were below the money-income poverty line. Poverty, at least on the surface, appears to be a major problem facing older people in America. Fully 15 percent of individuals sixty-five and older were earning less than $4,000 a year in 1983. There are a number of explanations for this phenomenon.

Not Providing for the Future

To some extent, we must admit that there are individuals who are poor when they are older because they did not save enough when they were younger. They did not start a retirement plan at an early enough age so they could be comfortable in their older years. Those who rely on Social Security alone for their retirement years can never expect to lead a truly comfortable life. Social Security wasn't designed to be a full retirement income program but, rather, as a supplement to private savings.

Being Crippled by Medical Bills

Many older individuals find themselves unable to make ends meet because they suffer from chronic illnesses that require constant attention and medical expenses. However, since the introduction of Medicare and Medicaid, this problem has been ameliorated for a large number of senior citizens. Further, many others take advantage of extensive private medical insurance in order to avoid being saddled with extraordinary expenses in case of extraordinary medical problems.

The Inability to Find Work Even When It Is Desired

Pressure not to hire older people in many companies and other work places makes it extremely difficult for senior citizens to work even when they want to. Union restrictions and minimum wage laws also make it difficult, if not impossible, for senior citizens to find full- or part-time work in lower-paying jobs that they might be perfectly happy to do if it weren't for the restrictions. Also, the Social Security program actually discourages retired people from making extra income. As of 1983, for every $2 that a Social Security recipient earns up to $6,600, he or she loses $1 of Social Security benefits. That is an effective tax rate of 50 percent, plus additional taxes, such as federal income tax, Social Security contributions, and state income taxes.

Pressure not to hire older people in many companies and other work places makes it extremely difficult for senior citizens to work even when they want to.

Statistics May Not Tell the Full Story

Unfortunately, the government statistics on incomes of older people are a very inaccurate measure of what their true standard of living is. The government statistics look only at money income; they ignore the value of all in-kind transfers from the government, such as food stamps, Medicare and Medicaid, public housing, and the like. Furthermore, money income data ignore completely the value of the implicit services that older people obtain from the homes they may own. A large number of retired people own their own homes and, indeed, may have paid for them completely. If you are seventy years old and live in a $60,000 house, you implicitly are receiving a stream of services from that house equal to what it would cost you to rent the same type of accommodations in the housing market. If, hypothetically, such a house could be rented for $400 a month, then the value of the housing services received by the owner-occupier of the house is $4,800 a year. This would be part of a retired couple's true or real income. Thus, to the extent that money income excludes the value of owner-occupied housing and the value of food stamps from the government, those money-income figures overstate the poverty problem of the aged.

What Do Senior Citizens Think about Their Own Situations?

As we mentioned, the statistics may not tell the true story of the plight of senior citizens in America. Two researchers, Alvin Rabushka and Bruce Jacobs, decided to find out how elderly people perceive their own situations. They interviewed a nationwide sample of elderly homeowners sixty years and over about their income, health, living conditions, and the like. The reason they chose homeowners is that 70 percent of the elderly own their own homes, and 87 percent of these own their homes "free and clear." The survey results were rather surprising. Only 11 percent fell below the government's official poverty line. Additionally, almost all the homeowners interviewed felt that their houses were adequate, and only 3 percent reported lack of money income as the reason they had to forego repairs. However, the authors point out that professional housing standards applied to these homes would show "anywhere from two to ten times as many housing problems as those acknowledged by the elderly themselves." (Rabushka and Jacobs did point out, however, that their survey sample from the rural South—about 30 percent of the national sample—showed a need for upgrading housing conditions there.)

In spite of their survey results, the authors were quick to agree that, although the conditions of the elderly may not be as bad as the media portray them, the majority of the elderly do need some kinds of help. They suggest voluntary home inspections, control of property taxes, and elimination of any mandatory retirement systems still in operation.[1]

THE TREND TOWARD ELDERLY RETIREMENT

For many people, the problem is not in continuing to work after age sixty-five but in knowing what to do upon early retirement—that is, at an age earlier than sixty-five. The average retirement age in the United States is 63½. In 1890, 68 percent of all men in the country age sixty-five were working; by 1976, only 21 percent of those age sixty-five worked. The trend toward earlier retirement is increasingly evident.

The trend toward early retirement points to one certainty: Those who decide to retire early must obviously have planned for that early retirement many years ago by providing for sufficient income to cover all those nonworking years. After all, if you decide to retire at fify-five and you live to at least age seventy, you need fifteen years of retirement income. You would have had to build up a pretty big nest egg in the form of a pension plan or some other retirement scheme. If you have any desire whatsoever to retire early (before sixty-five for men, sixty-two for women), there is no escaping the fact that, to do so, you will have to save more today. Do not plan on Social Security as a help to you; first, it would not start at age fifty-five, and second, it does not provide you with a very comfortable living standard (or, at least, it hasn't in the past).

To enjoy a long retirement period, you have to be equipped to take advantage of 100 percent leisure time. You might be ill-equipped if you failed to develop outside interests during your working years. Hence, it could be important for your happiness in retirement to lead some sort of balanced life before retirement. That is, at least moderate amounts of leisure activities should be included in your working time periods. The man or woman who spends sixty-hours a week working until age fifty-five and who hopes to enjoy a long retirement period on a large pension plan may be sadly disappointed, for his or her only interest will have been in work, not play. (A person can, however, develop new interests *after* retirement.) It is not surprising that some people who work their heads off while they are young end up working their entire lives because they become addicted to the excitement of a full day of work, at least five and sometimes six or seven days a week. Of course, there is nothing necessarily wrong with this; each of us has the right to pursue personal values and preferences. But if work is not what you think you want to do the rest of your life, it is wise to balance work with play while you're young. If you always put off doing what you would like to do during leisure time, you probably will never do it. Hobbies may sound corny to some, but they are an integral part of a life style that leads to a happy, fulfilling retirement, whether it be early or late.

1. Rabushka, Alvin, and Bruce Jacobs, *Old Folks at Home* (New York: The Free Press, 1979).

In sum, then, successful early retirement requires two ingredients:

1. A large savings program while you are working.
2. A personal development program for acquiring interests outside of work activities, to be expanded when retirement comes.

For many people, the problem is not in continuing to work after age sixty-five but in knowing what to do upon early retirement—that is, at an age earlier than sixty-five.

ALTERNATIVES TO EARLY RETIREMENT

Obviously, there are many alternatives to early retirement. You can work less and retire later in life. You do not have to work fifty weeks a year every year until you retire at age sixty-five. You can work thirty-five weeks a year, or forty, or even six months. It takes a very special job for that to be possible, but if that is what you really want in life, you can start your search right now to find the appropriate situation. You generally will not make as much money, but you will have more leisure time, which is as good in itself for most people. It has a value just as income does. Of course, here again you have to get just the right mix to suit yourself. If you work too little, you'll have too little money to make your leisure time satisfying by purchasing records, books, movie tickets, boats, restaurant meals, skis, trips, and so on.

STARTING A SECOND CAREER

Rather than retiring early and engaging only in leisure activities thereafter, many individuals seek a second career. This has been standard practice for individuals who join the armed forces at a very young age and retire after twenty or thirty years of service on a full pension. Many start a new career in perhaps an entirely different field than the one they worked in for the past several years. More than half of all federal government employees who retire as early as age fifty-five are gainfully employed thereafter, usually part-time. In deciding on a second career, it is necessary to do proper advance planning to avoid settling for the kinds of jobs associated with working pensioners—helper in the local store or night watchman. In other words, a long lead time is recommended for seeking a regular second job.

Many individuals in the business community retire and then work part-time as consultants to other businesspersons. Such jobs can be on a retainer or contract basis. Those who never were in business but always wanted to be can contact the United States Small Business Administration, Washington, D.C., to find out the risks and the possible benefits of going into business for oneself after an early retirement. A typical small-business venture that many older people go into is the purchase of a dry-cleaning establishment or some other such franchise where much of the advance planning has been taken care of by the national franchise management.

Financial Risks in Early Retirement

If you seek early retirement from your current career before private and public pension rights will give you a satisfactory standard of living, you clearly must seek a second career. Be aware, however, of the financial hazards you face.

Older employees, particularly those who work only part-time, are usually the first to be fired or laid off during a business downturn. You may also find that your physical strength is not as great as you had anticipated and that the job you took is too demanding. Your desire to move to a more pleasant climate may increase as you lose interest in your second career.

Hence, for most people, a second career is most enjoyable when it is undertaken for pleasure rather than financial necessity.

A Second Career without Pay—Volunteer Work

Individuals who are financially secure but desire to continue working may find tremendous satisfaction in the hundreds, indeed thousands, of volunteer programs throughout the nation. Some of them even pay modest amounts of money to the participants. The federal government has several major volunteer groups directed through an agency called ACTION. ACTION includes the Peace Corps, for overseas service; VISTA, for service in the United States; and a number of other smaller organizations. SCORE, of particular interest to senior citizens, is a service corps of retired executives that counsels small-business persons when

they are in trouble. Participants receive a modest expense allowance but no pay. To get information, write ACTION, Washington, D.C. 20525.

You can send for informative publications from the Administration on Aging, Department of Health and Human Services, Washington, D.C. 20201, which serves as a general source of information for volunteer groups and keeps tabs on state and local agencies. In addition, most states have their own agencies affiliated with the Administration on Aging that direct public volunteer programs.

A listing of other possible volunteer organizations would include colleges and universities, organizations of the aged, senior citizens centers, neighborhood-improvement centers, boards of education, churches, hospitals, and the Red Cross.

The decision to retire requires adequate knowledge of what expenses will be during retirement years.

THE COSTS OF RETIREMENT

The decision to retire requires adequate knowledge of what expenses will be during retirement years. Those, of course, also will be a function of where one desires to live. Living costs vary from place to place but, in general, are relatively the same except when the individual desires to live in a warm climate in an environment associated with a resort area, such as south Florida, Hawaii, and parts of California. Actually, most retired people stay in the community where they have spent their working years because that is where they have established relationships with the greatest number of people for the longest time. It is quite disruptive to move to a totally new environment where one knows no one and is unfamiliar with the physical surroundings. Most retired peole live in urban areas; the vast majority live in large cities or their suburbs; and, although few retired persons want to live in their children's households, a significant percent lives within driving distance of their offspring.

The Decision about Where to Live

Even if a decision is made to remain in a familiar community, there are still further decisions to face.

1. Should you stay in the family home even if it is too big?
2. Should you move to a smaller house or to an apartment that would require less expense and less upkeep?
3. Should you share a living arrangement with other retired people?

If the decision is made to relocate, then these decisions must be made.

1. Should you seek sunshine, even at a higher expense?
2. Would a planned community for retired persons be appropriate?
3. Would you like to go back to your old hometown?
4. Do you want to be within walking or driving distance of an offspring's house?
5. Do you want to move to a rural area?
6. Is a mobile home appropriate for you?

SOME MYTHS ABOUT OLD AGE

The notion that an aging person becomes less creative and less able to enjoy life has been contradicted through thousands of years of experience. A recent study of 738 successful individuals in the arts and sciences who lived to be well over seventy-eight years old revealed the following findings.

1. Historians and philosophers reached their peak in their sixties.
2. Botanists are most productive in their forties and sixties.
3. Inventors develop most of their patents in their sixties.
4. Historians, botanists, philosophers, geologists, and inventors achieved more in their seventies than they did in their thirties.

Pablo Casals died at the age of ninety-seven. He played the cello until the end and retained his vigor and creativity all along. When once asked for his recipe for growing old youthfully, he stated, "The secret of my good old age is this—I live. Very few people live." If you wish to get an idea of how other older individuals have continued to be creative and youthful well into their nineties, read Dr. Alex Comfort's *A Good Age* (New York: Crown, 1976).

Comfort's book probably marks the beginning of serious discussion on how individuals do not have to grow old "disgracefully." Agism, contends Comfort, is no different than sexism or racism; individuals should not be discriminated against by virtue of having lived a specified number of years.

A few of Comfort's ideas contradict standard notions about senior citizens.

1. **Leisure.** "Leisure is a con; it should mean time when you do what you yourself want to do. It gets sold as part of the unperson package, as time in which you are expected to do trivial and useless things for which you have to pay money."
2. **Retirement.** "Two weeks is about the ideal length of time to retire."
3. **Doctors.** "If you find one who thinks that you have to be infirm, crazy, impotent, or the like, by virtue of chronological age, change doctors."
4. **Brain.** "The human brain does not shrink, wilt, perish, or deteriorate with age. It normally continues to function well through as many as nine decades."

Comfort points out that there is an incredible amount of inaccurate data relating to older people. He confronts the attitude that most older people are constantly in bed because of illness. His statistics show that older people suffer fewer acute illnesses than younger ones—1.3 illnesses per year as opposed to 2.1 for all ages. He does agree that 81 percent of persons over sixty-five have some chronic problems compared to 54 percent of all below that age; however, the average chronic problem might be nothing more serious than hay fever or myopia. Further, a Duke University study found that 44 to 48 percent of those over sixty-five had no detectable deterioration in physical condition. In fact, some had improved over periods of from three to thirteen years.

The basic cause of physical deterioration in older people appears to be boredom, inactivity, and the belief that infirmity is to be expected. What is Comfort's conclusion about older people becoming physically handicapped? "Most of the handicaps of oldness in our society are social, conventional, and imaginary."

Most of the handicaps of oldness in our society are social, conventional, and imaginary.

SUMMARY

1. The percentage of the population over sixty-five has been rising as the nation's population growth rate has slowed down.
2. There may be discrimination against people over sixty-five in the job market.
3. Mandatory retirement seems to work against older citizens being able to lead productive lives.
4. There is, on the other hand, a trend toward earlier retirement for a significant part of the population.
5. Many individuals start second careers in their fifties and sixties.
6. There are many costs associated with retirement, not the least being the psychic costs of changing communities if a new environment is sought.
7. There are many myths about age, not the least of which is that older people cannot be creative or productive.

QUESTIONS FOR THOUGHT AND DISCUSSION

1. Why is the age distribution in the United States changing?
2. Will society be any different with an older population?
3. Discuss Alex Comfort's idea that "two weeks is about the ideal length of time to retire."

THINGS TO DO

Read Alex Comfort's *A Good Age*.

SELECTED READINGS

Barnes, John. *More Money for Your Retirement.* New York: Harper & Row, 1978.

Hefferan, Colien. "Retirement Income." *Family Economics Review,* Winter 1981, pp. 3–12.

Irwin, Robert. *The $125,000 Decision: The Older American's Guide to Selling a Home and Choosing Retirement Housing.* New York: McGraw-Hill, 1982.

LeClair, Robert T., *et al. Money and Retirement: How to Plan for Lifetime Financial Security.* Reading, Mass.: Addison-Wesley, 1981.

Nauheim, Ferd. *The Retirement Money Book: New Ways to Have More Income When You Retire.* New York: Acropolis Books, 1982.

Schultz, James H. *The Economics of Aging.* Belmont, Calif.: Wadsworth, 1976.

White House Conference Chartbook on Aging in America. Washington, D.C.: U.S. Government Printing Office, 1981.

Consumer ISSUE W

WILLS, TRUSTS, AND ESTATE PLANNING

GLOSSARY

ESTATE—The total property of whatever kind owned prior to the distribution of that property in accordance with the terms of a will (or, when there is no will, by the laws of inheritance in the state of domicile of the decedent).

ESTATE TAXES—Taxes based on the value of the assets, minus the liabilities, of an estate when transferred to the ownership of others. These taxes are paid by the donor, if he or she is living when this transfer takes place; or by the estate, if the donor is dead.

EXECUTOR/EXECUTRIX—The personal representative of the person who made a will. The executor/executrix takes charge of the estate, pays the debts, and so on.

INHERITANCE TAX—A tax assessed by the federal government or the state government (or both) on a certain portion of an estate upon the death of its owner.

INTESTATE—To have died without leaving a valid will.

JOINT TENANCY—Two or more people owning a percentage, but not a specific piece, of some form of property. When one owner dies, the surviving owner(s) assumes full ownership of the property.

PROBATE—Proving a will before a court having jurisdiction over the administration of the estate.

TENANCY BY THE ENTIRETY—Joint owners of property are husband and wife.

TENANCY IN COMMON—Because there are two or more owners of property, transactions involving the property are not legal unless all the owners give their signed permission.

TESTAMENTARY TRUST—A will or trust that bestows specific rights to specific individuals after the death of the person who created the will or trust.

TESTATE—To have died and left a valid will.

TESTATOR/TESTATRIX—A person who has made and/or left a will.

TRUSTEE—The person holding legal title to trust property.

WILL—A written document that allows a person to determine the disposition of his or her property at death.

Most individuals accumulate wealth throughout their lifetimes. At some point in their lives, they have more assets than liabilities; thus, their net worth is positive. For this reason, setting up wills, providing trusts, and engaging in careful estate planning are important to virtually everyone. In this Consumer Issue, we will examine why it is necessary to draw up a will. Then we will look at some of the more important trusts that can be created and the benefits and costs of doing so. Finally, we'll discuss the elements of estate planning and indicate ways in which federal and state estate taxes can be minimized. Appendix III contains salient points about wills.

WHAT IS A WILL?

A **will** is a legal document through which you dispose of your property or estate. Your **estate** consists of the difference between all your assets and all your liabilities. In addition, your will gives directions for the distribution of your estate; it specifies who shall receive what and how it should be used.

Generally, a will is ineffective prior to the death of the writer of the will. A will can be destroyed, canceled, or modified at any time by its writer. The person who makes out the will is called a **testator,** if a male, and a **testatrix,** if a female. Thus, if a person dies leaving a will, he or she is said to have died **testate.** On the other hand, if he or she dies without a will, that person is said to have died **intestate.**

WHY SHOULD YOU MAKE OUT A WILL?

If you should die intestate, the following things will occur, and each is an additional reason why everyone should make out at least a simple will.

1. You cannot name the person who will oversee the distribution of your estate. That person is called the **executor,** if a male, or the **executrix,** if a female.
2. You generally cannot name a guardian for your minor children or other dependents. This is particularly critical if both you and your spouse should die at the same time.
3. You lose the ability to direct the disposal of your property in order to maximize its benefits to your heirs.

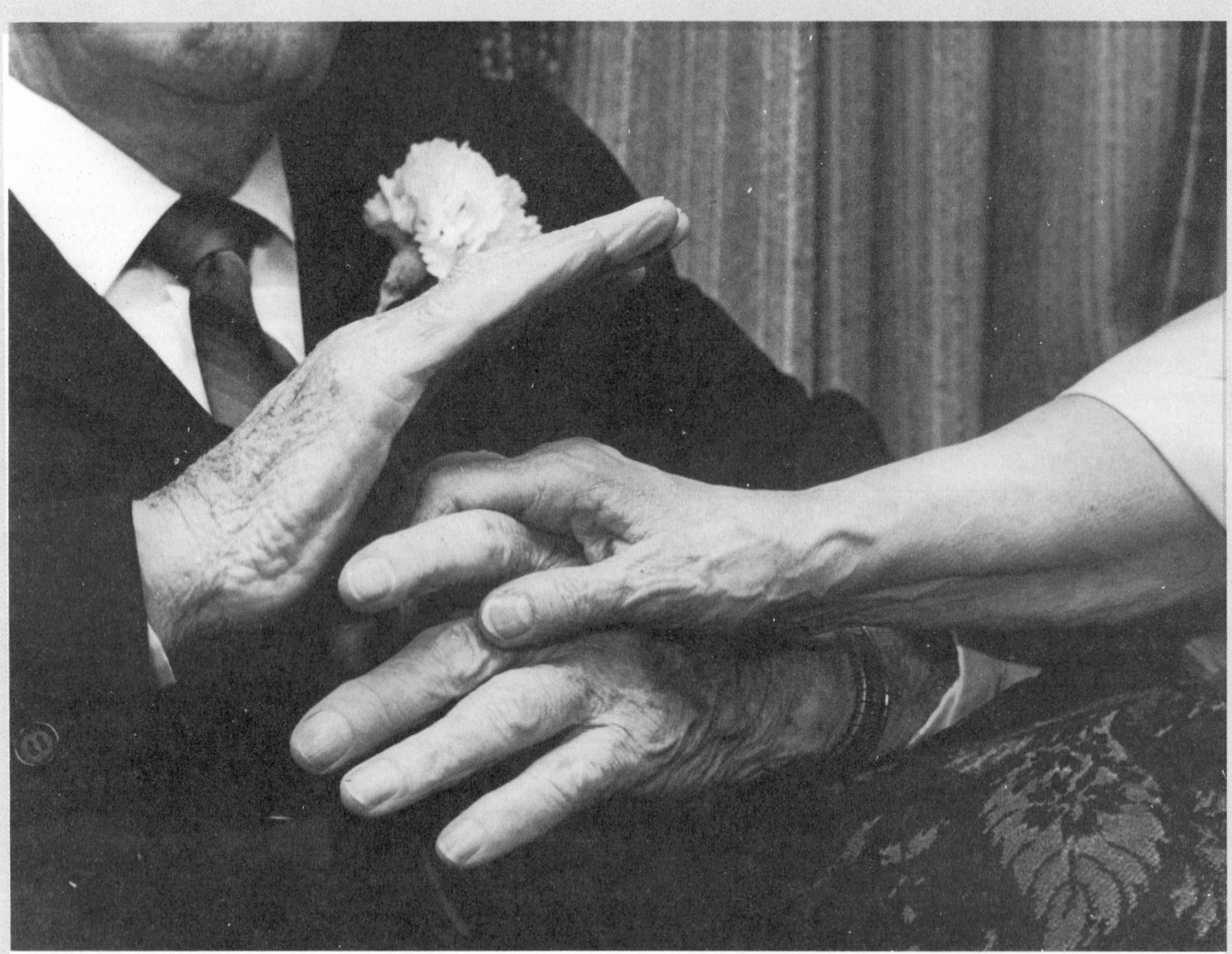

4. Your family and/or heirs will become unnecessarily involved in court procedures that could have been avoided with a valid will.
5. If you have no immediate family, persons in whom you have no particular interest may receive the bulk of your property.
6. The possibility of minimizing inheritance and estate taxes is eliminated.
7. Even if you have immediate family, the state will decide which percentage of your estate each individual will receive. You may have two offspring, one of whom is immensely rich, the other abysmally poor. Both may receive equal parts of your estate when you die if you do not have a will.
8. You cannot prevent your property from reverting to the state if you haven't named a person or persons legally qualified to inherit or claim it. (This is called *escheat.*)

What a Will Allows You to Do

Basically, a will allows you to decide the following:

1. Who gets your property.
2. How much each person or institution gets.
3. When that property will be received.
4. How the property can be safeguarded.
5. Who will handle its disposition.

Limitations on Disposition of Property by the Will

You cannot do just anything you want in a will. For example, it is generally impossible to eliminate completely your spouse from a will. In most states, the surviving spouse can elect to take the amount granted by state statutes for intestate situations. In other words, if state law says that the surviving spouse shall receive at least one-third of the estate and the will indicates that the spouse shall receive nothing, the surviving spouse usually will get the one-third amount. In a number of situations, however, it is possible to disinherit children.

Provisions in a will that are deemed against "public policy" can be invalidated by the courts. For example, a provision in a person's will to spend $20 million to erect a 300-foot-high statute of that person in place of an existing house in a suburban neighborhood would certainly not be held valid, even if it didn't violate local zoning ordinances. Provisions providing for bequests of property to individuals only if they remain unmarried throughout their lifetimes usually are held invalid since marriage is considered a "socially desirable" institution.

A Will Only Disposes of Certain Property

A will disposes of property that is not otherwise taken care of. There may be a large amount of property in a person's estate that does not pass to heirs through disposition of the will. For example, in most cases, life insurance proceeds automatically go to the beneficiary. If certain property is owned by two persons as joint tenants with the right of survivorship, then the survivor becomes sole owner of the property, no matter what the deceased's will states.

WHAT IS PROBATE?

Even though you have set up a will that explicitly states who should get what, how, when, and where, the will and your property must be **probated.** That is to say, it must be taken before a probate court in the appropriate jurisdiction. The court will make sure that the will has a genuine signature on it and that its execution will carry out your intent as precisely as possible. The person who has been named executor or executrix must satisfy what is usually called the surrogate's court in your area that all debts have been paid and that state and federal taxes also have been paid. Additionally, anyone who might have a claim on the estate has to have been notified before your will can be executed properly.

The procedure generally involves your attorney admitting the will to a probate court. Your attorney then issues letters testamentary to the executor or executrix named in the will. All parties are notified, and the required proof is submitted by the witnesses to the will to satisfy the court that the will is valid.

Because creditors usually have from four months to a year to make a claim, estates remain in the probate court for some time. The executor or executrix may attempt to settle federal estate taxes within nine months after your death; however, the IRS and state taxing authorities can take additional time to indicate their acceptance. Generally, it is only after all these things are completed that the distributions can be made from your estate. Furthermore, if any provision in the will is contested, it may remain in probate for many months, if not years; medium-sized estates of $50,000 or so often take at least a year to be probated. It is possible to reduce the amount of your assets that go through probate, but, unless you have virtually no net worth, it is impossible to avoid probate altogether.

JOINT OWNERSHIP

Two individuals, usually husband and wife, can own many of their assets jointly. Joint ownership can assume the following forms: **joint tenancy, tenancy by the entirety,** and **tenancy in common.**

Joint Tenancy

In a joint tenancy ownership arrangement, there are two or more owners. Each owns a percentage of an asset but not a specific part of it. Each joint owner can dispose of his or her share without the permission of other owners. When one owner dies, his or her share goes to the surviving owners.

Tenancy by the Entirety

This type of joint ownership is available only to husbands and wives. In an arrangement involving tenancy by the entirety, neither husband nor wife can dispose of his or her share of the assets without the permission of the other. When one spouse dies, entire ownership of the property is automatically assumed by the surviving spouse.

Tenancy in Common

In this arrangement, there may be two or more owners. Each may dispose of his or her share without the permission of the others. Unlike joint tenancy, tenancy in common has the share of a deceased owner going to his or her heirs. These heirs may or may not be the other owner or owners.

Why Is a Will Necessary?

In all these forms of joint ownership, it would appear that the deceased person's assets would pass on to the appropriate individuals without having to be probated. Note, though, that it is still necessary to have a will for the following reasons.

1. It is virtually impossible to put *all* property in joint ownership. All property not in joint ownership may not be dispersed upon its owner's death as he or she would have wanted. In other words, local intestacy law may disperse the property otherwise.

2. Without a will, property goes to the survivor outright in a joint ownership arrangement. A will, however, makes distribution more flexible. It can put "brakes" on surviving beneficiaries so they cannot spend their inheritances immediately.

3. If two co-owners die simultaneously and both lack wills, then property can be distributed under local intestacy law to heirs in a way that the deceased individuals may not have wished.

4. There may be no funds set aside for the payment of estate taxes or other debts if there is no will. Trouble may result when surviving co-owners refuse to cooperate.

TRUSTS

Generally, a trust is an arrangement whereby you leave your property to an individual, a bank, or a trust company to manage for the benefit of your heirs. Most trusts are set up because there are minor children surviving a parent or parents. The funds are usually invested by the **trustee** (the designated holder of the trust) in order to support and educate the children. After a period of time designated in the will or trust agreement, the remaining assets are distributed, usually to the beneficiaries of the trust.

The trustee has two principle responsibilities: to execute his or her *fiduciary* (or trust) responsibility prudently and in good faith and to preserve the principal in the trust and invest it so that the beneficiaries receive at least a reasonable rate of return. If the beneficiaries are dissatisfied with a trustee's performance, they usually can petition a state court for a change in the trust agreement or for a change in trustees. Since the trustee is responsible for managing the assets in the trust, care must be taken in selecting the trustee. Friends or relatives obviously will take a more personal interest in your trust than will an institution. Nonetheless, a professional trust company can offer you investment competence and continuity for the life of the trust. Perhaps it might be best to have co-trustees—a professional company, such as a trust department of a bank, or your lawyer and a close friend or relative.

Trusts can be created for anyone's benefit, including a spouse or a charity, and are not necessarily designed for the protection of children. For example, a surviving spouse may not have the interest or ability to manage the deceased spouse's estate; therefore, a trust agreement may be the most desirable method of arranging for use of the assets. Trusts also can be established while you are still living, and these can provide at least as many benefits as a trust created at death.

Life Insurance Trust

A life insurance trust is administered by a bank or any other trustee but not an insurance company. The trustee is named to manage the insurance proceeds after death for any heirs inexperienced in handling large sums of money.

Living Trust

A living trust permits you to make the income from your assets payable to yourself while you are alive or have them reinvested for your future benefit. This type of trust is not subject to probate. Note that many living trusts are subject to estate taxes.

Funded Trusts

With the funded trust, funds or assets other than life insurance can be put under the same expert management as the life insurance trust. This reduces estate administrative expenses and averts taxation. That is, taxes do not have to be paid first by a surviving spouse and then again by the children who would inherit the same funds from that person.

Testamentary Trust

A **testamentary trust** is tailor-made for you. In your will, for example, you can create a testamentary trust that makes certain your property will be managed expertly and used as you desire. The trustee, usually a bank, is given broad investment powers.

THE TAXATION OF WEALTH

In addition to all the taxes we've already discussed, the federal government also imposes gift and **estate taxes.** These so-called wealth taxes are based on the value of our assets, minus our liabilities, that we transfer to others while we are alive or at our death. The tax is imposed on the donor or testor, not the recipient of the wealth. Regardless of who pays it, the imposition of the tax reduces the value of the assets transferred.

The Economic Recovery Tax Act of 1981 significantly modified gift and estate taxation in this country. The deductions and credits granted under the new law exempt all but the extremely wealthy from the tax. The same unified tax rate applies to both, gifts or estates. A unified tax simply means that the transfer of wealth, either by gift (while alive) or estate (at death), is cumulatively subject to the same tax schedule as shown in Exhibit W–1. For instance, assume Mary gives Harry, a friend, $10,000 over the allowable donee exemption. In the accompanying chart, the dollar amount of the unified equivalent exemption shown in Column B will be reduced by $10,000 for Mary. If Mary dies in 1983, her unified exemption would be $265,000 ($275,000 unified exemption minus the $10,000 in excess of the donee exemption).

Estate and Gift Tax Provisions

The following provisions are effective for gifts made, or for estates of decedents dying, after December 31, 1981.

MARITAL DEDUCTION. An unlimited marital deduction is allowed for estate and gift tax purposes. Exhibit W–2 shows that no tax is due at the first partner's death because of the unlimited marital deduction. Compare this to the taxes due for a single person, and you'll see that this might be the only situation where being married is cheaper than being single.

ANNUAL GIFT-TAX EXCLUSION. The annual gift-tax exclusion is increased from $3,000 to $10,000 per donee ($6,000 to $20,000 if gift-splitting is elected). An unlimited exclusion for amounts paid for the benefit of a donee for medical expenses and school tuition is also provided.

The Numbers Are Small

In 1981, 98 percent of all estates will have paid no federal estate tax. In the future, the number of people paying estate and/or gift taxes will be even smaller. By 1987, an estimated 99.7 percent of all estates will be exempt.

State Inheritance and Estate Taxes

An *inheritance tax* is paid by those who receive the property; an estate tax is paid by the estate. Most states impose an inheritance tax, but some impose an estate tax instead. A few impose both. The state inheritance tax (or estate tax, if that is the case) usually is set at a lower rate than the federal estate tax. Note, though, that state exemptions usually are smaller than federal exemptions. Thus, the actual state tax due can be, and often is, considerably higher than the federal tax due.

State inheritance taxes are based on the value of the assets inherited by the individual. They are owed to the state in which the inherited assets are located rather than the state in which the person inheriting them lives. In many cases, the state tax varies not only with the value of the assets but also with the relationship of the recipient to the deceased.

The "Pick-Up" Tax

Most states have an added estate tax, which usually is called a "pick-up" tax. This tax is designed to ensure that an amount at least equal to the maximum allowable federal-estate-tax credit is charged. This tax does not, however, increase the *total* death taxes paid; it applies only when the amount due from other state death taxes is less than the allowable federal estate credit.

SUMMARY

1. Virtually everyone with any assets should have a will prepared; otherwise a person will die intestate.

EXHIBIT W–1
Unified Rate Schedule

UNIFIED SCHEDULE FOR 1983

If the amount with respect to which the tentative tax is to be computed is:	The tentative tax is
Not over $10,000	18% of such amount
Over $10,000 but not over $20,000	$1,800, plus 20% of the excess of such amount over $10,000.
Over $20,000 but not over $40,000	$3,800, plus 22% of the excess of such amount over $20,000.
Over $40,000 but not over $60,000	$8,200, plus 24% of the excess of such amount over $40,000.
Over $60,000 but not over $80,000	$13,000, plus 26% of the excess of such amount over $60,000.
Over $80,000 but not over $100,000	$18,200, plus 28% of the excess of such amount over $80,000.
Over $100,000 but not over $150,000	$23,800, plus 30% of the excess of such amount over $100,000.
Over $150,000 but not over $250,000	$38,800, plus 32% of the excess of such amount over $150,000.
Over $250,000 but not over $500,000	$70,800, plus 34% of the excess of such amount over $250,000.
Over $500,000 but not over $750,000	$155,800, plus 37% of the excess of such amount over $500,000.
Over $750,000 but not over $1,000,000	$248,300, plus 39% of the excess of such amount over $750,000.
Over $1,000,000 but not over $1,250,000	$345,800, plus 41% of the excess of such amount over $1,000,000.
Over $1,250,000 but not over $1,500,000	$448,300, plus 43% of the excess of such amount over $1,250,000.
Over $1,500,000 but not over $2,000,000	$555,800, plus 45% of the excess of such amount over $1,500,000.
Over $2,000,000 but not over $2,500,000	$780,800, plus 49% of the excess of such amount over $2,000,000.
Over $2,500,000 but not over $3,000,000	$1,025,800, plus 53% of the excess of such amount over $2,500,000.
Over $3,000,000 but not over $3,500,000	$1,290,800, plus 57% of the excess of such amount over $3,000,000.
Over $3,500,000	$1,575,800, plus 60% of the excess of such amount over $3,500,000.

UNIFIED CREDIT OR EXEMPTION

CALENDAR YEAR	COLUMN A Unified estate and gift tax credit increased to:	COLUMN B Unified equivalent exemption from estate and gift transfers of:
1981	$ 47,000	$175,625
1982	62,800	225,000
1983	79,300	275,000
1984	96,300	325,000
1985	121,800	400,000
1986	155,800	500,000
1987 and thereafter	192,800	600,000

MAXIMUM TAX REDUCED

CALENDAR YEAR	MAXIMUM RATE	FOR TRANSFERS OVER
1981	70%	$5,000,000
1982	65%	4,000,000
1983	60%	3,500,000
1984	55%	3,000,000
1984 and thereafter	50%	2,500,000

ADJUSTED GROSS ESTATE (After Subtracting Debts, Funeral Expenses, Administrative Costs, Etc.)	TAXES DUE AT FIRST PARTNER'S DEATH (Includes Marital Deduction)	TAXES DUE AT DEATH (Single Person)
$ 60,000	$ 0	$ 0
80,000	0	0
100,000	0	0
200,000	0	0
300,000	0	4,900
400,000	0	41,300
500,000	0	62,000
1,000,000	0	239,050

EXHIBIT W–2
Federal Estate Taxes in 1983

2. When you die intestate, you have no control over who oversees the distribution of your estate, who will be the guardian for minor children if your spouse is no longer living, or who will get what percentage of your estate.

3. A will allows you to designate who gets your property, how much each person or institution gets, when the property will be received, how the property can be safeguarded, and who will handle its disposition.

4. A will disposes of only certain amounts of property; for example, life insurance proceeds automatically go to the stated beneficiary.

5. A will must be probated—that is, taken to the appropriate court to demonstrate that all debts and taxes have been paid and that the will is valid.

6. Probate takes from four months to a year for relatively simple estates and wills and longer for more complicated and/or contested wills.

7. Joint ownership can assume the following forms: joint tenancy, tenancy by the entirety, and tenancy in common.

8. Even though property is held in common, a will is still necessary.

9. Many wills provide for at least part of the estate to go into a trust to be administered by a trustee for the benefit of the heirs of the deceased.

10. The trustee has two principal responsibilities: to execute his or her trust responsibility in good faith, and to preserve the principal in the trust and invest that principal wisely.

11. There are numerous types of trusts, including life insurance, living, funded, and testamentary.

12. The Economic Recovery Tax Act of 1981 greatly reduced and simplified the taxation of estates. All estate and gift taxes are now unified, and there are large credits for married individuals.

13. In addition to federal estate taxes, state inheritance and estate taxes must be paid in certain states.

QUESTIONS FOR THOUGHT AND DISCUSSION

1. What are the goals of estate planning?
2. Explain the major purpose of a will.
3. What happens when you die intestate?
4. What is the probate process?
5. What are the three forms of joint ownership? How do they differ from one another?

SELECTED READINGS

Cantor, Gilbert M. *How to Totally Avoid Estate Taxes.* New York: Enterprise Publishing, 1981.

Freilincher, Morton, *Estate Planning Handbook—with Forms.* Englewood Cliffs, N.J.: Prentice-Hall (latest edition).

Moody, William J. *How to Probate an Estate.* New York: Simon & Schuster, 1982.

Tax Angles in Writing Your Will. *Research Institute Recommendations,* Section 2, Personal and Business Tax Savings, May 2, 1980.

"What You Should Know about Wills," *Consumer Reports,* July 1980, pp. 434–40.

Whitney, Victor P. *The Essentials of Estate Planning.* New York: Van Nostrand Reinhold, 1982.

Appendix III:
HOW TO MAKE OUT YOUR WILL

GLOSSARY

ADMINISTRATIVE CLAUSES—Those clauses in a will that ensure that the instructions are carried out.

ATTESTATION CLAUSES—The clause that witnesses sign to validate a will.

LEGACY—A gift of property by will, usually a specific gift for a specific person.

TESTAMONIUM CLAUSE—The concluding clause of a will that indicates you are signing your name to approve it.

THE COMPOSITION OF A WILL

When you reach your state's legal age and if you have many assets, you should make out a will. While each will is different, most have at least five principal sections.

1. The opening recitation
2. The dispositive clauses
3. The administrative clauses
4. A testamonium clause
5. An attestation clause

Opening Recitation

This part of a will indicates who you are, where you live, and that you are of sound mind and competent to make a will. In addition, this section may revoke all previous wills, indicate that all debts and funeral expenses should be paid, and sometimes gives instructions as to how you should be buried.

Dispositive Clauses

This section indicates who should get what. In other words, it indicates **legacies,** of which there are four types: specific, general, demonstrative, and residuary.

SPECIFIC LEGACY. A particular piece of property in the estate is given to a particular person or institution; for example, you give your dog to your daughter.

GENERAL LEGACY. You give a specific amount of money to an individual or institution. Such a cash bequest is paid out of the general assets in the estate.

DEMONSTRATIVE LEGACY. A specific amount of money is bequeathed, along with the source of its payment; for example, $5,000 a year will go to the deceased's mother to be paid out of royalties on books the deceased has written.

RESIDUARY LEGACY. This bequest is payable out of the remainder of the estate after everything else has been paid, including the preceding three types of legacies and all debts and administrative expenses.

Administrative Clauses

The section of the will containing **administrative clauses** sets up the machinery for making sure your instructions are followed. In this section, you name your executors and the guardians for any minor children you have. The duties of an executor of executrix are described below.

Testamonium Clause

The **testamonium clause** concludes the will and indicates that you are signing your name to approve it. The will should not, however, be signed unless witnesses are present. An unwitnessed will may be no better than a blank piece of paper.

Attestation Clause

The **attestation clause** is signed by witnesses. It indicates that they know you signed the will of your own free will and were of sound mind when you did it. Witnesses must sign in the presence of each other, as well as in your presence.

THE IMPORTANT JOB OF THE EXECUTOR/EXECUTRIX

In your will, you must indicate who shall carry out your instructions. These persons or institutions are called your executors. Choosing an executor or executrix is a difficult task. You must be able to trust that person or institution to take a personal interest in seeing that your estate is properly handled after your death. Many states have limitations on who can be an executor or executrix. For example, Florida requires that the person either be a blood relative or a resident of the state of Florida; if you live in Florida, you could not name as executor or executrix for your estate a close friend who lived in California.

The Executor's or Executrix's Duties

It would be impossible to indicate all the duties the executor or executrix must perform, but here are some.

1. Managing the estate until it is settled, including
- **a.** Collecting debts due the estate.
- **b.** Managing real estate; arranging for maintenance and repairs.
- **c.** Registering securities in the name of the estate.
- **d.** Collecting insurance proceeds.
- **e.** Running the family business, if necessary.
- **f.** Arranging for the family's support during probate.
- **g.** Properly insuring assets.

2. Collecting all assets and necessary records, including
- **a.** Locating the will, insurance policies, real-estate papers, car registrations, and birth certificates.
- **b.** Filing claims for pension, Social Security, profit sharing, and veterans benefits.
- **c.** Taking possession of bank accounts, real estate, personal effects, and safe deposit boxes.
- **d.** Obtaining names, addresses, and Social Security numbers of all heirs.
- **e.** Making an inventory of all assets.
- **f.** Setting up records and books.

3. Determining the estate's obligations, including
- **a.** Determining which claims are legally due.
- **b.** Obtaining receipts for all claims paid.
- **c.** Checking on mortgages and other loans.

4. Computing and then paying all death taxes due, which requires
- **a.** Selecting the most beneficial tax alternatives.
- **b.** Deciding which assets to sell to provide necessary funds.
- **c.** Paying taxes on time to avoid penalties.
- **d.** Opposing what you think are unfair evaluations established by governmental taxing authorities.

5. Computing beneficiaries' shares and then distributing the estate, which involves
- **a.** Determining who gets particular items and settling family disputes.
- **b.** Transferring title to real estate and other property.
- **c.** Selling off assets to pay cash legacies.
- **d.** Paying final estate costs.
- **e.** Preparing accountings for the court's approval.

Given the amount of work involved in executing a will, you would hope that the executor or executrix would take a personal interest in the situation. A friend or relative might; but such a person might lack the necessary financial training to do so properly. That's why some people make a close relative or personal friend as one co-executor and name a professional trust company as another co-executor.

AVOIDING COMMON MISTAKES

Lawyers who handle estates and wills frequently encounter a number of related mistakes. Here are some of these mistakes and suggestions for avoiding them.

Writing Your Will Yourself

Handwritten wills (officially called holographic wills) are legal in less than 50 percent of the states. Even in states where they are legal, it is difficult to establish their validity. Oral wills are generally accepted only during combat, although some states recognize oral wills made during a final illness.

Disinheritance

If you desire to disinherit a particular family member (where it is possible to do so), you must state this explicitly in your will. Otherwise, the disinherited person may be able to persuade a court that you were not competent to make the will. You might want to write something like the following:

> After careful thought and reflection, I have decided and hence determined that it is better not to include a bequest to my niece, Martha.

Misunderstanding State Requirements

Each state has different requirements for a valid will. When you die, your permanent residence determines which state's laws apply. If you retire to California, make sure that the will you made in Minnesota is valid.

Not Keeping Your Will Up-to-Date

In many states, a will becomes invalid if it was drawn up before you either married or had children. Any change in marital status or family size should dictate that a new will is in order, with new specifications about dividing your estate.

Not Reappraising Your Executor or Executrix Regularly

What if you named as an executor a person who since has become mentally incompetent? What if you named as an executrix a woman who died? It will take much longer than usual to wind up an estate when such an event occurs. In any case, it is generally wise to name an alternate executor or executrix in case the first person you chose cannot or will not serve.

Not Specifying What Happens If an Heir Dies before You Do or Simultaneously

Air and automotive travel have increased the likelihood that several members of the same family may die in the same accident. If this happens, it is necessary that a second or even third beneficiary be listed in the will in case the previous one or ones are already dead. You might put a "delay clause" in all insurance policies and in the will; it would specify that the first listed beneficiary must survive you by at least thirty days, or the money will go to other heirs on the list.

Keeping Your Will in a Safe Deposit Box

In many states, your safe deposit box is sealed at your death and cannot be opened without a court order that may require time and expense.

Not Destroying an Old Will After Making a New One

A new will does not automatically invalidate an old one. The new one must specify that the person making the will revokes all former wills.

Omitting Too Much

Essentially, a will should dispose of the entire estate. In other words, wills should have a clause directing the disposal of residue and remainder.

A LETTER OF LAST INSTRUCTION

In addition to your will, you should have a separate letter of last instruction. The letter, which is opened at your death, should contain the following information.

1. The location of your will.
2. Instructions about your burial.
3. The location of all relevant documents, such as your Social Security card, marriage certificate, and birth certificate.
4. The location of all safe deposit boxes.
5. A list of your life insurance policies and where they are located.
6. Pension statements.
7. A list of all stocks and bonds, real and other property, and bank accounts, and their locations.
8. Any instructions concerning a business in which you might have been engaged.
9. A statement of reasons for not giving part of your estate to someone who normally would be expected to receive it.

A letter of last instruction is not a legal document. It does not replace a will and should not be considered a substitute for a valid will.

WHERE SHOULD YOU PUT YOUR WILL?

A will should be readily available upon the death of its maker. Therefore, once you will has been written, you should do at least one of the following:

1. Leave the original copy of the will with the attorney who drew it up. The attorney then will put it in a safe deposit box in the law offices or in a financial institution.
2. If you have a safe deposit box at home, you may keep the original copy of the will in it, but this is not often recommended.
3. You can keep the original copy of the will in your own safe deposit box in a financial institution. Many experts object to this idea, however, because a court order may be necessary for the box to be opened after your death.

4. If a professional trust company or financial institution has been named as an executor of the estate, that institution may keep the original copy of the will.

5. Some financial experts suggest that the husband's will be put in the wife's safe deposit box and the wife's will be put in the husband's safe deposit box.

Appendix IV: ESTATE PLANNING CONSIDERATIONS FOR WOMEN*

Because some married women often have not been as deeply involved with money matters as their husbands, it is important that they familiarize themselves with certain pertinent facts about family finances.

BASIC QUESTIONS FOR WHICH WOMEN MUST OBTAIN ANSWERS

1. How big is my husband's estate?
2. By how much will it be reduced because of estate taxes and administrative expenses?
3. Are all of his income taxes paid up to date? Have his returns been examined in the past years? Are there any risks and liabilities of which I should be aware?
4. What other potential claims (besides taxes) are there against his estate?
5. Are there any claims in dispute that would reduce his estate? Is my husband's executor in a conflict-of-interest position with respect to these disputed claims?
6. After the administration of the estate, will there be long-term debts held over, such as mortgages on the house?
7. What proportion of the principal of the estate and insurance policies comes directly to me and the children immediately or under powers of evasion of principal of trust if we do not have enough income to live on?
8. After all the current debts of the estate are paid off, what regular income will continue from the remaining assets if I keep them in their present form?
9. Should these assets be rearranged? If so, how?
10. Do I have a voice in making decisions on this asset rearrangement? If so, how?
11. Does my husband's will grant me certain responsibilities of trust, other than responsibilities of investment?
12. Will I have sufficient funds for educating and bringing the children up or must I provide these funds myself?
13. When my husband dies, are there any assets or income that I will obtain that will not go through his estate?
14. Will any of these assets or income be subject to income taxes or estate taxes at a later date?
15. Should I involve myself in the business my husband was running? If so, in what ways?
16. What if some of the children become involved in the family business and others do not? How do I avoid problems?
17. Do I live in a community-property state? If so, what are my new rights and responsibilities when my husband dies?
18. Do I have independent assets and sources of income apart from my job?
19. Can I file a joint return this year and the next two years following my husband's death? After that, do I become head of household? If so, for how long? What happens to my tax rate when I revert to a separate return?
20. What will my after-tax income be? Will I have enough to pay off debts and make separate provisions for my dependents?
21. Do I want to stay in the same house and try to live the same way I lived before? What are the tax considerations and other financial matters that might influence such a choice?
22. Shall I continue to work at the same job? Shall I go to work if I am not now working?
23. Do I now want to engage in volunteer activities or work with a nonprofit organization?
24. What should be my new estate plan after my husband's death?
25. Can I have confidence in the executor and trustee of my husband's estate? How can I check on them?
26. Will Social Security provide me with any benefits?

For further information on this subject, read Gustav Simon's *What Every Woman Doesn't Know* (New York: Macmillan Co., 1966) and also Paula Nelson's *The Joy of Money* (New York: Bantam Books, 1977).

*This short appendix draws heavily from information provided by Dr. K. P. Edwards, Brigham Young University.

INDEX OF GLOSSARY TERMS

INDEX

(Continuation of Credits)

Cooking Products; 342, 350, 351 Michael Rothstein, Jeroboam; 357, 359 Cathy Cheney, EKM-Nepenthe; 362, 363 Tim Jewett, EKM-Nepenthe; 366 Mimi Forsyth, Monkmeyer Press; 368 Tom Ballard, EKM-Nepenthe; 375, 377 Jeffrey Grosscup; 388, 389 Mike Valerie, Freelance Photographers Guild; 393 Russ Kline/Danbury Hospital, Photo Researchers; 402, 407, 414, 415, 419 Jeffrey Grosscup; 434 Jill Cannefax, EKM-Nepenthe; 441, 442 Evan Johnson, Jeroboam; 448, 449 Paul Conklin, Monkmeyer Press; 458 Tom Ballard, EKM-Nepenthe; 462, 463 Monkmeyer Press; 466, 467 Kent Reno, Jeroboam; 471, 481, 483 EKM-Nepenthe; 492, 493 Robert Burroughs, Jeroboam; 500 Paul Schmick, Monkmeyer Press; 508, 509 David S. Strickler, Monkmeyer Press; 516, 517 Robert Ginn, EKM-Nepenthe; 522 Randolph Falk, Jeroboam; 525 Jill Cannefax, EKM-Nepenthe; 528, 530 Steve Malone, Jeroboam; 534, 535 Richard Laird, Freelance Photographers Guild; 540 Jeffrey Grosscup; 542 Irene Bayer, Monkmeyer Press; 545, 546 EKM-Nepenthe

†